Frommer's

New York City
from $90 a Day

2004

by Brian Silverman

Here's what the critics say about Frommer's:

"Amazingly easy to use. Very portable, very complete."
—*Booklist*

"Detailed, accurate, and easy-to-read information for all price ranges."
—*Glamour Magazine*

"Hotel information is close to encyclopedic."
—*Des Moines Sunday Register*

"Frommer's Guides have a way of giving you a real feel for a place."
—*Knight Ridder Newspapers*

WILEY

Wiley Publishing, Inc.

About the Author

Brian Silverman has written about travel, food, sports, and music for publications such as *Saveur, Caribbean Travel & Life, Islands, American Way, The New Yorker,* and *The New York Times.* He is the author of several books including *Going, Going, Gone: The History, Lore, and Mystique of the Home Run* (HarperCollins), and co-editor of *The Twentieth Century Treasury of Sports* (Viking Books). Brian lives in New York, New York, with his wife and son.

Published by:

Wiley Publishing, Inc.

111 River St.
Hoboken, NJ 07030

ISBN 0-7645-3905-1

ISSN 8755-5433

Editor: Kathleen Warnock
Production Editor: Bethany André
Cartographer: Elizabeth Puhl
Photo Editor: Richard Fox
Production by Wiley Indianapolis Composition Services

Front cover photo: The Statue of Liberty
Back cover photo: A room at the Gershwin Hotel

For information on our other products and services or to obtain technical support, please contact our Customer Care Department within the U.S. at 800-762-2974, outside the U.S. at 317-572-3993 or fax 317-572-4002.

Wiley also publishes its books in a variety of electronic formats. Some content that appears in print may not be available in electronic formats.

Manufactured in the United States of America

5 4 3 2 1

Contents

5 Accommodations You Can Afford 98

6 Great Deals on Dining 133

7 Exploring New York City 191

8 Shopping for Big Apple Bargains 265

9 New York City After Dark 293

Index 333

List of Maps

An Invitation to the Reader

In researching this book, we discovered many wonderful places—hotels, restaurants, shops, and more. We're sure you'll find others. Please tell us about them, so we can share the information with your fellow travelers in upcoming editions. If you were disappointed with a recommendation, we'd love to know that, too. Please write to:

Frommer's New York City from $90 a Day 2004

Wiley Publishing, Inc. • 111 River St. • Hoboken, NJ 07030

An Additional Note

Please be advised that travel information is subject to change at any time—and this is especially true of prices. We therefore suggest that you write or call ahead for confirmation when making your travel plans. The authors, editors, and publisher cannot be held responsible for the experiences of readers while traveling. Your safety is important to us, however, so we encourage you to stay alert and be aware of your surroundings. Keep a close eye on cameras, purses, and wallets, all favorite targets of thieves and pickpockets.

Other Great Guides for Your Trip:

Frommer's New York City
Frommer's New York City with Kids
Frommer's Portable New York City
The Unofficial Guide to New York City
New York City For Dummies
Frommer's New York State

Frommer's Star Ratings, Icons & Abbreviations

Every hotel, restaurant, and attraction listing in this guide has been ranked for quality, value, service, amenities, and special features using a **star-rating system.** In country, state, and regional guides, we also rate towns and regions to help you narrow down your choices and budget your time accordingly. Hotels and restaurants are rated on a scale of zero (recommended) to three stars (exceptional). Attractions, shopping, nightlife, towns, and regions are rated according to the following scale: zero stars (recommended), one star (highly recommended), two stars (very highly recommended), and three stars (must-see).

In addition to the star-rating system, we also use **seven feature icons** that point you to the great deals, in-the-know advice, and unique experiences that separate travelers from tourists. Throughout the book, look for:

Finds	Special finds—those places only insiders know about
Fun Fact	Fun facts—details that make travelers more informed and their trips more fun
Kids	Best bets for kids and advice for the whole family
Moments	Special moments—those experiences that memories are made of
Overrated	Places or experiences not worth your time or money
Tips	Insider tips—great ways to save time and money
Value	Great values—where to get the best deals

The following **abbreviations** are used for credit cards:

AE	American Express	DISC	Discover	V	Visa
DC	Diners Club	MC	MasterCard		

Frommers.com

Now that you have the guidebook to a great trip, visit our website at **www.frommers.com** for travel information on more than 3,000 destinations. With features updated regularly, we give you instant access to the most current trip-planning information available. At Frommers.com, you'll also find the best prices on airfares, accommodations, and car rentals—and you can even book travel online through our travel booking partners. At Frommers.com, you'll also find the following:

- Online updates to our most popular guidebooks
- Vacation sweepstakes and contest giveaways
- Newsletter highlighting the hottest travel trends
- Online travel message boards with featured travel discussions

What's New in New York City

In these turbulent times of high security alerts, a roller-coaster economy, and serious international concerns, New York, showing its incredible resilience, continues to thrive and grow. Here are some of the changes you will find this year:

GETTING AROUND In May 2003, the Metropolitan Transit Authority (MTA) raised the cost of riding city **subways** and **buses** to $2 per ride (as well as raising the fares for multi-ride and unlimited Metro-Cards). Then a group of commuters sued the MTA over the hike, and a (subway-riding) judge ordered the agency to roll back the fares to $1.50. The MTA got an injunction to stop the rollback, and as this book goes to press, the stalemate continues. All references to bus and subway fares in this book will be given at the higher rate, and should you end up paying less per ride when you arrive, you won't be any happier about it than the native straphangers!

LOCAL LAWS In 2003, New York enacted a controversial and very tough **nonsmoking law** that prohibits smoking in all public places. That means you can't light up anywhere; not in restaurants, movie theaters, bowling alleys, arenas, auditoriums, nightclubs, or bars.

EXPLORING NEW YORK CITY A design concept for the redevelopment of the **World Trade Center** site (© 212/962-2300; www.renewnyc. com) was awarded to architect Daniel Libeskind for his "Memory Foundation" proposal. The proposal features five towers (the largest, at 1,776 feet, would be the tallest in the world), a Memorial Garden, a museum, cultural facilities, and hotel and office space. But construction of the project is years away; in the meantime, a **"Wall of Heroes"** was erected around the site, where you can pay your respects.

The newest museum in the city is the first cultural institution devoted to the history and evolution of human sexuality: the **Museum of Sex,** 233 Fifth Ave. (© **212/689-6337;** www. museumofsex.com).

The Skyscraper Museum, 2 West St. (© **212/968-1961;** www.sky scraper.org), moved into its permanent home on the ground floor of the Ritz-Carlton Hotel in Battery Park; while the **New York Transit Museum,** Boerum Place and Schermerhorn Street in Brooklyn (© **718/694-5100;** www.mta.nyc.ny.us/museum), completed a major renovation featuring a new art gallery, a classroom for children's workshops, a computer lab, and a reference library.

The **Museum of Modern Art,** 11 W. 53rd St., is still under renovation and is not expected to reopen until early 2005. Until then, the museum's temporary home, **MoMA QNS,** 45–20 33rd St. in Queens (© **212/ 708-9480;** www.moma.org), will continue to feature a full exhibition schedule.

The new four-story, 70,000-square-foot east wing of the **Museum** of Jewish Heritage: A Living Memorial to the Holocaust, 18 1st Place (© 212/509-6130; www.mjh nyc.org), is scheduled to open in late 2003. The wing will feature a state-of-the-art theater, memorial garden, extended gallery space, classrooms, and a resource center and library.

The **Morgan Library,** 29 E. 36th St. (© 212/685-0610; www.morgan library.org), will be closed for renovations during the life of this book.

The **AOL Time-Warner Center** at Columbus Circle is scheduled for completion in late 2003. One of its tenants will be **Jazz at Lincoln Center** (© 212/258-9800; www.jazzat lincolncenter.org). The $115 million, 100,000-square-foot facility will be the first performing arts center designed specifically for jazz.

DINING OUT   Despite the slow economy, restaurants continue to open in all price ranges. Danny Meyer, *restaurateur extraordinaire,* the man behind Union Square Café and Gramercy Park Tavern, opened a more wallet-friendly restaurant, **Blue Smoke,** 116 E. 27th St. (© 212/447-7733; www.bluesmoke.com), where barbecue reigns supreme.

In 2003, hamburger wars broke out in New York. The war was not about who had the best hamburger, but who had the most expensive. The winner was Daniel Boulud's **db Bistro Moderne,** which featured a $50 hamburger, made with ground short ribs, foie gras,

and shaved black truffles. For a good burger for a *lot* less, head to the new burger joint called, appropriately, **Burger Joint,** in the lobby of the Le Parker Meridien hotel, 118 W. 57th St. (© 212/708-7460), where you can get possibly the best burger in the city for just $4.95.

After being closed for renovations for a year, the storied 100-year-old saloon, **P.J. Clarke's,** 915 Third Ave., (© 212/317-1616; www.pjclarkes. com), reopened under new ownership but with all the original detail in place. Don't miss the oddly priced $8.10 hamburger.

The Upper West Side has been the beneficiary of a spate of new budget restaurants, the best of which is the remarkable **Celeste,** 502 Amsterdam Ave. (© 212/874-4559), which features fresh, original Italian dishes and perfect pizza cooked in the restaurant's own wood-burning oven.

On the Upper East Side, pizza also shines at **Nick's Family-Style Restaurant and Pizzeria,** 1814 Second Ave. (© 212/987-5700). But the antipasto and pastas are also excellent, making this much more than just your ordinary pizzeria.

In Harlem, new restaurants are opening at a record pace. One is **La Fonda Boricua,** 169 E. 106th St. (© 212/410-7292), which serves possibly the best Puerto Rican food in the city in a stylish, sophisticated setting.

⌐Tips   **Here Come the Elephants!**

No, it's not the annual march of the pachyderms through the Midtown Tunnel when the circus comes to town. For the first time, the Republican National Committee has chosen New York City as the site for its **Republican National Convention,** beginning August 30, 2004. If you are visiting around then, keep in mind that hotels, restaurants, and attractions will be booked *well* in advance, so plan accordingly. More than 50,000 delegates, support staff, and members of the media will be in town, occupying some 22,000 hotel rooms, so expect massive crowds throughout Manhattan, gridlock, demonstrations, and high(er) security.

> *Tips* **Dial ALL Those Digits!**
>
> As of 2003, when you're making a local call in New York City, you must dial "1" and the area code, even to calls in the same area code. If you're *in* 212, you still have to dial 1 + 212 and the regular seven-digit number.

Finally, the best ice cream in New York, along with one of the best views of Manhattan, can be found at the new **Brooklyn Ice Cream Factory,** at the Fulton Ferry Landing Pier, Brooklyn Heights (© **718/246-3963**).

AFTER DARK In September 2003, the **Zankel Concert Hall,** 881 Seventh Ave. (© **212/247-7800**), a 650-seat auditorium below Carnegie Hall, opened; the new venue will feature performances from a diverse range of artists, from Brazilian musician Caetano Veloso to the Romanian Takacs Quartet.

With the Republicans in residence at Madison Square Garden from mid-July to late August 2004, the arena's regular summer tenants, the WNBA's New York Liberty, will be playing part of the season at another Manhattan landmark: Radio City Music Hall. Instead of Rockettes, you'll see the Rockets (Houston, that is) and the Stars (San Antonio Silver Stars). Radio City has a much smaller capacity than MSG, so if your summer plans include a basketball game, call or e-mail well in advance for tickets (© 212/564/9622; www.nyliberty.com).

1

The Best of the Big Apple

New York is the concentrate of art and commerce and sport and religion and enter-tainment and finance, bringing to a single compact arena the gladiator, the evan-gelist, the promoter, the actor, the trader and the merchant. It carries on its lapel the unexpungeable odor of the long past, so that no matter where you sit in New York you feel the vibrations of great times and tall deeds, of queer people and events and undertakings.

New York is nothing like Paris; it is nothing like London; and it is not Spokane multiplied by sixty, or Detroit multiplied by four. It is by all odds the loftiest of cities.

—E.B. White

Novelist and essayist E.B. White wrote these words in 1948; and in the 56 years since then, his description of New York remains accurate. And though the grandeur and importance of New York has not changed, New York is constantly changing. Restaurants and nightclubs become trendy overnight, and then die under the weight of their own popularity. (As the philosopher Yogi Berra said: "Nobody goes there anymore; it's too crowded.") Broadway shows, exercise fads, city politics, even neighborhoods are all subject to the same Big Apple fickleness.

But within this ebb and flow lies the answer to why we New Yorkers persist in loving our city so, despite the high rents, the noise, the crowds, the cab driv-ers who don't know Lincoln Center from the Lower East Side, and the more stark realities of high-security-alert days and living in the shadow of great tragedy. Nowhere else is the challenge so tough, the pace so relentless, the stim-uli so ever changing and insistent—and the payoff so rewarding. It is why we go on; it is why we proudly persist in living our vibrant lives here.

Come witness New York's resilience for yourself—it's reason enough to visit.

1 How This Guide Can Save You Money

New York City is perpetually short on space and overflowing with people. It's a situation that turns the economy of supply and demand in the seller's favor, with vendors charging what the market will bear. The result has been stratospheric prices, some of the high-est in the country. If you're used to getting a simple, comfortable motel room for $60 or so, get set for a shock.

That's the bad news—but there's plenty of good news, too. You *can* stay in New York City comfortably, eat well, and see and do everything you want without blowing your budget. There are plenty of great deals for the intrepid traveler who knows where to look for value and discounts. And there are more travel and hotel bar-gains now than there have been in years—if you know where to look.

You've already taken the first step: buying this book. I've done the initial legwork, scouring the city and loading

On New York

The only credential the city asked was the boldness to dream. For those who did, it unlocked its gates and its treasures, not caring who they were and where they came from.

—Moss Hart

the pages that follow with money-saving advice, the top values and bargains, and the kind of New York travel know-how that comes only with years of research and experience.

Accommodations will be your biggest hurdle, although visitors have regained their bargaining power in the post-9/11 world. Every other aspect of New York is manageable if you look before you leap, which is how regular New Yorkers manage. The city tends to snag people who, exhausted, sit down at the first restaurant they see and end up with a huge bill—or those who stumble into a chic boutique to buy a souvenir that can be had for a fraction of the price with a little effort. Keep an eye on the goal, and you'll see New York has more affordable culinary and bargain hunters' delights than you'll have time to enjoy.

With average museum admissions hovering around 10 bucks a pop and guided bus tours starting at $30 for the basic look-see, you could spend a fortune on sightseeing and activities—but you don't have to. Start perusing these pages, and you'll find more to see and do for free and on the cheap than you could squeeze into one vacation (or two or three or four). I'm not suggesting that you skip everything that has a price tag; certain New York experiences shouldn't be missed. But read the pages that follow and you'll know what's worth your hard-earned dough—and what's not.

THE NEW-YORK-FROM-$90-A-DAY PREMISE

The idea is this: With good planning and a watchful eye, you can keep your basic daily costs—accommodations and three meals—down to as little as $90. This budget model works best for two adults traveling together who have at least $180 a day to work with and can share a double room. (Single rooms are less cost-efficient.) This way, if you aim for accommodations that cost around $120 for a double—a reasonable budget—you'll be left with about $30 per person per day for food (less drinks and tips). Snare a room for less—doable in this economic climate, especially in a less busy season or if you're willing to share a bathroom—and you'll have more left over from your $180-per-day budget for dining.

In defining this premise, we assume you want to travel comfortably, with your own room rather than a hostel bunk (even if it does mean a shared bathroom), and dining on good food. This book will serve you well even if you don't need to keep your two-person budget to a strict $180 a day, but you want to get the most for your money. It will, on the other side of the coin, also meet your needs if you want to travel on the ultracheap—for less than $90 a day—by staying in hostels and eating super-inexpensively.

Sightseeing, transportation, and entertainment are all extra. But I've got plenty of suggestions on how to keep those costs down, too. What you choose for entertainment will have a huge effect on your overall budget. If you go to nightclubs every night, you'll come home with a lighter wallet than if you spend time taking in free concerts or browsing galleries. If you seek top-name entertainment on Broadway or the cabaret circuit, you'll pay more than if you take a risk on tomorrow's stars at an Off-Broadway show or a no-cover bar. Only you know how much money you have to spend—but if you follow my advice,

you'll be able to make informed decisions so that it's money well spent.

Even if you stick with freebies, the Big Apple guarantees a memorable time. After all, to the late, great Quentin Crisp, every flat surface in New York is a stage—and you're guaranteed a nonstop show.

2 Cheap Thrills: Frommer's Favorite Free & Affordable Experiences

- **Best Attraction:** If you have time to do only one thing on your visit to New York, sail to the **Statue of Liberty.** No other monument embodies the nation's, and the world's, notion of political freedom and economic potential more than Lady Liberty. It is also the ultimate symbol of New York; the personification of the city's vast diversity and tolerance. *Note:* At press time, visitors can tour the grounds only at Liberty Island; the statue itself had not yet reopened to visitors. Whether this status will change is unknown at press time. Even if it doesn't, standing at the feet of Lady Liberty makes a more-than-worthwhile journey, especially in these reflective, patriotic days. See p. 210.
- **Best Building: Empire State Building.** Like the Statue of Liberty, the Empire State Building, once again the tallest building in New York, is one of the city's definitive icons.

  Runners-up include the Art Deco masterpiece, the **Chrysler Building,** and the triangular **Flatiron Building.** See chapter 7.
- **Best Street:** This was a tough choice. Fifth Avenue has the reputation, but has lost some luster the past few years with the proliferation of chain and theme stores, so my pick is **Broadway.** Beginning at the southern tip of the island downtown, Broadway runs from

Wall Street, up through Chinatown, SoHo, and Greenwich Village, past the Flatiron building at 23rd Street, into the heart of Times Square, and then up to Columbus Circle, past Lincoln Center and the Upper West Side, all the way to the northern tip of the island. No street captures the diversity of Manhattan better than Broadway.
- **Best Bridge:** Manhattan has five major bridges connecting the island to other shores, and the most historic and fascinating is the **Brooklyn Bridge.** For a close-up look at what was a marvel of civic engineering when it was built in 1883, and a real New York experience, walk across the bridge from Manhattan to Brooklyn. See p. 203.
- **Best Historic Building:** Despite all the modern steel and glass skyscrapers in New York, there are still many historic marvels standing, and the best of those is the beaux arts gem, Grand Central Terminal. This railroad station, built in 1913, was restored in the 1990s to recapture its initial brilliance. Even if you don't have to catch a train, make sure you visit. See p. 205.
- **Best Museum: American Museum of Natural History.** You could spend your entire visit to New York at this 4-square-block museum and not run out of things

to see. From the famed dinosaur halls to the newly renovated *Hall of Ocean Life,* the Museum of Natural History houses the world's greatest natural science collection. See p. 202.

- **Best Art Museum: Metropolitan Museum of Art.** Not just the best art museum in New York, but the best in North America. The number of masterworks here is mind-boggling. See p. 206.
- **Best Park:** Though New York has many very wonderful parks, there is no real competition here. **Central Park** is one of the world's greatest urban refuges; a center of calm and tranquility amongst the noise and bustle that is Manhattan. See p. 237.
- **Best Place to Take the Kids:** Again, **Central Park.** With a carousel, a zoo, two ice-skating rinks, and numerous playgrounds and ball fields, Central Park is a children's wonderland.
- **Best Neighborhood to Stroll:** Though I'm partial to the Upper West Side, I have to give the nod to **Greenwich Village.** With its historic streets, hidden cafes, cozy restaurants, and eccentric characters, Greenwich Village is a constant but pleasant barrage on the senses. See chapter 4.
- **Best Jogging Path: The Reservoir in Central Park.** Also known as Jacqueline Kennedy Onassis Reservoir, this 1½ mile path is the preferred path of presidential candidates, among others. See chapter 7.
- **Best Parade:** New York is famous for its parades, notably the Macy's Thanksgiving Day Parade and the St. Patrick's Day Parade, but the best parade in New York is the lesser-known **West Indian-American Day Parade.** Held on Eastern Parkway in Brooklyn, this is the biggest parade in the city. The music—calypso, soca, reggae, and Latin, the carnival costumes, and incredible Caribbean food make this an unforgettable experience. If you are lucky enough to be here on Labor Day, don't miss it. See chapter 2.

- **Best Street Festival: Ninth Avenue International Food Festival.** For one weekend in the middle of May, the Ninth Avenue Food Festival is the perfect illustration of ethnic diversity in the city. You'll be able to taste foods from restaurants and cuisines from Afghani to Peruvian. See chapter 2.
- **Best New Year's Eve Celebration: Fireworks in Central Park.** Avoid the madness of Times Square and head to **Central Park** where, at midnight, fireworks are set off and a midnight running race commences. See chapter 2.
- **Best Free Event:** Perennial favorites **SummerStage** in Central Park, now drowning in corporate sponsorship and slowly becoming a "paid" event; and **Shakespeare in the Park,** which is becoming more of a showcase for the celebrity of the moment; are losing their luster, leaving **Lincoln Center Out of Doors** as the winner. I've seen many great performances at the 4-week festival each August, on the plaza of Lincoln Center, including jazz great Sonny Rollins, the traditional Spanish dance troupe, Danzas Espanolas, and a children's sing-along my son still talks fondly about. There is something for everyone at this wonderful free event. See chapter 9.
- **Best Performance Space:** There are few greater spaces in the world than **Carnegie Hall.** Visually and acoustically brilliant, Carnegie Hall attracts an amazing array of

talent. But remember: Never ask a New Yorker how you get there. (Practice, practice, practice!) See p. 305.

- **Best Jazz Club: Village Vanguard.** The acoustics and sight lines aren't great, but you can't do better for finding consistently good-quality jazz. The Vanguard is a New York institution. See p. 317.
- **Best Budget Jazz Club: Smoke.** This cozy Upper West Side jazz club is emerging as one of the best in the city. There's no cover charge Sunday through Thursday, with Tuesday, for the tremendous

"Hammond Organ" night and Wednesday, for the "Hot Pants Funk Sextet," not to be missed. See p. 316.

- **Best Underground Musicians:** You can hear a wide variety of music by undiscovered talent in subway stations, much of it very good. My favorite is **Classic Soul,** a melodious doo wop group. Try to catch them, or others, at one of the major subway stations like Columbus Circle, 34th Street, Times Square, or Union Square. For more on underground musicians, see chapter 9.

3 Best Low-Cost Hotel Bets

You'll likely spend more than you like on a hotel room; it's a fact of life in the big city. But New York has a wealth of wallet-friendly choices for bargain hunters who know where to look. For the details on these and other affordable hotels, see chapter 5.

- **Best Overall Value—Downtown:** It's hard to beat the **Cosmopolitan Hotel–TriBeCa,** 95 W. Broadway (© **888/895-9400;** www.cosmohotel.com), for value. Each of the small, comfy, modern rooms comes with its own petite but immaculate private bathroom for as little as $119 a night. The high-rent neighborhood is hip as can be and subway-convenient to the rest of the city. See p. 99.

  Also of note is the **New York City Howard Johnson Express Inn,** 135 E. Houston St. (© **800/406-1411** or 212/358-8844; www.hojo.com), which has introduced reliable hotel comforts to the gentrified Lower East Side. This new-in-2002 hotel has newly outfitted rooms and a friendly staff, both nicer than they have to be for the money. See p. 100.
- **Best Overall Value—Midtown:** The **Super 8 Hotel Times Square,**

59 W. 46th St. (© **800/567-7720;** www.applecorehotels.com). With its combination of location, quality, comforts, and space, at rates that are a bargain in any town, much less the Big Apple—as low as $89 double, with breakfast—this one is hard to beat. See p. 119.

The **Chelsea Savoy,** 204 W. 23rd St. (© **866/929-9353;** www.chelseasavoynyc.com), is another great choice, offering reliable comforts for an affordable price—no small thing in a hotel market where "budget" goes hand in hand with "quirky." The hallways are attractive and wide, the elevators are swift and silent, and the rooms have big closets and roomy, well-kept bathrooms with lots of counter space. See p. 105.

- **Best Overall Value—Uptown:** The **Hotel Newton,** 2528 Broadway (© **888/HOTEL-58;** www.newyorkhotel.com), doesn't expect you to put up with a tiny room or myriad inconveniences because you aren't spending a fortune. With rates starting at $85 double, you'll get more than your money's worth here—and you'll save an additional 10% if you're a AAA member. See p. 126.

The **Comfort Inn—Central Park West,** 31 W. 71st St. (© 800/ 228-5150; www.comfortinn. com), can be the best deal in town if you book at the right time. It's loaded with comforts and is in one of the city's best residential neighborhoods. You can sometimes find rates as low as $72 double—with breakfast! See p. 124.

- **Best Value for Bargain Hunters Who Don't Mind Sharing:** If you're willing to share a bathroom, you'll be pleased with the **Larchmont Hotel,** in the loveliest part of Greenwich Village at 27 W. 11th St. (© 212/989-9333; www.larchmonthotel.com). See p. 104.

- **Best Value for Bargain Hunters Who Do Mind Sharing:** Kudos to **SoHotel,** 341 Broome St. (© 212/ 226-1482; www.pioneerhotel. com), which has done something no one else has managed: offer clean, friendly accommodations with private bathrooms for just $77 double year-round. The staff is professional, the decor is more attractive than most hotels in the shoestring category, and the edge-of-Chinatown location is safe and convenient. See p. 99.

- **Best for Bargain Hunters Willing to Compromise: Chelsea Lodge,** 318 W. 20th St. (© 800/ 373-1116; www.chelsealodge. com), offers the perfect compromise: You'll have an in-room sink and shower, so all you have to share is a toilet in the hall. If you're willing to do that, you'll find yourself in one of the cutest, cleanest, most comfortable hotels in New York—and at one of the cheapest rates in town. One of my all-time budget favorites! See p. 104.

- **Best Service for the Budget-Minded:** The staff at the **Broadway Inn,** 264 W. 46th St. (© 800/ 826-6300; www.broadwayinn. com), might be the most helpful in the city. They're so committed to making their guests feel welcome that they give you a hot line number to call when you're out and about if you need directions, advice on where to eat, or any other assistance. And you thought New Yorkers weren't friendly! See p. 112.

- **Best for Creative Spirits:** Reminiscent of Warhol's Factory at the height of its creativity and style, the supercool **Gershwin Hotel,** 7 E. 27th St. (© 212/545-8000; www.gershwinhotel.com), is the winner in this category. Billy Name is the house photog; what more do I need to say? See p. 110.

- **Best for Families:** On the Upper West Side, one of the city's most kid-friendly residential neighborhoods, is **The Milburn,** 242 W. 76th St. (© 800/833-9622; www.milburnhotel.com), which offers the best value-for-dollar ratio on suites in town. A queen-size sleeper sofa in the living room makes the junior and one-bedroom suites large enough to accommodate four, and a kitchenette with microwave, minifridge, and coffeemaker means you can save on breakfast bills. Kids under 13 stay free. See p. 128.

- **Best for the Style-Conscious:** The **Habitat Hotel,** 130 E. 57th St. (© 800/497-6028; www. habitatny.com), is carving out a niche as the "upscale budget" choice among style-conscious consumers. The narrow rooms are fresh and outfitted with flair, and the neighborhood is about as high fashion as it gets. See p. 121.

Site Seeing: The Big Apple on the Web

The New York Convention & Visitors Bureau's official site, **www.nyc visit.com**, is an excellent resource offering information on the city, from trip-planning basics to tips on where to take the kids. But there's far more to be learned about New York in cyberspace.

Citysearch (www.newyork.citysearch.com) is the city's hippest general-information site, with reviews and listings for restaurants, shopping, hotels, attractions, and nightlife. It's not as up-to-the-minute as it used to be, but it's still an excellent source for current happenings. Beware the search engine: If you're looking for a specific restaurant or shop, you're best off heading to the "Restaurants" or "Shopping" page and searching from there—and it still may take a few tries to find what you're looking for.

New York Today (www.nytoday.com) is the online arts, leisure, and entertainment arm of the *New York Times.* The *Times* created this site for those of us who wanted access to their excellent cultural coverage and restaurant reviews without having to wade through the main site (www.nytimes.com), which requires you to register.

Tops these days may be **New York Metro** ⭐ **(www.nymetro.com)**, the online arm of glossy weekly magazine *New York.* New York Metro is the most up-to-date site covering city happenings. (Although keep in mind that these things can change by the moment.) The site is strong in restaurant and shopping coverage; the magazine's shopping columnists update the site daily with news of sales and bargains.

All of the city's high-profile weeklies also maintain sites that are very useful for current happenings, including:

- *Time Out New York:* www.timeoutny.com
- *The Village Voice:* www.villagevoice.com
- *The New Yorker:* www.newyorker.com
- *Paper:* www.papermag.com
- *New York Press:* www.nypress.com

For more on these city-focused magazines, see "Publications" in "Orientation," in chapter 4.

Digital City New York (www.digitalcity.com/newyork) is much like Citysearch, and good for an alternative view. **About.com** also maintains a somewhat useful New York page at **www.gonyc.about.com**.

For the most up-to-date information on Lower Manhattan and Ground Zero, visit the website of the **Downtown Alliance,** the stellar Business Improvement District so productive in Lower Manhattan both before and after the September 11, 2001, terrorist attacks, at **www. downtownny.com**.

In addition, you'll find subject-specific sites listed in the appropriate chapters of this book.

Another excellent choice is **The Marcel,** 201 E. 24th St. (© **888/66-HOTEL;** www.nyc hotels.com), whose mod designer-outfitted rooms go for just $125, sometimes less—and the lounge downstairs is one of the hottest in town.

Fashionistas who don't mind sacrificing space for style might try for one of the handful of $95 rooms at Ian Schrager's super-hip **Hudson,** 356 W. 58th St. (© **800/444-4786;** www.ian schragerhotels.com). See p. 116.

- **Best for Gay & Lesbian Travelers:** New York is such a hub of gay life and culture that virtually all of the city's hotels welcome gay and lesbian visitors. But if you're looking for like-minded folks, try the fabulous Hollywood-themed **Chelsea Pines Inn,** 317 W. 14th St. (© **888/546-2700;** www. chelseapinesinn.com; see p. 105), or the more low-key but equally welcoming **Colonial House Inn,** 318 W. 22nd St. (© **800/689-3779;** www.colonialhouseinn. com; see p. 107).

- **Best Freebies:** The **Travel Inn,** 515 W. 42nd St. (© **800/869-4630;** www.newyorkhotel.com), wins on *two* counts. First is the free garage parking—a $25-a-day value at minimum for visitors driving to the city and free

in-and-out privileges. Summer visitors can take advantage of the rooftop swimming pool and sun deck. The **Skyline Hotel** (see directly below) offers similar value-minded perks. See p. 119.

- **Best for Travelers with Disabilities:** The comfortable, budget-minded **Skyline Hotel,** 725 Tenth Ave. (© **800/433-1982;** www.skylinehotelny.com), has seven generously sized wheelchair-accessible rooms, ramps, and fire-safety alarms for deaf and blind visitors, plus free parking. See p. 119.

- **Best Splurge:** The Art Deco–style **Hotel Metro,** 45 W. 35th St. (© **800/356-3870;** www.hotel metronyc.com), is a midpriced Midtown gem that feels much more expensive than it is, with stylish furnishings, marble bath-rooms, an attentive staff, and a rooftop terrace with the best view of the Empire State Building in town. You'll get a surprisingly good value for your dollar here, and free continental breakfast softens the blow. See p. 116.

4 Best Low-Cost Dining Bets

One of the joys of being in New York is that there's fabulous food at nearly every turn—and you don't have to whip out a platinum card to pay for it. Go ethnic—Chinese, Japanese, Jewish, Italian, Mexican, and much more—to indulge in the best cheap eats anywhere. For the details on these and other terrific affordable city restaurants, see chapter 6.

- **Best Newcomer: Celeste,** 502 Amsterdam Ave. (© **212/874-4559**). Small but special, Celeste's homemade pastas, special "frittis" (fried appetizers), and a wood-burning oven that turns out incredible pizzas make this a welcome addition to not only

the Upper West Side, but all Manhattan.

- **Best Chinese:** With all the culinary wonders that Chinatown has to offer, this is a tough choice. But **Joe's Shanghai,** 9 Pell St. (© **212/233-8888**), is the best of *many* good options. Now, how do they get the soup inside their famous soup dumplings? See p. 142.

- **Best Affordable French:** The charming, affordable Chelsea creperie **Rue des Crepes,** 104 Eighth Ave. (© **212/242-9900**), is my favorite in this category, thanks to a winning combination of food, setting, service, and low prices. See p. 163.

- **Best Affordable Italian: Lupa,** 170 Thompson St. (© 212/982-5089), a fantastic Roman-style trattoria and *salumeria* (Italian grocery store). Kudos to Batali for being the one celebrity chef in town who doesn't think you should have to spend a fortune on a first-class meal. See p. 158.

- **Best Diner:** The eclectic **Big Nick's Burger and Pizza Joint,** 2175 Broadway (© 212/362-9232), has offered culinary comfort any time of day or night for over 40 years. The varieties of burgers you can order are as mind-boggling as the collection of unidentifiable celebrity photos on the walls.

- **Best Burger: Burger Joint,** at Le Parker Meridien hotel, 118 W. 57th St. (© 212/708-7460). Who woulda thunk a fancy hotel like **Le Parker Meridien** would be the home to a place that serves great burgers at great prices?

- **Best Pizza: Patsy's Pizzeria,** 2287 First Ave. (© 212/534-9783). This great East Harlem pizzeria has been cranking out coal-oven pies since 1932. It was a favorite of Frank Sinatra, who used to have Patsy's pizzas shipped to him in Las Vegas. You can also order by the slice, but do it only if the pie is fresh out of the oven.

- **Best Early-Bird Dining Bargain:** French bistro and wine bar **Le Pere Pinard,** 175 Ludlow St. (© 212/777-4917), offers three courses—starter, entree, and dessert—for just $14 to diners who order between 5 and 7pm. It's an excellent deal, especially since you could spend that much on just a main course. Pair it with a glass of *vin* from the extensive, affordable list, and you have a memorable meal for 20 bucks. See p. 147.

- **Best Breakfast:** Uptown, head to **Good Enough To Eat,** but try to avoid weekends when the wait sometimes can last until lunch. See p. 184.

  Downtown, head to TriBeCa fave **Bubby's,** 120 Hudson St. (© 212/219-0666)—and don't be surprised if Harvey Keitel is chowing down on a monster-size omelet at the next table. See p. 140.

- **Best Late-Night Hangout:** Half authentic-French bistro, half all-American diner, **Florent,** 69 Gansevoort St. (© 212/989-5779), is the hipster crowd's favorite after-hours hangout. Thanks to its good food, great people-watching, and sense of humor, it's mine, too. See p. 158.

  In a neighborhood notoriously underserved in the late-night department, we-never-close **Pigalle,** 790 Eighth Ave. (© 212/489-2233), deserves props for offering affordable French fare to after-hours Theater District crowds. See p. 173.

- **Best Fast Food:** For value, it's hard to beat the terrific, health-minded Tex-Mex fare at local chain **Burritoville,** at 36 Water St. (© 212/747-1100) and throughout the city. See p. 138.

  It's also hard to beat **Emerald Planet,** 2 Great Jones St. (© 212/353-9727), whose wraps and smoothies are made with fresh ingredients and a world of ethnic influences. The Rockefeller Center location makes a delicious, healthful lunch stop during a day of Midtown sightseeing. See p. 158.

- **Best Old New York Experience: Eisenberg's Coffee Shop,** 174 Fifth Ave. (© 212/675-5096), has served the same retro fare since 1929—and prices are retro, too. New Yorkers consider this the best tuna salad in town, but the

Reuben is my ticket to culinary happiness. See p. 164.

In the *Noo Yawk* deli wars, **Katz's Delicatessen,** 205 E. Houston St. (C **212/254-2246**), is the choice among those who know their kreplach, knishes, and pastrami. No cutesy sandwiches here—just top-notch classics. The all-beef wieners are the best in a town known for its dogs. What's more, prices are a fraction of what those tourist-targeted Midtown delis charge. See p. 146.

- **Best for Families:** It's hard to beat **Virgil's Real BBQ,** 152 W. 44th St. (C **212/921-9494**), for eat-with-your-hands fun. See p. 175.

Kids of all ages love **Serendipity 3,** 225 E. 60th St. (C **212/838-3531**), a classic ice-cream parlor just like your childhood memories, but *better.* See p. 188. For more kid-friendly choices, see "Family-Friendly Restaurants," in chapter 6.

- **Best for Vegetarians:** A perennial favorite among vegetarians is the Asian-inspired fare at **Zen Palate,** 34 Union Square E. (C **212/614-9345**). See p. 166.

I prefer **Pongal,** 110 Lexington Ave. (C **212/696-9458**), which re-creates the flavorful vegetarian fare of southern India—and thanks to a daily visit from a rabbi, it's kosher, too! See p. 177.

- **Best Baked Goods and Sweets:** There's a lot of competition in this category, but the ultimate kudos go to Franco-Brussels import **Le Pain Quotidien,** 100 Grand St. (C **212/625-9009**), for its fresh-baked breads (baked in small batches five times daily) and scrumptious pastries and sweets, served in a SoHo-loft-goes-farmhouse setting. (You'll find locations in the Flatiron District and on the Upper West and Upper East Sides, too.) See p. 148.

- **Best Cheap Meal: Gray's Papaya,** 2090 Broadway (C **212/799-0243**). Though the $2.45 "recession special," two hot dogs and a fruit drink, is almost a $1 increase from the previous recession, it's still a bargain. But is it any good? Witness the lines out the door every day for lunch.

- **Best Ice Cream: Brooklyn Ice Cream Factory,** Fulton Ferry Landing Pier, Brooklyn (C **718/246-3963**). This is the perfect reward for a brisk walk across the Brooklyn Bridge. Have a rich, homemade ice cream with a view of the Manhattan skyline; a hard combination to beat.

- **Best Bagel: H&H Bagels,** 2239 Broadway (C **212/595-8003;** www.handhbagel.com). Competition is fierce in this category, but despite breaking the $1 barrier for the price for a bagel, H&H still makes the best. For more on bagels, see the box "Bagel Power" on p. 183.

- **Best 24-Hour Restaurant: Veselka,** 144 Second Ave. (C **212/228-9682**). This Ukrainian diner will meet almost all your food needs any time of day or night. If you want borscht at midnight, you can get it. If you want French toast at 4am, you can have it. It's a comfort to know they will make pretty much whatever you want when you want it. See p. 153.

- **Best All-You-Can-Eat Buffet: Charles' Southern Style Kitchen,** 2841 Frederick Douglass Blvd. (C **212/926-4313**). Not only is this Harlem restaurant the best all-you-can-eat buffet, it is also the best soul-food restaurant in the city. For $9.95 on weekdays, $11.95 on weekends, the down-home offerings here will tempt you to make an embarrassing number of visits to the buffet line. Come hungry!

2

Planning an Affordable Trip to New York City

In the pages that follow, you'll find everything you need to know to handle the practical details of planning your trip in advance—airlines and area airports, a calendar of events, resources for those with special needs, and much more—plus time-tested advice on how to save money at every turn.

1 65 Money-Saving Tips

Here are some tips to help you keep your travel costs down:

1. **Buy a package deal.** A package that includes transportation and hotel for one price might be the best bargain. In some cases, you'll get airfare, accommodations, and transportation to and from the airport, plus extras—maybe a sightseeing tour or restaurant and shopping discount coupons—for less than the cost of a room alone. For details on where to find the best packages, see "Money-Saving Package Deals" on p. 46.

2. **Order the discount-loaded *Entertainment* book.** Each annual edition, which sells for $15 (or $25 in retail stores), is packed with discounts on hotel stays (including top hotels at 50% off the rack rate), dining (including many two-for-one deals), and attractions and entertainment. You can preview discounts online. The coupons are good for the whole year, so you can use the book on multiple trips, or pass it on to friends visiting later in the year. To order, call © 888/213-SAVE or go to www.entertainment.com. Even if you don't buy it, visit the website; at press time, there were many

discounts ranging from restaurants to attractions, free for the printing.

3. **Buy a *New York for Less* guidebook.** The big value in this guide ($19.95) is its discount card, which offers hundreds of discounts from 20% to 50% at restaurants, attractions (including the Empire State Building), shops, theaters, and nightspots. The card is good for up to four people for up to 8 days and comes with a handbook detailing the places that honor *New York for Less.* It even includes a phone card that gives you $8 in free calls. To order, call © 888/463-6753 or 937/846-1411; or visit www.for-less.com, where you can also view a list of participating establishments.

4. **Check with NYC & Company for special offers.** The city's Convention & Visitors Bureau is very good about keeping visitors apprised of special offers. They offer programs and deals, from savings cards for discounts at shops and attractions to package deals. There's no telling what will be on offer, but check for the latest at www.nycvisit.com.

5. **Flash your AAA, AARP, military, senior, or student ID card.**

American Automobile Association membership is valuable for hotel discounts, often in the neighborhood of 10%, but may also score savings on Gray Line bus tours, harbor cruises, and the like. Seniors and students find a valid ID gets reduced admission to most attractions. Military and government folks should always ask about discounts; they can get as much as 40% off. Also check your corporate affiliations; a friend of mine who works at Kraft gets free admission to every cultural attraction that Philip Morris underwrites. The rule of thumb is to always ask.

WHEN TO GO

6. **Choose your season carefully.** How much you pay for your hotel room and airfare depends on the season. Prices can vary by hundreds of dollars, depending on the time of year. From January to mid-April is best for bargains, with summer from June to mid-August being second best. Spring and fall are the busiest, most expensive seasons, as is the Christmas season, but negotiating a decent rate is possible, especially in spring. Budget-minded travelers should skip Christmas and New Year's. Thanksgiving is a bargain hunter's delight for accommodations. For more on this, see "Money Matters" in "When to Go," later in this chapter.

GETTING TO NEW YORK CITY
AIR TRAVEL

7. **Plan ahead; be flexible.** You'll likely pay a lot less than full fare if you buy a 7-, 14-, or 21-day advance-purchase ticket. If you stay over Saturday or travel on Tuesday, Wednesday, or Thursday, you'll likely save even more. You can often save by opting for connecting flights rather than nonstop.

Sure, it's more time-consuming, but if saving money is your top priority, this can be a way to do it. Airlines won't generally volunteer this information, so be sure to ask.

8. **Always ask for the lowest fare.** Yes, reservations and travel agents should take for granted that you want the lowest possible fare—but they don't always do so. Be sure to ask specifically for the lowest fare. As with every aspect of your trip, ask about discounts for groups, seniors, children, and students.

9. **Consider all three airports when you're shopping.** Fares can be markedly different depending on which airport you fly into—LaGuardia, JFK, or Newark—and none of them are that far from Manhattan. Continental, for instance, almost always has cheaper flights into Newark because it's one of its hubs; United is another airline that often has cheaper prices into Newark. Even though it's in New Jersey, Newark can be more convenient to your Manhattan destination than the other airports, especially now that the Newark AirTrain links the airport to midtown Manhattan.

10. **Keep an eye out for airfare sales.** Check newspapers for advertised discounts or call the airlines and ask if any special deals are available. You'll almost never see a sale during July and August or during the Thanksgiving or Christmas seasons, but in periods of low-volume travel, you should be able to get a cross-country flight for $400 or less.

The lowest-priced fares are often nonrefundable, require a Saturday-night stay, and carry penalties for changing dates of travel. So, when you're quoted a fare, know exactly what the restrictions are before you commit.

11. **Try the discount carriers, too.** Don't forget to check with the no-frills airlines including jetBlue, AirTran, and Southwest (which flies into Long Island's MacArthur Airport, about 50 miles east of Manhattan). See p. 44 for a run-down of discount carriers that fly into area airports.

12. **Check for discounted fares with consolidators.** Also known as "bucket shops," consolidators are a good place to find low fares, often below even the airlines' discounted rates. Basically, these companies buy airfare in bulk and pass some of the savings on to you. Before you pay, ask for a confirmation number and then call the airline to confirm your seat. Be prepared to book with a different consolidator—and there are many—if the airline can't confirm your reservation. Also be aware that consolidator tickets are usually nonrefundable or come with stiff cancellation penalties.

I've found great deals at **Cheap Tickets** ☆ (☎ 888/922-8849; www.cheaptickets.com); I almost always do better by calling than I do on their website. **STA Travel** (☎ 800/329-9537; www.stravel.com), which recently acquired Council Travel, caters to young travelers, but offers discount fares to people of all ages. Other reliable consolidators include **1800FlyCheap.com** (☎ 800/359-2432; www.1800fly cheap.com); **TFI Tours International** (☎ 800/745-8000 or 212/736-1140; www.lowestairprice.com), which serves as a clearinghouse for unused seats; and "rebators" like **Travel Avenue** (☎ 800/333-3335; www.travelavenue.com), which rebate part of their commissions to you.

13. **Search the Internet for cheap fares.** You can tap into the same databases once accessible only to travel agents through sites like **Travelocity.com, Expedia.com,** and **Orbitz.com.** You might also check out **Qixo** (www.qixo.com), another search engine that allows you to search for flights and accommodations from some 20 airline and travel-planning sites (such as Travelocity) at once.

Going straight to the source can be an excellent strategy, since the major carriers frequently offer "Internet only" sales. A fare can pop up today that wasn't available yesterday, and won't be around tomorrow. Or check megasites that compile comprehensive lists of last-minute specials, notably **Smarter Living** (www.smarterliving.com) and **WebFlyer** (www.webflyer.com).

If you don't care who your carrier is, consider **Priceline** (www.priceline.com), which lets you "name your price" for airline tickets (as well as hotel rooms and rental cars). For airline tickets, you have to accept any flight between 6am and 10pm on the dates you've selected. Tickets are nonrefundable, and while they say no frequent-flier miles are awarded, we've been given them more than once.

A word of warning: Avoid on-line auctions. Sites that auction airline tickets and frequent-flier miles are the No. 1 perpetrators of Internet fraud, according to the National Consumers League.

14. **Sign up for e-mail notification of last-minute specials.** Each week, airlines send subscribers a list of discounted flights, usually leaving that Friday or Saturday and returning the next Monday or Tuesday. You can sign up at each airline's website; for URLs, see "By Plane" in "Getting There," later in this chapter.

Frommers.com: The Complete Travel Resource

For an excellent travel-planning resource, we highly recommend **Frommers.com** (www.frommers.com). We're a little biased, of course, but we guarantee that you'll find the travel tips, reviews, monthly vacation giveaways, and online-booking capabilities thoroughly indispensable. Among the special features are our popular **Message Boards,** where Frommer's readers post queries and share advice (sometimes even our authors show up to answer questions); **Frommers.com Newsletter,** for the latest travel bargains and insider travel secrets; and **Frommer's Destinations Section,** where you'll get expert travel tips, hotel and dining recommendations, and advice on the sights to see for more than 3,000 destinations around the globe. When your research is done, the **Online Reservations System** (www.frommers.com/book_a_trip) takes you to Frommer's preferred online partners for booking your vacation at affordable prices.

15. **Know when sales start.** You can often score the best online deal if you know when sales start, since last-minute deals may vanish in minutes. So, if you have a favorite site or airline, find out when last-minute deals are released to the public. (For example, Southwest's specials are posted every Tues at 12:01am CST.)

16. **Book a seat on a charter.** Most charter operators advertise and sell their seats through travel agents, making these local professionals your best source of information for flights. Before deciding to take a charter, check the restrictions: You might be asked to purchase a package tour, pay in advance, be amenable to a change in departure date, fly on an airline you're not familiar with, and/or pay stiff penalties if you cancel—as well as be understanding if the charter doesn't fill and is canceled up to 10 days before departure. Summer charters fill up more quickly and are almost sure to fly, but if you go with one, consider cancellation and baggage insurance.

OTHER TRANSPORTATION OPTIONS

17. **Consider taking a train or bus instead of flying.** Traveling by train or bus may be cheaper than flying. And if the cost of your train ticket is the same as an airline ticket, train travel still saves you money because you'll come into and out of Midtown without the additional cost of airport transfers. If you're as close to New York as Boston, Philly, or Washington, D.C., a train or bus can save time, now that Amtrak has added the new high-speed Acela trains. Your cheapest transportation method will always be the bus, but keep in mind that unless it's an express, it can take a lot of time.

18. **Have a flexible schedule when booking train travel, and always ask for the lowest fare.** When you're offered a fare, always ask if you can do better by traveling at different times or days. You can often save money by traveling at off-peak hours and on weekends. Don't forget to ask for discounts

for kids, seniors, passengers with disabilities, military personnel, or anything else that you think might qualify you for a lower fare.

19. **Keep an eye out for sales.** Go to www.amtrak.com and click on "Rail Sale," where you'll find discounts on select routes. Keep in mind, though, that if you buy a sale ticket, it is not refundable and cannot be exchanged. While you're online, check the "Savings & Promotions" page for discounted and/or value-added deals. **Greyhound** advertises sales at www.greyhound.com. They usually have a number of money-saving deals, ranging from "Friendly Savers" that let you travel for as little as $49 to free companion fares.

20. **Make reservations as soon as possible.** As with the airlines, discounts on buses and trains are often based on advanced purchase.

GETTING AROUND NEW YORK CITY

21. **Don't rent a car.** Driving is a nightmare and parking is ridiculously expensive. It's much easier to use public transportation.

22. **Take a bus or the subway from the airport.** You have to allot a bit more time, but public transportation offers great savings over taxis and car services. A shuttle bus connects JFK Airport to the A train, which whisks you into the city for $2. The M60 bus comes into Manhattan from LaGuardia for the same price. From Newark, regularly scheduled buses can drop you off around the city for around $10, and the AirTrain connects the airport with Manhattan for just $11.

23. **Use the subway and bus to get around the city.** The transit system is probably the city's best bargain. It's safe, relatively clean, quick, efficient, and cheap. Use taxis only late at night, when trains and buses can be few and far between, or when traveling a short distance in a group of three or four, when the fare might be less than multiple subway or bus fares.

24. **Buy a MetroCard.** If you're going to be in the city for a few days, or you're traveling in a group (up to four people can use a MetroCard at any given time), buy a $20 pay-per-ride MetroCard, which will get you 12 rides for the price of 10, and allow you to transfer within a 2-hour period of each ride you use. If you're going to do a lot of running around, consider a $7 daily **Fun Pass** or a $21 **7-Day MetroCard,** each of which allows unlimited rides for the life of the card. There's one strong caveat, however: Every person has to have his or her own unlimited-use MetroCard; you can't double-up as you can with pay-per-ride MetroCards.

25. **In the daytime, walk.** No other American city is more welcoming or so rewarding to explore on foot. Walking will save you money—and work off all the meals you'll no doubt buy with the savings.

ACCOMMODATIONS

26. **Stay uptown or downtown.** The advantages of a Midtown location are overrated, especially when saving money is your object. Manhattan is a petite island, and the subway can whisk you anywhere in minutes. You'll get the best value by staying in the neighborhoods where real New Yorkers live, such as Greenwich Village, Chelsea, Murray Hill, or—my favorite neighborhood for space-seekers and bargain hunters—the Upper West Side. These are the neighborhoods where real New

Yorkers hang out, too, so you won't want for good eats, nightlife, or Big Apple bustle.

27. **Visit over a weekend.** If your trip includes a weekend, you might save big. Business hotels tend to empty, and rooms that go for $300 or more Monday through Thursday can drop to as low as $150 or less once the execs have gone home. These deals are prevalent in the Financial District, but are often available in Midtown, too. See "Deal-Making with the Chains" on p. 106 for tips on packages.

28. **Watch for advertised discounts.** Scan ads in the travel section of your Sunday paper, which can be an excellent source for up-to-the-minute hotel deals. Also check the back of the travel section of the Sunday *New York Times,* where the best weekend deals and other hotel bargains are usually listed.

29. **Don't be afraid to bargain.** Always ask for a lower price than the first one quoted. Most rack rates include commissions for travel agents, which many hotels will cut if you make your own reservations and haggle a bit. Ask whether a less-expensive room is available than the first one mentioned or if any special rates apply: corporate, student, military, seniors. Mention membership in AAA, AARP, frequent-flier programs, corporate or military organizations, or unions, which might entitle you to deals. The chains, such as Best Western and Comfort Inn, tend to be good about trying to save you money, but reservations agents often won't volunteer the information; you have to pull it out of them.

30. **Dial direct.** When booking a room in a chain hotel, call the hotel's local line, as well as the toll-free number, and see where you get the best deal. The clerk who runs the place is more likely to know about booking patterns and will often grant deep discounts in order to fill up.

31. **Rely on a qualified professional.** Certain hotels give travel agents discounts in exchange for steering business their way, so if you're shy about bargaining, an agent may be better equipped to negotiate discounts for you.

32. **Shop online.** New York hotels often offer "Internet-only" deals that can save you 10% to 20% off what you'd pay if you booked by telephone. Also, hotels often advertise all of their available weekend and other package deals on their websites.

Also try such booking engines as **Travelocity.com, Expedia.com,** and **Orbitz.com.** I've found that Expedia, in particular, sometimes offers excellent rates you can't find elsewhere. Expedia requires you to pay up front, but you can usually cancel up to 72 hours in advance for a $25 fee. (Check the exact rules.)

Some of the discount reservations agencies (see tip 33) have sites that allow you to book online. **American Automobile Association** members may be able to score the best discounts by booking at **www.aaa.com**.

33. **Investigate reservations services.** These work like consolidators, buying up or reserving rooms in bulk, and then dealing them to customers at a profit. You can get 10% to 50% off; but remember, these discounts apply to rack rates, prices that people rarely end up paying. You may get a decent rate, but call the hotel directly to see if you can do better.

Start with **Quikbook** (© **800/789-9887** or 212/779-7666; www.quikbook.com), the best of the bunch since they book more than 100 hotels, require no prepayment, and allow you to make changes and cancellations (penalties depend on the hotel). Another good bet is **Hotel ConXions** (© 800/522-9991 or 212/840-8686; www.hotelconxions.com). Both Quikbook and Hotel ConXions have guaranteed room blocks in select properties, and can sometimes get you into a hotel that's otherwise sold out. You can also try the **Hotel Reservations Network,** also known as HotelDiscount!com (© 800/364-0801; www.180096 HOTEL.com or www.hotel discount.com), and **Accommodations Express** (© 800/950-4685; www.accommodationsexpress. com).

Important tips: Never just rely on a reservations service. Do a little homework; compare the rack rates to the discount rates to see what kind of deal you're getting. Always compare the rate a reservations service offers you with the rate direct from the hotel. If you're being offered a stay in a hotel I haven't recommended, do more research on it. It's not a deal if you end up at a dump.

34. **Take a chance with Priceline.** Tales abound of people who have scored luxury rooms for a $50 bid on the "name your price" site Priceline (**www.priceline.com**). If you're a gambler, Priceline can be a great way to win the budget war. You won't know the name of your hotel until it's bought and paid for, but you can choose your neighborhood and the class of hotel (from economy to deluxe), and Priceline guarantees that you'll stay in a nationally recognized, name-brand or independent hotel trusted for their quality, service, and amenities.

35. **If you find a rate that seems like a good value, book it early.** If somebody quotes you a good rate, don't assume it'll be waiting for you in a month, a week, or even a day. As hotels fill up and the number of empty rooms goes down, rates go up.

36. **If you find yourself without a room at the last minute, work it to your advantage.** I never recommend coming to town without reservations. But if you find yourself without a room, you might be able to strike a bargain. As the hours progress, the hotel becomes more anxious to fill empty rooms and will lower the rate to get your business. I've seen desk clerks sell $179 rooms for $79. But remember—this is a risky way to go, because if the hotel is full, you're out of luck.

37. **Be willing to share a bathroom.** For the best bargains, do as the Europeans do: Share a hall bathroom with your fellow travelers. Usually there are two or three bathrooms to a floor, often with separate rooms for the toilet and the shower and/or tub so all the facilities aren't tied up at once. If you're on a tight budget, you'll be able to stay at a nicer hotel than if you insist on a private bathroom. Many rooms have private sinks, so you can brush your teeth or wash your face in your room. A couple of very good bargain-rate places, the Chelsea Lodge and the Chelsea Pines Inn, have private in-room showers, so the only thing you have to share is the toilet.

38. **Consider a suite.** It sounds like a splurge, but if you're traveling with another couple or your family, a suite can be a bargain. They're cheaper than two hotel rooms. The living room almost always features a sofa bed, and

there's often a kitchenette where you can prepare coffee and light meals. Some places charge for more than two guests; some don't.

39. **If you're traveling with the kids, stay at a hotel that lets them stay for free.** Most hotels add a surcharge—from $10 to $30 per night—for each extra person beyond two sharing a room. So if you're traveling with kids, choose a hotel that lets them stay free. Age limits for free kid stays can range from 10 to 18. Even if the hotel usually charges for kids, it might be willing to drop this charge to draw you in, so do ask.

40. **Save on hotel tax by booking an apartment or home stay.** Booking a hosted or unhosted apartment stay can save you dollars on taxes. These agencies are able to charge just 8.625% sales tax, as opposed to 13¼% plus $2 per night for a regular hotel room. Even better: Tax is often included in the rates quoted by booking agencies; thus, a $130 room is just $130, while a regular hotel will charge you $149.23 per night for a $130 room. A tax loophole eliminated the tax on many 7-night or longer stays (which are classified as short-term leases rather than hotel stays). Be sure to get the specific rules at booking to avoid any surprises at bill time. See "Home Stay Sweet Home Stay," below, for recommended agencies.

41. **Look into group or long-stay discounts.** If you come as part of a group, you may be able to negotiate a bargain because the hotel can guarantee occupancy in a number of rooms. If you're planning a long stay (5–7 days or more), you might qualify for a discount, so be sure to ask.

42. **If you're on a shoestring budget, book a hostel bed.** You'll have no privacy—you'll share a room with fellow travelers and all facilities are common—but there's no arguing with the rate. The largest hostel in the **Hostelling International–American Youth Hostels** system houses travelers in bunk-bedded rooms for $29 to $35 per person per night. You'll save about $3 a night if you become an AYH member. Also consider the dorms at the **Chelsea Star,** the **Chelsea International Hostel, Chelsea Center Hostel,** the **Big Apple Hostel,** the East Village's **Whitehouse Hotel of New York,** Harlem's **Park View Hostel** and **Sugar Hill International House,** and the **Central Park Hostel & Inn.** See chapter 5 for listings. For additional hostel possibilities, surf to **The Hostel Handbook** (www.hostelhandbook.com) and **Hostels.com** on the Internet.

43. **Try the Y.** The Y isn't as cheap as hostel living, but the facilities are better. The **YMCA of Greater New York** (© 212/630-9600; www.ymcanyc.org) has eight residences throughout the city's five boroughs. You'll have a private room (some have private bathrooms) and access to the on-site fitness center—many feature state-of-the-art equipment, pools, and exercise classes—free. The Y is popular with families, older travelers, and singles. Contact the **West Side YMCA,** adjacent to Central Park at 5 W. 63rd St. (© 212/875-4100), and the **Vanderbilt Y,** 224 E. 47th St. (© 212/756-9600), as far in advance as possible, as these locations are popular. Manhattan locations are the most expensive, with prices starting around $80; if you can stay in Harlem, Brooklyn, or Queens, nightly rates start as low as $40. For information, visit

Finds Home Stay Sweet Home Stay

New York apartment or home stays can be a great way to go. They usually fall on the lower end of the price continuum and can range from spartan to splendid, and from a hosted bedroom in a private home to an unhosted, fully equipped apartment. No matter what, you can pretty much guarantee that you'll get more for your money than with a regular hotel room.

The city's best-kept accommodations secret is **Homestay New York** ✻ (✆ and fax **718/434-2071;** www.homestayny.com). Lovely owner Helayne Wagner can book you into a private room with a family (including her own) that welcomes travelers. Homes are in residential neighborhoods in Brooklyn, Queens, or Upper Manhattan, all within a half-hour of Midtown or downtown via subway or bus, and most are beautifully restored 19th- and early-20th-century houses. Not only can this save you money, it can be fun, too: Visitors are matched to hosts by age, interests, and occupation, and the hosts are more than happy to provide advice and assistance. You'll be the only in-house guest, so it's much like staying with a friend who delights in seeing you happy and enjoying the city.

Rates run $100 to $130 single or double, with shared or private bathroom depending on the home. Most rooms have TV, air-conditioning, and a small fridge, and towels are provided. Buffet breakfast is included; the price also often includes a welcome dinner, plus a farewell dinner if your stay lasts 5 or more days. Also included are free MetroCards and phone cards (values depend on the length of your stay), plus Broadway show information and discount coupons for live performances, comedy clubs, and other entertainment. In summer, guests staying 7 nights or more get a 3-hour evening cruise. With these extras, Homestay New York is an excellent value. Tax is included, which saves you an additional 13.25% plus $2 per night over what you'd pay in a hotel. Helayne also has access to theater discounts that you can't get on your own. A 3-night minimum is requested, and no credit cards are accepted. Children 3 and over are welcome.

A number of agencies can book you into a B&B room (hosted or unhosted) or a private apartment. The place to start is **Manhattan**

www.ymcanyc.org and click on "Guest Rooms & Group Rates."

44. **Dorm it.** At Columbia University, **International House,** 500 Riverside Dr. on the Upper West Side (✆ **212/316-8436** or 212/316-8473; www.ihouse-nyc.org), offers dormitory-style accommodations in July and August, priced at $40 or $45 depending on your length of stay (up to 20 nights);

you must be 18 or older to stay. International House has 11 guest rooms with private bathrooms and maid service, ranging from $110 to $150 for up to four people. These are especially reasonable if there are three or four of you, or if you're traveling in the autumn, when everybody else is charging an arm and a leg. Book well ahead.

Getaways ✩ (☏ **212/956-2010**; www.manhattangetaways.com). Judith Glynn maintains a beautifully kept and managed network of bed-and-breakfast rooms (from $105 nightly) and unhosted apartments (from $145) around the city. There's a 3-night minimum, and credit cards are accepted. Another decent bet is **A Hospitality Company** (☏ **800/987-1235** or 212/813-2244; www.hospitalityco.com), with more than 300 apartments they own and manage around Manhattan starting at $125 a night, or $675 weekly for a basic studio. These are rather sparsely furnished apartments and the company offers little in the way of service (it took me 5 days to get my TV fixed when I was displaced from home by renovation), but the apartments are clean and do the trick. There's no minimum stay, and credit cards are accepted. Optional cleaning services are available for longer stays. Additional agencies that can book you into a B&B room or a private apartment, with prices starting at $90 nightly, include **As You Like It** (☏ **800/277-0413** or 212/695-0191; www.furnapts.com), **Abode Apartment Rentals** (☏ **800/835-8880** or 212/472-2000; www.abodenyc.com), **CitySonnet** (☏ **212/614-3034**; www.citysonnet.com), **Manhattan Lodgings** (☏ **212/677-7616**; www.manhattanlodgings.com), and **New York Habitat** (☏ **212/255-8018**; www.nyhabitat.com).

Another advantage to booking a B&B or apartment accommodation is that taxes are lower, usually just 8¼% (as opposed to 13¼% plus $2 per night for a regular hotel room).

A few words of warning: If you go this route, keep in mind that you won't have the amenities that a hotel—even a budget hotel—can offer, such as maid service and tour planning. In fact, many accommodations called "B&Bs" don't even offer breakfast, so be sure to ask. You'll have a host on hand to offer personal assistance if you book through Homestay New York. I've received complaints about agencies that offer one thing and deliver another, so get all promises in writing and an exact total up front. Try to pay by credit card if possible, so you can dispute payment if the agency fails to live up to its promises.

45. **Make a spiritual connection.** Fully outfitted and maid-serviced guest rooms are offered at Columbia's **Union Theological Seminary** (☏ **212/280-1313**; www.uts.columbia.edu), for a pricey $130 to $175 per night.

More affordable accommodations are offered at **The House of the Redeemer,** a former Vanderbilt mansion on the Upper East Side, just steps from Museum Mile, at 7 E. 95th St. (☏ **212/289-0399**; www.houseoftheredeemer.org). This Episcopal worship center offers short-term accommodations (2–6 nights) to adult travelers of all faiths when groups are not in residence. Accommodations are $60 single, $75 double with hall bathroom, $100 double with private bathroom. Rooms are not available from late June to early September.

The Community of the Holy Spirit, an Episcopal monastic community of nuns, welcomes guests into their simple but neat private rooms (most with shared bathrooms) at **St. Hilda's House,** 621 W. 113th St. (© **212/932-8098;** www.chssisters.org). Rates are $65 single, $110 to $130 double, and $165 triple. Because this is a contemplative environment, it's best suited for visitors looking for the same. You are welcome to share meals with the sisters, but no meals are served and no guests are welcomed on Monday. Reserve well in advance, as these accommodations fill up early.

46. **Do as little business as possible through the hotel.** Any service the hotel offers will cost you dearly. You can find dry cleaners or other services in most areas of Manhattan. Find out before you dial whether your hotel imposes a surcharge on local or long-distance calls; it might be cheaper to use the pay phone in the lobby.

47. **If you're driving into the city and will need to garage your car, check parking rates with the hotel before you book.** Many hotels negotiate discounts at nearby garages. Choose a hotel that has a good rate, or you could pay a fortune to park (negating any savings you've earned by booking a cheap hotel).

DINING

48. **Book a room with a kitchenette.** This allows you to eat some meals in. Even if you only prepare breakfast, you're bound to save money this way.

49. **Stay at a hotel, guesthouse, or bed-and-breakfast that includes breakfast.** And be sure to confirm that it's included before you book, because some city guesthouses keep rates down by not offering breakfast. Ask what's included; the offering will most likely be a limited continental breakfast.

50. **Use any coupons you can get your hands on.** The New York Convention & Visitors Bureau offers a free visitor's guide that includes coupons in the back. Even if you order one in advance (see "Visitor Information," below), stop in at the local visitor centers, where the wall racks sometimes have coupons and advertisements for freebies, two-for-ones, and dining discounts. Also consider buying one or both of the discount/coupon books recommended in tips 2, 3, and 4 above. Before you leave home, check the deals offered through the **Playbill Online Theatre Club** (www.playbillclub.com), which often include a few dining discounts. If you use a dining discount coupon, remember to tip your waiter based on the full value of the meal; he's on a budget, too.

51. **Eat ethnic.** New York probably has the best collection of ethnic restaurants in the country, and the best offer first-class eats for low, low prices. Chinatown is always a good bet for top-quality meals for a pittance, as are the restaurants on East 6th Street east of Second Avenue, known as Little India. Jewish delis are first-rate in Manhattan—and the pastrami can keep you fueled for days.

52. **During warm weather, picnic.** New York is full of marvelous delis, greenmarkets, and gourmet groceries where you can assemble a delicious, affordable meal. The city is rich with parks that serve as great picnic spots: Battery Park, Bryant Park, and Union Square—and perhaps best of all, Central Park. If you don't feel like going

through the hassle of assembling a picnic at a grocery, try takeout, which will save you the cost of the tip you'd leave if you ate in.

53. **Eat street food.** Although dirty-water hot dogs and pretzels still have their appeal, New York's street-food offerings have expanded considerably. You'll find vendors all over the city hawking soups, gyros, falafels, baked potatoes with a variety of toppings, fresh fruit, and more. The best vendors congregate in high-end business districts, such as around Rockefeller Center in Midtown (vendors often line up just off Sixth Ave.; 50th St. is a hot corner) and in the Financial District. Sixth Avenue is lined with plazas where you can enjoy your alfresco lunch, and Lower Manhattan offers a wealth of even more pleasant open spaces.

54. **Order the prix-fixe special.** Fixed-price specials that include appetizers, side dishes, and dessert (as well as beverages in some cases) will almost always get you more bang for your buck. Just one example: Diners willing to eat between 5 and 7pm can have three courses for just $14 at authentic French wine bar **Le Pere Pinard** (p. 147). Also consider buffets like the great lunchtime one at **Salaam Bombay** (p. 141).

55. **Bring your own wine.** Some restaurants, even those with their own wine lists, will let you bring your own if you call and ask. At press time, places that are BYOB as policy include **Snack,** the **Zen Palate** in Union Square, **Afghan Kebab House,** the **Pink Tea Cup,** and just about any restaurant in Little India; all of these places are happy to open your bottle and provide glasses. (See chapter 6 for individual reviews.) However, *always* call and ask in advance.

(The only exception is Little India, where you can just arrive with a bottle or a six-pack and ask at the door.) If the answer is "no," be gracious and accept it. If the answer is "yes," ask whether a corkage fee is charged. See chapter 8 for tips on shops with good values on wine.

SIGHTSEEING

56. **Buy a CityPass.** CityPass may be New York's best sightseeing deal. Pay one price ($45, or $39 for kids 12–17) for admission to seven major attractions: The American Museum of Natural History (does not include Space Show); the Guggenheim Museum; the Empire State Building; the *Intrepid* Sea-Air-Space Museum; the Whitney Museum of American Art; MoMA QNS; and a 2-hour Circle Line cruise. If you purchased separate admission to each of these, you'd spend more than twice as much.

CityPass is not a coupon book. It contains actual tickets, so you can bypass ticket lines. This can save you hours, since sights like the Empire State Building often have lines of an hour or more.

CityPass is good for 9 days from the first time you use it. It's sold at all participating attractions and online at **www.citypass.net**. Your best bet is to buy it at the first attraction you visit because online orders rack up service and shipping fees. Start sightseeing at an attraction that's likely to have the shortest admission line, like the Guggenheim or the Whitney, or arrive before opening to avoid a wait. A preorder may be the way to go, however, if that's not convenient for you or you're starting your sightseeing on a weekend or during holiday time, when even those museums can have ugly ticket lines.

Value Museum & Entertainment Deals for Teens

High 5 Tickets to the Arts (☎ **212/HI5-TKTS;** www.high5tix.org) makes theater and culture more accessible for kids between the ages of 13 and 18. Teens can buy tickets for select theatrical performances and events for $5 each for weekend performances, or $5 for two (for the teen and a guest of any age) for Monday through Thursday performances. High 5 also offers discounted museum passes at the wallet-friendly price of two for $5 (for the teen and a guest of any age). Check the website for details on obtaining theater or museum tickets, which can usually be purchased with proof of age at any New York City Ticketmaster outlet or online. Also check the High 5 website for listings of free and nearly free events going on while you and your teen are in town.

Get more info by calling CityPass at ☎ **888/330-5008.** (CityPass is not sold over the phone.) The pricing and attraction list is confirmed through March 2004; call or check the website for updated information if your visit falls later in the year.

57. **Take advantage of freebies.** Many of the best things to do and see in Manhattan are free, from walking the Brooklyn Bridge to riding the Staten Island Ferry to exploring Central Park to attending TV show tapings. Additionally, some organizations offer free walking tours. Many museums and attractions that charge admission have free or pay-as-you-wish programs 1 day or evening a week. See "Where to Find Free Culture" (p. 218) and "Absolutely Free Walking Tours" (p. 248).

SHOPPING

58. **Ship major purchases home.** If you're buying high-ticket items, you can often save on the 8.25% New York sales tax by having items shipped home. Depending on the laws of your state, you can pay a lesser tax or skip the duty completely.

59. **Seek out sample sales.** Garment designers and manufacturers often sell off their newest items

(sometimes not even available in stores) for a song to raise quick cash; see "Scouring the Sample Sales" on p. 278.

60. **Do your homework and bargain on electronic equipment.** You'll notice a wealth of electronics stores throughout the Theater District, many trumpeting GOING OUT OF BUSINESS sales. These guys have been going out of business since the Stone Age. Trust me: The only way you'll do well is if you know your stuff. And play hard to get; I've seen prices tumble the closer I got to the door.

61. **Always ask for a better price on anything used or vintage.** It won't always work, but a lot of vintage, antiques, and collectibles dealers—even those with shops in high-rent districts such as SoHo and the Village—will drop their price if you're just savvy enough to ask. Always be polite, however, and don't push if you're told "no."

ENTERTAINMENT

62. **Buy discounted theater tickets through Playbill Online.** Joining Playbill's Online Theater Club (**www.playbillclub.com**) can yield substantial savings on advance-purchase theater tickets for Broadway and Off-Broadway

shows, including some of the top draws at press time. Becoming a member is free; all you have to do is register, and you'll have access to discounts that can range from a few dollars to as much as 50% off regular prices. The club also offers its members deals at some hotels as well as dining discounts, and you can sign up for e-mail updates on new offers. Other sites that offer similar services are **Theater-Mania** (**www.theatermania.com**) and **Broadway.com** (**www.broadway.com**), although the Broadway.com site wants a bit too much personal information for my taste. At TheaterMania, be sure to click on "TM Insider Deals" for instant discounts.

63. **Buy discounted same-day tickets at the TKTS booth.** If your heart is set on seeing a particular show, order your tickets well in advance. But if you're flexible, check out TKTS, which sells day-of-show tickets to plays on and Off-Broadway for 25% to 50% off face value, plus a $2.50 per-ticket service charge. In-the-know theatergoers skip the Theater District location for the far-less-crowded downtown booth, where you can also score matinee tickets a day in advance. For complete details, see "Top Ticket-Buying Tips" in chapter 9.

64. **Take advantage of free events.** Summertime is a great time to be in the city if you're a culture buff. Some of the city's top cultural organizations offer free outdoor events, from Shakespeare in the Park to the Metropolitan Opera. See "Park It! Shakespeare, Music & Other Free Fun" on p. 306.

But you don't have to wait until summer: Comb the listings in *Time Out New York, New York* magazine, the *New Yorker,* and the *New York Times* for free events ranging from dance performances to readings at Barnes & Noble. Or pick up a copy of **Club freeTime,** a monthly paper listing free events around Manhattan—usually 15 to 45 events per day, including movies, theater, dance, concerts, readings, and more. You can subscribe for $25 a year by calling ② **212/545-8900,** but there's no need to; there are short-term Internet subscriptions (1 week, $1.95; 1 month, $2.95; 3 months, $7.95), which score you the wealth of free listings, plus discounts to member events, including concerts and discussion groups. If you don't have Web access, you can pick up the current issue at many newsstands. Limited event listings and newsstand locations are online at **www.clubfreetime.com**.

65. Eschew high-priced, star performances for lesser-known, lower-priced surprises. Seeing the New York Philharmonic or a Broadway extravaganza is a must if you can afford it. But you'll save money—and maybe enjoy yourself more—by looking beyond the obvious. For instance, the nation's top music education institution, the Julliard School, offers a full slate of free and cheap events, from first-rate student concerts to lectures by celebrities of the performing-arts world. Smaller venues such as Bargemusic, the 92nd Street Y, and the Amato Opera Theatre offer intimate, only-in-New-York performances, sometimes by nationally known artists, at rock-bottom prices. Off- and Off-Off-Broadway theater is usually significantly less expensive than Broadway, and the quality doesn't have to suffer one bit.

2 Visitor Information

For information before you leave, your best source (besides this book, of course) is NYC & Company, the organization behind the **New York Convention & Visitors Bureau** (NYCVB), 810 Seventh Ave., New York, NY 10019. You can call © **800/ NYC-VISIT** or 212/397-8222 to order the **Official NYC Visitor Kit,** which has the *Official NYC Guide* detailing hotels, restaurants, theaters, attractions, events, and more; a fold-out map; a newsletter on the latest goings-on in the city; and brochures on attractions and services. It costs $5.95 to receive the packet (payable by credit card) in 7 to 10 days, $9.95 for rush delivery (3–4 business days) to U.S. addresses and international orders. (*Note:* I have received complaints that packages don't always strictly adhere to these time frames.)

Money-saving tip: Order the *Official NYC Guide,* the heart of the kit,

for free at **www.nycvisit.com** (click on "Visitors"). The site is also a great information source. To speak to a travel counselor, call © **212/484-1222.**

For visitor-center and information-desk locations once you arrive, see "Visitor Information" in "Orientation," in chapter 4.

Also check out "Site Seeing: The Big Apple on the Web" on p. 7. There you'll find details on the best online resources for planning your trip.

FOR U.K. VISITORS   Contact the **NYCVB Visitor Information Center,** 36 Southwark Bridge Rd., London, SE1 9EU (© **020/7202-6368**). You can order the Official NYC Visitor Kit by sending them an A5-size self-addressed envelope and 72p postage. For New York–bound travelers in the London area, the center also offers free travel-planning assistance.

3 Money

You never have to carry too much cash in New York, and while the city's pretty safe, it's best not to overstuff your wallet (but make sure you have at least $20 in taxi fare on hand).

ATMS

In most neighborhoods, you can find **ATMs** on every block. They're scarce in a few neighborhoods, like the East Village or Harlem. The city's biggest banks are Citibank, Chase, Fleet, and HSBC, which belong to the **Cirrus** (© **800/424-7787;** www.mastercard. com) and **PLUS** (© **800/843-7587;** www.visa.com/atms) networks. Expect to pay $1.50 or $2 each time you withdraw money from an ATM, in addition to what your home bank charges. Stay away from commercial machines, like those in hotel lobbies and corner delis, which often charge $3 or more per transaction. Avoid

poorly lit or out-of-the-way ATMs, especially at night.

Be sure you know your personal identification number (PIN) and be sure to find out your daily withdrawal limit before you depart. Also keep in mind that many banks impose a fee every time a card is used at a different bank's ATM. On top of this, the bank from which you withdraw cash may charge its own fee. To compare banks' ATM fees within the U.S., use www. bankrate.com.

TRAVELER'S CHECKS

Traveler's checks are something of an anachronism from the days before the ATM made cash accessible at any time. Traveler's checks used to be the only sound alternative to traveling with dangerously large amounts of cash. They were as reliable as currency, but, unlike cash, could be replaced if lost or stolen.

These days, traveler's checks are less necessary because most cities have 24-hour ATMs that allow you to withdraw small amounts of cash as needed. However, keep in mind that you will likely be charged an ATM withdrawal fee if the bank is not your own, so if you're withdrawing money every day, you might be better off with traveler's checks—provided that you don't mind showing identification every time you want to cash one.

You can get traveler's checks at almost any bank. **American Express** offers denominations of $20, $50, $100, $500, and (for cardholders only) $1,000. You'll pay a service charge ranging from 1% to 4%. You can also get American Express traveler's checks over the phone by calling © **800/221-7282;** Amex gold and platinum cardholders who use this number are exempt from the 1% fee. AAA members can obtain checks without a fee at most AAA offices.

Visa offers traveler's checks at Citibank locations nationwide, as well as at several other banks. The service charge ranges between 1.5% and 2%; checks come in denominations of $20, $50, $100, $500, and $1,000. Call © **800/732-1322** for information. **MasterCard** also offers traveler's checks. Call © **800/223-9920** for a location near you.

Foreign currency traveler's checks are useful if you're traveling to one country, or to the Euro zone; they're accepted at locations such as bed-and-breakfasts where dollar checks may not be, and they minimize the amount of math you have to do at your destination. **American Express** offers checks in Australian dollars, Canadian dollars,

British pounds, Euros, and Japanese yen. **Visa** checks come in Australian, Canadian, British, and Euro versions; **MasterCard** offers those four plus yen and South African rands.

If you choose to carry traveler's checks, be sure to keep a record of their serial numbers separate from your checks in the event that they are stolen or lost. You'll get a refund faster if you know the numbers.

CREDIT CARDS

American Express, MasterCard, and **Visa** are accepted almost everywhere in New York. **Carte Blanche** and **Diners Club** have made a comeback in hotel circles, and **Discover** is also popular (though don't count on it being accepted everywhere). Because New York has so many international visitors, cards like **enRoute, Eurocard,** and **JCB** are widely accepted, particularly at hotels. Budget travelers should remember that many of New York's most affordable restaurants accept cash only. See if they take credit cards *before* you order.

Credit cards are a safe way to carry money, they provide a convenient record of all your expenses, and they generally offer good exchange rates. You can also withdraw cash advances from your credit cards at banks or ATMs, provided you know your PIN. If you've forgotten yours, or didn't even know you had one, call the number on the back of your credit card and ask the bank to send it to you. It usually takes 5 to 7 business days, though some banks will provide the number over the phone if you tell them your mother's maiden name or some other personal information.

4 When to Go

Summer or winter, rain or shine, New York City always has fun things going on, so there's no real "best" time to go.

MONEY MATTERS Hotel prices are more flexible than they've been in years, but New York hotels are by no means throwing a fire sale. Therefore, if money is a big concern, you might want to follow these rough seasonal guidelines.

The least expensive time to visit is in winter, between the first of the year and early April. Sure, the weather can be awful, but hotels are suffering from the post-holiday blues, and rooms often go for a relative song. In the winter of 2003, for instance, rooms at the Comfort Inn–Central Park West were going for as little as $80 to $90 for AAA members. However, the occasional convention or event, such as February's annual Fashion Week, can sometimes throw a wrench in your winter savings plans.

Spring and autumn are traditionally the busiest, most expensive seasons after holiday time. Don't expect hotels to be handing you deals, but you might be able to negotiate a good rate. Spring is generally easier than fall; many hotels consider their peak season to be the last 4 months of the year.

The city is drawing more families these days, and they usually visit in the summer. Still, the prospect of heat and humidity keeps some people away, making July and the start of August a significantly cheaper time to visit.

Christmas is not a good time for budget-minded travelers. The first 2 weeks of December—the shopping weeks—are the worst when it comes to scoring an affordable room; that's when shoppers converge on the town to catch the holiday spirit and spend, spend, spend. Hotel prices go sky high, and the crowds can be intolerable. If you'd rather have more of the city to yourself, with better chances at discount Broadway-show tickets and easier access to attractions, you'll be happier visiting another time of year.

But Thanksgiving can be a great time to visit: Business travelers have gone home for the holiday, and the holiday shoppers haven't yet arrived. It's a little-known secret that most hotels away from the Thanksgiving Day Parade route have empty rooms

sitting, and they're usually willing to make great deals to fill them. Hotels practically give away hotel rooms for the week following Thanksgiving.

WEATHER   The worst weather in New York is during that long week or 10 days that arrives each summer between mid-July and mid-August, when temperatures go up to around 100°F with 90% humidity. You feel sticky, the streets smell, everyone's cranky, and the concrete canyons become furnaces. But summer has its compensations, such as wonderful free, open-air concerts and other events. And you might luck out, as the last few summers have been downright lovely. But if you are at all temperature sensitive, your odds of getting comfortable weather are better in June or September.

Another period when you might not like to stroll around is during January or February, when temperatures are commonly in the 20s and those concrete canyons turn into wind tunnels. The city looks gorgeous just after a snowfall, but the streets soon become an ugly, slushy mess. Again, you never know: Temperatures have regularly been in the 30s and mild 40s during the past few winters. If you hit the weather jackpot, you could have a bargain bonanza (see "Money Matters," above).

Fall and spring are the best times in New York (which is why they're the most expensive). From April to June and September to November, temperatures are mild and pleasant, and the light is beautiful. With the leaves changing in Central Park and just the hint of crispness in the air, October is fabulous—but expect to pay for the privilege of being here.

If you want to know how to pack, check the Weather Channel's online 10-day forecast at **www.weather.com**; I like to balance it against CNN's forecast at **www.cnn.com/weather**. You can also get the local weather by calling ✆ **212/976-1212.**

New York's Average Temperature & Rainfall

	Jan	Feb	Mar	Apr	May	June	July	Aug	Sept	Oct	Nov	Dec
Daily Temp. (°F)	38	40	48	61	71	80	85	84	77	67	54	42
Daily Temp. (°C)	3	4	9	16	22	27	29	29	25	19	12	6
Days of Precipitation	11	10	11	11	11	10	11	10	8	8	9	10

NEW YORK CITY CALENDAR OF EVENTS

The following is subject to change. Always confirm before you make plans around a specific event. Call the venue or the **NYCVB** at ✆ **212/484-1222**, go to **www.nycvisit. com**, or pick up a copy of **Time Out New York** for the latest details.

January

Restaurant Week. This twice-yearly event allows you to lunch for $20 at some of New York's finest restaurants. Call ✆ **212/484-1222** or check www.restaurantweek.com for the dates and restaurants. *Reserve immediately.* Late January or early February.

February

Chinese New Year. Chinatown rings in its own new year with 2 weeks of celebrations, including parades with dragon and lion dancers and costumes. The parade winds through Chinatown along Mott, Canal, and Bayard streets, and along East Broadway. Chinese New Year falls on January 22 in 2004 and is the Year of the Monkey. Call the **NYCVB** hot line at ✆ **212/484-1222** or the Asian American Business Development Center (✆ **212/966-0100**).

Valentine's Day Weddings atop the Empire State Building. You and your honey can become life-time members of the **Empire State Building** Wedding Club by getting hitched on the 80th floor observation deck on February 14, 2004. Just 15 lucky couples will be chosen based on "Why We Want to Get Married at the Empire State Building" essays, which are judged on originality, uniqueness, and style. The deadline is November 30; call ✆ **212/736-3100** or visit www.esb nyc.com for details.

Westminster Kennel Club Dog Show. The ultimate purebred-pooch fest. Some 30,000 dog fanciers congregate at **Madison Square Garden** for the 125th "World Series of Dogdom." All 2,500 dogs are American Kennel Club Champions of Record, competing for Best in Show. Call ✆ **800/455-3647** or visit www. westminsterkennelclub.org for info. Tickets are available through **Ticketmaster** (✆ **212/307-7171;** www. ticketmaster.com). February 10 and 11.

March

St. Patrick's Day Parade. More than 150,000 marchers join in the world's largest civilian parade, as Fifth Avenue from 44th to 86th streets rings with the sounds of bands and bagpipes, and an inordinate amount of beer is consumed (much of it green). The parade starts at 11am, but go extra early if you want a good spot. But beware of adolescents who have drunk too much of that green beer. Call ✆ **212/484-1222.** March 17.

April

Easter Parade. This isn't a traditional parade, *per se.* Once, New York's gentry came out to show off their tasteful but discreet toppings. Today, if you were planning to slip on a tasteful little number—you will *not* be the grandest lady along Fifth Avenue from 48th to 57th streets. It's more about flamboyant exhibitionism, with hats and costumes that get more outrageous every year—and anybody can join right in for free. The parade generally runs Easter Sunday from 10am to 3 or 4pm. Call ✆ **212/484-1222.** April 20.

New York International Auto Show. Hot wheels from all over the world whirl into the **Jacob K. Javits Convention Center** for the largest auto show in the United States. Many concept cars show up. Call ✆ **800/282-3336** or 212/216-2000, or visit www.autoshowny.com or www.javitscenter.com. One week in early or mid-April.

May

Bike New York: The Great Five Boro Bike Tour. The largest mass-participation cycling event in the United States attracts about 30,000 cyclists from all over the world. After a 42-mile ride through the five boroughs, finalists are greeted with a New York–style celebration of food and music. Call ✆ **212/932-BIKE** or visit www.bikenewyork.org to register. First or second Sunday in May.

Ninth Avenue International Food Festival. Spend the day sampling Italian sausages, homemade pirogi, spicy curries, and an assortment of other ethnic dishes. Street musicians, bands, and vendors add to the atmosphere at one of the city's best street fairs, stretching along Ninth Avenue from 37th to 57th streets. Call ✆ **212/484-1222.** One weekend in mid-May.

Fleet Week. About 10,000 Navy and Coast Guard personnel are "at liberty" in New York at the end of May. Usually from 1 to 4pm daily, you can visit the ships as they dock at the piers on the west side of Manhattan, and watch exhibitions by the Marines. Even if you don't

take in any of the events, you'll know it's Fleet Week because those 10,000 sailors invade Midtown in their white uniforms. It's simply wonderful—like *On the Town* come to life. Call ✆ **212/484-1222,** or visit http://fleetweek.navy.mil (the best source for a full list of events) or www.intrepidmuseum.org. Late May.

June

Museum Mile Festival. Fifth Avenue from 82nd to 102nd streets is closed to cars from 6 to 9pm as 20,000-plus strollers enjoy live music from Broadway tunes to string quartets, street entertainers from juggling to giant puppets, and free admission to nine Museum Mile institutions, including the Metropolitan Museum of Art and the Guggenheim. Call ✆ **212/606-2296** or any participating institutions for details. Usually the second Tuesday in June.

Lesbian and Gay Pride Week and March. A week of cheerful happenings precedes a parade commemorating the Stonewall Riot of June 27, 1969, which for many marks the beginning of the gay-liberation movement. Fifth Avenue goes wild as the LGBT community celebrates with bands, marching groups, floats, and plenty of panache. The parade starts on upper Fifth Avenue around 52nd Street and continues into the Village, where a street festival and a dance with fireworks cap the day. Call ✆ **212/807-7433** or check www.nycpride.org. Late June.

SummerStage. A summer-long festival of outdoor performances in **Central Park,** featuring world music, pop, folk, and jazz artists ranging from Boukman Eksperyans to Buckwheat Zydeco to the New York Grand Opera (always performing Verdi) to the Chinese Golden Dragon Acrobats. Performances are often free, but certain big-name events require tickets (usually less than $30). Call ℭ 212/360-2777 or visit www.summerstage.org. June through August.

Shakespeare in the Park. The Delacorte Theater in **Central Park** is the setting for first-rate free performances under the stars—including at least one Shakespeare production each season—often with stars on the stage. For details, see "Park It! Shakespeare, Music & Other Free Fun" on p. 306. Call ℭ 212/539-8750 or visit www. publictheater.org. June through August.

Restaurant Week. Lunch for only $20 at some of New York's finest restaurants. Participating places vary each year, so watch for the ads in the *New York Times,* call the NYCVB at ℭ 212/484-1222, or check www.restaurantweek.com for the schedule and participants, usually available by mid-May. *Reserve immediately.* One week in late June; some restaurants extend their offers to Labor Day.

July

Independence Day Harbor Festival and Fourth of July Fireworks Spectacular. Start the day amid the crowds at the Great July Fourth Festival in Lower Manhattan, and then catch Macy's fireworks over the East River (the best vantage point is from FDR Dr., which closes to traffic several hours before sunset). Call ℭ 212/484-1222 or Macy's Visitor Center at 212/494-2922. July 4th.

August

Lincoln Center Festival 2004. This series of free music and dance performances is held outdoors on the plazas of **Lincoln Center.** Call ℭ 212/546-2656, or visit www. lincolncenter.org for this year's

schedule (usually available in mid-July). Throughout August.

New York International Fringe Festival. Held in a variety of Lower East Side venues, this festival presents alternative and traditional theater, musicals, dance, comedy, and all manner of performance art. Hundreds of events are held over about 10 days in August. The quality can vary, and some performances push the envelope, but you'd be surprised at how many shows are *good.* Many aspire to be the next *Urinetown* (the musical that went from Fringe to Broadway). Call ℭ 888/FRINGE-NYC or 212/ 420-8777, or point your browser to www.fringenyc.org. Throughout August.

U.S. Open Tennis Championships. The Grand Slam event is held at the Arthur Ashe Stadium at the USTA National Tennis Center, the largest public tennis center in the world, at **Flushing Meadows Park** in Queens. Tickets go on sale in May or early June. The event sells out immediately, because many tickets are held by corporate sponsors who give them to customers. (It's worth it to check the list of sponsors to determine if anyone you know has a connection for tickets.) You can usually scalp tickets (an illegal practice) next to Shea Stadium. The last few matches are the most expensive, but you'll see more tennis early on, when your ticket allows you to wander the grounds and view several matches. Call ℭ 888/OPEN-TIX or 718/ 760-6200 in advance; visit www. usopen.org or www.usta.com for information. Two weeks around Labor Day.

Harlem Week. The world's largest black and Hispanic cultural festival actually spans almost the whole month to include the Black Film Festival, the Harlem Jazz and Music Festival, and the Taste of Harlem Food Festival. Expect a full slate of music, from gospel to hip-hop, and lots of other festivities. Visit www.harlemdiscover.com or call © 212/484-1222 for this year's schedule of events and locations. Throughout August.

Republican National Convention. For the first time the elephants, as opposed to the donkeys who last convened in New York in 1992, will be coming to New York to hold their national convention. The convention will start at the end of August, and over 50,000 people are expected to attend. If you are planning to visit the city during that time, be aware that security measures will be extra tight, especially around Madison Square Garden where the convention will be held, and what is normally a slow time for hotels and restaurants will be unusually busy. For more information call © 212/484-1200.

September

West Indian–American Day Parade. This Brooklyn event is New York's largest street celebration. Come for the costumes, pulsating rhythms (soca, calypso, reggae), colors, folklore, food (jerk chicken, oxtail soup, Caribbean soul food), and two million hip-shaking revelers. The route can change from year to year, but usually runs along Eastern Parkway from Utica Avenue to Grand Army Plaza (at the gateway to Prospect Park). Call © 212/484-1222 or 718/625-1515. Labor Day.

Broadway on Broadway. This free afternoon show features the songs and casts from virtually every Broadway show in the middle of Times Square. This event keeps getting bigger—and is usually broadcast on local TV—so you can expect the big stars. Call © 212/768-1560 or visit www.timessquarebid.org and click on "Events." One Sunday in mid-September.

New York Film Festival. Legendary hits *Pulp Fiction* and *Mean Streets* had their U.S. premieres at the Film Society of Lincoln Center's festival, a major stop on the film fest circuit. Screenings are held in Lincoln Center venues; advance tickets are advised, and a necessity for certain events (especially evening and weekend screenings). Call © 212/875-5600 for information, 212/875-5050 for tickets, or check www.filmlinc.com. Two weeks, late September to early October.

October

Feast of St. Francis. Animals from goldfish to elephants are blessed as thousands of *homo sapiens* look on at the **Cathedral of St. John the Divine.** A magical experience; pets, of course, are welcome. A fair follows. Buy tickets in advance because they can be hard to get. Call © 212/316-7540 or 212/662-7133 for tickets, or visit www.stjohndivine.org. First Sunday in October.

Ice Skating. Show off your skating style at the diminutive **Rockefeller Center** rink (© 212/332-7654), from mid-October to mid-March or early April (you'll skate under the Christmas tree for the month of Dec), or at the larger **Wollman Rink** in Central Park, on the east side between 62nd and 63rd streets (© 212/439-6900; www.wollmanskatingrink.com), and Lasker Rink, between 106th and 108th streets (© 212/534-7639). Both Central Park skating rinks usually close in early April.

Greenwich Village Halloween Parade. This is Halloween at its most outrageous. Drag queens and assorted other flamboyant types parade in wildly creative costumes. The parade route has changed over the years, but it generally starts after sunset at Spring Street and marches up Sixth Avenue to 23rd Street or Union Square. Call the *Village Voice* Parade hot line at ✆ **212/475-3333,** ext. 4044; point your browser to www.halloween-nyc. com; or check the papers for the route so you can watch—or participate, if you have the threads and the imagination. October 31.

November

New York City Marathon. Some 30,000 runners from around the world participate in the largest U.S. marathon, and more than a million fans cheer them on as they run through all five New York City boroughs and finish in Central Park. Call ✆ **212/423-2249** or 212/860-4455, or surf to www.nyrrc.org for applications. November 2 in 2003.

Radio City Music Hall Christmas Spectacular. A gaudy extravaganza, but a lot of fun nonetheless. Starring the Rockettes and a cast that includes live camels. After undergoing an extensive restoration for most of 1999, Radio City itself is a sight to see. For information, call ✆ **212/247-4777** or visit www. radiocity.com; buy tickets at the box office or Ticketmaster's **Radio City Hot Line** (✆ **212/307-1000**), or visit www.ticketmaster. com. Throughout November and December.

Macy's Thanksgiving Day Parade. The procession from Central Park West and 77th Street down Broadway to Herald Square continues to be a national tradition. Huge hot-air balloons of Rocky and Bullwinkle, Snoopy, the Pink Panther, Bart Simpson, and other cartoon favorites are the best part of the fun. The night before, you can see the big blow-up on Central Park West at 79th Street; call in advance to find out whether it will be open to the public. Call ✆ **212/484-1222** or Macy's Visitor Center at 212/494-2922. Thanksgiving Day.

Big Apple Circus. New York City's homegrown, not-for-profit circus is a favorite with children and everyone who's young at heart. Big Apple is committed to maintaining the classical circus tradition with sensitivity and only features animals that have a traditional working relationship with humans. A tent is pitched in **Damrosch Park** at **Lincoln Center.** Call ✆ **212/268-2500** or visit www.bigapplecircus.org. November through January.

December

Lighting of the Rockefeller Center Christmas Tree. Ice skating, singing, entertainment, and a crowd accompany the annual lighting ceremony. The tree stays lit around the clock until after the new year. Call ✆ **212/332-6868** or visit www.rockefellercenter.com for this year's date. Early December.

Holiday Trimmings. Stroll down Fifth Avenue and you'll see doormen dressed as wooden soldiers at **FAO Schwarz,** a 27-foot snowflake over the intersection outside **Tiffany's,** the **Cartier** building beribboned in red, wreaths warming the necks of the **New York Public Library**'s lions, and fanciful figures in the windows of **Saks Fifth Avenue** and **Lord & Taylor.** Madison Avenue between 55th and 60th streets is a good bet; **Sony Plaza** usually boasts some fabulous windows, as does **Barneys New York.** Throughout December.

Christmas Traditions. In addition to the **Radio City Music Hall Christmas Spectacular,** traditional holiday events include *A Christmas Carol* at **The Theater at Madison Square Garden** (✆ **212/465-6741** or www.thegarden.com; ✆ 212/307-7171 or www.ticketmaster.com), usually featuring a big name to draw in the crowds. Tchaikovsky's holiday favorite, *The Nutcracker* (✆ **212/870-5570;** www.nycballet.com), is performed by the New York City Ballet at **Lincoln Center.** At **Avery Fisher Hall** is the National Chorale's sing-along performances of Handel's *Messiah* (✆ **212/875-5030;** www.lincoln center.org) for a week before Christmas. Don't worry if the only words you know are "Alleluia, Alleluia!"—a lyrics sheet is given to ticket holders.

Lighting of the Hanukkah Menorah. Everything is done on a grand scale in New York, so it's no surprise that the world's largest menorah (32 ft. high) is at Manhattan's **Grand Army Plaza,** Fifth Avenue and 59th Street. Hanukkah celebrations begin at sunset on the first night of the holiday, with the lighting of the first of the giant electric candles. Early to mid-December.

New Year's Eve. The biggest party of them all happens in **Times Square,** where hundreds of thousands of raucous revelers count down in unison the year's final seconds until the new lighted ball drops at midnight at 1 Times Square. Hate to be a party pooper, but this one, in the cold surrounded by thousands of very drunk revelers, is a masochist's delight. Call ✆ **212/768-1560** or 212/484-1222, or visit www.timessquarebid.org. December 31.

Other year-end events include **fireworks** followed by the New York Road Runner's Club's annual **5K Midnight Run** in **Central Park;** call ✆ **212/860-4455** or visit www.nyrrc.org. Head to Brooklyn for the city's largest New Year's Eve **fireworks** celebration at Prospect Park; call **718/965-8999** or visit www.prospectpark.org.

The Cathedral of St. John the Divine is known for its annual **New Year's Eve Concert for Peace.** Past performers have included the Manhattan School of Music Chamber Sinfonia, Tony award–winning composer Jason Robert Brown *(Parade),* soprano Lauren Flanigan, and the Forces of Nature Dance Company. Call ✆ **212/316-7540** for information or 212/662-2133 for tickets, or go online to www.stjohndivine.org.

5 Travel Insurance

Check your existing insurance policies and credit-card coverage before you buy travel insurance. You may already be covered for lost luggage, canceled tickets, or medical expenses. The cost of travel insurance varies widely, depending on the cost and length of your trip, your age, your health, and the type of trip you're taking.

TRIP-CANCELLATION INSURANCE Trip-cancellation insurance helps you get your money back if you have to back out of a trip, if you have to go home early, or if your travel supplier goes bankrupt. Allowed reasons for cancellation can range from sickness to natural disasters to the State Department declaring your destination unsafe for travel. (Insurers usually won't cover vague fears, though, as many travelers discovered who tried to cancel their trips in October 2001 because they were wary of flying.) In this unstable world, trip-cancellation insurance is a good buy if you're getting tickets well in advance—who knows what the state of the world, or of your airline, will be in 9 months? Insurance policy details vary, so read the fine print—and especially make sure that your airline or cruise line is on the list of carriers covered in case of bankruptcy. For information, contact one of the following insurers: **Access America** (© 866/807-3982; www.accessamerica.com); **Travel Guard International** (© 800/826-4919; www.travelguard.com); **Travel Insured International** (© 800/243-3174; www.travelinsured.com); or **Travelex Insurance Services** (© 888/457-4602; www.travelex-insurance.com).

MEDICAL INSURANCE Most health-insurance policies cover you if you get sick away from home—but check, particularly if you're insured by an HMO.

LOST-LUGGAGE INSURANCE On domestic flights, checked baggage is covered up to $2,500 per ticketed passenger. If you plan to check items more valuable than the standard liability, see if your valuables are covered by your homeowner's policy, get baggage insurance as part of your comprehensive travel-insurance package, or buy Travel Guard's "BagTrak" product. Don't buy insurance at the airport, as it's usually overpriced. Be sure to take any valuables or irreplaceable items with you in your carry-on luggage, as many valuables (including books, money, and electronics) aren't covered by airline policies.

If your luggage is lost, immediately file a lost-luggage claim at the airport, detailing the luggage contents. For most airlines, you must report delayed, damaged, or lost baggage within 4 hours of arrival. The airlines are required to deliver luggage, once found, directly to your house or destination free of charge.

6 Health & Safety

WHAT TO DO IF YOU GET SICK AWAY FROM HOME

In most cases, your existing health plan will provide the coverage you need. But double-check; you may want to buy **travel medical insurance** instead. Bring your insurance ID card with you when you travel.

If you suffer from a chronic illness, consult your doctor before your departure. For conditions like epilepsy, diabetes, or heart problems, wear a **MedicAlert Identification Tag** (© 800/825-3785; www.medicalert. org), which will immediately alert doctors to your condition and give them access to your records through Medic Alert's 24-hour hot line.

Pack **prescription medications** in your carry-on luggage, and carry prescription medications in their original containers, with pharmacy labels—otherwise they won't make it through airport security. Also bring along copies of your prescriptions in case you lose your pills or run out. Don't forget an extra pair of contact lenses or prescription glasses.

7 Specialized Travel Resources

TRAVELERS WITH DISABILITIES

New York is more accessible to travelers with disabilities than ever. The city's bus system is wheelchair-friendly, and most of the major attractions are easily accessible. Even so, **always call first** to be sure that the places you want to go to are fully accessible.

Most hotels are ADA compliant, with suitable rooms for wheelchair-bound travelers as well as those with other disabilities. But before you book, **ask lots of questions based on your needs.** Many budget hotels are housed in older buildings that have had to be modified to meet requirements; still, elevators and bathrooms can be on the small side. If you have mobility issues, you'll probably do best to book into a newer hotel. You'll find links to New York's accessible accommodations, evaluated by people skilled to make such judgments, at **www.access-able.com** (click on "World Cities"). Some Broadway theaters and other venues provide total wheelchair accessibility; others provide partial accessibility. Many also offer lower-priced tickets for theatergoers with disabilities, though you'll need to check individual policies and reserve in advance.

Hospital Audiences, Inc. (© 212/575-7676; www.hospitalaudiences.org) arranges attendance and provides details about accessibility at cultural institutions as well as cultural events adapted for people with disabilities. Services include "Describe!," which allows visually impaired theatergoers to enjoy theater events; and the **HAI Hot Line** (© 212/575-7676), which offers accessibility information for hotels, restaurants, attractions, and much more. This organization also publishes *Access for All,* a guidebook on accessibility, available by calling © 212/575-7663 or by sending a $5 check to 548 Broadway, 3rd Floor, New York, NY 10012-3950.

Another good source is **Big Apple Greeter** (© 212/669-8159; www.bigapplegreeter.org). All of its employees are well versed in accessibility issues. They can provide a list of agencies that serve the city's disabled community, and sometimes have discounts to theater and music performances. Big Apple Greeter even offers one-to-one tours that pair volunteers with visitors with disabilities; they can introduce you to the public transportation system if you like. Reserve at least 1 week ahead.

GETTING AROUND Express Shuttle USA (© 800/451-0455 or 212/315-3006; www.graylinenewyork.com) operates minibuses with lifts from Newark airport to Midtown hotels by reservation; arrange pickup 3 or 4 days in advance. **Olympia Trails** (© 877/894-9155 or 212/964-6233; www.olympiabus.com) provides service from Newark International Airport, with half-price fares for travelers with disabilities. (Prepurchase your tickets to guarantee the discount fare, as drivers can't sell discounted tickets.) Not all buses are appropriately equipped, so call ahead for the daily schedule of accessible buses (press "0" [zero] to reach a real person).

A licensed ambulette company, **Upward Mobility Limousine Service** (© 718/645-7774; www.brainlink.com/~phil), is a wheelchair-accessible car service that can provide door-to-door airport shuttle service as well as taxi service anywhere in the metropolitan area. Arrange airport pickups with as much advance notice as possible.

Taxis are required to carry people who have folding wheelchairs and guide or therapy dogs. However, don't be surprised if they don't run each other down trying to get to you; even though you shouldn't have to, you may have to wait for a friendly (or fare-desperate) driver to come along.

Public buses are an inexpensive, easy way to get around New York. All buses' back doors are supposed to be equipped with wheelchair lifts (though the city has had complaints that not all are in working order). Buses also "kneel," lowering their front steps for people who have difficulty boarding. Passengers with disabilities pay half-price fares ($1). The **subway** isn't fully wheelchair accessible, but a list of about 30 accessible stations and a guide to wheelchair-accessible subway itineraries is on the MTA website. Call © 718/596-8585

for transit info, or go to www.mta.
info/ada/accessible.htm.

You're better off not trying to rent
your own car to get around the city.
But if you consider it the best mode of
transportation for you, **Wheelchair
Getaways** (© 800/379-3750 or 800/
344-5005; www.wheelchair-getaways.
com) rents specialized vans with
wheelchair lifts and features for travelers with disabilities throughout the
New York metropolitan area.

Many travel agencies offer custom-
ized tours and itineraries for travelers
with disabilities. **Flying Wheels Travel**
(© 507/451-5005; www.flyingwheels
travel.com) offers escorted tours and
cruises that emphasize sports and private tours in minivans with lifts. **Accessible Journeys** (© 800/846-4537 or
610/521-0339; www.disabilitytravel.
com) caters specifically to slow walkers
and wheelchair travelers and their families and friends.

Organizations that offer assistance
to travelers with disabilities include
the **Moss Rehab Hospital** (www.
mossresourcenet.org), which provides
a library of accessible-travel resources
online; the **Society for Accessible
Travel and Hospitality** (© 212/447-
7284; www.sath.org; annual membership fees: $45 adults, $30 seniors and
students), which offers a wealth of
travel resources for all types of disabilities and informed recommendations
on destinations, access guides, travel
agents, tour operators, vehicle rentals,
and companion services; and the
American Foundation for the Blind
(© 800/232-5463; www.afb.org),
which provides information on traveling with Seeing Eye dogs.

For more information specifically
targeted to travelers with disabilities,
the community website **iCan** (www.
icanonline.net/channels/travel/index.c
fm) has destination guides and several
regular columns on accessible travel.
Also check out the quarterly magazine
Emerging Horizons ($14.95 per year,

$19.95 outside the U.S.; www.emerg-
inghorizons.com); **Twin Peaks Press**
(© 360/694-2462; http://disability
bookshop.virtualave.net/blist84.htm),
offering travel-related books for travelers with special needs; and **Open
World Magazine,** published by the
Society for Accessible Travel and Hospitality (see above; subscription: $18
per year, $35 outside the U.S.).

FOR FAMILIES

As a result of the decrease in crime and
the increase in family-oriented entertainment (exemplified by the "new"
Times Square), city sidewalks are full
of pint-sized visitors. There are myriad
ways to keep them entertained, from
kid-oriented museums and theater to
theme park–style shopping and
restaurants.

While New York City offers
delights for the sophisticated traveler,
there's plenty to please the small fry; in
addition to museums just for them,
(p. 253), we note the hotels that are
the best bargains for families, and
restaurants where young folks are welcomed.

You can find good family-oriented
vacation advice on the Internet from
sites like the **Family Travel Network**
(www.familytravelnetwork.com);
**Traveling Internationally with Your
Kids** (www.travelwithyourkids.com),
a comprehensive site offering sound
advice for long-distance and international travel with children; and **Family Travel Files** (www.thefamilytravel
files.com), which offers an online
magazine and a directory of off-the-
beaten-path tours and tour operators
for families.

For the best places to stay and eat,
see "Affordable Family-Friendly
Hotels" in chapter 5 and "Family-
Friendly Restaurants" in chapter 6.
For sightseeing, check out "Especially
for Kids," in chapter 7. For more
extensive recommendations, you
might want a copy of *Frommer's New*

York City with Kids, dedicated to family visits to the Big Apple.

Good bets for the most timely information include the "Weekend" section of Friday's *New York Times,* which has a section dedicated to the best kid-friendly activities; the weekly *New York* magazine, which has a calendar of children's events in its "Cue" section; and *Time Out New York,* which also has a great weekly kids' section with a bit of an alternative bent. The *Big Apple Parents' Paper* is usually available for free at children's stores and other locations in Manhattan; you can also find good information from the folks behind the paper at **www. parentsknow.com**.

The first place to look for **babysitting** is in your hotel (ask about it when you reserve). Many hotels have services or will provide you with lists of sitters. Or you can call **The Baby Sitters' Guild** (✆ **212/682-0227**; www.baby sittersguild.com). The sitters are licensed, insured, and bonded, and can even take your child on outings.

FOR GAY & LESBIAN TRAVELERS

Gay and lesbian culture is as much a part of New York's basic identity as yellow cabs, high-rises, and Broadway theater. Indeed, in a city with one of the world's largest, loudest, and most powerful gay and lesbian populations, homosexuality is hardly seen as "alternative"—it's squarely in the mainstream. So city hotels tend to be neutral on the issue, and gay couples shouldn't have a problem; for gay-friendly accommodations, see "Best for Gay & Lesbian Travelers" under "Best Low-Cost Hotel Bets" in chapter 1. You'll want to see "The Gay & Lesbian Scene" in chapter 9 for nightlife suggestions.

The **International Gay & Lesbian Travel Association** (IGLTA; ✆ **800/ 448-8550** or 954/776-2626; www.

iglta.org) links travelers up with gay-friendly hoteliers as well as tour operators and airline representatives. **Now, Voyager** (✆ **800/255-6951;** www.nowvoyager.com), a San Francisco–based gay-owned travel service, is an excellent source for those who want assistance with trip planning. All over Manhattan, but especially in neighborhoods like the **West Village** (particularly Christopher St., famous as the main drag, so to speak, of New York gay male life) and **Chelsea** (Eighth Ave. from 16th to 23rd sts., and West 17th to 19th sts. from Fifth to Eighth aves.), shops, services, and restaurants have a lesbian and gay flavor. **The Oscar Wilde Bookshop,** 15 Christopher St. (✆ 212/255-8097; www.oscarwildebooks.com), is the city's best gay and lesbian bookstore, and a good source for information on the city's gay community.

The **Lesbian, Gay, Bisexual & Transgender Community Center** is at 208 W. 13th St., between Seventh and Eighth avenues (✆ **212/620- 7310;** www.gaycenter.org). The center is the meeting place for more than 400 organizations. You can check the online events calendar, which lists hundreds of happenings—lectures, dances, concerts, readings, films—or call. Their site offers links to gay-friendly hotels and guesthouses, plus tons of other information; the staff is also friendly and helpful.

Other good sources for lesbian and gay events are *HX* (www.hx.com), *New York Blade* (www.nyblade.com), *Next* (www.nextnyc.com), *Gay City News* (www.gaycitynews.com), and the *Village Voice* (www.villagevoice. com)—all free weeklies you can pick up in bars, clubs, stores, and sidewalk boxes throughout town. You'll also find lots of information on their websites. The glossy weekly *Time Out New York* (www.timeoutny.com)

boasts a terrific gay and lesbian section. The Lesbian, Gay, Bisexual & Transgender Community Center (see above) publishes a monthly guide listing events (also listed on their website).

In addition, there are lesbian and gay musical events, such as performances by the **New York City Gay Men's Chorus** (© 212/242-1777; www.nycgmc.org); health programs sponsored by the **Gay Men's Health Crisis** (GMHC; © **800/AIDS-NYC** or 212/807-6655; www.gmhc.org); the **Gay and Lesbian National Hotline** (© 212/989-0999; www.glnh. org), which offers peer counseling and information on upcoming events; and many other organizations.

FOR SENIOR TRAVELERS

Mention your senior status when you make your travel reservations, because all major airlines and many hotels offer discounts. Major airlines also offer coupons for domestic travel for seniors over age 60. Typically, a book of four coupons costs less than $700, which means you can fly anywhere in the continental United States for under $350 round-trip.

Also mention the fact that you're a senior when you first make your travel reservations. Both **Amtrak** (© **800/ USA-RAIL;** www.amtrak.com) and **Greyhound** (© 800/229-2424; www. greyhound.com) offer discounts to persons over 62, and most of the major domestic airlines offer discount programs for senior travelers.

Many hotels offer senior discounts; **Choice Hotels** (which include Comfort Inns, some of my favorite Midtown hotels; see chapter 5), for example, gives 30% off their published rates to anyone over 50, provided you book your room through their nationwide toll-free reservations number (that is, not directly with the hotels or through a travel agent). For a complete list of Choice Hotels, visit **www.hotelchoice.com.**

New York subway and bus fares are half price (75¢) for people 65 or older. Many museums and sights (and some theaters and performance halls) offer discounted entrance and tickets to seniors; so do ask for it. Always bring an ID card, especially if you've kept your youthful glow.

Members of **AARP** (formerly known as the American Association of Retired Persons), 601 E St. NW, Washington, DC 20049 (© **800/ 424-3410** or 202/434-2277; www. aarp.org), get discounts on hotels, airfares, and car rentals. AARP offers members a wide range of benefits, including *AARP: The Magazine* and a monthly newsletter. Anyone over 50 can join.

Many reliable agencies and organizations target the 50-plus market. **Elderhostel** (© 877/426-8056; www. elderhostel.org) arranges study programs for those aged 55 and over (and a spouse or companion of any age) in the U.S. Most courses last 5 to 7 days in the U.S. and many include airfare, accommodations in university dormitories or modest inns, meals, and tuition.

Recommended publications offering travel resources and discounts for seniors include the quarterly magazine *Travel 50 & Beyond* (www.travel50andbeyond.com); *Travel Unlimited: Uncommon Adventures for the Mature Traveler* (Avalon); *101 Tips for Mature Travelers,* available from Grand Circle Travel (© 800/221-2610 or 617/ 350-7500; www.gct.com); *The 50+ Traveler's Guidebook* (St. Martin's Press); and *Unbelievably Good Deals and Great Adventures That You Absolutely Can't Get Unless You're Over 50* (McGraw-Hill).

FOR STUDENTS

Many museums, sights, and theaters offer reduced admission to students, so don't forget to bring your student ID and valid proof of age.

Your best resource is the **Council on International Educational Exchange,** or **CIEE** (www.ciee.org). They can set you up with an International Student ID card, and their travel branch, **Council Travel Service** (© **800/226-8624;** www.council travel.com), the world's biggest student-travel agency, has joined with STA Travel (© **800/781-4040;** www. statravel.com) to get you discounts on plane tickets and the like. STA has offices at 254 Greene St., 10 Downing St. (Sixth Ave. at Bleecker St.; © **212/ 627-3111**); 30 Third Ave. (© **212/ 473-6100**); in Greenwich Village (© 212/254-2525); in Midtown at 205 E. 42nd St. (© **212/822-2700**); and locations at Columbia University, in Alfred Learner Hall, 2871 Broadway (© **212/854-0150**), and 2871 Broadway (© **212/865-2700**).

In Canada, **Travel CUTS** (© **866/ 246-9762** or 416/614-2887; www. travelcuts.com) offers similar services.

In London, **USIT World** (© **0171/ 730-3402;** www.usitworld.com/ index.html), opposite Victoria Station, is a specialist in student and youth travel.

Hostelling International–American Youth Hostels (© **202/783-6161;** www.hiayh.org) has its largest hostel in New York City at 891 Amsterdam Ave., at 103rd Street (© **212/ 932-2300;** www.hinewyork.org); see chapter 5 for a review. Reserve well ahead. You'll also find other, privately run hostels with cheap dorm beds in chapter 5. For additional hostelling choices in the city (and North America), order *The Hostel Handbook* by sending a check or money order for $5 (payable to Jim Williams) to The Hostel Handbook, Dept: HHB, 722 St. Nicholas Ave., New York, NY 10031. You can also find ordering information and a selection of listings at **www. hostelhandbook.com**. More info and recommendations can also be found online at **Hostels.com**.

8 The 21st-Century Traveler

INTERNET ACCESS AWAY FROM HOME

Travelers have any number of ways to check their e-mail and access the Internet on the road. Of course, using your own laptop—or even a PDA (personal digital assistant) or electronic organizer with a modem—gives you the most flexibility. But even if you don't have a computer, you can access your e-mail and even your office computer from cybercafes.

WITHOUT YOUR OWN COMPUTER

It's hard nowadays to find a city that *doesn't* have a few cybercafes. Although there's no definitive directory for cybercafes—these are independent businesses, after all—three places to start looking are at **www.cybercaptive.com**,

www.netcafeguide.com, and **www. cybercafe.com**.

Aside from formal cybercafes, most **youth hostels** nowadays have at least one computer you can get to the Internet on. And most **public libraries** across the world offer Internet access free or for a small charge. Avoid **hotel business centers,** which often charge exorbitant rates.

To retrieve your e-mail, ask your **Internet Service Provider (ISP)** if it has a Web-based interface tied to your existing e-mail account. If your ISP doesn't have such an interface, you can use the free **mail2web** service (www. mail2web.com) to view (but not reply to) your home e-mail. For more flexibility, you may want to open a free, Web-based e-mail account with **Yahoo! Mail** (http://mail.yahoo.com).

(Microsoft's Hotmail is another popular option, but Hotmail has severe spam problems.) Your home ISP may be able to forward your e-mail to the Web-based account automatically.

If you need to access files on your office computer, look into a service called **GoToMyPC** (www.gotomypc.com). The service provides a Web-based interface for you to access and manipulate a distant PC from anywhere—even a cybercafe—provided your "target" PC is on and has an always-on connection to the Internet (such as with Road Runner cable). The service offers top-quality security, but if you're worried about hackers, use your own laptop rather than a cybercafe to access the GoToMyPC system.

WITH YOUR OWN COMPUTER

Major Internet Service Providers (ISP) have **local access numbers** around the world, allowing you to go online by simply placing a local call. Check your ISP's website or call its toll-free number and ask how you can use your current account away from home, and how much it will cost.

Wherever you go, bring a **connection kit** of the right power and phone adapters, a spare phone cord, and a spare Ethernet network cable.

If you have an 802.11b/**Wi-fi** card for your computer, several commercial companies have made wireless service available in airports, hotel lobbies, and coffee shops, primarily in the U.S. **T-Mobile Hotspot** (www.t-mobile.com/hotspot) serves up wireless connections at more than 1,000 Starbucks coffee shops nationwide. **Boingo**

(www.boingo.com) and **Wayport** (www.wayport.com) have set up networks in airports and high-class hotel lobbies. IPass providers (see above) also give you access to a few hundred wireless hotel lobby setups. Best of all, you don't need to be staying at the Four Seasons to use the hotel's network; just set yourself up on a nice couch in the lobby. Unfortunately, the companies' pricing policies are byzantine, with a variety of monthly, per-connection, and per-minute plans.

Community-minded individuals have also set up **free wireless networks** in major cities around the world. These networks are spotty, but you get what you (don't) pay for. Each network has a home page explaining how to set up your computer for their particular system; start your explorations at www.personaltelco.net/index.cgi/WirelessCommunities.

USING A CELLPHONE ACROSS THE U.S.

Just because your cellphone works at home doesn't mean it'll work elsewhere in the country (thanks to our nation's fragmented cellphone system). It's a good bet that your phone will work in major cities. But take a look at your wireless company's coverage map on its website before heading out—T-Mobile, Sprint, and Nextel are particularly weak in rural areas. If you need to stay in touch at a destination where you know your phone won't work, **rent** a phone that does from **InTouch USA** (✆ **800/872-7626;** www.intouchglobal.com) or a rental-car location, but beware that you'll pay $1 a minute or more for airtime.

9 Getting There

BY PLANE

Three major airports serve New York City: **John F. Kennedy International Airport** (✆ **718/244-4444**) in Queens, about 15 miles (1 hr.) from

Midtown; **LaGuardia Airport** (✆ **718/533-3400**), also in Queens, about 8 miles (30 min.) from Midtown; and **Newark International Airport** (✆ **973/961-6000**) in New

Jersey, about 16 miles (45 min.) from Midtown. Information about all three airports is available online at **www.panynj.gov**; click on the "Airports" tab on the left.

Even though LaGuardia is the closest airport to Manhattan, it has a hideous reputation for chaos, in both ticket-desk lines and baggage claim. You may want to arrive and depart at JFK or Newark instead. (JFK has the best reputation for timeliness among New York–area airports.)

Almost every major domestic carrier serves a New York–area airport; most serve two or all three. Among them are **American** (✆ **800/433-7300;** www.aa.com), **America West** (✆ **800/235-9292;** www.americawest.com), **Continental** (✆ **800/525-0280;** www.continental.com), **Delta** (✆ **800/221-1212;** www.delta.com), **Northwest** (✆ **800/225-2525;** www.nwa.com), **United** (✆ **800/241-6522;** www.united.com), and **US Airways** (✆ **800/864-8331;** www.usairways.com).

In recent years, there has been rapid growth in the number of no-frills airlines serving New York. You might check out **AirTran** (✆ 800/247-8726; www.airtran.com); Chicago-based **ATA** (✆ 800/435-9282; www.ata.com); **Frontier** (✆ 800/432-1359; www.flyfrontier.com); **Midway** (✆ 800/446-4392; www.midwayair.com); **Midwest Express** (✆ 800/452-2022; www.midwestexpress.com); and **Spirit** (✆ 800/772-7117; www.spiritair.com); The JFK-based cheap-chic airline **jetBlue** ✭ (✆ 800/JETBLUE; www.jetblue.com) has taken New York by storm with its low fares and good service. The leading discount airline, **Southwest** (✆ 800/435-9792; www.iflyswa.com), flies into MacArthur (Islip) Airport on Long Island, 50 miles east of Manhattan.

Most major international carriers serve New York; see "Getting to the United States," in chapter 3, for details. For advice on getting the best airfare, see "65 Money-Saving Tips" at the beginning of this chapter.

GETTING THROUGH THE AIRPORT

With the federalization of airport security, security procedures at U.S. airports are more stable and consistent. Generally, you'll be fine if you arrive **1 hour** before a domestic flight; if you show up late, tell an airline employee and she'll probably whisk you to the front of the line.

Bring a **current, government-issued photo ID** such as a driver's license or passport, and if you've got an E-ticket, print out the **confirmation page;** you'll need to show it at the security checkpoint, and your ID at the ticket counter or the gate. (Children under 18 do not need photo IDs for domestic flights, but the adults checking in with them need them.)

Security lines are getting shorter than they were during 2002 and 2003, but some doozies remain. If you have trouble standing for long periods of time, tell an airline employee; the

---

Tips   Choosing Your NYC-Area Airport

It's more convenient to fly into Newark than JFK if your destination is Manhattan, and fares to Newark are often cheaper than those to the other airports. Newark is particularly convenient if your hotel is in Midtown West or downtown. Taxi fare into Manhattan is roughly equivalent to the fare from JFK—and now, with the new AirTrain in place (see "Transportation to & from the New York–Area Airports," below), Newark has the quickest and easiest-to-use public transportation link with Manhattan.

airline will provide a wheelchair. Speed up security by **not wearing metal objects** such as big belt buckles or clanky earrings. If you've got metallic body parts, a note from your doctor can prevent a long chat with the security screeners. Keep in mind that only **ticketed passengers** are allowed past security, except for folks escorting passengers with disabilities or children.

Federalization has stabilized **what you can carry on** and **what you can't.** The general rule is that sharp things are out, nail clippers are okay, and food and beverages must be passed through the X-ray machine—but that security screeners can't make you drink from your coffee cup. Bring food in your carry-on rather than checking it, as explosive-detection machines used on checked luggage have been known to mistake food (especially chocolate, for some reason) for bombs. Travelers in the U.S. are allowed one carry-on bag, plus a "personal item" such as a purse, briefcase, or laptop bag. Carry-on hoarders can stuff all sorts of things into a laptop bag; as long as it has a laptop in it, it's still considered a personal item. The Transportation Security Administration (TSA) has issued a list of restricted items; check its website (www.tsa.gov/public/index.jsp) for details.

In 2003, the TSA phased out **gate check-in** at all U.S. airports. Passengers with E-tickets and without checked bags can still beat the ticket-counter lines by using **electronic kiosks** or even **online check-in.** Ask your airline which alternatives are available, and if you're using a kiosk, bring the credit card you used to book the ticket. If you're checking bags, you will still be able to use most airlines' kiosks; call your airline for up-to-date information. **Curbside check-in** is a good way to avoid lines, although a few airlines still ban curbside check-in entirely; call before you go.

At press time, the TSA is also recommending that you **not lock your checked luggage** so screeners can search it by hand if necessary. The agency says to use plastic ties instead, which can be bought at hardware stores and can be easily cut off.

TRANSPORTATION TO & FROM THE NEW YORK–AREA AIRPORTS

For transportation information for all three airports (JFK, LaGuardia, and Newark), call **Air-Ride (© 800/247-7433)**, which offers recorded details on bus and shuttle companies and car services 24 hours a day; live operators staff the line Monday through Friday from 8am to 6pm EST. Similar information is online at **www.panynj.gov/airports**.

The Port Authority also runs staffed Ground Transportation Information counters on the baggage-claim level in each terminal at each airport, where you can get information and book transport. Most transportation companies have courtesy phones near the baggage-claim area.

Generally, travel time between the airports and midtown Manhattan by taxi or car is 45 to 60 minutes for JFK, 20 to 35 minutes for LaGuardia, and 35 to 50 minutes for Newark. Always allow extra time, especially during rush hour, peak holiday travel times, and if you're taking a bus.

SUBWAYS & PUBLIC BUSES

Taking the MTA to and from the airport can be a hassle, but it's the cheapest way to go—just $2 each way. However, keep in mind that the subways and buses that serve the airports involve multiple transfers and staircases; count on more hauling to your hotel (or a taxi fare) once you arrive in Manhattan. This won't work for travelers with lots of luggage, because you won't have anywhere to store it on the bus or subway. You might not want to take the bus or the subway if you're

Tips   Money-Saving Package Deals

Before you start your search for the lowest airfare, you may want to consider booking your flight as part of a travel package that allows you to buy airfare and accommodations (and sometimes extras like sightseeing tours and theater tickets) at a pay-one-price discount.

Here are a few tips to help you tell one package from another, and figure out which one is right for you:

- **Read this guide.** Research New York City. Compare the rack rates we've published to the discounted rates offered by the packagers. If you're being offered a stay in a hotel that we haven't recommended, do more research to learn about it, especially if it isn't a reliable franchise like Holiday Inn or Hyatt. It's not a deal if you end up at a dump.

- **Read the fine print.** Make sure you know *exactly* what's included in the package. Are hotel taxes and airport transfers included, or are they extra? Conversely, don't pay for a rental car you don't need— and you won't need one in New York. Before you commit, make sure you know how much flexibility you have, say, if your kid gets sick or your boss suddenly asks you to adjust your vacation schedule.

- **Use your best judgment.** If a deal appears to be too good to be true, it probably is. Go with a reputable firm with a proven track record. This is where your travel agent can come in handy; he or she should be knowledgeable about different packagers.

So how do you find a package deal?

The best place to start is the travel section of your Sunday newspaper. Check the ads in the back of travel magazines like *Travel Holiday, National Geographic Traveler,* and *Arthur Frommer's Budget Travel.*

A terrific source for Big Apple packages is **New York City Vacation Packages** (★ (© **888/692-8701** or 570/714-4692; www.nycvp.com), which can sell you a complete package including hotel, theater tickets, and more—usually for significantly less than if you booked those

---

traveling very early or very late, as you may have to go through some dicey neighborhoods.

For more subway and bus information, see "Getting Around" in chapter 4.

From/to JFK You can take the **A train** to JFK, which connects to one of two free **shuttle buses** that serve all the JFK terminals. Plan on 2 hours in each direction, maybe more if you're traveling at rush hour: The subway ride from Midtown takes about 75 minutes, and you'll need another 20 to 30 minutes for the shuttle ride to

your terminal; also be sure to factor in waiting time at both ends.

Upon exiting the terminal, pick up the shuttle bus (marked LONG TERM PARKING LOT); it takes you to the **Howard Beach station,** where you get the A train to Manhattan. Service is every 10 to 15 minutes during rush hour and every 20 minutes at midday, and the subway fare is $2. If you're traveling to JFK from Manhattan, take the A train that says FAR ROCKAWAY or ROCKAWAY PARK—*not* LEFFERTS BOULEVARD. Get off at the Howard Beach/JFK Airport station things separately. What's more, NYCVP can often build a package that includes otherwise sold-out tickets to Broadway shows like *The Lion King* and sporting events; they'll even book airport transportation and dining reservations for you if you wish.

One of the biggest packagers in the Northeast, **Liberty Travel** (© 888/271-1584; www.libertytravel.com), offers 2- to 7-night New York packages that usually include freebies like a Circle Line cruise or tickets to the Empire State Building, plus lots of good hotels at every price point.

The major airlines offering good-value packages to New York include **Continental Airlines Vacations** (© 800/301-3800; www.continental.covacations.com), **Delta Vacations** (© 800/654-6559; www.deltavacations.com), **US Airways Vacations** (© 800/422-3861; www.usairwaysvacations.com), **United Vacations** (© 888/854-3899; www.unitedvacations.com), **American Airlines Vacations** (© 800/321-2121; www.aavacations.com), and **Northwest WorldVacations** (© 800/800-1504; www.nwa.com/vacpkg). You may want to choose the airline that has frequent service to your hometown or the one on which you accumulate frequent-flier miles.

If you're a late planner, check out the discounted packages offered by **Site59.com.** Their last-minute getaways can save you up to 60% on your entire package, and can be booked anytime between 3 hours and 14 days in advance. Various combinations are available, including flight and hotel, land only (if you've already booked your flight or will be arriving by car), and others that include dining, entertainment, and more.

If you'd prefer to take the train rather than fly, check with **Amtrak Vacations** (© 800/321-8684; www.amtrak.com/savings/amtrakvacations.html) for all-inclusive ride-and-stay packages.

and connect to the shuttle bus, A or B, which goes to your terminal (they're clearly marked). The subway can actually be more reliable than taking a car or taxi at the height of rush hour.

From/to LaGuardia The **M60 bus** serves all LaGuardia terminals. When leaving LaGuardia, follow the GROUND TRANSPORTATION signs and look for the **M60** stop sign at the curb. The bus will take you to Broadway and 116th Street on Manhattan's west side, where you can transfer to a downtown bus or the 1 or 9 subway; you can also pick up the N subway into Manhattan by disembarking at the Astoria Boulevard station in Queens. The bus runs daily between 4am and 1am, leaving at half-hour intervals and taking 40 to 50 minutes. Be sure to allow at least 1¼ hours, however; you never know about traffic. *Money-saving tip:* Use a Metro-Card to pay your fare and you'll save the extra $2 it usually costs for the transfer. For the complete schedule and other pickup and drop-off points, visit **www.mta.nyc.ny.us/nyct**.

PRIVATE BUSES & SHUTTLES Buses and shuttle services provide a

Newark's New AirTrain: From Jersey to Manhattan in Minutes

AirTrain Newark now connects Newark International Airport with Manhattan via a speedy monorail/rail link.

Even though you have to make a connection, the system is fast, pleasant, and easy to use. Each arrivals terminal at Newark International Airport has a boarding station, so follow the signs once you collect your bags. All AirTrains head to **Newark International Airport Station,** where you transfer to a **NJ Transit** train. NJ Transit will deliver you to New York Penn Station, where you can pick up a cab to your hotel.

The whole process can have you in Manhattan in 20 minutes if you catch a quick connection. NJ Transit trains run two to three times an hour during peak travel times (once an hour during early and late hours); you can check the schedules on monitors before you leave the terminal, and again at the train station. Tickets can be purchased from vending machines at both the air terminal and the train station (no ticket is required to board the AirTrain). The one-way fare is $11.15 (children under 5 ride free). Once you arrive at Penn Station, a taxi can take you directly to your hotel.

The AirTrain is an excellent alternative to the taxi system, and so far, it's getting good reviews. Even if you have to wait 15 minutes or so to make a connection, you're likely to find the transfer from the airport to Manhattan is actually quicker than taking a cab, especially during rush hours, when it's easy to get stuck in bumper-to-bumper traffic.

On your return trip, the AirTrain is far more predictable than subjecting yourself to the whims of traffic. What's more, you can check your flight's status at the Newark International Airport Station—and, if you're flying on **Continental,** you can get your boarding pass, which allows you to skip the long lines at the terminal (although those with bags to check must still stand in line at the terminal and follow all security procedures).

Note that travelers heading to points beyond the city can also pick up Amtrak and other NJ Transit trains at Newark International Airport Station to their final destinations.

A word of warning: If you have mobility issues, mountains of luggage, or a bevy of small children to keep track of, you'll find it easier to rely on a taxi, car service, or shuttle that can offer you door-to-door transfers.

For more information on AirTrain Newark, call ℂ **888/EWR-INFO** or go online to **www.airtrainnewark.com.** For connection details, click on the links on the AirTrain website or contact **NJ Transit** (ℂ **800/626-RIDE; www.njtransit.com**) or **Amtrak** (ℂ **800/USA-RAIL; www.amtrak.com**).

comfortable and less expensive (but usually more time-consuming) option for airport transfers than do taxis and car services.

Super Shuttle serves all three airports; **New York Airport Service** serves JFK and LaGuardia; **Olympia Trails and Express Shuttle USA**

serves Newark. If you're not taking the AirTrain, these services are my favorite option for getting to and from Newark during peak travel times because the drivers usually take lesser-known surface streets that make the ride much quicker than if you go with a taxi or car, which will virtually always stick to the traffic-clogged main route.

Express Shuttle USA (© **800/451-0455** or 212/315-3006) vans depart Newark every 20 to 30 minutes between 7am and 11:30pm. They will drop you off at most hotels between 21st and 103rd streets in Manhattan. No reservation is required; just go to the ground-transportation desk or dial **24** on the Express Shuttle USA courtesy phone in the baggage-claim area. Service from mid-Manhattan to all three airports operates daily from 5am to 9pm; you must call a day in advance to arrange a hotel pickup. The regular one-way fare to and from Newark is $13, but you can save a few bucks by prepaying your round-trip at the airport.

The familiar blue vans of **Super Shuttle** (© **800/BLUE-VAN** or 212/258-3826; www.supershuttle.com) serve all three area airports, providing door-to-door service to Manhattan and points on Long Island every 15 to 30 minutes around the clock. As with Gray Line, you don't need to reserve your airport-to-Manhattan ride; just go to the ground-transportation desk or use the courtesy phone in baggage claim and ask for Super Shuttle. Hotel pickups for your return trip require 24 to 48 hours' notice; you can make your reservations online. Fares run $15 to $19 per person, depending on the airport, with discounts available for additional persons in the same party. **New York Airport Service** (© **718/875-8200;** www.nyairport service.com) buses travel from JFK and LaGuardia to the Port Authority Bus Terminal (42nd St. and Eighth

Ave.), Grand Central Terminal (Park Ave. between 41st and 42nd sts.), and to select Midtown hotels between 27th and 59th streets, plus the Jamaica LIRR Station in Queens, where you can pick up a train for Long Island. Follow the GROUND TRANSPORTATION signs to the curbside pickup or look for the uniformed agent. Buses depart the airport every 20 to 70 minutes (depending on your departure point and destination) between 6am and midnight. Buses to JFK and LaGuardia depart the Port Authority and Grand Central Terminal on the Park Avenue side every 15 to 30 minutes, depending on the time of day and the day of the week. To request direct shuttle service from your hotel, call the above number at least 24 hours in advance. One-way fare for JFK is $13, $23 round-trip; to and from LaGuardia, it's $10 one way, $17 round trip.

Olympia Airport Express (© **877/894-9155** or 212/964-6233; www. olympiabus.com) provides service every 5 to 30 minutes (depending on the time of day) from Newark International Airport to Penn Station (the pickup point is the northwest corner of 34th St. and Eighth Ave. and the drop-off point is the southwest corner), the Port Authority Bus Terminal (on 42nd St. between Eighth and Ninth aves.), and Grand Central Terminal (on 41st St. between Park and Lexington aves.). Passengers to and from the Grand Central Terminal location can connect to Olympia's Midtown shuttle vans, which service select Midtown hotels. Call for the exact schedule for your return trip to the airport. The fare runs $11 one way, $21 round-trip; it's $5 more if you connect to the hotel shuttle. Seniors and travelers with disabilities ride for $5.

TAXIS Taxis are a quick and convenient way to travel to and from the

Tips   Flying into Islip on Southwest

Southwest Airlines, the nation's leading discount carrier, flies into the New York area via Long Island MacArthur Airport, 50 miles east of Manhattan. If you're on one of these flights, your cheapest option is to pick up the shuttle that **Colonial Transportation** (✆ 631/589-3500; www.colonialtransportation.com) offers, which traverses the 3 miles from the airport to the Ronkonkoma Long Island Rail Road Station, and take the LIRR train to Manhattan. The shuttle fare is $5 per person, $1 for each additional family member accompanying a full-fare customer. From Ronkonkoma, it's about a 1½-hour train ride to Manhattan's Penn Station; the one-way fare is $9.50 at peak hours, $6.50 off-peak (half fare for seniors 65 or older and kids 5–11). You can also catch the Suffolk County Transit bus S-57 between the airport and the station Monday through Saturday for $1.50. Trains usually leave Ronkonkoma once or twice every hour, depending on the day and time. For more information, call ✆ **718/217-LIRR** or go online to **www.mta.nyc.ny.us/lirr**.

For more money but less hassle, you can catch the **Hampton Jitney** coach (✆ **631/283-4600**; www.hamptonjitney.com) to drop-off points on Midtown's east side. The cost is $25 per person, plus taxi fare from the terminal to the Hampton Jitney stop. They can explain the details and arrange for taxi transport (usually through Colonial Transportation, above).

Colonial Transportation (✆ **631/589-3500**; www.colonialtransportation.com), **Classic Transportation** (✆ **631/567-5100**; www.classictrans.com), and **Legends** (✆ **888/LEGENDS** or 718/788-1234; www.legendslimo.com) will pick you up at Islip Airport and deliver you to Manhattan via car, but expect to pay about $125 plus tolls and tip. Still, this may not be a bad deal if there are four of you and you have a lot of luggage. Be sure to arrange for it 24 hours in advance.

For additional options and the latest information, call **631/467-3210** or visit **www.macarthurairport.com**.

---

airports, but you'll pay for the convenience of door-to-door service. They're available at taxi stands outside the terminals, with dispatchers on hand during peak hours at JFK and LaGuardia, around the clock at Newark. Follow the GROUND TRANSPORTATION or TAXI signs. There may be a line, but it generally moves pretty quickly. Fares, whether fixed or metered, do not include bridge and tunnel tolls ($3.50–$6) or a tip for the cabbie (15%–20% is customary). They include all passengers and luggage—

never pay more than the metered or flat rate, except for tolls and a tip (from 8pm–6am, a 50¢ surcharge also applies on New York yellow cabs). Taxis have a limit of four passengers, so if there are more in your group, you'll have to take more than one cab. For more on taxis, see "Getting Around" in chapter 4. Cab fares from the airports to the city are as follows:

- **From JFK:** A flat rate of $35 to Manhattan (plus tolls and tip) is charged. The meter will not be turned on and the surcharge will not be added. The flat rate does not apply on trips from Manhattan to the airport.

- **From LaGuardia:** $16 to $26, metered, plus tolls and tip.
- **From Newark:** The dispatcher for New Jersey taxis gives you a slip of paper with a flat rate ranging from $30 to $38 (toll and tip extra), depending on where you're going in Manhattan, so be precise about your destination. New York yellow cabs aren't permitted to pick up passengers at Newark. The yellow-cab fare from Manhattan to Newark is the meter amount plus $10 and tolls (about $40–$50, perhaps a few dollars more with tip). New Jersey taxis aren't permitted to take passengers from Manhattan to Newark.

Note that a taxi fare increase was being discussed at press time, so fares may be higher by the time you arrive.

PRIVATE CAR SERVICES Private car companies provide 24-hour door-to-door airport transfers. The advantage they offer over taking a taxi is that you can arrange your pickup in advance and avoid the hassles of the taxi line. A taxi is virtually always cheaper from JFK thanks to the flat fare; otherwise, as a general rule of thumb, expect to pay a tad less with a car service during rush hour (because there's no ticking meter in bumper-to-bumper traffic), slightly more at other times.

Call at least 24 hours in advance (even earlier on holidays), and a driver will meet you near baggage claim (or at your hotel for a return trip). You'll probably be asked to leave a credit-card number to guarantee your ride. You'll likely be offered the choice of indoor or curbside pickup; indoor pickup is more expensive, but makes it easier to hook up with your driver (who usually waits in baggage claim holding a sign with your name on it). You can save a few dollars if you arrange for an outside pickup; call the dispatcher as soon as you land, then take your luggage to the waiting area, where you'll wait for the driver, which can take anywhere from 10 minutes to a half-hour. Besides the wait, the other disadvantage is that curbside can be chaos during prime deplaning hours.

Vehicles range from sedans to vans to limos and tend to be relatively clean and comfortable. Prices vary slightly by company and the size of car reserved, but expect a rate equivalent to taxi fare (except for the fare from JFK, as noted above) if you request a basic sedan and have only one stop; toll and tip policies are the same. Ask when booking what the fare will be and if you can use your credit card to pay for the ride so there are no surprises at drop-off time. There may be waiting charges tacked on if the driver has to wait an excessive amount of time for your plane to land, but the car companies will usually check on your flight beforehand to get an accurate landing time.

I've had the best luck with **Carmel** (© 800/922-7635 or 212/666-6666) and **Legends** (© 888/LEGENDS or 718/788-1234); **Allstate** (© 800/ 453-4099 or 212/333-3333) and

---

⌒Tips An Airport Warning

Never accept a car ride from the hustlers who hang out in the terminal halls. They're illegal, don't have proper insurance, and aren't safe. You can tell who they are because they'll approach you with a suspicious conspiratorial air and ask if you need a ride. Not from them, you don't. Sanctioned city cabs and car services wait outside the terminals.

Tips   **Getting to the Other Boroughs & the 'Burbs**

If you're traveling to a borough other than Manhattan, call **ETS Air Service** (© **718/221-5341**) for shared door-to-door service. For Long Island service, call **Classic Transportation** (© **631/567-5100**; www.classictrans. com) for car service, or **JFK Flyer** (© **516/766-6722**) for bus service. For service to Westchester County or Connecticut, contact **Connecticut Limousine** (© **800/472-5466** or 203/878-2222; www.ctlimo.com) or **Prime Time Shuttle of Connecticut** (© **800/377-8745**; www.primetimeshuttle.com).

If you're traveling to points in New Jersey from Newark Airport, call **Olympic Limousine** (© **800/822-9797** or 732/938-4300) for Ocean and Monmouth counties; the **Airporter** (© **800/385-4000** or 609/587-6600; www.goairporter.com) to Middlesex and Mercer counties, plus Bucks County, Penn.; or **State Shuttle** (© **800/427-3207** or 973/729-0030; www. stateshuttle.com) for destinations throughout New Jersey.

Additionally, **New York Airport Service** express buses (© **718/875-8200**; www.nyairportservice.com) serve the entire New York metropolitan region from JFK and LaGuardia, offering connections to the Long Island Rail Road; the Metro North Rail Road to Westchester County, upstate New York, and Connecticut; and New York's Port Authority, where you can pick up buses to points throughout New Jersey.

Tel-Aviv (© **800/222-9888** or 212/777-7777) also have reasonable reputations. (Keep in mind, though, that these services are only as good as the individual drivers—and sometimes there's a lemon in the bunch. If you have a problem, report it to the office.)

BY TRAIN

Amtrak (© **800/USA-RAIL;** www. amtrak.com) runs frequent service to New York City's **Penn Station,** on Seventh Avenue between 31st and 33rd streets, where you can pick up a taxi, subway, or bus.

If you're traveling to New York from a city along Amtrak's Northeast Corridor, Amtrak may be your best bet now that they've rolled out their new Acela trains, which cut travel time from D.C. down to 2½ hours, and travel time from Boston to 3 hours. Trains can also be less of a hassle, because they take you into Manhattan (thereby avoiding time-consuming and expensive airport transfers).

To get the best rates, book early (as much as 6 months in advance) and travel on weekends. See "65 Money-Saving Tips," at the beginning of this chapter, for more wallet-friendly advice, and check Amtrak's website for special discounted fares.

BY BUS

Buses arrive at the **Port Authority Terminal,** on Eighth Avenue between 40th and 42nd streets, where you can transfer to your hotel by taxi, subway, or bus. Buses can be slow and uncomfortable, but fares are usually much lower than trains and airlines.

Greyhound Bus Lines (© **800/229-9424;** www.greyhound.com) is the nation's biggest bus carrier. You'll find a list of their special fares and discounts on their Web page; ask about special deals if you call.

Peter Pan Lines (© **800/343-9999,** 212/564-8484, or 212/967-2900; www.peterpanbus.com) services the entire Northeast Corridor, from New Hampshire to Albany, N.Y., to Washington, D.C.; rates are low, and buses are much more comfortable than Greyhound's. For a complete list of bus carriers that serve Manhattan's Port Authority Bus Terminal, visit **www.panynj.gov/tbt/busline.HTM**.

Although the bus is likely to be the cheapest option, especially for East Coast short hauls, don't just assume. Always compare fares; sometimes, a full-fare bus ticket is no cheaper than the train. If you get lucky, you might even catch an airline fare sale that will make flying the most prudent option.

BY CAR

From the **New Jersey Turnpike** (I-95) and points west, there are three Hudson River crossings into the city's west side: the **Holland Tunnel** (lower Manhattan), the **Lincoln Tunnel** (Midtown), and the **George Washington Bridge** (Upper Manhattan). At press time, cars with only one passenger were prohibited from traveling from New Jersey through the Holland Tunnel during morning rush hour.

From **upstate New York,** take the **New York State Thruway** (I-87), which crosses the Hudson River on the Tappan Zee Bridge and becomes the **Major Deegan Expressway** (I-87) through the Bronx. For the East Side, continue to the Triborough Bridge and down FDR Drive. For the West Side, take the Cross Bronx Expressway (I-95) to the Henry Hudson Parkway or the Taconic State Parkway to the Saw Mill River Parkway to the Henry Hudson Parkway south.

From **New England,** the **New England Thruway** (I-95) connects with the **Bruckner Expressway** (I-278), which leads to the Triborough Bridge and FDR Drive on the East Side. For the West Side, take the Bruckner to the Cross Bronx Expressway (I-95) to the Henry Hudson Parkway south.

You'll have to pay tolls along some of these roads and at most crossings.

Once you arrive in Manhattan, park your car in a garage (expect to pay $20–$45 per day) and leave it. Don't use your car for traveling within the city. Public transportation, taxis, and walking will get you where you want to go much less stressfully.

10 Recommended Books & Films

For the definitive history of the birth of New York City to the end of the 19th century, there is no better read than *Gotham: A History of New York City to 1898,* by Edwin R. Burrows and Mike Wallace (Oxford University Press, 1998). Another recommended historical look at the growth of New York City, this one told in a breezy narrative tone, is *The Epic of New York City: A Narrative History,* by Edward Robb Ellis (Kodansha, 1997).

Luc Sante's *Low Life: Lures and Snares of Old New York* (Vintage Departures, 1992) details the bad old days of brothels, drug dens, and gambling saloons in New York in the early 20th century. A lively, fascinating read.

One of master biographer Robert Caro's early works, *The Power Broker: Robert Moses and the Fall of New York* (Random House, 1974), focuses on how master deal maker Robert Moses's vision transformed New York to what it became in the second half of the 20th century.

In *The Great Bridge: The Epic Story of the Building of the Brooklyn Bridge* (Simon & Schuster, 1983), author David McCullough devotes his estimable talents to the story of the Brooklyn Bridge.

The companion to the PBS series (see below) *New York,* by Ric Burns, Lisa Ades, and James Sanders (Knopf, 2001), uses lavish photographs and illustrations to show the growth of New York City.

There are not many places as cinematic as New York City. Filmmakers sometimes think of the city as a character itself. The list of movies in which New York plays a crucial role are too many to mention, but here are some of the top New York City movies:

Possibly the best New York City promotional film is the musical, *On The Town* with Gene Kelly and Frank Sinatra, about three sailors with 24-hours' leave spent exploring Gotham. Shot on location, all the landmarks, circa 1949, are captured in beautiful Technicolor.

Woody Allen is known as a New York filmmaker and proudly shoots all his films in the city. One of his best, and a good, but maybe a bit dated look at neurotic New York, is *Annie Hall.*

Following in Woody Allen's footsteps are director Rob Reiner and writer Nora Ephron, who made *When Harry Met Sally,* sort of a poor-man's *Annie Hall,* but a gorgeous cinematic tribute to New York. The famous "orgasm" scene was filmed in **Katz's Deli** (page 146).

"I love this dirty town," says Burt Lancaster in the gritty, crackling *Sweet Smell of Success.* In the beautifully black-and-white–photographed movie, Lancaster plays malicious gossip columnist J.J. Hunsecker, and Tony Curtis is perfectly despicable as the groveling publicist, Sidney Falco.

Another filmmaker identified with New York is Martin Scorsese. He has made many films in which New York played a central role, from *Mean Streets* to, most recently, *Gangs of New York,* which was actually filmed in Italy. But the one film where New York is a character, and not a very flattering one, is *Taxi Driver.* The Academy Award–nominated 1976 movie is tough and bloody, but to see images of seedy, grindhouse Times Square as it used to be before its recent reincarnation, there is no better film.

The best history of New York on video is the Ric Burns documentary, *New York,* which aired on PBS. The seven-disc, 14-hour DVD (also available on VHS) is a must see for anyone interested in the evolution of this great city.

3

For International Visitors

New York's global media profile might make it appear familiar, but movies and TV, music videos, and news images distort as much as they reflect. The gap between image and reality can make certain situations puzzling for the international—or even the domestic—visitor. This chapter will help prepare you for the more common issues that you might encounter.

1 Preparing for Your Trip

ENTRY REQUIREMENTS

Be sure to check with any U.S. embassy or consulate for the latest information, requirements, and travel advisories. You can obtain a visa application and other information online at the **U.S. State Department**'s website, **http://travel.state.gov**.

VISAS The U.S. State Department has a **Visa Waiver Program** allowing citizens of certain countries to enter the United States without a visa for stays of up to 90 days. At press time these included Andorra, Australia, Austria, Belgium, Brunei, Denmark, Finland, France, Germany, Iceland, Ireland, Italy, Japan, Liechtenstein, Luxembourg, Monaco, the Netherlands, New Zealand, Norway, Portugal, San Marino, Singapore, Slovenia, Spain, Sweden, Switzerland, and the United Kingdom. Citizens of these countries need only a valid passport and a round-trip air or cruise ticket in their possession upon arrival. If they first enter the United States, they may also visit Mexico, Canada, Bermuda, and/or the Caribbean islands and return to the United States without a visa. Further information is available from any U.S. embassy or consulate. Canadian citizens may enter the United States without visas; they need only proof of residence.

Citizens of all other countries must have (1) a valid passport that expires at least 6 months later than the end of their visit, and (2) a tourist visa, which may be obtained without charge from any U.S. consulate.

To obtain a visa, the traveler must submit a completed application form (either in person or by mail) with a 1½-inch-square photo, and must demonstrate binding ties to a residence abroad. Usually you can obtain a visa at once or within 24 hours, but it may take longer during the summer rush from June through August. If you cannot go in person, contact the nearest U.S. embassy or consulate for directions on applying by mail. Your travel agent or airline office may also be able to provide you with visa applications and instructions. The U.S. consulate or embassy that issues your visa will determine whether you will be issued a multiple- or single-entry visa and any restrictions regarding the length of your stay.

British subjects can get up-to-date visa information by calling the **U.S. Embassy Visa Information Line** (© **0891/200-290**) or by visiting the "Consular Services" section of the American Embassy London's website at www.usembassy.org.uk.

Irish citizens can get up-to-date visa information through the **Embassy of USA Dublin,** 42 Elgin Rd., Dublin 4, Ireland (*☎* **353/ 1-668-8777**), or by checking the "Consular Services" section of the website at www.usembassy.ie.

Australian citizens can get up-to-date visa information by contacting the **U.S. Embassy Canberra,** Moonah Place, Yarralumla, ACT 2600 (*☎* **02/6214-5600**), or by checking the U.S. Diplomatic Mission's website at http://usembassy-australia.state.gov/consular.

Citizens of **New Zealand** can get up-to-date visa information by contacting the **U.S. Embassy New Zealand,** 29 Fitzherbert Terr., Thorndon, Wellington (*☎* **644/472-2068**), or going to the "Services to New Zealanders" section of the website at http://usembassy.org.nz.

MEDICAL REQUIREMENTS

Unless you're arriving from an area known to be suffering from an epidemic (particularly cholera or yellow fever), inoculations or vaccinations are not required for entry into the United States. If you have a medical condition that requires **syringe-administered medications,** carry a valid, signed prescription from your physician—the Federal Aviation Administration (FAA) no longer allows airline passengers to pack syringes in their carry-on baggage without documented proof of medical need. If you have a disease that requires treatment with **narcotics,** you should also carry documented proof with you—smuggling narcotics aboard a plane is a serious offense that carries severe penalties in the U.S.

For **HIV-positive visitors,** requirements for entering the U.S. are somewhat vague and change frequently. According to *HIV and Immigrants: A Manual for AIDS Service Providers,* the Immigration and Naturalization Service (INS) doesn't require a medical exam for entry into the United States,

but INS officials may stop individuals because they look sick or because they are carrying AIDS/HIV medicine.

If an HIV-positive non-citizen applies for a non-immigrant visa, the question on the application regarding communicable diseases is tricky no matter which way it's answered. If the applicant checks "no," INS may deny the visa on the grounds that the applicant committed fraud. If the applicant checks "yes" or if INS suspects the person is HIV-positive, it will deny the visa unless the applicant asks for a special waiver for visitors. This waiver is for people visiting the United States for a short time, to attend a conference, for instance, to visit close relatives, or to receive medical treatment. For up-to-the-minute information, contact the Centers for Disease Control's **National Center for HIV** (*☎* **404/332-4559;** www.aidsinfo. nih.gov) or the **Gay Men's Health Crisis** (*☎* **212/367-1000;** www. gmhc.org).

DRIVER'S LICENSES Foreign driver's licenses are mostly recognized in the U.S., although you may want to get an international driver's license if your home license is not in English. (You don't need a car to get around New York City, anyway.)

PASSPORT INFORMATION

Safeguard your passport in an inconspicuous place like a money belt. Make a copy of the critical pages, including the passport number, and store it in a safe place, separate from the passport. If you lose your passport, contact the nearest consulate of your native country as soon as possible. Applications are downloadable from the websites listed below.

Note: The International Civil Aviation Organization (ICAO) has recommended that *every* individual who travels by air have his or her own passport. In response, many countries now require that children have their own passports to travel internationally, where before those under 16 or so may have been allowed to travel on a parent or guardian's passport.

FOR RESIDENTS OF CANADA

You can pick up a passport application at one of 28 regional passport offices or most travel agencies. Canadian children who travel must have their own passports. However, if you hold a valid Canadian passport issued before December 11, 2001, that bears the name of your child, the passport remains valid for you and your child until it expires. Passports cost C$85 for those 16 years and older (valid 5 years), C$35 for children 3 to 15 (valid 5 years), and C$20, for children under 3 (valid for 3 years). Applications, which must be accompanied by two identical passport-sized photographs and proof of Canadian citizenship, are available at travel agencies in Canada or from the central **Passport Office,** Department of Foreign Affairs and International Trade, Ottawa, ON K1A 0G3 (© **800/567-6868;** www. ppt.gc.ca/online_forms/index_e.asp). Processing takes 5 to 10 days if you apply in person, 3 weeks by mail.

FOR RESIDENTS OF THE UNITED KINGDOM

As a member of the European Union, you need only an identity card, not a passport, to travel to other EU countries. However, if you already possess a passport, it's always useful to carry it. To pick up an application for a standard 10-year passport (5-year passport for children under 16), visit the nearest Passport Office, major post office, or travel agency. You can also contact the **United Kingdom Passport Service** at © **0870/571-0410** or visit its website at www.passport.gov.uk. Passports are £33 for adults and £19 for children under 16, with an additional £30 fee if you apply in person at a Passport Office. Processing takes

about 2 weeks (1 week if you apply at the Passport Office).

FOR RESIDENTS OF IRELAND

You can apply for a 10-year passport, costing €57, at the **Passport Office,** Setanta Centre, Molesworth Street, Dublin 2 (© **01/671-1633;** www.irl gov.ie/iveagh). Those under age 18 and over 65 must apply for a €12 3-year passport. You can also apply at 1A South Mall, Cork (© **021/272-525**) or over the counter at most main post offices.

FOR RESIDENTS OF AUSTRALIA

You can pick up an application from your local post office or any branch of Passports Australia, but you must schedule an interview at the passport office to present your application materials. Call the **Australian Passport Information Service** at © **131-232,** or visit the government website at www.passports.gov.au. Passports for adults are A$144, and for those under 18, A$72.

FOR RESIDENTS OF NEW ZEALAND

You can pick up a passport application at any New Zealand Passports Office or download it from their website. Contact the **Passports Office** at © **0800/225-050** in New Zealand, or 04/474-8100, or log on to www. passports.govt.nz. Passports for adults are NZ$80, and for children under 16, NZ$40.

CUSTOMS
WHAT YOU CAN BRING IN

Every visitor over 21 years of age may bring in, free of duty: (1) 1 liter of wine or hard liquor; (2) 200 cigarettes, 100 cigars (but not from Cuba), or 3 pounds of smoking tobacco; and (3) $100 worth of gifts. These exemptions are for travelers who spend at least 72 hours in the United States and who have not claimed them within the preceding 6 months. It is forbidden to bring in foodstuffs (particularly fruit, cooked meats, and canned goods) and plants (vegetables, seeds, tropical plants, and the like). Foreign tourists may bring in or take out up to $10,000 in U.S. or foreign currency with no formalities; larger sums must be declared to U.S. Customs on entering or leaving, which includes filing form CM 4790. For more specific information, contact your nearest U.S. embassy or consulate, or the **U.S. Customs** office (✆ **202/927-1770** or www.customs.ustreas.gov).

Declare any medicines you are carrying and bring a letter or prescription from your doctor with you; you may bring in no more than you would normally use in the duration of your visit.

WHAT YOU CAN TAKE HOME

U.K. citizens returning from a non-EU country have a customs allowance of: 200 cigarettes; 50 cigars; 250g of smoking tobacco; 2 liters of still table wine; 1 liter of spirits or strong liqueurs (over 22% volume); 2 liters of fortified wine, sparkling wine, or other liqueurs; 60ml perfume; 250ml of toilet water; and £145 worth of all other goods, including gifts and souvenirs. People under 17 cannot have the tobacco or alcohol allowance. For more information, contact HM Customs & Excise at ✆ **0845/010-9000** (from outside the U.K., ✆ 020/8929-0152), or consult their website at www.hmce.gov.uk.

For a clear summary of **Canadian** rules, request the booklet *I Declare,* issued by the **Canada Customs and Revenue Agency** (✆ **800/461-9999** in Canada, or ✆ 204/983-3500; www.ccra-adrc.gc.ca). Canada allows its citizens a C$750 exemption, and you're allowed to bring back duty-free one carton of cigarettes, 1 can of tobacco, 40 imperial ounces of liquor, and 50 cigars. You're also allowed to mail gifts to Canada valued at less

than C$60 a day, if they're unsolicited and don't contain alcohol or tobacco (write on the package "Unsolicited gift, under $60 value"). All valuables should be declared on the Y-38 form before departure, including serial numbers of valuables you own, such as foreign cameras. *Note:* The $750 exemption can be used only once a year and only after an absence of 7 days.

The duty-free allowance in **Australia** is A$400 or, for those under 18, A$200. Citizens age 18 and over can bring in 250 cigarettes or 250 grams of loose tobacco, and 1,125 milliliters of alcohol. If you're returning with valuables you already own, such as foreign-made cameras, you should file form B263. A helpful brochure available from Australian consulates or Customs offices is *Know Before You Go.* For more information, call the **Australian Customs Service** at ✆ **1300/363-263,** or log on to www.customs.gov.au.

The duty-free allowance for **New Zealand** is NZ$700. Citizens over 17 can bring in 200 cigarettes, 50 cigars, or 250 grams of tobacco (or a mixture of all three if their combined weight doesn't exceed 250g); plus 4.5 liters of wine and beer, or 1.125 liters of liquor. New Zealand currency does not carry import or export restrictions. Fill out a certificate of export, listing the valuables you are taking out of the country; that way, you can bring them back without paying duty. Most questions are answered in a free pamphlet available at New Zealand consulates and Customs offices: *New Zealand Customs Guide for Travellers, Notice no. 4.* For more information, contact **New Zealand Customs,** The Customhouse, 17–21 Whitmore St., Box 2218, Wellington (✆ **0800/428-786** or 04/473-6099; www.customs. govt.nz).

HEALTH INSURANCE

Although it's not required of travelers, health insurance is recommended. Unlike many European countries, the

United States does not usually offer free or low-cost medical care to its citizens or visitors. Doctors and hospitals are expensive, and in most cases will require advance payment or proof of coverage before they render their services. Policies can cover everything from the loss or theft of your baggage and trip cancellation to the guarantee of bail in case you're arrested. Good policies will also cover the costs of an accident, repatriation, or death. Packages such as **Europ Assistance's "Worldwide Healthcare Plan"** are sold by European automobile clubs and travel agencies at attractive rates. **Worldwide Assistance Services, Inc.** (© 800/821-2828; www.worldwide assistance.com) is the agent for Europ Assistance in the United States.

Though lack of health insurance may prevent you from being admitted to a hospital in non-emergencies, don't worry about being left on a street corner to die: The American way is to fix you now and bill the living daylights out of you later.

INSURANCE FOR BRITISH TRAVELERS Most big travel agents offer their own insurance and will probably try to sell you their package when you book a holiday. **Britain's Consumers' Association** recommends that you insist on seeing the policy and reading the fine print before buying travel insurance. **The Association of British Insurers** (© 020/7600-3333; www.abi.org.uk) gives advice by phone and publishes *Holiday Insurance,* a free guide to policy provisions and prices. You might also shop around for better deals: Try **Columbus Direct** (© 020/7375-0011; www.columbusdirect.net).

INSURANCE FOR CANADIAN TRAVELERS Canadians should check with their provincial health plan offices or call **Health Canada** (© 613/957-2991; www.hc-sc.gc.ca) to find out the extent of their coverage and what documentation and receipts they must take home in case they are treated in the United States.

MONEY

CURRENCY The U.S. monetary system is very simple: The most common **bills** are the $1 (a "buck"), $5, $10, and $20 denominations. There are also $2 bills (seldom seen), $50 bills, and $100 bills (the last two are usually not welcome as payment for small purchases). All the paper money was recently redesigned, making the famous faces adorning them disproportionately large. The old-style bills are still legal tender.

There are seven denominations of coins: 1¢ (1 cent, or a penny); 5¢ (5 cents, or a nickel); 10¢ (10 cents, or a dime); 25¢ (25 cents, or a quarter); 50¢ (50 cents, or a half dollar); the gold "Sacagawea" coin worth $1; and, still in circulation, the Susan B. Anthony dollar coin. In New York City, you may receive dollar coins as change from MetroCard machines and at post offices.

CURRENCY EXCHANGE The foreign-exchange bureaus so common in Europe are rare even at airports in the United States and nonexistent outside major cities. You'll find them in New York's tourist areas like Times Square, but expect a lousy exchange rate. **American Express** (© 800/AXP-TRIP; www.american express.com) has many offices in the city, including 1185 Sixth Ave., at 47th Street (© 212/398-8585); at the New York Marriott Marquis hotel, 1535 Broadway, in the 8th-floor lobby (© 212/575-6580); on the mezzanine level at Macy's Herald Square, 34th Street and Broadway (© 212/695-8075); and at 374 Park Ave., at 53rd Street (© 212/421-8240). Visit http://travel.americanexpress.com/travel/personal/resources/tso to locate additional travel service offices.

> **Tips** **Getting the Best Exchange Rate**
>
> You'll actually get the best exchange rate for your national currency if you withdraw money from an ATM. But keep in mind that many banks impose a fee every time a card is used at an ATM (anywhere from $1–$3, depending on the ATM you choose and what your home bank is), so you may want to factor these fees in when you weigh your options.

Thomas Cook Currency Services (© 800/CURRENCY; www.us.thomascook.com) are at 1590 Broadway at 48th Street (© 212/265-6063); 1271 Broadway, at 32nd Street (© 212/679-4877); 317 Madison Ave. at 42nd Street (© 212/883-0401); 29 Broadway, south of Wall Street (© 212/363-6206); and 511 Madison Ave., at 53rd Street (© 212/753-2595).

TRAVELER'S CHECKS Though traveler's checks are widely accepted, make sure that they're denominated in U.S. dollars, as foreign-currency checks are often difficult to exchange. The three traveler's checks that are most widely recognized are **Visa, American Express,** and **Thomas Cook.** Record the numbers of the checks, and keep that information in a separate place in case they get lost or stolen. Most businesses are good about taking traveler's checks, but you're better off cashing them in at a bank (in small amounts, of course) and paying in cash. *Note:* You'll need identification, such as a driver's license or passport, to change a traveler's check.

CREDIT CARDS & ATMS Credit cards are the most widely used form of payment in the United States: **Visa** (Barclaycard in Britain), **MasterCard** (EuroCard in Europe, Access in Britain, Chargex in Canada), **American Express, Diners Club, Discover,** and **Carte Blanche.** There are, however, a handful of stores and restaurants, including some of the inexpensive ones listed in this book, that do not take credit cards, so be

sure to ask in advance. Most businesses display a sticker near their entrance to let you know which cards they accept. (*Note:* Businesses may require a minimum purchase, usually around $10, to use a credit card.)

You should bring at least one major credit card. You must have a credit or charge card to rent a car. Hotels and airlines usually require a credit-card imprint as a deposit against expenses, and in an emergency a credit card can be priceless.

You'll find **automated teller machines (ATMs)** on just about every block—at least in almost every town—across the country. Some ATMs will allow you to draw U.S. currency against your bank and credit cards. Check with your bank before leaving home, and remember that you will need a personal identification number (PIN) to do so. Most accept Visa, MasterCard, and American Express, as well as ATM cards from other U.S. banks. Expect to be charged up to $3 per transaction, however, if you're not using your own bank's ATM.

ATM cards with major credit card backing, known as "debit cards," are now a commonly acceptable form of payment in most stores and restaurants. Debit cards draw money directly from your checking account. Some stores enable you to receive "cash back" on your debit-card purchases as well.

SAFETY

Tourist areas in Manhattan are generally safe, and the city has experienced a dramatic drop in its crime rate over the last several years. Still, crime is a national problem, and U.S. urban areas tend to be less safe than those in Europe or Japan. Always stay alert, use your head, and trust your instincts. If you feel you're in an unsafe area or situation, you should leave as quickly as possible.

If you're in doubt about which neighborhoods are safe, don't hesitate to make inquiries with the hotel front-desk staff or the local tourist office.

Avoid deserted areas, especially at night, and don't go into parks after dark unless there's a concert or similar occasion that will attract a crowd.

Avoid carrying valuables on the street, and keep cameras or electronic equipment covered when not in use. If you're using a map, consult it inconspicuously—or study it before you leave your room. Hold onto your pocketbook, and place your billfold in an inside pocket. In theaters, restaurants, and other public places, keep your possessions in sight.

Always lock your room door. Hotels are open to the public, and in a large hotel, security may not be able to screen everyone who enters.

DRIVING An inviolable rule of thumb for New York: Don't even *think* of driving in the city. Like many cities, New York has its own arcane rules of the road, one-way streets, incomprehensible street-parking signs, and expensive parking garages. Public transportation—buses, subways, or taxis—will get you anywhere you want to go quickly and easily.

If you do drive to New York in a rental car, return it as soon as you arrive and rent another when you're ready to leave.

2 Getting to the United States

In addition to the domestic airlines listed in chapter 2, many international carriers serve John F. Kennedy International and Newark airports. **British Airways** (✆ **0845/77-333-77** or 0870/55-111-55 in the U.K., or 800/ AIRWAYS in the U.S.; www.british-airways.com) has daily service from London as well as direct flights from Manchester and Glasgow. **Virgin Atlantic** (✆ **01293/747-747** or 01293/511-581 in the U.K., or 800/862-8621 in the U.S.; www.virgin-atlantic.com) flies from London's Heathrow to New York.

Canadian readers might book flights on **Air Canada** (✆ **888/247-2262;** www.aircanada.ca), which offers direct service from Toronto, Montreal, Ottawa, and other cities.

Aer Lingus flies from Ireland to New York (✆ **0818/365000** in Ireland, 800/IRISH-AIR in the U.S.; www.aerlingus.ie). The following U.S. airlines fly to New York from most major European cities: **Continental** (✆ **0800/776-464** in the U.K., or 800/525-0280 in the U.S.; www.continental.com); **United** (✆ **0845/844-4777** in the U.K., or 800/864-8331 in the U.S.; www.ual.com); **American** (✆ **0208/572-5555** or 0845/778-9789 in the U.K., or 800/433-7300 in the U.S.; www.aa.com); and **Delta** (✆ **0800/414-767** in the U.K., or 800/221-4141 in the U.S.; www.delta.com).

Qantas (✆ **13-13-13** in Australia, 800/227-4500 in the U.S.; www.qantas.com.au) and **Air New Zealand** (✆ **0800/737-000** in New Zealand, 800/262-1234 in the U.S.; www.airnewzealand.co.nz) fly to the West Coast and will book you through to New York City on a partner airline.

For tips on finding the best fare to New York, see chapter 2, "Planning an Affordable Trip to New York City."

IMMIGRATION & CUSTOMS CLEARANCE Getting through immigration at the airport can take as

> ## Tips How to Save on International Airfares
>
> The idea of traveling abroad on a budget is something of an oxy-moron, especially when New York is your destination, but you can reduce the price of your airfare by a significant amount if you take the time to shop around.
>
> If you're on a tight budget and you're coming from Europe, consider traveling to New York between January and March. That's when airlines such as British Airways and Virgin Atlantic pull out all the stops to fill their post-holiday flights, and fares plummet. Hotels are also suffering the after-Christmas blues, and rooms often go for a relative song.
>
> If you're coming from anywhere else overseas, you can take advantage of the APEX (Advance Purchase Excursion) reductions offered by all major U.S. and European carriers. These usually require 7 to 21 days advance booking, cannot be canceled, and might come with significant change fees, but they'll save you hundreds of dollars over full-fare rates.
>
> Operated by the European Travel Network, **www.discount-tickets. com** is a great online source for regular and discounted airfares. You can use this site to compare rates and book accommodations, cars, and tours. Click on "Special Offers" for the latest package deals. Students should also try **USIT World** (© **0171/730-2101;** www.usitworld.com/index.html).
>
> Canadian travelers should check out the deals offered by **Travel CUTS** (© **866/246-9762;** www.travelcuts.com).
>
> For more money-saving airline advice, see "65 Money-Saving Tips," at the beginning of chapter 2.

long as 2 hours on some days, especially on summer weekends. This is especially true in the aftermath of the 9/11 terrorist attacks, with security being considerably beefed up at U.S. airports.

People traveling by air from Canada, Bermuda, and a few other countries can sometimes clear Customs and Immigration at the point of departure, which is much quicker.

3 If You're Traveling Beyond New York City

BY PLANE Some large airlines like Northwest and Delta offer travelers on their overseas flights special discount tickets called **Visit USA,** allowing mostly one-way travel from one U.S. destination to another at very low prices. These tickets are not on sale in the United States and must be purchased abroad in conjunction with your international ticket. This system is the best, easiest, and fastest way to see disparate parts of the United States at low cost. You should obtain information well in advance from your travel agent or the airline, since the conditions attached to these discount tickets can be changed without advance notice.

BY TRAIN If you're making a short hop to an East Coast city like Boston or Washington, D.C., rail is the best way to go. **Amtrak** (© **800/USA-RAIL;** www.amtrak.com) trains leave from New York's Penn Station, at Seventh Avenue and 34th Street. For more on Amtrak, see "Getting There" in chapter 2.

International visitors (excluding Canada) can buy a **USA Rail Pass,** good for 15 or 30 days of unlimited travel on Amtrak (℗ **800/USA-RAIL;** www.amtrak.com). The pass is available through many foreign travel agents. Prices in 2003 for a 15-day pass were $295 off-peak, $440 peak; a 30-day pass costs $385 off-peak, $550 peak. With a foreign passport, you can also buy passes at some Amtrak offices in the United States. Reservations are generally required and should be made for each part of your trip as early as possible. Regional rail passes are also available.

BY BUS Far from pleasant or speedy, buses nevertheless are your most economical option for traveling around the U.S. **Greyhound/Trailways** (℗ **800/229-9424** or 402/231-2222; www.greyhound.com) links destinations throughout the U.S., although smaller companies like **Peter Pan Bus Lines** (℗ **800/237-8747** or 413/781-2900; www.peterpanbus.com) offer better service to East Coast cities. Many companies offer discounts to students, travelers linking multiple destinations, or off-season travelers. For a list of bus carriers serving New York City, visit **www.panynj.gov/tbt/pabframe.HTM.**

Greyhound/Trailways also offers an **International Ameripass** that must be purchased before coming to the United States, or by phone through the Greyhound International Office at the Port Authority Bus Terminal in New York City (℗ **212/71-0492**). The pass can be obtained from foreign travel agents or through Greyhound's website (order at least 21 days before your departure to the U.S.) and costs less than the domestic version. 2003 passes cost as follows: 4 days ($160), 7 days ($219), 10 days ($269), 15 days ($329), 21 days ($379), 30 days ($439), 45 days ($489), or 60 days ($599). You can get more info on the pass at the website, or by calling ℗ **402/330-8552.** In addition, special rates are available for seniors and students.

FAST FACTS: For the International Traveler

Also see "Fast Facts: New York City," in chapter 4, for more city-specific information.

Automobile Rentals To rent a car in the United States, you need a valid driver's license, a passport, and a major credit card. The minimum age is usually 25, but some companies will rent to younger people and add a surcharge. It's a good idea to buy maximum insurance coverage unless you're positive your own auto or credit-card insurance is sufficient. All major car-rental agencies have branches in Manhattan; try **Hertz** (℗ **800/654-3131;** www.hertz.com), **National** (℗ **800/227-7368;** www.nationalcar.com), or **Avis** (℗ **800/230-4898;** www.avis.com). Car rental in New York City is *very* expensive.

Business Hours In general, **retail stores** are open Monday through Saturday from 10am to 6 or 7pm, Thursday from 10am to 8:30 or 9pm, and Sunday from noon to 5pm (see chapter 8). **Banks** tend to be open Monday through Friday from 9am to 3pm, and sometimes Saturday mornings.

Currency & Currency Exchange See "Money" under "Preparing for Your Trip," earlier in this chapter. For the latest market conversion rates, go online to **www.oanda.com** or **www.x-rates.com.**

Drinking Laws The legal age for purchase and consumption of alcoholic beverages is 21; proof of age is required and often requested at bars and clubs, so always bring ID. Liquor stores, the only retail outlets for wine and hard liquor in New York, are closed on Sundays, holidays, and election days while the polls are open. Beer can be purchased in grocery stores and delis Monday through Saturday and Sunday after noon. Last call at city bars is 4am, although many close earlier.

Do not carry open containers of alcohol in your car or any public area not zoned for alcohol consumption. The police can, and probably will, fine you on the spot. And nothing will ruin your trip faster than getting a citation for DUI ("driving under the influence").

Electricity Like Canada, the United States uses 110 to 120 volts AC (60 cycles), compared to 220 to 240 volts AC (50 cycles) in most of Europe, Australia, and New Zealand. If your small appliances use 220 to 240 volts, you'll need a 110-volt transformer and a plug adapter with two flat parallel pins here. Downward converters that change 220 to 240 volts to 110 to 120 volts are difficult to find in the United States, so bring one with you.

Embassies & Consulates All embassies are in Washington, D.C. Most countries have consulates general in New York as well as a mission to the United Nations. If your country isn't listed below, call directory information in Washington, D.C. (© **411** or 202/555-1212), or go online to **www.embassy.org/embassies** for the location and phone number.

Australia: Consulate General, 150 E. 42nd St., New York, NY 10117 (© **212/351-6500**). **Canada:** Consulate General, 1251 Ave. of the Americas, New York, NY 10020 (© **212/596-1628**; www.canada-ny.org). **Ireland:** Consulate General, 1251 Ave. of the Americas, New York, NY 10020-1175 (© **212/596-1628**). **Japan:** Consulate General, 299 Park Ave., 18th Floor, New York, NY 10171 (© **212/371-8222**; http://ny.cgj.org). **New Zealand:** Consulate General, 780 Third Ave., Suite 1904, New York, NY 10017 (© **212/832-4038**). **United Kingdom:** Consulate General, 845 Third Ave., New York, NY 10022 (© **212/745-0200**; www.britainusa.com/ny/).

Emergencies Call © **911** to report a fire, call the police, or get an ambulance anywhere in the United States. This is a toll-free call (no coins are required at public telephones).

If you have a medical emergency that doesn't require an ambulance, you can walk into a hospital's 24-hour emergency room (usually a separate entrance). For a list of hospitals, see "Fast Facts: New York City," in chapter 4. Because emergency rooms are often crowded, one of the walk-in medical centers listed under "What to Do if You Get Sick Away from Home" under "Health & Safety," in chapter 2, might be a better option.

Holidays Banks, government offices, post offices, and many stores, restaurants, and museums are closed on the following national holidays: January 1 (New Year's Day), the third Monday in January (Martin Luther King Jr. Day), the third Monday in February (Presidents' Day), the last Monday in May (Memorial Day), July 4th (Independence Day), the first Monday in September (Labor Day), the second Monday in October (Columbus Day), November 11 (Veterans' Day/Armistice Day), the fourth Thursday in November (Thanksgiving Day), and December 25 (Christmas).

Also, the Tuesday following the first Monday in November is Election Day and is a federal holiday in presidential-election years (next in 2004).

Legal Aid Most foreign tourists will probably never become involved with the American legal system. If you are stopped for a minor infraction (for example, speeding), never attempt to pay the fine directly to a police officer; this could be construed as bribery, a more serious crime. If it's a traffic infraction, do not get out of the car; stay seated with your hands on the wheel until the officer approaches. Pay fines by mail, or to the clerk of the court. If accused of a more serious offense, say and do nothing before consulting a lawyer. Everyone has the right to remain silent. Once arrested, a person can make one telephone call to a party of his or her choice. Call your embassy or consulate.

Mail Generally found at intersections, mailboxes are blue with a white eagle logo and carry the inscription U.S. MAIL. If your mail is addressed to a U.S. destination, don't forget to add the five-digit postal code (or ZIP code), after the two-letter abbreviation of the state to which the mail is addressed.

At press time, domestic postage rates were 22¢ for a postcard and 37¢ for a letter. For international mail, a first-class letter of up to 1 ounce costs 80¢ (60¢ to Canada and Mexico); a first-class postcard costs 70¢ (including Canada and Mexico); and a preprinted postal aerogramme costs 70¢. Point your browser to **www.usps.com** for U.S. postal information, or call ℂ **800/275-8777** for the nearest post office. Most branches are open Monday through Friday from 8am to 5 or 6pm, and Saturday from 9am to noon or 3pm.

Newspapers/Magazines In addition to the *New York Times* and other city papers, many newsstands carry a selection of international newspapers and magazines. For nearly all major newspapers and magazines from around the world, head to **Universal News & Magazines,** at 977 Eighth Ave., between 57th and 58th streets (ℂ **212/459-0932**), and 234 W. 42nd St., between Seventh and Eighth avenues (ℂ **212/221-1809**); or **Hotalings News Agency,** 142 W. 42nd St., between Broadway and Sixth Avenue (ℂ **212/974-9419**).

Taxes There is no value-added tax (VAT) at the national level, but every state, county, and city has the right to levy its own local tax on all purchases, including hotel and restaurant checks, airline tickets, and so on. Sales tax is usually not included in the price tags on merchandise but is added at the cash register. These taxes aren't refundable. In New York City, the **sales tax** is 8.625%. The **hotel tax** is 13.25% plus $2 per room per night (including sales tax). The **parking garage tax,** added to already high basic fees, is 18.25%.

Telephone & Fax The telephone system in the United States is run by private corporations, so rates, especially for long-distance and operator-assisted calls, can vary. Generally, hotel surcharges on long-distance and local calls are astronomical, so use a **public pay telephone,** which you'll find in most public buildings as well as hotel lobbies and on the street. Many convenience stores and newsstands sell **prepaid calling cards** in denominations up to $50; these can be the least expensive way to call

home. Many public phones at airports accept American Express, Master-
Card, and Visa credit cards. **Local calls** made from pay phones usually cost
25¢, though some hotel pay phones will charge 50¢.

Most long-distance and international calls can be dialed direct from
any phone. **For all calls within the United States and to Canada,** dial 1 followed by the area code and the seven-digit number. **For other international calls,** dial 011 followed by the country code, city code, and the
telephone number of the person you are calling. Some country and city
codes are as follows: **Australia** 61, Melbourne 3, Sydney 2; **Ireland** 353,
Dublin 1; **New Zealand** 64, Auckland 9, Wellington 4; **United Kingdom** 44,
Belfast 232, Birmingham 21, Glasgow 41, London 71 or 81. If you're calling the **United States** from another country, the country code is 01.

For **reversed-charge, collect, operator-assisted,** and **person-to-person
calls,** dial 0 (the number zero) followed by the area code and number you
want; an operator will then come on the line, and you should specify that
you are calling collect, or person-to-person, or both. If your operator-
assisted call is international, ask for the overseas operator.

For local and national directory assistance ("information"), dial ℂ **411.**

Most hotels have **fax machines** for guest use (be sure to ask about the
charge to use it), and many hotel rooms have in-room fax machines.
Receiving faxes is usually free (always ask first), but a less expensive way
to send faxes is at stores such as **The UPS Store,** a national chain of pack-
ing-service shops (look in the Yellow Pages under "Packing Services"), or
Kinko's, a chain of copy shops offering business services.

There are two kinds of telephone directories. The **White Pages** list private households and businesses in alphabetical order. The inside front
cover lists emergency numbers. The first few pages will tell you how to
make long-distance and international calls, and lists country and area
codes. Printed on yellow paper, the **Yellow Pages** list all local services,
businesses, industries, and houses of worship according to activity with an
index at the front or back. The Yellow Pages also include city plans or
detailed area maps, postal ZIP codes, and public transportation routes. A
useful online "yellow pages" for finding phone numbers and addresses in
New York and other U.S. cities is **www.smartpages.com**.

Time New York uses Eastern Standard Time (EST), which is 5 hours behind
Greenwich mean time (GMT).

Daylight saving time is in effect from the first Sunday in April through
the last Sunday in October. Daylight saving time moves the clock 1 hour
ahead. When daylight saving time is in effect, New York is 4 hours
behind GMT.

For the correct local time in New York, dial ℂ **212/976-1616.**

Tipping Tips are a very important part of certain workers' salaries, so it's
important that you leave appropriate gratuities. Tips aren't automatically
added to restaurant and hotel bills. In restaurants in New York City, you
can double the 8.625% tax to figure the appropriate tip.

Other tipping guidelines: 15% to 20% of the fare to taxi drivers; 10%
to 15% of the tab to bartenders; $1 to $2 per bag to bellhops; at least $1
per day to hotel maids; $1 per item to checkroom attendants; $1 to valet

parking attendants; and 15% to 20% to hairdressers. Tipping theater ushers, gas-station attendants, and fast-food employees isn't expected.

Toilets In general, you won't find public toilets or "restrooms" on the streets in New York, but they can be found in hotel lobbies, bars, restaurants, museums, department stores, or railway and bus stations. See "Restrooms" under "Fast Facts: New York City" at the end of chapter 4.

Traveler's Assistance **Travelers Aid** helps travelers with problems, including accidents, sickness, and lost or stolen luggage. There is an office on the second floor of the International Arrivals Building at JFK Airport (© **718/656-4870**), and in Newark Airport's Terminal B (© **973/623-5052**).

4

Getting to Know
New York City

This chapter gives you an insider's take on Manhattan's most distinctive neighborhoods and streets, tells you how to get around, and serves as a reference to everything from personal safety to libraries and liquor laws.

1 Orientation

VISITOR INFORMATION

INFORMATION OFFICES

- The **Times Square Visitors Center,** 1560 Broadway, between 46th and 47th streets (where Broadway meets Seventh Ave.), across from the TKTS booth (© **212/768-1560;** www.timessquarebid.org), is the city's top info stop. This attractive center features an info desk offering loads of information. There's also a Metropolitan Transportation Authority (MTA) desk that sells MetroCards, offers transit maps, and answers your questions on the transit system; a Broadway Ticket Center providing show information and selling full-price tickets; ATMs and currency-exchange machines; and computers with free Internet access. It's open daily from 8am to 8pm.
- The **New York Convention and Visitors Bureau** runs the **NYCVB Visitor Information Center** at 810 Seventh Ave., between 52nd and 53rd streets. In addition to information on attractions and a multilingual counselor, the center has interactive terminals that provide touch-screen access to visitor information via Citysearch and sell advance tickets to major attractions, which can save you from standing in long lines (you can also buy a CityPass using these; see p. 25). There's also an ATM, a gift shop, and phones that connect you directly with American Express card member services. The center is open Monday through Friday from 8:30am to 6pm, Saturday and Sunday from 9am to 5pm. For phone assistance, call © **212/484-1222.**

PUBLICATIONS

For comprehensive listings of films, concerts, performances, sports, museum and gallery exhibits, street fairs, and special events, the following are your best bets:

- The *New York Times* (www.nytimes.com or www.nytoday.com) features great arts and entertainment coverage, particularly in the Friday "Weekend" section and Sunday's "Arts & Leisure" section. Both days have full guides to the latest happenings in theater, music, dance, film, and the art world. Friday is good for cabaret, family fun, and general-interest events.
- *Time Out New York* (www.timeoutny.com) is an attractive, well-organized, and easy-to-use magazine. *TONY* features excellent coverage in categories from music, theater, and clubs (gay and straight) to museums, dance, book

and poetry readings, and kids' stuff. The regular "Check Out" section, unequaled in any other listings magazine, will fill you in on upcoming sample and closeout sales, crafts and antiques shows, and other shopping scoops. A new issue hits newsstands every Thursday.

- The famous free weekly *Village Voice* (**www.villagevoice.com**) is available late Tuesday downtown and early Wednesday elsewhere. From classical music to clubs, the arts and entertainment coverage couldn't be more extensive, and just about every music venue advertises its shows.

Other useful weeklies include the glossy *New York* magazine (**www.nymetro. com**), which offers restaurant reviews and whose "Cue" section is a selective guide to city arts and entertainment; the *New Yorker* (**www.newyorker.com**), which features "Goings On About Town" at the front of the magazine; and the *New York Press* (**www.nypress.com**), a free, weekly in the *Village Voice* vein. The monthly *Paper* (**www.papermag.com**) is a glossy alternamag that serves as good prep for those of you who want to experience the hipper side of the city.

CITY LAYOUT

Open the sheet map that comes with this book and you'll see the city is comprised of five boroughs: **Manhattan,** where most of the visitor action is; the **Bronx,** the only NYC borough on the mainland United States; **Queens,** where Kennedy and LaGuardia airports are located; **Brooklyn,** south of Queens, which is also on Long Island and is famed for its attitude, accent, and Atlantic-front Coney Island; and **Staten Island,** the least populous borough, bordering Upper New York Bay on one side and the Atlantic Ocean on the other.

It is Manhattan, the finger-shaped island pointing southwest off the mainland—surrounded by the Harlem River to the north, the Hudson River to the west, the East River (really an estuary) to the east, and Upper New York Bay to the south—that most visitors think of when they envision New York City. Despite the fact that it's the city's smallest borough (13½ miles long, 2¼ miles wide, 22 sq. miles), Manhattan contains the city's most famous attractions, buildings, and institutions. For that reason, almost all of the accommodations and restaurants in this book are in Manhattan.

In most of Manhattan, finding your way around is a snap because of the grid system by which the streets are numbered. If you can discern uptown and downtown, and East Side and West Side, you can find your way around pretty easily. In real terms, **uptown** means north of where you happen to be and **downtown** means south, although sometimes these labels have deeper meanings (generally speaking, "uptown" chic vs. "downtown" bohemianism).

Avenues run north and south (uptown and downtown). Most are numbered. **Fifth Avenue** divides the East Side from the West Side of town and serves as the eastern border of Central Park north of 59th Street. **First Avenue** is all the way east and **Twelfth Avenue** is all the way west. The three most important unnumbered avenues on the East Side you should know are between Third and Fifth avenues: **Madison** (east of Fifth), **Park** (east of Madison), and **Lexington** (east of Park, just west of Third). Important unnumbered avenues on the West Side are **Avenue of the Americas,** which all New Yorkers call Sixth Avenue; **Central Park West,** which is what Eighth Avenue north of 59th Street is called as it borders Central Park on the west (hence the name); **Columbus Avenue,** Ninth Avenue north of 59th Street; and **Amsterdam Avenue,** or Tenth Avenue north of 59th.

Broadway is the exception to the rule—it's the only major avenue that doesn't run uptown to downtown. It cuts a diagonal path across the island, from the northwest tip down to the southeast corner. As it crosses most major avenues, it creates **squares** (Times Sq., Herald Sq., and Union Sq., for example).

Streets run east to west (crosstown) and are numbered as they proceed uptown from Houston (*House*-ton) Street. To go uptown, walk north of, or to a higher-numbered street than, where you are. Downtown is south of (or a lower-numbered street than) your current location. If you can see a landmark like the Empire State Building, it's easy to determine uptown and downtown if you know what street you are on; remember that the Empire State Building is on 34th Street.

Fifth Avenue is the dividing line between the **East Side** and **West Side** of town (except below Washington Sq., where Broadway serves that function). On the east side of Fifth Avenue, streets are numbered with the distinction "East"; on the west side of Fifth Avenue, they are numbered "West." East 51st Street, for example, begins at Fifth Avenue and runs east to the East River, while West 51st Street begins at Fifth Avenue and runs west to the Hudson River.

If you're looking for a particular address, remember that even-numbered street addresses are on the south side of streets and odd-numbered addresses are on the north. Street addresses increase by about 50 per block starting at Fifth Avenue. For example, nos. 1 to 50 East are just about between Fifth and Madison avenues, while nos. 1 to 50 West are just about between Fifth and Sixth avenues. Traffic generally runs east on even-numbered streets and west on odd-numbered streets, with a few exceptions, like the major east-west thoroughfares—**14th, 23rd, 34th, 42nd, 57th, 72nd, 79th, 86th**—which have two-way traffic. Therefore, 28 W. 23rd St. is a short walk west of Fifth Avenue; 325 E. 35th St. would be a few blocks east of Fifth.

Avenue addresses are irregular. For example, 994 Second Ave. is at East 51st Street, but so is 320 Park Ave. Thus, it's quite important to know a building's cross street to find it. If you don't have the cross street and want to figure out the exact location using just the address, use the **Manhattan Address Locator**, later in this chapter.

Unfortunately, the rules don't apply to neighborhoods in Lower Manhattan, south of 14th Street—like Wall Street, Chinatown, SoHo, TriBeCa, the Village—since they sprang up before engineers devised this brilliant grid scheme. A good map is essential when exploring these areas.

STREET MAPS   You'll find a pullout map of Manhattan at the back of this book. There's also a decent one available for free as part of the **Official NYC**

⟨Tips **Orientation Tips**

I've indicated the cross streets for every destination in this book, but be sure to ask for the cross street (or avenue) if you call for an address.

When you give a taxi driver an address, always specify the cross streets. New Yorkers, even most cab drivers, probably wouldn't know where to find 284 E. 81st St., but they do know where to find 81st and Second. If you're heading to the Afghan Kebab House, for example, tell them that it's on Ninth Avenue between 51st and 52nd.

If you have only the numbered address on an avenue, you can figure out the cross street using the **Manhattan Address Locator** on p. 82.

Visitor Kit if you write ahead for information (see "Visitor Information," in chapter 2); you can also pick it up for free at the visitor centers listed above.

Even with all these freebies, I suggest investing in a map with more features if you want to zip around the city like a pro. **Hagstrom** maps are my favorites because they feature block-by-block street numbering—so instead of trying to guess the cross street for 125 Prince St., you can see that it's Greene Street. Hagstrom and other visitor-friendly maps are available at any good bookstore. You might also want to look for *The New York Map Guide: The Essential Guide to Manhattan* (Penguin), by Michael Middleditch, a 64-page book that maps the entire city, including attractions, restaurants, and nightlife spots.

Because there are always disruptions or changes in service, don't rely on any subway map that hasn't been printed by the Metropolitan Transit Authority; more on this in "Getting Around," later in this chapter.

MANHATTAN'S NEIGHBORHOODS IN BRIEF

Since they grew up over the course of hundreds of years, Manhattan's neighborhoods have multiple personalities and fluid boundaries. Still, it's relatively easy to agree upon what they stand for in general—so if you stop a New Yorker and ask him or her to point you to, say, the Upper West Side or the Flatiron District, they'll know where you want to go. From south to north, here is how I've defined Manhattan's neighborhoods throughout this book.

Downtown

Lower Manhattan: South Street Seaport & the Financial District Where New York City originated. Established by the Dutch in 1625 (the city's original name was Nieuw Amsterdam), New York's first settlements were here, on the southern tip of Manhattan; everything uptown was farmland and wilderness. While all that's changed, this is still the best place in the city to search for the past.

Lower Manhattan is everything south of Chambers Street. **Battery Park,** the point of departure for the Statue of Liberty, Ellis Island, and Staten Island, is on the south tip of the island. The **South Street Seaport,** now touristy but still a reminder of times when shipping was the lifeblood of the city, lies a bit north on the east coast; it's just south of the Brooklyn Bridge, which stands proudly as the ultimate engineering achievement of New York's 19th-century Industrial Age.

The rest of the area is the **Financial District,** but may even be more famous now as **Ground Zero.** Until

September 11, 2001, the Financial District was anchored by the **World Trade Center,** with the World Financial Center complex and Battery Park City to the west, and **Wall Street** running crosstown south and to the east. Now, a gaping hole sits where the Twin Towers and their five sister buildings stood.

Despite the devastation, the Financial District deserves to be celebrated as an incredible story of recovery. Within 6 months of that horrific day, the neighborhood was running pretty much normally.

Ground Zero has been cleaned, and recovery efforts officially ended in May 2002. In August of 2002, Governor George Pataki of New York, Governor James McGreevy of New Jersey, and New York Mayor Michael Bloomberg dedicated a viewing wall on the Church Street side of the site called the Wall of Heroes.

After a heated competition among ideas submitted by designers and architects, Daniel Libeskind's vision of a towering spire and a memorial wall was chosen by the committee to rebuild Ground Zero.

When and if that vision is ever realized is still up in the air, so to speak.

The surrounding area—including Wall Street, the South Street Seaport, and Battery Park—is open for business. **City Hall** remains the northern border of the district, abutting Chambers Street (look for City Hall Park on the map). Most of the streets of this neighborhood are narrow concrete canyons, with Broadway serving as the main uptown-downtown artery.

Most of the major subway lines congregate here before they end or head to Brooklyn (the exceptions: the B, D, F, J, M, Q, V, W, and Z lines cross into Brooklyn from the Lower East Side, over the Manhattan Bridge). All lines are running again; even the stop named "World Trade Center" on the E line is reopened (it actually lets you out to the north of the site). Any event can cause delays, so see "Getting Around" later this chapter for information on where to gather the latest subway information.

TriBeCa Bordered by the Hudson River to the west, the area north of Chambers Street, west of Broadway, and south of Canal Street is the *Tri*angle *Be*low *Ca*nal Street, or TriBeCa. Since the 1980s, as SoHo became saturated with chic, the spillover transformed TriBeCa into one of the city's hippest neighborhoods, where celebrities and families coexist in cast-iron warehouses converted into spacious, expensive loft apartments. Artists' lofts and galleries as well as hip antiques and design shops pepper the area, as do some of the city's best restaurants. Standing in the north shadow of the World Trade Center, TriBeCa suffered greatly in the wake of the disaster; however, it has recovered beautifully.

Actor Robert DeNiro gave the neighborhood a boost when he established the TriBeCa Film Center. Still, historic streets like White (especially the Federal-style building at no. 2) and Harrison (the stretch west from Greenwich St.) evoke a bygone, more human-scaled New York, as do a few holdout businesses and old-world pubs. This neighborhood seems to have brought together the old city and the new without bastardizing either. Because retail spaces are usually a few doors apart rather than right on top of one another, it manages to be more peaceful than other neighborhoods. It also happens to be home to one of my favorite budget hotels, the Cosmopolitan (p. 99).

The main uptown-downtown drag is **West Broadway** (2 blocks to the west of Broadway). Consider the Franklin Street subway station on the 1/9 line to be your gateway to the heart of the action. Take your map; the streets are a maze.

Chinatown New York City's most famous ethnic enclave is bursting past its traditional boundaries and encroaching on Little Italy. The former marshlands northeast of City Hall and below Canal Street, from Broadway to the Bowery, are where Chinese immigrants were forced to live in the 1870s. This booming neighborhood is a conglomeration of Asian populations. It offers tasty cheap eats in cuisines from Szechuan to Hunan to Cantonese to Vietnamese to Thai. Exotic shops offer strange foods, herbs, and souvenirs, as well as bargains on clothing and leather. Walking down Canal Street, peering into the myriad stores and watching crabs cut loose from their handlers at the exotic fish markets, is some of the city's best free entertainment.

The Canal Street (J, M, Z, N, R, 6, Q, W) station will get you to the heart of the action. The streets are crowded during the day and empty

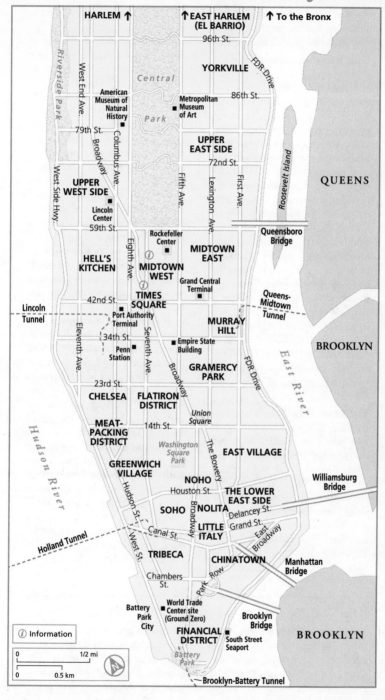

Manhattan Neighborhoods

HARLEM ↑   ↑ EAST HARLEM (EL BARRIO)   ↑ To the Bronx

96th St.

YORKVILLE

Riverside Park

West End Ave.

Central Park

American Museum of Natural History ■

86th St.

Metropolitan Museum of Art ■

79th St.

Columbus Ave.

Broadway

West Side Hwy.

UPPER EAST SIDE

72nd St.

Fifth Ave.

Lexington Ave.

First Ave.

Roosevelt Island

QUEENS

UPPER WEST SIDE

Lincoln Center ■

59th St.

Eighth Ave.

Rockefeller Center ■

MIDTOWN EAST

Queensboro Bridge

HELL'S KITCHEN

MIDTOWN WEST

TIMES SQUARE

ⓘ

ⓘ

Grand Central Terminal ■

42nd St.

Port Authority Terminal

Seventh Ave.

Queens-Midtown Tunnel

Lincoln Tunnel

Eleventh Ave.

34th St.

Penn Station ■

MURRAY HILL

Empire State Building ■

East River

BROOKLYN

Broadway

GRAMERCY PARK

FDR Drive

23rd St.

CHELSEA

FLATIRON DISTRICT

Union Square

MEAT-PACKING DISTRICT

14th St.

Washington Square Park

GREENWICH VILLAGE

EAST VILLAGE

Hudson River

Hudson St.

West St.

The Bowery

NOHO

Houston St.

SOHO

NOLITA

Broadway

THE LOWER EAST SIDE

Delancey St.

Williamsburg Bridge

LITTLE ITALY

Grand St.

East Broadway

Canal St.

Holland Tunnel

TRIBECA

CHINATOWN

Manhattan Bridge

Chambers St.

Park Row

Battery Park City

World Trade Center site (Ground Zero) ■

Brooklyn Bridge

FINANCIAL DISTRICT

South Street Seaport ■

BROOKLYN

Battery Park

ⓘ Information

| 0 | 1/2 mi |
| 0 | 0.5 km |

Ⓝ

Brooklyn-Battery Tunnel

out after around 9pm; they remain quite safe, but the neighborhood is more enjoyable during the bustle.

Little Italy Near Chinatown is Little Italy, traditionally the area east of Broadway between Houston and north of Canal Street. The community is shrinking today due to the encroachment of thriving Chinatown. It's now limited mainly to **Mulberry Street,** where you'll find most restaurants, and just a few off-shoots. With rents going up in the increasingly trendy Lower East Side, a few chic spots are moving in, further intruding upon the old-world landscape. Because the Grand Street subway station is scheduled to be closed until 2005 (except for one-stop shuttle service from the Broadway–Lafayette St. station), the best way to reach Little Italy is to walk east from the Spring Street station, on the no. 6 line, to Mulberry Street; turn south for Little Italy (you can't miss the year-round red, green, and white street decorations).

The Lower East Side The Lower East Side boasts the best of old and new New York: Witness the stretch of Houston between Forsyth and Allen streets, where Yoneh Shimmel's Knish Shop sits next to the city's newest film art-house, the Sunshine Cinema—and both are thriving. Some say that the Lower East Side has come full circle: Hipster 20-somethings have been drawn back to the neighborhood their immigrant grandparents worked to escape.

Of all the successive waves of immigrants and refugees who passed through this densely populated tenement neighborhood from the mid-19th century to the 1920s, eastern European Jews left the most lasting impression. Drugs and crime supplanted the Jewish communities, which first popped up between Houston and Canal streets, east of the Bowery, dragging the Lower East Side into the gutter—until recently. The neighborhood has experienced a renaissance over the last few years, and makes a fascinating stop for both nostalgia and nightlife hounds. Still, the blocks south of Houston can be grungy, so walk with confidence and care after dark.

There are some remnants of what was once the largest Jewish population in America along **Orchard Street,** where you'll find great bargain hunting in its many old-world fabric, clothing, and accessories stores still thriving between the club-clothes boutiques and trendy lounges. Keep in mind that many shops close early on Friday and all day on Saturday (the Jewish Sabbath). The expanding trendy set can be found in the blocks between Allen and Clinton streets south of Houston and north of Delancey, with more shops, bars, and restaurants popping up in the blocks to the east every day.

(Tips **Visiting the Lower East Side**

The **Lower East Side Business Improvement District** operates a visitor center at 261 Broome St., between Orchard and Allen streets (© **866/224-0206** or 212/226-9010), open daily from 10am to 4pm. Stop in for an Orchard Street Bargain District shopping guide, plus other information on this historic yet hip 'hood. You can also find shopping, dining, and nightlife directories online at **www.lowereastsideny.com**.

This area is not well served by the subway, so your best bet is to take the F train to Second Avenue and walk east on Houston; when you see Katz's Deli, you'll know you've arrived. You can also reach the neighborhood from the Delancey Street station on the F line, and the Essex Street station on the J, M, and Z lines.

SoHo & Nolita No relation to the London neighborhood of the same name, **SoHo** got its name as an abbreviation of "*So*uth of *Ho*uston Street." This fashionable neighborhood extends down to Canal Street, between Sixth Avenue to the west and Lafayette Street (1 block east of Broadway) to the east. It's accessible by subway: Take the N or R to Prince Street; the C, E, or 6 to Spring Street; or the F or V train to the Broadway–Lafayette stop (the B, D, and Q trains will not be serving Broadway–Lafayette during the life of this book due to Manhattan Bridge construction).

An industrial zone during the 19th century, SoHo retains the cast-iron architecture of the era, and in many places, cobblestone peeks out beneath the asphalt. In the early 1960s, cutting-edge artists began to occupy the drab, deteriorating buildings, turning it into the city's trendiest neighborhood. SoHo is now a prime example of urban gentrification and a major attraction thanks to its impeccably restored buildings, fashionable restaurants, and stylish boutiques. On weekends, the cobbled streets and narrow sidewalks are crowded with shoppers, with the prime action

between Broadway and Sullivan Street north of Grand Street.

Some critics claim that SoHo is a victim of its popularity—witness the departure of several imaginative galleries and independent boutiques for TriBeCa and Chelsea, as well as the influx of suburban chains like J. Crew and Victoria's Secret. However, SoHo is still one of the best shopping neighborhoods in the city, and few are more fun to browse. High-end peddlers set up along the boutique-lined sidewalks, hawking jewelry, coffee-table books, and their own art. At night, the neighborhood is a terrific, albeit pricey, dining and bar-hopping neighborhood (I recommend some affordable options in chapter 6).

In recent years, SoHo has been crawling east, taking over Mott and Mulberry streets—and Elizabeth Street in particular—north of Kenmare Street, an area now known as **Nolita** for its *No*rth of *Li*ttle It*a*ly location. Nolita is increasingly well known for its shopping. Some of the city's most promising clothing designers have set up shop, but don't expect bargains. Good, affordable restaurants abound, making the neighborhood well worth a browse. Taking the 6 to Spring Street will get you closest by subway, but it's a short walk east from SoHo proper.

The East Village & NoHo The **East Village,** which extends between 14th Street and Houston Street, from Broadway east to First Avenue and beyond to Alphabet City—avenues A, B, C, and D—is where the city's bohemia has gone.

Where to Check Your E-mail in the City That Never Sleeps

You don't have to be out of touch while you travel. There are ways to get your e-mail using any computer.

Your **Internet Service Provider** (ISP) may have a Web-based interface that lets you access your e-mail on computers other than your own. Just find out how it works before you leave home.

Or check out **www.mail2web.com**. This free service allows you to type in your e-mail address and password and retrieve your e-mail from any Web browser, as long as your home ISP hasn't blocked it with a firewall.

Or open a free mail account with a Web-based e-mail provider, such as **Hotmail (www.hotmail.com)** or **Yahoo! Mail (mail.yahoo.com)**. Your home ISP may be able to forward your home e-mail to the Web-based account.

All you'll need to check your e-mail away from home is a Web connection, available via your hotel's business center or cash-and-credit-card Internet-access machine (which many hotels now feature in the lobby), as well as Internet cafes and copy shops through the city. After logging on, point the browser to your ISP. Enter your user name and password, and you'll have access to your e-mail, usually for a few dollars an hour.

The **Times Square Visitors Center,** 1560 Broadway, between 46th and 47th streets (© **212/768-1560;** open daily 8am–8pm), has computer terminals that you can use to send e-mails courtesy of Yahoo!. You can even send an electronic postcard with a photo of yourself home to Mom.

Once, flower children tripped along St. Marks Place and listened to music at the Fillmore East; now the East Village is a mix of ethnic and trendy restaurants, upstart clothing designers and kitschy boutiques, punk-rock clubs (yep, still), and folk cafes—plus a half-dozen or so Off-Broadway theaters—all of which give the neighborhood a youthful vibe and a low-budget appeal for visitors and locals alike. In fact, you'll find the city's highest concentration of high-quality budget dining in these precincts.

The city has made a huge impact on the East Village, but there's still a seedy element that some won't find appealing—and some will. I love the East Village more than the West Village for its melting-pot vibe. Now yuppies and other ladder-climbing types make their homes alongside Russian immigrants who have lived in the neighborhood forever, and the cross-dressers and squatters who settled here in between. The neighborhood still embraces ethnic diversity, with elements of its Ukrainian and Irish heritage, while more recent immigrants have taken over 6th Street between First and Second avenues, now called "Little India."

The East Village isn't very subway accessible; unless you're traveling along 14th Street (the L line will drop you off at Third and First aves.), take the 4, 5, 6, N, R, Q, or W to 14th Street/Union Square; the N, R to 8th Street; or the 6 to Astor Place and walk east.

Open 24/7 in the heart of Times Square, **easyEverything** ⬥, 235 W. 42nd St., between Seventh and Eighth avenues (☎ 212/398-0775; **www. easyeverything.com**), is the first stateside branch of a worldwide web of Internet cafes. With 15-inch flat-screen monitors and superfast T-3 connections, this mammoth place makes accessing the Internet cheap through high volume: Access is available for $1 and up, the length of time that buys fluctuates depending on the occupancy at the time you log on. This generally works out to the cheapest Web time you can buy in the city.

CyberCafe (**www.cyber-cafe.com**)—in Times Square at 250 W. 49th St., between Broadway and Eighth Avenue (☎ 212/333-4109), and in SoHo at 273 Lafayette St., at Prince Street (☎ 212/334-5140)—is more expensive at $6.40 per half-hour, with a half-hour minimum (it's $3.20 for every subsequent 15 min.). But their T1 lines give you speedy access, and they offer a full range of other cyber, copy, fax, and printing services.

Kinko's (**www.kinkos.com**) charges 30¢ per minute ($15 per hr.) and is open at 100 Wall St., at Water Street (☎ 212/269-0024); near City Hall at 105 Duane St., between Broadway and Church Street (☎ 212/406-1220); 250 E. Houston St., between avenues A and B (☎ 212/253-9020); 21 Astor Place, between Broadway and Lafayette Street in the Village (☎ 212/228-9511); 245 Seventh Ave., at 24th Street (☎ 212/929-2679); 60 W. 40th St., between Fifth and Sixth avenues (☎ 212/921-1060); 221 W. 72nd St., at Broadway (☎ 212/362-5288); and about a billion other locations around town.

Until 1998 or so, **Alphabet City** resisted gentrification. No more. Bolstered by a major real estate boom, this way-east area of the East Village has blossomed. Bistros and smart shops are popping up on every corner. Nevertheless, the neighborhood can get deserted late at night, since it's generally the province of locals. It's far off the subway lines, so know where you're going if you venture here.

The southwestern section of the East Village, around Broadway and Lafayette between Bleecker and 4th streets, is called **NoHo** (for *No*rth of *Ho*uston), and has a completely different character. As you might have guessed, this area has developed more like its neighbor to the south, SoHo. Here you'll find trendy lounges, stylish restaurants, cutting-edge designers, and upscale antiques shops. NoHo is wonderful fun to browse; the Bleecker Street stop on the no. 6 line will land you in the heart of it, and the Broadway–Lafayette stop on the F/V line will drop you at its southern edge.

Greenwich Village Tree-lined streets crisscross and wind, following ancient streams and cow paths. Each block reveals yet another row of Greek Revival town houses, a well-preserved Federal-style house, or a peaceful courtyard or square. This is "the Village," from Broadway west to the Hudson River, bordered by Houston Street to the south and 14th Street to the north. It defies Manhattan's orderly grid system with streets that predate it, and unless you live here, it may be impossible to master the lay of the land—so take a map.

The Seventh Avenue line (1, 2, 3, 9) is the area's main subway artery, while the West 4th Street stop (where the A, C, and E lines meet the F and V lines) serves as its central hub. (Note that, due to rail work, the B, D, and Q subway trains will not be serving W. 4th St. during the life of this book.)

Nineteenth-century artists like Mark Twain, Edgar Allan Poe, Henry James, and Winslow Homer first gave the Village its reputation for embracing the unconventional. Artists like Edward Hopper and Jackson Pollock were drawn in, as well as writers like Eugene O'Neill, e.e. cummings, and Dylan Thomas. Radical thinkers from John Reed to Upton Sinclair basked in the neighborhood's liberal ethos, and beatniks Allen Ginsberg, Jack Kerouac, and William Burroughs dug the free-swinging atmosphere. Now the Village is the roost of choice for the young celebrity set, with the likes of Gwyneth Paltrow, and Matthew Broderick and Sarah Jessica Parker drawn by its historic, low-rise charms. Gentrification and escalating real-estate values conspire to push out the artistic element, but culture and counterculture still rub shoulders in cafes, jazz clubs, neighborhood bars, off-Broadway theaters, and an endless variety of tiny shops and restaurants. With a few charming and affordable hotels (see chapter 5), the Village makes a great base for visitors who prefer to avoid more touristy areas in favor of a quirkier, residential view of the city.

The Village is probably the most chameleon-like of Manhattan's neighborhoods. Some of the highest-priced real estate in the city runs along lower Fifth Avenue, which dead-ends at **Washington Square Park.** Serpentine **Bleecker Street** stretches through most of the neighborhood and is emblematic of the area's historical bent. The anything-goes attitude in the Village has fostered a large gay community around **Christopher Street** and Sheridan Square. The streets west of Seventh Avenue, an area known as the **West Village,** boast a more relaxed vibe and some of the city's most charming and historic brownstones. Three colleges—New York University, Parsons School of Design, and the New School for Social Research—keep the area thinking young, which explains the popularity of 8th Street, lined with shops selling cheap, hip clothes.

Streets are often crowded with weekend visitors (sometimes unkindly called "the B&T crowd," because they come to Manhattan via bridges and tunnels from Long Island and the mainland) and teenagers, especially on Bleecker, West 4th, 8th, and surrounding streets, and have been known to become increasingly sketchy west of Seventh Avenue in the late hours, especially on weekends. Keep an eye on your wallet when navigating the throngs. And Washington Square Park was cleaned up a couple of years back, but it's still best to stay out after dark.

Midtown

Chelsea & the Meat-Packing District Chelsea has come on strong in recent years as a hip address, especially for the gay community. A low-rise composite of town houses, tenements, lofts, and factories, the neighborhood comprises roughly the area west of Sixth Avenue from 14th to 30th streets. (Sixth Ave. below 23rd St. is considered part of the Flatiron District; see below.) Chelsea has also evolved into one of

---

Tips **Touring Tip**

If you'd like to tour a particular neighborhood with an expert, call **Big Apple Greeter** (© 212/669-8159; www.bigapplegreeter.org) at least 1 week ahead of your arrival. This nonprofit organization has specially trained volunteers who take visitors around town for a 2- to 4-hour tour of a specific neighborhood. And they say New York isn't friendly!

---

the city's best-value accommodations neighborhoods for travelers looking for something special as well as affordable (see chapter 5). Its main arteries are Seventh and Eighth avenues, and it's primarily served by the C, E and 1, 9 subway lines.

The **Chelsea Piers** sports complex to the far west and a host of shops (both unique boutiques and big names like Williams-Sonoma), well-priced bistros, and bars along the main drags have contributed to the area's rebirth. Even the Hotel Chelsea—the neighborhood's most famous architectural and literary landmark, where Thomas Wolfe and Arthur Miller wrote, Bob Dylan composed "Sad-Eyed Lady of the Low Land," Viva and Edie Sedgwick of Andy Warhol fame lived, and Sid Vicious killed girlfriend Nancy Spungeon—has undergone a renovation. Prices put it beyond reach of most budget travelers, but pop into the lobby if you're a pop-culture buff. You'll find a number of popular flea markets in parking lots along Sixth Avenue, between 24th and 27th streets, on the weekends.

One of the most recent trends in Chelsea has been the establishment of **West Chelsea** (from Ninth Ave. west) and the adjacent **Meat-Packing District** (south of West Chelsea in the far west Village, roughly from 17th St. to Little West 12th St.) as the style-setting neighborhoods for the 21st century. What SoHo was in the '60s, this industrial west world (dubbed "the Lower West Side" by *New York* magazine, and MePa by others) is today. New restaurants, cutting-edge shopping, and hot nightspots pop up daily in the still-beefy Meat-Packing District, while the area from West 22nd to West 29th streets between Tenth and Eleventh avenues is home to the cutting edge of today's art scene, with West 26th the unofficial "gallery row." This area is still quite industrial and in the early stages of transition. With galleries and bars in converted warehouses and meat lockers, browsing can be frustrating, and the sometimes-desolate streets a tad intimidating. Your best bet is to have a destination in mind, be it a restaurant, gallery, or nightclub, before you come.

The Flatiron District, Union Square & Gramercy Park These adjoining, and at some points, overlapping neighborhoods contain some of the city's most appealing streets. They have been rediscovered by New Yorkers and visitors alike, largely thanks to the boom-to-bust dot-com revolution of the last half-dozen or so years; the Flatiron District earned the nickname "Silicon Alley" during those heady times. These neighborhoods boast great shopping and dining, plus a central location that's hard to beat (and a handful of affordable hotels). The commercial spaces are often large expanses with witty designs and graceful columns.

The **Flatiron District** lies south of 23rd Street to 14th Street, between Broadway and Sixth Avenue, and centers around the historic Flatiron Building on 23rd (so named for its triangular shape) and Park Avenue South, which has become a sophisticated Restaurant Row. Below 23rd Street along Sixth Avenue (once known as the Ladies' Mile shopping district), discounters like Filene's Basement, Bed Bath & Beyond, and others have moved in. The shopping gets classier on Fifth Avenue, where you'll find a mix of national names and hip boutiques. Lined with Oriental carpet dealers and high-end fixture stores, Broadway has become the city's home-furnishings alley; its crowning jewel is the justifiably famous ABC Carpet & Home.

Union Square is the hub of the area; the N, R, 4, 5, 6, and L trains stop here, as do Q and W trains (until sometime in 2004), making it easy to reach. Long in the shadows of the more bustling (Times and Herald) and high-toned (Washington) squares, Union Square has experienced a renaissance in the last decade. Local businesses joined forces with the city to rid the park of drug dealers, and now it's a delightful place to spend an afternoon. Union Square is best known as the setting for New York's premier greenmarket every Monday, Wednesday, Friday, and Saturday. In-line skaters take over the space in the after-work hours. During the winter holidays, a series of booths and tents becomes a mini-mall for clothing, gifts, books, and ornaments. A number of hip and affordable restaurants rim the square, as do stores like Toys "R" Us, the city's best Barnes & Noble, and a Virgin Megastore.

From about 16th to 23rd streets, east from Park Avenue South to about Second Avenue, is the leafy, largely residential district known as **Gramercy Park.** The pity of the district is that so few can enjoy the park: Built by Samuel Ruggles in the 1830s to attract buyers to the area, it is the only private park in the city and locked to all but those who live on its perimeter (your windows have to look over the park for you to have a key). At the southern end of Lexington Avenue (at 21st St.), it is one of the most peaceful spots in the city. If you know someone who has a key, go there. Or book a room at the mid-priced Gramercy Park Hotel (p. 110), whose guests have park privileges.

At the northern edge, fronting the Flatiron Building on 23rd Street and Fifth Avenue, is lovely little **Madison Square.** Across from its northeast corner stood Stanford White's original Madison Square Garden (in whose roof garden White was murdered in 1906 by jealous millionaire Harry K. Thaw). It's now presided over by the New York Life Insurance Building, the New York State Supreme Court, and the Metropolitan Life Insurance Company, whose tower, at 700 feet, was the tallest in the world when it was built in 1909.

Midtown West & Times Square
Midtown West, the area from 34th to 59th streets west of Fifth Avenue to the Hudson River, encompasses several famous names: Madison Square Garden, the Garment District, Rockefeller Center, the Theater District, and Times Square. This is New York's tourism central, where you'll find the bright lights and bustle that draw people from all over the world. This is the city's biggest hotel neighborhood. While there are a lot of budget and mid-priced choices, rates can fluctuate dramatically, since this is where

everybody wants to stay; in periods of high demand, even "budget" hotels can price around the $200 mark. You're likely to find your best bargains elsewhere, especially in fall and the holiday season.

The 1, 2, 3, 9 subway line serves the massive neon station at the heart of Times Square, at 42nd Street between Broadway and Seventh Avenue, while the F, V line runs up Sixth Avenue to Rockefeller Center (B and D lines also serve Rockefeller Center, but travel only as far south as 34th St. until Manhattan Bridge work is complete in 2005). The N/R line cuts diagonally across the neighborhood, following the path of Broadway before heading up Seventh Avenue at 42nd Street (the Q and W trains also use this line until 2004). The A, C, E line serves the west side, running along Eighth Avenue.

If you know New York but haven't been here in a few years, you'll be quite surprised by the "new" **Times Square.** Longtime New Yorkers kvetch about the glory days of the peep-show-and-porn-shop Times Square that this cleaned-up version supplanted, but the truth is that it's a successful gentrification. Old theaters have come back to life as Broadway and children's playhouses, and scores of family-friendly restaurants and shops have opened (including the Virgin Megastore on Broadway). Plenty of businesses have moved in—MTV studios overlook Times Square at 1515 Broadway, and *Good Morning America* has its own studio at Broadway and 44th Street.

The lights have never been brighter, and Middle America has never been more welcome. Expect dense crowds; it's often tough just to make your way along the sidewalks.

Most of the Broadway theaters light up the streets just off Times Square, in the West 40s just east and west of Broadway. At the heart of the **Theater District,** where Broadway meets Seventh Avenue, is the TKTS booth, where crowds line up to buy discount tickets.

To the west, in the 40s and 50s between Eighth and Tenth avenues, is **Hell's Kitchen,** an area that is much nicer than its ghoulish name and one of my favorites in the city. The neighborhood resisted gentrification until the mid-1990s, but has grown into a charming, less touristy adjunct to the Theater District. Ninth Avenue has blossomed into one of the city's finest dining avenues; stroll along and you'll have a world of affordable cuisine to choose from, from American diner to hearty German to traditional Thai. Stylish boutiques and bars have also popped up in this area. Realtors tried to rename the area Clinton, but locals hold fast to Hell's Kitchen, clearly delighting in the increasing juxtaposition.

Unlike Times Square, **Rockefeller Center** has needed no renovation. Between 46th and 50th streets from Sixth Avenue east to Fifth, this Art Deco complex contains some of the city's great architectural gems, which house offices, a number of NBC studios (including *Saturday Night Live, Late Night with Conan O'Brien,* and

---

Impressions

I'm opposed to the redevelopment. I think there should be one neighborhood in New York where tourists are afraid to walk.
                                    —Fran Lebowitz on the "new" Times Square

Manhattan Address Locator

To locate avenue addresses, cancel the last figure, divide by 2, and add (or subtract) the key number below. The answer is the nearest numbered cross street, approximately.

Avenue A:	add 3	Eleventh Avenue:	add 15
Avenue B:	add 3	Amsterdam Avenue:	add 59
Avenue C:	add 3	Columbus Avenue:	add 59 or 60
First Avenue:	add 3	Lexington Avenue:	add 22
Second Avenue:	add 3	Madison Avenue:	add 27
Third Avenue:	add 10	Park Avenue:	add 34
Sixth Avenue:	subtract 12	Park Avenue South:	add 8
Eighth Avenue:	add 9	West End Avenue:	add 59
Ninth Avenue:	add 13	York Avenue:	add 4
Tenth Avenue:	add 14		

Note special instructions for finding address locations on the following:

Fifth Avenue

63 to 108:	add 11	For 776 to 1286: cancel last figure of
109 to 200:	add 13	house number and subtract 18 (do
201 to 400:	add 16	not divide house number by 2).
401 to 600:	add 18	For 1310 to 1494: cancel last figure of
601 to 775:	add 20	house number. For 1310, subtract 20
		and for every additional 20 street
		numbers, increase deduction by 1.

Seventh Avenue

1 to 1800:	add 12	above 1800:	add 20

Broadway

Anything from 1 to 754 is south of 8th Street, and hence a named street.

756 to 846:	subtract 29	above 953:	subtract 31
847 to 953:	subtract 25		

Central Park West

Cancel last figure and add 60.

Riverside Drive

Cancel last figure and

Up to 567:	add 72	568 and up:	add 78

the glass-walled *Today* show studio at 48th St.), and some boutiques. If you can negotiate the crowds, the winter holidays are a great time to be here, as ice skaters take over the central plaza, the huge Christmas tree twinkles against the night sky, and lines wind past the holiday windows of Saks Fifth Avenue, across the street.

Along Seventh Avenue south of 42nd Street is the **Garment District,** of little interest to tourists except for its sample sales, where some great new fashions are sold to serious bargain hunters willing to scour the racks (see chapter 8 for details). Other than that, it's a grim commercial area. Between Seventh and Eighth avenues and 31st and

33rd streets, **Penn Station** sits beneath ugly **Madison Square Garden,** where the Rangers, Knicks, and Liberty play. Taking up 34th Street between Sixth and Seventh avenues is **Macy's,** the world's largest department store; exit Macy's at the southeast corner and you'll find more famous-label shopping around **Herald Square.** The blocks around 32nd Street west of Fifth Avenue have developed into a Koreatown, with mid-priced hotels and Asian restaurants that offer some of the best-value stays and eats in Midtown.

Midtown West is also home to some of the city's most revered museums and institutions, including **Carnegie Hall,** the **Museum of Modern Art, Radio City Music Hall,** and the *Intrepid* **Sea-Air-Space Museum,** to name just a few.

Midtown East & Murray Hill Midtown East, the area including Fifth Avenue and everything east from 34th to 59th streets, is the more upscale side of Midtown. This side of town is short of subway trains, served mostly by the Lexington Avenue 4, 5, 6 lines.

Midtown East is where you'll find many of the city's grand hotels along Lexington Avenue and near the park at the top of Fifth. The stretch of **Fifth Avenue** from Saks at 49th Street extending to FAO Schwarz at 59th is home to the city's most high-profile haute shopping, including Tiffany & Co. and Bergdorf Goodman, but mid-priced names like Banana Republic and Liz Claiborne have moved in over the last 5 years. The stretch of 57th Street between Fifth and Lexington avenues is also known for high-fashion boutiques (Chanel, Hermès) and galleries, but change is underway since names like Levi's and Niketown have arrived. You'll find more spillover along **Madison Avenue,** a great strip for shoe shopping in particular.

Architectural highlights include the recently repolished **Chrysler Building,** with its stylized gargoyles glaring down on passersby; the beaux arts *tour de force* that is **Grand Central Terminal; St. Patrick's Cathedral;** and the glorious **Empire State Building.**

Far east, swank Sutton and Beekman places are enclaves of beautiful town houses and tiny pocket parks that look out over the East River. Along the river is the **United Nations,** which isn't officially in New York City, or even the United States, but on a parcel of land belonging to member nations.

Claiming territory east from Madison Avenue, **Murray Hill** begins somewhere north of 23rd Street (the line between it and Gramercy Park is fuzzy), and is most clearly recognizable north of 30th Street to 42nd Street. This brownstone-lined quarter is residential, notable for its handful of budget and mid-priced hotels. The stretch of Lexington Avenue in the high 20s is **Curry Hill,** and is a destination for inexpensive, good Indian and Pakistani food.

Uptown

The Upper West Side North of 59th Street and encompassing everything west of Central Park, the Upper West Side contains **Lincoln Center,** one of the world's premier performing-arts venues; the new **AOL Time Warner Center** with its upscale shops such as Hugo Boss, A/X Armani, and Sephora, restaurants, and the state-of-the-art Jazz at Lincoln Center; the **American Museum of Natural History,** whose renovated Dinosaur Halls and Rose Center for Earth and Space garner rave reviews; and a growing number of affordable hotels whose larger-than-Midtown rooms and nice residential location make them some of the best values—and some of my favorite places to stay—in the entire city.

Unlike the more stratified Upper East Side, the Upper West Side is home to an egalitarian mix of middle-class yuppiedom, laid-back wealth (lots of celebs and moneyed media types call Central Park West home), and ethnic families who were here before the gentrification.

The neighborhood runs all the way up to Harlem, around 125th Street, and includes **Morningside Heights,** where you'll find **Columbia University** and the perennial construction project known as the **Cathedral of St. John the Divine.** North of 59th Street is where Eighth Avenue becomes Central Park West, the eastern border of the neighborhood (and the western border of Central Park); Ninth Avenue becomes Columbus Avenue, lined with boutiques and cafes; and Tenth Avenue becomes Amsterdam Avenue, less charming than Columbus to the east and less trafficked than bustling Broadway (whose highlights are the gourmet food stores Zabar's and Fairway) to the west. Amsterdam in the 70s and 80s has blossomed into a restaurant-and-bar strip the last few years. You'll find Lincoln Center in the mid-60s, where Broadway crosscuts Amsterdam, to 125th Street.

Two subway lines serve the area: The 1, 2, 3, 9 line runs up Broadway, while the B and C trains go up Central Park West, stopping outside the Dakota (where John Lennon was shot and Yoko lives) at 72nd Street, and at the Museum of Natural History at 81st Street.

Upper East Side North of 59th Street and east of Central Park is some of the city's most expensive residential real estate. This is New York at its most gentrified: Walk along Fifth and Park avenues, especially between 60th and 80th streets, and you're sure to encounter some of the wizened WASPs and Chanel-suited socialites that make up the most rarefied of the city's population. Madison Avenue from 60th Street well into the 80s is the moneyed crowd's main shopping strip, in recent years vaunting ahead of Hong Kong's Causeway Bay to become the most expensive retail real estate *in the world.* The main attraction of this neighborhood is **Museum Mile,** the stretch of Fifth Avenue fronting Central Park that's home to no fewer than 10 cultural institutions, including Frank Lloyd Wright's **Guggenheim,** and anchored by the **Metropolitan Museum of Art.** But the elegant rows of town houses are worth a look: East 70th Street, from Madison to Lexington, is one of the world's most charming residential streets. If you want to see where real people live, move east to Third Avenue and beyond, called Yorkville, where affordable restaurants and street life start popping up.

A second subway line is in the works, but that's far in the future. For now, the Upper East Side is served by the crowded Lexington Avenue line (4, 5, 6 trains) and rather slow buses, so wear your walking shoes (or bring taxi fare) if you head here to explore.

Harlem Now that Bill Clinton has moved his post-presidential office—and more than a few Secret Service agents—into this uptown neighborhood, the world has again heard about Harlem, which has benefited from a dramatic image makeover in the last few years.

Harlem is really two areas: Harlem proper stretches from river to river, beginning at 125th Street on the West Side and 96th Street on the East Side. East of Fifth Avenue,

Finds Discovering Harlem

You'll find sightseeing, restaurants, arts, and nightlife information about Harlem in this book. But if you want to learn more, a great source is the **Harlem Association for Travel & Tourism** website at **www.hatt.org**.

Spanish Harlem (*El Barrio*) runs between East 100th and East 125th streets. Harlem proper is benefiting from the revitalization that has swept much of the city, with national retailers moving in, restaurants and nightspots opening, and visitors touring historic sites related to the Golden Age of African-American culture, when bands like the Count Basie and Duke Ellington orchestras played the Cotton Club and Sugar Cane Club, and literary giants like Langston Hughes and James Baldwin soaked up the scene. Some houses date back to when the area was a country retreat and represent some of the best brownstone mansions in the city. On **Sugar Hill** (from 143rd to 155th sts., between St. Nicholas and Edgecombe aves.) and **Striver's Row** (W. 139th St. between Adam Clayton Powell Jr. and Frederick Douglass blvds.) are a significant number of fine town houses. For cultural visits, there's the Morris-Jumel Mansion, the Schomburg Center, the Studio Museum, and the Apollo Theatre.

Do come to Harlem—it's one of the city's most vital, historic neighborhoods, and no other feels quite so energized. Your best bet is to take a guided tour (see "Affordable Sightseeing Tours," in chapter 7); if you come on your own, do it during the day. Don't wander without a plan, especially at night. If you head up after dark to a restaurant or club, be clear about where you're going and stay alert.

Washington Heights & Inwood
At the northern tip of Manhattan, Washington Heights (the area from 155th St. to Dyckman St., with adjacent Inwood running to the tip) is home to a large segment of Manhattan's Latino community, plus an increasing number of yuppies who don't mind trading a half-hour subway commute to Midtown for lower rents. **Fort Tryon Park** and **the Cloisters** are the two big reasons visitors come up this way. The Cloisters houses the Metropolitan Museum of Art's medieval collection, with excellent views across the Hudson to the Palisades.

2 Getting Around

Frankly, Manhattan's transportation systems are a marvel. It's miraculous that so many people can gather on this little island and move around on it. For the most part, you can get where you're going pretty easily using some combination of subways, buses, and cabs; this section will tell you how to do just that.

But between traffic gridlock and subway delays, sometimes you just can't get there from here—unless you walk. Walking can be the fastest way to navigate the island. During rush hours, you'll beat car traffic on foot, as taxis and buses stop and groan at gridlocked corners (don't even *try* going crosstown in a cab or bus in Midtown at midday). You'll also see a lot more by walking than by riding beneath the street or flying by in a cab. So pack comfortable shoes and hit the pavement—it's the best, cheapest, and most appealing way to experience the city.

BY SUBWAY

Run by the **Metropolitan Transit Authority (MTA),** the much-maligned sub-way system is actually the best way to travel around New York, especially during rush hours. Some three-and-a-half million people a day agree, as it's their pri-mary mode of transportation. The subway is quick, inexpensive, relatively safe, and pretty efficient, as well as being a genuine New York experience.

The subway runs 24 hours a day, 7 days a week. The rush-hour crushes are roughly from 8 to 9:30am and 5 to 6:30pm on weekdays; the rest of the time the trains are relatively uncrowded.

PAYING YOUR WAY

The venerable New York city token is now a thing of the past, having been elim-inated in 2003, so now you need a **MetroCard,** a magnetically encoded card that debits the fare when swiped through the turnstile (or the fare box on any city bus). Once you're in the system, you can transfer freely to any subway line that you can reach without exiting your station. MetroCards—not tokens—also allow you **free transfers** between the bus and subway within a 2-hour period.

MetroCards can be purchased primarily from ATM-style vending machines located in all stations or at one of the few remaining staffed station booths, where you can only pay with cash. The ATM-style vending machines accept cash, credit cards, and debit cards. You can also purchase MetroCards from a MetroCard merchant, such as most Rite-Aid drugstores or Hudson News at Penn Station and Grand Central Terminal; or at the MTA information desk at the Times Square Visitors Center, 1560 Broadway, between 46th and 47th streets.

MetroCards come in a few different configurations:

- **Pay-Per-Ride MetroCards,** which can be used for up to four people by swiping up to four times (bring the whole family). You can put any amount from $4 (two rides) to $80 on your card. Every time you put $10 on your Pay-Per-Ride MetroCard, you get an extra ride added to your total. (For example, if you buy a $10 MetroCard, you get six rides.) You can buy Pay-Per-Ride MetroCards in any denomination at any subway station at auto-mated MetroCard vending machines, which allow you to buy MetroCards using your major credit card. MetroCards are also available from shops and newsstands around town in $10 and $20 values. You can refill your card at

---

Tips **On the Sidewalks**

New Yorkers stride across wide, crowded pavements without any regard for the traffic light, weaving through crowds, dodging taxis and buses. **Never take your walking cues from the locals.** Wait for walk signals and always use crosswalks—don't jaywalk. Do otherwise and you could quickly end up as a flattened statistic.

Always pay attention to the traffic flow. Walk as if you're driving, stay-ing to the right. At intersections, keep an eye out for drivers who don't yield, turn without looking, or think a yellow traffic light means "Hurry up!" Unfortunately, most bicyclists seem to think that the traffic laws don't apply to them; they'll often blithely fly through red lights and dash the wrong way on one-way streets, so be on your guard.

For more safety tips, see "Playing It Safe," later in this chapter.

Tips **Fare Dilemma in NYC**

In May 2003, the Metropolitan Transit Authority (MTA) raised the cost of riding city subways and buses to $2 per ride (as well as raising the fares for the multi-ride and unlimited MetroCards). Then a group of commuters sued the MTA over the hike, and a (subway-riding) judge ordered the agency to roll back the fares to $1.50. The MTA got an injunction to stop the rollback, and as this book goes to press, the stalemate continues. All references to bus and subway fares in this book will be given at the higher rate, and should you end up paying less per ride when you arrive, you won't be any happier about it than the native straphangers!

---

any time until the expiration date on the card, usually about a year from the date of purchase, at any subway station.

- **Unlimited-Ride MetroCards,** which can't be used for more than one person at a time or more frequently than 18-minute intervals, are available in four values: the **daily Fun Pass,** which allows you a day's worth of unlimited subway and bus rides for $7; the **7-Day MetroCard,** for $21; and the **30-Day MetroCard,** for $70. Seven- and 30-day Unlimited-Ride MetroCards can be purchased at any subway station or from a MetroCard merchant. Fun Passes *cannot* be purchased at booths—you can only buy them at a MetroCard machine; from a MetroCard merchant; or at the MTA information desk at the Times Square Visitors Center. Unlimited-Ride MetroCards go into effect the first time you use them—so if you buy a card on Monday and don't begin to use it until Wednesday, Wednesday is when the clock starts ticking. A Fun Pass is good from the first time you use it until 3am the next day, while 7- and 30-day MetroCards run out at midnight on the last day. These MetroCards cannot be refilled; throw them out once they've expired and buy a new one.

Tips for using your MetroCard: The MetroCard swiping mechanisms at turnstiles are the source of much grousing among subway riders. If you swipe too fast or too slow, the turnstile will ask you to swipe again. If this happens, *do not move to a different turnstile,* or you may end up paying twice. If you've tried repeatedly and really can't make it work, tell the token-booth clerk; chances are good, though, that you'll get the movement down after a couple of uses.

If you're not sure how much money you have left, or when the card expires, use the station's MetroCard reader, usually near the station entrance or the token booth (on buses, the fare box will also provide you with this information).

To locate the nearest MetroCard merchant, or for any other MetroCard questions, call ℂ **800/METROCARD** or 212/METROCARD (ℂ 212/638-7622) Monday through Friday from 7am to 11pm, Saturday and Sunday from 9am to 5pm. Or go online to **www.mta.nyc.ny.us/metrocard**, which can give you a full rundown of MetroCard merchants in the tri-state (N.Y., N.J., and Conn.) area.

USING THE SYSTEM

As you can see from the full-color subway map on the inside back cover, the subway system basically mimics the lay of the land above ground, with most lines in Manhattan running north and south, and a few lines running east and west.

To go up and down the East Side of Manhattan (and to the Bronx and Brooklyn), take the 4, 5, or 6 train.

Subway Service Interruption Notes

Due to ongoing work by the Metropolitan Transit Authority (MTA) on the Manhattan Bridge through 2004, subway service will experience numerous interruptions during the life of this book.

Changes resulting from **Manhattan Bridge work** are clear. So far, the necessary rerouting of the B, D, and Q lines serving Sixth Avenue, Chinatown, Brooklyn, and Queens seems to be working out well. Here's a summary of the changes as they will affect visitors to Manhattan:

- Chinatown's Grand Street subway station is served only by a one-stop shuttle train that runs between SoHo's Broadway–Lafayette Street station and Grand Street. To reach Chinatown, either take the F train to Broadway–Lafayette Street (which is no longer served by the B, D, or Q trains) and change to the new gray S train to Grand Street; or take the N or R train to the Canal Street station instead.

- The 34th Street/Herald Square station is now the southern terminus of the B and D trains. For Sixth Avenue service below 34th Street, use the F train or the V train, which makes all F-train (local) stops in Manhattan along the Sixth Avenue line from Second Avenue at the south end to 47th–50th streets/Rockefeller Center before veering east to Queens.

- Q trains now run express along the N and R track (which runs along Broadway) instead of along their normal Sixth Avenue path in Manhattan, as does the new temporary (until 2004) W train. Both the Q and W trains stop at express stops only from 34th Street south.

The subway map featured on the inside back cover of this book was accurate at press time; however, service is always subject to change. Your best bet is to contact the **Metropolitan Transit Authority (MTA)** for the latest details; call ① **718/330-1234** or visit **www.mta.nyc.ny.us**, where you'll find system updates that are thorough, timely, and clear. Once you're in town, you can also stop at the MTA desk at the **Times Square Visitors Center,** 1560 Broadway, between 46th and 47th streets (where Broadway meets Seventh Ave.) to pick up the latest subway map. (You can also ask for one at any token booth, but they might not always be stocked.)

To travel up and down the West Side (and also to the Bronx and Brooklyn), take the 1, 2, 3, or 9 line; the A, C, E, or F line; or the B or D line.

The N, R, Q, and W lines first cut diagonally across town from east to west and then snake under Seventh Avenue before shooting out to Queens.

The crosstown S line, the Shuttle, runs back and forth between Times Square and Grand Central Terminal (as does the 7 line). Farther downtown, across 14th Street, the L line works its own crosstown magic.

Note: For service changes, see "Subway Service Interruption Notes," above.

Lines have assigned colors on subway maps and trains—red for the 1, 2, 3, 9 line; green for the 4, 5, and 6 trains; and so on—but nobody refers to them by color. Always use the number or letter when asking questions. Within Manhattan, the distinction between numbered trains that share the same line is usually that some are express and others are local. **Express trains** often skip about three stops for each one that they make; express stops are indicated on subway maps with a white (rather than solid) circle. Local stops usually come about 9 blocks apart.

Directions are almost always indicated using "Uptown" (northbound) and "Downtown" (southbound), so be sure to know what direction you want to head in. The outsides of some subway entrances are marked UPTOWN ONLY or DOWNTOWN ONLY; read carefully, as it's easy to head in the wrong direction. Once you're on the platform, check the signs overhead to make sure that the train you're waiting for will be traveling in the right direction. If you do make a mistake, it's a good idea to wait for an express station, like 14th Street or 42nd Street, so you can get off and change for the other direction without paying again.

The days of graffiti-covered cars are gone, but the stations—and an increasing number of trains—are not nearly as clean as they could be. Trains are air-conditioned (move to the next car if yours isn't), though during the dog days of summer the platforms can be sweltering. In theory, all subway cars have PA systems to allow you to hear the conductor's announcements, but they don't always work well. It's a good idea to move to a car with a working PA system in case sudden service changes are announced that you'll want to know about.

For **subway safety tips,** see "Playing It Safe," later in this chapter.

BY BUS

Less expensive than taxis and more pleasant than subways (they provide a mobile sightseeing window on Manhattan), MTA buses are a good transportation option. Their big drawback: They can get stuck in traffic, sometimes making it quicker to walk. They also stop every couple of blocks, rather than the eight or nine blocks that local subways traverse between stops. So for long distances, the subway is your best bet; but for short distances or traveling crosstown, try the bus.

Tips For More Bus & Subway Information

For transit information, call the Metropolitan Transit Authority's **MTA/New York City Transit Travel Information Center** at ✆ **718/330-1234.** Automated information is available 24 hours a day, and agents are on hand daily from 6am to 9pm. For online information, visit **www.mta.nyc. ny.us**; kudos to the MTA, because the information on the site is always current.

To request maps, call the Customer Assistance Line at ✆ **718/330-3322** (although recent service changes may not be reflected on printed maps). Riders with disabilities should direct inquiries to ✆ **718/596-8585;** hearing-impaired riders can call ✆ **718/596-8273.** For MetroCard information, call ✆ **212/638-7622** weekdays from 7 to 11am, weekends from 9am to 5pm, or go online to **www.mta.nyc.ny.us/metrocard**.

You can get bus and subway maps and additional information at most information centers (see "Visitor Information," earlier in this chapter). A helpful MTA transit information desk is located at the Times Square Visitors Center, 1560 Broadway, between 46th and 47th streets, where you can also buy MetroCards. Maps are sometimes available in subway stations (ask at the token booth), but rarely on buses.

Value Money-Saving Transit Tips: Free Transfers

If you pay your subway or bus fare with a **MetroCard,** you can transfer to another bus or to the subway (or from the subway to a bus) for up to 2 hours. You don't need to do anything special; just swipe your card at the turnstile, and the automated system keeps track.

If you use coins to board a bus and need to transfer to another line, request a free **transfer slip** that allows you to change to an intersecting bus route only (transfer points are listed on the transfer itself) within 1 hour of issue. Transfer slips cannot be used to enter the subway.

PAYING YOUR WAY

Like the subway fare, **bus fare** is $2, half price for seniors and riders with disabilities, free for children under 44 inches (up to three per adult). The fare is payable with a **MetroCard** or **exact change.** Bus drivers don't make change, and fare boxes don't accept dollar bills or pennies, so bring lots of quarters. You can't purchase MetroCards on the bus, so get them before you board; for details on where to get them, see "Paying Your Way" under "By Subway," above.

USING THE SYSTEM

You can't flag down a city bus—you have to wait at a bus stop. **Bus stops** are located every 2 or 3 blocks on the right-side corner of the street (facing the direction of traffic flow). They're marked by a curb painted yellow and a blue-and-white sign with a bus emblem and the route number or numbers. Guide-A-Ride boxes at most stops show a route map and a somewhat optimistic schedule.

Almost every major avenue has its own **bus route.** They run either north or south: downtown on Fifth, uptown on Madison, downtown on Lexington, uptown on Third, and so on. There are **crosstown buses** at strategic locations all around town: 8th Street (eastbound); 9th (westbound); 14th, 23rd, 34th, and 42nd (east- and westbound); 49th (eastbound); 50th (westbound); 57th (east- and westbound); 65th (eastbound across the West Side, through the park, and then north on Madison, continuing east on 68th to York Ave.); 67th (westbound on the East Side to Fifth Ave. and then south on Fifth, continuing west on 66th St. through the park and across the West Side to West End Ave.); and 79th, 86th, 96th, 116th, and 125th (east- and westbound). Some bus routes, however, are erratic: The M104, for example, starts at the East River, then turns at Eighth Avenue and goes up Broadway. The buses of the Fifth Avenue line go up Madison or Sixth and follow various routes around the city.

Most routes operate 24 hours a day, but service is infrequent at night. Some say that New York buses have a herding instinct: They come only in groups. During rush hour, main routes have "limited-stop" buses, identifiable by the orange card in the front window; they stop only at major cross streets.

To make sure the bus you're boarding goes where you're going, check the maps on the sign that's at every bus stop, get your hands on a route map (see "For More Bus & Subway Information," above), or *just ask.* The drivers are helpful, as long as you don't hold up the line too long.

While traveling, look out the window not only to take in the sights, but also to keep track of cross streets. You can signal for a stop by pressing the tape strip above and beside the windows and along the metal straps, about 1 block before you want to stop. Exit through the back doors (not the front door) by pushing on the yellow tape strip; the doors open automatically (pushing on the handles is useless). Most city buses are equipped with wheelchair lifts, making buses the preferable mode of public transportation for wheelchair-bound travelers (if you're in a seat that converts for wheelchair use, you'll be expected to vacate it if the bus stops to pick up a person in a chair); for more on this topic, see "Travelers with Disabilities," under "Specialized Travel Resources," in chapter 2. Buses also "kneel," lowering down to the curb to make boarding easier.

BY TAXI

If you don't want to deal with public transportation, finding an address that might be a few blocks from the subway station, or sharing your ride with three-and-a-half million other people, take a taxi. The biggest advantages are that cabs can be hailed on any street (provided you find an empty one—often simple, yet at other times nearly impossible) and will take you right to your destination.

Official New York City taxis, licensed by the Taxi and Limousine Commission, are yellow, with the rates printed on the door and a light with a medallion number on the roof. You can hail a taxi on any street. *Never* accept a ride from any other car except an official city yellow cab (private livery cars are not allowed to pick up fares on the street).

If you're planning to take taxis, be prepared to pay. The base fare on entering the cab is $2. The cost is 30¢ for every one-fifth mile or 20¢ per minute in stopped or very slow-moving traffic (or for waiting time). There's no extra charge for each passenger or for luggage. However, you must pay bridge or tunnel tolls (sometimes the driver will front the toll and add it to your bill at the end; most times, however, you pay the driver before the toll). You'll also pay a 50¢ night surcharge after 8pm and before 6am. A 15% to 20% tip is customary.

Note: Taxi drivers were lobbying for a fare increase at press time, and the mayor supports it, so don't be surprised if you find higher fares when you arrive.

Because it's going to cost you at least $2 just to get in the car, taxis are far more expensive than other forms of transportation. Visitors on a limited budget are generally better off relying on subways and buses, using taxis only late at night (after 11pm or midnight, when buses and subway trains start getting fewer and farther between) or to reach an out-of-the-way destination (maybe a bar or restaurant on the Lower East Side or the far East Village, neighborhoods not well served by the subway). You'll also get your money's worth out of a taxi at night, when there's little traffic to keep them from speeding you to your destination.

Although taxis are generally far more expensive than the subway or a bus, consider taking cabs for short hauls if there are three or four in your group. A taxi might not actually save you money, but you'll get door-to-door service for about the same price: It costs four people $6 to take the subway, which is no less than you'd pay for a short taxi ride from Times Square to the West Village, say, or from Carnegie Hall to your Murray Hill hotel. Skip taxis entirely at rush

---

Tips Taxi-Hailing Tips

When you're waiting on the street for a taxi, look at the **medallion light** on the top of the coming cabs. If the light is out, the taxi is in use. When the center part (the number) is lit, the taxi is available: Raise your hand to flag the cab. If all the lights are on, the driver is off-duty.

Note: A taxi can't take more than four people.

hour, when it's more convenient and cheaper to take the subway, because you don't want to end up stuck in traffic, delayed, and paying for unnecessary wait time.

Forget about hopping into the back seat and having some double-chinned, cigar-chomping driver slowly turn and ask, "Where to, Mac?" Nowadays most taxi drivers speak only an approximation of English and drive in engagingly exotic ways. Always wear your seat belt—taxis are required to provide them.

The TLC has posted a **Taxi Rider's Bill of Rights** in every cab. Drivers are required to take you anywhere in the five boroughs, to Nassau or Westchester counties, or to Newark Airport. They are supposed to know how to get you to any address in Manhattan and major points in the outer boroughs. They are required to provide air-conditioning and turn off the radio on demand, and they cannot smoke while you're in the cab. They are required to be polite.

You are allowed to dictate the route that is taken. It's a good idea to look at a map before you get in a taxi. Taxi drivers have been known to jack up the fare on visitors who don't know better by taking very circuitous routes. Know enough about where you're going to know that something's wrong if you hop in a cab at Sixth Avenue and 57th Street to go to the Empire State Building (Fifth Ave. and 34th St.), say, and you suddenly find yourself on Ninth Avenue.

On the other hand, listen to drivers who propose an alternate route. These guys spend 8 or 10 hours a day on these streets, and they know them well—where the worst traffic is, or where Con Ed has dug up an intersection. A knowledge-able driver will know how to get you to your destination quickly and efficiently.

Another important tip: Always make sure the meter is turned on at the start of the ride. You'll see the red readout register the initial $2 and start calculating the fare as you go. I've witnessed unscrupulous drivers hauling unsuspecting visitors around with the meter off, and then overcharging them at drop-off time.

Always ask for the receipt—it comes in handy if you need to make a complaint or if you leave something behind. It's a good idea to make a mental note of the driver's four-digit medallion number (usually posted on the divider between the front and back seats) just in case. You probably won't need it, but it's a good idea.

A taxi driver is obligated to take you to your desired destination. If the taxi driver is on duty and after giving your desired destination, the taxi driver refuses to take you there, write down the driver's name and medallion number and file a com-plaint with the Taxi and Limousine Commission.

For driver complaints and lost property, call the 24-hour Consumer Hot Line at ✆ **212/NYC-TAXI.** For details on getting to and from the local airports by taxi, see "By Plane" under "Getting There," in chapter 2. For further taxi infor-mation—including a complete rundown of your rights as a taxi rider—point your Web browser to **www.ci.nyc.ny.us/taxi**.

BY CAR

Forget driving yourself around the city. It's not worth it. Traffic is horrible, the streets have all the civility of the Wild West, street parking is nearly impossible (not to mention the security risks), and garage parking *will* cost you a fortune.

If you arrive in New York City by car, park it in a garage and leave it there. If you drive a rental car in, return it as soon as you arrive and rent another on the day you leave. Just about all of the major car-rental companies, including **National** (✆ 800/227-7368; www.nationalcar.com), **Hertz** (✆ 800/654-3131; www.hertz.com), and **Avis** (✆ 800/230-4898; www.avis.com), have multiple Manhattan locations.

TRAVELING FROM THE CITY TO THE SUBURBS

The **PATH** (✆ 800/234-7284; www.panynj.gov/path) system connects urban communities in New Jersey, including Hoboken and Newark, to Manhattan by subway-style trains. Stops in Manhattan are at Christopher and 9th streets, and along Sixth Avenue at 14th, 23rd, and 33rd streets. A new lower-Manhattan station, to replace the one destroyed underneath the World Trade Center, is not expected to be up and running until sometime in late 2004. The fare is $1.50.

New Jersey Transit (✆ 973/762-5100; www.njtransit.com) operates commuter trains from Penn Station, and buses from the Port Authority at Eighth Avenue and 42nd Street, to points throughout New Jersey.

The **Long Island Rail Road** (✆ 718/217-LIRR; www.mta.nyc.ny.us/lirr) runs from Penn Station, at Seventh Avenue between 31st and 33rd streets, to Queens and points beyond on Long Island.

Metro-North (✆ 800/METRO-INFO or 212/532-4900; www.mta.nyc.ny. us/mnr) departs from Grand Central Terminal, at 42nd Street and Lexington Avenue, for areas north of the city, including Westchester County, the lovely Hudson Valley, and Connecticut.

If you'd prefer to rely on substantially cheaper buses to reach your suburban destination, visit **www.panynj.gov/tbt/pabframe.HTM**, where you'll find a complete list of bus companies (in addition to NJ Transit, above) that service Manhattan's Port Authority bus terminal at Eighth Avenue and 42nd Street.

3 Playing It Safe

Sure, there's crime in New York City, but millions of people spend their lives here without being robbed and assaulted. In fact, New York is safer than any other large American city, and is listed by the FBI as somewhere around 150th in the nation for total crimes. While that's quite encouraging, it's still important to take precautions. Criminals are expert at spotting newcomers who appear disoriented or vulnerable.

Men should carry their wallets in their front pockets and women should keep hold of their purse straps. Cross camera and purse straps over one shoulder, across your front, and under the other arm. Never hang a purse on the back of a chair or on a hook in a bathroom stall; keep it in your lap or between your feet with one foot through a strap. Avoid carrying large amounts of cash. You might carry your money in several pockets so that if one is picked, the others might escape. Skip the flashy jewelry and keep valuables out of sight on the street.

Panhandlers are seldom dangerous and can usually be ignored (more aggressive pleas can be answered, "Not today."). If a stranger walks up to you on the street with a sob story ("I live in the suburbs and was attacked and don't have

---

Impressions

I like it here in New York. I like the idea of having to keep eyes in the back of your head all the time.

—John Cale

the money to get home. . . ."), it's likely a scam. You have every right to walk away. Be wary of an individual who "accidentally" falls in front of you or causes some other commotion, because he or she may be working with someone else who will take your wallet when you try to help. And remember: You *will* lose if you place a bet on a sidewalk card game or shell game.

Certain areas should be avoided late at night. I don't recommend going to the Lower East Side, Alphabet City in the far East Village, Harlem, or the Meat-Packing District unless you know where you're going. Don't be afraid to go, but head straight for your destination and don't wander onto deserted side streets. Times Square has been cleaned up, and there'll be crowds around until midnight, when theater- and moviegoers leave the area. Still, stick to the main streets, such as Broadway or Ninth Avenue, Midtown West's newest restaurant row. The areas south of Times Square are best avoided after dark, as they're largely abandoned once the business day ends. Take a cab or bus when visiting the Jacob Javits Center on 34th Street and the Hudson River. Don't wander the parks after dark, unless you're going to a performance; if that's the case, stick with the crowd.

If you plan on visiting the outer boroughs, go during the daylight hours. If the subway doesn't go directly to your destination, your best bet is to take a taxi. Don't wander the side streets; many areas in the outer boroughs are absolutely safe, but neighborhoods change quickly, and it's easy to get lost.

All this said, don't panic. New York has experienced a dramatic drop in crime and is safer than many other major U.S. cities these days, especially in the neighborhoods that visitors are prone to frequent. There's a good police presence on the street, so don't be afraid to stop an officer, or even a friendly-looking New Yorker (trust me—you can tell) if you need help getting your bearings.

SUBWAY SAFETY TIPS   In general, the subways are safe, especially in Manhattan. Still, stay alert and trust your instincts. Always keep a hand on your personal belongings.

When using the subway, *do not wait for trains near the edge of the platform* or on extreme ends of a station. During non-rush hours, wait for the train in view of the token-booth clerk or under the yellow DURING OFF HOURS TRAINS STOP HERE signs, and ride in the train operator's or conductor's car (usually in the center of the train; you'll see his or her head stick out of the window when the doors open). Choose crowded cars over empty ones—there's safety in numbers.

Avoid subways late at night, and take a cab after about 10 or 11pm— it's money well spent to avoid a long wait on a deserted platform. Or take the bus.

Tips **Top Safety Tips**

Trust your instincts, because they're usually right. You'll rarely be hassled, but it's always best to walk with a sense of purpose, and don't stop in the middle of the sidewalk to look at your map. If you find yourself on a deserted street that feels unsafe, it probably is; leave as quickly as possible. If you do find yourself accosted by someone with or without a weapon, remember to keep your anger in check and that the most reasonable response (maddening though it may be) is not to resist.

FAST FACTS: **New York City**

American Express Travel service offices are at many Manhattan locations, including 1185 Sixth Ave., at 47th Street (✆ **212/398-8585**); at the New York Marriott Marquis, 1535 Broadway, in the 8th-floor lobby (✆ **212/575-6580**); on the mezzanine level at Macy's Herald Square, 34th Street and Broadway (✆ **212/695-8075**); and at 374 Park Ave., at 53rd St. (✆ **212/421-8240**). Call ✆ **800/AXP-TRIP** or go online to **www.americanexpress.com** for other city locations or general information.

Area Codes There are four area codes in the city: two in Manhattan, the original **212** and the new **646,** and two in the outer boroughs, the original **718** and the new **347.** Also common is the **917** area code, which is assigned to cellphones, pagers, and a few land lines. *Note:* As of 2003, all calls between these area codes are local calls, but you'll have to dial 1 + the area code + the 7 digits for all calls, even ones in the same area code.

Doctors For emergencies requiring immediate attention, head to the nearest emergency room (see "Hospitals," below). New York also has several walk-in centers, like **DOCS at New York Healthcare,** 55 E. 34th St., between Park and Madison avenues (✆ **212/252-6001**), for non-emergency illnesses. The clinic, affiliated with Beth Israel Medical Center, is open Monday through Thursday from 8am to 8pm, Friday from 8am to 7pm, Saturday from 9am to 3pm, and Sunday from 9am to 2pm. The **NYU Downtown Hospital** offers referrals at ✆ **888/698-3362.**

Embassies/Consulates See "Fast Facts: For the International Traveler," in chapter 3.

Emergencies Dial ✆ **911** for fire, police, and ambulance. The **Poison Control Center** is at ✆ **800/222-1222** toll-free from any phone.

Hospitals The following hospitals have 24-hour emergency rooms. Don't forget your insurance card.

   Downtown: New York Downtown Hospital, 170 William St., between Beekman and Spruce streets (✆ 212/312-5063 or 212/312-5000); **St. Vincents Hospital and Medical Center,** 153 W. 11th St., at Seventh Avenue (✆ 212/604-7000); and **Beth Israel Medical Center,** First Avenue and 16th Street (✆ 212/420-2000).

   Midtown: Bellevue Hospital Center, 462 First Ave., at 27th Street (✆ 212/562-4141); **New York University Medical Center,** 560 First Ave., at 33rd Street (✆ 212/263-7300); and **Roosevelt Hospital,** 425 W. 59th St., between Ninth and Tenth avenues (✆ 212/523-6800).

   Upper West Side: St. Luke's Hospital Center, Amsterdam Avenue and 113th Street (✆ 212/523-3335); and **Columbia Presbyterian Medical Center,** 622 W. 168th St., between Broadway and Fort Washington Avenue (✆ 212/305-2500).

   Upper East Side: New York Presbyterian Hospital, 525 E. 68th St., at York Avenue (✆ 212/746-5050); **Lenox Hill Hospital,** 100 E. 77th St., between Park and Lexington avenues (✆ 212/434-2000); and **Mount Sinai Medical Center,** Fifth Avenue at 100th Street (✆ 212/241-6500).

Hot Lines The 24-hour **Rape and Sexual Abuse Hot Line** is ✆ 212/267-7273. The **Bias Crimes Hot Line** is ✆ 212/662-2427. The **LIFENET hot line** for suicide prevention, substance abuse, and other crises is ☎ 800/543-3638. For **Mental Health and Alcoholism Services Crisis Intervention,** call ☎ 212/219-5599. You can reach **Alcoholics Anonymous** at ☎ 212/870-3400 (general office) or 212/647-1680 (for alcoholics who need immediate counseling from a sober, recovering alcoholic). The **Domestic Violence Hot Line** is ☎ 800/621-4673. Other useful numbers are the **Crisis Help Line** ☎ 212/532-2400; **Samaritans' Suicide Prevention Line** ☎ 212/673-3000; to locate local **police** precincts ☎ 646/610-5000 or 718/610-5000; **Department of Consumer Affairs** ☎ 212/487-4444; and **taxi complaints** ☎ 212/NYC-TAXI or 212/676-1000. If you suspect your car was towed, call the **Department of Transportation TOWAWAY Help Line** at ☎ 212/869-2929.

Libraries The **New York Public Library** is on Fifth Avenue at 42nd Street (☎ 212/930-0830). This beaux arts beauty houses more than 38 million volumes, and the reading rooms have been restored to their former glory. More efficient and modern, if less charming, is the mid-Manhattan annex at 455 Fifth Ave., at 40th Street, across from the main library (☎ **212/340-0833**). For other branches, see the list online at **www.nypl.org.**

Liquor Laws The legal age to purchase and consume alcoholic beverages in New York is 21. Liquor and wine are sold only in licensed stores, which are closed on Sundays, holidays, and election days while the polls are open. Beer can be purchased in grocery stores and delis 24 hours a day, except Sundays before noon. Last call in bars is at 4am.

Newspapers/Magazines There are three major daily newspapers: the *New York Times,* the *Daily News,* and the *New York Post.* For details on where to find arts and entertainment listings, see "Publications," under "Visitor Information," earlier in this chapter.

If you want to find your hometown paper, visit **Universal News & Magazines,** at 234 W. 42nd St., between Seventh and Eighth avenues (☎ **212/221-1809**); and 977 Eighth Ave., between 57th and 58th streets (☎ **212/459-0932**); or **Hotalings News Agency,** 624 W. 52nd St., between Eleventh and Twelfth avenues (☎ **212/974-9419**).

Pharmacies **Duane Reade (www.duanereade.com)** has 24-hour pharmacies in Midtown at 224 W. 57th St., at Broadway (☎ **212/541-9708**); on the Upper West Side at 2465 Broadway, at 91st Street (☎ **212/799-3172**); and on the Upper East Side at 1279 Third Ave., at 74th Street (☎ **212/744-2668**).

Police Dial ☎ **911** in an emergency; otherwise, call ☎ **646/610-5000** or 718/610-5000 (NYPD headquarters) for the number of the nearest precinct.

Restrooms There are public restrooms at the visitor centers in Midtown (1560 Broadway, between 46th and 47th sts.; and 810 Seventh Ave., between 52nd and 53rd sts.). Grand Central Terminal, at 42nd Street between Park and Lexington avenues, also has clean restrooms. On the street, try Starbucks or another java chain—there's practically one on every block. The big bookstores are good for restrooms, too. You can also head to hotel lobbies (especially the big Midtown ones) and department stores like Macy's and Bloomingdale's. On the Lower East Side, stop into the Lower East Side BID Visitor Center, 261 Broome St., between Orchard and Allen streets (open Sun–Fri 10am–4pm, sometimes later).

Smoking Smoking is prohibited on public transportation, in the lobbies of hotels and office buildings, in taxis, in restaurants, in bars, and in most shops. In this town, if you want to smoke, take it outside.

Taxes **Sales tax** is 8.25% on meals, most goods, and some services, but is not charged on clothing and footwear under $110. **Hotel tax** is 13.25% plus $2 per room per night (including sales tax). **Parking-garage tax** is 18.25%.

Time For the correct time, dial ✆ **212/976-1616.**

Transit Information For information on getting to and from the airport, see "Getting There" in chapter 2, or call **Air-Ride** at ✆ **800/247-7433.** For information on subways and buses, call the **MTA** at ✆ **718/330-1234,** or see "Getting Around," earlier in this chapter.

Traveler's Assistance **Travelers Aid International (www.travelersaid.org)** helps distressed travelers with all kinds of problems, including accidents, sickness, and lost or stolen luggage. There is an office on the second floor of the International Arrivals Building at John F. Kennedy International Airport (✆ **718/656-4870**), and one in Newark International Airport's Terminal B (✆ **973/623-5052**).

Weather For the current temperature and next day's forecast, look in the upper-right corner of the front page of the *New York Times* or call ✆ **212/976-1212.** If you want to know how to pack before you arrive, point your browser to **www.cnn.com/weather** or **www.weather.com.**

5

Accommodations You Can Afford

After the economic boom of the late 1990s, the hotel industry in New York has come down to earth. In 2000, hotel occupancy was at a record high, 84%. But then the economy went sour, September 11 happened, and the bubble burst. In 2001, occupancy was down to around 72%, but rates remained high, hitting an astronomical average of $227. In 2002, occupancy rose slightly to 74% but rates fell to an average of $185. The downturn wasn't only economic; with all the new hotels built in better times, a glut of rooms meant increased competition for your business. So what wasn't so good for the industry was good for you. As of press time in 2003, many hotels were offering rates they hadn't offered in almost a decade.

With all those rooms to choose from, visitors have more bargaining power than they've had in years. Still, don't expect cheap. While the city does have a handful of good inexpensive hotels, it can be difficult to score a room with a private bathroom, nice furniture, closet space, and elevator—for $100 or less. Still, there are bargains if you know where to look.

To stay in New York on a tight budget, you must weigh what you're willing to spend versus what you're willing to put up with. If you only want to spend 100 or so bucks a night—a very budget-basic rate in this city—you're going to have to live with some inconveniences.

First, be aware that many of New York's budget hotels have **shared bathrooms.** There are a few exceptions—but in general, don't count on a double room with its own bathroom for less than $100.

Even if you're willing to spend a bit more, don't expect much in the way of **space,** New York's most coveted commodity. Don't be surprised if your hotel room isn't much bigger than the bed in it, the closet is a rack screwed to the wall, and the bathroom is the smallest you've ever seen. Pack light.

It's almost always more expensive to stay in the Theater District than in a residential **neighborhood** like Chelsea, Murray Hill, the Upper West Side, or Harlem; in fact, uptown has become a haven for travelers looking for the highest value-for-dollar ratio. Staying in a residential area is almost always quieter, and will give you better access to affordable restaurants where locals eat. Most travelers who choose residential areas end up thrilled with their advantages.

Remember: Hotel rooms are subject to **13.25% tax plus $2 per night,** unless otherwise noted.

HOW TO SAVE ON YOUR HOTEL ROOM

The **rates** quoted in the listings below are the rack rates (the maximum rates that a hotel charges). But rack rates are only guidelines, and there are ways around them. Before you start calling, review the "65 Money-Saving Tips" in chapter 2, including the box on p. 22, "Home Stay Sweet Home Stay," where you'll find time-tested advice on how to get the most for your accommodations dollar.

The hotels below have provided us with their best rate estimates for 2004, and all quoted rates were correct at press time. Be aware that **rates can change at any time,** subject to availability, seasonal fluctuations, and plain old increases. All bets are off at Christmas; expect everyone to charge over their rack rates.

1 TriBeCa

Cosmopolitan Hotel–Tribeca ★ *Value*   Hiding behind a plain-vanilla TriBeCa awning is one of the best hotel deals in Manhattan for travelers who insist on a private bathroom. Everything is budget but nice: The IKEA-ish furniture includes a work desk and an armoire (a few rooms have a dresser and hanging rack instead); for a few more bucks, you can have a love seat. Beds are comfy, and sheets and towels are of good quality. Rooms are small but make the most of the limited space, and the whole place is pristine. The two-level minilofts have lots of character, but expect to duck on the second level: Downstairs is the bathroom, TV, closet, desk, and club chair, while upstairs is a low-ceilinged bedroom. Management does a great job keeping everything fresh. The TriBeCa location is safe, hip, and subway-convenient; Ground Zero is a walk away (for better or worse). There's no room service, but a range of restaurants will deliver. In fact, all services are kept at a bare minimum to keep costs down, so you must be a low-maintenance guest to be happy here. If you are, this place is a great deal.

95 W. Broadway (at Chambers St.), New York, NY 10007. ✆ 888/895-9400 or 212/566-1900. Fax 212/566-6909. www.cosmohotel.com. 113 units. $119–$159 double. Inquire about discounts. AE, DC, MC, V. Parking $20, 1 block away. Subway: 1, 2, 3, 9 to Chambers St. *In room:* A/C, TV, dataport, ceiling fan.

2 On the Bowery

Off SoHo Suites Hotel *Value*   Once you had to put up with an industrial, edge-of-Chinatown neighborhood to enjoy Off SoHo Suites—a hotel with clean, welcoming rooms with full kitchen facilities at surprisingly low prices. But the neighborhood is getting nicer by the minute, and it's a stone's throw from the city's coolest dining, shopping, and nightlife: Nolita's Elizabeth Street is 2 blocks west, and the Lower East Side's Orchard and Ludlow streets are a half-dozen blocks east, not to mention Chinatown's nearby cheap eats. You'll get a lot for your dough: Each deluxe suite has a living and dining area with a pullout sofa, kitchen, private bathroom with hair dryer, and separate bedroom. In the economy suites, kitchens and bathrooms (with hair dryers) are shared with another room; if four of you are traveling, you can combine two economy suites into a sizable apartment. Everything is basic and the beds are a bit harder than you might like, but the whole place is nicely kept. Telephones have voice mail and dataports. *Note:* If you don't like a youth-oriented, gentrifying scene, stay elsewhere.

11 Rivington St. (between Chrystie St. and the Bowery), New York, NY 10002. ✆ 800/OFF-SOHO (633-7646) or 212/979-9808. Fax 212/979-9801. www.offsoho.com. 38 units (10 with shared bathroom). $66–$109 economy suite (2 people maximum); $89–$179 deluxe suite (4 people maximum). AE, MC, V. Parking $20 nearby. Subway: F to Second Ave., 6 to Spring St. Pets allowed (in deluxe suites only). **Amenities:** Cafe for breakfast and lunch; exercise room; access to nearby health club; activities desk; limited room service; dry cleaning/laundry; coin-op laundry. *In room:* A/C, TV w/free movies, dataport, kitchen with fridge and coffeemaker, hair dryer, iron.

SoHotel ★ *Finds*   Formerly the Pioneer, this is one of my favorite finds, and the little Euro-style hotel has done something no other Manhattan hotel has managed: It offers clean, quiet, friendly accommodations with private bathrooms for as little as $65 double (tax not included) on a year-round basis.

This older hotel (it claims to be the oldest in the city) has come into its own, and the friendly manager continues to make improvements. The same can be said for the neighborhood: The hotel is in a four-story walkup off a stretch of the Bowery, lined with restaurant suppliers, that was crusty and desolate a few years ago. But these days it's clean, safe, and convenient.

It's one level up to the lobby, which is older but bright and agreeable. Here you'll find a professional staff and morning coffee (the pot's usually on all day). Decorative painting adds an attractive flair to rooms, and hanging plants add color in the halls. Rooms have black linoleum floors, mix-and-match lamps and chairs, ceiling fans, and fresh and firm platform beds (which may be a tad too firm for some). Some have armoires, while others have a rack on the wall in lieu of a closet. Most rooms have a tiny but spotless bathroom with a shower stall (a handful have tubs). Shared-bathroom units (which have small sinks) are petite, but many spacious configurations are available, and the standard doubles are a good size. Room no. 11D is a family-friendly triple with two doubles and a twin and a sizable bathroom with a tub, while a room with three twins is a great configuration for friends. A few rooms have no windows, but they're blissfully silent and will even save you a few dollars. Ask for a renovated room (most are). Service is delightfully old-fashioned; a wake-up call consists of a clerk who'll knock on your door (BYO alarm and hair dryer if you'll want them).

341 Broome St. (between Elizabeth St. and the Bowery), New York, NY 10013. ℂ 212/226-1482. Fax 212/226-3525. www.pioneerhotel.com. 125 units (about 35 with shared bathroom). $55–$59 single or double with shared bathroom; $65–$89 double with private bathroom; $109–$129 triple, quad, or family room with private bathroom. Rates include tax. AE, DC, DISC, MC, V. Parking $10–$15 nearby. Subway: F to Second Ave., 6 to Spring St. **Amenities:** Free coffee in lobby. *In room:* A/C, TV, ceiling fan, no phone.

3 The Lower East Side

New York City Howard Johnson Express Inn ★★ *(Value* This new in 2002 hotel is a boon to travelers looking for quality at a great price, a trendy location, or both. It's the kind of hotel where recent college grads could put up their parents—*and* where they'd like to stay themselves.

The hotel sits on a wide thoroughfare next to a renovated Yiddish vaudeville house that houses a state-of-the-art movie complex. Bars, live-music clubs, restaurants, and offbeat shops abound on the surrounding blocks; East Village action is across Houston Street, and SoHo is to the west. The neighborhood may be on the cutting edge, but this HoJo is wonderfully predictable. In the second-floor lobby, we found a welcome bowl of Tootsie Rolls and a staff that's more attentive than most working in this price range. Rooms are small, but furnishings and textiles are attractive and of good quality: Mattresses are firm, work desks boast desk-level inputs and an ergonomic chair, and the granite bathrooms are nicer than those in some luxury hotels (some even have Jacuzzis).

Most rooms have queen beds, while some have two doubles; don't expect much elbowroom in either configuration. Those with room numbers ending in 01, 02, or 03 are the largest. Not much noise comes off of Houston, but request a back-facing or high-floor room for total quiet. Coffee's on all day in the lobby, and a basic continental breakfast (Danishes, donuts) is laid out in the morning.

135 E. Houston St. (at Forsyth St.), New York, NY 10002. ℂ 800/406-1411 or 212/358-8844. Fax 212/473-3500. www.hojo.com. 54 units. $109–$139 double. Rates include continental breakfast. Inquire about AAA, AARP, and corporate discounts. AE, DC, DISC, MC, V. Parking $29, 4 blocks away. Subway: F to Second Ave. **Amenities:** Dry cleaning/laundry. *In room:* A/C, TV, dataport, hair dryer, iron.

4 The East Village

East Village Bed & Coffee *Finds* **_Fair warning:_** This little guesthouse isn't for everyone. If you're turned off by the idea of staying behind a graffiti-covered facade in a space that's a work in progress, in an up-and-coming neighborhood, skip this one. But if you're an adventurous traveler who likes a communal vibe, and are willing to put up with a few eccentricities for a super deal, read on.

Friendly innkeeper Carlos Delfin has created a series of private guest rooms on two floors. All are small and basic, with little more than a high-quality bed and a work desk. Best is the sunlit French room, with queen bed and a chest of drawers. Also on the second floor are some very petite rooms, including the Mexican room, plus a common kitchen, living room with TV, and bathroom. Downstairs is a loftlike space with Carlos's workroom, office, and the main kitchen; a second bathroom; and two more Japanese-style bedrooms (with low ceilings and low platform beds) built as enclosed lofts over the main space (best for heavy sleepers). Furnishings are hodgepodge; everything is well worn but clean and comfortable—Carlos makes constant improvements—and a wonderful art collection brightens the mix. The back garden is open in warm weather. The Alphabet City neighborhood is gentrifying, but it's still the hinterlands as far as most visitors are concerned. Subways are a significant walk away, so use the money you save on your room to take cabs back late at night.

110 Ave. C (between 7th and 8th sts.), New York, NY 10009. *C* and fax 212/533-4175. Fax 212/979-9743. www.eastvillagebed.citysearch.com or www.bedandcoffee.com. 6 units (all with shared bathroom). $65–$80 single; $75–$90 double. Rates include tax. AE, MC, V. Subway: L to First Ave., 6 to Astor Place. **Amenities:** Common kitchen with coffee and tea; living room with TV/VCR; Internet connection for guest use; fax; free local calls from common phone. *In room:* A/C, no phone.

St. Mark's Hotel *★* This renovated hotel from the folks behind the Chelsea Savoy (p. 105) and Park Savoy (p. 118) is a welcome addition to the budget hotel scene. It's in a four-story walkup on St. Marks Place, the hot spot for the East Village's youth, lined with used-record stores, restaurants and bars, and a parade of tattooed hipsters. Folks in search of peace and quiet will abhor the location, but anybody interested in being at the heart of the action will love it.

In a city where dingy paint and 20-year-old carpet is the norm in budget hotels, St. Mark's pretty Parisian mural (in the stairwell leading up to the second-floor front desk), lighting, finished oak, and marble floors are a welcome sight. Rooms are basic and furnishings are simple, but even the smallest—one double bed—is a decent size and boasts new carpet, a firm bed, a TV, a phone with voice mail, and a tiled bathroom with a tiny sink, shower, and nice towels; butter-yellow walls and framed prints brighten most rooms. Services are minimal, but the staff is professional. There's no dedicated public space, but a pub sits on the ground level. Some of New York's best affordable restaurants are within shouting distance.

2 St. Marks Place (at Third Ave.), New York, NY 10003. *C* 212/674-0100 or 212/674-2192. Fax 212/420-0854. www.stmarkshotel.qpg.com. 67 units. $80–$110 single or double. No credit cards. Subway: 6 to Astor Place. *In room:* A/C, TV.

Second Home on Second Avenue *★* *Finds* Here's another guesthouse run by gregarious innkeeper Carlos Delfin, this one a big step up in quality, location, and price from his East Village Bed & Coffee (see above). It's a guesthouse for young, independent-minded travelers who prefer the restaurant- and club-heavy East Village. The rooms are large and eclectically furnished. Each is outfitted with two full beds, good closet space, a large TV with VCR, a CD player (unheard of in this price category), an alarm, and a phone (free local calls!) with answering machine in every room. If there are more than two of you, the suite, which has a separate living room with a leather sofa that pulls out into a queen bed and a big private bathroom, is a good bet. Bathrooms are older but clean. A nice, new common kitchen is fully outfitted and offers free coffee and tea.

A few words of caution: Don't expect lots in the way of service, as Carlos lives off-site. Rooms are on the third and fourth floors of a walk-up. The guesthouse is popular with European travelers, who tend to smoke; you may still want to stay elsewhere if the possibility bothers you.

221 Second Ave. (between E. 13th and 14th sts.), New York, NY 10003. (℃ and fax **212/677-3161**. www.second home.citysearch.com. 6 units (2 with private bathroom). $75–$145 single; $85–$175 double. Rates include tax. Extra person $20. 2-night minimum stay required. AE, MC, V. Parking about $20 nearby. Subway: L to Third Ave.; N, R, 4, 5, 6 to Union Sq. **Amenities:** Common kitchen. *In room:* A/C, TV/VCR, CD player.

Whitehouse Hotel of New York ⭐ *Value* This newly renovated, youth-oriented hotel is a wonderful addition because it offers private rooms at hostel prices, and the location is smashing. Rooms are tiny and plain, each with either a full bed or twins, so expect no perks; but everything is clean, well maintained, and relatively new. Good-quality linens and towels are provided. All rooms share simple shower-stall bathrooms off the hall. There's a lobby lounge with a TV, tables and chairs for lounging, a cafe area selling continental-style breakfast items, and friendly, grandfatherly service around the clock. A coin-op laundry and an Internet-access machine in the lobby add to the convenience. The city's best budget dining lines the East Village blocks; the heart of Greenwich Village is to the west, and SoHo and the Lower East Side are both just a 5-minute walk away. No smoking allowed, and no travelers under 18.

340 Bowery (between 2nd and Great Jones/3rd sts.), New York, NY 10012. (℃ **212/477-5623**. Fax 212/ 473-3150. www.whitehousehotelofny.com. 468 beds (all with shared bathroom). $30–$32 single; $60–$63 double; $80–$91 triple. Rates include tax. AE, DC, MC, V. Subway: 6 to Bleecker St. No children under 18 accepted. **Amenities:** Common kitchen w/microwave; Internet access machine and dataport in lobby; coin-op laundry; continental breakfast for a charge (daily 6–10am). *In room:* A/C.

5 Greenwich Village

Abingdon Guest House ⭐⭐ *Finds* Steve Austin and his partner Zachary Stass run this lovely guesthouse (and its downstairs coffee bar, **Brewbar**) in a retail-and-residential West Village neighborhood. Both men have an eye for style—the Abingdon is beautifully outfitted and professionally run. Accommodations with in-room bathrooms are pricey for most wallet-watching travelers (but worth the price if you feel like a splurge), but those with hall bathrooms are well priced—as low as $115, no more than $177—and still come with private bathrooms, just outside your room off the hall. All of the rooms are done in bold colors and outfitted with well-chosen art and furnishings. No matter which you choose, you'll get a quality mattress and linens, soft bathrobes, an alarm clock, a telephone with free local calls and your own answering machine (a splitter can be provided for your laptop), and maid service.

The neighborhood is terrific, with good restaurants and shops. The Abingdon is best for mature, independent travelers, because there's no regular staff on-site, and the area is geared to locals rather than tourists. The thoughtful style and privacy make it ideal for a romantic escape, but friends traveling won't feel out of place (in fact, two rooms feature two twin beds). It's a nonsmoking property.

13 Eighth Ave. (between W. 12th and Jane sts.), New York, NY 10014. (℃ **212/243-5384**. Fax 212/807-7473. www.abingdonguesthouse.com. 9 units. $137–$222 double. 4-night minimum on weekends, 2-night minimum

Abingdon Guest House **1**

Cosmopolitan Hotel—Tribeca **11**

East Village Bed & Coffee **6**

Larchmont Hotel **3**

New York City
Howard Johnson Express Inn **8**

Off SoHo Suites **9**

Second Home on Second Avenue **4**

SoHotel **10**

St. Mark's Hotel **5**

Washington Square Hotel **2**

Whitehouse Hotel of New York **7**

on weekdays. Rates $10 less for single travelers. Extra person $25. AE, DC, DISC, MC, V. Parking $20 nearby. Subway: A, C, E, L, 1, 2, 3, 9 to 14th St. **Amenities:** Coffee bar. *In room:* A/C, TV, dataport, hair dryer, iron, safe.

Larchmont Hotel *★★* *Value*   On a tree-lined block in a quiet part of the Village, this European-style hotel is a gem. If you're willing to share a bathroom, it's hard to do better for the money. The entire place has an air of warmth and sophistication. Each bright guest room is done in rattan and outfitted with a writing desk, a minilibrary, an alarm clock, a washbasin, and a few extras you normally have to pay a lot more for, such as bathrobes, slippers, and ceiling fans. Every floor has two shared bathrooms (with hair dryers) and a small kitchen. The management is constantly renovating, so everything feels clean and fresh. Those looking for a hip downtown base couldn't be better situated, because some of the city's best shopping, dining, and sightseeing—plus your choice of subway lines—is all close. A free continental breakfast that includes fresh-baked goods every morning is the crowning touch that makes the Larchmont a terrific deal. Book *well* in advance (the management suggests 6–7 weeks' lead time).

27 W. 11th St. (between Fifth and Sixth aves.), New York, NY 10011. *☎* 212/989-9333. Fax 212/989-9496. www.larchmonthotel.com. 58 units (all with shared bathroom). $70–$95 single; $90–$125 double. Rates include continental breakfast. Children under 13 stay free in parent's room. AE, MC, V. Parking $18 nearby. Subway: A, C, E, F, V to W. 4th St. (use 8th St. exit); F to 14th St. **Amenities:** Common kitchenette; tour desk; fax service; room service (10am–6pm). *In room:* A/C, TV, hair dryer, safe, washbasin, ceiling fan.

Washington Square Hotel   Popular with a young international crowd, this hotel sits behind a facade facing Washington Square Park (historically Henry James territory, now the heart of New York University). A marble-and-brass lobby leads to tiny rooms, each with a firm bed, a private bathroom, and a small closet with a pint-size safe. It's worth paying extra for a south-facing room on a high floor, because others can be dark. Both the Union Square Inn and Murray Hill's Thirty Thirty offer a bit more space and brand-new everything for a similar price; but the heart-of-campus location is ideal for travelers who want to be near Village restaurants, bars, and clubs. On-site is a very good restaurant and lounge, **North Square Lounge,** which draws locals with its stylish design, well-priced cocktails and bistro fare, and Sunday jazz brunch. The staff has been known to be terse, but service seems to be on an upswing.

103 Waverly Place (between Fifth and Sixth aves.), New York, NY 10011. *☎* 800/222-0418 or 212/777-9515. Fax 212/979-8373. www.wshotel.com. 170 units. $101–$131 single; $118–$151 double; $145–$188 quad. Rates include continental breakfast. Inquire about special rates and jazz packages. Rollaway $20 extra. AE, MC, V. Parking $20 nearby. Subway: A, C, E, F, V to W. 4th St. (use 3rd St. exit). **Amenities:** Restaurant; lounge; exercise room; dry cleaning/laundry. *In room:* A/C, TV, dataport, hair dryer, iron, safe.

6 Chelsea

Chelsea Lodge *★★* *Finds*   In a brownstone on a landmarked block, this small hotel is charming and a terrific value—arguably the best in the city for budget-minded travelers. The husband-and-wife owners, Paul and GG Weisenfeld, have put in an incredible effort: Renovations have restored original woodwork and created a country-in-the-city vibe with beautiful wallpapers and wainscoting, vintage furniture, and lovely touches like Hershey's Kisses on the pillows. The beds are the finest and best outfitted I've seen in this price category. Ongoing renovations show how much Paul and GG continue to care.

The only place with a similar grown-up sensibility for the same money is Greenwich Village's Larchmont (p. 104), but there, bathroom facilities are shared; at Chelsea Lodge, each room has its own sink and in-room shower stall, so you only have to share a toilet. The rooms are petite, the closets are small, and beds are full-size (queens wouldn't cut it). But considering the stylishness, the amenities—which include TV, a ceiling fan, a desk, and an alarm clock—and the neighborhood, you'd be hard-pressed to do better. Best for couples rather than shares. *Tip:* Try to book 2A, which is bigger than most, or one of the first-floor rooms, whose high ceilings make them feel more spacious.

318 W. 20th St. (between Eighth and Ninth aves.), New York, NY 10011. © 800/373-1116 or 212/243-4499. Fax 212/243-7852. www.chelsealodge.com. 24 units (all with semiprivate bathroom). $90 single; $105 double. AE, DC, DISC, MC, V. Parking about $20 nearby. Subway: 1, 9 to 18th St.; C, E to 23rd St. *In room:* A/C, TV, ceiling fan.

Chelsea Pines Inn ★★ *Value*   This inn caters largely to gay travelers, but all adult travelers are welcome as long as they'll be comfortable in a gay-oriented atmosphere. The inn straddles the border of the West Village, the heart of New York's gay community, and Chelsea, the hip neighborhood for the GLBT scene.

The rooms have comfortable furnishings, floral-print textiles, and a terrific collection of movie posters. Each room is dedicated to a Golden-Age-of-Hollywood star; the Paul Newman room boasts posters from movies such as *Hud* and *The Drowning Pool.* Rooms aren't big, but are well outfitted and arranged. Each has a minifridge, free HBO, a clock radio, and an answering machine; most have queen beds and daybeds for extra seating, and a half-dozen have breakfast areas with cafe tables and microwaves. Private bathrooms are bright and new; the cheapest (semiprivate) rooms have showers and sinks, so you just have to share a hall toilet. There's a payoff if you're willing to stay at the top of the five-story walkup: The Rock Hudson room sleeps four and has a terrific green-and-white bathroom with a skylight. The friendly staff mans the front desk around the clock, and continental breakfast is served in a cute breakfast room. There's also a greenhouselike enclosed patio and a backyard garden with blooming flowers.

317 W. 14th St. (between Eighth and Ninth aves.), New York, NY 10014. © 888/546-2700 or 212/929-1023. Fax 212/620-5646. www.chelseapinesinn.com. 23 units (15 with private bathroom). $89–$109 double with semiprivate bathroom, $119–$139 double with private bathroom; $129–$139 deluxe. Rates include expanded continental breakfast. Check website for specials. Extra person $20. 3-night minimum stay on weekends. AE, DC, DISC, MC, V. Parking $25 nearby. Subway: A, C, E to 14th St. Not appropriate for children. *In room:* A/C, TV, dataport, fridge, hair dryer, iron.

Chelsea Savoy Hotel ★★ *Kids*   The six-story Savoy was built from the ground up in 1995, so it isn't subject to the eccentricities of older hotels. The hallways are attractive and wide, the elevators swift and silent, and the cheery rooms of good size with big closets and roomy, immaculate bathrooms with tons of counter space. The reasonably priced quad rooms are suitable for a family of four (children stay free). Creature comforts abound: The rooms boast mattresses, furniture, and linens of high quality, plus the kinds of amenities you usually have to pay more for, like minifridges, in-room safes, and toiletries. Free continental breakfast makes a good value even better. Most rooms are street facing and sunny; corner rooms tend to be brightest but noisiest. Ask for a back-facing room if you crave total silence. The staff is young and helpful, and the increasingly hip neighborhood makes a good base for exploring both Midtown and downtown. A plain but pleasant sitting room off the lobby makes an excellent place to enjoy your morning coffee over a selection of newspapers and magazines.

204 W. 23rd St. (at Seventh Ave.), New York, NY 10011. © 866/929-9353 or 212/929-9353. Fax 212/741-6309. www.chelseasavoynyc.com. 90 units. $99–$115 single; $135–$175 double; $145–$195 quad. Rates include continental breakfast. Children stay free in parent's room. AE, MC, V. Parking $25 nearby. Subway: 1, 9 to 23rd St. *In room:* A/C, TV, dataport, fridge, hair dryer, iron, safe.

(Tips) Deal-Making with the Chains

Most hotels—particularly chains like Comfort Inn, Holiday Inn, and Best Western—are market-sensitive. Because they hate to see rooms sit empty, they'll often negotiate good rates at the last minute and in slow seasons.

The chains are also where you can ask for all kinds of discounts, from auto-club membership to senior status. And you might be able to take advantage of corporate or government rates or discounted weekend stays. Most chain hotels let the kids stay with parents for free. Ask for every possible kind of discount; if you find that you get an unhelpful reservation agent, call back and try again. And it's worth calling the hotel direct, where the front-desk staff will deal to keep their occupancy rate high.

Of course, there's no guarantee. Your chances of getting a deal aren't great if you're visiting in a busy season. But if you're willing to make a few extra calls, or spend some time surfing online—which might net you a 10% discount for booking online—you might get a deal at hotels that would otherwise be out of your price range.

Best Western's (© 800/528-1234; www.bestwestern.com) rack rates for their New York hotels are higher than you'd expect. At the **Best Western President Hotel,** in the Theater District at 234 W. 48th St. (© 800/826-4667 or 212/246-8800), doubles go for $129 to $229 but can drop to $99—a great deal on a centrally located hotel. Ditto for **Hampshire Hotels & Suites (www.bestnyhotels.com),** the company that manages this and chain hotels such as the **Quality Hotel on Broadway** (p. 128) and the **Comfort Inn–Central Park West** (p. 124), where rooms can go as low as $72 (with breakfast), as well as two Midtown Best Westerns and Howard Johnsons on Park Avenue; check their website for all the details.

At these and other franchised hotels—such as the ones run by **Apple Core Hotels** (© 800/567-7720; www.applecorehotels.com), a

Chelsea Star Hotel/Chelsea Suites   Industrial-chic hallways lead to private rooms that are minuscule and bare-bones basic at this Generation Y–targeted hotel—more hostel than hotel-like, with nothing more than a firm bed and an open closet. But they're spotless, the mattresses and linens are of good quality, and designer Rob Graf has infused them with enough style that they don't feel as dour as most supercheap sleeps. They're individually dressed in cheeky themes ranging from the Disco Room (graced by a *Fever*-era poster of Travolta in all his white-suited glory) to the Asian mod Madame Butterfly Room (tiny but lovely) to the glow-in-the-dark cosmos of the Orbit Room (complete with black light). Try to grab the Madonna Room, a relatively spacious quad where Mrs. Ritchie lived for a year in leaner days. The shared hallway bathrooms have showers only, but they're smart and clean. Shoestring travelers who don't mind snoozing with strangers can opt for a single bunk in one of the serviceable dorms.

For a bit more, you can have your own pad: a stylish, fully loaded apartment with an equipped kitchen, private bathroom, and TV in the furnished living management company that handles the **Comfort Inn Midtown** (p. 113), the **Ramada Inn Eastside** (p. 123), Manhattan's first **Red Roof Inn** (p. 118), the **Super 8 Hotel Times Square** (p. 119), and the **Best Western Manhattan,** 17 W. 32nd St. (© **212/736-1600**), doubles can go for as little as $89. Check with the franchiser directly if you're not quoted a good advance-booking rate, or go through the management company's online reservations system; their global 800 and online reservations systems will often garner you a better rate, which might include a promotion—or, at minimum, an "Internet User's Rate" that's 10% lower than the standard.

A good source for deals is **Choice Hotels** (© **800/4-CHOICE;** www.hotelchoice.com), which oversees Comfort Inn, Quality Hotel, and Clarion Hotel chains, all of which have terrific Manhattan branches.

Also try **Holiday Inn** (© **800/HOLIDAY;** www.holiday-inn.com), which has a handful of terrific hotels in Manhattan, all of which carry rack rates that are too high for most budget travelers. However, discounted weekend and slow-season rates can drop as low as $109 double at the **Holiday Inn Wall Street,** 15 Gold St. (© **212/232-7800;** www.holiday innwsd.com), New York's most high-tech hotel. Shoppers might like the **Holiday Inn Downtown/SoHo,** 138 Lafayette St. (© **212/966-8898;** www.holidayinn-nyc.com), straddling the border between Chinatown and SoHo.

Another hotel to try is the **Days Hotel Midtown,** 790 Eighth Ave., at 48th Street (© **800/544-8313** or 212/581-7000; www.daysinn.com). The bistro **Pigalle** (p. 173) gives it a better-than-budget flair, and the motel-like rooms are worth the $105-to-$130 rate you might be able to snare in slower seasons. Be sure to ask about senior, AAA, corporate, and promotional rates at all three (Choice, Holiday Inns, and Days Hotel), and check for online-booking discounts.

room. These are the best values in the house—and some of the best in Midtown—so book way ahead. *Tip:* The courtyard-facing apartments are quietest.

The Chelsea Star is a great addition to the budget hotel scene, but a word of warning: It is decidedly youth-oriented; mature travelers looking for standard amenities may be disappointed. The location—at the back door of Penn Station, more Midtown than Chelsea—may not be New York's finest, but it's cleaner and safer than ever, and cheap eateries and Irish pubs abound.

300 W. 30th St. (at Eighth Ave.), New York, NY 10001. © **877/827-6969** or 212/244-7827. Fax 212/279-9018. www.chelseastar.com or www.chelseasuites.com. 25 rooms (all with shared bathroom); 5 apts; 24 dorm beds. $59–$69 single; $79–$89 double; $89–$99 triple or quad. $25.50 per person in dorm. $159–$179 apt (sleeps up to 4). AE, DISC, MC, V. Parking about $25 nearby. Subway: A, C, E to 34th St./Penn Station. No children under 18 accepted. **Amenities:** Pay Internet PC; fax service; dry cleaning/laundry; shared pay phones. *In room:* A/C, no phone (TV, phone, and dataport in apts).

Colonial House Inn ⭒   This charming 1850 brownstone, on a pretty residential block in the heart of gay-friendly Chelsea, was the first permanent home of the Gay Men's Health Crisis. The four-story walk-up caters to a largely gay and lesbian clientele, but the friendly staff welcomes everyone. The place is beautifully maintained and professionally run. Rooms are small and basic but clean; all have radios, and those that share a hall bathroom (at a ratio of about three rooms per bathroom) have in-room sinks. Deluxe rooms—those with private bathrooms— have minifridges, and a few have working fireplaces. Both private and shared bathrooms are basic but nice. A terrific art collection brightens the public spaces. Book at least a month in advance for weekend stays. At parlor level is a breakfast room where a continental spread is put out from 8am to noon daily; coffee and tea are available all day. Rooms don't have hair dryers and irons, but the front desk will lend them. There's a nice roof deck split by a privacy fence (the area behind the fence is clothing optional). The neighborhood is chock-full of great restaurants and shopping, and offers easy access to the rest of the city.

318 W. 22nd St. (between Eighth and Ninth aves.), New York, NY 10011. © 800/689-3779 or 212/243-9669. Fax 212/633-1612. www.colonialhouseinn.com. 20 units (12 with shared bathroom). $80–$125 single or double with shared bathroom; $125–$140 double with private bathroom. Rates include expanded continental breakfast. 2-night minimum on weekends. Extra person $15. Weekly rates available. MC, V. Parking $20 nearby. Subway: C, E to 23rd St. **Amenities:** Internet-access PC in lounge; fax service. *In room:* A/C, TV, dataport.

SUPERCHEAP SLEEPS

Also consider the dorm beds ($25.50) at the **Chelsea Star Hotel** (see above).

Chelsea Center Hostel   Going strong since 1981, this small, pleasant hostel is ideal for travelers who prefer a laidback ambience and a good night's sleep over the standard hostel bustle. It's on two floors of a Chelsea brownstone. Rooms are bunk-bedded and hostel-simple, but everything is bright and clean, and rates include decent-quality sheets and blankets; each bed also has its own night light for late-night reading and writing. Plenty of top-flight dining and nightlife is nearby; there's no curfew, and the owners will be happy to point you in the right direction. One of the nicest perks is the light continental breakfast included in the rate; guests sit around their morning table to chat. There's also a common room, plus a garden for warm-weather relaxation. You can request a dorm bed at their eastside location, in the East Village (exact location provided upon booking).

313 W. 29th St. (just west of Eighth Ave.), New York, NY 10031. © 212/643-0214. www.chelseacenterhostel. com. 20 dorm beds in each location (all with shared bathroom). $30 dorm bed. Rate includes continental breakfast and tax. No credit cards. Subway: C, E to 23rd St. **Amenities:** Common kitchen and lounge rooms. *In room:* No phone.

Chelsea International Hostel   As hostels go, this is a good one. The only other private hostel in this league, both in terms of cleanliness and location, is the Big Apple Hostel (p. 120). The well-managed, well-maintained Chelsea International consists of a warren of low-rise buildings around a central courtyard, like a cottage complex. It's hugely popular with international travelers.

Accommodations and shared bathrooms are older and plain but fine; the shared rooms come with nice extras such as wall hooks, sinks, and in-room lockers big enough for most backpacks (BYO combination lock and towels). The miniscule private rooms have little more than a double bed and some shelf units, but you can call one your own for just 60 bucks. Some rooms have air-conditioning, so request one if it matters to you.

The two fully equipped common kitchens (with microwaves) are the best I've seen in a hostel, and free coffee, tea, sugar, and cream is on hand. The private courtyard has picnic tables and barbecues. There are also dining and lounge areas with TV, Internet-access machines, self-service laundry, and soda machines; free luggage storage is another plus. The neighborhood is great, the desk is attended 24 hours, and maintenance is on hand around the clock. At press time, free pizza was part of the package for Wednesday-night guests.

251 W. 20th St. (between Seventh and Eighth aves.), New York, NY 10011. ✆ **212/647-0010.** Fax 212/727-7289. www.chelseahostel.com. 288 dorm beds; 57 private units (all with shared bathroom). $25 dorm bed; $60 double. Rates include tax. AE, MC, V. Subway: 1, 9 to 18th St. **Amenities:** 2 kitchens; dining areas; Internet access; fax; coin-op laundry. *In room:* No phone.

7 Union Square, the Flatiron District & Gramercy Park

Carlton Arms   The motto here is THIS AIN'T NO HOLIDAY INN! The spirit of bohemianism and artistic freedom reigns in this backpacker's delight, where every room is a work of art by an artist given license to go hog wild. Think of this as the legendary Hotel Chelsea as it used to be. Some spaces are sublime, such as Robin Banks's Cartoon Room (#5B), Thias Charbonet's Underwater Room (#1A), Olivia Hamlin's super-realist 12A, the ocean-blue lobby (complete with fish in the TV), and the first-floor mosaic bathroom; others are simply bizarre. Whether you end up with a mermaid mural or a wall of teddy bears, you'll see why this is one of the most extraordinary hotels in the city.

But if you're looking for creature comforts, this is *not* the place for you. The cramped rooms are *very* basic. The beds are lumpy, and there's no air-conditioning. Each room has a sink, but you'll most likely end up sharing a bathroom with your fellow travelers (mainly students, international travelers, and existentialists). The place is clean, but there's no maid service. Still, the staff is friendly, and they'll be happy to take messages (rooms don't have phones; there's a pay phone in the lobby). The neighborhood isn't glitzy, but it's safe, quiet, residential, and overflowing with affordable restaurants. Reserve 1 to 2 months in advance, because despite the inconveniences, this place is almost always full.

160 E. 25th St. (between Lexington and Third aves.), New York, NY 10010. ✆ **212/679-0680** or 212/684-8337. www.carltonarms.com. 54 units (20 with private bathroom). $60–$90 single or double with shared bathroom; $99–$130 triple or quad with shared bathroom; $75–$100 single or double with private bathroom; $111–$140 triple or quad with private bathroom. 10% discount on 7-night stays paid upon arrival. MC, V. Subway: 6 to 23rd St. *In room:* No phone.

Chelsea Inn   The name may say Chelsea, but the east-of-Sixth-Avenue address is really Flatiron. It's still a great location, what with Union Square just a stone's throw in one direction and Chelsea in the other.

The inn is in two 19th-century brownstones, but don't expect too much. Staying here is like living in your own New York City tenement for a few days: The rooms feature a mix of thrift-store furniture, the beds in the twin rooms are little more than rollaways, and the quality of the mattresses is a crapshoot. Everything's faded, but the place is clean and well kept. More on the upside: Closets are big, bathrooms are fine, and all rooms feature a hot plate, minifridge, coffeemaker, cups and utensils, a safe, voice mail, and free coffee; those without a bathroom have their own sinks. Shared bathrooms are livened with murals, and you'll have to split yours with only one other room. If there's more than two of you, pair up two doubles that share a bathroom, and you can usually negotiate a discount. Groups of three or four will like no. 102, a spacious suite with a private bathroom, a dining table, and a kitchenette. The staff is accommodating, and deals are often available. It's a reasonable, well-priced budget choice.

46 W. 17th St. (between Fifth and Sixth aves.), New York, NY 10011. ✆ **800/640-6469** or 212/645-8989. Fax 212/645-1903. www.chelseainn.com. 26 units (18 with private bathroom). $109–$129 double with shared bathroom; $139–$159 double with private bathroom; $179–$259 suite (for up to 4). Check website

for available specials (as low as $79 at press time). AE, DISC, MC, V. Parking about $20 nearby. Subway: 4, 5, 6, N, R, Q, W to 14th St./Union Sq. *In room:* A/C, TV, fridge, minifridge, coffeemaker, safe.

Gershwin Hotel ☆ *Kids*   If you see glowing horns protruding from a lipstick-red facade, you're in the right place. This Warholesque hotel caters to up-and-coming artistic types—and names with an eye for good value—with its art collection and wild style. The lobby is a postmodern cartoon of kitschy furniture and pop art. The standard rooms are clean and bright, with Picasso-style wall murals, Philippe Starck–ish takes on motel furnishings, and more modern art. Superior rooms are best, worth the extra $10; all have a queen bed, two twins, or two doubles, plus a newish private bathroom with colorful tile. Families and groups of friends will love the family room, a two-room suite that nicely accommodates four with a queen bed in one room, two twins in the other.

One of the best things about the Gershwin is its great Factory-esque vibe: There's always something going on, whether it's live jazz, alt-rock, or stand-up comedy in the **Living Room;** nightly happy hour (7–9pm) in the **Red Room** beer bar; summer film screenings in the rooftop garden; or a show at the hotel's own art gallery (usually twice monthly). The hotel is more service-oriented than you usually see at this price level, and the staff is very professional.

7 E. 27th St. (between Fifth and Madison aves.), New York, NY 10016. ℂ **212/545-8000.** Fax 212/684-5546. www.gershwinhotel.com. 150 units. $99–$189 double (usually less than $150); $189–$219 family unit. Check website for discounts, 3rd-night-free specials, or other value-added packages. Extra person $10. AE, MC, V. Parking $25, 3 blocks away. Subway: N, R, 6 to 28th St. **Amenities:** Cafe (breakfast only); beer bar; tour desk; babysitting; dry cleaning/laundry; Internet-access PC. *In room:* A/C, TV, dataport, hair dryer, iron.

Gramercy Park Hotel   Opened in 1924, this old-world–style hotel has one of the best settings in the city. It's in one of New York's loveliest neighborhoods, on the edge of the private park—restricted to area residents and to hotel guests, who can also get a key—which gives Gramercy Park the air of a quiet London square.

Management has this dowager looking good. You'll still have to overlook the finer details, including ancient TVs and mix-and-match bathrooms updated haphazardly. But rooms are huge by city standards, and comfortable, and the hotel has an Old New York feel, due to an incredibly loyal staff, many of whom have worked here for generations. Each standard double has a king bed or two doubles, and some suites have pullout sofas that make them large enough to sleep six; all have big closets and fluffy towels in the roomy bathrooms. Request a park-facing room, which costs no more but features a great view and a small kitchenette (most suites have kitchenettes, too). A free continental breakfast, free Internet service, and a new fitness center are all very welcome new additions. Off the bustling lobby are a continental restaurant and a divey piano lounge with nightly entertainment that draws a young, retro-obsessed crowd.

2 Lexington Ave. (at 21st St.), New York, NY 10010. ℂ **800/221-4083** or 212/475-4320. Fax 212/505-0535. www.gramercyparkhotel.com. 509 units. $139–$160 single; $149–$170 double; $179–$210 suite. Extra person $10. Children under 12 stay free in parent's room. Rates include complimentary breakfast. AE, DC, DISC, MC, V. Parking $28 nearby. Subway: 6 to 23rd St. Pets accepted. **Amenities:** Restaurant; lounge; fitness center; salon; limited room service; in-room massage; dry cleaning/laundry. *In room:* A/C, TV, free Internet access, fridge, hair dryer.

Hotel 17   Hotel 17 has managed to garner a hip reputation; Madonna, David Bowie, and Maxwell have all been photographed in the eclectic, eccentric rooms. The neighborhood is great, the block is peaceful, and the individually decorated rooms are attractive (all have been freshened in the last year). Look beyond the stylish veneer and you'll find rooms that are cramped, dark, and basic—not for travelers looking for creature comforts. Each has its own sink, hair dryer, and alarm clock, and phones have recently been installed. The shared bathrooms are clean and have recently been renovated. The lobby has a funky, modern feel, but the security glass separating you from the staff detracts from the ambience. It's a decent deal, especially if you're the sort who requires some individuality in your lodgings. Expect lots of younger and international travelers, who don't mind the inconveniences and the lingering smell of smoke.

225 E. 17th St. (between Second and Third aves.), New York, NY 10003. ℭ 212/475-2845. Fax 212/677-8178. www.hotel17.citysearch.com. 120 units (all with shared bathroom). $60–$80 single; $60–$100 double; $85–$125 triple. MC, V. Parking about $20 nearby. Subway: 4, 5, 6 to 14th St.; L to Third Ave. No children under 18 accepted. **Amenities:** Coin-op laundry. *In room:* A/C, TV, hair dryer (no A/C or TV in singles).

The Marcel ★★ *Value*   Being budget-challenged doesn't mean you have to set-tle for boring. This Gramercy Park hotel offers style and a superhip scene at low, low prices. Thanks to designers Goodman Charlton, who love to infuse retro styles with futuristic freshness, the Marcel sits on the cutting edge style-wise. Fab faux *Mod Squad*–era Scandinavian stylings in the lobby lead to guest rooms boasting blond-wood built-ins that make clever use of limited space, and a bold geometric cushioned headboard adds a downright luxurious flair. The designer furnishings and textiles look and feel expensive, even if the lumpy-ish beds don't; still, budget travelers will be thrilled. And trust me—you're going to have to look long and hard for another hotel in town that supplies marble bathrooms, dual-line phones, and CD players at this price. Even if the service isn't fabulous or the little details aren't perfect, you should feel like you're getting a great deal here.

One of the strongest appeals of The Marcel is **Spread** (www.spreadnyc.com), a restaurant/lounge hybrid offering a small-plates menu, a sushi bar, cocktails, and a blast of an after-dark scene. The subterranean lounge **Coal** is an even more seductive space—just ask Natasha Richardson, who celebrated a birthday here.

201 E. 24th St. (at Third Ave.), New York, NY 10011. ℭ **888/66-HOTEL** (664-6835) or 212/696-3800. Fax 212/696-0077. www.nychotels.com. 97 units. $125–$175 double. AE, DISC, MC, V. Parking $24. Subway: 6 to 28th St. **Amenities:** Restaurant; lounge; coffee/cappuccino bar; limited room service; dry cleaning/laundry. *In room:* A/C, TV w/pay movies, CD player, dataport, hair dryer, iron.

Union Square Inn ★★ *Value*   A stone's throw east of Union Square on the fringe of the East Village, this unassuming hotel is a welcome addition. Rooms aren't as cheap as at sister hotel the Murray Hill Inn, but comforts are better-quality, every unit has a private bathroom, and everything feels fresh and new.

Four standard rooms are tiny twins with trundle beds; a handful in the deluxe category are spacious double/doubles that can accommodate more than two. Most fall in the moderate category, with one double bed and little room to spare—but you're not in the Big Apple to hang out in your room! All rooms boast terrific, brand-new pillow-top mattresses and good-quality sheets (probably the best bedding you'll find in this price category), cheery autumn-hued textiles and art, cute contemporary redwood furnishings, nice bedside lamps, and pretty all-new Italian-tile bathrooms. On the downside, all rooms lack views, open wall racks sub-stitute for closets, most bathrooms have shower only, halls are narrow, and there's no elevator—but those are minimal sacrifices considering the low prices.

Services are virtually nonexistent in order to keep costs down, but everything you'll need, from restaurants to dry cleaners to a slate of subway lines, is right at hand in the hip, central-to-everything location.

209 E. 14th St. (between Second and Third aves.), New York, NY 10003. ℭ 212/614-0500. Fax 212/614-0512. www.unionsquareinn.com or www.nyinns.com. 40 units. $99–$169 double. Rates include con-tinental breakfast. Extra person $20. AE, MC, V. Parking $25 nearby. Subway: L to Third Ave.; or 4, 5, 6, N, R to 14th St./Union Sq. **Amenities:** Coffee bar w/light meals. *In room:* A/C, TV, dataport.

8 Times Square & Midtown West

Americana Inn ★ *Value*   The cheapest hotel from the Empire Hotel Group—the people behind the Upper West Side's Newton and pricier properties—is a star in the budget category. Linoleum floors give the rooms a somewhat institutional quality, but the hotel is well run and immaculately kept. Rooms are spacious, with good-sized closets, private sinks, and an alarm built into the TV; the beds are the most comfortable I've found at this price. Most rooms come with a double bed or two twins; a few can accommodate three guests in two twin beds and a pullout sofa or three twins. One hall bathroom accommodates every three rooms or so; all are spacious and spotless, and the front desk lends hair dryers. Every floor has a kitchenette with microwave, stove, and fridge (BYO cooking utensils, or go plastic). The five-story building has an elevator (uncommon at this price), and four rooms are accessible for travelers with disabilities. Ask for a back-facing room away from the street noise.

69 W. 38th St. (at Sixth Ave.), New York, NY 10018. © **888/HOTEL-58** (468-3558) or 212/840-6700. Fax 212/840-1830. www.newyorkhotel.com. 50 units (all with shared bathroom). $65–$75 single; $75–$115 double. Check website for specials (winter rates as low as $60 double). Extra person $10. AE, MC, V. Parking $25–$35 nearby. Subway: B, D, F, V to 34th St. **Amenities:** Kitchenettes on each floor, safety-deposit boxes. *In room:* A/C, TV.

Broadway Inn ★★ *Finds*   More like a San Francisco B&B than a Theater District hotel, this lovely, welcoming inn is a charmer. The second-floor lobby sets the homey tone with bookcases, cushy seating, and cafe tables where free continental breakfast is served. The rooms are basic but comfy, outfitted in an appealing neo-Deco style with firm beds, good-quality linens and textiles, and nice bathrooms (about half have showers only). The place is impeccably kept. The standard doubles are fine for couples; if there's more than two of you or you're looking to stay a while, the suites—with pullout sofa, microwave, minifridge, and lots of closet space—are a great deal. Double-paned windows keep the rooms peaceful; still, ask for a back-facing one if you're extrasensitive.

The inn's biggest asset is its staff, whose members go above and beyond the call of duty to make guests happy; they'll even give you a hot-line number you can call for directions, advice, and other assistance while you're out. Service doesn't get any better in this price range. This gentrified corner of the Theater District makes a great base, especially for theatergoers. The inn has a loyal following, so reserve early. *Note:* There's no elevator in the four-story building, so overpackers and travelers with limited mobility should book elsewhere.

264 W. 46th St. (at Eighth Ave.), New York, NY 10036. © **800/826-6300** or 212/997-9200. Fax 212/768-2807. www.broadwayinn.com. 41 units, about half with shower only. $99–$139 single; $135–$225 double; $199–$299 suite. Rates include continental breakfast. Check the website for special deals (as low as $79 single, $99 double at press time). Extra person $10. Children under 12 stay free in parent's room. AE, DC, DISC, MC, V. Parking $20, 3 blocks away. Subway: A, C, E to 42nd St. **Amenities:** 2 nearby restaurants offer guest discounts; concierge; fax and copy service. *In room:* A/C, TV, dataport, fridge, hair dryer, iron.

Comfort Inn Manhattan   This centrally located hotel is a good choice for those who prefer to go with a national chain. It's on a block near some of Midtown's biggest attractions, including the Empire State Building and Macy's. This is a standard chain hotel, but the rooms are clean, well maintained, and large by Manhattan standards. In fact, Hotel Choice (Comfort Inn's parent company) presented this location its gold award for the quality of its professionalism, housekeeping, and hospitality. Nice extras include big closets, hair dryers, in-room safes, on-command movies, and voice mail on the phones. A number of rooms have microwaves and minifridges, and about 30 king-bedded rooms come with sleeper sofas. The lobby is attractive enough to invite lounging, and the front-desk staff is friendly and helpful. The expanded continental breakfast that's included in the rates is a big plus.

42 W. 35th St. (between Fifth and Sixth aves.), New York, NY 10001. © 800/228-5150 or 212/947-0200. Fax 212/594-3047. www.comfortinnmanhattan.com or www.comfortinn.com. 131 units. $99–$219 double. Rates include continental breakfast. Ask about senior, AAA, corporate, and other discounts. Extra person $15. Children under 19 stay free in parent's room. AE, DC, DISC, MC, V. Parking $18 nearby. Subway: B, D, F, N, Q, R, V, W to 34th St. **Amenities:** Restaurant; dry cleaning/laundry. *In room:* A/C, TV, dataport, hair dryer, iron.

Comfort Inn Midtown *(Value* Rates can climb in autumn or at Christmas, but low-season rates can make the rooms one of Midtown's best bargains. A mahogany-and-marble lobby leads to the petite but comfortable and nicely out-fitted guest rooms, which boast neo-Shaker furnishings, coffeemakers, blackout drapes, and marble-and-tile bathrooms; all rooms have tub/shower combinations. Every room previously in the "smoking allowed" category has been disinfected. Don't expect much in the way of service, but the location is excellent—steps from Times Square, Rockefeller Center, Broadway theaters, and a wealth of dining options.

129 W. 46th St. (between Sixth Ave. and Broadway), New York, NY 10036. © **800/567-7720** or 212/221-2600. Fax 212/790-2760. www.applecorehotels.com or www.comfortinn.com. 79 units. $89–$329 double. Rates include continental breakfast. Ask about senior, AAA, corporate, and other discounts; check www.comfortinn.com for online discounts. Extra person $10. Children under 14 stay free in parent's room. AE, DC, DISC, MC, V. Parking $20 nearby. Subway: 1, 2, 3, 9 to 42nd St./Times Sq.; N, R to 49th St.; B, D, F, V to 47–50th sts./Rockefeller Center. **Amenities:** Small fitness room; self-serve business center; dry cleaning/laundry. *In room:* A/C, TV, dataport, coffeemaker, hair dryer, iron.

Herald Square Hotel Presiding regally over the entrance, Philip Martiny's gilded sculpture *Winged Life* is emblematic of the new life in this older Man-hattan hotel. The owners took the Carrère & Hastings beaux arts building that was once home to *Life* magazine and reinvented it as a budget hotel with a sense of history. *Life* covers decorate the lobby and some of the rooms. The rooms are small and basic, with laminated furniture, fluorescent lighting, and good-sized but older bathrooms, plus voice mail and in-room safes. Still, if you're looking for a great location, this is a good bet (although I'd try the Portland Square, the Herald Square's sister hotel, first; see below). The hotel is popular with Euro-peans and other visitors who love the nearby shopping (Macy's, Lord & Taylor, the Manhattan Mall) and sightseeing (the Empire State Building). The friendly staff can arrange bus tours and airport transportation.

19 W. 31st St. (between Fifth Ave. and Broadway), New York, NY 10001. © 800/727-1888 or 212/279-4017. Fax 212/643-9208. www.heraldsquarehotel.com. 120 units (109 with private bathroom). $65–$99 single; $99–$120 double; $130–$140 triple or quad. Extra person $10. Children under 12 stay free in parent's room. AE, DISC, MC, V. Parking from $21 nearby. Subway: N, R to 28th St.; B, D, F, N, Q, R, V, W to 34th St. *In room:* A/C, TV, dataport, hair dryer, iron, safe.

Hotel Edison *(Kids* A big jump in prices means that the Edison is no longer one of the Theater District's best bargains, but it's still a reasonably good deal. A grand, block-long Art Deco–style lobby leads to rooms that have been nicely ren-ovated. Don't expect much more than the basics, but you will find a firm bed, decor that's more attractive than most in this category, and a clean tile bathroom. Most double rooms feature two twins or a full bed, but there are some queens; request one at booking and show up early for your best chance at one. The larger quad rooms, with two doubles, are the best reason to consider the Edison, especially if you're traveling with the kids. Off the lobby is the **Cafe Edison,** an

Midtown, Chelsea & Union Square Accommodations

Americana Inn **17**
Big Apple Hostel **8**
Broadway Inn **15**
Carlton Arms **30**
Chelsea Center Hostel **40**
Chelsea Inn **34**
Chelsea International Hostel **36**
Chelsea Lodge **38**
Chelsea Pines Inn **37**
Chelsea Savoy Hotel **35**
Chelsea Star Hotel/
  Chelsea Suites **41**
Colonial House Inn **39**
Comfort Inn Manhattan **18**
Comfort Inn Midtown **10**
Gershwin Hotel **28**
Gramercy Park Hotel **31**
Habitat Hotel **4**
Helmsley Middletowne **6**
Herald Square Hotel **22**
Hotel 17 **32**
Hotel Edison **11**
Hotel Grand Union **24**
Hotel Metro **19**
Hotel Wolcott **23**
Hudson **1**
La Quinta Inn **21**
Mayfair Hotel **12**
Murray Hill Inn **27**
New York Inn **14**
Park Savoy Hotel **2**
Pickwick Arms Hotel **5**
Portland Square Hotel **9**
Ramada Inn Eastside **26**
Red Roof Inn **20**
Skyline Hotel **13**
Super 8 Hotel Times Square **7**
The Marcel **29**
The Wyndham **3**
Thirty Thirty **25**
Travel Inn **16**
Union Square Inn **33**

old-style Polish deli that's a favorite among theater types and down-market ladies who lunch; **Sofia's,** a just-fine Italian restaurant; and the **Rum House Tavern,** which has a Caribbean flair and live entertainment most nights.

228 W. 47th St. (between Broadway and Eighth Ave.), New York, NY 10036. ℂ **800/637-7070** or 212/840-5000. Fax 212/596-6850. www.edisonhotelnyc.com. 780 units. $150–$170 single; $170–$200 double; $185–$230 triple or quad; $225–$275 suite. Extra person $15. AE, DC, DISC, MC, V. Parking $35. Subway: N, R to 49th St.; 1, 9 to 50th St. **Amenities:** 2 restaurants; cocktail lounge; exercise room; tour desk; dry cleaning/laundry. *In room:* A/C, TV, dataport.

Hotel Metro ✹✹ *(Kids)* One of my all-time favorites, the Metro is the best choice in Midtown for those who don't want to sacrifice style or comfort for affordability. This glamorous Art Deco–style jewel has larger rooms than you'd expect. They're outfitted with retro furnishings, playful fabrics, fluffy pillows, alarm clocks, and small but beautiful marble bathrooms. Only about half the bathrooms have tubs, but the others have huge shower stalls (junior suites have whirlpool tubs). The family room—a two-room suite with a second bedroom in lieu of a sitting area—is an ingenious invention, while families on tighter budgets can opt for a roomy double/double. There's a comfy, fire-lit library/lounge area off the lobby, where complimentary buffet breakfast is laid out and the coffeepot's on all day. The well-furnished rooftop terrace boasts a breathtaking view of the Empire State Building, and makes a great place to order up room service from the stylish and very good **Metro Grill.**

Prices skyrocket in fall, but it's relatively easy to score a rate between $150 and $180 through August, as long as you book well ahead; also check with airlines and other package operators for great-value package deals.

45 W. 35th St. (between Fifth and Sixth aves.), New York, NY 10001. ℂ **800/356-3870** or 212/947-2500. Fax 212/279-1310. www.hotelmetronyc.com. 179 units. $145–$250 double; $155–$300 triple or quad; $175–$350 family room; $210–$400 suite. Rates include continental breakfast. Check with airlines and other package operators for great-value package deals. Extra person $25. 1 child under 14 stays free in parent's room. AE, DC, MC, V. Parking $17 nearby. Subway: B, D, F, V, N, R to 34th St. **Amenities:** Restaurant; rooftop bar in summer; fitness room; salon; limited room service; dry cleaning/laundry. *In room:* A/C, TV, dataport, fridge, hair dryer, iron.

Hotel Wolcott Once one of the *grande dames* of Manhattan hotels, the Wolcott has been reinvented as a good-value option for bargain hunters. Only the lobby hints at its former grandeur; these days, the rooms are motel-standard, but they're rather large, well kept, and quite serviceable. Plusses include spacious bathrooms and phones with voice mail, plus minifridges in most rooms. On the downside, the decor is less than stylish and the closets tend to be small—but these are small sacrifices for prices this low. Some of the triples are poorly configured—but they're big enough for three, and come with two beds (as do the suites). What's more, the services—fitness room, business center, coin-op laundry, Nintendo, and TV Internet access in every room—far exceed most competitors in the budget category. All in all, you get your money's worth here.

4 W. 31st St. (at Fifth Ave.), New York, NY 10001. ℂ **212/268-2900.** Fax 212/563-0096. www.wolcott.com. 250 units. $99–$160 single or double; $115–$180 triple; $120–$220 junior suite for 2 or 3. Discounted AAA, AARP, and promo rates may be available. AE, MC, V. Parking $17 next door. Subway: B, D, F, V, N, R to 34th St. **Amenities:** Exercise room; tour desk; business center; coin-op laundry. *In room:* A/C, TV w/pay movies, dataport, fridge, hair dryer, video games, Internet access.

Hudson ✹ If you're a style hound on a budget, it's never too early to book one of the handful of cheap rooms at Hudson. This Ian Schrager hotel has become the white-hot center of the style universe, attracting an adoring crowd and star-studded events to its Philippe Starck–designed digs. The eye-popping hotel boasts an Ivy-League-on-Acid design that radiates energy. The ivy-draped lobby and the second-level "Private Park" deck—the best outdoor space in any Big Apple hotel—serve as the quad from which everything radiates, including the hot **Hudson Bar,** the classic-goes-Warhol **Library,** and the surprisingly afford- able cafeteria-style restaurant.

It's a good thing about the public spaces, because the handful of budget-friendly guest rooms are miniscule—think budget cabin on a Carnival cruise and you'll get the picture. There's no arguing with their beauty or luxury comforts, though: They were designed on the retro-romantic ocean liner model, with rich African Makore paneling, hardwood floors, beautifully made white-on-white beds, clever bedside lamps featuring translucent art by Francesco Clemente, a petite steel desk, and studded white-leather steamer trunk upholstery. Ultra-efficient appointments make even the smallest feel like a treat, but anybody who values spreading-out room over style should *definitely* book elsewhere.

356 W. 58th St. (between Eighth and Ninth aves.), New York, NY 10019. (C) 800/444-4786 or 212/554-6000. Fax 212/554-6139. www.ianschragerhotels.com. 1,000 units. $165–$295 double; $275–$345 studio. AE, DC, DISC, MC, V. Parking $46. Subway: 1, 9, A, B, C, D to 59th St./Columbus Circle. **Amenities:** Restaurant; 2 bars; 24-hr. fit- ness center; 24-hr. concierge; business center; room service (6:30am–midnight); dry cleaning/laundry; CD library. *In room:* A/C, TV w/pay movies, CD player, dataport and high-speed connectivity, minibar, hair dryer, safe.

Mayfair Hotel ⭐ Be prepared—the rooms here are *tiny*. The elevator is, too. That's it for the bad news. Now the good: The Mayfair is one of the Theater District's friendliest and best-kept budget hotels, and the location couldn't be bet- ter. Each room boasts a small but nice black-and-white tile bathroom (all but a few singles have tub/shower combos) and unstylish but perfectly nice decor. The wood-paneled lobby is more elegant than most in this price range; just off it is the cute French bistro **Le Garrick,** an attraction in its own right. A supernice staff is merely the icing on the cake. Don't be frightened off by the rack-rate range; while prices can soar in peak seasons, rates usually stay below $200, and it's easy to score a room for around $150 or less before the end of June. The ridiculous end of the price spectrum is charged only in autumn, when you *should* stay elsewhere.

242 W. 49th St. (between Broadway and Eighth Ave.), New York, NY 10019. (C) 800/55-MAYFAIR or 212/586-0300. Fax 212/307-5226. www.mayfairnewyork.com. 78 units. $100–$250 single or double ($100–$150 in most seasons). Corporate rates $10–$20 less; also check for low-season specials. AE, DC, MC, V. Parking $18 nearby. Subway: 1, 9, C, E to 50th St. **Amenities:** Restaurant; concierge. *In room:* A/C, TV, dat- aport, hair dryer, iron, safe.

New York Inn Don't expect much from this dingy little hotel on a still-ratty block of Eighth Avenue. But if you're committed to finding a room with private bathroom, TV, and phone in the Theater District for a low rate, this is probably your best choice—especially in the second half of the year, when prices sky- rocket at most neighboring budget hotels. A half-staircase leads up to the lobby, where you'll check in and proceed up a narrow staircase to three floors of rooms. Guest rooms are small and dark but have firm beds with relatively new spreads, new desktop TVs with cable, telephones with voice mail, and cramped bath- rooms with stall showers that could use some serious retiling. Maintenance is less than perfect, but everything is clean—frankly, as good as can be expected con- sidering the location and rate. I'd choose the St. Mark's Hotel (p. 101) first— but it's not in the heart of the Theater District. While this specific block is less than pretty, this area is gentrifying well, and great, affordable eats abound.

765 Eighth Ave. (between 46th and 47th sts.), New York, NY 10036. (C) 888/450-5555 or 212/247-5400. Fax 212/586-6201. www.newyorkinn.com. 40 units. $89–$130 single or double. Rates include continental breakfast and tax. AE, DISC, MC, V. Subway: C, E to 50th St. *In room:* A/C, TV, hair dryer.

Park Savoy Hotel The Park Savoy isn't as nice as its sibling, the Chelsea Savoy (p. 105), but the lower prices reflect the quality difference, making it a good deal. Rooms are basic, and a few were in need of a fresh coat of paint. All have voice mail and alarm clocks, most have walk-in closets, and a few have minifridges. All rooms have tiled private bathrooms that are petite (with showers only, no tubs) but attractive and clean. If your budget is tight, two of you can make do in the smallest rooms; the biggest ones can accommodate three or four in two double beds. Services are kept to a minimum to keep rates low, but there's a decent restaurant next door. Best of all is the convenient location—a block from Central Park and a stone's throw from Carnegie Hall, Lincoln Center, and the Columbus Circle subways, which give easy access to the rest of the city.

158 W. 58th St. (between Sixth and Seventh aves.), New York, NY 10019. © 212/245-5755. Fax 212/765-0668. 70 units. $95–$145 single or double. AE, MC, V. Parking $20 next door. Subway: A, B, C, D, 1, 9 to 59th St./Columbus Circle; N, R to 57th St. **Amenities:** Limited room service. *In room:* A/C, TV.

Portland Square Hotel Another Puchall family project (see the Herald Square Hotel, above), the Portland Square is a good Theater District bet for budget travelers. Some prefer this hotel to the comparable Herald Square: The public spaces have been renovated, and everything seems to be in good shape. The rooms are small, simple, and cheaply furnished (laminated furniture, fluorescent lighting), but clean. Ask for one with an extra-large bathroom; some are almost as big as the bedroom. Avoid the shared-bathroom singles if you can: The ratio is a high four rooms to a bathroom, some of the hall bathrooms were on the crusty side, and most of the shared bathrooms had a smoky odor. But the private bathrooms are a decent deal if money's tight. The staff is friendly and cooperative, but don't expect much in the way of service (that's one way they keep rates low).

132 W. 47th St. (between Sixth and Seventh aves.), New York, NY 10036. © **800/388-8988** or 212/382-0600. Fax 212/382-0684. www.portlandsquarehotel.com. 145 units (115 with private bathroom). $65–$75 single or double with shared bathroom; $99–$120 single with private bathroom; $125–$135 double with private bathroom; $135–$170 triple or quad with private bathroom. Extra person $10. AE, MC, V. Parking $24 across the street. Subway: B, D, F, V to 47th–50th sts./Rockefeller Center. **Amenities:** Luggage lockers. *In room:* A/C, TV, dataport.

Red Roof Inn ✦✦ Manhattan's first, and only Red Roof Inn offers relief from Midtown's high-priced hotel scene. The hotel occupies a former office building that was gutted and laid out fresh, allowing for more spacious rooms and bathrooms than you'll usually find in this price category. The lobby feels smart, and elevators are quiet and efficient. In-room amenities—including coffeemakers and TVs with on-screen Web access—are better than most competitors', and furnishings are new and comfortable. The location—on a bustling block lined with nice hotels and affordable Korean restaurants, just a stone's throw from the Empire State Building and Herald Square—is excellent.

The rack-rate range is ridiculous, but it's usually easy to score a room for less than $150 if you book well in advance. Be sure to compare the rates offered by Apple Core Hotel's reservation line (the management company) and those quoted on Red Roof's national reservation line and website, as they can vary significantly. Complimentary continental breakfast adds to the good value.

6 W. 32nd St. (between Broadway and Fifth Ave.), New York, NY 10001. © **800/567-7720**, 800/RED-ROOF, or 212/643-7100. Fax 212/643-7101. www.applecorehotels.com or www.redroof.com. 171 units. $89–$329 double (usually less than $159). Rates include continental breakfast. Children under 14 stay free in parent's room. AE, DC, DISC, MC, V. Parking $22. Subway: B, D, F, V, N, R to 34th St. **Amenities:** Breakfast room; wine-and-beer lounge; exercise room; concierge; business center; dry cleaning/laundry. *In room:* A/C, TV w/pay movies, dataport, fridge, coffeemaker, hair dryer, iron, video games, Internet access.

Skyline Hotel *Kids*   This nice, newly renovated motor hotel offers predictable comforts and some uncommon extras—inexpensive storage parking ($8 a day) and a lovely indoor pool—that make it a very good value. A pleasant lobby leads to motel-standard rooms that are a far cry from stylish, but are bigger than most in this price range. There are two room categories: standard, with two twin beds; and deluxe, with either a king bed with sofa or a queen bed. The deluxe with king and sofa is best for families. They boast decent-size closets, small work desks (in most), and double-paned windows that open to let fresh air in, and shut out a surprising amount of street noise when closed. Some rooms have brand-new bathrooms, but the older ones are still fine. Everything is very well kept. Another plus for the family is the pool, which has a nicely tiled deck and plush deck chairs; but it's open limited hours, so call ahead if it matters.

725 Tenth Ave. (at 49th St.), New York, NY 10019. © 800/433-1982 or 212/586-3400. Fax 212/582-4604. www.skylinehotelny.com. 230 units. $109–$179 standard; $139–$229 deluxe. Check website or inquire about special rates (as low as $89 at press time). Extra person $15. Children 14 and under stay free in parents' room. AE, DC, DISC, MC, V. Parking $8 (charge for in/out privileges). Subway: A, C, E to 50th St. Pets accepted with $200 deposit. **Amenities:** Restaurant (American/Italian); bar, big-screen TV, and live entertainment; indoor pool; Gray Line tour desk; Internet-access machine in lobby. *In room:* A/C, TV w/pay movies, video games, and Internet access, dataport, hair dryer, iron, safe.

Super 8 Hotel Times Square ★★ *Value*   The Super 8 folks, in alliance with Apple Core Hotels (the franchisee behind such hotels as the Comfort Inn Midtown and Red Roof Inn), have done a terrific job reinventing the former Hotel Wentworth into a bright, attractive hotel offering better-than-budget accommodations in the heart of Midtown. The Wentworth was built in 1902 as a hotel for women, so it boasts extra-large rooms (by New York standards), outfitted with a king or two doubles, and all-new bathrooms. Decor isn't what you'd call stylish, but it's attractive, with woods, pastel wallpaper, green carpeting, and floral spreads. All rooms are well outfitted with fridges, coffeemakers, small work desks, hair dryers, irons, and alarm clocks, plus Nintendo and on-screen e-mail access. Mom and Dad will love the family suite, which features a king in one room and two twins (in lieu of a sitting area) in the other; be flexible in your travel and you may be able to snare this suite for as little as $129.

The lobby is bright and elegant, and service is professional. Perks include a state-of-the-art exercise room and a breakfast room serving a continental meal that's included in the rate—for as little as $89 double! Even in high seasons, when Super 8 rates can climb into the mid-$100s, you'll still get your money's worth. In fact, Apple Core always keeps their hotels priced ahead of the curve.

59 W. 46th St. (between Fifth and Sixth aves.), New York, NY 10036. © 800/567-7720 or 212/719-2300. Fax 212/790-2760. www.applecorehotels.com or www.super8.com. 206 units. $89–$329 double (usually less than $179); family suite from $129. Rates include continental breakfast. Check for AAA, AARP, and other discounts. Children under 14 stay free in parent's room. AE, DC, DISC, MC, V. Parking $20 next door. Subway: B, D, F, V to 42nd St. **Amenities:** Breakfast room; exercise room; business center with computer, fax, copier; dry cleaning/laundry. *In room:* A/C, TV w/pay movies, dataport, fridge, coffeemaker, hair dryer, iron, video games, Internet access.

Travel Inn *Kids*   Extras like a huge outdoor pool and sun deck, a sunny, up-to-date fitness room, and free parking (with in-and-out privileges!) make the Travel Inn another terrific deal. Like the Skyline (see above), the Travel Inn may not be loaded with personality, but it offers the clean, bright regularity of a good chain hotel—an attractive trait in a city where "quirky" is the catchword at most affordable hotels. Rooms are oversize and comfortable, furnished with extra-firm beds and desks; even the smallest double is sizable and has a roomy bathroom, and double/doubles make affordable shares for families. A renovation over the last couple of years has made everything feel like new, even the tiled bathrooms. The neighborhood has gentrified and isn't as far off as you might think: Off-Broadway theaters and good restaurants are nearby, and it's a 10-minute walk to the Theater District. It's a good bet even if you don't have a car.

515 W. 42nd St. (just west of Tenth Ave.), New York, NY 10036. Ⓒ 888/HOTEL58 (468-3558), 800/869-4630, or 212/695-7171. Fax 212/967-5025. www.newyorkhotel.com. 160 units. $125–$250 double. AAA discounts available. Check website for Internet deals (as low as $105 at press time). Extra person $10. Children under 16 stay free in parent's room. AE, DC, DISC, MC, V. Free self-parking. Subway: A, C, E to 42nd St./Port Authority. **Amenities:** Coffee shop; outdoor pool; fitness center; tour desk; 24-hr. room service. *In room:* A/C, TV, dataport, hair dryer, iron.

The Wyndham ★ *(Finds)*   This hotel isn't part of the upscale chain of the same name; rather, it's a family-owned charmer that's one of Midtown's best hotel deals: perfectly located, on a great block steps away from Fifth Avenue and Central Park. The Wyndham is stuck in the '70s on all fronts, but its guest rooms are enormous, comfortable, and loaded with character. The hotel features a wild collection of wallpaper, from candy stripes to crushed velvets, so some rooms cross the ticky-tacky line. But others are lovely, with such details as rich Oriental carpets and well-worn libraries, and the eclectic art collection that lines the walls boasts some real gems. If you're put in a room that's not to your taste, just ask politely to see another one; the staff is usually willing to accommodate.

Most important, it's a great deal: The rooms are quite large and feature huge walk-in closets (the biggest I've seen). The surprisingly affordable suites also have full living rooms, dressing areas, and cold kitchenettes (fridge only). You'll need a two-bedroom suite if you bring the kids (only two guests are allowed in standard rooms or one-bedroom suites), but the rate is a steal considering the space. Don't expect an alarm clock, hair dryer, luxury toiletries, or other modern amenities. But at these prices, you can afford to invest in travel sizes.

42 W. 58th St. (between Fifth and Sixth aves.), New York, NY 10019. Ⓒ 800/257-1111 or 212/753-3500. Fax 212/754-5638. 212 units. $140–$175 single or double; $190–$250 1-bedroom suite; $335–$390 2-bedroom suite (up to 4 guests included in rate). AE, DC, MC, V. Parking $40 nearby. Subway: N, R to Fifth Ave.; B, Q to 57th St. **Amenities:** Restaurant with excellent cocktail lounge; salon; dry cleaning/laundry. *In room:* A/C, TV, dataport.

SUPERCHEAP SLEEPS

Big Apple Hostel ★   This is the nicest hostel in Midtown, if not in all of Manhattan. It's not fancy, but it's well run, spotlessly clean, and in the heart of the Theater District; many luxury hotels wish they had it so good. All dorm rooms are four-bedded; they're well spaced and well kept, with metal bunks and good mattresses with blankets and linens. Only guests in private rooms get towels, so dormers should bring their own. Private rooms are basic but better than most in hostels; all have phones (free local calls!), TVs, radio, and alarm, and some have a table and chairs. The shared bathrooms are better than average. There's a stocked kitchen with microwave, a backyard patio with barbecue, and a luggage storage room. It's popular with Japanese and other international travelers who like the location. It doesn't get much better at bargain-basement prices—much better than the better known Aladdin Hostel farther west on 45th Street.

119 W. 45th St. (between Sixth and Seventh aves.), New York, NY 10036. Ⓒ 212/302-2603. Fax 212/302-2605. www.bigapplehostel.com. 112 dorm beds; 11 private doubles. $28–$38.50 dorm bed; $78–$109 double. MC, V. Subway: N, R, S, 1, 2, 3, 7, 9 to Times Sq./42nd St. **Amenities:** Common kitchen. *In room:* Fans, no phone in dorm units.

9 Midtown East & Murray Hill

Habitat Hotel ⭐ Marketed as "upscale budget," this hotel features rooms dressed to appeal to travelers who are short on funds but big on style. They're well designed in a natural palette accented with black-and-white photos. Everything is better quality and more attractive than in most hotels in this price range, from the firm mattresses to the plush towels to the pedestal sinks in every room. The bathrooms are all new; choose between shared (one for every three to four rooms), private, or a semiprivate "minisuite" (two rooms sharing an adjacent bathroom—great for friends traveling together).

The only downside—and it may be a big one for couples—are the sleeping arrangements. A few queens are available (at the high end of the price spectrum), but most of the double rooms have a twin bed with a pullout trundle, which takes up most of the width of the room when it's open. Despite that drawback, rates are attractive, especially for the rooms with shared bathroom, considering the *Metropolitan Home* mindset and the A-1 location. You may prefer the option of private bathrooms at sister hotel Thirty Thirty (below), because they don't have the space limitations these have, but this hotel has a more thrilling location and a more exciting vibe thanks to the popular restaurant and bar, **Opia.** The four pricey penthouse deluxe rooms have queen beds, private bathrooms, microwaves, and minifridges—but if you're going to spend that much money, stay at the Waldorf instead.

The second-floor lobby is designer-stylish and professionally staffed, the bar scene hops, and the neighborhood is safe, chic, and super convenient—especially for shoppers, since Bloomingdale's is 2 blocks away. You won't even have to put on your shoes to visit Kenneth Cole, whose new boutique is just downstairs.

130 E. 57th St. (at Lexington Ave.), New York, NY 10022. ⓒ **800/497-6028** or 212/753-8841. Fax 212/838-4767. www.habitatny.com. 300 units (about 40 with private bathroom). $75–$115 single or double with shared bathroom; $135–$185 single or double with private bathroom; $240–$270 minisuite (2 rooms with shared bathroom); $325–$450 penthouse studio with private bathroom. Rates include continental breakfast. Inquire or check website for student rates and promotions (from $79 at press time). AE, DC, DISC, MC, V. Parking $25. Subway: 4, 5, 6 to 59th St.; E, F to Lexington Ave. **Amenities:** Restaurant/bar; tour desk. *In room:* A/C, TV, dataport.

Helmsley Middletowne ⭐ This value-laden member of the Helmsley chain (yes, as in Leona Helmsley) boasts little in the way of style, services, or amenities, but rooms and suites are large, comfortable, and well priced, and the location is fantastic—you usually have to spend more to stay in this 'hood. The hotel started life as an apartment building and still has the vibe. The lobby is virtually nonexistent, but the front-desk staff—most of whom have worked here for *years*—is brisk and friendly. Room decor is generic and furnishings are older, but beds are firm and everything is well kept. Each room has a refrigerator (usually with a wet bar), multiple-line phones, a dated but fine bathroom, and a wealth of closet space. The one- and two-bedroom suites are well priced and big enough to accommodate families. They also boast walk-in kitchenettes (some lack dishware, though, so request it or bring plastic); some have fireplaces and/or balconies as well. Business travelers can request an in-room fax machine. Not sexy but a nice choice in the midprice range.

148 E. 48th St. (between Third and Lexington aves.), New York, NY 10017. ⓒ **800/221-4982** or 212/755-3000. Fax 212/832-0261. www.helmsleyhotels.com. 192 units. $195–$205 double; from $235 1- or 2-bedroom suite. Rates include continental breakfast. Ask about packages. Children under 12 stay free in parent's room. AE, DC, MC, V. Parking $30. Subway: 6 to 51st St. **Amenities:** Restaurant; dry cleaning/laundry. *In room:* A/C, TV, fridge, hair dryer, iron, kitchenettes in suites.

Hotel Grand Union   This centrally located hotel is big with budget-minded international travelers. A pleasant white-on-white lobby leads to clean, spacious rooms with nice extras that are uncommon in this price category, like hair dryers and free HBO. Bad fluorescent lighting, unattractive furniture, and a lack of natural light dampen the mood—but considering the roominess, rates, and central-to-everything location, the Grand Union is a deal. A nicely configured quad with two twins and a queen in a separate alcove, no. 309 is a great bet for families. Most bathrooms have been outfitted in granite or tile; ask for a newly renovated one. The staff is helpful, there's a pleasant sitting room off the lobby, and an adjacent coffee shop is convenient for morning coffee or a quickie burger.

34 E. 32nd St. (between Madison and Park aves.), New York, NY 10016. © 212/683-5890. Fax 212/689-7397. www.hotelgrandunion.com. 95 units. $116–$138 single or double; $132–$158 twin or triple; $158–$190 quad. Call or check website for special rates (as low as $90 at press time). AE, DC, DISC, MC, V. Parking $22 nearby. Subway: 6 to 33rd St. **Amenities:** Coffee shop; tour desk; fax service. *In room:* A/C, TV, dataport, fridge, hair dryer.

Murray Hill Inn ★ *Value*   In a five-story walk-up in a pleasant neighborhood, the Murray Hill Inn is shoestring-basic—but there's no arguing with its cleanliness, key in judging accommodations in this price range. Rooms are tiny and outfitted with one or two beds with motel-standard bedspreads and furnishings, a wall rack, a phone, and small TV; most rooms with shared bathroom also have private sinks (request one when booking). These Euro-style rooms share the in-hall bathrooms that are new and spotless. Some of the doubles have an alcove that can accommodate a third traveler on a cot if you're on an extra-tight budget. Rooms with private bathrooms are the nicest; they're spacious, with new bathrooms and dataports on the telephones. Most have pullout sofas that can accommodate an extra traveler. Don't expect much in terms of facilities beyond a pleasant (if tiny) lobby, plus a sitting area with a vending machine, an ATM, and a luggage-storage area. The rooms with private bathrooms go fast, so book early; you can often deal on shared-bathroom units, though.

143 E. 30th St. (between Lexington and Third aves.), New York, NY 10016. © 888/996-6376 or 212/683-6900. Fax 212/545-0103. www.murrayhillinn.com. 50 units (10 with shared bathroom). $60–$65 single with shared bathroom; $75–$80 double with shared bathroom, $125 double with private bathroom. Ask about discounts and special rates (as low as $95 with private bathroom at press time). Extra person $20. Children under 12 stay free in parent's room. AE, MC, V. Parking about $25 nearby. Subway: 6 to 28th St. *In room:* A/C, TV.

Pickwick Arms Hotel *Value*   For a Midtown hotel on the East Side, this is like entering an economic time warp. The location couldn't be better. The older, sometimes astoundingly small rooms are spare (think monk's cell), but they're well kept, and the place is safe and well run. There are a few doubles and twins with private bathrooms (the larger deluxe twins can accommodate a rollaway), but the majority of rooms are singles with private, semiprivate, or shared hall bathrooms. Two friends traveling together can take advantage of the semiprivate situation: Two singles (each with sink, TV, desk, closet, and telephone) that share a bathroom can be had for the same price as a twin room. All of the bathrooms are worn-looking and have showers only, but they're clean. A renovation has spiffed up the halls and rooms. If you want a great location for a low price, this is the place. On site is a rooftop patio with skyline views, and an affordable restaurant serving three squares a day.

230 E. 51st St. (between Second and Third aves.), New York, NY 10022. © 800/742-5945 in the U.S., 800/874-0074 in Canada, or 212/355-0300. Fax 212/755-5029. www.pickwickarms.com. 320 units (200 with private bathroom). $69–$119 single; $140–$165 double or twin; $155–$165 triple. AE, DC, MC, V. Parking $30–$35 nearby. Subway: 6 to 51st St. **Amenities:** Restaurant, roof patio. *In room:* A/C, TV, dataport.

Ramada Inn Eastside The most affordable of the Apple Core Hotels (which also include the Red Roof Inn, the Comfort Inn Midtown, and the Super 8 Hotel), this former Quality Hotel fell under the Ramada banner in 2002. It's nothing special—small, basic rooms with older bathrooms—but a renovation has given them a fresh look in greens and beige. Its other features are the location, in quiet Murray Hill, which abounds with affordable restaurants; the value-added amenities, which include free continental breakfast, free local phone calls, business center, and fitness room; and the usually low rates. Don't expect anything in the way of service, but considering how expensive an average room has become, this hotel is a value. It's quite easy to score a room for $139 or less most of the year.

161 Lexington Ave. (at 30th St.), New York, NY 10016. (✆ 800/567-7720 or 212/545-1800. Fax 212/790-2760. www.applecorehotels.com. 96 units. $89–$209 double. Rates include continental breakfast. Inquire about seasonal/weekend discounts (as low as $79 at press time). Children under 13 stay free in parent's room. AE, DC, DISC, MC, V. Parking $20 nearby. Subway: 6 to 33rd St. **Amenities:** Coffee shop; business center, exercise room (both under renovation at press time). *In room:* A/C, TV w/pay movies, dataport, coffeemaker, hair dryer, iron, video games, Internet access.

Thirty Thirty ⭑⭑ *Value* This hotel is just right for bargain-hunting travelers looking for a splash of style for an affordable price. The building (which formerly housed the Martha Washington women's hotel and the nightclub Danceteria) has been gutted, renovated, and redone with brand-new everything. The design-conscious tone is set in the loftlike industrial-modern lobby. Pretty hallways lead to rooms that are mostly on the smallish side but do the trick for those who intend to spend their days out on the town rather than holed up here. They're done in a natural palette with a creative edge—purplish carpet, khaki bedspread, woven wallpaper—that comes together more attractively than you might expect. Configurations are split between twin/twins (great for friends), queens, and queen/queens (great for triples, budget-minded quads, or shares that want more spreading-out room). Features include cushioned headboards, firm mattresses, stylish bedside lamps, two-line phones, built-in wardrobes, and spacious, tiled bathrooms. No. 1135 is a large L-shaped queen with a nice granite bathroom. A few larger units have kitchenettes—try to book one if you're staying a while, as you'll appreciate the extra room and the fridge. There's no room service, but delivery is available from nearby restaurants, and we're told the hotel will be adding a restaurant soon.

30 E. 30th St. (between Madison and Park aves.), New York, NY 10016. (✆ 800/497-6028 or 212/689-1900. Fax 212/689-0023. www.thirtythirty-nyc.com. 240 units. $115–$175 double, $145–$195 double with kitchenette; $185–$245 quad. Call for last-minute deals, or check website for special promotions (as low as $99 at press time). AE, DC, DISC, MC, V. Parking $35, 1 block away. Subway: 6 to 28th St. Pets accepted with advance approval. **Amenities:** Concierge; dry cleaning/laundry. *In room:* A/C, TV, dataport, hair dryer.

10 The Upper West Side

Amsterdam Inn ⭑ *Value* This renovated five-story walk-up offers basic accommodations that add up to a great value in a terrific neighborhood. The private bathrooms are bigger and better at the Murray Hill Inn (p. 122), but you might be able to do better on the rates here, and if you're going to share a bathroom, these are in good shape. The inn's biggest assets are its Upper West Side location, its newness, its cleanliness, and its professional management.

The rooms are small and narrow, with a bed, a rack to hang your clothes on, a set of drawers with a TV on top, a side table with a lamp and a phone that requires a deposit to activate, and a sink if there's no private bathroom. The Euro-style rooms share the in-hall bathrooms at a ratio of about 2½ to 1. The bathrooms are new but have showers only. If you book a double, make sure it's a *real* double, with a double bed. The singles with trundles can (theoretically) accommodate two, but don't expect to have any space left over. Management seems willing to negotiate, so always ask for a lower rate.

340 Amsterdam Ave. (at 76th St.), New York, NY 10024. ℂ **212/579-7500.** Fax 212/579-6127. www.amsterdam inn.com. 25 units (12 with private bathroom). $60–$75 single with shared bathroom; $75–$95 bunk-bed twin or double with shared bathroom; $95–$115 double with private bathroom. Extra person $20. Children under 12 stay free in parent's room. AE, MC, V. Parking $20–$25 nearby. Subway: 1, 9 to 79th St. *In room:* A/C, TV.

Holmes Bed & Breakfast ★ *Finds*   This terrific, well-priced B&B is an excellent choice for independent-minded travelers who like a residential feel and a little personality in their lodgings. Four guest rooms are available on two floors of a nicely maintained brownstone on a tree-lined block in the heart of the Upper West Side. Owner Marguerite Holmes is an accomplished artist; not only do her terrific multigenre paintings (which run the gamut from pastoral scenes to impressive abstracts) fill the hallways and guest rooms, but her creative eye has turned what could be very basic accommodations into something really special.

Each well-maintained room has cable TV (a couple have a VCR), a well-chosen mix of vintage furnishings and original art, good-quality bedding, and a direct-dial phone. The two rooms with private bathrooms each have a fridge, coffeemaker, microwave, and toaster oven, while the two shared-bathroom units share a pantry kitchenette. The Cranberry Room is the nicest; it boasts a marble bathroom with shower, generous closet space, and a terrace, while the Blueberry Room has a private bathroom with a tub and a sleeper sofa that can sleep a third person. The two shared-bathroom units share an older but nice bathroom.

There's no formal breakfast serving, but a cupboard is stocked with help-yourself breakfast items. A friendly resident innkeeper is on hand and glad to help if you need advice or assistance. Smoking is not allowed.

W. 91st St. (off Amsterdam Ave.), New York, NY 10024. ℂ **917/838-4808.** Fax 212/769-2348. www.holmes nyc.com. 4 units (2 with shared bathroom). $90–$115 double. Rates include morning breakfast items. Discounts on weekly and monthly stays Jan–Mar. AE, DC, MC, V. Subway: 1, 2, 3, 9 to 96th St. *In room:* A/C, TV, kitchenette w/fridge, toaster oven, microwave.

Hotel Belleclaire   This beaux arts hotel boasts a great Upper West Side location and renovated, stylish guest rooms that are larger than most, but could use a little more attention to detail. Still, the accommodations do the job, and the management seems intent on pleasing. The rooms have small, freshly tiled bathrooms with tub/shower combos (six have roll-in showers to accommodate travelers with disabilities). Cushioned headboards, nice fabric-covered cubes for modular seating, small TVs, minifridges, and alarm clocks are the main amenities. Closets are small. The shared-bathroom units are the same but have in-room sinks and share hall bathrooms at a ratio of 3 to 1. The family suite features two attached, semiprivate bedrooms with a bathroom, a minifridge, and a big walk-in closet. A well-equipped fitness center was recently added. This is a perfectly decent choice in a first-class residential neighborhood.

250 W. 77th St. (at Broadway), New York, NY 10024. ℂ **877/HOTEL-BC** (468-3522) or 212/362-7700. Fax 212/ 362-1004. www.hotelbelleclaire.com. 189 units (39 with shared bathroom). $109 double with shared bathroom; $169–$189 double with private bathroom; $229 family suite. Ask about AAA, corporate, group, and other discounts. AE, DC, DISC, MC, V. Parking $25 nearby. Subway: 1, 9 to 79th St. **Amenities:** Fitness center; tour desk; fax; dry cleaning/laundry. *In room:* A/C, TV w/pay movies and games, dataport, fridge, hair dryer, iron.

Upper West Side Accommodations

Amsterdam Inn **7**

Central Park Hostel & Inn **2**

Holmes Bed & Breakfast **5**

Hostelling International– New York **1**

Hotel Belleclaire **6**

Hotel Newton **3**

Hotel Olcott **9**

The Milburn **8**

Quality Hotel on Broadway **4**

Hotel Newton ★ (*Value*)   Finally—an inexpensive hotel that's *nice*. Unlike many of its peers, the Newton doesn't scream "budget!" at every turn, or require you to have the attitude of a college student to put up with it. As you enter the pretty lobby, a uniformed staff that's attentive and professional greets you.

The rooms are large, with good, firm beds, work desks, and new bathrooms, plus roomy closets in most (a few have wall racks only). Some are big enough to accommodate families with two doubles or two queen beds. Each suite features two queen beds in the bedroom, a sofa in the sitting room, plus niceties like a microwave, minifridge, and iron, making them worth the few extra dollars. The bigger rooms and suites have been upgraded with cherrywood furnishings, but even the older laminated furniture is much nicer than you usually see in this price range. The AAA-approved hotel really is impeccably kept. The 96th Street express subway stop is just a block away. The neighborhood boasts lots of affordable restaurants, and a cute diner in the same block provides room service.

2528 Broadway (between 94th and 95th sts.), New York, NY 10025. (*C*) **888/HOTEL-58** (468-3558) or 212/678-6500. Fax 212/678-6758. www.newyorkhotel.com. 110 units. $85–$160 double or junior suite. AAA, corporate, senior, and group rates available; check website for Internet deals (from $75 double at press time). Extra person $10. Children under 15 stay free in parent's room. AE, DC, DISC, MC, V. Parking $20 nearby. Subway: 1, 2, 3, 9 to 96th St. **Amenities:** 24-hr. room service. *In room:* A/C, TV, hair dryer.

Hotel Olcott (*Value*)   This old dowager remains one of New York's best budget bargains. About half of this residential hotel houses permanent and long-term residents, but the rest is open to out-of-towners. The studios and suites are a steal. The apartments are stylish, for the 1970s, but they're maintained with care, and even the studios are bigger than most NYC apartments (the suites are enormous). The discount furnishings are not pretty, but they're comfortable. Every apartment has a big bathroom and a kitchenette with minifridge, hot plate with kettle, toaster, and basic dishes and utensils; studios generally have dining tables for two and suites have four-tops. Phones have voice mail. Suites have TV only in the living room and sofas don't pull out, but the friendly management will lend you a cot (or even an additional bed) if you're bringing the family or sharing with friends. Ask for a renovated room when you book; most of the suites and about half of the studios have brand-new, bright-white kitchenettes and freshly laid tile in the bathroom.

The Olcott is steps from Central Park on one of Manhattan's most high-class blocks (the Dakota apartment building is just doors away). Nearby Columbus Avenue bustles with boutiques and restaurants, and just off the surprisingly sophisticated lobby is **Dallas BBQ** for cheap eats and bathtub-size cocktails.

27 W. 72nd St. (between Columbus Ave. and Central Park W.), New York, NY 10023. (*C*) **212/877-4200.** Fax 212/580-0511. www.hotelolcott.com. 200 units. $130 studio double ($840 weekly); $150 suite ($980 weekly); $1,600 weekly 2-bedroom suite (sleeps up to 4). Extra person $15. MC, V (check or money-order deposit required to guarantee room). Parking $35, 4 blocks away. Subway: B, C to 72nd St. **Amenities:** Restaurant; bar. *In room:* A/C, TV, dataport, kitchenette w/fridge.

The Milburn ★ (*Kids*)   On a quiet Upper West Side street, The Milburn offers reasonably priced rooms and suites with kitchenettes in the same neighborhood—at about half the price. These suites are an excellent value. Every suite is rife with amenities, including a dining area, a bathroom, a kitchenette (with free coffee), two-line phones, and more. Junior and one-bedroom suites boast a pull-out queen sofa, an extra TV, a CD player, and a desk. Don't expect much from

Kids Affordable Family-Friendly Hotels

The best way for families on a budget to save is to bunk together in a larger room with two double or queen beds. Some hotels have sweet suite deals that allow the kids to sleep on a pullout sofa in the living room, thus giving everybody a little well-deserved privacy.

Chelsea Savoy Hotel (p. 105)   These attractive, affordable rooms are large and comfy enough to accommodate four. Big closets and roomy, immaculate bathrooms with tons of counter space make sharing even easier. Children stay free, and continental breakfast is included.

Gershwin Hotel (p. 110)   This funky Flatiron District hotel looks like the domain of the artsy crowd, but it suits families extremely well. Parents in search of a high space-to-dollar ratio will love the family room, a two-room suite that accommodates Mom and Dad in a queen bed in one bedroom, two kids in two twins in the adjacent one.

Hotel Edison (p. 113)   Quads can accommodate four in two double beds, and value-priced suites with pullout sofas offer even more space. The nearly 1,000-room hotel bustles around the clock with families and tour groups from around the world, so you can feel comfortable allowing the kids to act like kids here. A coffee shop/deli serves wallet-friendly meals.

Hotel Metro (p. 116)   This Art Deco–inspired hotel is an excellent choice for families who want more in the way of room, service, and comforts thanks to the hotel's "family room": a two-room suite with a second bedroom in lieu of a sitting area. This configuration gives mom and dad privacy, and kids their own real beds.

Hotel Olcott (p. 126)   Every one-bedroom apartment has a stocked kitchenette, dining table, and space to spread out. Sofas don't pull out, but the bedroom usually has two queens, and the management will lend you a cot or extra bed for the living room if you prefer. Central Park is steps away, and a barbecue joint in the building serves affordable family meals.

The Milburn (p. 128)   This Upper West Sider is a real suite deal for any visitor, but their kids-under-12-stay-free policy makes it a stellar choice for families. Every room has a fully outfitted kitchenette (with microwave) and a dining area. The one-bedroom suites are a bargain, and a pullout queen sofa in the living room makes them comfortable for families. The neighborhood is kid-friendly, and Central Park is an easy walk away.

Skyline Hotel (p. 119) and **Travel Inn** (p. 119)   If you're driving, take advantage of the low-cost or, at Travel Inn, free parking at these two motor hotels. And you'll like the family-size rooms, and the kids will love the pools (a rarity in affordable hotels). *And* children stay free (under 14 at the Skyline, under 16 at the Travel Inn).

the decor, but everything is attractive and in good shape. The conscientious management keeps the whole place spotless and in good order. In fact, what makes the Milburn a find is that it's more service-oriented than most hotels in this price range: The friendly staff will do everything from providing free copy, fax, and e-mail services to picking up your laundry at the dry cleaner next door. All in all, this is a great choice for bargain hunters—especially families, for whom rollaways and cribs are on hand.

242 W. 76th St. (between Broadway and West End Ave.), New York, NY 10023. ℭ 800/833-9622 or 212/362-1006. Fax 212/721-5476. www.milburnhotel.com. 114 units. $129–$179 studio double; $149–$185 junior suite, $169–$239 1-bedroom suite. Check website for seasonal specials (as low as $99 at press time). Extra person $10. Children under 13 stay free in parent's room. AE, DC, MC, V. Parking $20–$29. Subway: 1, 9 to 79th St. **Amenities:** Fitness room; access to nearby health club; business services; coin-op laundry; free video library. *In room:* A/C, TV/VCR (Sony PlayStation on request), dataport, kitchenette w/ifridge and coffeemaker, hair dryer, iron, safe, CD player in suites.

Quality Hotel on Broadway *Value*   Stay at this reliable, freshly renovated hotel if you like lots of space; some rooms are large enough for two doubles or a king bed. Rooms feature dark-wood, hotel-standard furnishings that include a work desk with a good ergonomic chair; an armoire holds the TV and good drawer space. Each room has an alarm clock, two phones with voice mail and free local calls, and a makeup mirror in the bathroom. Some also have a minifridge or a kitchenette; request one when you book. Most bathrooms have spacious granite countertops. A library-style sitting room is off the lobby. The location is terrific—cheaper than staying on the Upper West Side in the 70s and 80s, but just as nice neighborhood-wise, surrounded by affordable restaurants and 2 blocks from an express subway station that will whisk you to Times Square in two stops. Best of all, the online discount deals can be stellar (as low as $70 at press time).

215 W. 94th St. (at Broadway), New York, NY 10025. ℭ 800/228-5151 or 212/866-6400. Fax 212/866-1357. www.bestnyhotels.com. 350 units. $119–$149 single or double; $179–$219 junior suite (sleeps 2 or 3). Ask about senior, AAA, corporate, and promotional discounts; check www.hotelchoice.com for online-booking discounts (as low as $70 at press time). Extra person $15. Children under 18 stay free in parent's room. AE, DC, DISC, MC, V. Parking $17. Subway: 1, 2, 3, 9 to 96th St. **Amenities:** Restaurant; concierge; coin-op laundry; dry cleaning/laundry; fax service. *In room:* A/C, TV, dataport, coffeemaker, hair dryer, iron.

SUPERCHEAP SLEEPS

Central Park Hostel & Inn   There's really no inn here—just a hostel. Run by the folks behind the Amsterdam, Murray Hill, and Union Square inns, this cheap choice offers everything clean, fresh, and of decent quality; mattresses, pillows, and linens are better than in most hostels (BYO towels). The shared bathrooms are brand-new (shared at a ratio of about 10 beds to a bathroom). Each floor has a locker area and the building is generally bright and sunny; the front desk is staffed around the clock, morning coffee and munchies are available at the corner deli, and a basement rec room and TV lounge with Internet access machine was in the works at press time.

Now the downside: Most dorm rooms have one too many bunk beds; there's barely any floor space for luggage. Columbia University is helping by building student housing throughout the area, but the location is still sketchy. It's separated from virtually all commercial activity (along Broadway and Amsterdam Ave.) by a major housing project. Luckily, the B and C trains' stops are at the end of the block. I'd try another city hostel first—the Big Apple (p. 120), Chelsea Center (p. 108), and Chelsea International (p. 108) are as clean and much better located.

19 W. 103rd St. (between Central Park W. and Manhattan Ave.), New York, NY 10025. (©) **877/PARK-BED** (727-5233) or 212/678-0491. Fax 212/678-0453. www.centralparkhostel.com. 150 dorm beds. $26–$36 dorm bed; $75–$85 private twin. Rates include tax. Inquire about discounted rates. No credit cards. Subway: B, C to 103rd St. *In room:* A/C, no phone.

Hostelling International–New York Staying here is like going back to college—a very international college, with clocks set for six different time zones behind the front desk and a backpack-toting clientele from around the globe. Beds are cheap, but expect to bunk it (upper or lower?) with people you don't know in rooms of 4, 6, 8, or 12. Everything is extremely basic, but the mattresses are firm and the shared bathrooms are nicely kept. There are four rooms with one double and two bunk beds that have private bathrooms. The well-managed hostel feels like a student union, with bulletin boards and listings of events posted; a coffee bar with an ample menu and pleasant seating; two TV rooms; a game room; and a library with bill- and credit-card–operated Internet access computers. There's also a common kitchen, vending machines, a coin-op laundry, a terrace, and a yard with picnic tables and barbecues in summer. The neighborhood has improved over the years, but it's still a little sketchy; 1 block over is much nicer Broadway, lined with affordable restaurants and shops.

891 Amsterdam Ave. (at 103rd St.), New York, NY 10025. (©) **800/909-4776** or 212/932-2300. Fax 212/932-2574. www.hinewyork.org. 624 beds; 4 units with private bathroom. $29–$38 dorm bed; $120–$135 for family room (sleeps up to 4) or private quad. Travelers must be 18 or older. AE, DC, MC, V. Subway: 1, 9 to 103rd St. **Amenities:** Coffee bar; access to nearby health club; game room; activities desk; coin-op laundry. *In room:* A/C, locker (BYO lock), no phone.

11 Harlem

Urban Jem Guest House ★ This B&B is the best place to stay in Harlem. Jane Alex Mendelson, a refugee from the corporate world, has successfully reinvented herself as an innkeeper. In the Mount Morris Historic District, her renovated 1878 brownstone is graced with fine woodwork and beautiful original (nonworking) fireplaces. The house is a work in progress, so don't expect perfection; there's still plenty to be done, and the furnishings are largely an odds-and-ends mix. But the accommodations offer good value. The second floor has two guest rooms with firm queen beds, new private bathrooms, and spacious kitchenettes with stove, minifridge, microwave, and the basic tools for preparing and serving a meal. On the third floor are two nice rooms that share a hall bathroom and fully equipped kitchen: one a pretty bedroom with a queen bed, the other a spacious room with two foldout futon sofa beds. They can also be combined into a two-bedroom suite, which gives you a whole floor to yourself. Every room has a phone, and local calls are free.

You can pay an extra $7.50 for daily maid service (the trash is taken out daily); otherwise, sheets and towels are changed weekly. Jane is friendly and helpful and can provide lots of neighborhood information. The bustling urban neighborhood has welcomed the inn, and it makes a good starting point for exploring jazz-, gospel-, and history-rich Harlem. Midtown is about a half-hour subway ride away, but Jane recommends taking a cab back after 11pm or so.

Bed-and-Breakfasting in Brooklyn

Leafy, lovely brownstone Brooklyn is the best-kept secret for B&B-loving budget travelers. The neighborhoods are jewels; these are some of the most desirable areas in the city for folks who don't want to hassle with the bustle of Manhattan. What's more, they're safe and subway-convenient, with Manhattan just 15 to 30 minutes away via subway. Each boasts a good selection of affordable restaurants catering to a local crowd.

The historic neighborhood of Park Slope is the heart of brownstone Brooklyn, and home to **Bed & Breakfast on the Park,** 113 Prospect Park W. (© **718/499-6115;** www.bbnyc.com). Housed in an 1895 Victorian town house across the street from Prospect Park, this inn has two beautifully outfitted shared-bathroom units ($125 or $150 double). A sumptuous breakfast is served in the formal dining room. Six more rooms with private bathrooms are available for guests who are looking to splurge. However, be aware that there is a 10% service charge added to all bills.

Another excellent choice is **Akwaaba Mansion,** 347 MacDonough St. (© **718/455-5958;** www.akwaaba.com), a meticulously restored 1860s Italianate villa in Bedford-Stuyvesant, outfitted with Afrocentric elegance. Four suites are available in the 18-room home, each with private bathroom with either a claw-foot or a Jacuzzi tub, for $120 to $150 double—including a hearty, Southern-style breakfast. The innkeepers are a lovely and helpful couple who love welcoming guests into their home; they also operate an affordably elegant restaurant with live jazz on Friday and Saturday nights, plus an all-you-can-eat Sunday brunch for just $11.95, just down the street.

In Carroll Gardens is the **Baisley House Bed-and-Breakfast,** 294 Hoyt St. (© **718/935-1959;** www.virtualcities.com/ons/ny/n/nyn1901.htm), a Victorian mansion that offers three guest rooms: one single and two doubles, each with shared bathroom, all including cable TV with VCR and a full breakfast. There's an opulent drawing room for lounging, plus an English-style garden out back. Rates are $95 to $150 double.

Also consider **Garden Green Bed-and-Breakfast,** 641 Carlton Ave. (© **718/783-5717;** www.virtualcities.com/ons/ny/n/nyn7601.htm), in the Prospect Heights section of brownstone Brooklyn, near Park Slope, the Brooklyn Museum of Art, and Prospect Park. Two double rooms (one with a full-size bed, one with two twins) share a hall bathroom, while a full-floor garden apartment—the best value of the three—boasts a queen bed, a sleeper sofa, a kitchen, and access to the lovely garden out back. Rates run an affordable $95 to $135 single or double; breakfast is not served.

Be prepared for a 2-night minimum at any bed-and-breakfast.

ACCOMMODATIONS ■

Central Park
 Hostel & Inn **17**
Hostelling International
 New York **16**
Park View Hotel **9**
Sugar Hill International
 House **2**
Urban Jem Guest House **6**
West Side Inn **13**

DINING ◆

Absolute Bagels **14**
Africa Restaurant #1 **8**
Bayou **5**
Charles Southern Style
 Kitchen **1**
Columbia Bagels **11**
Hungarian Pastry Shop **12**
La Fonda Boricua **15**
Miss Mamie's
 Spoonbread Too **10**
Papaya King **4**
Patsy's Pizzeria **7**
Sylvia's **3**
Tom's Restaurant **11**
V&T Pizzeria **12**

2005 Fifth Ave. (between 124th and 125th sts.). ✆ **212/831-6029.** Fax 212/831-6940. www.urbanjem.com. 4 units (2 with shared bathroom that can be combined into a suite). $90–$200 single or double. Rates include continental breakfast upon request. Extra person $15. 2-night minimum on weekends or holidays. AE, DISC, MC, V. Subway: 2, 3 or 4, 5, 6 to 125th St. **Amenities:** Self-serve laundry (small fee). *In room:* A/C, TV, CD player, dataport, kitchenette w/fridge and microwave, hair dryer, iron.

SUPERCHEAP SLEEPS

Sugar Hill International House   This intimate hostel is a good choice for people looking for a quiet, nonsmoking hostel. It's in two brownstones in the Sugar Hill Historic District, a residential, predominantly African-American section of Harlem. Owner Jim Williams has been here since 1984, and he and his partners have literally written the book on hostelling—or one of them, anyway: *The Hostel Handbook,* a guide to hostels across North America with an accompanying website (www.hostelhandbook.com).

Hand-hewn bunk beds fill spacious, high-ceilinged rooms accommodating six to eight; a few highly coveted double rooms are available on a first-come, first-served basis. Accommodations are hostel basic: You'll get a mattress, pillow, and linens (BYO towels), plus plenty of floor space for your stuff; you can store valuables in a safe in the main office. Bathrooms are older but well kept, and divided into toilet, shower, and sink sections for easy sharing. The buildings are works in progress, but the place is well kept and well run. The owners are very friendly and helpful, long-term staff lives on-site, and security is tight: A passport ID is required for check-in (required at most private hostels these days), you will be assigned a code for the front door and provided with a key for your specific dorm, and no guests are allowed. One dorm is for women only. There's a common kitchen with a fridge, a cooktop, and basic tools; takeout is available, and St. Nick's Pub is across the street for genuine Harlem jazz.

722 St. Nicholas Ave. (between 146th and 147th sts.), New York, NY 10031. ✆ **212/926-7030**. www.sugar hillhostel.com. 25 dorm beds. $25 single dorm bed; $60 bunk-bed twin. No credit cards. Subway: A, B, C, D to 145th St. **Amenities:** Free Internet access; kitchen. *In room:* No phone.

6

Great Deals on Dining

Without a doubt, New York is the best restaurant town in the country. Other cities might have particular specialties—Paris has better bistros, Hong Kong better Chinese, Los Angeles better Mexican—but no culinary capital spans the globe as successfully as NYC.

The sheer variety is astounding. That's due in part to New York's vibrant immigrant mix. Let a newcomer arrive and see that his or her native foods aren't being served and *zap!*—there's a restaurant, cafe, or grocery to fill the void. Yet we New Yorkers can be fickle: One moment a restaurant is hot, the next it's passé. Do call ahead to see if it's still there!

But eating in New York ain't cheap. The primary cause? The high rents, which are reflected in your tab. Wherever you're from, New York's restaurants will seem *expensive*. Yet as you peruse this chapter, you'll see that values abound—especially if you eat ethnic and venture beyond tourist zones into the neighborhoods where real New Yorkers eat, such as Chinatown, the Upper West Side, and the East Village. But even if you're not venturing beyond Times Square, I've included inexpensive restaurants in every neighborhood.

For ideas on how to save, revisit the dining section in "65 Money-Saving Tips," in chapter 2.

RESERVATIONS Reservations are always a good idea, and a virtual necessity if your party consists of more than two people. Do yourself a favor and make them, so you won't be disappointed. If you're booking dinner on a weekend night, call a few days to a week in advance; even farther in advance never hurts, especially if you're set on a certain dining hour.

But lots of restaurants, especially at the affordable end of the spectrum, don't take reservations. One of the ways they're able to keep prices down is by packing people in as quickly as possible. This means that the best cheap and midpriced restaurants often have a wait. Your best bet is to go early or late. Often, you can get in more quickly on a weeknight. Or go knowing that you'll have to wait; there are worse things than sipping a glass of wine or a margarita at the bar.

THE LOWDOWN ON SMOKING After the tough new nonsmoking laws are imposed in 2003, basically you will not be able to light up in any restaurant anywhere in the city. There will be a select few restaurants that will get special exemptions, but at press time, names of those restaurants were not available.

TIPPING Tipping is easy in New York. Double the 8.625% sales tax and voilà! Happy waitperson. If you check your coat, leave a dollar per item for the checkroom attendant.

1 Restaurants by Cuisine

AFRICAN
African Restaurant #1 (Harlem, p. 189)

Africa #2 ✦ (Midtown West, p. 170)

AMERICAN

All State Cafe (Upper West Side, p. 179)

Bendix Diner (East Village, p. 151)

Big Nick's Burger and Pizza Joint ✦ (Upper West Side, p. 182)

Bubby's ✦✦ (TriBeCa, p. 140)

Burger Joint ✦ (Midtown West, p. 179)

Chat 'n' Chew (Union Square, p. 164)

Corner Bistro (Greenwich Village, p. 156)

EJ's Luncheonette (Greenwich Village, Upper East and Upper West Sides, p. 156)

Empire Diner (Chelsea, p. 160)

ESPN Zone (Times Square, p. 174)

Fanelli's Cafe (SoHo, p. 148)

Gray's Papaya (Greenwich Village, p. 160; Upper West Side, p. 179; Upper East Side, p. 188)

Good Enough To Eat ✦ (Upper West Side, p. 184)

Hard Rock Cafe (Midtown West, p. 174)

Jackson Hole (Midtown East, Murray Hill, Upper East and Upper West Sides, p. 187)

Jekyll & Hyde Club (Midtown West, p. 174)

Joe Allen ✦✦ (Midtown West/Times Square, p. 171)

Johny's Grill & Luncheonette (Chelsea, p. 162)

Kitchenette (TriBeCa, p. 141)

Lyric Diner (Gramercy Park, p. 165)

Manhattan Chili Co. ✦ (Midtown West/Times Square, p. 173)

Mars 2112 (Midtown West, p. 174)

Old Town Bar & Restaurant ✦ (Flatiron District, p. 165)

Papaya King (Times Square, p. 177; Upper East Side, p. 188; Harlem, p. 190)

Paul's Palace ✦ (East Village, p. 152)

Peter Luger Steakhouse ✦ (Brooklyn, p. 190)

Popover Cafe (Upper West Side, p. 185)

Prime Burger (Midtown East, p. 178)

Route 66 Cafe (Midtown West, p. 175)

Serendipity 3 (Upper East Side, p. 188)

Tom's Restaurant (Upper West Side, p. 186)

Vynl ✦ (Midtown West, p. 176)

Walker's ✦ (TriBeCa, p. 141)

ASIAN FUSION/PAN-ASIAN

Republic (Union Square, p. 165)

Rice ✦ (Nolita, p. 149)

Zen Palate ✦ (Union Square, Midtown West, Upper West Side, p. 166)

BELGIAN

B. Frites (Midtown West, p. 176)

Le Pain Quotidien ✦✦ (SoHo, Flatiron District, Midtown East, Upper East and Upper West Sides, p. 148)

Petite Abeille (Chelsea, p. 162; TriBeCa, Greenwich Village, p. 154)

BRAZILIAN

Brazil Grill ✦ (Midtown West, p. 170)

Rice 'n' Beans (Midtown West, p. 174)

BRITISH

A Salt & Battery (Greenwich Village, p. 156)

Christer's (Midtown East, p. 178)

Puck Fair (Nolita/SoHo, p. 149)

Tea & Sympathy (Greenwich Village, p. 159)

CHINESE

Flor de Mayo (Upper West Side, p. 184)

Funky Broome ✦ (Chinatown, p. 142)

Grand Sichuan International ✦ (Chelsea, Midtown West, p. 162)

Joe's Shanghai ✿✿ (Chinatown,
Midtown West, p. 142)

New Big Wong ✿ (Chinatown,
p. 142)

New York Noodletown ✿✿
(Chinatown, p. 143)

Sweet-n-Tart Cafe (Chinatown,
p. 144)

CONTEMPORARY AMERICAN

AKA Cafe (Lower East Side,
p. 144)

CREOLE

Bayou ✿ (Harlem, p. 189)

FRENCH

Florent (Meat-Packing District,
p. 158)

Franklin Station Café ✿ (TriBeCa,
p. 140)

La Bonne Soupe ✿ (Midtown
West, p. 171)

L'Express (Flatiron District/Union
Square, p. 164)

Le Pain Quotidien ✿✿ (SoHo,
Flatiron District, Midtown East,
Upper East and Upper West
Sides, p. 148)

Le Pere Pinard ✿ (Lower East
Side, p. 147)

Le Zinc ✿✿✿ (TriBeCa, p. 141)

Pigalle ✿ (Midtown West, p. 173)

Rue des Crepes ✿✿ (Chelsea,
p. 163)

GERMAN

Hallo! Berlin ✿ (Midtown West,
p. 171)

Knödel (Midtown East, p. 178)

GOURMET SANDWICHES/ CAFE/TAKEOUT

Absolute Bagels (Upper West Side,
p. 179)

Amy's Bread (Midtown West,
p. 176; Chelsea, p. 163; Upper
East Side, p. 189)

Antique Cafe ✿ (Chelsea, p. 160)

Caffé Roma ✿ (Little Italy, p. 144)

Columbia Bagels (Upper West
Side, p. 183)

Dean & Deluca (Greenwich
Village, p. 160; SoHo, p. 150;
Midtown West, p. 177)

Eisenberg's Coffee Shop (Flatiron
District, p. 164)

Emerald Planet ✿ (Greenwich
Village, Midtown West, p. 158)

Ess-A-Bagel (Midtown East,
p. 183)

F&B ✿ (Chelsea, p. 161)

Ferrara (Little Italy, p. 144)

H&H Bagels ✿ (Upper West Side,
p. 179; Midtown West, p. 167;
Upper East Side, p. 183)

Housing Works Used Books Cafe
✿ (SoHo, p. 150)

Hungarian Pastry Shop (Upper
West Side, p. 187)

Island Burgers & Shakes (Midtown
West, p. 171)

Le Pain Quotidien ✿✿ (SoHo,
Flatiron District, Midtown East,
Upper East and Upper West
Sides, p. 148)

Little Pie Company (Chelsea,
p. 163; Midtown East, p. 178)

Mangia (Financial District,
Midtown East, Midtown West,
p. 138)

Mike's Take-Away (Midtown East,
p. 178)

Murray's Bagels (Greenwich
Village, p. 183)

P&W's Sandwich & More Shop
(Upper West Side, p. 187)

Silver Moon Bakery (Upper West
Side, p. 187)

Xando/Cosí (locations all over the
city, p. 186)

Yura & Company (Upper East
Side, p. 188)

GREEK

Johny's Grill & Luncheonette
(Chelsea, p. 162)

Snack (SoHo, p. 149)

ICE CREAM

Brooklyn Ice Cream Factory ✿
(Brooklyn, p. 190)

Chinatown Ice Cream Factory
(Chinatown, p. 143)

Nyonya ⭐ (Chinatown, p. 143)

MEXICAN/TEX-MEX

Burritoville ⭐ (locations all over the city, p. 138)

Gabriela's ⭐⭐ (Upper West Side, p. 184)

Los Dos Rancheros Mexicanos (Midtown West, p. 172)

Manhattan Chili Co. ⭐ (Midtown West/Times Square, p. 173)

Mexican Radio (SoHo, p. 148)

Noche Mexicana ⭐ (Upper West Side, p. 185)

Taco & Tortilla King (Gramercy Park, p. 166)

Tajin Restaurant (Financial District, p. 138)

MIDDLE EASTERN

Afghan Kebab House (Midtown West, p. 167)

Bereket ⭐ (Lower East Side, p. 146)

Lemon Tree Cafe (Midtown West, p. 172)

Moustache (Greenwich Village, East Village, p. 159)

PIZZA

Big Nick's Burger and Pizza Joint ⭐ (Upper West Side, p. 182)

Grimaldi's Pizzeria ⭐ (Brooklyn, p. 157)

John's Pizzeria (Times Square, original in Greenwich Village and locations on the Upper West and Upper East Sides, p. 157

Lil' Frankie's Pizza (East Village, p. 154)

Lombardi's (SoHo/Little Italy, p. 157)

Nick's Family-Style Restaurant and Pizzeria ⭐ (Upper East Side, p. 188)

Patsy's Pizzeria ⭐⭐ (Harlem, p. 157)

Pintaile's Pizza (Union Square, p. 167; Upper East Side, p. 188)

Totonno's Pizzeria Napolitano (Upper East Side, p. 189)

Two Boots (East Village and Greenwich Village, p. 154; Midtown East, p. 156)

V&T Pizzeria (Upper West Side, p. 186)

SEAFOOD

New York Noodletown ⭐⭐ (Chinatown, p. 143)

SOUTHERN/SOUL FOOD/ BARBECUE

Acme Bar & Grill (NoHo, p. 150)

Blue Smoke ⭐ (Flatiron District, p. 163)

Charles' Southern Style Kitchen ⭐ (Harlem, p. 189)

Miss Mamie's Spoonbread Too ⭐ (Harlem, p. 190)

The Pink Tea Cup (Greenwich Village, p. 159)

Sylvia's (Harlem, p. 189)

Virgil's Real BBQ ⭐⭐ (Times Square, p. 175)

THAI

Chanpen (Midtown West, p. 170)

Siam Inn ⭐ (Midtown West, p. 175)

TIBETAN

Tsampa (East Village, p. 153)

UKRAINIAN

Veselka ⭐ (East Village, p. 153)

VEGETARIAN/HEALTH-CONSCIOUS

Angelica Kitchen (East Village, p. 150)

Pongal ⭐ (Murray Hill, p. 177)

The Pump (Murray Hill, Midtown West, p. 178)

Tiengarden (Lower East Side, p. 147)

Tsampa (East Village, p. 153)

Zen Palate ⭐ (Union Square, Midtown West, Upper West Side, p. 166)

VIETNAMESE

Nha Trang ⭐ (Chinatown, p. 143)

Saigon Grill ⭐ (Upper West Side, p. 185)

2 The Financial District

If you'd like to chow down where George Washington once did (it's a splurge), consider the beautifully restored, Revolutionary-era **Fraunces Tavern** (p. 220).

Burritoville ★ *Value* TEX-MEX   This bright, cheerful minichain serves up the best "fast food" in the city. In fact, its fare doesn't deserve to be called fast food. This is forward-thinking Mexican, prepared with healthy ingredients—fresh produce, brown rice, and black beans—using no lard, preservatives, or canned goods. Even the tortillas are pressed every day. Options range from well-stuffed tacos and quesadillas to only-at-Burritoville creations such as a spicy white-chicken chili with cumin, salad burritos, and a number of wraps. The menu offers a wealth of options for vegetarians, as well as anyone looking for a quick, healthy bite. Another nice thing is their flexibility—you can make substitutions and special requests easily, and usually without an extra charge. *Tip:* The green salsa is hot; the red salsa (made with open-flame-roasted tomatoes) is not.

In addition to this location (a short walk from Battery Park and the Statue of Liberty and Staten Island ferry landings), a second lower-Manhattan location is in the Financial District at 20 John St., between Broadway and Nassau (© **212/766-2020**). There are 11 more Burritovilles throughout the city, most with good table seating that makes Burritoville more attractive and comfortable than your average fast-food joint.

36 Water St. (just north of Broad St.). © 212/747-1100. www.burritoville.com. Reservations not accepted. Main courses $4.50–$9. AE, DISC, MC, V. Daily 11am–10pm. Subway: 2, 3 to Wall St.; 1, 9 to South Ferry.

Mangia MEDITERRANEAN/CAFE   This gourmet cafeteria is an ideal place to take a break while sightseeing. Between the giant salad and soup bars, the sandwich and hot-entree counters, and expansive cappuccino-and-pastry counter, even the most finicky eater will have a hard time deciding what to eat. Everything is freshly prepared and beautifully presented. The soups and stews are particularly good (there are a number of daily choices), and a cup goes well with a fresh-baked pizzette (a minipizza). Pay-by-the-pound salad bars don't get any better than this, hot-meal choices (such as grilled mahimahi or cumin-marinated lamb kebab) are cooked to order, and sandwiches are made as you watch. It's packed with Wall Streeters between noon and 2pm, but things move quickly and there's enough seating that usually no one has to wait. Come in for a late breakfast or an afternoon snack and you'll virtually have the place to yourself. At press time, Mangia was in the process of adding a sit-down section with waiter service in addition to the cafeteria. In addition to Wall Street, Mangia has two cafeteria-style cafes in Midtown that offer similar, if not quite such expansive, menus.

40 Wall St. (between Nassau and William sts.). © 212/425-4040. www.mangianet.com. Reservations not accepted. Soups and salads $3.50–$5; sandwiches and main courses $6–$14 (most less than $10). AE, DC, DISC, MC, V. Mon–Fri 7am–5pm (waiter service available 11:30am–4pm). Subway: 2, 3, 4, 5 to Wall St.; J, M, Z to Broad St. Also at 50 W. 57th St. (between Fifth and Sixth aves.; © 212/582-5554; Mon–Fri 7am–8pm; Sat 8:30am–6pm; subway: B, Q to 57th St.); 16 E. 48th St. (between Fifth and Madison aves.; © 212/754-0637; Mon–Fri 7am–6pm; subway: B, D, F, Q to 47th–50th sts./Rockefeller Center.).

Tajin Restaurant *Value* MEXICAN   This Mexican luncheonette is a favorite among Wall Streeters, who love the bullish portions of south-of-the-border cooking at low prices. Tostadas might be the best deal: Crisp tortillas come piled with traditional fillings, including your choice of chicken and beef, for $2.95. The enchiladas are fresh-made and saucy; try the spinach-and-mushroom version,

Financial District, TriBeCa, Chinatown & Little Italy Dining

Bubby's **12**
Burritoville **17, 19, 22**
Caffe Roma **2**
Chinatown Ice Cream Factory **7**
Ferrara **3**
Franklin Station Café **13**
Funky Broome **1**
Joe's Shanghai **9**
Kitchenette **18**
Le Zinc **15**

Mangia **20**
New Big Wong **5**
New York Noodletown **8**
Nha Trang **10**
Nyonya **4**
Petite Abeille **14**
Salaam Bombay **16**
Sweet-n-Tart Café **6**
Tajin Restaurant **21**
Walkers **11**

topped with cheese and salsa verde. There's always something interesting on the "specials" board. Come early, before you begin your sightseeing, to launch your day with huevos rancheros, *huevos con chorizo* (eggs with sausage), or a breakfast burrito stuffed with scrambled eggs, potatoes, green pepper, onions, and a touch of jalapeño. The small dining room is spare but not unpleasant. Food comes on real plates but with plastic forks. Service can be a tad gruff on occasion, but it's generally fine. There may be a short line for a table at the height of the lunch hour (noon–1:30pm), but it moves very quickly.

85 Greenwich St. (south of Rector St.). © 212/509-5017. Reservations not accepted. Main courses 65¢–$6 at breakfast, $5–$10 at lunch and dinner. AE, MC, V. Mon–Fri 7am–9pm; Sat 9am–5pm. Subway: 1, 9 to Rector St.

3 TriBeCa

In addition to the choices below, **Burritoville** (p. 138) is at 144 Chambers St., at Hudson Street (© **212/964-5048**). There's a branch of the Belgian cafe **Petite Abeille** (p. 162) at 134 W. Broadway, between Duane and Thomas streets (© **212/791-1360**).

Bubby's ★★ AMERICAN   How do we love Bubby's? Let us count the ways: for the sublime macaroni and cheese, for divine garlic burger and fries (accompanied by Bubby's own "wup-ass" ketchup), for the homemade meatloaf with cider gravy and garlic mashies. Then there's the roasted rosemary chicken and chipotle-crusted Black Angus steak, and the classic cocktails the bartender makes. Bubby's is known for its generous portions and fresh-from-the-field greens, as well as big, home-style breakfasts that draw big crowds and long lines for the weekend brunch. The high-ceilinged, brick-walled, loftlike space is very homey *and* very TriBeCa. The wait staff doesn't neglect the non-celebs, even though the regular clientele includes the likes of Harvey Keitel and other downtown luminaries. Best of all are Bubby's pies: baked fresh daily, a half dozen from which to choose (along with another half-dozen homemade cakes), and topped with fresh-made whipped cream.

120 Hudson St. (at N. Moore St.). © 212/219-0666. www.bubbys.com. Reservations recommended for dinner (not accepted for brunch). Main courses $2–$7 at breakfast, brunch, and lunch; $9–$19 at dinner. AE, DC, DISC, MC, V. Mon–Thurs 8am–11pm; Fri 8am–midnight; Sat 9am–4:30pm and 6pm–midnight; Sun 9am–10pm. Subway: 1, 9 to Franklin St.

Franklin Station Café FRENCH/MALAYSIAN ★   This charming brick-walled cafe is a winner for affordable Malaysian noodle and curry bowls and French-inspired sandwiches. The dishes on the handwritten-and-illustrated menu are prepared by the kitchen with all-natural ingredients. Sandwiches are simple but satisfying creations such as home-baked ham with honey mustard, lettuce, and tomato; mozzarella with basil, vine-ripened tomato, and extra-virgin olive oil; smoked salmon with mascarpone and chives; and tuna salad with jalapeño. For warm and cozy, you can't do better than one of the noodle bowls, such as tom yum shrimp, with sprouts, pineapple, and cucumber in a hot-and-sour broth; or seafood udon, with helpings of squid, shrimp, and salmon in a milder vegetable broth. For a more substantial meal, check the blackboard for such specials as Chilean sea bass in cardamom sauce. Service is friendly and efficient, wine and beer is available, and the desserts (a scrumptious fresh-baked tart and banana or carrot-raisin cake are usually among the choices) are well priced and pleasing. Omelets dominate the morning menu. It's a great choice for a casual meal, especially if you're heading to a performance at the nearby Knitting Factory.

222 W. Broadway (at Franklin St.). © 212/274-8525. www.franklinstation.com. Reservations not accepted. Breakfast $4.50–$7.50; sandwiches $6.50–$7; Malaysian specialties and noodle bowls $7–$13.50; house specials $10.50–$16.50. AE, DC, MC, V. Daily 8am–11pm. Subway: 1, 9 to Franklin St.; 2, 3 to Chambers St.

Kitchenette AMERICAN HOME COOKING   This TriBeCa luncheonette has become a prime contender on the comfort-food circuit, thanks to Hungry Man–size breakfasts and just-like-home cooking. The little room has the feel of a New England diner, with folk art on the walls and country-rustic chairs at the tables. Expect high-cholesterol breakfasts and hearty salads and sandwiches. Weekly lunchtime blue-plate specials include shepherd's pie with mashed-potato crust on Tuesday and gooey four-cheese mac and cheese on Friday (specials are subject to change). Everything is well prepared and filling. Service is sit-down at breakfast, but lunch is more cafeteria-style, with orders taken at the counter.

80 W. Broadway (at Warren St.). © 212/267-6740. www.kitchenettenyc.com. Main courses $4.50–$7 at breakfast, $5.25–$9.25 at lunch and brunch, $9.50–$17 at dinner. AE ($20 minimum). Mon–Fri 7:30am–4:30pm; Sat–Sun 9am–4:30pm. Subway: 1, 2, 3, 9 to Chambers St.

Le Zinc ★★★ *Value* FRENCH BISTRO   The new restaurant from David and Karen Waltuck (the team behind glorious, big-ticket Chanterelle) is this affordable and authentic French bistro. Despite its TriBeCa address, Le Zinc is unfussy and unpretentious, boasting genuine warmth and creative bistro cuisine. The space is open and comfortable, with big, well-spaced tables, banquette seating, unframed art posters glazed into the walls, and soft, sexy lighting.

The menu features bistro favorites with gentle accents, some of which reach beyond France to Eastern Europe, Asia, and even New Orleans. Winning choices include a skate wing browned in butter and capers; Grandma Gaby's Hungarian stuffed cabbage; mussels in snail butter; an excellent duck, foie gras, and pistachio terrine from the charcuterie; rib steak and frites; and a thick, juicy bacon cheeseburger. Reservations aren't taken, but any wait is worth it—put yourself in the competent hands of the bartenders at the mahogany bar. The crowd is grown-up and easygoing. This is a real winner—and reason enough to visit TriBeCa.

139 Duane St. (between W. Broadway and Church St.). © 212/513-0001. www.lezincnyc.com. Reservations not accepted. Main courses $3–$7 at breakfast, $7–$16 at lunch, $10–$21 at dinner. AE, DISC, MC, V. Sun–Thurs 8am–1am; Fri–Sat 8am–3am. Subway: 1, 2, 3, 9 to Chambers St.

Salaam Bombay ★ PAN-INDIAN   Salaam Bombay is much more attractive than most curry houses, and the Pan-Indian cuisine is a cut above the standard fare. Dinner is more expensive than Indian should be, but the daily $12.95 all-you-can-eat lunch is a bargain for travelers willing to make lunch their main mealtime; it's a freshly prepared, top-quality spread—you'll watch the tandoori chef pulling fresh-baked *naan* (flatbread) from the clay oven. There are a dozen or so fresh-made meat and vegetarian dishes, as well as all the traditional accompaniments. The location is convenient for a sightseeing break.

The room is romantically low-lit and formally outfitted in the evening, and service is attentive, so dinner is worth the expense if you care to splurge.

317 Greenwich St. (between Duane and Reade sts.). © 212/226-9400. www.salaambombay.com. Main courses $9–$18; daily all-you-can-eat buffet lunch $12.95. AE, DC, DISC, MC, V. Sun–Fri 11:30am–3pm; Sun–Thurs 5–10:30pm; Fri–Sat 5–11pm. Subway: 1, 2, 3, 9 to Chambers St.

Walker's ★ AMERICAN   Down-to-earth as ever, Walker's is an old holdout from pre-fabulous TriBeCa. The space is charming, with a tin ceiling, a long wooden bar, oldies on the sound system, friendly bartenders, cozy tables, and low prices. The meat-and-potatoes fare includes an 8-ounce sirloin burger, a delicious grilled rib eye, and well-roasted organic chicken with mashies among an extensive list of entrees and specials, plus crisp, fresh salads. The fried oysters with Cajun aioli make a great starter. Low lighting sets a nice dinnertime mood, and service is friendly and attentive enough, as long as you're not in a hurry.

16 N. Moore St. (at Varick St.). ℭ **212/941-0142.** Reservations accepted for dinner. Main courses $8–$15 at dinner. AE, DC, DISC, MC, V. Daily noon–1am (bar usually open to 4am). Subway: 1, 9 to Franklin St.; 2, 3 to Chambers St.

4 Chinatown & Little Italy

Funky Broome ✪ CHINESE/CANTONESE This neon-bright Chinese joint straddles the Nolita/Chinatown border geographically and in attitude—and the crowd, a mix of hipsters and Chinese nationals, loves the fusion. The mind-set is evident in the playful decor and the mainly Cantonese menu. The kitchen keeps preparations authentic, but presentations are a joy: Rice is served in a section of bamboo, and miniwoks are presented over an open flame to keep the contents sizzling (the pork with enoki mushrooms is my favorite). There's a wealth of seafood, poultry, stir-fry, sizzling, and vegetarian dishes, ranging from favorites like General Tso's chicken to wild offerings like marinated goose intestines and stir-fried conch with sweet peas and jellyfish for the more adventuresome. It's a great place to try Chinatown eats without having to surmount a language barrier.

176 Mott St. (at Broome St.). ℭ **212/941-8628.** Reservations accepted. Main courses $3.50–$16 (most less than $12). AE, MC, V. Sun–Thurs 11:30am–11pm; Fri–Sat 11:30am–midnight. Subway: 6 to Spring St.

Joe's Shanghai ✪✪ CHINESE/SHANGHAI Tucked away on a little side street off the Bowery is this Chinatown institution, which serves up authentic cuisine. The stars of the extensive menu are the soup dumplings, quivering steamed pockets filled with broth and your choice of pork or crab, accompanied by a side of seasoned soy. Listed as "steamed buns" (item nos. 1 and 2), these culinary marvels never disappoint. Neither does the rest of the Shanghai-inspired menu, which boasts such main courses as whole yellowfish bathed in spicy sauce; and an excellent "mock duck," a saucy bean-curd dish similar to Japanese *yuba* that's a hit with vegetarians and carnivores alike. The room is set mostly with round tables of 10 or so, and you'll be asked if you're willing to share. It's a great way to watch and learn from your neighbors (many of whom are Chinese), who are usually happy to tell you what they're eating. If you want a private table, expect a wait. *Note:* The Midtown location is geared more to Western diners, and is more expensive across the board, but it takes major credit cards.

9 Pell St. (between Bowery and Mott sts.). ℭ **212/233-8888.** Reservations recommended for 10 or more. Main courses $4.25–$17. No credit cards. Daily 11am–11pm. Subway: N, R, Q, W, 6 to Canal St.; F to Delancey St. Also at 24 W. 56th St. (between Fifth and Sixth aves.; ℭ **212/333-3868**; subway: B, Q to 57th St.).

New Big Wong ✪ CHINESE/CANTONESE There's nothing new about New Big Wong and that's a good thing. Why mess with success? For over 30 years, Big Wong has been an institution for workers from the nearby courthouses and Chinese families feasting on congee (rice porridge) and fried crullers for breakfast (for more see the box, "Breakfast, Not Brunch!" on p. 161). They come not only for the congee, but for the superb roasted meats (pork and duck seen hanging in the window), the comforting noodle soups, and the terrific barbecued ribs. This is simple, down-home, Cantonese food: lo mein, chow fun, and bok choy in oyster sauce, cooked lovingly and so very cheap. If you don't mind sharing a table, Big Wong is a must at any time of day.

Tips **Sweet, Not Sour**

To help cool my palate after a spicy Asian meal, one of my favorite stops in Chinatown is the **Chinatown Ice Cream Factory,** 65 Bayard St., between Mott and Elizabeth streets (© **212/608-4170**). The ice cream is made on the premises and is a contender for best in the city. But what separates the Chinatown Ice Cream Factory from all the others are the exotic Asian-inspired flavors such as ginger, mango, almond cookie, litchi, green tea, and the incredible red bean. If you have room after your Chinatown feast, don't miss it.

---

67 Mott St. (between Canal and Bayard sts.). © 212/964-1452. Appetizers $1.50–$5; congee $1.50–$6; soups $3–$5; Cantonese noodles $5.25–$11. No credit cards. Open daily 8:30am–9pm. Subway N, R, 6, to Canal St.

New York Noodletown ★★ CHINESE/SEAFOOD   So what if the fluorescent-lit room has all the ambience of a school cafeteria? The food is fabulous. The mushroom soup is a lunch in itself, thick with earthy chunks of shiitakes, vegetables, and noodles. Another appetizer that can serve as a meal is the hacked roast duck in noodle soup. The kitchen excels at seafood preparations, so be sure to try at least one: Looking like a snow-dusted plate of meaty fish, the salt-baked squid is sublime. The quick-woked Chinese broccoli or the crisp sautéed baby bok choy are great accompaniments. Other special dishes are various sandy pot casseroles: hearty, flavorful affairs slow-simmered in clay vessels. Unlike most of its neighbors, New York Noodletown keeps very long hours, which makes it the best late-night bet in the neighborhood, too.

28½ Bowery (at Bayard St.). © 212/349-0923. Reservations accepted. Main courses $4–$13. No credit cards. Daily 9am–3:30am. Subway: N, R, 6 to Canal St.

Nha Trang ★ VIETNAMESE   The decor may be standard-issue, Chinatown (glass-topped tables, linoleum floors, mirrored walls), but this friendly, bustling place serves up the best Vietnamese fare in Chinatown. A plate of six crispy, finger-size spring rolls is a nice way to start; the slightly spicy pork-and-shrimp filling is offset by the wrapping of lettuce, cucumber, and mint. The *pho* noodle soup comes in a quart-size bowl brimming with bright vegetables and meats and seafood. But my favorite dish is the simple barbecued pork chops—sliced paper-thin, soaked in a soy/sugar cane marinade, and grilled to utter perfection. Everything is well prepared, though, and your waiter will be glad to help you design a meal to suit your tastes.

If there's a line and you don't want to wait, head a couple of blocks over to the nice second location, **Nha Trang Centre,** which accepts credit cards.

87 Baxter St. (between Canal and Bayard sts.). © 212/233-5948. Reservations accepted. Main courses $4–$12.50. No credit cards. Daily 11am–9:30pm. Subway: N, R, 6 to Canal St. Also at 148 Centre St. (at Walker St.; © 212/941-9292; MC, V; subway: N, R, 6 to Canal St.).

Nyonya ★ *Finds* MALAYSIAN   You won't find many Malaysian restaurants in New York, but this is one of the best. This spacious, bustling restaurant designed like a south-Asian Tiki hut offers efficient, friendly service, but it's the huge portions of exotic, spicy food that are the real treat. Coconut milk, curry, and chili-pepper–laden dishes are staples of Malaysian cuisine. The Malaysian national dish, *roti canai,* an Indian pancake with a curry-chicken dipping sauce, is outstanding. The noodle soups are meals in themselves; *prawn mee,* egg noodles,

---

Espresso, Anyone?

With the encroachment of Chinatown upon what was formerly Little Italy north of Canal Street, the neighborhood made famous in movies like *The Godfather* has lost much of its appeal. More importantly, the quality restaurants are gone. Though there are still many Italian restaurants, especially along Mulberry Street, there are none I can in good conscience recommend. Sadly, the street has become a tourist trap with waiters trying to lure customers off the streets by waving menus at them. I do recommend the appetizing combination of a dinner in Chinatown at an Asian restaurant followed by coffee and a pastry at one of Little Italy's *pasticcerias*. My favorite is **Caffé Roma** ⭐, 385 Broome St., on the corner of Mulberry (© 212/226-8413). The cannolis (try the chocolate-covered one) and tiramisu are spectacular. Open from 8am to midnight daily. Another you might try is **Ferrara**, 195 Grand St., between Mott and Mulberry streets (© 212/226-6150). Founded in 1892, the pasticceria claims to be America's first espresso bar. Cafe seating is available, so you can enjoy instant, sweet gratification. Open daily from 8am to midnight (to 1am on Sat).

---

shredded pork, and large shrimp in a spicy shrimp broth was sinus-clearing, while the curry spareribs were nothing short of spectacular. Even the drinks and desserts are exotic, including *sooi pooi* drink (sour plum) and *pulut hitam,* creamy black glutinous rice with coconut milk. But vegans beware: There's not much on the menu for you here; most dishes are prepared in either a meat or fish broth.

194 Grand St. (between Mulberry and Mott sts.). © 212/334-3669. Appetizers $2.25–$8; noodle soups $4.25–$6; main dishes $5.25–$16. No credit cards. Sun–Thurs 11am–11:30pm; Fri–Sat 11am–midnight. Subway 6 to Spring St.

Sweet-n-Tart Cafe *(Value* CHINESE   Supercheap, there's almost nothing over $6—and, considering the prices, the quality is stellar. Rarely is Chinese food described as airy and light, but this is, especially the noodle soups. The scallion pancake is beautifully seasoned, and the Taiwan-style salt-baked chicken, served on broth-soaked rice, is a don't-miss. There are plenty of familiar dishes—fried rice, lo mein, pan-fried dumplings, and the like—but this is also a good bet for adventurous diners who'd like to try something new, be it shredded jellyfish, chicken with sea cucumber, or broiled frog. Consider the quail eggs with lotus seed in a light, peppery broth. Sweet-n-Tart's specialty is *tong shui*, a broth or gelatin made with herbal, nut, or fruit essences. Served cold or hot, they're taken as invigorating medicinal tonics. You can have yours at any time during the meal, but I've found they offer a clean, fresh finish.

There's zero ambience, but it's pleasant enough, and the service is some of the best I've experienced in Chinatown. No alcohol is served, but the servers keep your glass filled with tea, and a juicer blends papaya and other fresh-fruit shakes.

76 Mott St. (just south of Canal St.). © 212/334-8088. Reservations not accepted. Main courses $4–$10. No credit cards. Sun–Thurs 9am–11pm; Fri–Sat 9am–midnight. Subway: N, R, 6 to Canal St.

5 The Lower East Side

AKA Cafe CONTEMPORARY AMERICAN/LATIN AMERICAN   This bare-bones sibling to the much-pricier 71 Clinton Fresh Food down the block serves similarly creative and well-prepared cuisine with a Latin flair for less than

A Salt & Battery **11**
Acme Bar & Grill **22**
AKA Café **37**
Angelica Kitchen **2**
Bendix Diner **3**
Bereket **31**
Bombay Dining **8**
Burritoville **14**
Café Habana **30**
Cucina de Pesce **20**
Dean & Deluca **27**
Dean & Deluca Café **1**
Emerald Planet **23**
Fanelli's Café **28**
Frank **10**

Frutti de Mare **21**
Gandhi **6**
Housing Works
  Used Books Café **26**
Jeollado **33**
Katz's Delicatessen **35**
Le Pain Quotidien **42**
Le Pere Pinard **36**
Lil' Frankie's Pizza **32**
Lombardi's Pizza **40**
Mexican Radio **41**
Mitali East **7**
Moustache **5**
Otafuku **17**
Paul's **12**

Puck Fair **25**
Rice **39**
Rose of India **9**
Sapporo East **4**
Second Avenue Deli **15**
Snack **29**
Soba-Ya **16**
Tiengarden **38**
Tsampa **18**
Two Boots **34**
Two Boots to GoGo **24**
Veselka **13**
Village Yokocho **19**

half the price. The menu is small, but budget diners with adventurous palates will love the rich and flavorful oyster soup, seasoned with white wine, aromatic veggies, smoked bacon, and quinoa; inventive empanadas, corn-bread pastries stuffed with fillings like roast turkey and smoked pumpkin; the pressed Cuban sandwich, made with Smithfield ham, Swiss, and pickled peppers; and my favorite, supertender braised pork with celery-root purée in a carrot-cumin broth. Portions are small, so order one more dish than you think you'll need. I'm less enamored with the fruity martinis than many, but there's an affordable and nicely chosen by-the-glass wine list, plus a full bar. "Super bueno" *dulce de leche* makes the perfect finish. The room is decor-free, but service is friendly.

49 Clinton St. (between Stanton and Rivington sts.). ℂ 212/979-6096. Reservations recommended. Main courses $5–$12. AE, MC, V. Mon–Fri noon–4:30pm; Mon–Sat 6pm–midnight. Subway: F, J, M, Z to Delancey/Essex sts.

Bereket ★ *Value* MIDDLE EASTERN/TURKISH This popular kebab house has undergone an expansion that more than doubled the number of tables and upgraded its hole-in-the-wall ambience to shiny diner-style decor—and the quality of their grilled meats is as excellent as ever. Order at the counter, where you'll see the kebabs displayed behind glass, waiting to hit the grill, and then snare a table as your plate is being prepared. The *kofte*, ground lamb with spices, is a favorite, but you won't go wrong with any of the choices. Complete dinners— two skewers of your choice, rice, and salad—are a steal for a 10 spot, especially the mixed grill, which features chicken, *shish* (beef), and *doner* (lamb) kebabs. Vegetarians have a lot to choose from, including excellently herbed hummus, falafel, great *piyaz* (white-bean salad with chopped onions and parsley), and babaganoush. Everything is freshly prepared in-house, and the counter staff is friendly and accommodating. No alcohol is served, but Turkish coffee should provide the necessary jolt.

187 E. Houston St. (at Orchard St.). ℂ 212/475-7700. Reservations not accepted. Main courses $3.50–$13.50. No credit cards. Open daily 24 hr. Subway: F to Second Ave.

Katz's Delicatessen ★★ *Value* JEWISH DELI Arguably the city's best Jew-ish deli. The motto is, "There's Nothing More New York than Katz's," and it's spot-on. Founded in 1888, this cavernous, brightly lit place is suitably *Noo Yawk,* with dill pickles, Dr. Brown's cream soda, and old-world attitude to spare. You are handed a ticket as you come in, and it's marked by the server for each item you buy; you can choose to sit in the waiter-serviced area, or grab a tray and stand in line to order your meal. (Tip the carver who prepares your sand-wich and gives you a slice of whatever you've ordered on a small plate while he's at work.)

All of Katz's traditional eats are first-rate: matzo-ball and chicken-noodle soups, potato knishes, cheese blintzes, egg creams (made with Katz's very own seltzer), and all-beef hot dogs. There's no faulting the pastrami—smoked to perfection and piled high on rye—or the dry-cured roast beef, either. All of the well-stuffed sandwiches are substantially cheaper than you'll find at any other deli in town. What's more, Katz's is one of the only delis cool enough to let you split one with your travel partner without adding a bogus $2 to $3 "sharing" charge.

Note: A great New York souvenir is a Katz's T-shirt, admonishing the wearer to "Send a Salami to Your Boy in the Army!"

205 E. Houston St. (at Ludlow St.). ℂ 212/254-2246. Reservations not accepted. Sandwiches $2.15–$10; other main courses $5–$17.50. AE, MC, V ($20 minimum). Sun–Tues 8am–10pm; Wed–Thurs 8am–11pm; Fri–Sat 8am–2:30am. Subway: F to Second Ave.

Le Pere Pinard ★ *Finds* FRENCH BISTRO/WINE BAR   This authentic
French wine bar and bistro is a charming slice of Le Marais, with high ceilings,
burnished brick walls, well-spaced tables with mix-and-match chairs, and an
authentic come-as-you-are air. Everything is well worn in a comfortable way.
The kitchen specializes in the Gallic version of comfort food: steak frites, shell
steak with Roquefort sauce, shepherd's pie with a delightfully cheesy crust, a terrific *brandade* (a dish of salt fish puréed with olive oil, milk, and garlic), and a
charcuterie and cheese plate—the perfect match for the sublime crusty-on-the-
outside, soft-in-the-middle bread that accompanies every meal. Greens are fresh
and well prepared; even a simple mesclun salad wears a just-right vinaigrette.

There's a wonderful and affordable wine selection by the bottle, carafe, and
glass. Service is attentive in an easygoing way. I've eaten here plenty, and both
food and service are consistently good. There's also a pleasant garden in warm
weather. Attention diners happy to eat on the early side (before 7pm): The pre-
theater meal—three courses for $14—is a stellar deal.

175 Ludlow St. (south of Houston St.). ℂ 212/777-4917. Reservations recommended. Main courses
$11.50–$19.50; pre-theater menu daily 5–7pm, $14 for 3 courses. AE. Mon–Thurs 5pm–midnight; Fri
5pm–1am; Sat 11am–1am; Sun 11am–midnight. Subway: F to Second Ave.

Tiengarden VEGAN   This petite restaurant serves up first-rate vegan fare. As
with much vegetarian fare, the emphasis is on Asian flavors and spices. The
kitchen uses all-natural ingredients, with no preservatives, MSG, or egg or dairy.
Veggies are always fresh and never overcooked. Among my favorites are the spicy
organic tofu with shiitakes, bell peppers, and soy in a zippy Szechuan sauce; the
steaming noodle soups, made with a clear mushroom stock and your choice of
wheat, rice, or udon noodles; and the herbed home fries. I'm not a fan of faux
meats, but these are some of the best in town. No beer or wine—but lest it all
sound too austere, the vegan cakes and cookies are downright devilish.

170 Allen St. (1½ blocks south of Houston St.). ℂ 212/388-1364. Main courses $5–$10.50; lunch specials
$5–$6 (until 4pm). No credit cards. Mon–Sat noon–4pm and 5–10pm. Subway: F to Second Ave.

6 SoHo & Nolita

Also consider **Lombardi's Pizza,** 32 Spring St., between Mott and Mulberry
streets (ℂ **212/941-7994;** see the box "Pizza New York Style" on p. 157).

Cafe Habana LATIN AMERICAN   This is a sleek update of a typical Hispanic luncheonette. It's hip without being the least bit pretentious, and what the
food may lack in authenticity it more than makes up for in quality and flavor:
Shrimps are big and hearty; pork is moist and flavorful; cilantro and other spices
are fresh and aromatic. Winning starters include *pozole,* hominy corn stew with
shredded chicken or pork in a clear broth that you season to taste with oregano,
chile, and lime; and the hugely popular Mexican corn on the cob, which is skew-
ered, coated with lime juice and grated cheese, sprinkled with chile powder, and
grilled into a messy but sweet popcorny treat. Main courses include the ultra-
moist roast pork (perfect with a squeeze of lime) and *camarones al ajillo,* shrimp
in spicy garlic sauce. Most everything comes with your choice of red or black
beans and rice. Wine and a handful of Mexican beers are served, but I really
enjoyed the not-too-sweet red hibiscus tea.

The room is narrow and tables are petite (especially those for two), but a middle aisle keeps the place from feeling too crowded, and service is easygoing and
friendly. Don't be surprised if there's a wait for a table.

17 Prince St. (at Elizabeth St.). (C) **212/625-2001.** Reservations not accepted. Main courses $5–$15. AE, MC, V. Daily 9am–midnight. Subway: B, D, F, Q to Broadway/Lafayette St.; 6 to Spring St.

Fanelli's Cafe AMERICAN   Once upon a time, SoHo consisted of a few galleries, some artists living in loft space no one wanted, a few Italian bakeries, and Fanelli's. It couldn't be more different now: The galleries have given way to Banana Republic, the bakeries have moved over for Balthazar, and people pay millions for the lofts. Thankfully, Fanelli's remains. This is a classic New York pub, with a long bar propped up by regulars, and a corner door and pressed-tin ceiling that have locked in the 1847 atmosphere. The giant burgers are great, the pastas are fresh, and the beer is served in pint glasses. The daring will give the mussels a shot. Wine? House red. The Bloody Marys are a godsend for a hangover (white wine is the secret ingredient). If you're coming for dinner, especially on a weekend, your best bet is to arrive before 7pm, which is when the noise level really starts to escalate.

94 Prince St. (at Mercer St.). (C) 212/226-9412. Reservations not accepted. Main courses $6–$15 (most less than $12). AE, MC, V. Sun–Thurs 10am–12:30am; Fri–Sat 10am–1am. Subway: N, R to Prince St.

Le Pain Quotidien ★★ FRENCH/BELGIAN/BAKERY CAFE   This airy neoclassical-goes-farmhouse cafe offers a sophisticated, casual meal at a bargain-basement price. Take a seat at a table for two or cozy up to one of the generous and comfy common tables (the one in the sunlit front room is best). The light menu is comprised mostly of beautiful sandwiches and salads. Excellent choices include the open-faced beef carpaccio sandwich dressed with basil, Parmesan, and virgin olive oil on dark country bread; Paris ham with three mustards on crusty French; and a board of fine French cheeses—brie, chavignol, Gruyère—and your choice of walnut bread, rye, wheat, or a baguette. All are garnished with seasonal greens and fresh herbs. Salads are a good value because they come piled high and accompanied by a plate of French bread. Soups are homemade, hearty, and warming. Breads are baked five times daily in small batches. Save room for dessert—fruit tarts, pies, brownies, cookies, brioches—or stop just for a sweet and a cappuccino; the warm Belgian waffle sprinkled with powdered sugar and fresh blueberries makes a light-as-air choice. Tables are waiter-serviced, but an up-front counter serves walk-ins and takeout.

100 Grand St. (between Mercer and Greene sts.). (C) 212/625-9009. www.painquotidien.com. Reservations not accepted. Breakfast $3–$7.50; sandwiches and salads $7.50–$18 (most less than $12). No credit cards. Daily 8am–7pm. Subway: N, R to Canal St. Also at ABC Carpet & Home, 38 E. 19th St. (between Broadway and Park Ave. S.; (C) 212/625-9009; subway: 4, 5, 6, N, R, L to 14th St./Union Sq.); 50 W. 72nd St. (between Columbus Ave. and Central Park W.; (C) 212/712-9700; subway: B, C to 72 St.); 833 Lexington Ave. (between 63rd and 64th sts.; (C) 212/755-5810; subway: 4, 5, 6 to 59th St.; N, R to Lexington Ave.); 1336 First Ave. (between 71st and 72nd sts.; (C) 212/717-4800; subway: 6 to 68th St.); 1131 Madison Ave. (between 84th and 85th sts.; (C) 212/327-4900; subway: 4, 5, 6 to 86th St.).

Mexican Radio MEXICAN   The hip SoHo-goes-south-of-the-border decor—mango walls, candles, folk art, rough-hewn furniture—creates an artsy-rustic atmosphere in which to dig into good Old Mexico fare. The multicolored corn chips (not free; $2.50) come with a fresh, tangy salsa. Main choices range from well-stuffed burritos to fajita platters. Fans shouldn't pass on the chocolatey mole (one of the best in the city). Another winner is the *carnitas,* tender shredded pork soaked in a marinade of oranges, lemons, limes, and garlic, then grilled with a pepper salsa and served with fresh-made white-corn tortillas. The spice meter is turned up high, so ask your friendly waiter to point you to the cooler dishes if you shy away from fiery spices. The margaritas are terrific. ***Beware:*** The room can get *loud* as weekend evenings wear on.

19 Cleveland Place (just south of intersection of Spring and Lafayette sts.). ℂ 212/343-0140. Reservations accepted for parties of 6 or more. Main courses $8–$16. AE, MC, V. Sun–Thurs noon–11:30pm; Fri–Sat noon–midnight. Subway: 6 to Spring St.

Puck Fair *Finds* BRITISH   This pub looks as if it could have been lifted whole-sale from a corner in London and plunked down this side of the pond. It's gen-uine, but a young crowd and a hip soundtrack make it feel fresh (unlike Fanelli's, which is an old-time institution). Twenty beers are on tap (including Guinness), and the kitchen serves up good pub grub: chicken potpie, bangers and mash, beef-stuffed cottage pie topped with the fluffy mashies, Guinness-battered fish and chips, and "toasties" (hot sandwiches) filled with your choices of cheese, ham, mushrooms, and Irish sausage. A nice yellowfin tuna niçoise adds a nou-veau edge to the menu. The best tables are on the mezzanine; come post-lunch or for early dinner to try to snare one.

298 Lafayette St. (just south of Houston St.). ℂ 212/431-1200. www.puckfair.citysearch.com. Main courses $6–$10 at brunch, $8–$17 at dinner (most $8–$13). AE, MC, V. Daily noon–4am. Subway: F, S to Broadway/Lafayette St.; N, R to Prince St.

Rice ★ *Value* PAN-ASIAN/INDO-CARIBBEAN   This sleek restaurant has a Japanese vibe and an affordable seasonal menu built around—you guessed it—rice. Pick your grain from the seven choices, which range from brown to Bhutanese red or Thai black, and pair it with any of 10 toppings. Vietnamese-grilled lemon grass chicken goes well with short-grain Japanese or sticky rice, while Jamaican jerk chicken wings are an ideal match for yellow rice and peas. Basmati is a must for the warm lentil salad or Indian curry. If you're not sure, go with the pairing suggestions on the short but appealing menu. Thick Portuguese soup, flavored with potatoes and distinctive caraway-flavored rice, is a vegan's delight; it pairs up well with grilled eggplant maki or rice balls topped with tomato-cumin sauce for a vegetarian meal for about $10. Rice bowls come small or large to suit your appetite, but all portions tend to be on the daintier side.

A word of warning: Like so many affordable downtown restaurants, the din-ing room is tiny, so come early to snare a table along the comfortable banquette; otherwise, you may end up perched at postage-stamp–size high tables on the opposite wall. Rice is best for twosomes at dinnertime, as only two tables can accommodate larger parties. A takeout outlet is in the adjacent storefront.

227 Mott St. (between Prince and Spring sts.). ℂ 212/226-5775. Reservations not accepted. Main courses $6–$13. No credit cards. Daily noon–midnight. Subway: 6 to Spring St.

Snack GREEK   This SoHo newcomer draws a chic crowd with its beautifully prepared Hellenic eats. Tables are tiny and seating is tight, but a tin ceiling, Art Nouveau light fixtures, and shelves lined with Greek grocery goods transform the storefront dining room into a charmer. Even with paper plates and plastic utensils, this place is atmospheric enough to enjoy a wallet-friendly date (you're welcome to BYO wine or beer). The menu is traditional Greek, and the kitchen usually strikes gold. The *taramosalata* (carp roe dip) and *spanikopitakia* (spinach squares) are wonderful. Dressed with fresh tomatoes, roasted red onions, and a roasted tomato aioli and served on fresh, crusty *ciabatta,* the braised lamb sand-wich is terrific. If the wait is too long at lunch, order to go and head down the block to the park, where tables and benches come in handy for alfresco dining.

105 Thompson St. (between Prince and Spring sts.). ℂ 212/925-1040. Reservations not accepted. Main courses $6–$14. No credit cards. Sun–Mon 11am–8:30pm; Tues–Sat 11am–10:30pm. Subway: C, E to Spring St.

QUICK BITES

If you need a coffee break, head to **Housing Works Used Books Cafe** ⚐, 126 Crosby St. (1 block east of Broadway), south of Houston Street (☎ **212/334-3324;** www.housingworksubc.com). This attractive and airy used-book shop (whose proceeds support AIDS charities) has a cafe that serves coffee and tea, salads, sandwiches, sweets, and other light bites. There are tables where you can pull up a chair, and you're welcome to read while you nosh. Beer and wine are served, and such events as readings and wine tastings are held in the evenings.

Dean & Deluca also has a walk-up cafe for coffee, sandwiches, and sweets at the front of their store at 560 Broadway, at Prince Street (☎ **212/431-1691**).

7 The East Village & NoHo

In addition to the choices below, a great choice for wallet-friendly Middle Eastern fare is **Moustache** (p. 159), at 265 E. 10th St., between First Avenue and Avenue A (☎ **212/228-2022**). There's also an East Village branch of Sapporo (p. 175) called **Sapporo East,** on the corner of First Avenue and 10th Street (☎ **212/260-1330**), with a good sushi bar in addition to the cheap-eats Japanese menu offered here and at the sushi-less Theater District location.

Burritoville (p. 138) is at 141 Second Ave., between St. Marks Place and 9th Street (☎ **212/260-3300**). Additionally, a second location of British chippery **A Salt & Battery** (p. 156) is at 80 Second Ave., between 4th and 5th streets (☎ **212/254-6610**). Also consider the kosher **Second Avenue Deli**, 156 Second Ave., at 10th Street (☎ **212/677-0606**), for Jewish deli fare extraordinaire.

Acme Bar & Grill *Kids* SOUTHERN/BARBECUE   Acme's motto is AN OKAY PLACE TO EAT. This NoHo joint is divey in a pleasing way, with a good-natured staff, a Louisiana roadhouse theme, and the ambience of a well-worn neighborhood favorite. Acme serves up platters of Southern cooking and barbecue, including po' boys, crawfish, jambalaya, seafood gumbo, thick-cut pork chops, chicken-fried steak, baby back ribs—good, cheap, filling eats. Kids are welcome, and there are plenty of choices for them on the menu. The restaurant is a hot-sauce lover's delight, with dozens of bottles lining the walls. Fresh-baked corn bread starts the meal, and a range of beers is available.

9 Great Jones St. (at Lafayette St.). ☎ 212/420-1934. Reservations accepted for parties of 8 or more. Main courses $6–$14 at lunch, $7–$16 at dinner; fixed-price weekend brunch $10 (includes coffee and tea, plus juice, Bloody Mary, beer, or mimosa). AE, DC, DISC, MC, V. Mon–Thurs 11:30am–midnight; Fri–Sat 11am–1am; Sun 11am–11pm. Subway: 6 to Bleecker St.

Angelica Kitchen ORGANIC VEGETARIAN   This cheerful restaurant is serious about vegan cuisine. The kitchen prepares everything fresh daily; they guarantee at least 95% of all ingredients are organically grown. But good-for-you (and good-for-the-environment) doesn't have to mean boring—this is flavorful, beautifully prepared cuisine served in a country-kitchen–style setting. Salads spill over with sprouts and crisp veggies and are crowned with homemade dressings. The Dragon Bowls, a specialty, are heaping portions of rice, beans, tofu, and steamed vegetables. The daily specials feature the best of what's fresh and in season in such dishes as fiery three-bean chili, slow-simmered with sun-dried tomatoes and a blend of chili peppers; baked tempeh in a sourdough baguette dressed in mushroom gravy; and lemon-herb baked tofu layered with roasted vegetables and fresh pesto on mixed-grain bread. Breads and desserts are fresh-baked and similarly wholesome (and made without eggs, of course).

300 E. 12th St. (just east of Second Ave.). ℂ **212/228-2909.** Reservations accepted for parties of 6 or more. Main courses $6–$14.50. No credit cards. Daily 11:30am–10:30pm. Subway: L, N, R, 4, 5, 6 to 14th St./ Union Sq.

Bendix Diner AMERICAN DINER   For the same reason that it's just plain wrong to order healthy at Big Boy, it's nutty to go for the gentler side of the menu at this funky diner. Ignore the Thai dishes and indulge in the all-American grub. The burgers are served deluxe with a heap of fries, the chili con carne (over rice with onions, peppers, and cheese) is heavy with beef and beans, and the meatloaf and mashed potatoes are better than Ma used to make. The chicken-noodle soup, with its richer-than-usual broth (no bouillon cubes here) is fabulous. Breakfast is available any time, and it's as hearty and wholesome as you'd expect. Sunday brunch gets alarmingly crowded, so bring a chunk of the *Times* to tide you over.

167 First Ave. (between 10th and 11th sts.). ℂ **212/260-4220.** Main courses $4.50–$15 (most under $10). AE, MC, V. Sun–Tues 8am–11pm; Wed–Sat 8am–1am. Subway: L to First Ave.

Cucina di Pesce *Value* ITALIAN   This crowded East Village stalwart—left over from the neighborhood's pre-trendy days—is legendary for its value. It's charming, too, if a little loud. The focus is on old-world basics like lasagna, marinara-topped pasta, shrimp scampi, and veal Marsala. Every once in a while somebody in the kitchen goes too far with a shellfish-and-mollusk combo, but by and large the offerings satisfy. The wide selection of pastas (fettuccine primavera, linguine with clam sauce) is always fresh-made and properly sauced, the veal tender, and the calamari well seasoned and crisp. The great-meal/low-price combo means that the place can be a mob scene (so to speak), but free mussels marinara at the bar makes the wait easier to take. Try to snare a seat in the garden if the weather suits. As for wine, stick with the house red, or opt for beer instead.

Note: If the wait is too long, head across the street to **Frutti di Mare,** 84 E. 4th St., at Second Avenue (ℂ **212/979-2034**), which offers up basically the same schtick, minus the mussels at the bar.

87 E. 4th St. (between Second and Third aves.). ℂ **212/260-6800.** www.cucinadipesce.com. Main courses $8–$13 (specials may be slightly higher); 3-course pre-theater dinner with glass of wine $10 (daily 3–6:30pm). No credit cards. Daily 2:30pm–midnight. Subway: F to Second Ave.

Frank ★★ *Value* ITALIAN   This home-style restaurant serves straight-from-the-boot cuisine. The menu is small but satisfying, focusing on what the kitchen does well: Rigatoni al ragu wears a meat-and-tomato "gravy" slow-cooked to perfection. It appears again on the house specialty, the *polpettone*—literally "the big meatball"—a beautifully seasoned mound of beef with a potato-and-pancetta gratin that's better than dessert in my book. The spaghetti with garlic and extra-virgin olive oil is simple, but the pasta is al dente and tossed to perfection with just the right bit of finely grated cheese; anchovy lovers should go with the fishy version. There's homemade gnocchi and ravioli, plus spiced meatloaf. The wine list is well priced, with a good selection by the glass.

The young waitstaff is easygoing and earnest, and the brick-walled room is dimly lit and attractive in a cozy way. On the downside, the tables are so close together that you can't help but overhear your neighbors' conversation; the open kitchen can make the dining room rather smoky at times; and there's often a wait (**Vera,** the bar at Frank's, offers a place to unwind with a glass of wine). But these minor inconveniences are well worth it for the marvelous payoff that is Frank fare.

Dining Zone: Little India

East 6th Street between First and Second avenues in the East Village is called "Little India," thanks to the dozen or more Indian restaurants that line the block (Subway: F to Second Ave.). Dining here isn't exactly high style; the restaurants offer decent food at discount prices, sometimes accompanied by live sitar music. It's fun to grab a bottle of wine or a six-pack (many of Little India's restaurants don't serve alcohol, but will often let you bring in your own) and cruise the strip. In warm weather, each usually stations a hawker out front to convince you that theirs is *so* much better than the competition's (and sometimes offer a discount coupon).

Some people speculate that there's just one big kitchen behind East 6th, but a few of the strip's restaurants deserve special attention. **Bombay Dining,** at 320 E. 6th St. (© **212/260-8229**), is a standout, serving excellent *samosa* (vegetable-and-meat patties), *pakora* (banana fritters), and *papadum* (crispy bean wafers with coarse peppercorns). Also try **Gandhi,** 345 E. 6th St. (© **212/614-9718**), for a touch of low-light romance; **Mitali East,** 334 E. 6th St. (© **212/533-2508**), the king of curry; and **Rose of India,** 308 E. 6th St. (© **212/533-5011**), most notable for the pure spectacle of its every-day-is-Christmas decor.

88 Second Ave. (between 5th and 6th sts.). © 212/420-0202. Reservations accepted only for parties of 8 or more. Main courses $9–$14. No credit cards. Mon–Thurs 10:30am–4pm and 5pm–12:45am; Fri–Sat 10:30am–4pm and 5pm–1:45am; Sun 10:30am–11:45pm. Subway: 6 to Astor Place.

Jeollado (*Value* ASIAN/SUSHI Sushi chef Kirjin Kim expanded to this cavernous space, which he named after his South Korean hometown. Just like its plain-Jane sister joint, Sandobe Sushi, Jeollado offers one of the best price-to-quality ratios in the city for sushi lovers. Take it from this sushi hound: You'll pay significantly more—and wait just as long—for sushi of this high quality anywhere else. The fresh fish is generously and expertly cut. The sushi combos are a good-value starting point; supplement with some sea-salty *edamame* (soybean pods) and one or two of the creative house rolls, such as the Hawaiian (ruby-red tuna and real crab meat). The Korean side of the menu features Korean pancakes, teriyaki and noodle dishes, and *bibimbop* (spiced vegetables served over rice). Service can be slow, the room can get loud, and it's almost always packed, but the efficient servers turn the tables over quickly, and the payoff is worth it.

Note: If you're in the neighborhood, Kim's original no-decor **Sandobe Sushi,** 330 E. 11th St., between First and Second avenues (© **212/780-0328**), still offers excellent sushi-meal deals at similarly low prices.

116 E. 4th St. (between First and Second aves.). © 212/260-7696. Reservations not accepted. Sushi rolls $3.40–$11.75; sushi combos $9.75–$17.75; nonsushi entrees $8–$15. No credit cards. Daily 5pm–1am. Subway: F to Second Ave.

Paul's Palace (★ *Value* AMERICAN This neighborhood diner serves some of the best burgers in the city. Every burger is a half-pounder, made from 100% pure beef or turkey. Both versions are thick, juicy, and delicious. Variations run the gamut from a slate of cheeseburgers (American, Swiss, mozzarella, cheddar, Monterey Jack, blue) to concoctions like the Texas (topped with a fried egg) and the Eastsider (a bacon cheeseburger with ham, mushrooms, tomatoes, and onions). If you're in the mood for something else, consider a Philly cheese-steak, a tuna melt, or any one of a dozen omelets. Fries are crisp and yummy. A better-than-average selection of beers is on hand, while egg creams, milk shakes, and root-beer floats offer old-fashioned comfort.

131 Second Ave. (between 7th St. and St. Marks Place). (212/529-3033 or 212/529-3097. Reservations not accepted. Burgers and main courses $2.30–$10.60. No credit cards. Sun–Thurs 11am–midnight; Fri–Sat 11am–1am. Subway: 6 to Astor Place.

Soba-Ya ★★ *Finds* JAPANESE NOODLES   Soba-Ya has a loyal following, but the masses haven't discovered it yet. That makes it easy to walk in and enjoy an affordable, healthy meal without a wait. Go with one of the special starters, which might be grilled shiitakes or luscious *toro* (tuna belly) sashimi, then move on to one of the house specialties: generous, steaming noodle bowls. They come with *soba* (thin buckwheat) or *udon* (a very thick noodle much like pasta) and in a number of combinations. A menu with descriptions and pictures makes it easy for noodle novices to order. I love the *nabeyaki,* an udon bowl with shrimp tempura, and the excellent-quality *una-don,* broiled eel over rice. Cold soba dishes topped with your choice of ingredients are also available. Everything is beautifully presented, and there's a lengthy list of sakes. The lovely blond-wood dining room is blessed with a soothing, Zen-like vibe and attentive service.

229 E. 9th St. (between Second and Third aves.). (212/533-6966. Reservations not accepted. Main courses $6.50–$14. AE, DC, DISC, MC, V. Daily noon–4pm and 5:30–10:30pm. Subway: 6 to Astor Place.

Tsampa *Finds* TIBETAN/VEGETARIAN   The Tibetan food served here is light, wholesome, and vegetarian-friendly, prepared with mostly organic produce, but not strictly vegetarian. Some of the dishes are a bit bland (skip the curry), but most are flavorfully spiced. Start with an order of *momo,* Tibet's signature dish. Momo are steamed or fried dumplings stuffed with your choice of ingredients—from chicken and veggies to tofu and chives—served with a pair of spicy red and green hot sauces. A baked udon noodle dish makes a pleasing follow-up, as does the whole grilled fish and the *sherpa khala,* baby potatoes sautéed with chicken, greens, garlic, and ginger served with Tibetan bread. A candlelit ambience and mature service makes Tsampa a good bet for budget-friendly romance.

212 E. 9th St. (between Second and Third aves.). (212/614-3226. Reservations accepted. Main courses $9–$16 (most less than $13). AE, MC, V. Daily 5–11:30pm. Subway: 6 to Astor Place.

Veselka ★ UKRAINIAN DINER   Whenever the craving hits for Eastern European fare at old-world prices, Veselka fits the bill 24 hours a day with divine *pirogi* (small, doughy envelopes filled with potatoes, cheese, or sauerkraut), *kasha varnishkes* (cracked buckwheat and noodles with mushroom sauce), stuffed cabbage, grilled Polish kielbasa, fresh-made potato pancakes, and classic soups like a sublime borscht. Breakfast is special here (see the box "Breakfast, Not Brunch!" on p. 161). The Christmas borscht, which hits the menu in early December and stays through January, is a simple but divine rendering of the Eastern European classic. But if all you want is a burger, don't worry—it's a classic, too. Save room for the delicious house-made desserts.

The atmosphere in the diner is comfortable, modern, and appealing, with an artsy slant. Regional beers from the Ukraine and Poland and a nice selection of wines from California and South America add a sophisticated touch. No wonder Veselka surpasses its status as a popular after-hours hangout with club kids and other night owls to be a favorite at any hour.

144 Second Ave. (at 9th St.). ℂ 212/228-9682. Reservations not accepted. Main courses $5–$13. AE, DC, DISC, MC, V. Daily 24 hrs. Subway: 6 to Astor Place.

Village Yokocho (Value) JAPANESE/KOREAN BARBECUE   Village Yokocho is about as authentic as Japanese restaurants get. When you enter this second-floor spot, you feel like you're stepping into a Tokyo yakitori bar, complete with a hip clientele that's a mix of Japanese and in-the-know Americans. Between the regular menu and the specials, the choices are vast. Dishes run the gamut from dumplings and yakisoba noodles to exotica such as deep-fried squid eggs. The broiled-eel bowl is finer quality than you'll get at many restaurants and a deal at $8. The yakitori skewers, both meat and veggie choices grilled over an open flame, are excellent. Korean dishes include oxtail soup and *bibinbop,* a rice bowl topped with veggies, ground beef, and a fried egg. The specials change depending on the season, but you might find soft-shell crab in ponzu sauce, broiled yellowtail with teriyaki sauce, and any number of sashimi appetizers. There's a big, affordable sake menu as well as several beers.

8 Stuyvesant St. (at Third Ave. and E. 9th St.), 2nd floor. ℂ 212/598-3041. Reservations not accepted. Main courses $4–$12. AE, MC, V. Sun–Wed 5pm–3am; Thurs–Sat 5pm–4am. Subway: 6 to Astor Place.

QUICK BITES
Adventuresome diners should seek out **Otafuku,** 236 E. 9th St., between Second and Third avenues (ℂ **212/353-8503**). Run by two Japanese women, this tiny takeout specializes in *okonomiyaki,* a Japanese pancake made with egg and flour, blended with shredded cabbage and either meat or seafood, then grilled on a hot plate and topped with a traditional sauce and curly dried bonito flakes. *Okonomiyaki* means, "cook what you like," and you can choose your ingredients: beef, pork, shrimp, or squid. It's a delicious, filling, and healthy one-dish meal that's also dirt cheap—I defy you to spend $10 here. There are no tables, but you can take your food to the Starbucks across Third Avenue, which has plenty of outdoor seating, or head to a bench in Union Square Park a few blocks north.

You'll find better-than-average, thin-crust pizza at **Lil' Frankie's Pizza,** 19 First Ave., between 1st and 2nd streets (ℂ **212/420-4900**). Try the Sicilian with the salted anchovies; you'll never scorn an anchovy pizza again. If you like your pizza on the funky side, head to the original **Two Boots** ★, 37–45 Ave. A, between 2nd and 3rd streets (ℂ **212/505-2276** or 212/254-1919; www.twoboots.com). The East Village location also boasts two entertainment spaces: The **Pioneer Theater** (ℂ **212/254-3300**), hosting independent films; and the **Den of Cin** at Two Boots Video (ℂ **212/254-1441**), a lounge hosting cult films, music, comedy, and other entertainment. Call or check the website for a schedule.

8 Greenwich Village & the Meat-Packing District

In addition to the choices below, there's an outpost of the coffeehouse/sandwich bar **Xando/Cosí** (p. 186) at 504 Sixth Ave., at 13th Street (ℂ **212/462-4188**). There's also a **Burritoville** (p. 138) at 298 Bleecker St., near Seventh Avenue (ℂ **212/633-9249**). The ultrafresh, supercheap **Go Sushi** (p. 177) is at 3 Greenwich Ave. (Sixth Ave. at 8th St.; ℂ **212/366-9272**). There's also a branch of the Belgian **Petite Abeille** (p. 162) in the West Village at 466 Hudson St., at Barrow Street (ℂ **212/741-6479**), and another at 200 W. 14th St., between Ninth and Tenth avenues (ℂ **212/727-1505**). The original and best **John's Pizzeria** ★

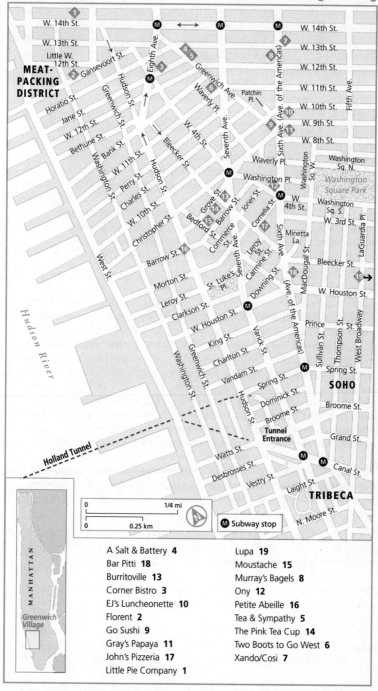

Map labels:
MEAT-PACKING DISTRICT
Hudson River
Washington Square Park
SOHO
TRIBECA
MANHATTAN
Greenwich Village
Holland Tunnel
Tunnel Entrance

Streets: W. 14th St., W. 13th St., Little W. 12th St., W. 12th St., W. 11th St., W. 10th St., W. 9th St., W. 8th St., Gansevoort St., Horatio St., Jane St., W. 12th St., Bethune St., Bank St., W. 11th St., Perry St., Charles St., W. 10th St., Christopher St., Eighth Ave., Hudson St., Greenwich St., Washington St., West St., Bleecker St., W. 4th St., Greenwich Ave., Waverly Pl., Seventh Ave., Sixth Ave. (Ave. of the Americas), Fifth Ave., Patchin Pl., Washington Sq. N., Washington Sq. S., W. 3rd St., LaGuardia Pl., Waverly Pl., Washington Pl., W. 4th St., Grove St., Barrow St., Jones St., Cornelia St., Bedford St., Commerce St., Leroy St., Carmine St., Downing St., Minetta La., MacDougal St., Bleecker St., W. Houston St., Barrow St., Morton St., St. Luke's Pl., Leroy St., Clarkson St., W. Houston St., King St., Charlton St., Vandam St., Varick St., Spring St., Dominick St., Broome St., Prince St., Sullivan St., Thompson St., West Broadway, Spring St., Broome St., Grand St., Watts St., Desbrosses St., Vestry St., Laight St., Canal St., N. Moore St.

0   1/4 mi
0   0.25 km

Ⓜ Subway stop

A Salt & Battery 4
Bar Pitti 18
Burritoville 13
Corner Bistro 3
EJ's Luncheonette 10
Florent 2
Go Sushi 9
Gray's Papaya 11
John's Pizzeria 17
Little Pie Company 1

Lupa 19
Moustache 15
Murray's Bagels 8
Ony 12
Petite Abeille 16
Tea & Sympathy 5
The Pink Tea Cup 14
Two Boots to Go West 6
Xando/Cosi 7

is at 278 Bleecker St., between Sixth and Seventh avenues (© **212/243-1680**); see the box "Pizza New York Style" on p. 157. Two spinoffs from the popular Two Boots pizzerias can be found in Greenwich Village at **Two Boots to Go West,** 201 W. 11th St., at Seventh Avenue (© **212/633-9096**), or **Two Boots to Go-Go,** 74 Bleecker St., at Broadway (© **212/777-1033**).

Also you'll find **Murray's Bagels** at 500 Sixth Ave., between 12th and 13th streets (© **212/466-2830**); see the box "Bagel Power" on p. 183.

A Salt & Battery BRITISH   Adjacent to tearoom Tea & Sympathy (see below) and a shop selling Cadbury Flake bars, Hob Nob biscuits, and other English groceries and trinkets, this is this newest addition to Nicky Perry's burgeoning Pax Brittania. This shop is so genuine that they serve the goods wrapped in newspaper. Stick with the traditional varieties (halibut, cod) and you'll enjoy the real thing (crisp-battered outside, flaky and greaseless inside). The room is tiny, with no more than six or eight seats, so come at an off hour or be prepared to wait—but it's worth it. English beers are available, of course.

112 Greenwich Ave. (between 12th and 13th sts.). © 212/691-2713. www.asaltandbattery.com. Reservations not accepted. Main courses $5–$13. AE, MC, V. Daily noon–10pm. Subway: A, C, E, 1, 2, 3, 9 to 14th St. Also at 80 Second Ave. (between 4th and 5th sts.; © 212/254-6610; subway: F to Second Ave.).

Bar Pitti ⭐ ⟨Value⟩ TUSCAN ITALIAN   This indoor/outdoor trattoria is a hip sidewalk scene, and one of downtown's best dining bargains. Waiting for a table can be a chore, but all is forgiven once you take a seat, thanks to authentic, affordably priced cuisine and some of the friendliest waiters in town. Despite the packed seating, Bar Pitti wins you over with Italian charm—it's the kind of place where the waiter brings over the list of daily specials on a blackboard, and if you want more cheese, a block of Parmesan and a grater suddenly appear. Peruse the menu, but don't get your heart set on anything until you see the board, which boasts the best of what the kitchen has to offer; on my last visit, they wowed me with fabulous veal meatballs. Winners off the regular menu, which focuses heavily on pastas and panini, include excellent beef carpaccio; grilled country bread with prosciutto, garlic, and olive oil; and spinach-and-ricotta ravioli in a creamy sage and Parmesan sauce. The all-Italian wine list is high-priced compared to the menu, but you'll find a few good-value choices.

268 Sixth Ave. (between Bleecker and Houston sts.). © 212/982-3300. Reservations accepted for parties of 4 or more. Main courses $7.50–$16 (some specials may be higher). No credit cards. Daily noon–midnight. Subway: A, C, E, F, V to W. 4th St. (use 3rd St. exit).

Corner Bistro BURGERS   This old-time neighborhood bar serves up what some people (including *The Daily Show*'s Jon Stewart) consider to be the best burger in the city. Its well-charred, beefy burgers are deservedly famous—and you'd be hard-pressed to dine so well for so little anywhere else. The top of the line is the bistro burger, with bacon, cheese, lettuce, and tomato, for 5 bucks. The thin, crispy fries, served up on a paper plate, are an appropriate accompaniment. Head elsewhere if you want something besides a burger, because the other offerings are limited and half-hearted, except for the chili. Service can be slow, but why bother being in a rush at an atmospheric neighborhood locale like this?

331 W. 4th St. (at Jane St., near Eighth Ave.). © 212/242-9502. Reservations not accepted. Burgers and sandwiches $2.50–$6. No credit cards. Mon–Sat 11am–3:30am; Sun noon–3:30am. Subway: A, C, E to 14th St.

EJ's Luncheonette ⟨Kids⟩ AMERICAN DINER   This retro diner is popular with all Village types, including yuppies and their kids, who come for hearty

Value Pizza New York Style

Once the domain of countless first-rate pizzerias, Manhattan's pizza offerings have noticeably dropped in quality. The proliferation of national chains into the market has lowered pizza standards. Still, there is plenty of good pizza to be found. Don't be tempted by imitations; when it comes to pizza, search out the real deal. In alphabetical order, these are some of the best pizzerias in Manhattan.

Grimaldi's. 19 Old Fulton St., between Front and Water streets (© 718/858-4300). If you need incentive to walk across the Brooklyn Bridge, Grimaldi's, in Brooklyn Heights, provides it. The pizza is so good, made in a coal oven with a flavorful sauce and homemade mozzarella, you might run across the bridge to get to it. Be warned: It can get very crowded at dinnertime, so pick your spots here.

John's. 278 Bleecker St., near Seventh Avenue S. (© 212/243-1680). Expansion (there are now four outlets in the city) has slightly diminished the luster of John's, but the pizza is still a cut above all the rest. Thin-crusted and cooked in a coal oven with the proper ratio of tomato sauce to cheese, John's has a very loyal following. Though the quality at all of the locations is good, the original Bleecker Street location is the most old-world romantic and my favorite.

Lombardi's. 32 Spring St., between Mulberry and Mott streets (© 212/941-7994). Claiming to be New York's first "licensed" pizzeria, Lombardi's opened in 1905 and still uses a generations-old Neopolitan family pizza recipe. The coal oven kicks out perfectly cooked pies, some topped with ingredients such as pancetta (Italian bacon), homemade sausage, and even freshly shucked clams. It's hard to go wrong here, no matter what topping. A garden in the back makes it even more inviting during warm weather.

Patsy's. 2287 First Ave., between 117th and 118th streets (© 212/534-9783). My favorite and also the favorite of Frank Sinatra, who liked it so much he had its pies flown out to Las Vegas. The coal oven here has been burning since 1932, and though this East Harlem neighborhood has had its ups and downs, the quality of pizza has never wavered. Try the marinara pizza, a pie with fresh marinara sauce but no cheese that's so good you won't miss the mozzarella. Unlike the other pizzerias here, you can order by the slice at Patsy's. Don't be fooled by imitators; this is the original and the best.

American fare in a 1950s setting—vinyl booths, Formica tabletops, a soda fountain, and a lunch counter with stools that spin. The menu features a large selection of breakfasts so good you won't be ashamed of indulging in a stack of banana-pecan pancakes for dinner. There's also a terrific selection of burgers (including a great veggie version), sandwiches, salads, and main dishes such as meatloaf with mashed potatoes. Everything is better than you'd expect, and service is friendly. Don't miss the amazing sweet-potato fries. Weekend brunch is a big deal at all three locations, but expect a wait.

432 Sixth Ave. (between 9th and 10th sts.). ✆ **212/473-5555.** Reservations not accepted. Main courses $4–$12. AE. Sun–Thurs 8:30am–10:30pm; Fri–Sat 8:30am–11pm. Subway: A, C, E, F, V to W. 4th St. (use 8th St. exit). Also at 447 Amsterdam Ave. (between 81st and 82nd sts.; ✆ **212/873-3444;** subway: 1, 9 to 79th St.); 1271 Third Ave. (at 73rd St.; ✆ **212/472-0600;** subway: 6 to 77th St.).

Emerald Planet ⭐ INTERNATIONAL/WRAPS   This San Francisco import led the charge to bury the sandwich and replace it with the wrap, a phenomenon that has reached every mall in America by now. The Emerald Planet ideology is simple: You can eat wraps at every meal, from bacon and eggs (the Omaha) in the morning to fresh grilled veggies with goat cheese (the Sonoma) at noon to jerk chicken, mango salsa, and jasmine rice (the Kingston) at dinner. All ingredients are fresh, and the emphasis is on healthy.

2 Great Jones St. (at Broadway). ✆ 212/353-9727. www.emeraldplanet.citysearch.com. Wraps $5–$8; smoothies $4–$5. AE, MC, V. Mon–Fri 9am–10pm; Sat noon–10pm; Sun noon–8pm. Subway: 6 to Bleecker St.; N, R to 8th St. Also at 30 Rockefeller Plaza, lower concourse level (down the hall from the skating rink; ✆ 212/218-1133; subway: B, D, F, Q to 47th–50th sts./Rockefeller Center).

Florent _Kids_ DINER/FRENCH BISTRO   In the heart of the Meat-Packing District, Florent, the nearly 24-hour French bistro dressed up as a '50s-style diner, is a perennial hot spot no matter what time of day; a children's menu makes this the perfect place to bring the kids for lunch or early dinner. But it's after the clubs close when the joint really jumps. Tables are tightly packed, almost uncomfortably so in some cases, but it's all part of the late-night festivities. This place has a real sense of humor (check out the menu boards above the bar) and a CD catalog full of the latest indie sounds, all adding to the hipster fun. The food's good, too: The grilled chicken with herbs and mustard sauce is a winner, moist and flavorful, as is the French onion soup crowned with melted Gruyère. There are always diner faves like burgers and chili, in addition to Gallic standards like _moules frites;_ and the comfort-food specialties such as chicken potpie make regular appearances. The fries are light, crispy, and addictive.

69 Gansevoort St. (2 blocks south of 14th St. and 1 block west of Ninth Ave., between Greenwich and Washington sts.). ✆ 212/989-5779. www.restaurantflorent.com. Reservations recommended for dinner. Main courses $4.50–$14.50 at brunch and lunch, $8–$20.50 at dinner (most less than $15); 2-course fixed-price lunches $8.25–$11.95; 3-course fixed-price dinner $18.95 before 7:30pm, $20.95 7:30pm–midnight. No credit cards. Mon–Thurs 9am–5am; Fri–Sun 24 hrs. Subway: A, C, E, L to 14th St.

Lupa ⭐⭐ _Value_ CENTRAL ITALIAN   Mario Batali, the man behind the acclaimed and expensive Babbo and the Food Network's "Molto Mario," operates this Roman-style trattoria. Reservations are taken for the back room only, and I advise you to get them, as it's quieter and more civilized. The front room is for walk-ins; it's loud and cramped and you'll probably have to wait unless you come early, but the food is worth it.

Don't be scared off by the all-Italian menu; the butcher-coated waiter will steer you through the language and preparations. It's a short list, but one that boasts lots of treats. As always with Mario, the pastas stand out: The _bucatini all'amatriciana,_ a classic Italian tube pasta in a smoky tomato sauce made from hog jowl (bacon), is divine, as is the ricotta gnocchi with Italian sausage and fennel. Don't miss an opportunity to start with the _prosciutto di carpegna_ with roasted figs, an ideal marriage of salt and sweet; it's easy to build a value-packed meal from the list of antipasti. Among the main courses, the classic saltimbocca was a disappointment, but the oven-roasted littleneck clams with sweet _soppressata_ (salami) was a joy. The wine list is massive and superaffordable.

170 Thompson St. (between Houston and Bleecker sts.). © **212/982-5089.** www.luparestaurant.com. Reservations highly recommended. Antipasti $5–$12; main courses $9–$17; 4-course prix fixe $30 at lunch, $45 at dinner (only for parties of 7 or more). AE, DC, MC, V. Daily noon–2:45pm and 5:30–11:30pm. Subway: 1, 9 to Houston St.

Moustache ⟨Value⟩ MIDDLE EASTERN

Moustache (pronounced moo-*stahsh*) is the sort of exotic neighborhood spot that's just right. On a side street in the West Village, this charming hole-in-the-wall boasts a Middle Eastern vibe and fare that's both palate-pleasing and wallet-friendly. Delicately seasoned dishes bear little resemblance to the food at your average falafel joint. Expect subtly flavored hummus, tabbouleh, and spinach-chickpea-tomato salad (or a large plate of all three); oven-roasted "pitzas," thin, matzolike pita crusts topped with spicy minced lamb and other ingredients; and—best of all—homemade pita bread, which puts any of those store-bought Frisbees to shame. Moustache is hugely popular, so don't be surprised if there's a line—but it's worth the wait.

90 Bedford St. (between Barrow and Grove sts.). © **212/229-2220.** Reservations not accepted. Main courses $5–$12. No credit cards. Daily noon–midnight (last order at 11pm). Subway: 1, 9 to Christopher St. Also at 265 E. 10th St. (between First Ave. and Ave. A; © **212/228-2022;** subway: L to First Ave.).

Ony JAPANESE NOODLES

This smart, stylish noodle shop is a welcome addition to a less-than-attractive stretch of Sixth Avenue. The specialty is *men-chanko,* a ramen-noodle soup served in a soy, miso, or tomato broth with your choice of fresh ingredients, from chicken and shrimp to tofu to kimchee and fresh vegetables—or all of the above. Menchanko arrives piping hot at your table in a large metal bowl, with both chopsticks and a ladle for easy sipping and slurping. A handful of other noodle dishes are also on hand, including udon bowls and cold soba (buckwheat) noodle dishes, plus a short sushi-roll menu— but this place is all about the noodles. The room is attractive, and service professional. Pony up to the sleek noodle bar if you're in a hurry.

357 Sixth Ave. (between W. 4th St. and Washington Place). © **212/414-8429.** Reservations not accepted. Noodle bowls $7.75–$9.75; sushi $4.50–$11. AE, MC, V. Daily 11am–1am. Subway: A, C, E, F, V to W. 4th St. (use 3rd St. exit).

The Pink Tea Cup ⟨Value⟩ SOUL FOOD

This simple soul-food joint has been serving smothered pork chops, fried chicken, barbecue, and other hearty fare to New Yorkers since 1954. Portions are large, and every dinner comes with your choice of two vegetables, soup *and* salad, bread, and Jell-O or bread pudding for dessert. Tops among the main courses are the chicken and dumplings, in a thick, flavorful broth. If you're in the mood for something simpler, opt for a fried-catfish or roast-beef sandwich, or a satisfying burger (served with pie and coffee for just $5.50). Spend a couple extra dollars on a side of macaroni and cheese—you won't be disappointed. Another worthy extra: the coconut cake. Service is efficient and attentive, and the old-fashioned jukebox boasts selections from R&B legends. Feel free to bring your own beer or wine. ***One word of warning:*** The restroom sits at the bottom of a tiny, vertigo-inducing spiral staircase.

42 Grove St. (between Bleecker and Bedford sts.). © **212/807-6755.** www.thepinkteacup.com. Reservations not accepted. Breakfast $4–$9.25; sandwiches and burger combos $3–$9.25; complete dinners (including soup, salad, and dessert) $9.25–$15.25. No credit cards. Mon–Thurs 8am–midnight; Fri–Sun 8am–1am. Subway: 1, 9 to Christopher St.

Tea & Sympathy BRITISH

When Londoner Nicky Perry moved to New York, she was disappointed to find no proper British tearoom, so she opened her own. Tea & Sympathy seems transplanted wholesale from Greenwich or

Highgate, complete with an oddball collection of creamers and teapots, snappy British waitstaff, and plenty of charm. Elbow room is at a minimum and the place is usually packed, but it's worth the squeeze for the full afternoon tea, which comes on a tiered tray with crust-off finger sandwiches like chicken salad and egg and 'cress, scones with jam and Devonshire cream, and cakes and cookies for a sugary finish. The menu also features such traditional British comforts as shepherd's pie, bangers and mash, and a chicken-and-leek pie. Anglophiles line up for the Sunday dinner—roast beef and Yorkshire pudding, of course. For dessert, try the treacle pudding, ginger cake, or yummy sherry trifle.

108 Greenwich Ave. (between 12th and 13th sts.). ℂ 212/807-8329 or 212/989-9735. www.teaand sympathynewyork.com. Reservations not accepted. Main courses $5.50–$12 at lunch and brunch, $10.50–$17 at dinner; full afternoon tea $19 ($35 for 2). MC, V. Daily 11:30am–10pm. Subway: 1, 2, 3, 9, A, C, E to 14th St.

QUICK BITES

There's a downtown location of Upper West Side classic **Gray's Papaya,** 402 Sixth Ave., at 8th Street (ℂ **212/260-3532**). Hot dogs are just as cheap, but beware: Don't eat more than two. They're rather greasy.

Gourmet grocer **Dean & Deluca** has a cafe at 11th Street and University Place (ℂ **212/473-1908**), a great stop for a sandwich or cafe au lait and pastry.

9 Chelsea

In addition to the choices below, **Burritoville** (p. 138) is at 264 W. 23rd St., between Seventh and Eighth avenues (ℂ **212/367-9844**).

Antique Cafe ✦ CAFE   I love the atmosphere and the beautifully prepared food at this brick-walled cafe, named for the flea markets that fill the nearby Sixth Avenue parking lots on weekends (see chapter 8). The cafe is always fragrant with the aroma of fresh-baked goods. There's no printed menu; instead, the day's bill of fare features whatever's fresh, including homemade soups, bounteous salads, gourmet sandwiches that run the gamut from roast beef to peanut-butter-and-jelly, quiche, and pastries and cappuccino. Making regular appearances are a terrific bruschetta with melted Swiss, mushroom, and onion ($3.50); a dynamite haddock chowder ($3.75); a London-broil salad boasting a beautiful cut, tomatoes, red onions, and cilantro over mixed greens ($6.25); and a simple, healthy chicken paella with salad ($6). Order at the friendly counter and take a seat at one of the small cafe tables indoors or out, or take your food over to Madison Square Park.

101 W. 25th St. (just west of Sixth Ave.). ℂ 212/675-1663. All items less than $8. No credit cards. Daily 7:30am–6:30pm. Subway: F to 23rd St.

Empire Diner AMERICAN DINER *(Overrated)*   This throwback to the all-American diner looks like an Airstream camper plunked down on the corner. This classic joint boasts an Art Deco vibe, honest coffee, and great mashed potatoes. The food is diner fare: eggs, omelets, burgers, sandwiches, and a nice turkey platter. Frankly, I think it's overrated—you'll find better breakfast fare elsewhere—but there's no denying its status as a fixture on the late-night scene. If you want quiet, go early. If you want an eyeful, wait for the after-hours crowd; 1 to 3am offers the best people-watching. There's live music courtesy of a regular pianist. When the weather's warm, a pleasing sidewalk cafe appears, and the limited traffic this far West keeps the soot-and-fumes factor down.

210 Tenth Ave. (at 22nd St.). ℂ 212/243-2736. Reservations not accepted. Main courses $9–$18. AE, DC, DISC, MC, V. Daily 24 hr. Subway: C, E to 23rd St.

Tips Breakfast, Not Brunch!

Brunch has always been a pet peeve of mine. I mean, what is it really but a slightly fancier version of breakfast at inflated prices? It's not served until mid-morning—and only on weekends . . . what a scam! I'll take breakfast over brunch any day—especially on weekends. Here are some of my favorite restaurants for the morning meal:

Bubby's ★. 120 Hudson St., at North Moore Street (© **212/219-0666;** www.bubbys.com). I don't usually order grits north of the Mason-Dixon line, but I make an exception at Bubby's. They are the perfect complement to Bubby's Breakfast: two eggs, toast, bacon, and a cup of Joe. Open at 8am Monday through Friday and 9am Saturday and Sunday. See p. 140.

EJ's Luncheonette. 447 Amsterdam Ave., between 81st and 82nd streets (© **212/873-3444**), and two other locations. The Greek diners that served cheap breakfasts were everywhere when I first moved to Manhattan, but most have gone the way of the Checker cab; they're practically extinct. In their place you will find retro diners like EJ's that try to replicate the legendary breakfasts of those diners. And in reality, the breakfasts at the retro diners, though not as cheap, are better than I remember. At EJ's, the banana-pecan pancakes are so good you might want to return and have them for dinner. Opens at 8:30am daily. See p. 156.

Good Enough To Eat ★. 483 Amsterdam Ave., between 83rd and 84th streets (© **212/496-0163;** www.citysearch.com/nyc/goodenough). The wait for breakfast on weekends at this Upper West Side institution is ridiculous. So go during the week, when you can gorge on pumpkin French toast; a "Wall Street" omelet, baked honey-mustard glazed ham with Vermont cheddar, or "Peter Paul" pancakes, filled with Belgian chocolate chips and topped with roasted coconut. I'm getting hungry writing this! Opens at 8am Monday through Friday and 9am Saturday and Sunday. See p. 184.

New Big Wong ★. 67 Mott St., between Canal and Bayard streets (© **212/964-1452**). No eggs. No coffee. No pancakes. Can it be breakfast? You bet it is! You'll find a breakfast of a hot bowl of congee, rice porridge with pork, beef, or shrimp accompanied with a fried cruller and tea served in a glass, unusual but eminently satisfying. Big Wong is a breakfast favorite among the residents of Chinatown. Opens daily at 8:30am. See p. 142.

Veselka ★. 144 Second Ave., at 9th Street (© **212/228-9682**). The Greek diner might be extinct in Manhattan, but this Ukranian diner lives on. And we are grateful, because New York wouldn't be the same without Veselka's buckwheat pancakes and cheese blintzes. Open 24 hours. See p. 153.

F&B ★ *Finds* INTERNATIONAL/GOURMET SANDWICHES Budget-minded New Yorkers have rejoiced at the arrival of F&B, which serves a global menu of European street food (Danish and German hot dogs, Swedish meatballs,

Belgian frites, New Orleans beignets) in a stylish powder-blue space. The signature dog comes in a variety of styles, from the Great Dane, a Danish dog dressed with rémoulade, roast onions, marinated cucumber slices, Danish mustard, and ketchup on a toasted bun; to Pups in a Blanket, adorable minidogs in puff pastry served with honey mustard. A veggie dog is also available. The warm beignets come brushed with powdered sugar and your choice of dips, including chocolate, maple syrup, and crème anglaise. The crispy twice-cooked frites come accompanied with your choice of a range of flavored butters, oils, and dips, including a yummy garlic aioli. You can wash it down with Belgian-style beers, ciders, wine, and even champagne. Delivery is available if you're staying in the area.

269 W. 23rd St. (between Seventh and Eighth aves.). ℂ 646/486-4441. Reservations not accepted. Main courses $1.50–$10. AE, MC, V. Daily 11am–11pm. Subway: C, E to 23rd St.

Grand Sichuan International ⭐ _Value_ SZECHUAN CHINESE Grand Sichuan serves up real Chinese here in Chelsea. This comfortable spot has garnered raves for its authentic Szechuan cuisine. Spicy-food lovers will be thrilled, as the kitchen excels at dishes that are intensely spiced but not numbing—a balance that few Chinatown kitchens can achieve. The flavors are complex and strong, especially in such choices as Szechuan wontons in red oil, Chairman Mao's pork with chestnuts, and my favorite, boneless whole fish with pine nuts in a modified sweet-and-sour sauce. The house bean curd in spicy sauce is another winner, but only for those with a high tolerance for hot. The staff will be happy to recommend milder dishes.

229 Ninth Ave. (at 24th St.). ℂ 212/620-5200. Reservations accepted for parties of 3 or more. Main courses $3.25–$14. AE, DC, MC, V. Daily 11:30am–11pm. Subway: C, E to 23rd St. Also at 745 Ninth Ave. (between 50th and 51st sts.; ℂ 212/582-2288; subway: C, E to 50th St.).

Johny's Grill & Luncheonette _Value_ GREEK/AMERICAN DINER This neighborhood greasy spoon offers up cheap eats and a dose of local color. Johny has been running the grill for over 25 years; his dad makes the soups and specials from the kitchen in the back. The personal-size pita pizzas are incredible, with the grilled chicken the best among the terrific choices. To order like an insider, sidle up to the long counter and use the burger code (not on the menu—it's secret code among Johny and his regulars): a "full house" is a burger with the works (lettuce, tomato, onion, and pickle), while a "deluxe" is a full house plus fries. Other specialties include grilled sandwiches like the Big Mo (roast beef, coleslaw, and cheese) or the Florentine (grilled chicken, spinach, and feta cheese). Both the TV and radio are usually on, and Johny usually knows the score.

124 W. 25th St. (between Sixth and Seventh aves.). ℂ 212/243-6230. Breakfast $1.25–$4.50; sandwiches, burgers, and salads $2.50–$6. No credit cards. Mon–Sat 8am–3:45pm. Subway: 1, 9, F to 23rd St.

Petite Abeille BELGIAN This delightful cafe serves Belgian fare to a loyal local crowd that returns each day for morning pastries, quiches, salads, sandwiches, and sweets. Start with a fresh-from-the-oven _pain au chocolat_ or cream-cheese croissant, and return at lunch for a fresh-baked quiche; panini bread dressed with Black-Forest ham, Swiss cheese, and pineapple; a beautiful niçoise salad; or a traditional Belgian dish like _les carbonnades à la Flamande,_ a classic Belgian stew. In addition to a first-rate espresso bar, a full selection of Samantha and Looza Nectar juices are on hand.

107 W. 18th St. (at Sixth Ave.). ℂ 212/604-9350 or 212/367-9062. Main courses $5.25–$11.25 (most under $8). AE, MC, V. Mon–Fri 7am–7pm; Sat–Sun 9am–5pm. Subway: F to 14th St. Also at 400 W. 14th St. (between

Ninth and Tenth aves.; ℂ 212/727-1505; subway: A, C, E to 14th St.); 466 Hudson St. (at Barrow St.; ℂ 212/741-6479; subway: 1, 9 to Christopher St.); 134 W. Broadway (between Duane and Thomas sts.; ℂ 212/791-1360; subway: 1, 2, 3, 9 to Chambers St.).

Rue des Crepes ★★ *Value* FRENCH   Seldom do decor, quality, and service come together so well in such an affordable restaurant. Evoking a Parisian cafe with muraled walls, tiled floors, Art Nouveau lamps, and petite tables, the dining room is comfortable and romantic. Chef Michael Kalajian, a Culinary Institute of America graduate and former student of four-star chef Charlie Palmer, whips up light-as-air buckwheat (and cholesterol-free) crepes and folds them around a host of savory fillings, from classics like turkey and brie to spicy Moroccan *merguez* sausage accompanied by white beans and roasted garlic. Vegetarian options are available, including yummy homemade hummus and roasted veggies. Soups and salads are also served; sandwiches are prepared on fresh baguettes from Amy's Bread, and pre-prepared ones are ready to go in the take-out case. Dessert crepes come with your choice of fillings; my favorite is the "Sidewalk," a classic preparation with butter, sugar, lemon, and chocolate, but fresh-fruit and fat-free vanilla-cream options are on hand for waist-watchers. You'll order at the counter, but a server takes over from there. Beer and wine are available. ***Money-saving tip:*** Check the website for a 10%-off coupon.

104 Eighth Ave. (between 15th and 16th sts.). ℂ 212/242-9900. www.ruedescrepes.com. Reservations not accepted. Main courses $6–$9. AE, MC, V. Sun–Thurs 11am–11pm; Fri–Sat 11am–1am. Subway: A, C, E to 14th St.

QUICK BITES

At Chelsea Market, 75 Ninth Ave., between 15th and 16th streets, a second branch of **Amy's Bread** (ℂ 212/462-4338) has cafe tables where you can enjoy a light bite for breakfast or lunch.

There's also the wonderful **Little Pie Company** at 407 W. 14th St., west of Ninth Avenue (ℂ 212/414-2324), where you can sit at a table or pull up a stool at the counter and dig in to one of the classic pies and cakes, which many consider New York's best; the sour-cream apple is divine.

10 The Flatiron District, Union Square & Gramercy Park

In addition to the choices below, you can find **Xando/Cosí** (p. 186) at 841 Broadway, at 13th Street (ℂ 212/614-8544), and 257 Park Ave. S., between 20th and 21st streets (ℂ 212/598-9300). For baked goods and sandwiches and salads, try **Le Pain Quotidien** ★★ (p. 148) at ABC Carpet & Home, 38 E. 19th St., between Broadway and Park Avenue South (ℂ 212/625-9009).

Blue Smoke ★ *Finds* BARBECUE/SOUTHERN   Leave it to Danny Meyer, the impresario behind classic restaurants like the Union Square Café and the Gramercy Tavern, to create a restaurant where you can order a smoked bologna sandwich. For many, that might be a culinary risk; for Meyer, it is another triumph. The big chunk of smoked homemade bologna is nothing like what you used to throw between two slices of bread. Meyer claims that Blue Smoke was his effort to replicate the barbecue he grew up on in St. Louis. He even had a high-tech smoker built to slowly, lovingly cook the meats. The ribs come in three varieties: Memphis baby backs, salt and pepper dry rubbed, and St. Louis spare ribs, all tender to the bone, with the St. Louis variety, glazed in a mild barbecue sauce, the clear winner. Though the meats are the attraction, the side dishes are as good as I've tasted anywhere, especially the collard greens, speckled with pieces of pork, and the slow-cooked green beans, oozing with flavor. The house Blue Smoke Ale is the perfect hearty complement to the rich food.

116 E. 27th St. (between Park and Lexington aves.). ⟨ℂ⟩ **212/447-7733.** www.bluesmoke.com. Reservations suggested. Main courses $10–$22. AE, DC, DISC, MC, V. Open daily 11:30am–11pm, Late-night menu Wed–Sat 11pm–1am. Subway: 6 to 28th St.

Chat 'n' Chew AMERICAN   Looking for a place to get a square meal that won't break the bank or leave you hungry? Then head to this hole-in-the-wall that excels at down-home cooking. In fact, the space is so down-homey it's on the brink of becoming a theme restaurant, but the chow's the real thing. Look for honey-dipped fried chicken, roast turkey with all the fixin's, barbecue pork chops with skin-on mashed potatoes, and mac 'n' cheese as crispy on the outside as it is gooey on the inside. There are a few unnecessary nods to contemporary tastes—if you're looking for grilled tuna, you don't belong here—but the only real misstep is the meatloaf, which is a disappointment. Weekend brunch sees such standards as oatmeal with brown sugar and omelets with honey-baked ham on the side. Portions are all large, service is snappy, and beer's available. Desserts are of the Duncan Hines layer-cake variety, and the soda fountain serves up everything from egg creams to Häagen-Dazs shakes. The crowd mainly consists of the young and hip (who can afford to throw caution to the wind when it comes to calories), but everyone will feel perfectly welcome.

10 E. 16th St. (between Fifth Ave. and Union Sq. W.). ⟨ℂ⟩ **212/243-1616.** www.chatnchew.citysearch.com. Reservations not accepted. Sandwiches and salads $6–$11; main courses $7–$14. AE, MC, V. Mon–Fri 11:30am–midnight; Sat 10:30am–midnight; Sun 10:30am–11pm. Subway: L, N, R, Q, W, 4, 5, 6 to 14th St./Union Sq.

Eisenberg's Coffee Shop *Finds* SANDWICHES   Eisenberg's has always been, and remains, the real deal. This old-world luncheonette has been dishing up the same eggs/bacon/burgers/sandwiches since 1929, at pretty much the same prices—adjusted for inflation, of course, but still welcomingly wallet-friendly.

One of the best things about Eisenberg's is the staff, some of whom have seemingly been there since the Eisenhower era. More likely than not, you'll be greeted with a growled "Hiya, sweetheart," or a gravelly "What'll it be, love?" Pony up to the long counter or nab one of the four or five tables and place your order. Is this the best tuna in town as often proclaimed? Decide for yourself. Or try the egg or chicken salad. Either way, you won't go wrong. Morning diners can choose from a number of egg dishes, including a Western omelet or pastrami and eggs. The egg cream—that frothy mix of milk, chocolate syrup, and real from-the-bottle seltzer—is the real deal. Service is fast and efficient.

174 Fifth Ave. (at 22nd St.). ⟨ℂ⟩ **212/675-5096.** Reservations not accepted. Main courses $2.25–$7.25. No credit cards. Mon–Fri 6am–5pm; Sat 7:30am–4pm. Subway: N, R to 23rd St.

L'Express FRENCH   This round-the-clock French bistro is a favorite of New Yorkers for affordable anytime fare. The service is friendly and attentive, and the mood-lit room comfortable and romantic in the evening; the food is respectable, if not fabulous. I like the appetizers best, especially the escargots in butter and herbs, the onion tart, *boudin noir* (blood sausage) with caramelized apples and mashed potato, and the good house paté. Among the mains are a roasted half-chicken, a juicy lamb burger, and roasted rabbit in Dijon-mustard sauce; skip the boeuf bourguignon, which is hiding a poor cut. Wines are somewhat pricey, averaging $7 a glass, but a large selection of imported beers is on hand, including Trappist ales. The dense, gooey French bread that comes with every meal is worth the price of a meal. Daytime diners will feel perfectly welcome to camp out for a couple of hours, nursing a cup of tea and delving into a good book.

249 Park Ave. S. (at 20th St.). ℂ 212/254-5858. Reservations accepted for parties of 5 or more only. Main courses $2–$7.50 at breakfast, $5–$15 at lunch, $9–$18 at dinner (most less than $15). AE, MC, V. Open daily 24 hr. Subway: 6 to 23rd St.

Lyric Diner AMERICAN   Want to know where the good diners are? Follow the cops. On the east side, you'll find 'em at the Lyric, which dishes out good, straightforward diner fare in a clean, bright, well-lit space. Expect all the diner standards: hot open sandwiches, Monte Cristos and Reubens, burgers, and stuffed baked potatoes. Breakfast is served 'round the clock, of course.

283 Third Ave. (at 22nd St.). ℂ 212/213-2222. Reservations not accepted. Breakfast (served all day) $2.75–$11 (most less than $7); sandwiches and salads $2.25–$11; dinner $10–$18 (including soup or salad). AE, MC, V. Open daily 24 hr. Subway: 6 to 23rd St.

Molly's Pub & Restaurant Sheeben IRISH   Molly's is a real-deal Irish pub, complete with Tudor detailing, a fireplace creating a warm and toasty ambience, and a back room with checked tablecloths, photos covering every inch of wall space, and waitresses bringing you three types of mustard with your corned beef and cabbage. The menu also features lamb stew, beer-battered fish and chips, and a perfect shepherd's pie, as well as a good burger and entree-size salads. Sandwiches come with fries; dinners come with salad and Irish soda bread. The jukebox features familiar tunes and is set at a pleasant volume. Tuck into a genuine Irish breakfast on weekends, complete with white and black puddings (baked beans $1.25 extra).

287 Third Ave. (between 22nd and 23rd sts.). ℂ 212/889-3361. www.mollys.citysearch.com. Reservations not accepted. Main courses $9–$13 at brunch; $6.50–$16 at lunch (most less than $12); $8–$19 at dinner (most less than $14). AE, DC, DISC, MC, V. Mon–Wed 11:30am–midnight; Thurs–Sun 11:30am–2am (bar until 4am). Subway: 6 to 23rd St.

Old Town Bar & Restaurant ✦ AMERICAN   If you've watched TV at all over the last couple of decades, this place should look familiar: It was featured in the old *Late Night with David Letterman* intro, starred as Riff's Bar in *Mad About You*, and appeared in such movies as *The Devil's Own, Bullets Over Broadway,* and *The Last Days of Disco.* But this is no stage set—it's a genuine tin-ceilinged 19th-century bar serving up good pub grub, lots of beers on tap, and a sense of history. Sure, there are salads on the menu, but everybody comes for the burgers. Whether you go low-fat turkey or bacon-chili-cheddar, they're perfect every time. You have your choice of sides, but go with the shoestring fries. Other good choices include Buffalo wings, fiery bowls of chili with cheddar cheese and sour cream, and a Herculean Caesar salad slathered with mayo and topped with anchovies. Food comes up from the basement kitchen courtesy of ancient dumbwaiters behind the bar, where equally crusty bartenders would rather *not* make you a Cosmopolitan, thank you very much.

45 E. 18th St. (between Broadway and Park Ave. S.). ℂ 212/529-6732. Reservations not accepted. Main courses $6–$12. AE, MC, V. Mon–Fri 11:30am–midnight; Sat–Sun 12:30pm–midnight. Subway: L, N, R, Q, W, 4, 5, 6 to 14th St./Union Sq.

Republic PAN-ASIAN/NOODLES   Proving once and for all that you don't have to sacrifice style for wallet-friendly prices, this chic noodle joint serves up affordable food in a neighborhood where it's getting harder to find an affordable meal. Cushionless, backless benches pulled up to pine-and-steel tables don't encourage lingering, but that's the point: This is the kind of place that knows how to make you feel happy and get you out the door quickly. The Chinese, Vietnamese, and Thai-inspired noodle menu attracts a stream of on-the-go customers. For a one-bowl meal, try the spicy coconut chicken (chicken slices in coconut milk, lime juice, lemon grass, and galangal) or spicy beef (rare beef with wheat noodles spiced with chiles, garlic, and lemon grass). Service is friendly. The long, curving bar is perfect for solitary diners in the daytime and during the early-dinner hour; later, it livens up with a crowd who come to enjoy such libations as the Sake Dragon (sake and Chambord) and Fuji apple Cosmopolitan.

37 Union Sq. W. (between 16th and 17th sts.). ℂ **212/627-7172.** Reservations accepted for parties of 10 or more. Main courses $7–$9. AE, DISC, MC, V. Sun–Wed 11:30am–11pm; Thurs–Sat 11:30am–11:30pm. Subway: L, N, R, Q, W, 4, 5, 6 to 14th St./Union Sq.

Taco & Tortilla King *Value* TEX-MEX   This low-profile sleeper is little more than a lunch counter, but the authentic food can't be beat. Sit down to a couple of tacos and you'll think you've been transported to one of those gourmet Mexican joints your friends in Southern California keep raving about. The kitchen won me over with the basics: fresh-made guacamole infused with lime, and flour tortillas made from scratch and baked on the premises. All the staples, from well-stuffed burritos to sizzling fajitas, are authentically prepared, hearty, and satisfying; a good portion of the offerings can be prepared meatless for vegetarians. It's an all-around winner for a fast meal at an unbeatable price.

285 Third Ave. (between 22nd and 23rd sts.). ℂ **212/679-8882** or 212/481-3930. A la carte items 99¢–$5.60; sandwiches $2.30–$6.80; combo plates $4.90; by-the-lb. fajitas $13–$18. AE, MC, V ($15 minimum). Mon–Fri 11am–11:30pm; Sat–Sun 11:30am–11pm. Subway: 6 to 23rd St.

Via Emilia ★ *Value* EMILIA-ROMAGNA ITALIAN   This candlelit, brick-walled trattoria is a haven for budget diners in the high-priced Park Avenue South area. The menu is simple but satisfying, with an emphasis on house-made pastas—as you might expect from a restaurant that emphasizes the cuisine of Emilia-Romagna. The specialty is tortellini; the *tortellini in brodo,* meat-stuffed tortellini in a chicken broth, is a great way to start your meal. Other starters include fresh-grilled squid or thin-sliced tenderloin carpaccio, served with shaved Parmesan and leafy arugula. There's not a dud among the pastas, all of which are oversize, none exceeding $12. There's also a handful of non-pasta entrees, including veal scallopine in an aromatic sauce with diced asparagus, and the *cosciotto d'agnello,* a thinly sliced leg of lamb with mushrooms, cannelloni beans, and tomatoes, like a lighter, Italian cassoulet. Wines are well priced, too, and service is better than you'd expect at a restaurant this affordable.

240 Park Ave. S. (between 19th and 20th sts.). ℂ **212/505-3072.** Reservations not accepted. Main courses $7.50–$15. No credit cards. Mon–Sat 5–11pm. Subway: N, R, 6 to 23rd St.

Zen Palate ★ PAN-ASIAN/VEGETARIAN   Zen Palate has adopted the healthy, less-is-more approach to Asian cuisine. Each location shares the same Japanese-influenced postmodern decor, with teak and patinated copper; the Union Square flagship is a standout, with a counter downstairs for on-the-run eaters and a warren of spare but attractive dining rooms upstairs, including some with Japanese-style seating.

Tofu is king here, but you're not limited to it. Stars on the wide-ranging menu include taro spring rolls and basil moo-shu rolls for something creative, as well as veggie dumplings and buns for a more traditional Asian choice. Despite the good-for-you approach, main courses such as Rose Petals (homemade soy pasta in a sweet rice-ginger sauce with garden vegetables) and Curry Supreme (with tofu, potatoes, and carrots) are very flavorful, and some will particularly appeal to spicy-food lovers. Even more affordable casual grazing dishes are served in the all-day gourmet shop downstairs. All in all, a good bet for health-minded diners.

And as an added attraction, you're welcome to BYOB with no corkage fee in the upstairs dining room at this location.

34 Union Sq. E. (at 16th St.). (℃ 212/614-9345. www.zenpalate.com. Reservations accepted. Main courses $7–$17.50 ($3–$8 in gourmet shop). AE, MC, V. Mon–Sat 11am–10:45pm; Sun noon–10:45pm. Subway: L, N, R, Q, W, 4, 5, 6 to 14th St./Union Sq. Also at 663 Ninth Ave. (at 46th St.; (℃ 212/582-1669; subway: A, C, E to 42nd St.); 2170 Broadway (between 76th and 77th sts.; (℃ 212/501-7768; subway: 1, 9 to 79th St.).

QUICK BITES

Pintaile's Pizza, 124 Fourth Ave., between 12th and 13th streets ((℃ **212/ 475-4977;** www.pintailespizza.com), dresses their crisp organic crusts with layers of plum tomatoes, extra-virgin olive oil, and other fresh ingredients. This new branch of the East Side favorite even has lots of seating for in-house eating.

11 Times Square & Midtown West

Check out the Asian-nouvelle vegetarian cuisine at **Zen Palate** (p. 166), at 663 Ninth Ave., at 46th Street ((℃ 212/582-1669). **Joe's Shanghai** (p. 142) has a Midtown branch at 24 W. 56th St., west of Fifth Avenue ((℃ **212/333-3868**), offering soup dumplings and other dishes—but expect to pay a bit more here than in Chinatown. An outpost of **Grand Sichuan International** (p. 162) dishes up killer Szechuan fare at 745 Ninth Ave., between 50th and 51st streets ((℃ **212/582-2288**). A branch of the ultrafresh, cheap eat-in/takeout sushi joint, **Go Sushi** (p. 177), is at 756 Ninth Ave., at 51st Street ((℃ **212/459-2288**).

There's a cafeteria-style **Mangia** (p. 138) at 50 W. 57th St., between Fifth and Sixth avenues ((℃ **212/582-5882**). Two nice branches of **Burritoville** (p. 138) are at 352 W. 39th St., at Ninth Avenue ((℃ **212/563-9088**), and 625 Ninth Ave., at 44th Street ((℃ **212/333-5352**).

Also consider **Emerald Planet** (p. 158), on the lower concourse at 30 Rockefeller Plaza ((℃ **212/218-1133**), for wraps and yummy smoothies. Healthy eaters will enjoy the all-natural eats at **The Pump** (p. 178), 40 W. 55th St., between Fifth and Sixth avenues ((℃ **212/246-6844**), too. There is a very nice outlet of **John's Pizza** in Times Square, 260 W. 44th St., between Seventh and Eighth avenues ((℃ **212/391-7560**); see the box "Pizza New York Style" on p. 157.

If you're over by the *Intrepid,* stop into the sister location of **H&H Bagels,** 639 W. 46th St., at Twelfth Avenue ((℃ **212/595-8000**), to sample incredible fresh-baked bagels; see the box "Bagel Power" on p. 183.

Afghan Kebab House MIDDLE EASTERN *Value* You'll find Afghan Kebab Houses all over the city. Are they related? Who knows, but I like this one the best for heaping plates of first-rate Middle Eastern fare. Kebabs are the first order of business: All are pleasing, but my favorite is the *sultani,* chunks of ground lamb marinated in aromatic spices and broiled over wood charcoal with green peppers and tomatoes. The *tikka kebabs*—lamb and beef—are impressive, as is the chicken korma, slow-cooked with fresh onions, tomatoes, peppers, and fresh herbs. All plates come with amazingly aromatic brown Indian basmati rice and flat Afghan bread. The room is simple and well worn but evocative, with Oriental carpets serving as table runners, and service is attentive.

764 Ninth Ave. (between 51st and 52nd sts.). (℃ 212/307-1612 or 212/307-1629. Reservations accepted. Main courses $10–$16 (most less than $12). AE, DC, DISC, MC, V. Daily 11:30am–10:30pm. Subway: C, E to 50th St.

Midtown, Chelsea & Union Square Dining

UPPER EAST SIDE

MIDTOWN EAST

Rockefeller Center

Grand Central Terminal

New York Public Library

MURRAY HILL

Empire State Bldg.

Madison Square Park

FLATIRON DISTRICT

GRAMERCY PARK

United Nations

Peter Cooper Village

Stuyvesant Town

Los Dos Rancheros Mexicanos **33**
Lyric Diner **53**
Mandoo Bar **60**
Mangia **66, 78**
Manhattan Chili Co. **6, 26**
Mars 2112 **16**
Molly's Pub & Restaurant Sheeben **53**
Old Town Bar & Restaurant **47**
Papaya King **29**
Petite Abeille **41**
Pigalle **18**
Pintaile's **43**
Pongal **57**
Prime Burger **69**
Republic **46**
Rice 'n' Beans **13**
Route 66 Café **3**
Rue des Crepes **40**
Sapporo **17**
Serendipity 3 **80**
Siam Inn **14**
Stage Deli **5**
Taco & Tortilla King **53**
The Pump **59, 75**
Via Emilia **50**
Virgil's Real BBQ **25**
Vynl **7**
Won Jo **61**
Xando/Cosi **43, 49 ,58, 70**
Zen Palate **22, 44**

M Subway stop

Upper Manhattan

Uptown

Midtown

Downtown

Africa #2 ★ *Finds* AFRICAN   Visiting this roomy restaurant in the middle of midtown Manhattan, you'll feel like you've left New York and made your way into the heart of Senegal. Decorated haphazardly with African art, the relaxed atmosphere and leisurely pace is seemingly a continent away from most New York restaurants. Then there is the food: Senegalese and typically spicy. The *poisson frite*—fried fish with shrimp, salad, and plantains—is spectacular, as is the chicken with couscous; the grilled half chicken rubbed with peppery spices, served over aromatic couscous, and covered with sweet sautéed onions; and the *dakhine*, lamb stewed in a rich peanut sauce with onions and beans. No alcohol is served, but try the tangy homemade ginger beer or the refreshing sorrel drink. If you are lucky, Senegalese music videos will be playing on the television while you eat.

346 W. 53rd St. (between Eighth and Ninth aves.). ✆ 212/399-7166. Main courses lunch $7–$8; dinner $7–$11. No credit cards. Daily 12:30pm–midnight. Subway: C, E to 50th St.

Brazil Grill ★ BRAZILIAN   The Theater District is loaded with overpriced tourist traps, and many affordable restaurants feel dowdy or downscale. So where can you go for a nice pre- (or post-) theater dinner that won't break the bank? Try the Brazil Grill, where the tables are spacious, the staff is charming, cobalt-blue accents add a touch of elegance, and the menu showcases the sunny flavors of Brazil. The prix fixe is a great deal: three courses for $19.95. The broader menu offers lots of country cooking to satisfy the meat-and-potatoes crowd (sizzling beef skewers with peppers and onions), while diners with more adventurous palates might try the spicy *camarao baiana* (shrimp sautéed with palm oil and served in a sauce of coconut milk, tomatoes, and garlic). Portions are generous, and main courses come with ample sides of rice and beans. The wine list offers affordable choices, including an array of wines by the glass for $5 to $6. Don't miss the incredible *doce de leite*, a rich and creamy caramel confection, for dessert.

787 Eighth Ave. (at 48th St.). ✆ 212/307-9449. www.brazilgrill.citysearch.com. Reservations recommended, especially pre-theater. Main courses $10.95–$21.95; 3-course prix-fixe dinner $19.95. AE, DC, MC, V. Daily noon–midnight. Subway: 1, 2 C, E to 50th St.

Chanpen THAI   This charming restaurant serves Thai food at Chinatown prices. It's a tad cheaper than nearby Siam Inn (p. 175), especially at lunch, when Siam Inn caters to a middle-management crowd; Chanpen's lunch specials are values that draw savvy worker bees from throughout the neighborhood. In addition to the prices, you'll be pleased by the bright dining room, the pleasant and attentive service, and the classic preparations of familiar Thai favorites.

761 Ninth Ave. (at 51st St.). ✆ 212/586-6808. AE, MC, V. Reservations accepted for dinner Sun–Thurs only. Main courses $8–$15; lunch special (Mon–Fri 11:30am–3pm) $7–$8. AE, MC, V. Sun–Thurs 11:30am–11pm; Fri–Sat 11:30am–midnight. Subway: C, E to 50th St.

44 Southwest ★ *Finds* ITALIAN   This mom-and-pop restaurant serves up the best Italian food in Midtown for the money. It's simple but charming, with an original tin ceiling, red-checkered tablecloths, and soft lighting; the result is a romantic first-date ambience (very *Lady and the Tramp* sharing spaghetti). The dishes are generously portioned and very satisfying. Pastas are perfectly al dente; I especially love the thick and hearty meat sauce on the linguine Bolognese. The chicken Parmesan is classically yummy, and personal pizzas arrive with wonderfully chewy crusts. The wine list is affordable and the service attentive, making 44 Southwest a winner on all fronts for wallet-watching visitors.

621 Ninth Ave. (at 44th St.). ✆ 212/315-4582 or 212/315-4681. Reservations accepted (recommended for pre-theater dining). Main courses $8–$14. AE, MC, V. Sun–Thurs noon–11pm; Fri–Sat noon–midnight. Subway: A, C, E to 42nd St.

Hallo! Berlin ⭐ GERMAN   Hallo! Berlin bills itself as "New York's Wurst Restaurant"—and indeed it is. If wurst is best in your book, don't miss it. Hallo! Berlin is straight outta Deutschland, serving up eight varieties of sausage, from boiled beef-and-pork knockwurst to pan-fried veal bavarianwurst and beef currywurst. Sandwiches come with all the fixings, including red cabbage, sauerkraut, onions, and mustard, but I prefer the combo, which lets me choose two kinds of sausage (substitute spaetzle for German fries for maximum satisfaction). There's also a terrific Wiener schnitzel. The potato pancakes make a great starter; one generous order is enough for a few friends to share. A big bowl of lentil, split-pea, or potato soup with cut-up wurst and bread and butter makes a satisfying lunch for just $5. The main location is petite and pleasant, with efficient table service and a couple of taps pouring German brews, while the Tenth Avenue location is a full-scale beer hall well equipped for larger parties.

402 W. 51st St. (just west of Ninth Ave.). ℭ 212/541-6248. Reservations not accepted. Sandwiches $3–$3.75; main courses (with soup) $6.50–$15; lunch specials (until 5pm) $5.25–$6.50. MC, V. Mon–Sat 11am–11pm; Sun 4–11pm. Subway: C, E to 50th St. Also at 626 Tenth Ave. (at 44th St.; ℭ 212/977-1944; subway: A, C, E to 42nd St./Port Authority).

Island Burgers & Shakes ⓥalue GOURMET BURGERS/SANDWICHES   This aisle-size diner glows with the colors of a California surf shop. As the name implies, folks come for the Goliath-size burgers—either beef hamburgers or, the specialty of the house, *churrascos* (flattened grilled chicken breasts). Innovation strikes with the more than 40 toppings: Choose anything from the horseradish, sour cream, and black-pepper burger to the Hobie's (with black-pepper sauce, blue cheese, onion, and bacon). Choose your own bread from a selection ranging from soft sourdough to crusty ciabatta. Island Burgers doesn't serve fries; you're meant to eat these fellows with their tasty dirty potato chips. You can also opt for a baked potato slathered in butter and sour cream. Thick shakes and cookies are available to satisfy your sweet tooth, while health-minded diners have a selection of hearty entree-size salads from which to choose; the Caesar is a delightful rendering of the classic.

766 Ninth Ave. (between 51st and 52nd sts.). ℭ 212/307-7934. www.island.citysearch.com. Reservations not accepted. Sandwiches and main-course salads $6.50–$9.50. No credit cards. Sun–Thurs noon–10:30pm; Fri–Sat noon–11pm. Subway: C, E to 50th St.

Joe Allen ⭐⭐ AMERICAN PUB   This Restaurant Row pub is a glorious throwback to yesteryear, when theater types went to places like Sardi's and Lüchow's—and yep, Joe Allen. Joe Allen is still going strong; don't be surprised if you spot a stage star or two. The straightforward pub food is reliable and well priced, and served at big, comfortable tables (the kind that restaurant managers don't order anymore because they take up too much room) covered with red-checked cloths. The meatloaf is terrific, but you can't go wrong with the chili, the Greek salad, the burgers, or anything that comes with mashed potatoes. More than 30 beers are available, and some good wines by the glass. The staff is a congenial and neighborhood-appropriate mix of career waiters and aspiring thespians. You'll enjoy perusing the walls covered with posters and other memorabilia from legendary Broadway flops.

326 W. 46th St. (between Eighth and Ninth aves.). ℭ 212/581-6464. Reservations recommended (a must for pre-theater dining). Main courses $9–$22 (most less than $17). MC, V. Mon–Tues and Thurs–Fri noon–11:45pm; Wed and Sat–Sun 11:30am–11:45pm. Subway: A, C, E to 42nd St./Port Authority.

La Bonne Soupe ⭐ ⓚids FRENCH BISTRO   This slice of Paris has been around forever, and for gourmet at good prices, it's still hard to beat it. You'll

---

Tips **The Midtown Deli News**

If you're in Midtown and looking for one of the Big Apple's quintessential delis, head to the **Stage Deli,** 834 Seventh Ave., between 53rd and
54th streets (℡ **212/245-7850;** www.stagedeli.com), known for its
celebrity sandwiches, from the Joe DiMaggio (corned beef, pastrami,
chopped liver, and Bermuda onion) to the Julia Roberts (chicken salad,
hard-boiled egg, lettuce, and tomato); or the **Carnegie Deli,** 854 Seventh
Ave., at 55th Street (℡ **212/757-2245;** www.carnegiedeli.com), for pastrami, corned beef, and cheesecake. *Note:* These landmarks specialize in
tourist-target pricing, with sandwiches coming in between $12 and $20.
You get your money's worth—they're more than most mortals can consume in one sitting—but you'll be charged $2 to $3 to split one with your
travel partner. Head down to **Katz's** (p. 146) or up to **Barney Greengrass**
(p. 182) for less touristy, less expensive deli experiences.

---

even see French natives elbow-to-elbow in the newly renovated dining room.
"Les bonnes soupes" are satisfying noontime meals of salad, bread, a big bowl of
soup (mushroom and barley with lamb is a favorite), dessert (chocolate mousse,
crème caramel, or ice cream), and wine or coffee—a great bargain at just $13.95.
The menu also features entree-size salads (including a good niçoise), burgers,
and bistro fare like omelets, quiche Lorraine, croque monsieur, and fancier fare
like steak frites and filet mignon *au poivre.* Rounding out the menu are French
fondues: Emmethal cheese, beef, and creamy chocolate to finish off the meal;
the silky-smooth chocolate mousse is yummy. A kids' menu is available, offering
a burger or chicken and fries, plus dessert, for $10.25. Bon appétit!

48 W. 55th St. (between Fifth and Sixth aves.). ℡ 212/586-7650. www.labonnesoupe.com. Reservations
recommended for parties of 3 or more. Main courses $9–$19.25 (most less than $15); "les bonnes soupes"
fixed price $13.95; 3-course fixed price $20 at lunch and dinner. AE, DC, MC, V. Mon–Sat 11:30am–midnight;
Sun 11:30am–11pm. Subway: E, F to Fifth Ave.; B, Q to 57th St.

Lemon Tree Cafe *Value* MIDDLE EASTERN   Lemon Tree is bare-bones
decor-wise, with institutional furnishings and a few posters of Egypt or Syria dis-
tracting you from the fake-wood paneling and linoleum floor. But the food is
fresh, tasty, and plentiful. All pita sandwiches come overstuffed with lettuce,
tomato, cabbage, onion, and tahini sauce. The falafel is top notch. Veggie platters are light and delicious, particularly the lemony hummus, babaganoush, and
tabbouleh. The grilled meat platters (served with salad and rice) are huge. Service
can be slow and quirky, but it's worth putting up with for the great meal deal.

769 Ninth Ave. (between 51st and 52nd sts.). ℡ 212/245-0818. Reservations not accepted. Sandwiches
$2.50–$4; platters $5–$9. AE, DISC, MC, V ($20 minimum). Daily 11am–11pm. Subway: C, E to 50th St.

Los Dos Rancheros Mexicanos *Finds* MEXICAN   Authentic with a no-frills
decor; tables with paper menus beneath the glass, plastic cups, and cheap
dishes—but murals and a Wurlitzer jukebox pumping out Latin pop add charm.
The Pueblo-style food isn't for the faint of heart: The famous moles are extra-
rich; the house-made salsas are hot, hot, hot; and barbecued goat, tripe soup,
and tongue tacos are among the specialties. But even the less adventurous will
dig in to the enchiladas (don't pass up the beef), burritos, and other choices with
gusto. Everything is affordable and well prepared; soft, fresh corn tortillas are
served with almost every dish. Service is attentive, and Mexican beers are available.

Check the wall behind the open kitchen for the specials. The south-of–Port Authority neighborhood can be desolate at night, so go earlier rather than later.

507 Ninth Ave. (at 38th St.). © 212/868-7780. Reservations not accepted. Tacos $2–$3; burritos and sand-wiches $4–$7; platters $7–$12. No credit cards. Daily 11am–10:30pm. Subway: A, C, E to 42nd St./ Port Authority.

Mandoo Bar *Finds* KOREAN   When you think of Korean food, you usually think of barbecue cooked at your table. But not all Korean food is alike. Mandoo Bar is a dumpling house, which specializes in all manner of fresh dumplings. I love the *mool mandoo,* broiled dumplings stuffed with vegetables and meat, and the baby mandoo, bite-size dumplings of beef, pork, and leek. The menu also offers fried-noodle dishes, including great pad Thai and Korean-style noodle soups; fried rice and *bibimbop* with veggies and beef; and *pajeon,* a Korean pancake with seafood. Plenty of meatless options are on hand. The room is plain but pleasant, with long blond-wood tables and benches that speak to Mandoo Bar as a quick-bite kind of place. Service is brisk and efficient, in a friendly way. Beer and wine are available. Don't be surprised if there's a lunchtime wait, when ravenous shoppers descend from Macy's, but the line moves quickly.

2 W. 32nd St. (just west of Fifth Ave.). © 212/279-3075. Reservations not accepted. Main courses $6–$14. AE, DC, MC, V. Daily 11:30am–11pm. Subway: B, D, F, N, Q, R, V, W to 34th St./Herald Sq.

Manhattan Chili Co. ★ *Kids* TEX-MEX/AMERICAN   This big, festive Theater District restaurant adjacent to David Letterman's Ed Sullivan Theater is a great choice for a casual, affordable meal, especially if you have kids. The hearty chili bowls are geared to young palates. The extensive list of chili choices is marked by spice level, from traditional Abilene with ground beef, tomatoes, basil, and red wine (mild enough for tenderfeet) to the Texas Chain Gang, which adds jalapeños to the mix for those who prefer hot. There's even a three-chili sampler plate. In addition, expect favorites like nachos, chicken wings, big salads, and generous burritos and burgers. It's hard to go wrong here—even vegetarians have lots to choose from. A fun place to eat!

1697 Broadway (between 53rd and 54th sts.). © 212/246-6555. www.manhattanchilico.com. Reservations accepted. Chili bowls $10; main courses $11–$16; Sat–Sun brunch $10.95. AE, DISC, MC, V. Sun–Mon 11:30am–11pm; Tues–Sat 11:30am–midnight. Subway: B, D, E to Seventh Ave.; 1, 9 to 50th St. Also at 1500 Broadway (entrance on 43rd St.; © 212/730-8666; subway: N, R, S, 1, 2, 3, 7, 9 to 42nd St./Times Sq.).

Pigalle ★ FRENCH BRASSERIE   This brasserie is a wonderful Theater District choice, thanks to its winning combination of high-quality fare, low prices, and location—not to mention 24-hour service that makes it the best place to satisfy post-anything munchies. The beautifully designed room by Nancy Mah boasts all the trimmings of a traditional brasserie—zinc-topped bar, colorful rattan, soft ochre lighting—with a designer edge. The room is big, airy, and comfortable, great for couples and larger parties alike. The menu offers true-to-form versions of brasserie fare, including onion soup gratinée, *classique* cassoulet, duck confit, and steak au poivre. Stick to the classics and you'll enjoy yourself. Also check out the inspired cocktail menu, reason enough to come in. The Violet Martini is perfectly shaken with Grey Goose and a hint of violet essence, then dressed with a single purple petal. **Note:** If you're going pre-theater, make it clear from the moment you sit.

790 Eighth Ave. (at 48th St.), adjacent to the Days Hotel. © 212/489-2233. Reservations recommended. Main courses $6.50–$14 at breakfast and lunch, $8–$18 at dinner. AE, DC, DISC, MC, V. Daily 24 hrs. Subway: C, E to 50th St.

Kids Family-Friendly Restaurants

While it's always smart to call ahead to make sure a restaurant has kids' menus and high chairs, you can count on the following to be especially accommodating. Additionally, you and the kids might also consider **Acme Bar & Grill** (p. 150), **Florent** (p. 158), and **Artie's Delicatessen** (p. 182). And don't forget the pizzerias, **John's** (p. 157) and **Lombardi's** (p. 157).

Among the city's theme restaurants, take the kids to the **Hard Rock Cafe,** 221 W. 57th St., between Broadway and Seventh Avenue (© **212/ 489-6565;** www.hardrockcafe.com). **Mars 2112,** 1633 Broadway, at 51st Street (© **212/582-2112;** www.mars2112.com), boasts costumed characters and a "rocket ride" to the dining area from street level, as well as a video arcade that can keep the kids busy for hours (or until you run out of quarters). Little groovy ghoulies will love the thrills and chills of the **Jekyll & Hyde Club,** 1409 Sixth Ave., between 57th and 58th streets (© **212/541-9509;** www.eerie.com), while sports-minded kids can drag their baseball dads and soccer moms to the **ESPN Zone,** 1472 Broadway, at 42nd Street (© **212/921-3776;** www.espnzone.com). Here are some other choices for the whole family:

EJ's Luncheonette (p. 156). There's a kids' menu featuring peanut-butter-and-jelly sandwiches along with downsized versions of the classics. Order up a milk shake on the side, and your kid will be in hog heaven.

Good Enough To Eat (p. 184). Comfort food for kids like macaroni and cheese, pizza, and great desserts.

Manhattan Chili Co. (p. 173). Expect kid-friendly nachos, chicken wings, not-too-hot bowls of thick and meaty chili, and other faves like burritos and burgers.

Serendipity 3 (p. 188). Kids of all ages will love this whimsical restaurant and ice-cream shop, which serves up a huge menu of American favorites, followed up by colossal ice-cream treats.

Virgil's Real BBQ (p. 175). This pleasing Times Square barbecue joint welcomes kids with open arms—and Junior will be more than happy, I'm sure, to be *allowed* to eat with his hands.

Rice 'n' Beans BRAZILIAN   This cool, dark, hallway-size restaurant dishes up bold-flavored, stick-to-your-ribs fare that'll make you want to stand up and samba. Among the highlights are *feijoada,* the national dish of Brazil, a hearty stew of black beans, pork ribs, and linguica (Portuguese sausage); and a roasted chicken seasoned with tomato and cilantro. Prices have climbed a bit in recent years, but big eaters will still get a bang for their buck. The best bargain is the restaurant's namesake: For less than $10 you get a large plate mounded with rice, beans, mixed vegetables, collard greens, and plantains—a vegetarian's delight. Portions are monstrous. The weekday lunch specials—full meals with rice, beans, plantains, and your choice of roasted or sautéed chicken, beef stew, thin-cut sautéed pork chops, or the day's fried fish—are a steal. *Be forewarned:* Service can be slow at times and ambience is almost nonexistent.

744 Ninth Ave. (between 50th and 51st sts.). ℭ **212/265-4444**. Reservations not accepted. Full plates $5–$8.25 at lunch, $6–$17 at dinner. AE, DISC, MC, V. Sun–Thurs 11am–10pm; Fri–Sat 11am–10:30pm. Subway: C, E to 50th St.

Route 66 Cafe AMERICAN DINER   Here's a good bet for straightforward American eats. The brick-walled room is light, bright, and spacious, making it a nice place to enjoy a casual, affordable meal. Expect an extensive menu with diner standards, from waffles, eggs, and bagels to burgers, salads, triple-decker sandwiches, meatloaf, and pastas. The food satisfies and isn't as overpriced as most Theater District fare. Service is friendly and a juice bar adds a healthy twist.

858 Ninth Ave. (between 55th and 56th sts.). ℭ **212/977-7600**. Reservations not accepted. Breakfast $3.75–$7.75; sandwiches and salads $4.70–$10; dinner entrees $10–$22 (most less than $15). AE, DC, DISC, MC, V. Daily 7:30am–midnight. Subway: A, B, C, D, 1, 9 to 59th St./Columbus Circle.

Sapporo ★ JAPANESE   Comfort food doesn't get any better than a big ramen or fried-rice bowl from Sapporo. This no-frills restaurant serves up good, cheap Japanese eats, and the mostly Japanese crowd is testimony to its authenticity. Sapporo is famous for their *gyoza,* pork-filled dumplings that are pan-fried and served with a soy, rice-vinegar, and chile-oil dipping sauce. Other choices include *chahan,* lightly fried Japanese rice with veggies, egg, fish cake, and your choice of pork or chicken; sweet beef and tofu sukiyaki; fried pork cutlets; and any of the huge noodle bowls. Some of the servers speak little English, so just point to your choice, and don't hesitate to ask for silverware if you prefer it to chopsticks. Beer and sake are served, and there's a sushi bar at the East Village location.

152 W. 49th St. (between Sixth and Seventh aves.). ℭ **212/869-8972**. Reservations not accepted. Main courses $6–$9. No credit cards. Mon–Sat 11am–11pm; Sun 11am–10pm. Subway: N, R to 49th St. Sapporo East at 245 E. 10th St. (also at First Ave.; ℭ **212/260-1330**; subway: L to First Ave.).

Siam Inn ★ THAI   Situated on an unremarkable stretch of Eighth Avenue, Siam Inn is an attractive outpost of good Thai food. All your favorites are here, well prepared and served by a brightly attired and courteous staff. *Tom kah gai soup* (with chicken, mushrooms, and coconut milk), chicken satay with peanut sauce, and light, flaky curry puffs all make good starters. Among noteworthy entrees are the *masaman* and red curries (the former rich and peanutty, the latter quite spicy), spicy sautéed squid with fresh basil and chiles, and perfect pad Thai. Unlike many of the drab restaurants in this neighborhood, the decor is pretty and pleasing—black tables and chairs, cushy rugs, and soft lighting.

854 Eighth Ave. (between 51st and 52nd sts.). ℭ **212/757-4006**. www.siaminn.com. Reservations suggested. Main courses $8–$12 at lunch, $8–$16 at dinner. AE, DC, MC, V. Mon–Fri noon–11:30pm; Sat–Sun 4–11:30pm. Subway: C, E to 50th St.

Virgil's Real BBQ ★★ *Kids* BARBECUE   Virgil's may look like a theme-park version of a down-home barbecue joint, but this place takes its barbecue seriously. The meat is house-smoked with a blend of hickory, oak, and fruitwood chips, and almost every regional school is represented, from Carolina pulled pork to Texas beef brisket to Memphis ribs. You may not consider this contest-winning chow if you're from barbecue country, but for New York, it's not bad. I love to start with the barbecued shrimp, accompanied by mustard slaw, and a plate of buttermilk onion rings with blue cheese for dipping. The ribs are first rate, and the chicken is moist and tender—go for a combo if you just can't choose. Burgers, sandwiches, and other entrees (chicken-fried steak, anyone?)

are also available if you can't face up to all that meat 'n' sauce. And cast that corn bread aside for a full order of buttermilk biscuits, which come with maple butter so good it's like dessert. Don't worry about making a mess; when you're through eating, you get a hot towel for washing up. The bar offers a huge selection of on-tap and bottled brews.

152 W. 44th St. (between Sixth and Seventh aves.). ℂ **212/921-9494**. www.virgilsbbq.com. Reservations recommended. Sandwiches $6–$11; main courses and barbecue platters $13–$26 (most less than $19). AE, DC, DISC, MC, V. Sun–Mon 11:30am–11pm; Tues–Sat 11:30am–midnight. Subway: 1, 2, 3, 7, 9, N, R to 42nd St./Times Sq.

Vynl ✿ AMERICAN DINER   Vynl adds a hip quotient to the traditional diner formula with Lucite and Bakelite decor, a collection of action figures through the ages (from Captain and Tennille to Tyson Beckford), a 1970s-to-now soundtrack, and an affordable menu in a gatefold album cover (ours were from Lionel Richie and Three Dog Night). But Vynl isn't all veneer—the food is terrific. The brioche French toast with sautéed apples and caramel sauce is a great way to launch a weekend. For daytime and evening, the fare runs the gamut from diner fare to Asian-accented dishes including Thai curries, a veggie stir-fry, and Chinese chicken salad. Service is friendly and attentive. Pay with a credit card so you can sign the bill with the coolest pen in town (yours to purchase, if you wish).

824 Ninth Ave. (at 54th St.). ℂ **212/974-2003**. Reservations not accepted. Main courses $4.50–$11. AE, MC, V. Mon–Tues 11:30am–11pm; Wed–Fri 11:30am–midnight; Sat 9:30am–midnight; Sun 9:30am–11pm. Subway: C, E to 50th St.

Won Jo ✿✿ KOREAN BARBECUE/JAPANESE   This round-the-clock Korean barbecue is a good bet for first-timers and purists alike. The menu at this brightly lit restaurant is massive, but barbecue is the way to go. All the cuts of meat are high quality (shrimp is available, too), and the table barbecues come with six side dishes (including kimchee), plus rice, dipping sauce, and lettuce leaves for wrapping barbecued meats. This is an interactive meal; you'll cook everything at your table's built-in grill. Unlike some neighboring joints, the food isn't blazingly spiced, but it's still piquant. The staff may not speak the best English, but they're happy to walk novices through the steps. It's a feast that's particularly fun with a crowd—Asian pop blares through the speakers, and groups keep the place hopping, especially on weekends—but couples will be well contented, too. The sushi, teriyaki, and *bibimbop* (Korean hot-pot dishes) are well prepared, too.

23 W. 32nd St. (between Broadway and Fifth Ave.). ℂ **212/695-5815**. Reservations not accepted. Full barbecue dinners $17–$20; main courses $8–$27 (most less than $12). AE, MC, V. Daily 24 hr. Subway: B, D, F, N, R, Q, W to 34th St.

QUICK BITES

Amy's Bread, 672 Ninth Ave., between 46th and 47th streets (ℂ **212/977-2670;** www.amysbread.com), makes a great daytime stop. The brick-walled bakery/cafe serves up fresh-baked pastries, quiches, sandwiches made on some of the city's best bread, homemade soups, and excellent sweets (including divine old-fashioned layer cake), as well as cappuccino. Pastries are $1 to $4, sandwiches $3 to $6. A few tables are on hand in addition to the takeout counter.

Little more than a jazzy, neon-lit storefront, **B. Frites,** 1657 Broadway, between 51st and 52nd streets (ℂ **212/767-0858**), is a purveyor of authentic Belgian fries. You can choose from at least a dozen sauces, ranging from traditional mayo to herb-seasoned tomato purée. The $7.55 soup-and-fries combo (tax included) is a great deal at lunch.

Papaya King is at 255 W. 43rd St., just off Eighth Avenue (© **212/944-4590**). The two-all-beef-franks-and-an-all-natural-fruit-drink combo is a bargain at $4.30.

Gourmet grocer **Dean & Deluca** runs a bustling, airy cafe at 9 Rockefeller Center, at 49th Street, across from the *Today* show studio (© **212/664-1363**).

12 Midtown East & Murray Hill

In addition to the listings below, there's a cafeteria-style branch of **Mangia** (p. 138) at 16 E. 48th St., east of Fifth Avenue (© **212/754-0637**); and a **Burritoville** (p. 138) at 866 Third Ave. (actually on 52nd St. between Lexington and Third aves.; © **212/980-4111**). **Jackson Hole** (p. 187) is at 521 Third Ave., at 36th Street (© **212/679-3264**), for burgers and other affordable diner fare. Additionally, there are two area outposts of the coffeehouse/sandwich bar **Xando/Cosí** (p. 186): at 461 Park Ave. S., at 31st Street (© **212/634-3467**); and 320 Park Ave., at 51st Street (© **212/754-6144**).

Also consider **Le Pain Quotidien,** at 833 Lexington Ave. (between 63rd and 64th sts.; © **212/755-5810**) and the scrumptious **Ess-A-Bagel** at 831 Third Ave. (at 51st St.; © **212/980-1010**); see the box "Bagel Power" on p. 183.

Go Sushi (Value) JAPANESE/SUSHI This bright, attractive chain of eat-in/takeout joints serves up excellent sushi for wallet-watching fans. It's boxed in bento-style containers, but everything is prepared fresh by a bevy of chefs behind the counter, so you never have to worry about quality; you can also place orders if what you desire is not ready-made. In addition to sashimi, nigiri, and cut-roll choices, you can choose from a selection of fresh-made noodle bowls as well as bentos with teriyaki or tempura. I know locals who eat at Go Sushi three times a week. All in all, it's a wallet-friendly choice for a quick, healthy meal. No alcohol is served.

982 Second Ave. (at 52nd St.). © 212/593-3883. Reservations not accepted. A la carte sushi $1.50–$2; rolls $3.80–$9 (most less than $6); sushi combos and bentos $5–$17 (most less than $10); noodle soups $5.50–$6.50. AE, MC, V. Daily 11:30am–11:10pm. Subway: 6 to 51st St. Also at 511 Third Ave. (between 34th and 35th sts.; © 212/679-1999; subway: 6 to 33rd St.); 756 Ninth Ave. (at 51st St.; © 212/459-2288; subway: C, E to 50th St.); 3 Greenwich Ave. (Sixth Ave. at 8th St.; © 212/366-9272; subway: A, C, E, F, V, S to W. 4th St.).

Katsu-Hama (Finds) JAPANESE Even if you've never dined on Japanese cuisine, give this restaurant a try. It specializes in *katsu*, breaded and cleanly fried cutlets, usually pork, friendly to American palates. Katsu-Hama also katsus chicken, prawns, and potatoes ("cream croquettes") in addition to moist pork tenderloin. Dinners start at $8.95 and come with as much rice, miso, and cabbage salad as you can eat. Japanese curries and skewers (yakitori) are also on hand, and there's a kids' menu. The butter-yellow room features modern art and comfy seating. Service is welcoming, knowledgeable, and generous with seconds. Beer and a short but good sake selection are on hand. It's an excellent value offering a more pleasing all-around dining experience than most in this price range.

11 E. 47th St. (between Fifth and Madison aves.). © 212/758-5909. www.katsuhama.com. Reservations accepted. Main courses and complete meals $7–$16. AE, DC, DISC, MC, V. Mon–Thurs 11:30am–3pm and 5–10:30pm; Fri 11:30am–10:30pm; Sat–Sun 11:30am–9:30pm. Subway: B, D, F, V to 47th–50th sts./Rockefeller Center.

Pongal ★ (Value) VEGETARIAN/INDIAN A standout on Curry Hill, the stretch of Lexington in the 20s that's home to a number of Indian restaurants. Pongal specializes in the vegetarian cuisine of southern India, and also happens

Moments Grand Dining at Grand Central

The lower concourse of **Grand Central Terminal** ★★, 42nd Street at Park Avenue, is a haven of cheap eats—and the setting is an architecture-lover's delight. Head downstairs and you'll find everything from bratwurst to sushi. Standouts include **Junior's,** a branch of the Brooklyn stalwart, serving deli sandwiches, burgers, and their world-famous cheesecake in a waiter-serviced dining area. (With a few exceptions, most of the outlets are takeout counters; there's abundant seating at the center of the concourse.) **Mike's Take-Away** serves up soups, salads, and sandwiches, including a mushroom stew in winter. **Little Pie Company** serves up the Big Apple's best pies, plus fresh-baked muffins and the concourse's best coffee. **Cafe Spice Express** serves terrific Indian fare, while **Christer's** and **Knödel** specialize, respectively, in fish and chips and German-style brats, wieners, and sausages. There's also an outpost of pizzeria **Two Boots.** If you want beer or wine, visit one of the two **bar cars,** which sit near tracks 105 and 112. For the best soft ice cream north of the Jersey shore, try **Custard Beach.** For a complete list of vendors, check out www.grandcentralterminal.com.

to be kosher (only in New York!). And you don't have to be a vegetarian to love this place. The hearty dishes are always freshly prepared to order by the conscientious kitchen. Ingredients are top-quality, vegetables and legume dishes never overcooked, and the well-spiced sauces outstanding. The specialty is *dosai,* a large golden crepe filled with onions, potatoes, and other goodies, accompanied by coconut chutney and flavorful sauce. The food is very cheap, with nothing priced over $10. The restaurant is low-lit and attractive, with a pleasing ambience, making it a nice choice for a special night on the town. Service can be slow on occasion, so have patience and don't be shy about waiving down your waiter.

110 Lexington Ave. (between 27th and 28th sts.). ☎ 212/696-9458. www.pongal.org. Reservations not accepted. Main courses $6–$11 (most less than $9). DC, DISC, MC, V. Mon–Fri noon–3pm and 5–10pm; Sat–Sun noon–10pm. Subway: 6 to 28th St.

Prime Burger AMERICAN/HAMBURGERS Across the street from St. Patrick's Cathedral, this no-frills coffee shop is a heavenly find in a high-priced 'hood. The juicy burgers and well-stuffed sandwiches are tasty, the fries crispy and generous. The front seats, which might remind you of old wooden grammar-school desks, are great fun—especially when business-suited New Yorkers take their places at these oddities. A great stop during a day of Fifth Avenue shopping.

5 E. 51st St. (between Fifth and Madison aves.). ☎ 212/759-4729. Reservations not accepted. Main courses $3.25–$9. No credit cards. Mon–Fri 6am–6:30pm; Sat 6am–5pm. Subway: 6 to 51st St.

The Pump HEALTH-CONSCIOUS Here's a terrific stop for diners watching their figures as well as their wallets. An appealing mix of retro-cute and future-chic, with a counter in back and a few tables, The Pump espouses a philosophy that eating right doesn't have to mean boring. Everything is low-fat and high in protein but doesn't sacrifice flavor for healthfulness. This is casual food with natural ingredients: salads, sandwiches, "supercharged" combo platters, fresh juices, and high-protein and health shakes. Although they serve up a great nature burger (a blend of brown rice, sunflower seeds, herbs, and veggies), The

Pump isn't a vegetarian restaurant; lean beef, turkey, and chicken are served. Because they cater to a workout crowd that needs energy, portions are substantial. Salad dressings are fat-free, using tahini and honey mustard, and pizzas are prepared with nonfat mozzarella, low-sodium tomato sauce, and whole-wheat crust. At breakfast, eggs, pancakes, and potatoes are baked, never fried—so you can indulge in a steak-and-egg sandwich (served on a whole-wheat pita).

113 E. 31st St. (between Park and Lexington aves.). (C) 212/213-5733. www.thepumpenergyfood.com. Reservations not accepted. Breakfast $3.75–$8.50; sandwiches and salads $4.75–$7; full plates $8–$14. AE, MC, V. Mon–Thurs 9:30am–9:30pm; Fri 9:30am–8pm; Sat 11am–6:30pm. Subway: 6 to 33rd St. Also at 40 W. 55th St. (between Fifth and Sixth aves.; (C) 212/246-6844; subway: F to 57th St.).

QUICK BITES

Burger Joint ★, at Le Parker Meridien hotel, 118 W. 57th St. ((C) 212/708-7460). Who woulda thunk that a fancy hotel like **Le Parker Meridien** would be the home to a place called Burger Joint that serves great burgers at great prices ($5.95 for a cheeseburger). Will wonders never cease?

13 The Upper West Side

For good burgers and diner fare, visit **EJ's Luncheonette** (p. 156), 447 Amsterdam Ave., between 81st and 82nd streets ((C) 212/873-3444) or **Jackson Hole** (p. 187), 517 Columbus Ave., at 85th St. ((C) 212/362-5177). Vegetarians and health-minded diners might also consider **Zen Palate** (p. 166), 2170 Broadway, between 76th and 77th streets ((C) 212/501-7768).

For French baked goods, sandwiches, and salads of a divine order, also consider **Le Pain Quotidien** ★ (p. 148), at 50 W. 72nd St., between Columbus Avenue and Central Park West ((C) 212/712-9700).

You'll find some of the best bagels in New York on the Upper West Side, including **H&H Bagels,** 2239 Broadway, at 80th Street ((C) 212/595-8003); **Absolute Bagels,** 2788 Broadway, between 106th and 107th streets ((C) 212/932-2105); and **Columbia Bagels,** 2788 Broadway, at 110th Street ((C) 212/222-3200); for more information, see the box "Bagel Power" on p. 183.

Near Lincoln Center, **John's Pizzeria,** 48 W. 65th St., between Broadway and Central Park West ((C) 212/721-7001), serves up one of the city's best pies in a nice brick-walled dining room; see the box "Pizza New York Style on p. 157. What would the Upper West Side be without its own **Burritoville** (p. 138)—or two? There's one at 166 W. 72nd St., near Broadway ((C) 212/580-7700), and at 451 Amsterdam Ave., between 81st and 82nd streets ((C) 212/787-8181).

For one of the most satisfying meal deals in the city, head for the original **Gray's Papaya** 2090 Broadway, at 72nd Street ((C) 212/799-0243). Try the "recession special": $2.45 for two beef dogs and a fruit drink. The good thing is that at Gray's, there is always a recession.

All State Cafe *Finds* AMERICAN   This subterranean pub is one of Manhattan's undiscovered treasures—a classic neighborhood "snugger." It's easy to miss, and the regulars like it that way. The All State attracts a crowd drawn in by the casual ambience, the outstanding jukebox, and the superior burgers. If you're not in the burger mood, dig in to a variety of fresh salads and sandwiches, plus main courses like homemade fusilli with sautéed shrimp and scallops in a shiitake-mushroom sauce. The dining room behind the bar has casual, rough-hewn tables and chairs and an easygoing ambience; a fireplace makes it inviting in cold weather. Draft beers, a wine list featuring affordable labels from the United States and Australia, and a full bar round out the comfortable picture.

Absolute Bagels **1**

All State Café **23**

Amy's Bread **32**

Artie's Delicatessen **14**

Bardolino **36**

Barney Greengrass,
the Sturgeon King **10**

Big Nick's Burger Joint/
Pizza Joint **19**

Burritoville **15, 25, 35, 42**

Café con Leche **6, 17**

Celeste **12**

Columbia Bagels **1**

EJ's Luncheonette **16, 34**

Flor de Mayo **5**

Gabriela's **7, 22**

Good Enough to Eat **13**

Gray's Papaya **24**

H&H Bagel **18**

Hungarian Pastry Shop **3**

Jackson Hole **11, 31, 38, 45**

John's Pizzeria **27, 30**

Le Pain Quotidien **26, 29, 33, 39**

Nick's Family-Style
Restaurant and Pizzeria **44**

P&W's Sandwich
& More Shop **3**

Papaya King **41**

Pintaile's Pizza **41**

Popover Café **9**

Saigon Grill **8**

Serendipity 3 **28**

Silver Moon Bakery **2**

Tom's Restaurant **1**

Totonno's Pizzeria
Napolitano **37**

V&T Pizzeria **3**

Xando/Cosi **21**

Yura & Company **43**

Zen Palate **20**

Ⓜ Subway stop

250 W. 72nd St. (between Broadway and West End Ave.). © **212/874-1883.** Reservations not accepted. Main courses $10–$14. No credit cards. Daily 11:30am–4am (sometimes earlier; food nightly until 12:45am). Subway: 1, 2, 3, 9 to 72nd St.

Artie's Delicatessen JEWISH DELI Artie's opened in 1999 but already has the vibe of an institution. What's more, it's as good as many of the best delis in Manhattan (I prefer it over tourist traps like the Carnegie and the Stage), and far more cheery. In other words, Artie's is tourist-friendly, but in a good way; even New Yorkers appreciate it. All of your favorites are here—from corned beef to chopped liver to tongue on rye—and arrive at your table in top form. The pastrami is everything it should be, and the chicken soup with kreplach is a sore throat's worst nightmare. Artie's chili dogs deserve special note—they may be the best in town. Burgers, omelets, and salads are also on hand. Nostalgia-inducing desserts include Jell-O, baked apple, New York black-and-white cookies, very good homemade ruggelach, and sliced birthday cake every day ("No birthday necessary—song not included").

2290 Broadway (between 82nd and 83rd sts.). © **212/579-5959.** www.arties.com. Reservations not accepted. Main courses $6–$12 at breakfast, $6–$17 at lunch and dinner. AE, DISC, MC, V. Sun–Thurs 9am–11pm; Fri–Sat 9am–11:30pm. Subway: 1, 9 to 86th St.

Barney Greengrass, the Sturgeon King JEWISH DELI This daytime-only deli, going strong since 1908, is different from other delis; it's small and quiet, with an emphasis on smoked fish and service that's friendly rather than attitude-laden. It's a legend for its high-quality salmon (sable, gravlax, Nova Scotia, kippered, lox, pastrami—you choose), whitefish, and sturgeon (of course). But meat-lovers won't be disappointed: The triple-deckers are terrific (and much cheaper than at Midtown's delis), and the chicken liver inspired a raging, months-long debate among restaurant critics a few years back.

541 Amsterdam Ave. (between 86th and 87th sts.). © **212/724-4707.** Reservations not accepted. Breakfast $3.50–$14; sandwiches $2.50–$16 (most less than $10); smoked fish platters $16–$36 (most less than $22). No credit cards. Tues–Fri 8:30am–4pm (takeout 8am–6pm); Sat–Sun 8:30am–5pm (takeout 8am–6pm). Subway: 1, 9 to 86th St.

Big Nick's Burger and Pizza Joint (Kids) AMERICAN/PIZZA A neighborhood landmark since 1962, Big Nick's menu seems to have grown each year of its existence. Trying to decide if you want the Madrid burger, with olives, feta, and pimentos, with or without buffalo meat; a slice of Hawaiian pizza; or just an order of the spinach pie can be exhausting. If reading the menu is too much for you, peruse the numerous photos of celebrities who have supposedly chowed at Big Nick's over the years, or just keep your eyes on the non-stop "Three Stooges" marathon playing on the restaurant's televisions. Whatever you do, you'll never forget your Big Nick's experience. With all those diversions, it's a great place to take the kids; they'll never be bored.

2175 Broadway (at 77th St.). © **212/362-9238.** www.bignicksnyc.com. Reservations not accepted. Main courses $3.50–$19 (most less than $10). MC, V. Daily 24 hr. Subway: 1, 9 to 79th St.

Cafe con Leche (Value) LATIN AMERICAN This longtime favorite serves up terrific Cuban-style fare in a bright, comfortable, upscale luncheonette setting. All of the staples of Latin-Caribbean cuisine are here, including pressed sandwiches; empanadas (the meat-filled are best); terrific *ropa vieja* (Cuban-style slow-cooked and shredded beef); oxtail stew; and a wonderful paella, bursting with seafood and famous as the house specialty. Dishes come with your choice of red or black beans and yellow or white rice. Sprinkle some of their homemade

Bagel Power

Bagels are a quintessential New York food. People here are very loyal to their favorite bagels, and discussions about who makes the best bagel in New York often can lead to heated arguments. I have my favorite (see chapter 1, "Best Low-Cost Dining Bets"), but you won't go wrong with a bagel from any of the places I've listed below.

Absolute Bagels. 2708 Broadway, between 106th and 107th streets (*©* 212/932-2105). A new player on the scene and chief competitor to Columbia Bagels (see below). Their egg bagels, hot out of the oven, melt in your mouth, and their whitefish salad is perfectly smoky though not overpowering.

Columbia Bagels. 2836 Broadway, at 110th Street (*©* 212/222-3200). They say that their bagels are so good they named a university after them. And they are good; certainly good enough to keep Columbia students well fed and very happy. The homemade cheese spreads are also excellent.

Ess-A-Bagel. 359 First Ave., at 21st Street (*©* 212/260-2252; www.ess-a-bagel.com). When it comes to size, Ess-A-Bagel's are the best of the biggest; plump, chewy, and oh-so satisfying.

H&H Bagels. 2239 Broadway, at 80th Street (*©* 212/595-8003; www.handhbagel.com). Long reputed to be the best bagel in New York, and maybe as a result the owners arrogantly raised the price to the blasphemous rate of $1 a bagel. But they are very good, though some complain they are a bit too sweet. There's only takeout here, which means constantly fresh bagels . . . a good thing for the bagel aficionado.

Murray's Bagels. 500 Sixth Ave., between 12th and 13th streets (*©* 212/462-2830). There's nothing like a soft, warm bagel to begin your day, and Murray's does them very well indeed. Their smoked fish goes perfectly on their bagels.

garlic or pepper sauce on your food—if you dare. The café con leche is worthy of the restaurant's name. For a special treat, try the batidas, fresh milk shakes made from tropical fruits in flavors like papaya, piña colada, and mango.

424 Amsterdam Ave. (between 80th and 81st sts.). *©* 212/595-7000. Reservations not accepted. Main courses $5–$15 (most less than $10). AE, MC, V. Daily 8am–11pm. Also at 726 Amsterdam Ave. (between 95th and 96th sts.; *©* 212/595-7000; subway: 1, 2, 3, 9 to 96th St.).

Celeste ★★ *Finds* ITALIAN   In the land of smoked fish and Chinese restaurants, this new Italian restaurant is a welcome addition to the Upper West Side dining scene. Tiny but charming, Celeste features its own wood-burning pizza oven, which churns out thin-crust, simple but delicious pizzas. But pizza is not the only attraction; the "fritti" (fried) course is unique; the *fritto misto de pesce* (fried mixed seafood) is delectable, but really special are the fried zucchini blossoms, usually available in the summer and fall. The fresh pastas are better than the dried pasta; I never thought the fresh egg noodles with cabbage, shrimp, and sheep's cheese would work, but it was delicious. Not on the menu, but usually available, are artisanal plates of rare Italian cheeses served with homemade jams.

Though the main courses are also good, stick with the pizzas, antipasto, frittis, and pastas. For dessert, try the gelato; the pistachio was the best I've had in New York. The restaurant has been "discovered," so go early or go late—or expect a wait.

502 Amsterdam Ave. (between 84th and 85th sts). © **212/874-4559**. Reservations not accepted. Pizzas $10–$12; antipasto $7–$10; pastas $10; main courses $14–$16. No credit cards. Mon–Sat 5–11pm; Sun noon–3:30pm. Subway 1, 9 to 86th St.

Flor de Mayo ⭐ *Finds* LATIN AMERICAN/CHINESE   Cuban/Chinese cuisine is a New York phenomenon that started in the late 1950s when Cubans of Chinese heritage immigrated to New York after the revolution. Most of the immigrants took up residence on the Upper West Side, and Cuban/Chinese restaurants flourished. Many have disappeared, but the best one, Flor de Mayo, remains and is so popular that a new branch opened farther south on Amsterdam Avenue. The kitchen excels at both sides of the menu. The best dish on the massive menu is the half *la brasa* chicken lunch special, beautifully spiced and slow-roasted until it's fork tender and falling off the bone, served with a giant pile of fried rice, bounteous with roast pork, shrimp, and veggies. Offered Monday through Saturday until 4:30pm, the whole meal is just $6.95, and it's enough to fortify you for the day. Service and atmosphere is reminiscent of Chinatown: efficient and lightning-quick. My favorite combo: the hearty, noodles, greens, shrimp, and pork-laden Chinese soup with an order of yellow rice and black beans.

2651 Broadway (between 100th and 101st sts.). © **212/663-5520** or 212/595-2525. Reservations not accepted. Main courses $4.50–$19 (most under $10); lunch specials $5–$7 (Mon–Sat to 4:30pm). AE, MC, V ($15 minimum). Daily noon–midnight. Subway: 1, 9 to 103rd St. Also at 484 Amsterdam Ave. (between 83rd and 84th sts.; © **212/787-3388**; Subway: 1, 9 to 86th St).

Gabriela's ⭐⭐ *Value* MEXICAN   Until chef/owner Garbriela Hernandez opened her restaurant almost 10 years ago, authentic Mexican food was difficult to find on the Upper West Side, not to mention most of New York City. Flavors of her native Guadalajara are prominent here; this is not your typical combination taco restaurant. Gabriela's roast chicken, a blend of Yucatán spices and a slow-roasting rotisserie, results in some of the tenderest, juiciest chicken in town—and at $7 for a half chicken with two sides (plenty for all but the biggest eaters) and $13 for a whole, it's one of the city's best bargains, too. All of the specialties on the extensive menu are well prepared, generously portioned, and satisfying. The *pozole*, a traditional hominy-and-chicken and pork stew, is a treat, while the fresh, chunky, perfectly limed guacamole is some of the best I've had. I'm partial to the original, uptown restaurant, where the dining room is large, bright, and pretty, with a pleasing south-of-the-border flair, and the service is quick and attentive. Try one of Gabriela's yummy fruit shakes (both mango and papaya are good bets) or tall *agua frescas* (fresh-fruit drinks), which come in a variety of tropical flavors; beer, wine, and margaritas are served, too.

685 Amsterdam Ave., at 93rd St. (© **212/961-0574**). www.gabrielas.com. Reservations accepted for parties of 6 or more. Main courses $5–$9 at lunch, $7–$20 at brunch and dinner (most less than $15); early dinner specials $9.95, includes glass of wine or frozen margarita (Mon–Fri 4–7pm); Sat–Sun 3:30–6:30pm). AE, DC, MC, V. Mon–Thurs 11:30am–11pm; Fri–Sat 11:30am–midnight; Sun 11:30am–10pm. Subway: 1, 2, 3, 9 to 96th St. Also at 315 Amsterdam Ave. (at 75th St.; © **212/875-8532**; Subway: 1, 2, 3, 9 to 72nd St.).

Good Enough To Eat ⭐ *Kids* AMERICAN   For 23 years, the crowds have been lining up on weekends outside Good Enough To Eat to experience chef/owner Carrie Levin's incredible breakfasts (see the box "Breakfast, Not Brunch!" on p. 161); as a result, lunch and dinner at the restaurant have been somewhat overlooked, which is too bad, because those meals can be as good as the breakfasts.

The restaurant's cow motif, the cozy throw pillows, and farmhouse knick-knacks imply hearty, home-cooked food; and that is what is done best here. Don't waver from ordering the mainstays: meatloaf with gravy and mashed potatoes; traditional turkey dinner with cranberry relish, gravy, and corn-bread stuffing; macaroni and cheese; griddled corn bread; Vermont spinach salad; and the barbecue sandwich, roasted chicken with barbecue sauce and homemade potato chips. And save room for the homemade desserts; though the selection is often overwhelming, I can never resist the coconut cake. This is food you loved as a kid, one reason why the kids will love it as well. There are only 20 tables here, so expect a wait on weekends during the day or for dinner after 6pm.

483 Amsterdam Ave. (between 83rd and 84th sts.). ℂ 212/496-0163. www.citysearch.com/nyc/good enough. Breakfast $4.50–$9; lunch $8.50–$15; dinner $8.50–$23 (most under $18). AE, MC, V. Breakfast Mon–Fri 8am–4pm, Sat–Sun 9am–4pm; lunch Mon–Fri 11:30am–4pm; dinner Mon–Thurs 5:30–10:30pm, Fri–Sat 5:30–11pm, Sun 5:30–10pm. Subway: 1, 9 to 86th St.

Noche Mexicana ★ *Finds* MEXICAN   This tiny, new Mexican restaurant serves some of the best tamales in New York. Wrapped in cornhusks, as a good tamale should be, they come in two varieties: in a red mole sauce with shredded chicken or in a green tomatillo sauce with shredded pork. There are three tamales in each order, which costs only $5, making it a cheap and almost perfect lunch. The burritos are authentic and meals unto themselves. The *tinga* burrito, shredded chicken in a tomato-and-onion chipotle sauce, is my favorite. Each is stuffed with rice, beans, and guacamole. Don't get fancy here; stick with the tamales, burritos, and soft tacos, the best being the taco *al pastor,* a taco stuffed with pork marinated with pineapple and onions.

852 Amsterdam Ave. (between 101st and 102nd sts.). ℂ 212/662-6900 or 212/662-7400. Burritos $6–$7.50; tacos $2; tamales $5; Mexican dishes $8.50–$9.50. AE, DISC, MC, V. Sun–Thurs 10am–11pm; Fri–Sat 10am–midnight. Subway: 1, 9 to 103rd St.

Popover Cafe *Kids* HOME-STYLE AMERICAN   The first thing people usually call Popover's is kid-friendly, a nod to its child-size burger, PBJ sandwiches, and decor that's chockablock with teddy bears. But grownups will like it just as much. Everybody gets addicted to the fluffy popovers with strawberry butter or preserves. The full dinner entrees are a bit pricey, but Popover's forte is comfort food that makes hearty and affordable breakfasts and lunches: omelets and scrambles, chili and soups, and salads and sandwiches. A bowl of one of the day's homemade soups (vegetarian three-bean and split-pea are two of my favorites) accompanied by a popover makes a more-than-satisfying lunch for a few dollars. Service is warm and welcoming; in fact, eating here feels like stepping into somebody's big, old, hospitable New England home. Well worth a stop. Beware the crowds at brunch, however, which can ruin the mood.

551 Amsterdam Ave. (between 86th and 87th sts.). ℂ 212/595-8555. Reservations not accepted. Main courses $6–$11 at breakfast and brunch, $9–$15 at lunch, $8.50–$21 at dinner (most less than $15). AE, MC, V. Mon–Fri 8am–10pm; Sat–Sun 9am–10pm. Subway: 1, 9 to 86th St.

Saigon Grill ★ *Value* VIETNAMESE   This cafeterialike restaurant isn't very fancy, but the artistry in the food preparation, along with whopping portions at bargain-basement prices, more than makes up for the too-bright lighting and uncomfortable seating. I always judge Vietnamese restaurants by their salads, and Saigon Grill's are outstanding. The *goi du du,* shredded green papaya salad with grilled beef and crushed peanuts, is a Vietnamese specialty and is done perfectly here. But my favorite salad is the bean-curd and baby-green salad, fresh mesclun greens with slivers of fried bean curd topped by crushed peanuts in a spicy *nuac cham* sauce. The soups can be meals here; *pho bo* is comforting, with oxtail stock and thin slices of rare beef, while the *canh chua* (hot-and-sour soups) will help clear your sinuses. The curries are popular here, but I prefer the basil dishes, in particular the basil prawns: jumbo shrimp with vegetables and Thai basil in a spicy fish sauce. If you crave noodles, try the *bun xao*, stir-fried rice noodles with shredded vegetables, egg, and crushed peanuts with your choice of chicken, shrimp, beef, or vegetarian. Come with a group and be prepared to share; there will be more than enough for everyone.

620 Amsterdam Ave. (at 90th St.) ℂ 212/875-9072. Lunch special $4.95–$7.50; soups $2.95–$6.50; main courses $8–$14 (most under $10). AE, DISC, DC, MC, V. Daily 11am–midnight. Subway 1, 9 to 86th St.

Tom's Restaurant AMERICAN DINER   Tom's would be just any other diner if it weren't for its famous connections: This is the restaurant that served as the exterior for Monk's on *Seinfeld* and inspired Suzanne Vega to write "Tom's Diner." It's worth a pilgrimage if you're a Jerry fan or if you're in the neighborhood. It's popular with Columbia University students, thanks to its long hours and cheap coffee-shop fare. Expect the standards, from three-egg omelets to tuna salad. The '70s-era waitstaff emits the requisite attitude and won't think twice of rushing you when it's crowded.

2880 Broadway (at 112th St.). ℂ 212/864-6137. Reservations not accepted. Main courses $3–$10. No credit cards. Sun–Wed 6am–1:30am; Thurs–Sat 24 hr. Subway: 1, 9 to 110th St.

Xando/Cosi GOURMET SANDWICHES/CAFE/TAKEOUT   City coffeehouse chain Xando met sandwich maker Cosí, and it's a match made in heaven. The stars of the menu are Cosí's sandwiches, baked-on-the-premises pocket breads filled with your choice of mix-and-match fillings and spreads, plus combos for those who can't decide. Smoked Nova salmon with goat cheese and cucumber is one of my favorites, but I also love the tandoori chicken with roasted red peppers, and the tomato, basil, and mozzarella. The kitchen bakes personal pizzas on yummy Cosí bread as well, with such toppings as goat cheese and roasted red peppers. The Xando side of the equation serves up drinks; wine, beer, and coffee cocktails like the Mocha Kiss (Irish cream, Kahlúa, Grand Marnier, and mocha coffee). In a coffeehouse version of s'mores, all of the necessary ingredients—chocolate, graham crackers, and giant marshmallows—are served in a pupu platter tray, and you fire your own over the open flame. The setting is *Friends*-reminiscent coffeehouse style, with bright colors and comfy IKEA-ish furniture. If you see a crowd, don't despair; there's additional seating downstairs.

2160 Broadway (at 76th St.). ℂ 212/595-5616. www.xandocosi.com. Reservations not accepted. Soups and salads $2.50–$8; sandwiches and pizzas $6–$9. AE, MC, V. Sun–Thurs 7am–midnight; Fri–Sat 7am–2am. Subway: 1, 2, 3, 9 to 72nd St. Also at 841 Broadway (at 13th St.; ℂ 212/614-8544; subway: 4, 5, 6, L, N, R to 14th St./Union Sq.); 504 Sixth Ave. (at 13th St.; ℂ 212/462-4188; subway: F to 14th St.); 257 Park Ave. S. (at 21st St.; ℂ 212/505-7978; subway: 6 to 23rd St.); 461 Park Ave. S. (at 31st St.; ℂ 212/634-3479; subway: 6 to 33rd St.); 320 Park Ave. (at 51st St.; ℂ 212/754-6144; subway: 6 to 51st St.). Call ℂ 212/653-1600 or visit website for additional sandwich-bar-only locations.

QUICK BITES

Farther uptown, the place to go is **V&T Pizzeria** ⍟, 1024 Amsterdam Ave., between 110th and 111th streets (ℂ 212/666-8051 or 212/663-1708). This is a sit-down (or carryout) restaurant with red-checked tablecloths and traditional pies with red sauce and a chewy crust. V&T caters to a Columbia University crowd, so prices stay low—how can you *not* splurge on one of the mascarpone-filled cannolis for dessert, right?

After pizza at the V&T, head next door to the lovely, worn **Hungarian Pastry Shop,** 1030 Amsterdam Ave., between 110th and 111th streets (© **212/866-4230**)—a landmark for 40 years. It's an ideal stop for coffee and pastry or a plateful of crumbly, buttery cookies. For something more substantial, head next door to **P&W's Sandwich & More Shop** (© **212/222-2245**), specializing in homemade soups, bagels, made-to-order sandwiches, by-the-pound salads, and the like. There are no tables, but you're welcome to pick up your food and take it over to the pastry shop to enjoy. If you're staying in the area and your room has kitchen facilities, P&W's also makes a good spot at which to stock up on supplies like milk, cereal, peanut butter, coffee, paper plates, plastic utensils, and the like.

Silver Moon Bakery, 2740 Broadway, at 105th Street (© **212/866-4717**), is bright, airy, and alive with fresh-baked pastry smells. Come by for a first-rate java fix and a fresh-from-the-oven brioche, a muffin, or other baked goods.

14 The Upper East Side

There's also a branch of **EJ's Luncheonette** (p. 156), the retro all-American diner, at 1271 Third Ave., at 73rd Street (© **212/472-0600**).

Burritoville (p. 138) is at 1489 First Ave., between 77th and 78th streets (© **212/472-8800**), and 1606 Third Ave., between 90th and 91st streets (© **212/410-2255**).

John's Pizzeria (p. 157) has a location at 408 E. 64th St. (between First and York aves.; © **212/935-2895**); see the box "Pizza New York Style," on p. 157.

For baked goods and sandwiches and salads, consider **Le Pain Quotidien** ★★ (p. 148), which has three Upper East Side locations: 833 Lexington Ave., between 63rd and 64th streets (© **212/755-5810**); 1336 First Ave., between 71st and 72nd streets (© **212/717-4800**); and an easy walk from Museum Mile at 1131 Madison Ave., between 84th and 85th streets (© **212/327-4900**).

Bardolino *Value* ITALIAN *Shhh*—don't tell Bardolino, but they should be charging more. This trattoria prepares terrific pastas in a romantic atmosphere. On my last visit, I enjoyed a traditional Caesar, followed by a fantastic penne alla vodka with peas and prosciutto in a lightly creamy pink sauce—so good I dream about it when I'm hungry. Other choices include fusilli *norcia,* in a tomato sauce with hot and sweet Italian sausage; and a first-rate puttanesca. The wine list is well priced and pleasing. This is the kind of solicitous service you usually have to pay twice as much to enjoy. The fixed-price meal deals at weekend brunch, lunch, and early dinner make an already excellent value even better.

1496 Second Ave. (at 78th St.). © 212/734-9050 or 212/734-9395. Reservations accepted. Pastas $7–$11; main courses $11–$13 (specials may be slightly higher); 2-course fixed-price lunch $5.95 (daily to 3:45pm); weekend brunch $7.95 (with mimosa or juice); 2-course fixed-price dinner $9.95 (daily 4–7pm). AE, DC, MC, V. Mon–Fri noon–11:30pm; Sat–Sun 11am–11:30pm. Subway: 6 to 77th St.

Jackson Hole *Kids* AMERICAN The "home of the 7-oz. burger" has been satisfying the hunger pangs of New Yorkers with all-American diner food at low prices since 1972. There's no faulting the juicy burger, which comes in more than 30 topping combos, all piled high on a hefty beef or turkey patty, or a marinated and grilled chicken breast. The Eastsider—a bacon-cheese version topped with ham, mushrooms, tomatoes, and fried onions—is actually trademarked. Hearty salads, blue-plate specials, and stuffed baked potatoes are also on hand, and eggs, omelets, and fluffy pancakes are served all day. This location has garden dining.

232 E. 64th St. (between Second and Third aves.). © 212/371-7187. www.jacksonholeburgers.com. Reservations not accepted. Sandwiches and main courses $5–$14 (most less than $10). AE, MC, V. Mon–Thurs

10:30am–1am; Fri–Sat 10:30am–1:30am; Sun 10:30am–midnight. Subway: 6 to 68th St. Also at 521 Third Ave. (at 35th St.; ℂ 212/679-3264; subway: 6 to 33rd St.); 1611 Second Ave. (between 83rd and 84th sts.; ℂ 212/737-8788; subway: 4, 5, 6 to 86th St.); 1270 Madison Ave. (at 91st St.; ℂ 212/427-2820; subway: 6 to 96th St.); 517 Columbus Ave. (at 85th St.; ℂ 212/362-5177; subway: B, C to 86th St.).

Nick's Family-Style Restaurant and Pizzeria ⭐ *Kids* ITALIAN   Since 1994, Nick Angelis has wowed them in Forest Hills, Queens with his pizzas. In 2003, he took his act to Manhattan, where the pizza is garnering equally high praise. The pizza is thin-crust, with the proper proportions of creamy, homemade mozzarella and fresh tomato sauce. But this is much more than a pizzeria; try the light, lemony baked clams or "Josephine's" perfectly breaded eggplant parmigiana. If you dare combine pizza with a calzone, this is the place; Nick's calzone, stuffed with ricotta and mozzarella cheese, is spectacular. The *orechhiette* with broccoli rabe and sausage is the pasta winner, while the filet of sole oreganato Livornese with mussels is the standout main course. Save room for an extra-large cannoli for dessert; the shell is perfectly flaky and the filling ultra-creamy. Full orders are enough to feed two or three and are a great bargain for a group, but half orders are also available. The room is comfortable and far from fancy. Go early or be prepared to wait.

1814 Second Ave. (at 94th St.). ℂ 212/987-5700. Pizzas $11–$13; Macaroni half orders $5–$11, full orders $11–$22; main courses half order $7.50–$11, full orders $15–$22. AE, DC, DISC, MC, V. Sun–Thurs 11:30am–11pm, Sat–Sun 11:30am–midnight. Subway: 6 to 96th St.

Serendipity 3 *Kids* AMERICAN   You'd never guess that this whimsical place was once a favored stop for Pop guru Andy Warhol. Wonders never cease—and neither does the confection at this delightful restaurant and sweet shop. Serendipity's small front-room curiosity shop overflows with odd objects, from jigsaw puzzles to silly jewelry. But the real action is behind the shop, where the quintessential American soda fountain reigns supreme. Happy people gather at marble-topped ice-cream-parlor tables for burgers and foot-long hot dogs, meat-loaf with mashed potatoes and gravy, and salads and sandwiches with cute names like "The Catcher in the Rye" (their own twist on the BLT, with chicken and Russian dressing—on rye, of course). What they're really there for are the desserts. The restaurant's signature is Frozen Hot Chocolate, a slushie version of everybody's cold-weather favorite; other crowd pleasers include dark double devil mousse, celestial carrot cake, lemon icebox pie, and anything with hot fudge. Serendipity is a charmer to be appreciated by adults and kids alike.

225 E. 60th St. (between Second and Third aves.). ℂ 212/838-3531. www.serendipity3.com. Reservations accepted for lunch and dinner (not just dessert). Main courses $7–$18; sweets and sundaes $5–$17 (most under $10). AE, DC, DISC, MC, V. Sun–Thurs 11:30am–midnight; Fri 11:30am–1am; Sat 11:30am–2am. Subway: N, R to Lexington Ave.; 4, 5, 6 to 59th St.

QUICK BITES

The original **Papaya King**, 179 E. 86th St., at Third Avenue (ℂ 212/369-0648), is Gray's Papaya's chief rival. It's not as good and a bit more expensive, but they still cook a pretty fair hot dog here.

For more refined tastes, there's **Yura & Company**, 6045 Third Ave., at 92nd Street (ℂ 212/860-8060), one of the Upper East Side's best-kept secrets. This gourmet bakery/cafe serves good coffee, scones, and muffins, and a selection of foods that are perfect for a Central Park picnic (the 90th St. entrance is a few blocks away). Or you can opt for table service in the country-style dining room, a cute spot for breakfast or a well-made sandwich. Good angel-food cake, too.

Pintaile's Pizza, at 26 E. 91st St., between Fifth and Madison avenues (ℂ 212/722-1967; open daily 11am–9:30pm), dresses their organic crusts with tomatoes, extra-virgin olive oil, and fresh ingredients. Pintaile's is also at 1237 Second Ave., between 64th and 65th streets (© **212/752-6222;** open daily 11am–10:30pm).

For a more traditional pie, head to **Totonno's Pizzeria Napolitano,** 1544 Second Ave., between 80th and 81st streets (© **212/327-2800**). Recently opened on the Upper East Side scene for coffee and pastry is **Amy's Bread** (p. 189), 972 Lexington Ave., between 70th and 71st streets (© **212/537-0270**).

15 Harlem

Also consider **Patsy's Pizzeria** (see the box "Pizza New York Style" on p. 157). **Sylvia's,** 328 Lenox Ave., between 126th and 127th streets (© **212/996-0660**), once the best soul-food restaurant in Harlem, has turned into a tourist trap. If you are determined to go, make it for the Sunday gospel brunch, which is an absolute joy.

There is an extension of Africa #1 (p. 189) called **African Restaurant #1,** at 247 W. 116th St., between Seventh and Eighth avenues (© **212/666-9400**) with the same menu and the same exotic ambience.

Bayou ✹ CREOLE   This intimate, casually sophisticated Creole restaurant is a symbol of Harlem's renaissance. The room is stylish in a trend-defying way, with burnished yellow walls, big oak tables, a mahogany bar, and dim lighting. The well-prepared food is pure New Orleans: shrimp and okra gumbo, cornmeal-fried oysters, sautéed chicken livers, and shrimp rémoulade with deviled eggs. Shrimp Creole and crawfish étouffée are both served in their own piquant sauces over rice. Farm-raised catfish is marinated and sliced thin, then deep-fried in cornmeal until the outside is perfectly crisp, while the inside stays moist and flaky. Salads are crisp and bounteous. Service is extremely attentive and professional. An affordable wine list and well-priced desserts and starters make Bayou a good value, to boot. The fine glass of Pinot Noir I had would've been $8 anywhere below 96th Street; here, it was just $6. Desserts are divine; don't pass up the bread pudding, made with fresh peaches and a scrumptious bourbon sauce.

308 Lenox Ave. (between 125th and 126th sts.). © 212/426-3800. www.bayouinharlem.com. Reservations recommended for dinner. Main courses $8–$15 at lunch, $9–$23 at dinner (most less than $18); Sun brunch $14–$21 (includes starter and mimosa or Bloody Mary). AE, DC, MC, V. Lunch: Mon–Fri 11:30am–4pm; Dinner Mon–Thu 6–10pm, Fri–Sat 6–11pm; Brunch Sun 12–4pm. Happy Hour Mon–Thu 5–7pm.

Charles' Southern-Style Kitchen ✹ *Finds* SOUL FOOD   Nothing fancy about this place, just a brightly-lit, 25-seater on a not-very-attractive block in upper Harlem. But you don't come for fancy; you come for soul food at its simplest and freshest. And you better come hungry. The all-you-can-eat buffet features crunchy, incredibly moist pan-fried chicken, ribs in a tangy sauce with meat falling off the bone, smoky stewed oxtails in a thick brown onion gravy, macaroni and cheese, collard greens with bits of smoked turkey, black-eyed peas, and corn bread warm and not overly sweet. Desserts are made fresh daily; I had an incredible slice of carrot cake on my last visit. The beverage choices are limited to lemonade or ice tea, so BYOB of something stronger. Brave the long journey uptown; you'll not regret the experience. Opening hours, however, can be erratic, so call ahead before you make the trek.

2841 Eighth Ave. (between 151st and 152nd sts.). © 877/813-2920 or 212/926-4313. All-you-can-eat-buffet lunch $7; dinner $10 Mon–Thurs, $12 Fri–Sun. AE, MC, V. Sun 1–8pm; Mon 4pm–midnight; Tues–Sat noon–4am. Subway: D to 115th St.

La Fonda Boricua ★ *Finds* PUERTO RICAN   The food of Puerto Rico is vastly underrated, and the best of that cuisine can be found here in the heart of El Barrio. Was that singer Marc Anthony sitting across from New York Yankee Bernie Williams? This stylish, 75-seat former diner is a hangout for leaders of the local Latino community and beyond: politicians, artists, writers, musicians, and ballplayers who convene for delicious Puerto Rican staples such as tender, succulent octopus salad; crispy *chicharrones* of pork; slightly smoky *arroz con pollo;* garlic-laden *lechon asado* (roasted pork shoulder); thinly pounded citrus-marinated steak smothered with onions, rice, and beans in many varieties; and that artery-clogging favorite, *mofongo* (fried mashed plantains with garlic and crispy pieces of pork rind). They also come for the creative vibes encouraged by the owners, Jorge and Roberto Ayala, who have adorned the restaurant with paintings from local artists, promote impromptu jams from visiting musicians, and foster an atmosphere of Latino sophistication. The portions are more than generous and the prices easily affordable. The only disappointment was the lack of variety for dessert; flan, though excellent, was the only option.

169 E. 106th St. (between Third and Lexington aves.). ℂ 212/410-7292. Lunch $5–$8; dinner $7–$10. No credit cards. Daily 10am–10pm. Subway: 6 to 103rd St.

Miss Mamie's Spoonbread Too ★ *Finds* SOUTHERN   Entering this bright, strawberry-curtained charmer is like stepping straight into South Carolina. Take a seat at one of the retro Formica-topped tables and nibble from the plate of corn bread as you peruse the menu of Southern classics: fried chicken, barbecue shrimp (great sauce!), and short ribs falling off the bone and topped with a perfect gravy (zesty but not too peppery). If you can't choose, try the sampler plate, a "smorgasbord of Southern delights." Every entree comes with your choice of two sides, including macaroni and cheese, collard greens, candied yams, and better-than-mom-makes potato salad. Save room for dessert, which follows the traditional line with sweet-potato pie, banana pudding, and home-baked cobblers and cakes. Service is charming and attentive; beer and wine are available.

366 W. 110th St. (between Columbus and Manhattan aves.). ℂ 212/865-6744. Reservations not accepted. Main courses $7–$15. MC, V. Mon–Sat noon–10:30pm; Sun 11am–10:30pm. Subway: 2, 3 to 125th St. Also at 547 Lenox Ave. (between 137th and 138th sts.; ℂ 212/690-3100; subway: 2, 3 to 135th St.).

QUICK BITES
Papaya King has another location at 121 W. 125th St., between Lenox Avenue and Adam Clayton Powell Boulevard (ℂ **212/665-5732**). The two-all-beef-franks-and-an-all-natural-fruit-drink combo is a bargain at $4.30.

16 Brooklyn
QUICK BITES
Consider dropping in on **Peter Luger Steakhouse** ★, 178 Broadway, at Driggs Avenue, Williamsburg (ℂ **718/387-7400**). Not for a steak—that's beyond your budget if you are reading this book—but for the "Luger-Burger," one of the best in the city, which goes for a paltry $5.95; fries, cheese, or bacon are extra.

Satisfy your sweet tooth at the **Brooklyn Ice Cream Factory** ★, Fulton Ferry Landing Pier, Brooklyn Heights (ℂ **718/246-3963**) for the best ice cream in the city and a great view of the Manhattan skyline. And don't forget about **Grimaldi's Pizzeria,** 19 Old Fulton St., between Front and Water streets (ℂ **718/858-4300**), one of the best pizzerias in the city; see "Pizza New York Style" on p. 157.

If this is your first trip to New York, face facts: It will be impossible to take in the entire city. Because New York is almost unfathomably big and constantly changing, you could live your whole life here and still make fascinating daily discoveries. This chapter is designed to give you an overview so you can narrow your choices to the itinerary that best captures your needs and interests.

Decide on a few things you absolutely must see and do, and then let the city take you on its own ride. Inevitably, you'll be blown off course by unplanned diversions that are as much fun as what you meant to see.

1 Sights & Attractions by Neighborhood

MANHATTAN
EAST VILLAGE & NOHO
Merchant's House Museum ✦
(p. 233)

THE FLATIRON DISTRICT/
UNION SQUARE
Center for Jewish History (p. 215)
Flatiron Building (p. 232)
Theodore Roosevelt Birthplace
(p. 230)
Union Square Park (p. 246)

GREENWICH VILLAGE
Forbes Magazine Galleries (p. 217)
Washington Square Park (p. 246)

HARLEM
Abyssinian Baptist Church ✦
(p. 235)
Astor Row Houses (p. 231)
Jumel Terrace Historic District
(p. 231)
Morris-Jumel Mansion ✦ (p. 231)
Mother A.M.E. Zion Church
(p. 236)
Schomburg Center for Research in
Black Culture (p. 229)
Strivers' Row (p. 231)
Studio Museum in Harlem
(p. 230)

Sugar Hill (p. 231)
Sylvan Terrace (p. 231)

LOWER EAST SIDE
Lower East Side Tenement
Museum ✦ (p. 222)

LOWER MANHATTAN/
FINANCIAL DISTRICT/
NEW YORK HARBOR
Battery Park ✦✦ (p. 244)
Bowling Green Park (p. 245)
Brooklyn Bridge ✦✦ (p. 203)
Castle Clinton National
Monument (p. 245)
Ellis Island ✦✦ (p. 204)
Federal Hall National Memorial
(p. 217)
Fraunces Tavern Museum (p. 220)
Museum of American Financial
History (p. 223)
Museum of Jewish Heritage—
A Living Memorial to the
Holocaust ✦ (p. 223)
National Museum of the American
Indian (p. 227)
New York City Police Museum
(p. 228)
New York Stock Exchange ✦✦
(p. 211)

Downtown Attractions

Midtown Attractions

Uptown Attractions

American Folk Art Museum:
Eva & Morris Feld Gallery **20**

American Museum of
Natural History **25**

The Ansonia **23**

Asia Society **15**

Cathedral of St. John the Divine **1**

Central Park Zoo **18**

Children's Museum
of Manhattan **26**

Cooper-Hewitt
National Design Museum **6**

The Dakota **22**

El Museo del Barrio **3**

The Frick Collection **14**

Gracie Mansion **11**

Guggenheim Museum **8**

Jewish Museum **5**

Lasker Rink **2**

Lincoln Center **21**

Metropolitan Museum of Art **12**

Mount Vernon Hotel
Museum & Garden **16**

Museum of the
City of New York **4**

National Academy of Design **7**

Neue Galerie **9**

New York Historical Society **24**

92nd Street Y **10**

Rose Center for
Earth and Space **25**

Temple Emanu-El **17**

Tisch Children's Zoo **18**

Whitney Museum of
American Art **13**

Wollman Rink **19**

E. 106th St.
E. 105th St.
E. 104th St.
E. 103rd St.
E. 102nd St.
E. 101st St.
E. 100th St.
E. 99th St.
E. 98th St.
E. 97th St.
E. 96th St.
E. 95th St.
E. 94th St.
E. 93rd St.
E. 92nd St.
E. 91st St.
E. 90th St.
E. 89th St.
E. 88th St.
E. 87th St.
E. 86th St.
E. 85th St.
E. 84th St.
E. 83rd St.
E. 82nd St.
E. 81st St.
E. 80th St.
E. 79th St.
E. 78th St.
E. 77th St.
E. 76th St.
E. 75th St.
E. 74th St.
E. 73rd St.
E. 72nd St.
E. 71st St.
E. 70th St.
E. 69th St.
E. 68th St.
E. 67th St.
E. 66th St.
E. 65th St.
E. 64th St.
E. 63rd St.
E. 62nd St.
E. 61st St.
E. 60th St.
E. 59th St.

Mount Sinai
Hospital

MUSEUM MILE

Fifth Ave.
Madison Ave.
Park Ave.
Lexington Ave.
Third Ave.
Second Ave.
First Ave.
York Ave.
East End Ave.

The
Reservoir

Transverse

The
Great
Lawn

Metropolitan
Museum of Art

Transverse

PARK

Transverse

Central
Park
Zoo

Wollman
Rink

Central Park South

UPPER EAST
SIDE

FDR Dr.

CARL SCHURZ
PARK

East River

ROOSEVELT ISLAND

Ward's Island Footbridge

WARD'S ISLAND
PARK

WARD'S
ISLAND

Upper
Manhattan

Uptown

Midtown

Downtown

0   1/4 mi
0   0.25 km

From Lower
Level

To
Upper
Level

Sutton Pl.

Roosevelt Island Tram

Queensboro Bridge

Tips **Alert: Subway Access Update**

Changes in normal subway service happen almost every weekend. Stops are skipped, routes changed . . . it's enough to frustrate a veteran New York subway rider. I *strongly* recommend you check with the **Metropolitan Transit Authority** at ℂ **718/330-1234** or **www.mta.nyc.ny.us** before you plan your travel routes; your hotel concierge or any token-booth clerk should also be able to assist you.

MARBLE HILL

Kingsbridge Rd.

Baker Field

87

Fordham Rd.

New York Botanical Garden

Bronx Zoo

0   1/2 mi
0   0.5 km

M Subway stop

Isham Park

Inwood Hill Park

207th St.

Dyckman St.

Nagle Ave.

Tenth Ave.

9A

Fort Tryon Park

Henry Hudson Pkwy.

Riverside Dr.

Broadway

Audubon Ave.

Amsterdam Ave.

University Ave.

Grand Concourse

95   1

W. 181st St.

Cross Bronx Expwy.

Claremont Park

J. Hood Wright Park

St. Nicholas

87

THE BRONX

George Washington Bridge

Fort Washington Park

Harlem River Dr.

Grand Concourse

John Mullaly Park

Broadway

Macombs Dam Park

E. 161st St.

Franz Sigel Park

Yankee Stadium

Melrose Ave.

Westchester Ave.

W.155th St.

Trinity Park

Jackie Robinson Park

Young Park

E. 149th St.

St. Mary's Park

Hamilton Heights/ Sugar Hill Historic District

Broadway

Amsterdam Ave.

Convent Ave.

St. Nicholas

W. 145th St.

Major Deegan Expwy.

Third Ave.

Willis Ave.

ATTRACTIONS
Abyssinian Baptist Church **7**
Astor Row Houses **10**
Cathedral of
    St. John the Divine **15**
The Cloisters **2**
Dyckman Farmhouse Museum **1**
Jumel Terrace Historic District **3**
Morris–Jumel Mansion **4**
Mother A.M.E. Zion Church **8**
Schomburg Center for
    Research in Black Culture **9**
Strivers' Row **6**
Studio Museum in Harlem **12**
Sugar Hill **5**
Sylvan Terrace **4**

NIGHTLIFE
Apollo Theatre **13**
Lenox Lounge **11**
Showmans Cafe **14**

Hudson River

9A

Riverside Dr.

W. 135th St.

St. Nicholas Park

Douglass Blvd.

Adam Clayton Powell Jr. Blvd.

Malcolm X Blvd.

W. 138th St.

E. 138th St.

87

Bruckner Blvd.

Fifth Ave.

Harlem River Park

Henry Hudson Pkwy.

Sakura Park

W. 125th St.

Broadway

Morningside Park

Frederick

St. Nicholas

Lenox Ave./

Marcus Garvey Park

Triborough Bridge

Randall's Island Park

Columbia University

Kingsbridge

Adam Clayton Powell Jr. Blvd.

Mount Morris Historic District

W. 116th St.

Thomas Jefferson Park

278

Triborough Bridge

15

W. 110th St. (Cathedral Pkwy.)

Harlem Meer

E. 110th St.

E. 110th St. Recreation Pier

WARD'S ISLAND

W.

106th St.

E. 106th

St.

FDR Dr.

Ward's Island Park

West End Ave.

Broadway

Amsterdam Ave.

Columbus Ave.

Manhattan Ave.

Central Park West

Central Park

Fifth Ave.

Madison Ave.

Park Ave.

Lexington Ave.

Third Ave.

Second Ave.

First Ave.

Harlem River

East River

97th St. Transverse

M Subway stop

QUEENS

Upper Manhattan

Uptown

Midtown

Downtown

Tips **Advance-Planning Tip**

If you're planning your itinerary around specific attractions, make sure they'll be open while you're in town. This is also a good way to check current programming, such as museum schedules, and prioritize your time—there will always be more to see and do than you'll have time for.

Also, if you're planning on hitting many major attractions while you're in town, consider buying the **CityPass,** which can save you fully half on regular admission to such attractions as the Museum of Natural History, the Empire State Building, and others; see p. 25 for details.

Museum of Sex (p. 226)
Museum of the City of New York (p. 226)
National Academy of Design (p. 227)
Neue Galerie New York (p. 227)
92nd Street Y ✿ (p. 21 and p. 249)
Temple Emanu-El (p. 236)
Tisch Children's Zoo (p. 242)
Whitney Museum of American Art ✿✿ (p. 213)

UPPER MANHATTAN
The Cloisters ✿ (p. 216)

UPPER WEST SIDE
American Folk Art Museum, Eva and Morris Feld Gallery (p. 215)
American Museum of Natural History ✿✿✿ (p. 202)
The Ansonia (p. 232)
Cathedral of St. John the Divine ✿ (p. 235)
Central Park ✿✿✿ (p. 237)
Children's Museum of Manhattan ✿ (p. 253)
The Dakota (p. 232)
New-York Historical Society ✿ (p. 228)
Rose Center for Earth and Space ✿ (p. 202)
Wollman Rink ✿ (p. 243)

OUTER BOROUGHS
THE BRONX
Arthur Avenue (p. 257)
Bronx Zoo Wildlife Conservation Park ✿✿✿ (p. 255)

Edgar Allan Poe Cottage (p. 233)
New York Botanical Garden ✿ (p. 256)
Wave Hill ✿ (p. 256)
Yankee Stadium (p. 263)

BROOKLYN
Brooklyn Botanic Garden ✿ (p. 258)
Brooklyn Bridge ✿✿ (p. 203)
Brooklyn Heights Historic District ✿ (p. 260)
Brooklyn Museum of Art ✿✿ (p. 258)
Brooklyn Tabernacle ✿ (p. 259)
Coney Island (p. 259)
Grand Army Plaza (p. 257)
New York Aquarium (p. 259)
New York Transit Museum (p. 259)
Prospect Park ✿✿ (p. 260)

QUEENS
American Museum of the Moving Image ✿ (p. 261)
Flushing Meadows–Corona Park (p. 254)
Isamu Noguchi Garden Museum ✿ (p. 262)
MoMA QNS ✿ (p. 208)
Museum for African Art (p. 262)
New York Hall of Science ✿ (p. 254)
P.S. 1 Contemporary Art Center (p. 262)
Queens Museum of Art (p. 262)
Shea Stadium (p. 263)
Socrates Sculpture Park (p. 263)

2 Suggested Itineraries

If you're a first-time visitor and you'd like a blueprint with which to begin planning your time, consider the following 5-day game plan. Mix and match as you will!

Day 1   Start your day off just like the city itself did: At Manhattan's southern tip, New York's oldest precinct. Leave early to catch the first ferry to the **Statue of Liberty** ★★★ and **Ellis Island** ★★. This will occupy your morning.

Once back on the mainland, pop over to the downtown **TKTS booth** at South Street Seaport (the line is usually shorter than at Times Sq.) to pick up some half-price tickets for a **Broadway** or **Off-Broadway show** (something's always available for the evening, or tomorrow afternoon if you prefer a matinee).

After lunch, you might want to visit the Wall of Heroes surrounding **Ground Zero.** You can also pay your respects to the victims of the WTC attack in waterfront **Battery Park** ★★, where the bronze sphere that stood on the World Trade Center plaza between the Twin Towers now stands, bearing its war wounds, as a temporary memorial to the victims of the September 11, 2001, terrorist attacks.

Or, hop the subway to Brooklyn (the A/C line will whisk you from Manhattan to High St. in minutes) and stroll back to the 212 area code over the **Brooklyn Bridge** ★★, which offers one of my favorite views of the Manhattan skyline.

Or use the time to enjoy one of Lower Manhattan's many historic or cultural attractions, such as the moving **Museum of Jewish Heritage—a Living Memorial to the Holocaust** ★; surprisingly diminutive **Wall Street** ★★; or the **National Museum of the American Indian,** housed in the stunning 1907 beaux-arts **U.S. Customs House,** worth a visit for the architecture alone.

Head back to your hotel to freshen up so you can enjoy a leisurely dinner at one of the city's many fantastic and inexpensive restaurants.

Day 2   Spend most of the day at one of the big museums like the **Metropolitan Museum of Art** ★★★ or the **American Museum of Natural History** ★★★. You could spend a week at either, so you might want to take a Highlights Tour. Don't miss the new Harrison Ford–narrated Space Show at the Natural History Museum's **Rose Center for Earth and Space** ★.

After you've had enough museum going (you'll give out before you exhaust these collections), head into **Central Park** ★★★; both museums sit right on its fringe. If you still have some energy left, you might stroll out of the south end to do a bit of window-shopping on **Fifth Avenue.** Plan on dinner at one of the city's ethnic enclaves (see chapter 6 for recommendations).

Day 3   Start with the 3-hour **Circle Line Sightseeing Cruise** ★★, which circumnavigates Manhattan and offers a fascinating perspective on the island. In the afternoon, explore one or two of the downtown neighborhoods—perhaps the cast-iron canyons of **SoHo,** the 19th-century streets of **Greenwich Village,** or exotic **Chinatown.** Walk the thoroughfares, poke your head into shops, or sit at a cafe and watch the world go by. If you prefer to have a guide, schedule a **guided walking tour** (see "Affordable Sightseeing Tours," later in this chapter).

Stay downtown for the evening, catching dinner in a stylish (or authentically old-world) restaurant and following up with some out-on-the-town time, perhaps in a live-music or comedy venue, a dance club, a hipper-than-thou cocktail lounge, or a neighborhood tavern (see chapter 9 for recommendations). Or, if you've had enough of downtown, head uptown for some down-home cooking in Harlem, and then some jazz at **Smoke.**

Day 4   Head to **Rockefeller Center** ✦✦ to start your day with Matt and Katie outside the *Today* show studio, or to score standby tickets for Conan O'Brien. Make your way to the **Empire State Building** ✦✦✦ to see the view from the 86th floor of New York's ultimate landmark skyscraper.

Once you're done, head to **Grand Central Terminal** ✦ (a pleasant walk on a nice day) to admire the marvelous beaux-arts monument to modern transportation, and to have lunch. Head for the **food concourse,** which boasts a wealth of wallet-friendly full-service and casual options (see chapter 6).

Spend the afternoon browsing one or two of the smaller museums—maybe the *Intrepid* Sea-Air-Space Museum, the **Frick Collection** ✦✦, or the **Whitney.** Afterwards, enjoy another evening at the theater; or, if it's summer, catch one of the city's free alfresco entertainment events (see chapter 9). Or catch a **baseball game;** the Yankees or the Mets are likely to be in residence (sometimes both); you might get lucky and get some bleacher seats.

Day 5   Use the morning to explore one of the major attractions you've missed thus far. If you spent day 2 at the Met, spend today at the **American Museum of Natural History** ✦✦✦. Or go see Frank Lloyd Wright's iconic **Guggenheim Museum** ✦. Tour that nerve center of international relations, the **United Nations.** Or, if you haven't seen **Central Park** ✦✦✦ yet, go now.

After lunch, take stock: What haven't you done yet that you don't want to miss? What do you want to do more of? Perhaps a bit of shopping (see chapter 8), or a visit to a museum that focuses on your interests, such as the **International Center of Photography** ✦, the **Museum of Arts and Design** ✦, or the **Museum of Television & Radio.** You're becoming a pro at exploring the city by now, so take the bull by the horns and make the most of your afternoon.

In the evening, celebrate the end of a great vacation with some live music. Splurge on a night of jazz at one of the Big Apple's legendary clubs, or take in a night of laughs at one of the city's comedy clubs, such as the **Comedy Cellar.** If you're the party type, don your glad rags and dance the night away at one of the city's outrageous clubs. No matter what you choose, make it a night to remember!

3 The Top Attractions

In addition to the choices below, don't forget **Central Park** ✦✦✦, the great green swath that is, by virtue of its existence, New York City's greatest marvel. Central Park is so big and multifaceted that it earns its own section (p. 237).

American Museum of Natural History ✦✦✦   This is one of the hottest museum tickets in town, thanks to the $210 million **Rose Center for Earth and Space** ✦, whose planetarium sphere hosts the show "Are We Alone?"—the most technologically advanced sky show on the planet. Prepare to be blown away. The show is short—less than a half-hour—but phenomenal. **Buy your tickets in advance** in order to guarantee admission (they're available online); you can also buy tickets in advance for a specific IMAX film or exhibition, such as the Butterfly Conservatory (see below), which I recommend, especially during peak seasons and for weekend visits; otherwise, you might miss out.

Start your tour of the museum at the Rose Center. Afterwards, follow the Cosmic Pathway, which spirals around the sphere and down to the main level, chronicling the 15-billion-year evolution of the universe. (The sphere itself is used to create a point-of-reference scale that puts the universe into better perspective.) Other must-sees include the Big Bang Theater, which re-creates the birth of the universe; the Hall of the Universe, with its very own 15½-ton meteorite; and the Hall of Planet Earth, which focuses on the geologic processes of our home planet (great volcano display!). All in all, you'll need at least 2 hours to fully explore the Rose Center. *Tip:* Friday night is a great time to visit, as the center isn't overcrowded, the sounds of live jazz fill the Hall of the Universe, you can get a snack, and bathed in blue light, the sphere looks magical.

The rest of the 4-square-block museum is nothing to sneeze at. Founded in 1869, it houses the world's greatest natural-science collection in a group of buildings made of towers and turrets, pink granite, and red brick overflowing with neo-Gothic charm. The diversity is astounding: some 36 million specimens ranging from microscopic organisms to the world's largest cut gem, the Brazilian Princess Topaz (21,005 carats). If you don't have a lot of time, you can see the best of the best on free **Highlights Tours** offered daily every hour at 15 minutes after the hour from 10:15am to 3:15pm. Free daily **Spotlight Tours,** thematic tours that change monthly, are also offered; stop by an information desk for the schedule. **Audio Expeditions,** high-tech audio tours that allow you to access narration in the order you choose, are available to help you make sense of it all.

If you see only one exhibit, see the **dinosaurs** ⭐, on the fourth floor. Start in the **Orientation Room,** where a video gives an overview of the 500 million years of evolutionary history that led to you. Continue to the **Vertebrate Origins Room,** where models of ancient fish and turtles hang overhead, with plenty of interactive exhibits and kid-level displays to keep young minds fascinated. Next come the great **dinosaur halls,** with mammoth, spectacularly reconstructed skeletons and more interactive displays. **Mammals and Their Extinct Relatives** brings home what you've learned in the previous halls, showing how yesterday's prehistoric monsters have evolved into today's modern animals.

The **Hall of Biodiversity** is an impressive multimedia exhibit, but its doom-and-gloom story about the future of rainforests and other natural habitats might be too much for the little ones. Kids 5 and older should head to the **Discovery Room,** with lots of hands-on exhibits and experiments. (Be prepared, Mom and Dad; there seems to be a gift shop filled with fuzzy stuffed animals at every turn.)

The museum excels at **special exhibitions,** so check to see what's on while you're in town. The **Butterfly Conservatory** ⭐, a walk-in enclosure housing nearly 500 free-flying tropical butterflies, has developed into a can't-miss fixture from October through May; check to see if it's in the house while you're in town.

Central Park W. (between 77th and 81st sts.). ℂ 212/769-5100 for information, or 212/769-5200 for tickets (tickets can also be ordered online). www.amnh.org. Suggested admission $10 adults, $7.50 seniors and students, $6 children 2–12. Space Show and museum admission $19 adults, $14 seniors and students, $11.50 children under 12. Additional charges for IMAX movies and some special exhibitions. Daily 10am–5:45pm; Rose Center open Fri to 8:45pm. Subway: B, C to 81st St.; 1, 9 to 79th St.

Brooklyn Bridge ⭐⭐ *(Moments)*   Its Gothic-inspired stone pylons and steel-cable webs have moved poets like Walt Whitman and Hart Crane to sing the praises of this great span, the first to connect Manhattan to Brooklyn. Begun in 1867 and completed in 1883, the beautiful Brooklyn Bridge is the city's best-known symbol of the age of growth that seized the city during the late 19th century. Walk across the bridge and imagine the awe that New Yorkers felt at seeing two boroughs joined by this monumental span. It's still astounding.

Designed by John Roebling, this massive engineering feat was plagued by death and disaster. Roebling was fatally injured in 1869 when a ferry rammed a waterfront piling. His son, Washington, who was subsequently put in charge, contracted the bends in 1872 working underwater, and oversaw the rest of the construction with a telescope from his bed at the edge of the East River (his wife relayed his instructions to the workers). Washington refused to attend the 1883 opening ceremonies, having had a bitter disagreement with the company that financed the construction. Though it was declared the "eighth wonder of the world" upon its completion, the bridge's troubles were not over: Twelve pedestrians were killed in a stampede when a rumor of its imminent collapse spread like wildfire on the day it opened. Things are usually calmer now.

Walking the Bridge: This is one of my all-time favorite New York activities, although there's no doubt that the Lower Manhattan views from the bridge now have a painful resonance. A wide wood-plank pedestrian walkway is elevated above the traffic, making it a relatively peaceful, and popular, walk. It's a great vantage point from which to contemplate the New York skyline.

There's a sidewalk entrance on Park Row, just across from City Hall Park (take the 4, 5, or 6 train to Brooklyn Bridge/City Hall). But why do this walk *away* from Manhattan? For Manhattan skyline views, take an A or C train to High Street, one stop into Brooklyn. From there, you'll be on the bridge in no time: Come above ground, then walk through the little park to Cadman Plaza East and head down the slope (left) to the stairwell that will take you up to the footpath. (Following Prospect Place under the bridge, turning right onto Cadman Plaza E., will also take you directly to the stairwell.) It's about a 20- to 40-minute stroll over the bridge to Manhattan (there are benches along the way). The footpath will deposit you right at City Hall Park.

Tip: The perfect complement to your stroll over the Brooklyn Bridge is a stop for pizza at **Grimaldi's** (see "Pizza New York Style," in chapter 6), followed by delicious homemade ice cream at the **Brooklyn Ice Cream Factory** (② **718/ 246-3963**), at the Fulton Ferry Fire Boat House and in the shadow of the bridge. The pizza and ice cream will fortify you for your return stroll.

Subway: A, C to High St.; 4, 5, 6 to Brooklyn Bridge–City Hall.

Ellis Island ★★   Roughly 40% of Americans can trace their heritage back to an ancestor who came through here. For the 62 years when it was America's main entry point for immigrants (1892–1954), Ellis Island processed some 12 million people. The greeting was often brusque—especially in the early years when as many as 12,000 came through in a single day. The **Immigration Museum** skillfully relates the story of Ellis Island and immigration in America by placing the emphasis on personal experience.

It's difficult to leave the museum unmoved. Today you enter the Main Building's baggage room, just as the immigrants did, and then climb the stairs to the **Registry Room,** with its vaulted tiled ceiling, where millions waited anxiously for medical and legal processing. A step-by-step account of the immigrants' voyage is detailed in the exhibit, with haunting photos and oral histories. What might be the most poignant exhibit is **"Treasures from Home,"** 1,000 objects and photos donated by descendants of immigrants, including family heirlooms, religious articles, and clothing and jewelry. Outside, the **American Immigrant Wall of Honor** commemorates the names of more than 500,000 immigrants and their families, from Myles Standish to Jay Leno. You can research your own family's history at the **American Family Immigration History Center;** start your research at home at www.ellisislandrecords.org. You might also make time to see the award-winning short film *Island of Hope, Island of Tears,* which plays on a continuous loop in two theaters. Short live performances are also often part of the day's events.

Touring Tips: Ferries run daily to Ellis Island and Liberty Island from Battery Park and Liberty State Park (in New Jersey) at frequent intervals; see the Statue of Liberty listing (p. 210) for details.

In New York Harbor. ✆ 212/363-3200 (general info), or 212/269-5755 (ticket/ferry info). www.nps.gov/elis or www.ellisisland.org. Free admission (ferry ticket charge). Daily 9:30am–5:50pm (last ferry departs around 3:30pm). For subway and ferry details, see the Statue of Liberty listing on p. 210 (ferry trip includes stops at both sights).

Empire State Building ★★★

It took 60,000 tons of steel, 10 million bricks, 2½ million feet of electrical wire, 120 miles of pipe, and 7 million man-hours to build. King Kong climbed it in 1933. A plane slammed into it in 1945. The World Trade Center superseded it in 1970 as the island's tallest building. On September 11, 2001, it regained its status as New York City's tallest building after 31 years of taking second place. Through it all, the Empire State Building has remained one of the city's favorite landmarks, and its signature high-rise. Completed in 1931, the limestone-and-stainless-steel streamline deco dazzler climbs 102 stories (1,454 ft.) and now harbors the offices of fashion firms, and, in its upper reaches, a jumble of broadcast equipment.

Always a conversation piece, the Empire State Building glows every night, bathed in colored floodlights to commemorate events of significance—red, white, and blue for Independence Day; green for St. Patrick's Day; red, black, and green for Martin Luther King Day; blue and white for Hanukkah; even lavender and white for Gay Pride Day (you can find a lighting schedule online). The silver spire can be seen from all over the city. On a lovely day, stand at the base of the Flatiron Building (p. 232) and gaze up Fifth; the crisp, gleaming deco tower jumps out, soaring above the sooty office buildings that surround it.

But the views that keep nearly three million visitors a year coming are the ones from the 86th- and 102nd-floor **observatories.** The lower one is best—you can walk out on a windy deck and look through coin-operated viewers (bring quarters!) over what, on a clear day, can be as much as an 80-mile radius. The panorama is magnificent. The higher observation deck is glass-enclosed and cramped.

Light fog can create an admirably moody effect, but it goes without saying that a clear day is best. Dusk brings the most remarkable views and the biggest crowds. Consider going in the morning, when the light is still low on the horizon, keeping glare to a minimum. Starry nights are pure magic.

In your haste to go up, don't rush through the beautiful marble **lobby** without pausing to admire its features, which include a wonderful streamline mural.

Time-saving tip: If you don't mind spending about $1 more per ticket—you can avoid ticket lines by buying advance tickets online. It's money well spent in the busy seasons. Place your order well before you leave home.

350 Fifth Ave. (at 34th St.). ✆ 212/736-3100. www.esbnyc.com. Observatory admission $10 adults, $9 seniors and children 12–17, $4 children 5–11, free for children under 5. Mon–Fri 10am–midnight; Sat–Sun 9:30am–midnight; tickets sold until 11:25pm. Subway: B, D, F, N, R, V, Q, W to 34th St.; 6 to 33rd St.

Grand Central Terminal ★★

The 1913 landmark (designed by Warren & Wetmore with Reed & Stem) has been restored to its position as one of the most magnificent public spaces in the country. The restoration, done by Beyer Blinder Belle in 1998, is a triumph. Their work has reanimated the genius of the station's original intent: to inspire those who pass through with feelings of civic pride and appreciation for Western architectural traditions. In short, they've put the "grand" back into Grand Central.

Come and visit, even if you're not catching a train. If you arrive and leave by subway, be sure to exit the station, walking a couple of blocks south, to about 40th Street, before turning to admire Jules-Alexis Coutan's neoclassical sculpture *Transportation* over the south entrance, with a majestic Mercury, the Roman god of commerce and travel, as its central figure.

The greatest visual impact comes when you enter the vast **main concourse.** The high windows again allow sunlight to penetrate the space, glinting off the half-acre Tennessee marble floor. The brass clock over the central kiosk gleams, as do the gold- and nickel-plated chandeliers piercing the side archways. The **sky ceiling,** again a brilliant greenish blue, depicts the constellations of the winter sky above New York. They're lit with 59 stars, surrounded by 24-carat gold and emitting light fed through fiber-optic cables, their intensities replicating the magnitude of the stars as seen from Earth. On the east end of the main concourse is a grand **marble staircase** where there had never been one before, but as the original plans had always intended.

This beaux-arts splendor serves as a hub of activity as well. New retail shops and restaurants have taken over the mezzanine and lower levels. Off the main concourse at street level, there's a mix of specialty shops and national retailers, as well as the truly grand **Grand Central Market** for gourmet foods (see chapter 8). The **New York Transit Museum Gallery Annex & Store,** in the shuttle passage, houses city transit-related exhibitions and an excellent gift shop (p. 259). The **lower concourse** houses a food court that's a budget diner's delight, offering everything from bratwurst to New York–style cheesecake, as well as the famous **Oyster Bar & Restaurant** (✆ 212/490-6650).

The **Municipal Art Society** (✆ 212/935-3960; www.mas.org) offers a free walking tour of Grand Central Terminal on Wednesday at 12:30pm, which meets at the information booth on the Grand Concourse. The **Grand Central Partnership** (✆ 212/697-1245) runs its own free tour every Friday at 12:30pm, which meets in front of the Whitney Museum at Philip Morris gallery, at 42nd Street and Park Avenue. Call to confirm before you set out to meet either tour.

42nd St. at Park Ave. ✆ 212/340-2210 (events hot line). www.grandcentralterminal.com. Subway: S, 4, 5, 6, 7 to 42nd St./Grand Central.

Metropolitan Museum of Art ★★★ The Metropolitan Museum of Art draws some five million people a year, more than any other attraction in the city. No wonder: This place is magnificent. At 1.6 million square feet, this is the largest museum in the Western Hemisphere. Nearly all the world's cultures through the ages are on display—from Egyptian mummies to ancient Greek statuary to Islamic carvings to Renaissance paintings to Native American masks to 20th-century decorative arts—and masterpieces are the rule. You could go once a week for a lifetime and find something new on each visit.

So unless you plan on spending your entire vacation here (some people do), you cannot see the entire collection. My recommendation is to give it one good, long day. One way to get an overview is to take the **Museum Highlights Tour,** offered every day (usually 10:15am–3:15pm). Even some New Yorkers who've spent many hours in the museum could profit from this once-over. Visit the museum's website for a schedule of this and subject-specific walking tours (Old Master Paintings, American Period Rooms, Arts of China, Islamic Art, and so on); you can also get a schedule of the day's tours at the Visitor Services desk when you arrive. A daily schedule of free **Gallery Talks** is available as well.

Moments Evening Events at the Met

On **Friday and Saturday evenings,** the Met remains open for art viewing and cocktails in the Great Hall Balcony Bar (5–8pm) and live classical music. A slate of after-hours programs (gallery talks, tours) changes by the week; call for schedule. The restaurant stays open until 10pm (last reservation at 8:30pm); dinner is usually accompanied by piano music.

The least overwhelming way to see the Met on your own is to pick up a map at the round desk in the entry hall and concentrate on what you like, whether it's 17th-century paintings, American furniture, or the art of the South Pacific. Highlights include the American Wing's **Garden Court,** with its 19th-century sculpture; the ground-level **Costume Hall;** and the **Frank Lloyd Wright room.** The beautifully renovated **Roman and Greek galleries** are overwhelming, but in a marvelous way, as is the collection of later **Chinese art.** The highlight of the **Egyptian collection** is the **Temple of Dendur,** in a dramatic, specially built glass-walled gallery with Central Park views. The **Greek Galleries,** which at last fully realize McKim, Mead & White's grand neoclassical plans of 1917, and the **Ancient Near East Galleries** are particularly of note. But it all depends on what your interests are. Don't forget the marvelous **special exhibitions,** which can range from "Jade in Ancient Costa Rica" to "Cubism and Fashion."

To purchase tickets for concerts and lectures, call ℰ **212/570-3949** (Mon–Sat 9:30am–5pm). The roof garden is worth visiting from spring to autumn, offering peaceful views over Central Park and the city.

Money-saving tip: The Met's medieval collections are housed in Upper Manhattan at the **Cloisters** ✮ (p. 216); admission is included with your Met ticket purchase, but seeing both satisfactorily in a single day is more than only the most die-hard budget travelers should try to accomplish. If you're committed to seeing both on one ticket, start at the Cloisters at opening time on a Friday or Saturday (the Met's extended-hour days, so you can maximize your time), then move downtown to the main museum in the afternoon.

Fifth Ave. at 82nd St. ℰ **212/535-7710.** www.metmuseum.org. Admission (includes same-day entrance to the Cloisters) $12 adults, $7 seniors and students, free for children under 12 when accompanied by an adult. Sun and Tues–Thurs 9:30am–5:30pm; Fri–Sat 9:30am–9pm. No strollers allowed Sun (back carriers available at 81st St. entrance coat-check area). Subway: 4, 5, 6 to 86th St.

Museum of Modern Art/MoMA QNS ✮ The Museum of Modern Art (or MoMA to its friends) boasts the world's greatest collection of painting and sculpture from the late 19th century to the present, everything from Monet's *Water Lilies* and Klimt's *The Kiss* to masterworks by Frida Kahlo, Edward Hopper, Andy Warhol, Robert Rauschenberg, and others. Top that off with an extensive collection of drawings, photography, architectural models and modern furniture, iconic design objects ranging from tableware to sports cars, and film and video (including the world's largest collection of D.W. Griffith films), and you have quite a museum. If you're into modernism, this is the place to be.

Here's the Bad News: MoMA will be closed while you're in town. The museum is undergoing a $650 million renovation of its West 53rd Street building, under the guidance of architect Yoshio Taniguchi, that will double the exhibit space when the project is complete in 2005.

Tips Avoiding the Crowds at Big Apple Museums

Many of the city's top museums—including the Natural History Museum, the Met, the Guggenheim, and the Whitney—have late hours on Friday and/or Saturday nights. Take advantage of them. You'll largely have the place to yourself by 5 or 6pm—which, in most cases, leaves you hours left to explore, unfettered by crowds or screaming kids. The other option, as I've stressed through the book, is to avoid weekends and come early on weekdays, preferably when the doors open.

Here's the Good News: The museum has opened temporary exhibit space called **MoMA QNS** in the old Swingline stapler factory in Long Island City. The spectacularly renovated 45,000-square-foot gallery exhibits highlights of the collection, among them van Gogh's *Starry Night,* Picasso's *Les Demoiselles d'Avignon,* and Warhol's *Gold Marilyn Monroe.* Workshops, a limited program schedule, and special exhibitions will also be part of the fun: April through July of 2004 will feature the program, "Photography, Fashion and Film," while July through October there will be a program on landscape design. Yes—it's definitely worth a short subway ride to Queens. Getting there is quick and easy; in fact, from Midtown, you can be here quicker than you can get to the Village. Also consider visiting the MoMA affiliate **P.S. 1 Contemporary Art Center** (p. 262), also in Long Island City, while you're there. You might consider making a day of it: The **Queens Artlink** (www.moma.org/qal) is a free weekend arts shuttle, running Saturday and Sunday from 10:30am to 5:30pm and linking five top-flight art institutions in the area, including MoMA QNS, P.S. 1, the **Isamu Noguchi Garden Museum** ✦ (p. 262), the **American Museum of the Moving Image** ✦ (p. 261), and the **Socrates Sculpture Park** (p. 263).

45–20 33rd St., Long Island City, Queens. ✆ **212/708-9400.** www.moma.org. Admission $12 adults, $8.50 seniors and students, free for children under 16 accompanied by an adult; pay what you wish Sat–Sun. Mon–Thurs 10am–5pm; Fri 10am–7:45pm; closed Tue–Wed. Subway: 7 to 33rd St. (MoMA QNS is across the street).

Rockefeller Center ✦✦ *(Moments)* A streamline masterpiece, Rockefeller Center is one of New York's central gathering spots. A prime example of the city's skyscraper spirit, it was erected in the 1930s, when the city was deep in the Depression as well as its most passionate Art Deco phase. Designated a National Historic Landmark in 1988, it's the world's largest privately owned business-and-entertainment center, with 18 buildings on 21 acres.

For a dramatic approach to the entire complex, start at Fifth Avenue between 49th and 50th streets. The builders purposely created the gentle slope of the Promenade, known here as the **Channel Gardens** because it's flanked to the south by La Maison Française and to the north by the British Building. You'll also find a number of shops along here, including a branch of the **Metropolitan Museum of Art Store,** a good stop for elegant gifts (some quite affordable). The Promenade leads to the **Lower Plaza,** home to the famous ice-skating rink and alfresco dining in summer in the shadow of Paul Manship's gilded bronze statue *Prometheus.* All around the flags of the United Nations' member countries flap in the breeze. Just behind *Prometheus,* in December and early January, towers the city's majestic official Christmas tree.

The **Rink at Rockefeller Plaza** ☆ (✆ **212/332-7654;** www.rockefeller center.com) is tiny but romantic, especially during the holidays, when the Christmas tree's lights twinkle. It's open from mid-October to mid-March, and you'll skate under the tree from early December through the holiday season.

The focal point of this "city within a city" is the **GE Building** ☆, at 30 Rockefeller Plaza, a 70-story showpiece. It's still one of the city's most impressive buildings; walk through for a look at the granite-and-marble lobby, lined with sepia-toned murals by José Maria Sert. You can pick up a walking-tour brochure highlighting the center's art and architecture at the main information desk. **NBC** maintains studios throughout the complex. Shows like *Saturday Night Live, Dateline NBC,* and *Late Night with Conan O'Brien* originate in the GE Building (see "Talk of the Town: Free TV Tapings," on p. 251, for tips on getting tickets). NBC's ***Today* show** is broadcast live on weekdays from 7 to 10am from the glass-enclosed studio on the corner of 49th Street and Rockefeller Plaza; come early if you want a visible spot, and bring your HI MOM! sign.

The 70-minute **NBC Studio Tour** (✆ **212/664-3700;** www.shopnbc.com/ nbcstore/default.aspx) will take you behind the scenes, but it's not worth the expenditure for wallet-watching budget travelers ($17.50 adults, $15 seniors and kids 6–16). If you're committed to the notion, you can reserve your tickets for either tour in advance or buy them right up to tour time at the **NBC Experience** store, on Rockefeller Plaza at 49th Street.

Other notable buildings include the **International Building,** on Fifth Avenue between 50th and 51st streets, worth a look for its Atlas statue; and the **McGraw-Hill Building,** on Sixth Avenue between 48th and 49th streets, with its 50-foot sun triangle on the plaza. Designed by Donald Deskey, the restored **Radio City Music Hall** ☆, 1260 Sixth Ave., at 50th Street (✆ **212/247-4777;** www.radiocity.com), is one of the city's largest indoor theaters, with 6,200 seats, but its true grandeur derives from its Art Deco appointments. From the distant seats, the stage's proscenium arch evokes a faraway sun setting on the horizon. The men's and women's lounges are also splendid. The theater hosts the annual **Christmas Spectacular,** starring the Rockettes. The 1-hour **Stage Door Tour,** offered Monday through Saturday, is $16 for adults, $10 for children under 12.

Between 48th and 50th sts., from Fifth to Sixth aves. ✆ 212/332-6868. www.rockefellercenter.com. Subway: B, D, F, V to 47th–50th sts./Rockefeller Center.

Solomon R. Guggenheim Museum ☆ It's been called a bun, a snail, a concrete tornado, and even a giant wedding cake. Whatever simile you choose, Frank Lloyd Wright's only New York building, completed in 1959, is best summed up as a brilliant work of architecture—so brilliant that it competes with the art for your attention. If you're looking for the city's best modern art, head to MoMA or the Whitney first; come to the Guggenheim to see the house.

It's easy to see the bulk of what's on display in 2 to 4 hours. Inside, a spiraling rotunda circles over a slowly inclined ramp that leads you past changing exhibits. Usually the progression is counterintuitive: from the first floor up, rather than from the sixth floor down. Permanent exhibits of 19th- and 20th-century art, including Kandinsky, Klee, Picasso, and French Impressionists, occupy a stark annex called the **Tower Galleries,** an addition accessible at every level that some critics claimed made the original look like a toilet bowl backed by a water tank (judge for yourself—I think there may be something to that).

The Guggenheim runs some special programs, including free daily docent-led **tours,** lectures, family films, avant-garde screenings for grown-ups, curator-led gallery tours on select Friday afternoons, and the **World Beat Jazz Series,** which resounds through the rotunda on Friday and Saturday from 5 to 8pm.

1071 Fifth Ave. (at 88th St.). ⓒ 212/423-3500. www.guggenheim.org. Admission $12 adults, $8 seniors and students, free for children under 12; pay as you wish Fri 6–8pm. Sun–Wed 9am–6pm; Fri–Sat 9am–8pm. Subway: 4, 5, 6 to 86th St.

Staten Island Ferry ★★ *Value*   Here's New York's best freebie—especially if you just want to glimpse the Statue of Liberty and not climb her steps. You get an hour-long excursion (round-trip) into the world's biggest harbor. This is not strictly a sightseeing ride, but commuter transportation to and from Staten Island (remember Melanie Griffith in *Working Girl?*). During business hours you'll share the boat with working stiffs reading papers and drinking coffee, blissfully unaware of the sights outside.

You, however, should go on deck and enjoy the busy harbor traffic. The old orange-and-green boats usually have open decks along the sides or at the bow and stern; try to catch one of these boats if you can, because the newer white boats don't have decks. Grab a seat on the right side of the boat for the best view. On the way out of Manhattan, you'll pass the Statue of Liberty, Ellis Island, and from the left side of the boat, Governor's Island; you'll see the Verrazano Narrows Bridge spanning the distance from Brooklyn to Staten Island in the distance.

When the boat arrives at St. George, Staten Island, everyone must disembark. Follow the boat-loading sign on your right as you get off; you'll circle around to the next loading dock. It's all well worth the time spent.

Departs from the Whitehall Ferry Terminal at the southern tip of Manhattan. ⓒ 718/815-BOAT. www.ci.nyc. ny.us/html/dot. Free admission ($3 for car transport on select ferries). 24 hrs.; every 20–30 min. weekdays, less frequently off-peak and weekend hours. Subway: N, R to Whitehall St.; 4, 5 to Bowling Green; 1, 9 to South Ferry (ride in 1 of the 1st 5 cars).

Statue of Liberty ★★★ *Kids*   For the millions who came by ship to America in the last century—as tourists or immigrants—Lady Liberty, standing in the Upper Bay, was their first glimpse of America. No monument so embodies the nation's, and the world's, notion of freedom and economic potential. Even if you don't make it to Liberty Island, you can get a glimpse from Battery Park, from the New Jersey side of the bay, or from the Staten Island Ferry (see above).

Proposed by French statesman Edouard de Laboulaye as a gift from France to the United States commemorating the two nations' friendship, the statue was designed by sculptor Frédéric-Auguste Bartholdi with the help of Alexandre-Gustave Eiffel (of the famed Paris tower), and unveiled on October 28, 1886. Despite the fact that Joseph Pulitzer had to make a mighty effort to attract donations on this side of the Atlantic for her pedestal (designed by American Richard Morris Hunt), more than a million people watched as the French tricolor veil was pulled away. After nearly 100 years of wind, rain, and exposure to the harsh sea air, Lady Liberty received a successful $150 million face-lift in time for its centennial celebration on July 4, 1986. Feted in fireworks, Miss Liberty became more of a city icon than ever before.

Touring Tips: Ferries leave daily every half-hour to 45 minutes from 9am to about 3:30pm (their clock), with more frequent ferries in the morning and extended hours in summer. Try to go early on a weekday to avoid the crowds that swarm in the afternoon, on weekends, and on holidays.

Tips **Lady Liberty Touring Updates**

At press time, **only the grounds of Liberty Island were open to the public.** Whether and when the pedestal, museum, and/or the body of the statue itself will reopen was unknown at this writing, but the close-up view from the grounds is breathtaking enough to make the journey worthwhile.

If the statue does reopen, be sure to arrive by noon if your heart's set on experiencing everything. And keep in mind that, for the last few years, the National Park Service has instituted a "crown" policy during the peak **summer** season: Visitors who want to walk up to the crown must be on one of the **first two ferries of the day.** At other times, you must be on line to climb to the crown by 2pm; otherwise, you will not be allowed up.

These and all policies regarding access to the Statue of Liberty and Ellis Island are subject to change at any time. *Please* call or check the website (**www.nps.gov/stli**) for the latest access information.

A stop at **Ellis Island** ★★ (p. 204) is included in the fare, but if you catch the last ferry, you can only visit the statue or Ellis Island, not both.

You can **buy ferry tickets in advance** via www.statueoflibertyferry.com, which will allow you to board the boat without standing in the ticket line; however, there is a service charge. Even if you've purchased tickets, arrive as much as 30 minutes before your desired ferry time to allow for increased security procedures. The ferry ride takes about 20 minutes.

Once on Liberty Island, you'll start to get an idea of the statue's immensity: She weighs 225 tons and measures 152 feet from foot to flame. Her nose alone is 4½ feet long, and her index finger is 8 feet long.

Note that access to the statue itself was severely restricted at this writing; see "Lady Liberty Touring Updates" (below) for details.

If the statue does reopen to the public, you may have to wait as long as 3 hours to walk up into the crown. If it's summer, or you're not in shape, you may want to skip it: It's a grueling 354 steps (the equivalent of 22 stories) to the crown, or you can take the elevator the first 10 stories up (a shortcut I endorse). But even if you take the elevator, the interior is stifling once the temperature starts to climb. You don't have to go all the way up to the crown; there are **observation decks** at different levels, including one at the top of the pedestal that's reachable by elevator. Even if you don't go inside, a stroll around the base is an extraordinary experience, and the views of the Manhattan skyline are stellar.

On Liberty Island in New York Harbor. © **212/363-3200** (general info), or 212/269-5755 (ticket/ferry info). www.nps.gov/stli or www.statueoflibertyferry.com. Free admission; ferry ticket to Statue of Liberty and Ellis Island $10 adults, $8 seniors, $3 children 3–17. Daily 9am–5pm (last ferry departs around 4pm); extended hours in summer. Subway: 4, 5 to Bowling Green; 1, 9 to South Ferry. Walk south through Battery Park to Castle Clinton, the fort housing the ferry-ticket booth.

Wall Street & the New York Stock Exchange ★★ *Value* Wall Street—it's an iconic name, and the world's prime hub for bulls and bears everywhere. This 18th-century lane (you'll be surprised at how little it is) is appropriately monumental, lined with neoclassical towers that reach as far skyward as the dreams of investors who built it into the world's most famous financial market.

What's Happening in Times Square

There's no doubt that Times Square has evolved into something very different than it was a decade ago, when it had a deservedly sleazy reputation. Yet there is much debate whether the old was better than the new. For the real New Yorker, there is not much to offer here; the restaurants aren't very good, the crowds are stifling, and the shops are unimaginative major chains. The area has become a sterile Disney-fied celebration of kitsch. Still, the neon spectacle is something everyone should witness before returning home. If you are interested in spending more time in the area, here are some of its attractions:

ABC's *Good Morning America* has set up a street-facing studio at Broadway and 44th Street (across from **MTV**'s own); **NASDAQ**'s eight-story billboard—the world's largest video screen, at Broadway and 43rd—has joined the landscape; and World Wrestling Entertainment spent a mint restoring the landmark Paramount Building and installing a 47,500-square-foot entertainment complex. Take note of the WWE's marquee: Between the restored historic scrollwork is a full-color sign that incorporates the latest in LED and fiber-optic technology. A handful of upper-end new hotels in the heart of the action means that thousands more visitors can stay right on (or just off) the Great White Way—as long as they're willing to shell out big-time to do it.

ESPN Zone (1472 Broadway; ☏ **212/921-ESPN**), **Planet Hollywood** (Broadway and 45th St.; ☏ **212/333-7827**), and **B.B. King Blues Club & Grill** (237 W. 42nd St.; ☏ **212/997-4144**) all joined the pack in the 21st century, reinvigorating the notion of themed dining and nightlife. The rockin' **Virgin Megastore** at 1540 Broadway (☏ **212/921-1020**) has a major presence (see chapter 8), as does **MTV**, which draws loads of *Total Request Live* fans to Broadway and 45th Street every weekday afternoon.

Forty-Second Street between Seventh and Eighth avenues, the former porn paradise, has been rebuilt from scratch as a family-oriented entertainment mecca. In addition to a spate of renovated theaters—including the **New Victory** (see "Kids Take the Stage: Family-Friendly Theater," in chapter 9), the **New Amsterdam** (home to *The Lion King*), and the former Selwyn, reinvented as the **American Airlines Theatre** and now home of the Roundabout Theater—the neon-bright block is chock-full with retail and amusements, including **Madame Tussaud's New York**; the multilevel, state-of-the-art **Broadway City** ☏ video arcade; two 20-plus-screen movie complexes; and plenty of mall-familiar shopping and dining, including the **Museum Company** and a **Yankees Clubhouse Shop** (where you can purchase tickets).

At the heart of the action is the **New York Stock Exchange (NYSE),** the world's largest securities trader, where you can watch the billions change hands and get an idea of how the money merchants work. NYSE came into being in 1792, when merchants met daily under a buttonwood tree to pass off to each other the U.S. bonds that had been sold to fund the Revolutionary War. By 1903, they were trading stocks of publicly held companies in this Corinthian-columned beaux-arts "temple" designed by George Post. About 3,000 companies are listed on the exchange, trading nearly 314 billion shares valued at about $16 trillion. Until September 11, 2001, visitors could acquire free tickets to tour a small interactive museum and watch the action on the trading floor from the glass-lined, mezzanine-level observation gallery. However, the facility has been closed to the public since the terrorist attack. The website says it is closed "indefinitely."

20 Broad St. (between Wall St. and Exchange Place). © 212/656-5165. www.nyse.com. Free admission. Call or visit Web site to see if building has re-opened to public for tours. Subway: J, M, Z to Broad St.; 2, 3, 4, 5 to Wall St.

Whitney Museum of American Art ★★

Arguably the finest collection of 20th-century American art belongs to the Whitney, thanks to the efforts of Gertrude Vanderbilt Whitney. A sculptor herself, she organized exhibitions by American artists shunned by traditional academies, assembled a sizable personal collection, and founded the museum in 1930 in Greenwich Village.

Today's museum is an imposing presence on Madison Avenue—an inverted, three-tiered pyramid of concrete and gray granite with seven seemingly random windows designed by Marcel Breuer, a leader of the Bauhaus movement. The rotating permanent collection consists of a selection of major works by Edward Hopper, George Bellows, Georgia O'Keeffe, Roy Lichtenstein, Jasper Johns, and other significant artists. The second floor is devoted to works from its permanent collection from 1900 to 1950, while the rest is dedicated to rotating exhibits.

Shows are usually all well curated and more edgy than what you'd see at MoMA or the Guggenheim, though not as left-of-mainstream as what you'll find at the New Museum. Topics range from topical surveys, such as "American Art in the Age of Technology" and "The Warhol Look: Glamour Style Fashion," to in-depth retrospectives of famous or lesser-known movements (such as Fluxus, the movement that spawned Yoko Ono, among others) and artists (Mark Rothko, Keith Haring, Duane Hanson, Bob Thompson). The next **Whitney Biennial** is scheduled for spring 2004. Biennials serve as the premier launching pad for new American artists working on the vanguard in every media.

Free **gallery tours** are offered daily, and music, screenings, and lectures fill the calendar. The Whitney is also notable for having the best museum restaurant in town: **Sarabeth's at the Whitney,** worth a visit in its own right.

For details on the **Whitney Museum of American Art at Philip Morris,** the petite Midtown annex, which you can visit for free, see p. 231.

945 Madison Ave. (at 75th St.). © 877/WHITNEY or 212/570-3676. www.whitney.org. Admission $12 adults, $9.50 seniors and students, free for children under 12; pay as you wish Fri 6–9pm. Tues–Thurs and Sat–Sun 11am–6pm; Fri 1–9pm. Subway: 6 to 77th St.

World Trade Center site (Ground Zero) *Moments*

The World Trade Center dominated lower Manhattan. The record-breaking complex occupied 16 acres, and its 12 million square feet of office space housed more than 350 firms and organizations. About 50,000 people worked there, and some 70,000 others (tourists and businesspeople) visited each day. The vast complex included, in addition to two 110-story towers—one of which rewarded visitors with breathtaking views from the Top of the World observation deck, more than 1,350 feet in the air—five additional buildings (including a hotel), a huge plaza rich with outdoor sculpture, a vast underground shopping mall, and a full slate of restaurants, including the spectacular Windows on the World, the city's ultimate special-occasion restaurant.

Then the first plane hit the north tower, Tower 1, at 8:45am on Tuesday, September 11, 2001. By 10:30am, it was all gone, along with nearly 3,000 lives.

Clean-up and recovery efforts officially ended in May 2002. In August of 2002, Governor George Pataki of New York, Governor James McGreevy of New Jersey, and New York Mayor Michael Bloomberg dedicated a viewing wall on the Church Street side of the site, called the **Wall of Heroes.** On the wall are the names of those who lost their lives that day, along with the history of the site, including photos of the construction of the World Trade Center in the late 1960s and stories of how, after it opened in 1972, it changed the New York skyline and downtown. Almost 2 years removed from the horrific events of that September day, a walk along the Wall of Heroes remains a painfully moving experience.

The future of the site is still in question. After a heated competition where proposals by designers and architects were submitted, Daniel Libeskind's vision of a towering spire and a memorial void was chosen. When and if that vision is ever realized is still very much up in the air.

On March 11, 2002, a temporary victims' memorial was in place at **Battery Park** (p. 244): The bronze sphere that once stood on the World Trade Center plaza between the Twin Towers now stands witness, bearing its war wounds, until a permanent one can be erected. Additionally, the gates of **Trinity Church** (p. 237) will continue to serve as an impromptu memorial, brimming with tokens of remembrance and blessing left by visitors from around the world.

Bounded by Church, Barclay, Liberty, and West sts. ℂ 212/484-1222. www.nycvisit.com or www.southst seaport.org for viewing information; www.downtowny.com for Lower Manhattan area information and rebuilding updates. Subway: C, E to World Trade Center; N, R to Cortlandt St.

4 More Manhattan Museums

In 1978, New York's finest cultural institutions on Fifth Avenue from 82nd to 104th streets formed a consortium called **Museum Mile,** the name New York City gave to the stretch several years later. The "mile" begins at the **Metropolitan Museum of Art** ✿✿✿ (see "The Top Attractions," above) and moves north to **El Museo del Barrio.** However, even the smallest museums require some time; so don't plan on just popping into a few as you stroll along. Your best bet is to head directly to the museum that's tops on your list, then proceed to your second choice if you have time. If you're heading to the Metropolitan, you'll only see a portion of the collection there in a full day.

For the **Brooklyn Museum of Art** ✿✿, the **New York Transit Museum,** the **American Museum of the Moving Image** ✿, the **Queens Museum of Art,** the **Isamu Noguchi Garden Museum** ✿, and the **P.S. 1 Contemporary Art Center,** see "Highlights of the Outer Boroughs" (p. 255).

If you're traveling with the kids, consider the museums in "Especially for Kids" (p. 253), which include the **Children's Museum of Manhattan** ✿, the **Sony Wonder Technology Lab,** and the **New York Hall of Science** ✿.

If you're interested in historic-house museums, see "In Search of Historic Homes" (p. 233).

Also, don't forget to see what's on at the **New York Public Library** ✿✿, which regularly holds excellent free exhibitions; see p. 232. Set to open in 2004 is the **Rubin Museum of Art** at 138 W. 17th Street, at Seventh Avenue. The museum, located on the site of the original Barney's department store, will feature over

25,000 square feet of gallery and event space. Permanent collections will include over 1,200 pieces of Himalayan art.

American Folk Art Museum ★★ It's been open 2 years and New Yorkers still can't stop raving about the new home of the American Folk Art Museum. Designed by Tod Williams Billie Tsien Architects, this gorgeous, ultra-modern boutique museum has been called by *House & Garden* no less than the city's greatest new museum and best work of architecture since Frank Lloyd Wright built the Guggenheim in 1959, while *New York* magazine called it "brilliant" and "a tour de force." Not only is it a stunning structure, but it also heralds American folk art into the top echelon of museum-worthy art.

The new building quadruples the museum's exhibit space to 30,000 square feet. The modified open-plan interior features an extraordinary collection of traditional works from the 18th century to the self-taught artists and craftspeople of the present, reflecting the breadth and vitality of the American folk-art tradition. A splendid variety of quilts, in particular, makes the textiles collection the museum's most popular. Look for "The Perfect Game: America Looks at Baseball," running from January 24 to June 17, 2004. The book- and gift shop is outstanding, filled with one-of-a-kind objects.

The original Lincoln Center location is now the **Eva and Morris Feld Gallery,** which displays art from the permanent collection, including new acquisitions. There's also a second gift gallery here.

45 W. 53rd St. (between Fifth and Sixth aves.). ℂ **212/265-1040.** www.folkartmuseum.org. Admission $9 adults, $5 seniors and students, free for children under 12, free to all Fri 6–8pm. Tues–Thurs and Sat–Sun 10am–6pm; Fri 10am–8pm. Eva and Morris Feld Gallery: 2 Lincoln Sq. (Columbus Ave. between 65th and 66th sts., across from Lincoln Center). ℂ **212/595-9533.** Free admission. Tues–Sun 11am–7:30pm; Mon 11am–6pm. Subway: 1, 9 to 66th St.

Asia Society The Asia Society was founded in 1956 by John D. Rockefeller III with the goal of increasing understanding between Americans and Asians through art exhibits, lectures, films, performances, and conferences. The society is a leader in presenting contemporary Asian and Asian-American art. Now, after a $30 million renovation that doubled the exhibition space was completed in 2001, the society's headquarters is bigger, smarter, and better than ever. Never has so much of the core collection, comprised of Rockefeller's Pan-Asian acquisitions dating from 2000 B.C. to the 19th century, been on display before. Well-curated temporary exhibits run the gamut from "The New Way of Tea," exploring Japan's elaborate tea ceremony, to "Through Afghan Eyes: A Culture in Conflict, 1987–1995," a study in photographs and video. The mammoth calendar of events runs the gamut from films to lectures to discussions featuring experts in Pan-Asian and global politics, business, and more.

725 Park Ave. (at 70th St.). ℂ **212/288-6400.** www.asiasociety.org. Gallery admission $7 adults, $5 seniors and students, free for children under 16, free to all Fri 6–9pm. Tues–Thurs and Sat–Sun 11am–6pm; Fri 11am–9pm. Subway: 6 to 68th St./Hunter College.

Center for Jewish History *Finds* This 125,000-square-foot complex is the largest repository of Jewish history, art, and literature in the Diaspora. It unites five of America's leading institutions of Jewish scholarship: the **American Jewish Historical Society** (www.ajhs.org), the national archives of the Jewish people in the Americas; the **Leo Baeck Institute** (www.lbi.org), documenting the history of German-speaking Jewry from the 17th century until the Nazis; the **Yeshiva University Museum** (www.yu.edu/museum), which includes general-interest exhibits, plus a collection of Judaica objects confiscated by the Nazis; the

YIVO Institute for Jewish Research (www.yivoinstitute.org), focusing on exhibits exploring the diversity of the Jewish experience; and the **American Sephardi Federation** (www.asfonline.org), representing the spiritual, cultural, and social traditions of the American Sephardic communities (Jews from Southern Europe, North Africa, and the Middle East). This union represents about 100 million archival documents, 500,000 books, and thousands of objects of art and ephemera, ranging from Thomas Jefferson's letter denouncing anti-Semitism to memorabilia of famous Jewish athletes.

The main gallery space is the Yeshiva Museum, which comprises four galleries, an outdoor sculpture garden, and a children's workshop; a range of exhibits also showcase holdings belonging to the other institutions. A central feature is the **Reading Room,** home to stacks accessible by serious researchers and lay historians alike, as well as the **Center Genealogy Institute,** which offers assistance in family-history research. Another huge component of the center is its 250-seat home to a packed schedule of events. There's also a kosher cafe.

15 W. 16th St. (between Fifth and Sixth aves.). ℂ **212/294-8301.** www.cjh.org. Admission to Yeshiva University Museum $6 adults, $4 seniors and students, free to all other facilities. Yeshiva University Museum Sun and Tues–Wed 11am–5pm; Thurs 11am–8pm. Reading Room and Genealogy Institute Mon–Thurs 9:30am–4:30pm; Fri by appt. All other galleries Mon–Thurs 9am–5pm; Fri 9am–4pm. Subway: 4, 5, 6, N, R, L, Q, W to 14th St./Union Sq.; F, V to 14th St.

The Cloisters ⭐ If it weren't for this branch of the Metropolitan Museum of Art, many New Yorkers would never get to the northernmost point in Manhattan. This remote yet lovely spot is devoted to the art and architecture of medieval Europe. Atop a cliff overlooking the Hudson River, you'll find a 12th-century chapter house, parts of five cloisters from medieval monasteries, a Romanesque chapel, and a 12th-century Spanish apse brought intact from Europe. Surrounded by peaceful gardens, this is the one place on the island that can even approximate the kind of solitude suitable to such a collection. Inside you'll find extraordinary works that include the famed Unicorn tapestries, sculpture, illuminated manuscripts, stained glass, ivory, and precious metal work.

Despite its remoteness, the Cloisters are extremely popular, especially in fine weather, so try to schedule your visit on a weekday. A free guided **Highlights Tour** is offered Tuesday through Friday at 3pm and Sunday at noon; gallery talks are also a regular feature. **Garden Tours** are offered Tuesday through Sunday at 1pm in May, June, September, and October; lectures and other programming are on Sunday from noon to 2pm; medieval-music concerts are held in the 12th-century Spanish chapel.

At the north end of Fort Tryon Park. ℂ **212/923-3700.** www.metmuseum.org. Suggested admission (includes same-day entrance to the Metropolitan Museum of Art) $12 adults, $7 seniors and students, free for children under 12. Nov–Feb Tues–Sun 9:30am–4:45pm; Mar–Oct Tues–Sun 9:30am–5:15pm. Subway: A to 190th St., then a 10-min. walk north along Margaret Corbin Dr., or pick up the M4 bus at the station (1 stop to Cloisters). Bus: M4 Madison Ave. (Fort Tryon Park–The Cloisters).

Cooper-Hewitt National Design Museum ⭐ Part of the Smithsonian Institution, the Cooper-Hewitt is in the Carnegie Mansion, built by Andrew Carnegie in 1901 and renovated in 1996. Some 11,000 square feet of space is devoted to changing exhibits that are well conceived, engaging, and educational. Shows are both historic and contemporary in nature, and topics range from "The Work of Charles and Ray Eames: A Legacy of Invention" to "The Architecture of Reassurance: Designing the Disney Theme Parks."

Note the Art Nouveau–style copper-and-glass canopy above the entrance. And visit the garden, ringed with Central Park benches from various eras.

2 E. 91st St. (at Fifth Ave.). © **212/849-8400**. www.si.edu/ndm. Admission $8 adults, $5 seniors and students, free for children under 12, free to all Tues 5–9pm. Tues 10am–9pm; Wed–Sat 10am–5pm; Sun noon–5pm. Subway: 4, 5, 6 to 86th St.

Dahesh Museum of Art *(Value)*   If you consider yourself a classicist, this small museum is for you. It's dedicated to 19th- and early-20th-century European academic art, a continuation of Renaissance, baroque, and rococo traditions that were overshadowed by the arrival of Impressionism. (If you're not familiar with this academic school, expect lots of painstaking renditions of historical subjects and pastoral life.) Artists represented include Jean-Léon Gérôme, Lord Leighton, and Edwin Long, whose *Love's Labour Lost* is a cornerstone of the collection.

601 Fifth Ave. (between 48th and 49th sts.), 2nd floor. © **212/759-0606**. www.daheshmuseum.org. Free admission. Tues–Sat 11am–6pm. Subway: B, D, F, V to 47th–50th sts./Rockefeller Center.

El Museo del Barrio   What started in 1969 with a display in a school classroom is today the only museum in America dedicated to Puerto Rican, Caribbean, and Latin American art. The northernmost Museum Mile institution has a permanent exhibit ranging from pre-Columbian artifacts to photographic art and video. The display of *santos de palo,* wood-carved religious figurines, is worth noting, as is "Taíno, Ancient Voyagers of the Caribbean," dedicated to the cultures that Columbus encountered when he landed in the "New World." The changing exhibitions focus on 20th-century artists and contemporary subjects.

1230 Fifth Ave. (at 104th St.). © **212/831-7272**. www.elmuseo.org. Suggested admission $5 adults, $3 seniors and students, free for children under 12. Wed–Sun 11am–5pm. Subway: 6 to 103rd St.

Federal Hall National Memorial *(Value)*   Fronted by 32-foot fluted marble Doric columns, this 1842 neoclassical temple is most famous for what happened here while the site was occupied by the 18th-century City Hall. Peter Zenger, publisher of the outspoken *Weekly Journal,* stood trial in 1735 for "seditious libel" against Royal Governor William Cosby. Defended brilliantly by Alexander Hamilton, Zenger's eventual acquittal (based on the grounds that anything you printed that was true, even if it wasn't very nice, couldn't be construed as libel) set the precedent for freedom of the press, later guaranteed in the Bill of Rights, which was drafted and signed inside this building. New York's first major rebellion against British authority also occurred here, when the Stamp Act Congress met in 1765 to protest King George III's policy of "taxation without representation." J.Q.A. Ward's 1883 statue of George Washington on the steps commemorates the spot of the first presidential inauguration, in 1789. Congress met here after the revolution, when New York was briefly the nation's capital.

Call ahead if you'd like to hook up with one of the 20- to 30-minute guided tours (I recommend it), which usually take place between 12:30 and 3:30pm.

26 Wall St. (at Nassau St.). © **212/825-6888**. www.nps.gov/feha. Free admission. Mon–Fri 9am–5pm. Subway: 4, 5 to Wall St.

Forbes Magazine Galleries *(Kids)*   The late publishing magnate Malcolm Forbes may have been a self-described "capitalist tool," but he had esoteric, almost childish, tastes. With its model boats, toy soldiers, old Monopoly games, trophies, miniature rooms, presidential memorabilia, and Fabergé eggs, this is a great little museum for you and the kids. Personal anecdotes explain why certain objects attracted Forbes's attention and turn the collection into an interesting biographical portrait. The Picture and Autograph Galleries, where you can find Abraham Lincoln's Emancipation Proclamation, are also intriguing.

(Value **Where to Find Free Culture**

New York's gargantuan stash of museums, galleries, and attractions makes this city one of the cultural capitals of the world. But the cost of this culture can be high, especially because many museums now charge $10 or more. But don't get discouraged; there are ways around these steep fees.

Some city attractions are free all the time. Some set aside an afternoon, an evening, or a day during the week when you can explore at no charge. Others offer "pay what you wish" times, be it $1 or the full admission price.

Most museums keep pretty solid schedules, but it's always a good idea to call ahead and confirm free and "pay what you wish" times—because these, like everything else, are always subject to change.

ALWAYS FREE

- Abyssinian Baptist Church (p. 235)
- American Folk Art Museum's Eva and Morris Feld Gallery (p. 215)
- Brooklyn Tabernacle (p. 259)
- Center for Jewish History (all galleries except Yeshiva University Museum; p. 215)
- Dahesh Museum of Art (p. 217)
- Federal Hall National Memorial (p. 217)
- Forbes Magazine Galleries (p. 217)
- Mother A.M.E. Zion Church (p. 236)
- National Museum of the American Indian (p. 227)
- New York City Police Museum (p. 228)
- New York Public Library (p. 232)
- New York Stock Exchange (p. 211)
- New York Transit Museum's Gallery Annex (p. 259)
- St. Patrick's Cathedral (p. 236)
- Schomburg Center for Research in Black Culture (p. 229)
- Socrates Sculpture Park (p. 263)
- Sony Wonder Technology Lab (p. 254)
- South Street Seaport (charge for museum admission; p. 230)
- Staten Island Ferry (p. 210)
- Temple Emanu-El (p. 236)
- Trinity Church ($2 donation requested for noonday concerts; p. 237)
- Whitney Museum of American Art at Philip Morris (p. 231)
- Zenith Media Lounge at the New Museum of Contemporary Art (p. 228)

SOMETIMES FREE (OR PAY WHAT YOU WISH)

- Museum of Arts and Design: Thursday from 6 to 8pm; regular admission $7.50 (p. 223)
- American Folk Art Museum: Friday 6 to 8pm; regular admission $9 (p. 215)

- **Asia Society:** Friday 6 to 9pm; regular admission $7 (p. 215)
- **Bronx Zoo Wildlife Conservation Park:** All day Wednesday; regular admission $9 (p. 255)
- **Brooklyn Botanic Garden:** All day Tuesday and Saturday from 10am to noon year-round, plus all day Wednesday, Thursday, and Friday from mid-November to mid-March; regular admission $3 (p. 258)
- **Brooklyn Museum of Art:** First Saturday of the month from 5 to 11pm; regular admission $6 (p. 258)
- **Children's Museum of the Arts:** Thursday from 4 to 6pm; regular admission $5 (p. 254)
- **Cooper-Hewitt National Design Museum:** Tuesday from 5 to 9pm; regular admission $8 (p. 216)
- **The Jewish Museum:** Tuesday from 5 to 8pm; regular admission $8 (p. 221)
- **MoMA QNS:** Friday from 4:30 to 8:15pm; regular admission $12 (p. 208)
- **New York Hall of Science:** Thursday and Friday from 2 to 5pm; regular admission $7.50 (p. 254)
- **New York Transit Museum:** Seniors enter free Tuesday from noon to 4pm; regular senior admission $1.50 (p. 259)
- **Solomon R. Guggenheim Museum:** Friday from 6 to 8pm; regular admission $12 (p. 209)
- **Studio Museum in Harlem:** First Saturday of the month; regular admission $5 (p. 230)
- **Wave Hill:** All day Tuesday and Saturday mornings in summer, every day in winter; regular admission $4 (p. 256)
- **Whitney Museum of American Art:** Friday from 6 to 9pm; regular admission $10 (p. 213)

ALMOST FREE (ADMISSION OF $3 OR LESS)

- **Brooklyn Botanic Garden:** $3 (p. 258)
- **Cathedral of St. John the Divine:** $2 ($3 for guided tour; p. 235)
- **Edgar Allan Poe Cottage:** $2 (p. 233)
- **Fraunces Tavern Museum:** $3 (p. 220)
- **Morris-Jumel Mansion:** $3 (p. 231)
- **Museum of American Financial History:** $2 (p. 223)
- **New Museum of Contemporary Art:** Thursday from 6 to 8pm, $3; regular admission $6 (p. 227)
- **New York Botanical Garden:** $3 (p. 256)
- **New York Transit Museum:** $3 (p. 259)
- **Prospect Park Wildlife Conservation Center:** $2.50 (p. 260)
- **Scandinavia House:** $3 (p. 229)
- **Theodore Roosevelt Birthplace:** $3 (p. 230)

62 Fifth Ave. (at 12th St.). (℮) **212/206-5548**. www.forbes.com/forbescollection. Free admission. Tues–Wed and Fri–Sat 10am–4pm (hours vary, call ahead). Subway: L, N, R, 4, 5, 6 to 14th St./Union Sq.

Fraunces Tavern Museum   This petite museum of early American history and culture is most famous for the Long Room, in which George Washington made his farewell to his soldiers at the end of the American Revolution, but it also houses exhibits such as "Colonists, Revolutionaries, Builders: Freemasons in America." Built in 1907, this replica of the original 1717 tavern is nevertheless a wonderful example of New York's pre-Revolutionary architectural style.

One of the best ways to experience Fraunces Tavern is to dine there. The restaurant serves lunch and dinner Monday through Saturday. The tavern has been painstakingly re-created and the fare significantly upscaled since the Revolutionary War days—as have entree prices, which are in the low $20s. The fare is mainly American, but the menu includes some West Indian dishes in honor of 18th-century restaurateur Samuel Fraunces. For a more cost-efficient but equally atmospheric experience, stop by for a drink in the bar.

54 Pearl St. (near Broad St.). (℮) **212/425-1778**, or 212/968-1776 for restaurant reservations. www.fraunces tavernmuseum.org. Admission $3 adults, $2 students and seniors, free for children under 6. Mon–Fri 10am–4:45pm. Restaurant Mon–Fri 6:30am–9:30pm (last seating); Sat noon–5pm (tavern/bar area only) and 5–9:30pm (dining room). Subway: N, R to Whitehall St.; 2, 3 to Wall St.; 4, 5 to Bowling Green.

The Frick Collection ★★   Henry Clay Frick could afford to be an avid collector of European art after amassing a fortune in the coke and steel industries at the turn of the 20th century. To house his treasures and himself, he hired Carrère & Hastings to build this 18th-century French-style mansion (1914).

Most appealing about the Frick is its intimate size and setting. This is a living testament to New York's Gilded Age—the interior still feels like a private home (albeit a really rich guy's home) with beautiful paintings. Come here to see the classics by Titian, Bellini, Rembrandt, Turner, Vermeer, El Greco, and Goya, to name only a few. A highlight is the **Fragonard Room,** graced with the rococo series *The Progress of Love.* The portrait of Montesquieu by Whistler is stunning. Sculpture, furniture, Chinese vases, and French enamels complement the paintings. Included in the price of admission, the AcousticGuide audio tour is useful because it allows you to follow your own path rather than a proscribed route. A free 22-minute **video** presentation is screened in the Music Room every half-hour from 10am to 4:30pm (from 1:30 on Sun).

In addition to the permanent collection, the Frick regularly mounts small, well-focused temporary exhibitions. In the fall of 2003, the museum will feature "The Drawings of Francois Boucher," demonstrating the 18th-century artist's extraordinary technique as a draftsman; "A Beautiful and Gracious Manner: The Art of Parmigianino" will run through the winter of 2004. Free **chamber-music concerts** are held twice a month, generally every other Sunday at 5pm in fall and winter, select Thursdays at 5:45pm in warm weather, as well as once-a-month **lectures,** select Wednesdays at 5:30pm. Call or visit the website for the current schedule and ticket information.

1 E. 70th St. (at Fifth Ave.). (℮) **212/288-0700**. www.frick.org. Admission $10 adults, $5 seniors and students. Children under 10 not admitted; children 10–16 must be accompanied by an adult. Tues–Sat 10am–6pm; Sun 1–6pm. Closed all major holidays. Subway: 6 to 68th St./Hunter College.

International Center of Photography ★ *Finds*   The state-of-the-art gallery space is ideal for viewing exhibitions of the museum's 50,000-plus prints, as well as visiting shows. The emphasis is on contemporary photographic works, but historically important photographers aren't ignored.

1133 Sixth Ave. (at 43rd St.). ℭ **212/857-0000.** www.icp.org. Admission $9 adults, $6 seniors and students. Tues–Thurs 10am–5pm; Fri 10am–8pm; Sat–Sun 10am–6pm. Subway: B, D, F, V to 42nd St.

Intrepid **Sea-Air-Space Museum** *Kids* The most astonishing thing about the aircraft carrier USS *Intrepid* is how it can be so big and so small simultaneously. It's a few football fields long, weighs 40,000 tons, and holds 40 aircraft. But stand there and think about landing an A-12 jet on the deck and suddenly it's minuscule. In the passageways below, you'll find it isn't quite the roomiest of vessels. Now a National Historic Landmark, the exhibit also includes the destroyer USS *Edson,* and the submarine USS *Growler,* the only intact strategic missile submarine open to the public anywhere, as well as a collection of vintage and modern aircraft, including the A-12 Blackbird, the world's fastest spy plane.

Kids just love this place. They—and you—can climb inside a replica of a Revolutionary War submarine, sit in an A-6 Intruder cockpit, and follow the progress of America's astronauts as they work in space. There are even navy flight simulators in the Technologies Hall. Look for family-oriented activities and events at least one Saturday a month.

The interactive exhibit "All Hands on Deck," teaches kids and adults how things work on ships, and there's a recently added AH-1 Cobra attack helicopter. The action-packed *Intrepid Wings* shows aircraft carrier take-offs and recoveries in the new Allison and Howard Lutnick Theater; the film runs throughout the day. "Remembering 9-11" recalls those lost, both civilians and rescuers. The grand visitor center, opened in 2000, makes for an impressive entrance, and the museum store is well stocked; goods include NYPD and FDNY logo gear. But dress warmly for a winter visit—it's almost impossible to heat an aircraft carrier.

Pier 86 (W. 46th St. at Twelfth Ave.). ℭ **212/245-0072.** www.intrepidmuseum.org. Admission $14 adults; $10 veterans, seniors, and students; $7 children 6–11; $2 children 2–5. $5 extra for flight-simulator rides. Apr–Sept Mon–Fri 10am–5pm, Sat–Sun 10am–7pm; Oct–Mar Tues–Sun 10am–5pm. Last admission 1 hr. before closing. Subway: A, C, E to 42nd St./Port Authority. Bus: M42 crosstown.

Japan Society The Japan Society was founded in 1907 to foster cultural understanding and enlightened relations between East and West, and does so admirably. The society's U.S. headquarters, housed in a striking modern building by Junzo Yoshimuro (1971), mounts exhibits of Japanese art in a serene gallery. Changing displays have included "Japanese Theater in the World" and "Frank Lloyd Wright and the Art of Japan: The Architect's Other Passion"; and late in 2003 "Isamu Noguchi and Modern Japanese Ceramics: Close Embrace of the Earth." The tranquil, elegant building also features a bamboo-pond garden as well as a 278-seat auditorium that hosts a wide variety of performances, from contemporary Japanese dance and music to *butoh* dance and kabuki. The extensive program schedule also features lectures, gallery talks, films, and classes throughout the year; call or check the website for current programming.

333 E. 47th St. (between First and Second aves.). ℭ **212/832-1155.** www.japansociety.org. Admission $5 adults, $3 seniors and students. Gallery: Tues–Fri 11am–6pm; Sat–Sun 11am–5pm. Subway: E, V to Lexington Ave.; 6 to 51st St.

The Jewish Museum Housed in a Gothic-style mansion renovated in 1993 by AIA Gold Medal winner Kevin Roche, this museum now has the world-class space it deserves to showcase its collections, which chronicle 4,000 years of Jewish history. The permanent exhibit, "Culture and Continuity: The Jewish Journey," tells the story of the Jewish experience from ancient times through today. Artifacts include daily objects that might have served the authors of the books of Genesis, Psalms, and Job, and an assemblage of Torahs. A collection of classic TV and radio programs is available for viewing through the Goodkind Resource Center (as any fan of television's golden age knows, its finest comic moments were Jewish comedy). The scope of the exhibit is phenomenal, and its story an enlightening—and intense—one. A random-access audio guide is geared to families (free with admission). In addition to the in-house shop, don't miss the Jewish Museum Design Shop in the adjacent brownstone. *Money-saving tip:* Check the website for online admission discounts (50% off at press time).

1109 Fifth Ave. (at 92nd St.). ✆ 212/423-3200. www.thejewishmuseum.org. Admission $8 adults, $5.50 seniors and students, free for children under 12; pay what you wish Thurs 5–8pm. Sun 10am–5:45pm; Mon–Wed 11am–5:45pm; Thurs 11am–8pm; Fri 11am–3pm. Subway: 4, 5 to 86th St.; 6 to 96th St.

Lower East Side Tenement Museum ✪ This museum is the first-ever National Trust for Historic Preservation site that was not the home of someone rich or famous. It's a five-story tenement that 10,000 people from 25 countries called home between 1863 and 1935—people who had come to the United States looking for the American dream. The museum tells the story of the immigration boom of the late 19th and early 20th centuries, when the Lower East Side was considered the "Gateway to America." A visit here is a good follow-up to an Ellis Island trip—what happened to the people who passed through that way station?

The only way to see the museum is by guided tour. Two tenement tours, held on all open days and lasting an hour, offer an exploration of the museum: **Piecing It Together: Immigrants in the Garment Industry,** which focuses on the apartment and the lives of its turn-of-the-20th-century tenants, an immigrant Jewish family named Levine from Poland; and **Getting By: Weathering the Great Depressions of 1873 and 1929,** featuring the homes of the German-Jewish Gumpertz family and the Sicilian-Catholic Baldizzi family, respectively. A guide leads you into each dingy urban time capsule, where several apartments have been restored to their lived-in condition, and recounts the stories of the families who occupied them. You can pair them for an in-depth look at the museum.

These tours are not really for kids, who won't enjoy the serious tone and "don't touch" policy. Much better for them is the 45-minute, weekends-only **Confino Family Apartment** tour, a living-history program geared to families, which allows kids to converse with an interpreter playing teenage immigrant Victoria Confino (ca. 1916); kids can handle whatever they like and try on period clothes.

The hour-long **Streets Where We Lived** neighborhood-heritage walking tour is offered on weekends from April to December. Small permanent and rotating exhibits, including photos, videos, and a model tenement, are housed in the Visitor Center and exhibition space in the tenement building at 97 Orchard St. Special tours and programs are sometimes on the schedule.

Tours are limited in number and sell out quickly, so it pays to buy tickets in advance, which you can do online, or over the phone by calling **Ticketweb** at ✆ **800/965-4827.** Note that the potential acquisition of a neighboring tenement at 99 Orchard St. may change programming, so confirm schedules.

Visitor Center at 90 Orchard St. (at Broome St.). ✆ 212/431-0233. www.tenement.org. Tenement and walking tours $9 adults, $7 seniors and students; Confino Apartment $8 adults, $6 seniors and students. Tenement tours depart every 40 min. Tues–Fri 1–4pm; Sat–Sun every half-hour 11am–4:45pm. Confino Apartment tour Sat–Sun hourly noon–3pm. Walking tour Apr–Dec Sat–Sun 1 and 2:30pm. Subway: F to Delancey St.; J, M, Z to Essex St.

Mount Vernon Hotel Museum & Garden *Finds*   It's a pleasant shock to find such a little-known jewel on this thoroughly modern block. This survivor from the early American republic was built as a carriage house for Abigail Adams Smith, daughter of President John Adams, and her husband, William Stephens Smith, in 1799. It's been restored by the Colonial Dames of America to its early-19th-century condition, when the house served as the Mount Vernon Hotel—a country hotel for overnights away from the city. On a guided tour you can explore nine period rooms, outfitted in Federal style, as well as the grounds, planted as a late-18th-century garden would be. An orientation center offers a scale model of the building as it looked in 1799 and screens a video on New York City in the early 19th century. Special events take place throughout the year.

421 E. 61st St. (between First and York aves.). (C) **212/838-6878.** Admission $4 adults, $3 seniors, free for children under 12. Tues–Sun 11am–4pm (last tour 3:15pm). Closed Aug. Subway: N, R to Lexington Ave.; 4, 5, 6 to 59th St.

Museum of American Financial History   Real money buffs (and who among us isn't?) may want to make a stop here. The exhibits housed in this Smithsonian-affiliate museum include numismatic and vintage ticker-tape displays; murals and photos depicting historic Wall Street scenes; and interactive financial news terminals, so little bulls and bears can learn how to keep up with the market. Temporary installations have run the gamut from "Morgan," a chronicle of the lasting influence of J. Pierpont Morgan, to "High Notes," an oddly compelling exhibit of high-denomination currency.

28 Broadway (just north of Bowling Green Park). (C) **877/98-FINANCE,** 212/908-4110, or 212/908-4519. www.financialhistory.org. Admission $2. Tues–Sat 10am–4pm. Subway: 4, 5 to Bowling Green; J, M to Broad St.; 2, 3 to Wall St.

Museum of Arts and Design ✿ *Finds*   Formerly called the American Craft Museum, this small but aesthetically pleasing museum is the nation's top showcase for contemporary crafts. The collection focuses on objects that are prime examples of form and function, ranging from jewelry to baskets to vessels to furniture. You'll see a strong emphasis on material as well as craft, whether it be fiber, ceramics, or metal. Special exhibitions can range from expressionist clay sculpture to fine bookbinding, and can celebrate movements or single artisans. Or just take your chances and stop in—you're unlikely to be disappointed. Stop into the gorgeous shop even if you don't make it into the museum (p. 288).

40 W. 53rd St. (between Fifth and Sixth aves.). (C) **212/956-3535.** www.americancraftmuseum.org. Admission $8 adults, $5 students and seniors, free for children under 12; pay as you wish Thurs 6–8pm. Tues–Wed and Fri–Sun 10am–6pm; Thurs 10am–8pm. Subway: E, V to Fifth Ave.

Museum of Jewish Heritage—A Living Memorial to the Holocaust ✿   In the south end of Battery Park City, the Museum of Jewish Heritage occupies a six-sided building designed by award-winning architect Kevin Roche, with a six-tier roof alluding to the Star of David and the six million murdered in the Holocaust. The permanent exhibits ("Jewish Life a Century Ago," "The War Against the Jews," and "Jewish Renewal") recount the daily prewar lives, the horror that destroyed them, and the renewal experienced by European and immigrant Jews in the years from the late 19th century to the present. The museum's power derives from the way it tells that story: through the objects, photographs, documents, and, most poignantly, the videotaped testimonies of Holocaust victims, survivors, and their families, all chronicled by Steven

Art for Art's Sake: The Gallery Scene

Manhattan has more than 500 private art galleries, selling everything from old masters to tomorrow's news. Galleries are free to the public, generally Tuesday through Saturday from 10am to 6pm. Nobody will expect you to buy—it's all about looking.

The best way to choose where to browse is by perusing the "Art Guide" in the Friday "Weekend" section of the *New York Times,* or the Sunday "Arts & Leisure" section; the "Cue" section of *New York* magazine; the Art section in *Time Out New York;* or the *New Yorker*'s "Goings on About Town." You can find the latest listings at **www.ny metro.com**, whose Arts page gives you access to *New York* magazine's listings; **www.newyork.citysearch.com** (click on "Arts"); **www.artnet. com**; and **www.galleryguide.org**. An excellent source—more for practicals on the galleries and the artists and genres—is **www.artincontext. org**. The *Gallery Guide* is available at most galleries.

I suggest picking a gallery or a show in a neighborhood that suits your taste, and start browsing. I've listed a few starting points in the neighborhoods below—uptown in Midtown East and on the Upper East Side; Chelsea, Manhattan's *avant* gallery row; and downtown, mainly in SoHo, hub for the modern-art establishment. This list doesn't begin to scratch the surface; there are many more galleries as well as concentrations of galleries in areas like the East Village, TriBeCa, and Brooklyn (the Art in Context site is a good way to locate them).

When choosing a browsing territory, keep in mind that uptown galleries tend to be more traditional, downtown galleries more contemporary, and far west Chelsea galleries the most cutting-edge. Museum-quality works dominate uptown, while raw talent and emerging artists are most common in west Chelsea. But you'll find constant surprises in all neighborhoods.

UPTOWN   Uptown galleries are clustered in and around the crossroads of Fifth Avenue and 57th Street and on and off Madison Avenue in the 60s, 70s, and 80s. These blue-chip galleries maintain their white-glove demeanor. They include **Hirschl & Adler Galleries,** 21 E. 70th St. (© 212/ 535-8810; www.hirschlandadler.com), for 18th- to 20th-century European and American painting and decorative arts; powerhouses **Gagosian Gallery,** 980 Madison Ave. (© 212/744-2313; www.gagosian. com), and **Pace Wildenstein,** 32 E. 57th St. (© 212/421-3292), whose focus is on classic modernism, representing such artists as Barbara Hepworth and Claes Oldenburg; **Margo Feiden Galleries,** 699 Madison Ave. (© 212/677-5330; www.alhirschfeld.com), the authorized representative of the works of the late Al Hirschfeld; **James Cohan Gallery,** 41 W.

Spielberg's Survivors of the Shoah Visual History Foundation. Thursday evenings are dedicated to panel discussions, performances, and music, while Sundays are for family programs and workshops; a film series is also a regular part of the calendar. A new East Wing that will triple the exhibition and events space and add a Family History Center was slated for completion in fall 2003.

57th St. (© 212/755-7171; www.jamescohan.com), strong in modern photography; **Mary Boone Gallery,** 745 Fifth Ave. (© 212/752-2929), known for such artists as Ross Bleckner and Nancy Ellison; **Richard L. Feigen & Co.,** 34 E. 69th St. (© 212/628-0700; www.rlfeigen.com); and **Wildenstein,** the classical big brother of Pace Wildenstein, 19 E. 64th St. (© 212/879-0500; www.wildenstein.com), specializing in big-ticket works: old masters, Impressionism, and Renaissance paintings and drawings.

CHELSEA The West 20s between Tenth and Eleventh avenues are home to the avant-garde, with West 26th serving as the unofficial "gallery row." Most galleries are not in storefronts but in the large spaces of multistory former garages and warehouses. Galleries worth seeking out include **Paula Cooper,** 534 W. 21st St. (© 212/255-1105), specializing in conceptual and minimal art; **George Billis Gallery,** 511 W. 25th St., 9F (© 212/645-2621; www.georgebillis.com), who shows works by emerging artists like still-life modernist Tom Gregg and *avant*-photographer Matt Ernst; **Gagosian Gallery,** 555 W. 24th St. (© 212/741-1111; www.gagosian.com), shows such major modern artists as Richard Serra and Julian Schnabel; **Cheim & Read,** 547 W. 25th St. (© 212/242-7727), which often shows works by such high-profile pop artists as Diane Arbus, Larry Clark, Robert Mapplethorpe, and Nan Goldin; **DCA Gallery,** 525 W. 22nd St. (© 212/255-5511; www.dcagallery.com), specializing in contemporary Danish artists; and **Alexander and Bonin,** 132 Tenth Ave. (© 212/367-7474; www.alexanderandbonin.com), which mounts excellent solo exhibitions by artists from the Americas and Europe.

SOHO SoHo remains colorful, if less edgy than it used to be, with the action centered around West Broadway. Start with **Bronwyn Keenan,** 3 Crosby St. (© 212/431-5083), who's known for a keen eye for emerging talent; **Peter Blum Gallery,** 99 Wooster St. (© 212/343-0441), who showcased Kim Sooja, a Korean artist who uses traditional Korean bedcovers to comment on the promise of wedded bliss; **Lehmann Maupin,** 39 Greene St. (© 212/965-0753), whose exhibitions run the gamut from unknowns to contemporary masters like Ross Bleckner; **O. K. Harris,** 383 W. Broadway (© 212/431-3600; www.okharris.com), which shows a wide and fascinating variety of contemporary painting, sculpture, and photography; and **Louis K. Meisel,** 141 Prince St. (© 212/677-1340; www.meiselgallery.com), specializing in photo realism and American pinup art (yep, Petty and Vargas girls).

While advance tickets are not usually necessary, you may want to purchase them to guarantee admission; call © 212/945-0039. Audio tours narrated by Meryl Streep and Itzhak Perlman are available for an additional $5.

Money-saving tip: Check the website for a $2-off admission coupon (available at press time), which you'll need to print out and bring with you.

18 First Place (at Battery Place), Battery Park City. (*) 212/509-6130. www.mjhnyc.org. Admission $7 adults, $5 seniors and students, free for children under 5. Sun–Wed 10am–5:45pm; Thurs 9am–8pm; Fri and eves of Jewish holidays 10am–3pm. Subway: 4, 5 to Bowling Green.

Museum of Sex *Finds* How many cities can claim their own Museum of Sex? Not too darn many! This one debuted in 2002, and despite its provocative title, offers a studied, historical look at the history of sex in our culture. The first exhibit, "NYC Sex: How New York City Transformed Sex in America," is scheduled to run through 2003. To enter the exhibit, you are given a scarlet X to wear as a ticket. An audio tour with headphones and commentary by such notables as Xaviera Hollander (The Happy Hooker) and Vanessa Del Rio (erotic video superstar) explain what you are seeing: details of 19th-century New York brothels, stag films from the early 1900s, videos of strippers Gypsy Rose Lee and Blaze Starr and 1970s porn queen Linda Lovelace, displays of condom cases from the 1930s, the development of gay and lesbian erotica, and S&M toys such as a genuine cat o' nine tails are some of the highlights. And if you pine for the Times Square of old, there is even a video of what it was like during the peep show glory years of the 1970s. This is not your ordinary museum gift shop; how about a $1,375 snakeskin whip as a souvenir to show all your friends back home? Many of the displays are very graphic, so the museum may not be for everyone. Go for an afternoon quickie and you save $5 on the steep $17 admission. The museum has recently added walking tours; see the website for more information.

233 Fifth Ave. (at 27th St). (*) 866/MOSEX NYC. www.museumofsex.com. Admission $17 adults, $14 students and seniors, $12 before 2, Mon–Fri. No one under 18 admitted. Subway: N, R to 28th St.

Museum of Television & Radio If you can resist the allure of this museum, I'd wager you've spent the last 70 years in a bubble. You can watch and hear the great personalities of TV and radio—from Uncle Miltie to Johnny Carson to Jerry Seinfeld—at a private console. You can conduct computer searches to pick out the great moments of history, viewing almost anything that made its way onto the airwaves, from the Beatles' appearance on *The Ed Sullivan Show* to the crumbling of the Berlin Wall. The collection consists of 75,000 programs and commercials, only a fraction of which are available for instant viewing (call at least a week in advance to arrange for a specific reel); you're allowed to watch up to four shows in one sitting. Selected programs are also presented in two theaters and two screening rooms.

25 W. 52nd St. (between Fifth and Sixth aves.). (*) 212/621-6800 or 212/621-6600. www.mtr.org. Admission $10 adults, $8 seniors and students, $5 children under 13. Tues–Sun noon–6pm (Thurs until 8pm, Fri theater programs until 9pm). Subway: B, D, F, V to 47th–50th sts./Rockefeller Center; E, V to 53rd St.

Museum of the City of New York A wide variety of objects—costumes, photographs, prints, maps, dioramas, and memorabilia—trace the history of New York City from its beginnings as a Dutch colony in the 16th century to its present-day prominence. Two outstanding exhibits are the re-creation of John D. Rockefeller's master bedroom and dressing room, and the space devoted to "Broadway!" a history of New York theater. Kids will love "New York Toy Stories," a permanent exhibit of toys and dolls owned and adored by centuries of New York children. The "Painting the Town: Cityscapes of New York" exhibit explores the changing cityscape from 1809 to 1997, and carries new profundity in the wake of the September 11, 2001, terrorist attacks. Check for a schedule of other exhibits relating to the terrorist attack, as part of the museum's "Project September 11."

1220 Fifth Ave. (at 103rd St.). (*) 212/534-1672. www.mcny.org. Suggested admission $7 adults; $4 seniors, students, and children; $12 families. Wed–Sat 10am–5pm; Sun noon–5pm. Subway: 6 to 103rd St.

National Academy of Design   Founded in 1825 and housed in a land-marked beaux-arts town house, the National Academy is one of the oldest art institutions in the country and is dedicated to preserving the academic tradition. It has three components: a fine-arts school; an honorary professional association of artists; and a museum, which mounts exhibits from its large collection on such themes as "Art in the Age of Queen Victoria" and "The Watercolors of Charles Hawthorne." The Annual Exhibition is the nation's oldest juried show.

1083 Fifth Ave. (between 89th and 90th sts.). © 212/369-4880. www.nationalacademy.org. Admission $8 adults, $4.50 seniors, $5 students. Wed–Thurs noon–5pm; Fri 11am–6pm; Sat–Sun 11am–5pm. Subway: 4, 5, 6, to 86th St.

National Museum of the American Indian, George Gustav Heye Center _Value_   This collection represents the Smithsonian Institution's Native People holdings. It's housed in New York until its new home on the Mall in Washington, D.C., is completed sometime this year. Until then, enjoy items spanning more than 10,000 years of native heritage, collected a century ago mainly by New York millionaire George Gustav Heye. About 70% of the collection is dedicated to the natives of North America and Hawaii; the rest represents the cultures of Mexico and Central and South America. There's a wealth of material, but it's not as well organized as it could be. The museum also hosts temporary themed exhibitions and interpretive programs plus free storytelling, music, and dance presentations.

The museum is housed in the 1907 beaux-arts **U.S. Customs House** ⚑, designed by Cass Gilbert and a National Historic Landmark. The statues lining the front of this granite structure personify _Asia_ (pondering philosophically), _America_ (bright-eyed and bushy-tailed), _Europe_ (decadent, whose time has passed), and _Africa_ (sleeping) by Daniel Chester French (of Lincoln Memorial fame). The most interesting, if unintentional, sculptural statement—keeping in mind the building's current purpose—is the giant seated woman to the left of the entrance representing America and surrounded by references to Native America: Mayan pictographs adorning her throne, Quetzalcoatl under her foot, and the plains Indian scouting out from over her shoulder. Inside, the oval rotunda designed by Raphael Guastavino was frescoed by Reginald Marsh to glorify the shipping industry (and, by extension, the Customs office once housed here).

1 Bowling Green (between State and Whitehall sts.). © 212/514-3700. www.nmai.si.edu. Free admission. Daily 10am–5pm. Subway: 4, 5 to Bowling Green; N, R to Whitehall.

Neue Galerie New York _Finds_   This museum is dedicated to German and Austrian art and design, with a focus on the early 20th century. The collection features painting, works on paper, decorative arts, and other media from such artists as Klimt, Kokoschka, Kandinsky, Klee, and leaders of the Wiener Werkstätte decorative arts and Bauhaus movements such as Adolf Loos and Mies van der Rohe. Once occupied by Mrs. Cornelius Vanderbilt III, the landmark-designated 1914 Carrère & Hastings building (they built the New York Public Library as well) is worth a look. **Cafe Sabarsky** is modeled on a Viennese cafe, so museumgoers in need of a snack break can expect a fine Linzer torte.

1048 Fifth Ave. (at 86th St.). © 212/628-6200. www.neuegalerie.org. Admission $10 adults, $7 seniors. Fri–Mon 11am–7pm. Subway: 4, 5, 6 to 86th St.

New Museum of Contemporary Art ⚑   This contemporary-arts museum has moved closer to the mainstream in recent years, but it's only a safety margin in from the edge as far as most of us are concerned. Expect adventurous and well-curated exhibitions. The 2004 exhibition calendar had not been announced at press time, but previous schedules have included "Portrait of the Lost Boys," New Zealander Jacqueline Fraser's moving narrative made of sumptuous fabric and fragile wire sculptures that examines the high incidence of suicide among teenage boys in New Zealand; the experimental film and slide projections of Brazilian artist Hélio Oiticica; and Belgian artist Wim Devoye's *Cloaca,* a fascinating sculptural installation using an array of laboratory glassware, electric pumps, computer monitors, and plastic tubing to both scientifically and artistically replicate the organic function of the human digestive system. The **Zenith Media Lounge,** a digital and media-arts technology space housing rotating installations, is free to the public. In 2005, the museum will move to a new 60,000-square-foot, $35 million home on the Bowery at Prince Street.

583 Broadway (between Houston and Prince sts.). (C) 212/219-1222. www.newmuseum.org. Admission $6 adults, $3 seniors and college students; $3 for adults Thurs 6–8pm; always free to visitors 18 and under. Tues–Sun noon–6pm; Thurs noon–8pm (Zenith Media Lounge to 6:30pm). Subway: N, R to Prince St.; F, S to Broadway/Lafayette St.

New York City Fire Museum ★ *Kids* Housed in a 1904 firehouse, the former quarters of FDNY Engine Co. 30, this museum houses one of the country's most extensive collections of fire-service memorabilia from the 18th century to the present. It's also the best place to pay tribute to the 343 heroic firefighters who lost their lives in the World Trade Center disaster. Expect changing exhibits relating to the September 11, 2001, terrorist attacks. Other displays range from vintage fire marks to fire trucks to the gear and tools of modern firefighters. Also look for leather hoses, fireboats, and Currier & Ives prints, plus a new exhibit on fire safety and burn prevention geared to families. Real firefighters are almost always on hand to share stories and fire-safety information. The retail store sells FDNY logo wear and souvenirs. Call ahead for details on scheduling a guided tour.

278 Spring St. (between Varick and Hudson sts.). (C) 212/691-1303. www.nycfiremuseum.org. Admission $4 adults, $2 seniors and students, $1 children under 12. Tues–Sat 10am–5pm; Sun 10am–4pm. Subway: C, E to Spring St.

New York City Police Museum *Kids* Newly opened in this Lower Manhattan location in early 2002, this small museum tells the story of the NYPD and offers a look at the present-day world of law enforcement through the eyes of NYPD officers. Exhibits include arrest records of famous criminals, fingerprinting and forensic art stations, and crime-fighting weapons galore.

100 Old Slip (at South St., 2 blocks south of Wall St.). (C) 212/480-3100. www.nycpolicemuseum.org. Free admission (donation suggested). Tues–Sat 10am–5pm. Subway: N, R to Whitehall St.; 2, 3 to Wall St.

New-York Historical Society ★ Launched in 1804, the New-York Historical Society is a major repository of American history, culture, and art, with a focus on New York. The neoclassical edifice near the Museum of Natural History has emerged from the renovation tent. Now open on the fourth floor is the Henry Luce III Center for the Study of American Culture, a state-of-the-art facility and gallery of fine and decorative arts, which displays more than 40,000 objects amassed over 200 years—including paintings, sculpture, Tiffany lamps, textiles, furniture, even carriages—that had been in storage for decades. Also look for paintings from Hudson River School artists Thomas Cole, Asher Durand, and Frederic Church, including Cole's five-part masterpiece, *The Course of Empire.* Of particular interest to scholars and ephemera buffs are the extensive Library Collections, which include books, manuscripts, maps, newspapers, photographs, and more documents chronicling the American experience. (An appointment may be necessary to view some or all of the Library Collections, so call ahead.)

Also of note are the society's temporary exhibits; a series called "History Responds" was one of the best in the city dealing with the September 11, 2001, terrorist attacks and its aftermath. World Trade Center–related exhibits are likely to continue, so interested visitors should be sure to check the exhibition schedule.

An extensive calendar of public programs runs the gamut from family story hours to Irving Berlin music nights to lectures by such luminaries as Ric Burns and Susan Sontag to expert-led walks through Manhattan neighborhoods.

2 W. 77th St. (at Central Park W.). (© 212/873-3400. www.nyhistory.org. Admission $6 adults, $4 seniors and students, free for children 12 and under. Tues–Sun 11am–6pm. Subway: B, C to 81st St.; 1, 9 to 79th St.

Scandinavia House: The Nordic Center in America *Finds*   Dedicated to both the shared and unique cultures of Denmark, Finland, Iceland, Norway, and Sweden, Scandinavia House features two floors of galleries and an outdoor sculpture terrace display rotating art and design exhibits that can range from "Scandia: Important Early Maps of the Northern Regions" to "Strictly Swedish: An Exhibition of Contemporary Design." The rest of the space, including the 168-seat Victor Borge Hall, is dedicated to a calendar full of lectures, film screenings, music and drama performances, and scholarly presentations, all of a Nordic ilk. The exquisite modern building—designed to showcase Scandinavian materials and aesthetics—is worth a look in itself, especially if you're a modern-architecture buff. Guided tours are offered Tuesdays and Thursdays at 2pm and last a half-hour; they're free, but reservations are recommended.

The shop is a riot of fine Scandinavian design, and the excellent **AQ Café** serves up Swedish meatballs and other Scandinavian delicacies.

58 Park Ave. (between 37th and 38th sts.). (© 212/879-9779. www.scandinaviahouse.org. Suggested admission to 3rd- and 4th-floor galleries $3, $2 seniors and students; free admission to other spaces. Exhibitions Tues–Sun noon–6pm; cafe Mon–Sat 10am–5pm; store Mon–Sat 10am–6pm. Subway: 6 to 33rd St.; 4, 5, 6, 7, S to 42nd St./Grand Central.

Schomburg Center for Research in Black Culture *Value*   Arturo Alfonso Schomburg, a black Puerto Rican, set himself to accumulating materials about blacks in America, and his massive collection is now housed and preserved at this research branch of the New York Public Library. The Exhibition Hall, the Latimer/Edison Gallery, and the Reading Room host exhibits related to black culture, such as "Lest We Forget: The Triumph over Slavery" and "Masterpieces of African Motherhood." A rich calendar of talks and performing-arts events is part of the continuing program. Make an appointment for a guided tour so you can see the 1930s murals by Harlem Renaissance artist Aaron Douglas; it'll be worth your while. Academics and others interested in a more complete look at the center's holdings can preview what's available online. Call to inquire about current exhibitions and information on tours and public programs.

515 Malcolm X Blvd. (Lenox Ave., between 135th and 136th sts.). (© 212/491-2200. www.nypl.org. Free admission. Gallery Mon–Sat 10am–6pm; Sun 1–5pm. Subway: 2, 3 to 135th St.

Skyscraper Museum   Wowed by the sheer verticality in this town? Awed by the architectural marvel that is the high-rise? You're not alone. If you'd like to learn more about the technology, culture, and sheer muscle behind it all, seek out this formerly itinerant museum, which moved into its first permanent home in the spring of 2003 in a brand-new 38-story Skidmore, Owings & Merrill tower that also houses the Ritz-Carlton Battery Park hotel. The new space comprises two galleries, one housing a permanent exhibition dedicated to the evolution of Manhattan's commercial skyline, the other to changing shows.

2 West St., Battery Park City. ✆ 212/968-1961. www.skyscraper.org. Subway: 4, 5 to Bowling Green.

South Street Seaport & Museum *Kids*   This landmark district encompasses 11 blocks of historic buildings, a museum, several piers, shops, and restaurants.

You can explore most of the Seaport on your own. It's an odd place. The 18th- and 19th-century buildings lining the cobbled streets and alleyways are beautifully restored but have a theme-park air about them, no doubt due to the mall-familiar shops housed within. The height of the Seaport's cheesiness is Pier 17, a barge converted into a mall, complete with food court and jewelry kiosks.

Despite its rampant commercialism, the Seaport is worth a look. There's a good amount of history to be discovered here, most of it around the **South Street Seaport Museum,** a fitting tribute to the sea commerce that once thrived here.

In addition to the galleries—which house paintings and prints, ship models, scrimshaw, and nautical designs, as well as exhibitions—there are a number of historic ships berthed at the pier, including the 1911 *Peking* and the 1893 Gloucester fishing schooner *Lettie G. Howard.* The museum also offers a number of guided **walking tours;** call or check **www.southstseaport.org** for details.

Even **Pier 17** has its merits. Head up to the third-level deck overlooking the East River, where the wooden chairs will have you thinking about what it was like to cross the Atlantic on the *Normandie.* From here, you can see south to the Statue of Liberty, north to the Brooklyn Bridge, and across to Brooklyn Heights.

At the gateway to the Seaport, at Fulton and Water streets, is the *Titanic* **Memorial Lighthouse,** a monument to those who lost their lives when the ocean liner sank on April 15, 1912. It was erected overlooking the East River in 1913 and moved to this spot in 1968, just after the historic district was so designated.

A variety of events take place year-round, ranging from street performers to concerts to fireworks; check the website or dial ✆ **212/SEA-PORT.**

At Water and South sts.; museum Visitor Center is at 12 Fulton St. ✆ 212/748-8600 or 212/SEA-PORT. www. southstseaport.org or www.southstreetseaport.com. Museum admission $5. Museum Apr–Sept Fri–Wed 10am–6pm, Thurs 10am–8pm; Oct–Mar Wed–Mon 10am–5pm. Subway: 2, 3, 4, 5 to Fulton St. (walk east, or downslope, on Fulton St. to Water St.).

Studio Museum in Harlem   The small but lovely museum is devoted to 19th- and 20th-century African-American art as well as 20th-century African and Caribbean art and traditional African art and artifacts. Rotating exhibitions are a big part of the museum's focus, such as "Smithsonian African-American Photography: The First 100 Years, 1842–1942"; the silk-screens and lithographs of Jacob Lawrence; and an annual exhibition of works by emerging artists as part of its Artists-in-Residence program. There's also a small sculpture garden, a good gift shop, and a full calendar of special events.

144 W. 125th St. (between Lenox Ave. and Adam Clayton Powell Blvd.). ✆ 212/864-4500. www.studio museuminharlem.org. Admission $5 adults, $3 seniors, $1 children under 12, free for all on lst Sat of the month. Sun and Wed–Fri noon–6pm; Sat 10am–6pm. Subway: 2, 3 to 125th St.

Theodore Roosevelt Birthplace   This National Historic Site is a reconstruction on the same site as the brownstone where Theodore Roosevelt was born on October 27, 1858, and lived his first 14 years. Period rooms appear as they did in Teddy's youth. The powder-blue parlor is in the rococo-revival style popular at the time, the dining room boasts horsehair-covered chairs, and the nursery has a window that leads to a small gymnasium built to help the frail Teddy get stronger. There's also a collection of Roosevelt memorabilia.

28 E. 20th St. (between Broadway and Park Ave. S.). © **212/260-1616.** www.nps.gov/thrb. Admission $3 adults, free for children under 18 and National Park Passport holders. Mon–Fri 9am–5pm (tours hourly from 10am–4pm). Subway: N, R to Broadway/23rd St.; 6 to 23rd St.

Whitney Museum of American Art at Philip Morris *Value*   This Midtown branch of the Whitney Museum of American Art (p. 213) features an airy sculpture court and a petite gallery that hosts changing exhibits, usually the works of living contemporary artists. Well worth peeking into if you happen to be in the neighborhood; I popped in recently and found a wonderful exhibition that juxtaposed the organic-inspired sculptures and drawings of Isamu Noguchi and Ellsworth Kelly. Free gallery talks are offered Wednesday and Friday at 1pm.

120 Park Ave. (at 42nd St., opposite Grand Central Terminal). © **917/663-2453.** www.whitney.org. Free admission. Gallery Mon–Wed and Fri 11am–6pm; Thurs 11am–7:30pm. Sculpture Court Mon–Sat 7:30am–9:30pm; Sun 11am–7pm. Subway: S, 4, 5, 6, 7 to 42nd St./Grand Central.

5 Skyscrapers & Other Architectural Highlights

For details on the **Empire State Building** ★★★, see p. 205; **Grand Central Terminal** ★★, see p. 205; **Rockefeller Center** ★★, see p. 208; the **U.S. Customs House,** p. 245; and the **Brooklyn Bridge** ★★, p. 203. "Places of Worship," below, covers **St. Patrick's Cathedral, Temple Emanu-El,** and the **Cathedral of St. John the Divine** ★.

In addition to the landmarks below, architecture buffs may want to seek out the **Lever House,** at 390 Park Ave., between 53rd and 54th streets, and the **Seagram Building** (1958), at 375 Park Ave., which are the city's best examples of the glass-and-steel International style, with the latter designed by master architect Mies van der Rohe himself. Also in Midtown East is the **Sony Building,** at

---

Fun Fact **Harlem's Architectural Treasures**

Originally conceived as a suburb for 19th-century Manhattan's moneyed set, Harlem has always had more than its share of historic treasures. Pay a call on the **Astor Row Houses,** 130th Street between Fifth and Lenox avenues, a series of 28 town houses built in the early 1880s by the Astors, graced with wooden porches, yards, and ornamental ironwork.

Equally impressive is **Strivers' Row,** West 139th Street between Adam Clayton Powell Jr. and Frederick Douglass boulevards, where hardly a brick has changed among the McKim, Mead & White neo-Italian Renaissance town houses since 1890. Once the original white owners had moved out, these houses attracted the cream of Harlem, "strivers" like Eubie Blake and W. C. Handy.

Handsome brownstones, town houses, and row houses are atop **Sugar Hill,** 145th to 155th streets, between St. Nicholas and Edgecombe avenues, named for the "sweet life" enjoyed by its residents. In the early 20th century, such prominent blacks as W.E.B. DuBois, Thurgood Marshall, and Roy Wilkins lived in the building at 409 Edgecombe Ave.

While you're uptown, don't miss the **Jumel Terrace Historic District,** west of St. Nicholas Avenue between 160th and 162nd streets. Of particular note is **Sylvan Terrace,** which feels more like a Hudson River town than a part of Harlem. A walk along it will lead you to the **Morris-Jumel Mansion** ★ (see "In Search of Historic Homes," below).

550 Madison Ave., designed in 1984 by Philip Johnson with a rose-granite facade and a playful Chippendale-style top that puts it a cut above the rest on the block.

The Upper West Side is home to two of the city's prime examples of residential architecture. On Broadway, between 73rd and 74th streets, is **The Ansonia,** looking like a flamboyant architectural wedding cake. This splendid beaux-arts building has been home to the likes of Stravinsky, Toscanini, and Caruso, thanks to its virtually soundproof apartments. (It was also the spot where members of the Chicago White Sox plotted to throw the 1919 World Series.) Even more notable is **The Dakota,** at 72nd Street and Central Park West. Legend has it that the angular 1884 apartment house—accented with gables, dormers, and oriel windows that give it a brooding appeal—earned its name when its developer, Edward S. Clark, was teased by friends that he was building so far north of the city that he might as well be building in the Dakotas. One of the building's most famous residents, John Lennon, was gunned down outside the 72nd Street entrance on December 8, 1980; Yoko Ono still lives there.

Chrysler Building ★★   Built as Chrysler Corporation headquarters in 1930, this is perhaps the 20th century's most romantic architectural achievement, especially at night, when the lights in its triangular openings play off its steely crown. As you admire its facade, be sure to note the gargoyles reaching out from the upper floors, looking for all the world like streamline-Gothic hood ornaments.

There's a fascinating tale behind this building. While it was under construction, architect William Van Alen hid his final plans for the spire that now tops it. Working at a furious pace in the last days of construction, the workers assembled the elegant pointy top in secrecy—and then they raised it right through what people had assumed was going to be the roof, and for a brief moment it was the world's tallest building (a distinction taken by the Empire State Building a few months later). The observation deck closed long ago, but you can visit its lavish ground-floor interior, which is Art Deco to the max. The ceiling mural depicting airplanes and other marvels of the first decades of the 20th century evince the bright promise of technology. The elevators are works of art, covered in exotic woods (especially note the lotus-shaped marquetry on the doors).

405 Lexington Ave. (at 42nd St.). Subway: S, 4, 5, 6, 7 to 42nd St./Grand Central.

Flatiron Building   This triangular masterpiece was one of the first skyscrapers. Its knife-blade wedge shape is the only way the building could fill the triangular property at the intersection of Fifth Avenue and Broadway, and that coincidence created one of the city's most distinctive buildings. Built in 1902 and fronted with limestone and terra cotta, the Flatiron measures only 6 feet across at its narrow end. It was originally named the Fuller Building, then later "Burnham's Folly," because folks were certain that architect Daniel Burnham's 21-story structure would fall down. It didn't. There's no observation deck, and the building mainly houses publishing offices, but there are a few shops on the ground floor. The building's existence has served to name the neighborhood around it—the Flatiron District, home to a bevy of smart restaurants and shops.

175 Fifth Ave. (at 23rd St.). Subway: N, R to 23rd St.

New York Public Library ★★ *Value*   The New York Public Library, adjacent to Bryant Park (p. 245) and designed by Carrère & Hastings (1911), is one of the country's finest examples of beaux-arts architecture, a majestic structure of white Vermont marble with Corinthian columns and allegorical statues. Before climbing the broad flight of steps to the Fifth Avenue entrance, take note of the

Finds **In Search of Historic Homes**

New York's appetite for change often means that older architecture is torn down so that money-earning high-rises can go up. Surprisingly, the city maintains a fine collection of often-overlooked historic houses that are more than a tale of architecture—they're the stories of the people who passed their lives in buildings that range from humble to magnificent.

The **Historic House Trust of New York City** preserves 19 houses in all five boroughs. Those worth seeking out include the **Morris-Jumel Mansion** ✮, in Harlem at 65 Jumel Terrace (at 160th St. east of St. Nicholas Ave.; ✆ **212/923-8008**; open Wed–Sun 10am–4pm; admission $3, $2 seniors and students), a grand colonial mansion built in the Palladian style around 1765 and now Manhattan's oldest surviving house. The **Edgar Allan Poe Cottage,** 2460 Grand Concourse, at East Kingsbridge Road, the Bronx (✆ **718/881-8900;** www.bronxhistoricalsociety. org; open Sat 10am–4pm, Sun 1–5pm; admission $2), was the final home of the poet and author, who moved his wife here because he thought the "country air" would be good for her tuberculosis. Among the works he penned in residence (1846–49) are "The Bells" and "Annabel Lee." The house is outfitted with period furnishings and exhibits on Poe's life and times.

The **Merchant's House Museum** ✮, 29 E. 4th St. between Lafayette Street and Bowery in NoHo (✆ **212/777-1089;** www.merchantshouse. com; open Thurs–Mon 1–5pm; admission $5, $3 for seniors and students), is a rare jewel: a perfectly preserved 19th-century home, complete with intact interiors, whose last resident is said to have been the inspiration for Catherine Sloper in Henry James's *Washington Square.* The house is a prime example of Greek Revival architecture. Seven rooms are outfitted with the belongings of the original inhabitants, offering a prime look at domesticity in the 19th century.

Each of the others has its own fascinating story, and admission is generally around $2 or $3. A brochure listing the locations and touring details of all 19 of the historic homes is available by calling ✆ **212/360-8282;** recorded information is available at ✆ **212/360-3448.** You'll find information online at **www.preserve.org/hht** (click on "Things to Do," then "Attractions").

famous lion sculptures—*Fortitude* on the right and *Patience* on the left. At Christmastime they don natty wreaths to keep warm.

This library is actually the **Humanities and Social Sciences Library,** only one of the research libraries in the New York Public Library system. The interior is one of the finest in the city and features **Astor Hall,** with arched marble ceilings and grand staircases. The **Main Reading Rooms** have now reopened after a massive restoration and modernization that brought them back to their stately glory and moved them into the computer age (goodbye, card catalogs!).

Even if you don't stop in to peruse the periodicals, you may want to check out one of the excellent rotating **exhibitions;** look for "Ninety From the Nineties:

A Decade of Printing" in late 2003. Call or check the site to see what's on while you're in town. There's also a full calendar of **lecture programs,** with past speakers ranging from Tom Stoppard to Cokie Roberts; popular speakers often sell out, so it's a good idea to purchase tickets in advance.

Fifth Ave. and 42nd St. ℭ **212/869-8089** (exhibits and events), or 212/661-7220 (library hours). www. nypl.org. Free admission to exhibitions. Mon and Thurs–Sat 10am–6pm; Tues–Wed 11am–7:30pm. Subway: B, D, F, V to 42nd St.; S, 4, 5, 6, 7 to Grand Central/42nd St.

United Nations   The U.N. headquarters occupies 18 acres of international territory—neither New York City nor the United States has jurisdiction here— along the East River from 42nd to 48th streets. Designed by an international team of architects (led by American Wallace K. Harrison and including Le Corbusier), the complex along the East River weds the 39-story glass slab Secretariat with the free-form General Assembly on grounds donated by John D. Rockefeller Jr. One hundred eighty nations use the facilities to arbitrate worldwide disputes.

Guided tours last 45 minutes to an hour and take you to the General Assembly Hall and the Security Council Chamber, and introduce the history and activities of the United Nations and its related organizations. Along the tour you'll see donated objects and artwork, including charred artifacts that survived the atomic bombs at Hiroshima and Nagasaki, stained-glass windows by Chagall, a replica of the first *Sputnik,* and a colorful mosaic called *The Golden Rule,* based on a Norman Rockwell drawing, which was a gift from the United States in 1985.

If you take the time to wander the landscaped **grounds,** you'll be rewarded with lovely views and some surprises. The monument *Good Defeats Evil,* donated by the Soviet Union in 1990, fashioned a contemporary St. George slaying a dragon from parts of Russian and American missiles. At press time, the **Delegates' Dining Room** was closed to the public for lunch; feel free to call ℭ **212/963-7625** to see if it has reopened to visitors.

At First Ave. and 46th St. ℭ **212/963-8687.** www.un.org/tours. Guided tours $10 adults, $7.50 seniors, $6.50 high school and college students, $5.50 children 5–14. Children under 5 not admitted. Daily tours every half-hour 9:30am–4:45pm; closed weekends Jan–Feb; limited schedule may be in effect during the general debate (late Sept to mid-Oct). Subway: S, 4, 5, 6, 7 to 42nd St./Grand Central.

Moments   **A View from (next to) the Bridge**

Want to enjoy a little-known, but spectacular view of the New York skyline? Go for a ride on the **Roosevelt Island Tram** (ℭ 212/832-4543 ex.1). This is the same tram that King Kong "attacks" in the Universal Studio Theme Park in Florida, and the same tram you have probably seen in countless movies, most recently *Spiderman* The Tram originates at 59th Street and Second Avenue, costs $2 each way, ($2 round trip for seniors) and takes four minutes to traverse the East River to Roosevelt Island, where there are a series of apartment complexes and parks. During those four minutes you will be treated to a gorgeous view down the East River and the East Side skyline with views of the United Nations; and four bridges: the Queensboro, Williamsburg, Manhattan, and Brooklyn Bridge. On a clear day you might even spot Lady Liberty. And don't worry, despite what you've seen the movies, the tram is safe and your friendly neighborhood Spiderman has everything under control. The Tram operates daily 6am until 2:30am and until 3:30am on weekends.

Woolworth Building ⭐ This soaring "Cathedral of Commerce" cost Frank W. Woolworth $13.5 million worth of nickels and dimes in 1913. Designed by Cass Gilbert, it was the world's tallest edifice until 1930, when the Chrysler Building surpassed it. At its opening, President Woodrow Wilson pressed a button from the White House that illuminated the building's 80,000 electric light bulbs. The neo-Gothic architecture is rife with spires, gargoyles, flying buttresses, vaulted ceilings, 16th-century–style stone-as-lace traceries, turrets, and a churchlike interior.

Step into the marble entrance arcade to view the mosaic Byzantine-style ceiling and gold-leafed neo-Gothic cornices. The corbels (carved figures under the crossbeams) in the lobby include portraits of the building's engineer Gunwald Aus measuring a girder (above the staircase to the left of the main door), Gilbert holding a model of the building, and Woolworth counting coins (both above the left-hand corridor of elevators). Stand near the security guard's podium and crane your neck for a glimpse of Paul Jennewein's murals of *Commerce* and *Labor*, half hidden on the mezzanine. Cross Broadway for the best view of the exterior.

233 Broadway (at Park Place, near City Hall Park). Subway: 2, 3 to Park Place; N, R to City Hall.

6 Places of Worship

New York has an incredible range of religious institutions, notable for their history, architecture, and/or inspirational music. I've listed two of Harlem's premier gospel institutions below; if you would rather go to one of these gospel services in the company of a guide, see "Affordable Sightseeing Tours," on p. 247. Those who would like to hear the rousing gospel of the multiple Grammy Award–winning **Brooklyn Tabernacle Choir** should see p. 259.

If you do plan to attend a gospel service, be prepared to stay for the entire 1½- to 2-hour service. It is impolite to exit early. (Services are extremely popular, so you'll find it just plain difficult to leave before the end, anyway.)

Abyssinian Baptist Church ⭐ The most famous of Harlem's more than 400 houses of worship is this Baptist church, founded downtown in 1808 by African-American and Ethiopian merchants. It was moved uptown to Harlem back in the 1920s by Adam Clayton Powell Sr., who built it into the largest Protestant congregation in America. His son, Adam Clayton Powell Jr. (for whom the adjoining boulevard was named), carried on his tradition, and also became a U.S. congressman. Abyssinian is now the domain of the activist-minded Rev. Calvin O. Butts, whom the Chamber of Commerce has declared a "Living Treasure." The Sunday-morning services—at 9 and 11am—offer a wonderful opportunity to experience the Harlem gospel tradition.

132 Odell Clark Place (W. 138th St., between Adam Clayton Powell Blvd. and Lenox Ave.). © 212/862-7474. www.abyssinian.org. Subway: 2, 3, B, C to 135th St.

Cathedral of St. John the Divine ⭐ The world's largest Gothic cathedral has been a work in progress since 1892. Its sheer size is amazing enough—a nave that stretches two football fields and a seating capacity of 5,000—but keep in mind that there is no steel structural support. The church is being built using Gothic engineering; blocks of granite and limestone are carved by master masons and their apprentices—which may explain why construction is still ongoing, more than 100 years after it began, with no end in sight. That's precisely what makes this place so wonderful: Finishing isn't necessarily the point. A December 2001 fire destroyed the north transept, which housed the gift shop. But this phoenix rose from the ashes; the cathedral was reopened to visitors within a month, even though the scent of charred wood was still in the air.

Though the seat of the Episcopal Diocese of New York, St. John's embraces an interfaith tradition. Each chapel is dedicated to a different national, ethnic, or social group. The genocide memorial in the Missionary chapel—dedicated to the victims of the Ottoman Empire in Armenia (1915–23), of the Holocaust (1939–45), and in Bosnia-Herzegovina since 1992—moved me to tears, as did the FDNY memorial in the Labor chapel. Although it was originally conceived to honor 12 firefighters killed in 1966, hundreds of personal note cards and trinkets of remembrance have evolved it into a moving tribute to the 343 firefighting heroes murdered in the September 11, 2001, terrorist attacks.

You can explore the cathedral on your own, or on the **Public Tour,** offered 6 days a week; also inquire about periodic (usually twice-monthly) **Vertical Tours,** which take you on a hike up the 11-flight circular staircase to the top, for spectacular views. St. John the Divine is also known for presenting outstanding workshops, musical events, and important speakers. The free **New Year's Eve concert** draws thousands of New Yorkers; so, too, does its annual **Blessing of the Animals,** held in early October (see "Calendar of Events," in chapter 2). To hear the pipe organ in action, attend the weekly **Choral Evensong and Organ Meditation** service Sunday at 6pm.

1047 Amsterdam Ave. (at 112th St.). ✆ **212/316-7540,** 212/932-7347 (tour information and reservations), or 212/662-2133 (event information and tickets). www.stjohndivine.org. Suggested admission $2; tour $3; vertical tour $10. Mon–Sat 7am–6pm; Sun 7am–8pm. Tours offered Tues–Sat 11am; Sun 1pm. Worship services Mon–Sat 8 and 8:30am (morning prayer and holy Eucharist), 12:15pm, and 5:30pm (1st Thurs service 7:15am); Sun 8, 9, and 11am and 6pm; AIDS memorial service 4th Sat of the month at 1pm. Subway: B, C, 1, 9 to Cathedral Pkwy.

Mother A.M.E. Zion Church   Another of Harlem's great gospel churches is this African Methodist Episcopal house of worship, the first black church to be founded in New York State. Established on John Street in Lower Manhattan in 1796, Mother A.M.E. was known as the "Freedom Church" for the central role it played in the Underground Railroad. Among the escaped slaves the church hid was Frederick Douglass; other famous congregants have included Sojourner Truth and Paul Robeson. Rousing Sunday services are at 11am.

140–7 W. 137th St. (between Adam Clayton Powell Blvd. and Lenox Ave.). ✆ **212/234-1544.** www.mother africanmethodistezchurch.com. Subway: 2, 3 or B, C to 135th St.

St. Patrick's Cathedral   This Gothic white-marble and stone structure is the largest Catholic cathedral in the United States, as well as the seat of the Archdiocese of New York. Designed by James Renwick, begun in 1859, and consecrated in 1879, St. Patrick's wasn't completed until 1906. Irish Catholics picked one of the city's WASPiest neighborhoods for St. Patrick's. If you don't wish to attend Mass, you can pop in between services to get a look at the impressive interior. The St. Michael and St. Louis altar came from Tiffany and Co. (also on Fifth Ave.), while the St. Elizabeth altar—honoring Mother Elizabeth Seton, the first American-born saint—was designed by Paolo Medici of Rome.

Fifth Ave. (between 50th and 51st sts.). ✆ **212/753-2261.** www.ny-archdiocese.org/pastoral/cathedral_ about.html. Free admission. Sun–Fri 7am–8:30pm; Sat 8am–8:30pm. Mass Mon–Fri 7, 7:30, 8, and 8:30am, noon, and 12:30, 1, and 5:30pm; Sat 8 and 8:30am, noon, and 12:30 and 5:30pm; Sun 7, 8, 9, and 10:15am (Cardinal's Mass), noon, and 1, 4, and 5:30pm; holy days 7, 7:30, 8, 8:30, 9, 11, and 11:30am, noon, and 12:30, 1, 5:30, and 6:30pm. Subway: B, D, F, V to 47th–50th sts./Rockefeller Center.

Temple Emanu-El   Many of New York's most prominent families are members of this Reform congregation—the first established in New York City. The largest house of Jewish worship in the world is a blend of Moorish and

Romanesque styles, symbolizing the mingling of Eastern and Western cultures. The temple houses a remarkable collection of Judaica in the Herbert & Eileen Bernard Museum, including a collection of Hanukkah lamps ranging from the 14th to the 20th centuries. Three galleries also tell the story of the congregation from 1845 to the present. Free **tours** are given after services Saturday at noon. Inquire for a schedule of lectures, films, music, and symposiums.

1 E. 65th St. (at Fifth Ave.). ✆ **212/744-1400**. www.emanuelnyc.org. Free admission. Daily 10am–5pm. Services Sun–Thurs 5:30pm; Fri 5:15pm; Sat 10:30am. Subway: N, R to Fifth Ave.; 6 to 68th St.

Trinity Church   Serving God and Mammon, this Wall Street house of worship—with neo-Gothic flying buttresses, stained-glass windows, and vaulted ceilings—was designed by Richard Upjohn and consecrated in 1846. At that time, its 280-foot spire dominated the skyline. Its main doors, embellished with biblical scenes, were inspired in part by Ghiberti's famed doors on Florence's Baptistery. The historic church stood strong while office towers crumbled around it on September 11, 2001. The gates to the historic church serve as an impromptu memorial to the victims of the September 11, 2001, terrorist attacks, with countless tokens of remembrance left by both locals and visitors alike.

The church runs a brief free **tour** daily at 2pm (a second Sun tour follows the 11:15am Eucharist); groups of five or more should call ✆ **212/602-0872** to reserve. There's a small museum at the end of the left aisle displaying documents (including the 1697 church charter from William III), photographs, replicas of the Hamilton-Burr duel pistols, and other items. Surrounding the church is a churchyard whose monuments read like a history book: a tribute to martyrs of the American Revolution, Alexander Hamilton, Robert Fulton, and many more. Lined with benches, this makes a wonderful picnic spot on warm days.

Also part of Trinity Church is **St. Paul's Chapel,** at Broadway and Fulton Street, New York's only surviving pre-Revolutionary church, and a transition shelter for homeless men until it was transformed into a relief center after the September 11, 2001, terrorist attacks; it returned to its former duties in mid-2002. Built by Thomas McBean, with a templelike portico and Ionic columns supporting a massive pediment, the chapel resembles London's St. Martin-in-the-Fields. In the small graveyard, 18th- and early-19th-century notables rest in peace and modern businesspeople sit for lunch.

Trinity holds its **Noonday Concert series** of chamber music and orchestral concerts Monday and Thursday at 1pm; call ✆ **212/602-0747** or visit the website for a schedule, and to see if programming has resumed at St. Paul's.

At Broadway and Wall St. ✆ **212/602-0800**, 212/602-0872, or 212/602-0747 (concert information). www. trinitywallstreet.org. Free admission and tours; $2 suggested donation for noonday concerts. Museum Mon–Fri 9–11:45am and 1–3:45pm; Sat 10am–3:45pm; Sun 1–3:45pm. Services Mon–Fri 8:15am, 12:05, and 5:15pm (additional Healing Service Thurs at 12:30pm); Sat 8:45am; Sun 9 and 11:15am (also 8am Eucharist service at St. Paul's Chapel, between Vesey and Fulton sts.). Subway: 4, 5 to Wall St.

7 Central Park ✮✮✮ & Other Places to Play

CENTRAL PARK

Without the miracle of civic planning that is Central Park, Manhattan would be an unbroken block of buildings. Instead, in the middle of Gotham, an 843-acre retreat provides an escape valve and tranquilizer for millions of New Yorkers.

While you're here, take advantage of the park's many charms—not the least of which is its layout. Frederick Law Olmsted and Calvert Vaux won a competition with a plan that marries flowing paths with sinewy bridges, integrating them into the natural landscape with its rocky outcroppings, man-made lakes, and wooded pockets. The park's construction, between 1859 and 1870, provided employment during a depression and drew the city's population into the upper reaches of the island, which at that time were still quite rural. Nevertheless, designers predicted the hustle and bustle to come, and hid traffic from the eyes and ears of park-goers by building roads that are largely hidden from the bucolic view.

On just about any day, Central Park is crowded with New Yorkers and visitors alike. On nice days, especially weekend days, it's the city's party central. Families come to play in the snow or the sun, depending on the season; in-line skaters come to fly through the crisp air and twirl in front of the band shell; couples come to stroll or paddle the lake; dog owners come to hike and throw Frisbees to Bowser; and just about everybody comes to sunbathe at the first sign of summer. On beautiful days, the crowds are part of the appeal—folks come here to peel off their urban armor and relax, and the common goal puts a general feeling of camaraderie in the air. On these days, the people-watching is more compelling than anywhere else in the city. But even on the most crowded days, there's always somewhere to get away from it all, if you just want a little peace and quiet, and a moment to commune with nature.

ORIENTATION & GETTING THERE   Look at your map—that great green swath in the center of Manhattan is Central Park. It runs from 59th Street (also known as Central Park South) at the south end to 110th Street at the north end, and from Fifth Avenue on the east side to Central Park West (the equivalent of Eighth Ave.) on the west side. A 6-mile rolling road, **Central Park Drive,** circles the park, and has a lane set aside for bikers, joggers, and in-line skaters. A number of **transverse (crosstown) roads** cross the park at major points—at 65th, 79th, 86th, and 97th streets—but they're built down a level, largely out of view, to minimize intrusion on the bucolic nature of the park.

A number of subway stops and lines serve the park. To reach the southernmost entrance on the west side, take an A, B, C, D, 1, or 9 to 59th Street/Columbus Circle. To reach the southeast corner, take the N, R to Fifth Avenue; from this stop, it's an easy walk to the Information Center in the **Dairy** (© 212/794-6564; open daily 11am–5pm, to 4pm in winter), mid-park at about 65th Street. Here you can ask questions, pick up information, and purchase a good park map.

If your time for exploring is limited, I suggest entering the park at 72nd or 79th streets (subway: B, C to 72nd St. or 81st St./Museum of Natural History). From here, you can pick up information at the visitor center at **Belvedere Castle** (© 212/772-0210; open Tues–Sun 10am–5pm, to 4pm in winter), midpark at 79th Street. There's also a visitor center at the **Charles A. Dana Discovery Center** (© 212/860-1370; open daily 11am–5pm, to 4pm in winter), at the northeast corner of the park at Harlem Meer, at 110th Street between Fifth and

---

Moments **Central Park in the Snow**

There are not many sights as lovely as Central Park after a fresh snow. It's as if the city noise completely disappeared, creating an absolutely special, magical feeling. If you are lucky enough to be in New York during a snowfall, head up to Central Park and experience the magic.

Central Park

Lenox avenues (subway: 2, 3 to 110th St.). The Dana Center is an environmental center hosting workshops, exhibits, music programs, and park tours, and lends fishing poles for fishing in Harlem Meer (park policy is catch-and-release).

Food carts and vendors are at all of the park's main gathering points, so finding a bite is never a problem. You'll also find food counters at the **Conservatory,** on the east side of the park, north of the 72nd Street entrance; and at **The Boat House,** on the lake near 72nd Street and Park Drive North, which also offers a full-service menu (✆ **212/517-2233**).

GUIDED WALKS   The **Central Park Conservancy** offers a slate of free walking tours; call ✆ **212/360-2726** or check **www.centralparknyc.org** for the current schedule (click on the "Walking Tours" button on the left). The Dana Center hosts ranger-guided tours on occasion (call ✆ **800/201-PARK** or 212/ 860-1370 for the schedule).

FOR FURTHER INFORMATION   Call the main number at ✆ **212/360-3444** for recorded information, or 212/310-6600 or 212/628-1036 to speak to a live person. Call ✆ **888/NY-PARKS** for events information. The park also has two websites: The city parks department's site at **www.centralpark.org**, and the Central Park Conservancy's site at **www.centralparknyc.org**, each of which features maps and a rundown of attractions and activities. For a park **emergency,** dial ✆ **800/201-PARK,** which will link you to the park rangers.

SAFETY TIP   Even though the park has the lowest crime rate of any of the city's precincts, keep your wits about you, especially in the more remote northern end. It's a good idea to avoid the park entirely after dark, unless you're heading to one of the restaurants for dinner or to a SummerStage or Shakespeare in the Park event (see chapter 9), when you should stick with the crowds.

EXPLORING THE PARK

The best way to see Central Park is to wander along the park's 58 miles of winding pedestrian paths, keeping in mind the following highlights.

Before starting your stroll, stop by the **Information Center** in the Dairy (✆ **212/794-6464;** open daily 11am–5pm, to 4pm in winter), midpark in a 19th-century–style building overlooking Wollman Rink at about 65th Street, to get a good park map and other information on sights and events.

The southern part of Central Park is more formally designed and heavily visited than the relatively rugged and remote northern end. Not far from the Dairy is the **carousel,** with 58 hand-carved horses (✆ **212/879-0244;** open daily 10:30am–6pm, to 5pm in winter; rides are 90¢); the zoo (see the listing for "Central Park Zoo"); and the Wollman Rink for roller- or ice-skating (see "Activities," below).

The **Mall,** a long, formal walkway lined with elms shading benches and sculptures of sometimes-forgotten writers, leads to the focal point of Central Park, **Bethesda Fountain** ⋆ (along the 72nd St. transverse road). **Bethesda Terrace** and its sculpted entryway border a large **lake** where dogs fetch sticks, boaters glide by, and anglers try their luck at catching carp, perch, catfish, and bass. You can rent a rowboat at or take a gondola ride from **Loeb Boathouse,** on the eastern end of the lake (see "Activities," below). Boats of another kind are at **Conservatory Water** (on the east side at 73rd St.), a stone-walled pond flanked by statues of both **Hans Christian Andersen** and **Alice in Wonderland.** On Saturday at 10am, die-hard yachtsmen race remote-controlled sailboats in fierce competitions following Olympic regulations. (Sorry, model boats aren't for rent.)

Tips **Softball for the Stars**

Every spring and summer, Central Park is home to many softball leagues. One of the oldest and most celebrated is the Broadway Show League, which plays at Hecksher Fields, around 63rd Street on the west side of the park. The league features representatives from all the major Broadway productions; in 2002, *The Producers* beat out the team from *42nd Street* to capture their second consecutive league championship. The co-ed games, which are open for all to watch, can get pretty intense, and you might be surprised who you see out there shagging flies; Al Pacino, Matthew Broderick, and Robert Redford have all played in the league. I once witnessed Edie Falco slide headfirst into second base. And yes, she was safe.

Sheep Meadow on the southwestern side of the park is a designated quiet zone, where Frisbee throwing and kite flying are as energetic as things get. Another respite is **Strawberry Fields** ⭐, at 72nd Street on the west side. This memorial to John Lennon, who was murdered across the street at The Dakota apartment building, is a gorgeous garden centered around an Italian mosaic bearing the title of this Beatle's most famous solo song, and his lifelong message: IMAGINE. In keeping with its goal of promoting world peace, the garden has 161 varieties of plants, donated by each of the 161 nations in existence when it was designed in 1985. This is a wonderful place for peaceful contemplation.

Bow Bridge, a graceful lacework of cast iron designed by Calvert Vaux, crosses over the lake and leads to the most bucolic area of Central Park, the **Ramble.** This dense 38-acre woodland with spiraling paths, rocky outcroppings, and a stream is the best spot for bird watching and feeling as if you've discovered an unimaginably leafy forest right in the middle of the city.

North of the Ramble, **Belvedere Castle** ⭐ is home to the **Henry Luce Nature Observatory** (✆ 212/772-0210), worth a visit if you're with children. From the castle, set on Vista Rock (the park's highest point at 135 ft.), you can look down on the **Great Lawn,** where softball players and sun worshipers compete for coveted greenery, and the **Delacorte Theater,** home to Shakespeare in the Park (p. 306). The small **Shakespeare Garden** south of the theater is scruffy, but it does have plants, herbs, and trees mentioned by the playwright. Behind Belvedere Castle is the **Swedish Cottage Marionette Theatre** ⭐ (✆ 212/988-9093), hosting marionette plays for children.

Continue north along the east side of the Great Lawn, parallel to East Drive. Near the glass-enclosed back of the **Metropolitan Museum of Art** ⭐⭐⭐ (p. 206) is **Cleopatra's Needle,** a 69-foot obelisk originally erected in Heliopolis around 1475 B.C. It was given to the city by the khedive of Egypt in 1880. (The khedive bestowed a similar obelisk, which now sits on the Embankment of the Thames, to the city of London.)

North of the 86th Street Transverse Road is the **Jacqueline Kennedy Onassis Reservoir,** so named after the death of the First Lady, who lived nearby and often enjoyed a run along the 1½-mile jogging track around the reservoir.

North of the reservoir is my favorite part of the park. It's much less traversed, and in some areas, absolutely tranquil. The **North Meadow** (at 96th St.) features 12 baseball and softball fields; it's here that the Harlem Little League, which made it to the Little League World Series in 2002, plays many of their games, so you might just spot the next Jeter out there. Sadly, the North Meadow is circled by a not very attractive fence, and 6 months of the year that fence is locked and the Meadow closed. An unfortunate recent trend in Central Park has been the proliferation of fences. They have become so prevalent that at times you get the feeling you are not really in a park, but a museum.

North of the North Meadow, at the northeast end of the park, is the **Conservatory Garden** ✿ (at 105th St. and Fifth Ave.), Central Park's only formal garden, with a magnificent display of flowers and trees reflected in calm pools of water. (The gates to the garden once fronted the Fifth Ave. mansion of Cornelius Vanderbilt II.) **The Lasker Rink and Pool** (☎ **212/534-7639**) is the only swimming pool in Central Park; and in the winter it converts to a skating rink, offering a less hectic alternative to Wollman Rink (see "Activities" below). **Harlem Meer** and its boathouse were recently renovated and look beautiful. The boathouse now berths the **Charles A. Dana Discovery Center,** near 110th Street between Fifth and Lenox avenues (☎ **212/860-1370**), where children learn about the environment and borrow fishing poles for catch-and-release at no charge. **The Pool** (at W. 100th St.), possibly the most idyllic spot in all of Central Park, was recently renovated and features willows, grassy banks, and a small pond populated by some very well-fed ducks. You might even spot an egret and a hawk or two lurking around here.

GOING TO THE ZOO

Central Park Zoo ✿ *Kids* It has been a decade since the zoo in Central Park was renovated, making it both more human and more humane. Sea lions frolic in the central pool area. The gigantic, graceful polar bears (one of whom, by the way, made himself a true New Yorker when he began regular visits with a shrink) glide back and forth across a watery pool that has glass walls, through which you can observe very large paws doing very smooth strokes. The monkeys seem to regard those on the other side of the fence with knowing disdain. In the hot and humid Tropic Zone, large, colorful birds swoop around in freedom, sometimes landing next to nonplused visitors.

The indoor Tropic Zone is a real highlight; its steamy rainforest is home to everything from black-and-white Colobus monkeys to emerald tree boa constrictors to a leaf-cutter ant farm; look for the dart poison frog exhibit, which is very cool. So is the large penguin enclosure in the Polar Circle, which is better than the one at San Diego's Sea World. In the Temperate Territory, look for the Asian red pandas (cousins to the black-and-white ones), which look like beautiful raccoons. Despite their pool and piles of ice, the polar bears still look sad.

The entire zoo is good for short attention spans; you can cover the whole thing in 1½ to 3 hours, depending on the size of the crowds and how long you like to linger. It's also very kid-friendly, with lots of well-written and -illustrated placards that older kids can understand. For the littlest ones, there's the $6 million **Tisch Children's Zoo.** With sheep, llamas, potbellied pigs, and more, this petting zoo and playground is a real blast for the 5-and-under set.

830 Fifth Ave. (at 64th St., just inside Central Park). ☎ 212/861-6030. www.wcs.org/zoos. Admission $6 adults, $1.25 seniors, $1.50 children 3–12, free for children under 3. Apr–Oct Mon–Fri 10am–5pm; Sat–Sun 10am–5:30pm. Nov–Mar daily 10am–4:30pm. Subway: N, R to Fifth Ave.

ACTIVITIES

The 6-mile rolling road circling the park, **Central Park Drive,** has a lane for bikers, joggers, and in-line skaters. The best time to use it is when the park is closed to traffic: Monday through Friday from 10am to 3pm (except Thanksgiving to New Year's) and 7 to 10pm. It's also closed from 7pm Friday to 6am Monday, but when the weather is nice, the crowds can be hellish.

BIKING Off-road mountain biking isn't permitted; stay on Central Park Drive or your bike may be confiscated by park police.

You can rent 3- and 10-speed bikes as well as tandems in Central Park at the **Loeb Boathouse,** midpark near 72nd Street and Park Drive North, just in from Fifth Avenue (𝄐 **212/517-2233** or 212/517-3623), for $9 to $20 an hour, with a complete selection of kids' bikes, cruisers, tandems, and the like ($200 deposit required); at **Metro Bicycles,** 1311 Lexington Ave., at 88th Street (𝄐 **212/ 427-4450**), for about $7 an hour, or $35 a day; and at **Toga Bike Shop,** 110 West End Ave., at 64th Street (𝄐 **212/799-9625;** www.togabikes.com), for $30 a day. No matter where you rent, be prepared to leave a credit-card deposit.

BOATING March through November, gondola rides and rowboat rentals are available at the **Loeb Boathouse,** midpark near 74th Street and Park Drive North, just in from Fifth Avenue (𝄐 **212/517-2233** or 212/517-3623). Rowboats are $10 for the first hour, $2.50 every 15 minutes thereafter, and a $30 deposit is required; reservations are accepted.

HORSE-DRAWN CARRIAGE RIDES At the entrance to the park at 59th Street and Central Park South, you'll see a line of **horse-drawn carriages** waiting to take passengers through the park or along certain of the city's streets. Horses belong on city streets as much as chamber pots belong in our homes. You won't need me to tell you how forlorn most of these horses look—skip it.

ICE-SKATING **Wollman Rink** ⊛, on the east side of the park between 62nd and 63rd streets (𝄐 **212/439-6900;** www.wollmanskatingrink.com), is the city's best outdoor skating spot, more spacious than the rink at Rockefeller Center. It's open for skating from mid-October to mid-April, depending on the weather. Rates are $8.50 for adults, $4.25 for seniors and kids under 12, and skate rental is $4.75; lockers are available (locks are $6.75). **Lasker Rink** (𝄐 **212/534-7639)** on the east side around 106th Street, is a less-expensive alternative to the much-more-crowded Wollman Rink. It's open November through March. Rates are $4.50 for adults, $2.25 for kids under 12; skate rental is $4.75.

IN-LINE SKATING Central Park is the city's most popular place for blading. See the beginning of this section for details on Central Park Drive, the main drag for skaters. On weekends, head to West Drive at 67th Street, behind Tavern on the Green, where you'll find trick skaters weaving through an NYRSA slalom course at full speed, or the Mall in front of the band shell (above Bethesda Fountain) for twirling to tunes. In summer, **Wollman Rink** converts to a hotshot roller rink, with half-pipes and lessons available (see "Ice-Skating," above).

You can rent skates for $20 a day from **Blades Board and Skate,** 120 W. 72nd St., between Broadway and Columbus Avenue (𝄐 **212/787-3911;** www. blades.com). Wollman Rink (see above) also rents in-line skates for park use at similar rates.

PLAYGROUNDS Nineteen Adventure Playgrounds are scattered throughout the park, perfect for jumping, sliding, swinging, and digging. At Central Park

West and 81st Street is the **Diana Ross Playground** ⚡, voted the city's best by *New York* magazine. Also on the west side is the **Spector Playground,** at 85th Street and Central Park West, and, farther north, the **Wild West Playground** at 93rd Street. On the east side is the **Rustic Playground,** at 67th Street and Fifth Avenue, a delightfully landscaped space rife with islands, bridges, and slides; and the **Pat Hoffman Friedman Playground,** behind the Metropolitan Museum of Art at East 79th Street, is geared toward older toddlers.

RUNNING   Marathoners and wannabes run in Central Park along the 6-mile **Central Park Drive,** which circles the park (run toward traffic to avoid being mowed down by wayward cyclists and in-line skaters). For a shorter loop, try the midpark 1.5-mile track around the **Jacqueline Kennedy Onassis Reservoir** (keep your eyes ready for spotting Madonna and other famous bodies). It's safest to jog only during daylight hours and where everybody else does. Avoid the small walks in the Ramble and at the north end of the park.

SWIMMING   **Lasker Pool,** around 106th Street on the east side (✆ **212/534-7639**), is the only pool in Central Park. It is open from July 1 to Labor Day weekend. Rates are $4 for adults, $2 for kids under 12. Bring a towel.

OTHER PARKS

For parks in Brooklyn and Queens, see "Highlights of the Outer Boroughs" (p. 255). For more information on these and other city parks, go online to **nyc parks.completeinet.net.**

Tips Running the City

Here, as suggested by the **New York Road Runner's Club,** are the five best running routes in Manhattan.

Central Park Reservoir: Bill Clinton jogged this 1½-mile flat dirt track during the 1992 Democratic convention. It's possibly the most famous running route in the world. Wonder if we'll see Dubya running around it when the Republicans come to town in 2004?

The **Loop** in Central Park: I used to run past Madonna and her male bodyguards when she was a frequenter of the 6-mile loop. Now I see Howard Stern jogging, no bodyguards in sight, but usually with a female companion or two.

East River: Entering on 63rd St. and York Avenue and running up to 125th Street and back is a 6-mile jog where you will pass Gracie Mansion, high-rises overlooking the river, and fishermen testing the river waters.

Hudson River South: Entering at Chelsea Piers at West 23rd Street and continuing down to Battery Park City is approximately a 5-mile run. In the warm months it's a carnival downtown, with in-line skaters, kayakers, musicians, and cyclists crowding the slim downtown park.

Hudson River North: Entering at Riverbank State Park at 145th Street on the Hudson River and running down lovely Riverside Park, passing the 79th Street Boat Basin, and ending at the Intrepid Sea-Air-Space Museum is approximately a 6-mile run.

Battery Park ⭐⭐ As you traverse Manhattan's concrete canyons, it's easy to forget you're on an island. But at Manhattan's southernmost tip, you get the real sense that just past Liberty, Ellis, and Staten islands is the Atlantic Ocean.

The 21-acre park is named for the cannons built to defend residents after the American Revolution. **Castle Clinton National Monument** (the place to purchase tickets for the Statue of Liberty and Ellis Island ferry) was built as a fort before the War of 1812, though it was never used as such. The 22-ton **bronze sphere** by Fritz Koenig that was recovered from the rubble of the World Trade Center, where it stood between the Twin Towers as a symbol of global peace, now stands—severely damaged but still whole—in the park as a temporary memorial to the victims of the World Trade Center terrorist attack. This may be the finest place in the city to pay tribute to those who were lost.

You'll likely recognize Battery Park for the role it played in *Desperately Seeking Susan*. Besides the T-shirt vendors and hot-dog carts, you'll find several statues and memorials throughout the park. This is quite the civilized park, with lots of STAY OFF THE GRASS! signs and Wall Streeters eating sandwiches on the park benches. Pull up your own bench for a good view across the harbor.

From State St. to New York Harbor. Subway: N, R to Whitehall St.; 1, 9 to South Ferry; 4, 5 to Bowling Green.

Bowling Green Park This patch of green at the end of Broadway is most notable for its early history. This is most likely the spot where, in 1626, Peter Minuit gave beads and other trinkets worth about 60 guilders ($24) to a group of Indians, and then claimed he had bought Manhattan. The local Indians didn't think they owned this island because Manhattan was considered communal hunting ground, so it isn't clear what the Indians thought the trinkets meant. Either (a) they thought the exchange was a way of closing an agreement to extend the shared hunting use to this funny-looking group of pale people with yellow beards; or (b) they were selling land that they didn't own in the first place, thus performing the first shrewd real-estate deal of the Financial District.

When George III repealed the Stamp Act in 1770, New Yorkers raised a statue of him here, although today it's just another lunch spot for stockbrokers. The statue lasted 5 years, until the day the Declaration of Independence was read to the public in front of City Hall (now Federal Hall) and a crowd rushed down Broadway to topple the statue, chop it up, melt it down, and transform it into 42,000 bullets, which they later used to shoot the British.

With the demise of the World Trade Center, the lower Manhattan **TKTS booth,** officially named the **Downtown Theatre Centre,** has relocated to Bowling Green Park Plaza. This is the place to pick up same-day discounted tickets for a Broadway or Off-Broadway show; the line is usually shorter here than it is at the Times Square location. For details, see p. 297.

On the fringe of the park is the stunning 1907 beaux-arts **U.S. Customs House,** currently housing the National Museum of the American Indian (p. 227).

From State St. to New York Harbor. Subway: 4, 5 to Bowling Green; N, R to Whitehall St.

Bryant Park ⭐ Another success story in urban redevelopment, Bryant Park is the latest incarnation of a 4-acre site that was, at various times, a graveyard and a reservoir. Named for poet and *New York Evening Post* editor William

Cullen Bryant (look for his statue on the east end), the park rests atop the New York Public Library's underground stacks. Another notable statue is a squat and evocative stone portrait of Gertrude Stein.

This simple green swath is welcome relief from Midtown's concrete, taxi-choked jungle, and good weather attracts brown-baggers from neighboring office buildings. Just behind the library is **Bryant Park Grill** (© 212/840-6500; www.bryantpark.org/amenities/dining.php), a gorgeous, airy bistro with spectacular views but merely decent food. The grill's two summer alfresco restaurants— **The Terrace,** on the Grill's roof, and the **Cafe** are extremely pleasant on a nice day.

In the summer of 2002, **Le Carrousel** opened; it's a working merry-go-round created to complement the park's French classical style. It's not as big as the Central Park Carrousel, but it's utterly charming, with 14 different animals that revolve to the sounds of French cabaret music. Le Carrousel is open year-round, weather permitting, from 11am to 7pm, and costs $1.50 to ride.

Additionally, the park plays host to New York's **Seventh on Sixth** fashion shows, set up in billowy white tents (open to the trade only) in the spring and fall.

In the summer, HBO sponsors the **Bryant Park Summer Film Festival,** in which a classic film—*Dr. Zhivago, Viva Las Vegas,* and the like—is shown on a 20-by-50-foot screen under the stars every Monday evening at sunset. Admission is free; just bring a blanket and a picnic. Rain dates are Tuesdays. For the current schedule, call © 212/512-5700 or visit www.hbobryantpark film.com.

Behind the New York Public Library, at Sixth Ave. between 40th and 42nd sts. www.bryantpark.org. Subway: B, D, F, V to 42nd St.; 7 to Fifth Ave.

Union Square Park   Reclaimed from drug dealers and abject ruin in the late '80s, Union Square Park is now one of the city's best assets. This patch of green is the focal point of the fashionable Flatiron and Gramercy Park neighborhoods. Don't miss the grand equestrian statue of George Washington at the south end, or the bronze statue (by Bartholdi, the sculptor of the Statue of Liberty) of the marquis de Lafayette at the eastern end, gracefully glancing toward France.

This charming square is the site of New York's premier **Greenmarket.** Every Monday, Wednesday, Friday, and Saturday, vendors hawk fresh veggies and fruits, organic baked goods, cider, wine, and even fresh fish and lobsters in booths that flank the north and west sides of the square. Fresh-cut flowers and plants are also for sale, as are books and postcards. During summer and fall, you can graze the bazaar and assemble a cheap and healthy lunch to munch under the trees or at the picnic tables at the park's north end. Musical acts play the small pavilion at the north end of the park, and in-line skaters take over the market space in the after-work hours. A **cafe** is open at the north end of the park in warm weather.

From 14th to 17th sts., between Park Ave. S. and Broadway. Subway: 4, 5, 6, L, N, R, Q, W to 14th St./ Union Sq.

Washington Square Park   You'll be hard-pressed to find much "park" in this mostly concrete square—a burial ground in the late 18th century—but it's undeniably the focal point of Greenwich Village. Chess players, skateboarders, street musicians, New York University students, couples, the occasional film crew, and not a few homeless people compete for attention throughout the day and most of the night. (If anyone issues a challenge to play you in the ancient and complex Chinese game of Go, don't take them up on it—you'll lose money.)

The lively scene belies a macabre past. Once marshland traversed by Minetta Brook, it became in 1797 a potter's field, and the remains of some 10,000 bodies are buried here. In the early 1800s, the square, or the infamous Hanging Elm in the northwest corner where MacDougal Street meets the park, was used for public executions. It wasn't until the 1830s that the Greek Revival town houses on **Washington Square North** known as "The Row" (note especially nos. 21–26) attracted the elite. Stanford White designed Washington Arch (1891–92) to commemorate the centenary of George Washington's inauguration as president. While in the neighborhood, peek down MacDougal Alley and Washington Mews, both lined with delightful old carriage houses.

At the southern end of Fifth Ave. (where it intersects Waverly Place between MacDougal and Wooster sts.). Subway: A, C, E, F, V to West 4th St./Washington Sq.

8 Affordable Sightseeing Tours

Reservations are required on some of the tours listed below, but even if they're not, it's always best to call ahead to confirm prices, times, and meeting places.

HARBOR CRUISES

Circle Line Sightseeing Cruises ★★   Circle Line is the only tour company that circumnavigates the entire 35 miles around Manhattan, and I love this ride. The **Full Island** cruise takes 3 hours and passes by the Statue of Liberty, Ellis Island, the Brooklyn Bridge, the United Nations, Yankee Stadium, the George Washington Bridge, and more, including Manhattan's wild northern tip. The panorama is riveting, and the commentary isn't bad. The big boats are basic but fine, with lots of deck room for everybody to enjoy the view. Snacks, soft drinks, coffee, and beer are available onboard for purchase.

If 3 hours is more than you or the kids can handle, go for either the 1½-hour **Semi-Circle** or **Sunset/Harbor Lights** cruise, both of which show you the highlights of the skyline. There's also a 1-hour **Seaport Liberty** version that sticks close to the south end of the island. But of all the tours, the kids might like **The Beast** best, a thrill-a-minute speedboat ride offered in summer only.

In addition, a number of adults-only **Live Music and DJ Cruises** sail regularly from the seaport from May through September ($20–$40 per person). Depending on the night of the week, you can groove to the sounds of jazz, Latin, gospel, dance tunes, or blues as you sail along the skyline.

Departing from Pier 83, at W. 42nd St. and Twelfth Ave. Also departing from Pier 16 at South St. Seaport, 207 Front St. ℂ 212/563-3200. www.circleline.com, www.ridethebeast.com, and www.seaportmusiccruises.com. Sightseeing cruises $17–$25 adults, $16–$20 seniors, $10–$12 children 12 and under. Subway to Pier 83: A, C, E to 42nd St. Subway to Pier 16: J, M, Z, 2, 3, 4, 5 to Fulton St.

SPECIALTY TOURS
MUSEUMS & CULTURAL ORGANIZATIONS

In addition to the choices below, those interested in touring the Financial District with a guide should also consider the **World of Finance Walking Tour** offered Fridays at 10am by the Museum of American Financial History; see p. 223.

Value   Absolutely Free Walking Tours

A number of neighborhood organizations and Business Improvement Districts (BIDs) offer free guided walks of their neighborhoods. For travelers on a budget, these introductory freebies are well worth taking advantage of:

The **Municipal Art Society** (✆ **212/935-3960**; www.mas.org) offers a free walking tour of Grand Central Terminal on Wednesday at 12:30pm, which meets at the information booth on the Grand Concourse. The **Grand Central Partnership** (✆ **212/697-1245**) runs its own free tour every Friday at 12:30pm, meeting outside the station in front of the Whitney Museum at Philip Morris gallery, at 42nd Street and Park Avenue. It's a real joy now that Grand Central has been restored. Call to confirm the schedule and meeting spot before you set out to meet either tour.

The Alliance for Downtown New York, the Business Improvement District in charge of Lower Manhattan, offers a free 90-minute **Wall Street Walking Tour** ✦ every Thursday and Saturday at noon, rain or shine. This guided tour explores the history and architecture of the nation's first capital and the world center of finance. Stops include the New York Stock Exchange, Trinity Church, Federal Hall National Monument, and other sites of historic and cultural importance. Tours meet on the steps of the U.S. Customs House (p. 245), at 1 Bowling Green (subway: 4, 5 to Bowling Green). Reservations are not required (unless you're a group), but you can call ✆ **212/606-4064** or visit **www.downtownny.com** to confirm the schedule.

The **Orchard Street Bargain District Tour** (✆ **866/224-0206** or 212/226-9010; www.lowereastsideny.com) explores the history and retail culture of this neighborhood. This is a good bet for bargain-hunters, who will learn about the old-world shops and newer outlet stores in this discount-shopping destination. The free tours are given Sunday at 11am from April to December, rain or shine, and no reservation is required. Meet up with the guide in front of Katz's Delicatessen, 205 E. Houston St., at Ludlow Street.

If you're looking to tour a specific neighborhood with an expert guide, call **Big Apple Greeter** (✆ **212/669-8159**; www.bigapplegreeter. org). This nonprofit organization consists of specially trained New Yorkers who volunteer to take visitors around town for a free 2- to 4-hour tour of a particular neighborhood. Reservations must be made in advance, preferably at least 1 week ahead of your arrival. Big Apple Greeter is also well suited to accommodate travelers with disabilities; see "Specialized Travel Resources" in chapter 2 for details.

The **Municipal Art Society** ✦ (✆ 212/439-1049 or 212/935-3960; www.mas.org) offers excellent historical and architectural walking tours aimed at intelligent, individualistic travelers. A highly qualified guide who gives insights into the significance of buildings, neighborhoods, and history leads each tour. Topics range from the urban history of Greenwich Village to "Mies and the Moderns," examining the architectural legacy of Mies van der Rohe, to an examination of the "new" Times Square. Weekday walking tours cost $12; weekend tours cost $15. Reservations may be required depending on the tour, so call ahead. A full schedule is available online or by calling © **212/439-1049.**

The **92nd Street Y** ★ (© **212/415-5500** or 212/415-5628; www.92ndsty.org) offers a variety of walking and bus tours, many featuring funky themes or behind-the-scenes visits. Subjects can range from "Diplomat for a Day at the U.N." to "Secrets of the Chelsea Hotel," from "Artists of the Meat-Packing District" to "Jewish Harlem." Prices range from $20 to $60 (sometimes more for bus tours), but many include ferry rides, afternoon tea, dinner, or whatever suits the program. Guides are experts on their subjects, ranging from historians to an East Village poet, mystic, and art critic (for "Allen Ginsberg's New York" and "East Village Night Spots"), and many routes travel into the outer boroughs; some day trips even reach beyond the city. Advance registration is required for all walking and bus tours. Schedules are planned a few months in advance, so check the website for tours that might interest you.

INDEPENDENT OPERATORS

One of the most highly praised sightseeing organizations in New York is **Big Onion Walking Tours** ★ (© **212/439-1090;** www.bigonion.com). Enthusiastic Big Onion guides (all hold degrees in American history) peel back the layers of history to reveal the city's secrets. The 2-hour tours are offered mostly on weekends, and subjects include the "The Bowery," "Presidential New York," "Irish New York," "Central Park," "Greenwich Village in Twilight," "Historic Harlem," "Jewish Ellis Island," "Brooklyn Bridge & Brooklyn Heights at Twilight," and historic takes on Lower Manhattan. One of the most popular is the "Multiethnic Eating Tour" of the Lower East Side, where you munch on everything from dim sum and dill pickles to fresh mozzarella. Tour prices range from $12 to $18 for adults, $10 to $16 for students and seniors. No reservations are necessary, but Big Onion *recommends that you call to verify schedules.*

All tours from **Joyce Gold History Tours of New York** ★ (© **212/242-5762;** www.nyctours.com) are offered by Joyce Gold herself, an instructor of Manhattan history at New York University and the New School, who has been conducting walks around New York since 1975. Her tours can cut to the core of this town; Joyce is full of fascinating stories about Manhattan and its people. Tours are arranged around themes like "The Colonial Settlers of Wall Street," "The Genius and Elegance of Gramercy Park," "Downtown Graveyards," "The Old Jewish Lower East Side," "Historic Harlem," and "TriBeCa: The Creative Explosion." Tours are offered most weekends March through December and last from 2 to 4 hours, and the price is $12 per person; no reservations are required. Private tours can be arranged year-round, either for individuals or groups.

Behind the scenes is the focus of **Adventure on a Shoestring** ★★ (© **212/265-2663**), which offers 90-minute public walking tours on weekends (and some weekdays and holidays) year-round for just $5. One of the earliest entrants in the now-burgeoning walking-tour market, Howard Goldberg has provided unique views of New York since 1963, exploring Manhattan's neighborhoods with a breezy, man-of-the-people style. Tours run the gamut from historical and architectural walks of artsy SoHo, elegant Sutton Place, or little-known

Roosevelt Island to themed walks like "A Salute to Jacqueline Kennedy Onassis" and "Greenwich Village Ghosts Galore." Most tours focus on Manhattan, but Mr. Goldberg occasionally leads tours to Astoria, Queens, home to the largest Greek population outside of Greece; the fascinating Russian quarter of Little Odessa, Brooklyn; and other ethic enclaves. This is one of the best budget bargains in New York. Walks go on regardless of the weather. Call for reservations.

Alfred Pommer has conducted **New York City Cultural Walking Tours** (© 212/979-2388; www.nycwalk.com) in nearly every Manhattan neighborhood for over 15 years. He focuses on history and architecture, making the past come alive via photographs and stories. A number of his tours focus on specific subjects, such as "Gargoyles in Manhattan." His 2½-hour tours take place most Sundays at 2pm. The charge is $10 per person, and no reservation is needed; just show up at the assigned spot. Mr. Pommer also offers weekday walking tours that cost $20 per person and require reservations; call © 212/334-2211, ext. 101, or go to www.imar.com/nycwalk. Private tours are available at $35 per hour for individuals or groups.

Self-proclaimed "radical historian" Bruce Kayton leads unconventional **Radical Walking Tours** (© 718/492-0069; www.he.net/~radtours) to conventional tourist sights. A tour of Harlem covers the Black Panthers, the Communist Party, and Malcolm X, in addition to the Apollo Theatre and the Schomburg Center; and a visit to the Lower East Side focuses on radical Jews such as Abraham Cahan (founder of the *Jewish Daily Forward* in 1897) and the Rosenbergs. Two Greenwich Village tours are offered, of course. His newest is the "Non-Jerry Seinfeld Upper West Side Tour." Most tours cost $10 and last 2½ to 4½ hours; no reservations are required.

Would you like to cruise by Monica and Chandler's apartment building? How about the courthouse where the prosecutors of *Law & Order* fight the good fight? **On Location Tours** (© 212/239-1124 or 212/935-0168; www.sceneontv.com) offers narrated minibus tours on their **Manhattan TV Tour;** tickets are $20 for adults, $10 for kids 6 to 9, free for 5 and under. Or, if you want to see Carrie Bradshaw's Big Apple, take the 2½-hour *Sex in the City* **Tour;** tickets cost $30. Most tours take place on Saturdays and depart from the Times Square Visitors Center, at noon and 2:30pm, respectively. There's a 3-hour *Sopranos* **Tour** that will take you to New Jersey for $35. Reservations are a must.

Recommended by the Harlem Travel and Tourism Association, **A La Carte New York Tours** (© 212/828-7360; www.alacartecity.com) also offers a slate of walking, bus, architecture, jazz, Apollo Theatre, and gospel tours of the Upper Manhattan neighborhood. Prices run from $15 to $75, depending on the options you choose. All guides are licensed and extremely knowledgeable.

New York Like a Native ⭑ (© 718/393-7537; www.nylikeanative.com) offers the city's best introduction to Brooklyn. The tours focus mainly on the best of brownstone Brooklyn, and you can choose from a 2½-hour version ($13), or an extended 4½-hour version ($35); the longer tour includes lunch, but you must cover your own bus and subway fares. Tours are generally offered on Saturdays April through December, and meet at the Brooklyn Library on Grand Army Plaza (subway: 2, 3 to Grand Army Plaza). *Prepaid reservations are required;* visit the website or call © 212/239-1124 to order.

9 Talk of the Town: Free TV Tapings

The trick to getting tickets for TV tapings in this city is to be from out of town. Visitors have a much better chance than we New Yorkers; producers are gun-shy about filling their audiences with obnoxious locals and see everybody who's not from New York as being from the heartland—their target TV audience.

If your heart's set on getting tickets to a show, request them as early as possible—6 months ahead isn't too early. You're usually asked to send a postcard. Always include the number of tickets you want, your preferred dates of attendance (be as flexible as you can), and your address *and* phone number. Tickets are always free. The shows tend to be pretty good about trying to meet your specific date requests, but don't be surprised if Ricki or Montel are far more responsive than, say, Dave Letterman. And even if you send in your request early, don't be surprised if tickets arrive as late as 1 or 2 weeks before tape date.

If you come to town without any tickets, all hope is not lost. Because they know that not every ticket holder will make it, many studios give out standby tickets on the day of taping. If you can get up early and don't mind standing in line for a couple (or a few) hours, you may get one. Now, the bad news: Only one standby ticket per person is allowed, so everybody who wants to get in has to get up at the crack of dawn and stand in line. And even if you get your hands on a standby ticket, it doesn't guarantee admission; they usually start seating standbys only after the regular ticket holders are in. Still, chances are good.

For additional information on getting tickets, call the NYCVB at © 212/484-1222. And remember—you don't need a ticket to be on the *Today* show.

If you attend a taping, bring a sweater! As anybody who watches Letterman knows, it's *cold* in those studios. And bring ID, as proof of age may be required.

Change of Heart   The syndicated dating show has relocated to the Big Apple, for better or worse. To score audience tickets, call © 877/485-7144, or fill out the online ticket request form at www.changeofheart.warnerbros.com.

Emeril Live   If you haven't seen enough of superstar chef Emeril Lagasse, you can try to catch a taping of his show. Scoring tickets is no easy recipe; they're only available through the Food Network through periodic ticket lotteries. The best way to get in is to sign up for the weekly newsletter at FoodTV.com (click on "Newsletter" on the left-hand scroll bar), which announces ticket lotteries.

The Daily Show with Jon Stewart   Comedy Central's irreverent, often hilarious mock newscast tapes every Monday through Thursday at 5:45pm, at 513 W. 54th St. Make your advance ticket requests by phone at © 212/586-2477, or check with them for any cancellation tickets for the upcoming week; the line is open Monday through Thursday from 10:30am to 4pm for tickets.

Good Morning America   Fans of ABC's weekday-morning show can join Diane Sawyer and Charlie Gibson in their street-facing studio at Broadway and 44th Street as part of the live audience. To witness the 7 to 9am broadcast, fill out the online request at www.abcnews.go.com/sections/GMA (click on "GMA Tickets"), or call © 212/580-5176 during business hours.

Last Call with Carson Daly   Tapings of the MTV heartthrob's NBC late-night gabfest are much like a grown-up TRL, without the countdown or screaming sweet 16s. Tapings are on select weeknights at 7 and/or 9pm. You can reserve up to four tickets by calling © 212/664-3056. Standby tickets are distributed on the day of taping at 9am outside 30 Rockefeller Plaza, on the 49th Street side of the building, on a first-come, first-served basis (**read:** Come early if you actually want to get one). Note that a standby ticket does not guarantee admission.

Late Night with Conan O'Brien Conan tix might not have quite the cachet of a Dave ticket, but they're a very hot commodity—so start planning now. Tapings are Tuesday through Friday at 5:30pm (arrive by 4:45pm), and you must be 16 or older to attend. You can reserve up to four tickets by calling ☎ **212/664-3056.** Standby tickets are distributed on the day of taping at 9am outside 30 Rockefeller Plaza, on the 49th Street side of the building (under the NBC Studios awning), on a first-come, first-served basis.

The Late Show with David Letterman Here's the most in-demand TV ticket in town. Tapings are Monday through Thursday at 5:30pm (arrive by 4:15pm), with a second taping Thursday at 8pm (arrive by 6:45pm). You must be 18 or older to attend. Send your postcard 6 to 9 months in advance (two tickets max; one request only, or all will be disregarded), to *Late Show* Tickets, Ed Sullivan Theater, 1697 Broadway, New York, NY 10019. You can also register at www.cbs.com/latenight/lateshow (click on "Get Tickets") to be notified of tickets that may become available for specific dates you select over the next 3 months. On tape days, there are no standby lines anymore; call ☎ **212/247-6497** at 11am for up to two standby tickets; start dialing early, because the machine will kick in as soon as all standbys are gone. If you do get through, you may have to answer a trivia question about the show to score tickets.

Live! with Regis and Kelly Tapings with Regis Philbin and Kelly Ripa are Monday through Friday at 9am at the ABC Studios at 7 Lincoln Sq. (Columbus Ave. and W. 67th St.) on the Upper West Side. You must be 10 or older to attend (under 18s must be accompanied by a parent). Send your postcard (four tickets max) at least a *full year* in advance to *Live!* Tickets, Ansonia Station, P.O. Box 230777, New York, NY 10023-0777 (☎ **212/456-3054**). Standby tickets are sometimes available. Arrive at the studio no later than 7am and request a standby number; standby tickets are handed out on a first-come, first-served basis.

The Ricki Lake Show Tickets can be requested by calling ☎ **800/GO-RICKI,** or filling out the online form at www.ricki.com. You can also use this line, or register on the website, to volunteer yourself as a guest for shows such as "I'm a 30-Year-Old Virgin—Will You Be My First?" or "Stop Being Naked Around My Man!" You must be 18 or older to attend.

Saturday Night Live SNL tapings are Saturday at 11:30pm from fall to late spring (arrival time 10pm); there's also a dress rehearsal at 8pm (arrival time 7pm). You must be 16 or older to attend. Tickets are so in demand that the lottery system for advance tickets is usually suspended. However, you can try for standby tickets on the day of the taping, which are distributed at 7am outside 30 Rockefeller Plaza, on the 49th Street side of the building, on a first-come, first-served basis; only one ticket per person will be issued. If you want to try your luck with advanced tickets, call ☎ **212/664-3056** *as far in advance of your arrival in New York as possible* to determine the current ticket-request procedure.

The Today Show Anybody can be on TV with Katie, Matt, and weatherman Al Roker. All you have to do is show up outside *Today*'s glass-walled studio at Rockefeller Center, on the southwest corner of 49th Street and Rockefeller Plaza, with your very own HI, MOM! sign. Tapings are Monday through Friday from 7 to 10am, but come at the crack of dawn if your heart's set on being in front. Who knows? If it's a nice day, you may even get to chat with Katie, Matt, or Al in a segment. Come extra early to attend a Friday Summer Concert Series show.

Total Request Live   The countdown show that made Carson Daly a household name is broadcast live from MTV's second-floor glass-walled studio at 1515 Broadway, at 44th Street in Times Square, weekdays at 3:30pm. Crowds start gathering below at all hours, depending on the drawing power of the day's guest. Audience tickets can sometimes be reserved by calling the **TRL Ticket Reservation Hot Line** at ℂ **212/398-8549;** you must be between the ages of 16 and 24 to attend. If you're not able to score reservations, arrive by 2pm (preferably earlier) if you want a prayer of making it into the in-studio audience; a producer usually roams the crowd asking music-trivia questions and giving away standby tickets for correct answers. And don't forget to make your WE LOVE YOU, CARSON! signs large enough to be captured on camera. You may also be able to watch or participate in other tapings; stop into the MTV Store on the corner of 44th and Broadway, where flyers for tapings and events are sometimes stacked next to the register.

The View   ABC's popular girl-power gabfest tapes live Monday through Friday at 11am (ticket holders must arrive by 9:30am). Requests, which should be made 12 to 16 weeks in advance, can be submitted online (www.abc.go.com/theview) or via postcard to Tickets, *The View,* 320 W. 66th St., New York, NY 10023. Because exact date requests are not usually accommodated, try standby: Arrive at the studio before 10am and put your name on the standby list; earlier is better, because tickets are handed out on a first-come, first-served basis. You must be 18 or older to attend.

10 Especially for Kids

Some of New York's sights and attractions are designed specifically with kids in mind. But many of those I've discussed in the rest of this chapter are terrific for kids as well as adults; I've also included cross-references to the best of them.

Probably the best place to entertain the kids is in **Central Park** ✦✦✦, which has kid-friendly diversions galore (p. 237). For general tips and additional resources, see "For Families" under "Specialized Travel Resources," in chapter 2.

MUSEUMS

In addition to the museums specifically for kids, also consider the following: The **American Museum of Natural History** ✦✦✦ (p. 202), whose dinosaur displays are guaranteed to wow both you and the kids; the *Intrepid* **Sea-Air-Space Museum** (p. 221), on a battleship with an amazing collection of vintage and high-tech airplanes; the **Forbes Magazine Galleries** (p. 217), whose collection includes a number of vintage toys and games; the **New York City Police Museum** (p. 228); the **New York City Fire Museum** ✦ (p. 228), housed in a real firehouse; the **American Museum of the Moving Image** ✦ (p. 261), where you and the kids can learn how movies are made; the **Lower East Side Tenement Museum** ✦ (p. 222), whose weekend living-history program really intrigues school-age kids; the **New York Transit Museum** (p. 259), where kids can explore vintage subway cars and other hands-on exhibits; and the **South Street Seaport & Museum** (p. 230), which little ones will love for its theme park–like atmosphere and old boats bobbing in the harbor.

Children's Museum of Manhattan ✦   Designed for ages 2 to 12, this museum is strictly hands-on. Interactive exhibits and activity centers encourage self-discovery—and a recent expansion means there's now even more to keep the kids learning. The Time Warner Media Center takes children through the world of animation and helps them produce their own videos. The Body Odyssey is a many, scientific journey through the body. This isn't just a museum for the 5-and-up set—there are exhibits designed for babies and toddlers, too. The busy schedule also includes daily art classes and storytellers, and a full slate of entertainment on weekends. Look for *Art Inside Out,* an interactive exhibit dedicated to introducing families to art and museums and featuring a video-making installation from photographer and Weimaraner-lover William Wegman, among others, to run from October 2002 through the end of 2003.

212 W. 83rd St. (between Broadway and Amsterdam Ave.). © 212/721-1234. www.cmom.org. Admission $6 adults and children, $3 seniors. Wed–Sun and school holidays 10am–5pm. Subway: 1, 9 to 86th St.

Children's Museum of the Arts   Interactive workshop programs for children ages 1 to 12 and their families are the attraction here. Kids dabble in puppet making and computer drawing or join in singalongs and live performances. Also look for rotating exhibitions of the museum's permanent collection, featuring WPA work; and the Piccolo Spoleto Festival through July 2003. Call or check the website for the current exhibition and activities schedule.

182 Lafayette St. (between Broome and Grand sts.). © 212/941-9198 or 212/274-0986. www.cmany.org. Admission $6 for visitors 1–65; pay what you wish Thurs 4–6pm. Wed and Fri–Sun noon–5pm; Thurs noon–6pm. Subway: 6 to Spring St.

New York Hall of Science ★   Children will love this huge, hands-on museum, which bills itself as "New York's Only Science Playground." This place is amazing for school-age kids. Exhibits let them be engulfed by a giant soap bubble, float on air in an antigravity mirror, compose music by dancing in front of light beams, and explore the world of microbes. There are even video machines that kids can use to retrieve astronomical images, including pictures taken by the *Galileo* in orbit around Jupiter. There's a Preschool Discovery Place for the really little ones. But best of all is the summertime **Outdoor Science Playground** ★ for kids 6 and older—ostensibly lessons in physics, but really just a great excuse to laugh, jump, and play on jungle gyms, slides, seesaws, spinners, and more.

The museum is located in **Flushing Meadows–Corona Park,** where kids can enjoy even more fun beyond the Hall of Science. Not only are there more than 1,200 acres of park and playgrounds, there's a zoo, a carousel, an indoor ice-skating rink, an outdoor pool, and bike and boat rentals. Kids and grown-ups will love getting an up-close look at the Unisphere steel globe, which was not really destroyed in *Men in Black.* The park is also home to the **Queens Museum of Art** (p. 262) as well as Shea Stadium and the U.S. Open Tennis Center.

4701 111th St., in Flushing Meadows–Corona Park, Queens. © 718/699-0005. www.nyhallsci.org. Admission $7.50 adults, $5 seniors and children 4–17; free to all Thurs–Fri 2–5pm. Extra $2 for Science Playground. Mon–Wed 9:30am–2pm (Tues–Wed to 5pm in summer); Thurs–Sun 9:30am–5pm. Subway: 7 to 111th St.

Sony Wonder Technology Lab   Kids and adults love this four-level high-tech science-and-technology center, which explores communications and technology. You can experiment with robotics, explore the body through medical imaging, edit a video, mix a song, design a video game, and save the day at an environmental command center. The lab also features the first high-definition interactive theater in the United States. Admission is free; this place is popular, however, so make reservations in advance. Reservations can be made up to 2 weeks in advance by calling © 212/833-5414 on Monday, Wednesday, or Friday between 11am and 4pm. Otherwise, you may not get in, or you may get tickets that require you to return at a different time.

Sony Plaza, 550 Madison Ave. (at 56th St.). © 212/833-8100, or 212/833-5414 for reservations. www.sonywondertechlab.com. Free admission. Tues–Wed, and Fri–Sun 10am–6pm; Thurs 10am–8pm; last entrance 30 min. before closing. Subway: E, V or N, R to Fifth Ave.; 4, 5, 6 to 59th St.

OTHER KID-FRIENDLY DIVERSIONS

In addition to the choices below, don't forget New York's theme restaurants, which are playgrounds unto themselves for kids; see "Family-Friendly Restaurants" in chapter 6. For kid-friendly theater, see "Kids Take the Stage: Family-Friendly Theater " in chapter 9.

ZOOS & AQUARIUMS Bigger kids will love the **Bronx Zoo** ✯✯✯ (see below), while the **Central Park Zoo** ✯ with its Tisch Children's Zoo (p. 242) is suitable for younger kids. At the **New York Aquarium** at Coney Island (p. 259), kids can touch starfish and sea urchins and watch bottlenose dolphins and California sea lions stunt-swim in the outdoor aqua theater. Brooklyn's **Prospect Park** ✯✯ (p. 260) also boasts a wonderful little zoo.

SKY-HIGH VIEW Kids of all ages can't help but turn dizzy with delight at incredible views from atop the **Empire State Building** ✯✯✯ (p. 205).

ARCADES **Lazer Park,** in Times Square at 1560 Broadway (entrance at 163 W. 46th St.; © **212/398-3060;** www.lazerpark.com), has amusements ranging from old-fashioned pinball to virtual-reality games and a laser-tag arena. Even better is the brand-new **Broadway City** ✯, 241 W. 42nd St., between Seventh and Eighth avenues (© **212/997-9797;** www.broadwaycity.com), a neon-bright, multilevel interactive game center designed on a Big Apple theme where you could lose your kids (and a year's supply of quarters) for an entire day.

SPECIAL EVENTS Children's eyes grow wide at the march of **parades** (especially Macy's Thanksgiving Day Parade), **circuses** (Big Apple, Ringling Bros. and Barnum & Bailey), and **holiday shows** (the Rockettes' Christmas and Easter performances). See "Calendar of Events," in chapter 2, for details.

11 Highlights of the Outer Boroughs

THE BRONX

In addition to the choices below, literary buffs might also want to visit the **Edgar Allan Poe Cottage,** the final home for the author of *The Raven, The Tell-Tale Heart,* and other masterworks. See "In Search of Historic Homes" (p. 233).

Bronx Zoo Wildlife Conservation Park ✯✯✯ *Kids* Founded in 1899, the Bronx Zoo is the largest metropolitan animal park in the United States, with more than 4,000 animals on 265 acres. This is an extremely progressive zoo as zoos go—most of the cages have been replaced by more natural settings, ongoing improvements keep it feeling fresh and up-to-date, and it's far more bucolic than you might expect. I think it's one of the city's best attractions.

One of the most impressive exhibits is the **Wild Asia Complex.** This zoo-within-a-zoo comprises the **Wild Asia Plaza** education center; **Jungle World,** an indoor re-creation of Asian forests with birds, lizards, gibbons, and leopards; and the **Bengali Express Monorail** (open May–Oct), which takes you on a narrated ride high above free-roaming Siberian tigers, Asian elephants, Indian rhinoceroses, and other nonnative New Yorkers (keep your eyes peeled—the animals aren't as interested in seeing you). The **Himalayan Highlands** is home to some 17 extremely rare snow leopards, as well as red pandas and white-naped cranes. The 6½-acre **Congo Gorilla Forest** is home to Western lowland gorillas, okapi, red river hogs, and other African rainforest animals.

The **Children's Zoo** (open Apr–Oct) allows young humans to learn about their wildlife counterparts. Kids can compare their leaps to those of a bullfrog, slide into a turtle shell, climb into a heron's nest, see with the eyes of an owl, and hear with the acute ears of a fox. There's also a petting zoo. Camel rides are another part of the summertime picture, as is the **Butterfly Zone** and the **Skyfari** aerial tram (each an extra $2 charge).

If the natural settings and breeding programs aren't enough to keep zoo residents entertained, they can choose to ogle the two million annual visitors. But there are ways to beat the crowds. Try to visit on a weekday or on a nice winter's day. In summer, come early, before the heat of the day sends the animals back into their enclosures. Expect to spend an entire day here—you'll need it.

Getting There: Liberty Lines' BxM11 express bus, which makes stops on Madison Avenue, will take you to the zoo; call ℂ **718/652-8400.** By subway, take the 2 train to Pelham Parkway and walk west to the Bronxdale entrance.

Fordham Rd. and Bronx River Pkwy., the Bronx. ℂ **718/367-1010.** www.wcs.org/zoos. Admission $9 adults, $6 seniors and children 2–12, discounted admission Nov–Mar; free Wed year-round. There may be nominal additional charges for some exhibits. Nov–Mar daily 10am–4:30pm (extended hours for Holiday Lights late Nov to early Jan); Apr–Oct Mon–Fri 10am–5pm, Sat–Sun 10am–5:30pm.

New York Botanical Garden ⭐ A National Historic Landmark, the 250-acre New York Botanical Garden was founded in 1891 and today is one of America's foremost public gardens. The setting is spectacular—a natural terrain of rock outcroppings, a river with cascading waterfall, hills, ponds, and wetlands.

Highlights of the Botanical Garden are the 27 **specialty gardens** (the Peggy Rockefeller formal rose garden, the Nancy Bryan Luce herb garden, and the rock garden are my favorites), an **orchid collection,** and 40 acres of **uncut forest** as close as New York gets to its virgin state. The **Enid A. Haupt Conservatory,** a stunning series of Victorian glass pavilions that recall London's Crystal Palace, shelters a collection of tropical, subtropical, and desert plants as well as seasonal flower shows. There's also a **Children's Adventure Garden.** Natural exhibits are augmented by year-round educational programs, musical events, bird-watching excursions, lectures, special family programs, and many more activities. Snuff Mill, once used to grind tobacco, has a charming cafe on the banks of the Bronx River. There are so many ways to see the garden—tram, golf cart, walking tours—that it's best to call or check the website for more information.

Getting There: Take Metro North (ℂ **800/METRO-INFO** or 212/532-4900; www.mta.nyc.ny.us/mnr) from Grand Central Terminal to the New York Botanical Garden station; it's a 20-minute ride. By subway, take the D or 4 train to Bedford Park, then bus Bx26 or walk southeast on Bedford Park Boulevard for 8 blocks. The garden operates a shuttle to and from Manhattan April through October on Fridays and weekends, Saturdays only in November and December. Round-trip shuttle and garden tickets are $15 for adults, $12 for seniors and students, $9 for children 2 to 12; call ℂ **718/817-8779** for reservations.

200th St. and Southern Blvd., the Bronx. ℂ **718/817-8700.** www.nybg.org. Admission $3 adults, $2 seniors and students, $1 children 2–12. Extra charges for Everett Children's Adventure Garden, Enid A. Haupt Conservatory, T.H. Everett Rock Garden, Native Plant Garden, and narrated tram tour; entire Garden Passport package is $10 adults, $7.50 seniors and students, $4 children 2–12. Apr–Oct Tues–Sun and Mon holidays 10am–6pm; Nov–Mar Tues–Sun and Mon holidays 10am–4pm.

Wave Hill ⭐ *Finds* Formerly a private estate with panoramic views of the Hudson River and the Palisades, Wave Hill has, at various times, been home to a British U.N. ambassador as well as Mark Twain and Theodore Roosevelt. Set in a bucolic neighborhood that doesn't look anything like you'd expect from the Bronx, its 28 gorgeous acres were bequeathed to the city of New York for use as a public garden that is now one of the most beautiful spots in the city. It's a

Finds Arthur Avenue

Not far from the Bronx Zoo and Botanical Gardens is **Arthur Avenue** ⭐, the Little Italy of the Bronx. Unlike the Little Italy of downtown Manhattan, this one is the real deal. It's also the perfect complement to a day spent at the Zoo or the Botanical Gardens. From Fordham Road, walk south and you will begin to smell the aroma of freshly baked bread, cured sausages, tomato sauce, and sidewalk clam bars. By the time you hit 187th Street, your mouth will be watering and you won't know which market, restaurant, or pizzeria to try first. Some of the neighborhood standouts include **Mario's Restaurant** (© 718/584-1188), where the Neapolitan pizza is magnificent and the ziti with broccoli unforgettable; **Mike's Deli** (© 718/295-5033), in the Arthur Avenue Retail market, makes almost perfect mozzarella and sandwiches like "Big Mike's Combo," a fresh-baked hero with mortadella, salami, capiccola, and provolone; and **Egidio's Pastry** (© 718/295-6077), for espresso, cappuccino, and cannoli. Try to visit mid-week rather than on a weekend when it is less crowded. *Directions:* Take the 4 or D train to Fordham Road, and from there the 12 bus east; or take 2 or 5 train to Pelham Parkway, and the 12 bus west; alternately, you can take the Metro North Harlem Line to Fordham Road, then the shuttle bus to Belmont and Bronx Zoo.

---

wonderful place to commune with nature along wooded paths and in herb and flower gardens, where horticulturists have labeled all of the plants. Benches are positioned for quiet contemplation and spectacular views. It's a great spot for taking in the Hudson River vibe without having to travel to Westchester to visit the Rockefeller estate. Programs range from horticulture and environmental education to landscape history and forestry to dance performances and concerts. A new Visitor and Horticultural Center designed by Robert A.M. Stern is currently under construction, and should make this hidden jewel shine even brighter.

Getting There: Take the 1 or 9 subway to 231st Street, then take the Bx7 or Bx10 bus to the 252nd Street stop; or take the A subway to 207th Street and pick up the Bx7 to 252nd Street. From the 252nd Street stop, walk west across the parkway bridge and turn left; at 249th Street, turn right. Metro North trains (© 212/532-4900) travel from Grand Central to the Riverdale station; from there, it's a pleasant 5-block uphill walk to Wave Hill.

675 W. 252nd St. (at Independence Ave.), the Bronx. © 718/549-3200. www.wavehill.org. Admission $4 adults, $2 seniors and students; free in winter and Sat mornings and Tues in summer. Tues–Sun 9am–4:30pm; extended hours in summer (call ahead).

BROOKLYN

For details on walking the **Brooklyn Bridge** ⭐⭐, see p. 204.

It's easy to link visits to the Brooklyn Botanic Garden, the Brooklyn Museum of Art, and Prospect Park, because they're an easy walk from one another, just off **Grand Army Plaza.** Designed by Frederick Law Olmsted and Calvert Vaux as a suitably grand entrance to their Prospect Park, it boasts a grand Civil War memorial arch designed by John H. Duncan (1892–1901) and the main **Brooklyn Public Library,** an Art Deco masterpiece completed in 1941 (the garden and museum are just on the other side of the library, down Eastern Pkwy.). The entire area is a half-hour subway ride from midtown Manhattan.

Brooklyn Botanic Garden ⭐ Down the street from the Brooklyn Museum of Art (see below) is the most popular botanic garden in the city. This 52-acre sanctuary is at its most spectacular in May, when the deep-pink blossoms of cherry trees are abloom. Well worth seeing is the **Cranford Rose Garden,** one of the largest and finest in the country; the **Shakespeare Garden,** an English garden featuring plants mentioned in his writings; a **Children's Garden;** the **Osborne Garden,** a 3-acre formal garden; the **Fragrance Garden,** designed for the blind but appreciated by all noses; and the extraordinary **Japanese Hill-and-Pond Garden.** The renowned **C.V. Starr Bonsai Museum** is home to the world's oldest and largest collection of bonsai, while the impressive $2.5 million Steinhardt Conservatory holds the garden's extensive indoor-plant collection.

1000 Washington Ave. (at Eastern Pkwy.), Brooklyn. ℂ **718/623-7200.** www.bbg.org. Admission $3 adults, $1.50 seniors and students, free for children under 16; free to all Tues and Sat 10am–noon year-round and Wed–Fri mid-Nov to mid-Mar. Apr–Sept Tues–Fri 8am–6pm, Sat–Sun 10am–6pm; Oct–Mar Tues–Fri 8am–4:30pm, Sat–Sun 10am–4:30pm. Subway: Q to Prospect Park; 2, 3 to Eastern Pkwy./Brooklyn Museum.

Brooklyn Museum of Art ⭐⭐ One of the nation's premier art institutions, the Brooklyn Museum of Art rocketed back into the public consciousness in 1999 with the controversial "Sensation: Young British Artists from the Saatchi Collection," which drew international media attention and record crowds who came to see just what an artist—and a few conservative politicians—could make out of a little elephant dung.

Indeed, the museum is best known for its consistently remarkable exhibitions—which ranged from "The Last Expression: Art and Auschwitz" to "Pulp Art: From the Collection of Robert Lesser" in mid-2003 alone—as well as its excellent permanent collection. The museum's grand beaux-arts building, designed by McKim, Mead & White (1897), befits its outstanding holdings, most notably the Egyptian, Classical, and Ancient Middle Eastern collection of sculpture, wall reliefs, and mummies. The decorative-arts collection includes 28 American period rooms from 1675 to 1928 (the Moorish-style smoking room from John D. Rockefeller's 54th St. mansion is my favorite). Other highlights are the African and Asian arts galleries, dozens of works by Rodin, a good costumes and textiles collection, and a diverse collection of both American and European painting and sculpture that includes works by Homer, O'Keeffe, Monet, Cézanne, and Degas. Look for more terrific exhibits on the 2003–04 calendar.

200 Eastern Pkwy. (at Washington Ave.), Brooklyn. ℂ **718/638-5000.** www.brooklynmuseum.org. Suggested admission $6 adults, $3 seniors and students, free for children under 12; free 1st Sat of the month 11am–11pm. Wed–Fri 10am–5pm; 1st Sat of the month 11am–11pm, each Sat thereafter 11am–6pm; Sun 11am–6pm. Subway: 2, 3 to Eastern Pkwy./Brooklyn Museum.

⟮*Value* An Arts Party Grows in Brooklyn

First Saturday is the Brooklyn Museum of Art's popular program that takes place (you guessed it) the first Saturday of each month. It runs from 5 to 11pm and includes free admission and a slate of live music, films, dancing, talks, and other entertainment that can get esoteric—think karaoke, poetry, silent film, experimental jazz, and disco. On a recent Saturday, events included an Irish dance performance, a panel discussion on black photographers, a screening of *Hair,* and a dance party featuring a funk-and-soul DJ. As only-in-New-York events go, First Saturday is a good one—you can always count on a full slate of cool.

Brooklyn Tabernacle   Under the direction of passionate orator Pastor Jim Cymbala and his choral-director wife Carol, this nondenominational Christian revival church has grown into one of the largest—a congregation of nearly 10,000—and most renowned churches in the nation. Folks come from all over the world to see the 275-voice, four-time Grammy Award–winning **Brooklyn Tabernacle Choir,** one of the nation's most celebrated gospel choirs.

Brooklyn Tabernacle relocated to Smith Street, in the heart of downtown Brooklyn, in mid-2002. The gloriously renovated house of worship seats nearly 4,000 for each service. Still, come early for a prime seat, especially when the choir sings (at the noon and 4pm Sun services).

17 Smith St. (between Fulton and Livingston sts.), Brooklyn. ℂ 718/290-2000. www.brooklyntabernacle.org. Services Sun 9am, noon, and 4pm; Tues 7pm. Subway: 1, 2 to Hoyt St.; 4, 5 to Borough Hall; A, C, F to Jay St./Borough Hall; M, N, R to Lawrence St./Metro Tech.

New York Aquarium *(Kids)*   Because of the long subway ride (about an hour from midtown Manhattan) and its proximity to the Coney Island boardwalk, this one is really for summer. The aquarium is home to hundreds of sea creatures. Taking center stage are Atlantic bottlenose dolphins and California sea lions that perform daily during summer at the **Aquatheater.** Also in the spotlight are Pacific octopuses, sharks, and a brand-new sea horse exhibit. Black-footed penguins, sea otters, and a variety of seals live at the **Sea Cliffs exhibit,** a re-creation of a Pacific coastal habitat. My favorites are the beautiful beluga whales, which exude buckets of aquatic charm. Children love the hands-on exhibits at **Discovery Cove.** There's an indoor ocean-view cafeteria and an outdoor snack bar, plus picnic tables.

If you've made the trip out, check out the human exhibits on **Coney Island**'s 2¾-mile boardwalk. Not much is left from its heyday, and it can be a little eerie when the crowds aren't around. But you can still use the beach, drop some cash at an arcade, and ride the wooden **Cyclone** roller coaster (still a terrifying ride, if only because it seems so . . . rickety). Also treat yourself to a **Nathan's Famous** hot dog, just off the boardwalk at Surf and Stillwell avenues. This is the original—where the term "hot dog" was coined in 1906.

502 Surf Ave. (at W. 8th St.), Coney Island, Brooklyn. ℂ 718/265-3400. www.nyaquarium.com. Admission $11 adults, $7 seniors and children 2–12. Open daily 10am–4:30pm. Subway: D, F to W. 8th St., Brooklyn.

New York Transit Museum *(Kids)*   Under renovation at press time, this underground museum was scheduled to reopen in 2003. It's housed in a decommissioned subway station, and is a wonderful place to spend an hour or so. The museum is small but well done, with multimedia exhibits exploring the history of the subway from its groundbreaking (Mar 24, 1900) to the present. Kids and parents will enjoy the interactive elements and the vintage subway cars, wooden turnstiles, and station mosaics of yesteryear. New at reopening will be "On the Streets: New York's Trolleys and Buses." It's a minor but remarkable tribute to an important development in the city's history.

Remaining open throughout renovation is the **Gallery Annex & Store at Grand Central Station,** which houses rotating exhibitions and a transit-themed gift shop (see "Museum Stores," in chapter 8). A second museum store, and a travel-information kiosk, is at the **Times Square Visitors Center;** see chapter 4.

Boerum Place and Schermerhorn St., Brooklyn. ℂ 718/694-5100. www.mta.info/museum. Admission $3 adults, $1.50 seniors and children 3–17; free for seniors Tues noon–4pm. Mon–Fri 10am–4pm; Sat–Sun noon–5pm. Subway: A, C, F to Jay St.; N, R to Court St.; 2, 3, 4, 5 to Borough Hall. **Gallery Annex:** In Grand Central Terminal (on the main level, in the shuttle passage next to the Station Masters' office), 42nd St. and Lexington Ave. ℂ 212/878-0106. Subway: 4, 5, 6, 7, S to 42nd St./Grand Central.

Prospect Park ⭐⭐ Designed by Frederick Law Olmsted and Calvert Vaux after their success with Central Park, this 562 acres of woodland, meadows, bluffs, and ponds is considered their masterpiece by many.

The best approach is from Grand Army Plaza, presided over by the **Soldiers' and Sailors' Memorial Arch** (1892) honoring Union veterans. For the best view of the landscape, follow the path to Meadowport Arch and proceed through to the Long Meadow, following the path that loops around it (about an hour's walk). Other highlights include the 1857 Italianate mansion **Litchfield Villa** on Prospect Park West; the **Friends' Cemetery** Quaker burial ground (where Montgomery Clift is eternally prone—sorry, it's fenced off to browsers); the wonderful 1906 beaux-arts **boathouse;** the 1912 **carousel,** with white wooden horses salvaged from a Coney Island merry-go-round (open Apr–Oct; rides 50¢); and **Lefferts Homestead Children's Historic House Museum** (✆ 718/965-7777), a 1783 Dutch farmhouse with a museum of period furniture and exhibits geared to kids (open Apr–Nov Fri–Sun 1–4pm). There's a map at the park entrance that you can use to get your bearings.

On the east side of the park is the **Prospect Park Wildlife Zoo** (✆ 718/ 399-7339). This is a thoroughly modern children's zoo where kids can walk among wallabies, explore a prairie-dog town, and much more.

At Grand Army Plaza, bounded by Prospect Park W., Parkside Ave., and Flatbush Ave., Brooklyn. ✆ 718/965-8951, or 718/965-8999 for events information. www.prospectpark.org. Zoo admission $2.50 adults, $1.25 seniors, 50¢ children 3–12. Zoo Apr–Oct Mon–Fri 10am–5pm, Sat–Sun 10am–5:30pm; Nov–Mar daily 10am–4:30pm. Subway: 2, 3 to Grand Army Plaza (walk down Plaza St. W. 3 blocks to Prospect Park W. and the entrance) or Eastern Pkwy./Brooklyn Museum.

BROOKLYN HEIGHTS HISTORIC DISTRICT

Just across the Brooklyn Bridge is **Brooklyn Heights** ⭐, a peaceful neighborhood of tree-lined streets, more than 600 historic houses built before 1860, landmark churches, and restaurants. Even with its magnificent promenade providing sweeping views of Lower Manhattan's ragged skyline, it feels more like its own village than part of the larger urban expanse.

This is where Walt Whitman wrote *Leaves of Grass.* In the 19th century, abolitionist Henry Ward Beecher railed against slavery at **Plymouth Church of the Pilgrims** on Orange Street between Henry and Hicks streets. If you walk down **Willow Street** between Clark and Pierrepont, you'll see three houses (nos. 108–112) in the Queen Anne style that was fashionable in the late 19th century, as well as a trio of Federal-style houses (nos. 155–159) built before 1829. Also visit **Montague Street,** the main drag of Brooklyn Heights, full of cafes and shops. On Water Street, under the Brooklyn Bridge, is the **River Café** (✆ 718/522-5200; www.rivercafe.com), where a drink or dinner at twilight as the lights of Manhattan begin to flicker on will offer an unforgettable view. And don't forget about **Grimaldi's Pizzeria,** near the water on historic Old Fulton Street, and the **Brooklyn Ice Cream Factory,** on Front Street (see chapter 6).

GETTING THERE Bounded by the East River, Fulton Street, Court Street, and Atlantic Avenue, the Brooklyn Heights Historic District is one of the most easily accessible sights beyond Manhattan. The neighborhood is reachable via several subway trains: the A, C, F to Jay Street; the 2, 3, 4, 5 to Clark Street or Borough Hall; and the N, R to Court Street. *Note:* Status of the N, R, and C lines was unknown at press time, but all other above-mentioned service is normal.

It's easy to link a walk around Brooklyn Heights and along its promenade with a walk over the **Brooklyn Bridge** ⭐⭐ (p. 204), a tour that makes for a lovely afternoon. Take a 2 or 3 train to **Clark Street** (the first stop in Brooklyn). Turn right out of the station and walk toward the water, where you'll see the start of the **Brooklyn Promenade.** Stroll along the promenade for the now-heart-breaking views of Lower Manhattan and the multimillion-dollar brownstones, or park yourself on a bench to contemplate.

The promenade ends at Columbia Heights and Orange Street. To head to the bridge from here, turn left and walk toward the Watchtower Building. Before heading downslope, turn right immediately after the playground onto Middagh Street. After 4 or 5 blocks, you'll reach a busy thoroughfare, Cadman Plaza West. Cross the street and follow the walkway through **Cadman Plaza Park;** veer left at the fork. At Cadman Plaza East, turn left (downslope) toward the underpass, where you'll find the stairwell up to the Brooklyn Bridge footpath on your left.

QUEENS

In summer 2002, the **Museum of Modern Art** ⭑ closed its midtown Manhattan campus for a 3-year renovation, opening an exhibit space in Long Island City called **MoMA QNS** ⭑ (p. 208). This 45,000-square-foot exhibition space is already a rousing success, showcasing many of the finest works in the museum's collection, offering popular touring exhibits, and making the quick and easy subway ride out to Queens more than worthwhile.

When you head to MoMA QNS, consider making a day of it. **Queens Artlink** (www.moma.org/qal) is a free weekend arts shuttle, running Saturday and Sunday from 11:30am to 5:30pm and linking all of the institutions below (except the Queens Museum of Art). You can also catch a weekend ride on the **Long Island City Art Loop,** a free shuttle bus between the Noguchi Museum, the Socrates Sculpture Park, and P.S. 1, Saturday and Sunday between noon and 6pm. Any participating institution can answer questions about the shuttles.

For details on the **New York Hall of Science** ⭑ and **Flushing Meadows–Corona Park** (home to the Queens Museum of Art), see p. 254.

American Museum of the Moving Image ⭑ _Kids_   Head here if you truly love movies. Unlike Manhattan's Museum of Television & Radio (p. 226), which is more of a library, this is a thought-provoking museum examining how moving images—film, video, and digital—are made, marketed, and shown. It's housed in part of the Kaufman Astoria Studios, which once were host to W.C. Fields and the Marx Brothers, and more recently have been used by Martin Scorsese (*The Age of Innocence*), Bill Cosby (his *Cosby* TV series), and *Sesame Street.*

The museum's core exhibit, **"Behind the Screen,"** is an engaging two-floor installation that takes you step-by-step through the process of making, marketing, and exhibiting moving images. There are more than 1,000 artifacts, from technological gadgetry to costumes, and interactive exhibits where you can try your hand at sound-effects editing or create animated shorts, among other simulations. Special-effects benchmarks, from the mechanical mouth of *Jaws* to the blending of past and present in *Forrest Gump,* are explored and explained. And in a nod to nostalgia, memorabilia that wasn't swept up by the Planet Hollywood chain is displayed, including a Hopalong Cassidy lunchbox, an E.T. doll, celebrity coloring books, and Dean Martin and Jerry Lewis puppets. Also on display are sets from *Seinfeld.* Even better are the daily hands-on demonstrations, where you can watch film editors, animators, and the like at work.

"Insiders' Hour" tours are offered every day at 2pm. The museum also hosts **free film and video screenings,** often accompanied by artist appearances, lectures, or discussions. Seminars often feature film and TV pros discussing their craft; past guests have included Spike Lee, Terry Gilliam, Chuck Jones, and Atom Egoyan, so it's worth seeing if someone's on while you're in town. There's a terrific gift shop chock-full of affordable movie- and TV-themed gifts, too.

35th Ave. at 36th St., Astoria, Queens. (℡) 718/784-0077 or 718/784-4777. www.ammi.org. Admission $8.50 adults, $5.50 seniors and college students, $4.50 children 5–18. Tues–Fri noon–5pm; Sat–Sun 11am–6pm (evening screenings Sat–Sun at 6:30pm). Subway: R to Steinway St.; N to Broadway.

Isamu Noguchi Garden Museum ★ *Finds*

No place in the city is more Zen than this marvelous indoor/outdoor garden museum showcasing the work of Japanese American sculptor Isamu Noguchi (1904–88). Unfortunately, the original building in Long Island City, built in 1927 and purchased by Noguchi in 1975, has been closed for renovation and is scheduled to open later in 2003, but at press time, no official announcement had been made. Until the renovations are complete, the museum has established temporary exhibition space in nearby Sunnyside, Queens. Before heading out, however, check the website or call to confirm where the museum will be located. In Sunnyside, space is limited to indoor exhibitions; it's still worth visiting to see a beautifully curated collection of the artist's masterworks in stone, metal, wood, and clay. You'll even see theater sets, furniture, and models for public gardens and playgrounds that Noguchi designed. A free guided tour is offered at 2pm. The museum shop will continue to sell Noguchi's Akari lamps as well as books, cards, posters, and the like.

Temporary site: 36–01 43rd Ave. (at 36th St.), Sunnyside, Queens. Subway: 7 to 33rd St. Walk north to 36th St., turn left, and go 1 block to 43rd Ave. Original location, returning 2003: 32–37 Vernon Blvd. (at 33rd Rd.), Long Island City, Queens. Subway: N to Broadway. Walk west on Broadway toward Manhattan until Broadway ends at Vernon Blvd.; turn left on Vernon and go 2 blocks. (℡) 718/204-7088. www.noguchi.org. Suggested admission $4 adults, $2 seniors and students. Wed–Fri 10am–5pm; Sat–Sun 11am–6pm. Subway: 7 to 33rd St. Walk north to 36th St., turn left, and go 1 block to 43rd Ave.

Museum for African Art *Finds*

This captivating museum is a leading organizer of temporary—and usually excellent—exhibits dedicated to historic and contemporary African art and culture. In September 2002, the museum moved out of SoHo into a long-term temporary home in Long Island City (the same building where the Isamu Noguchi Museum is temporarily housed), which it will occupy until its Museum Mile home is ready on Fifth Avenue between 109th and 110th streets. Weekend and evening programs include music and dance performances, art-making workshops, family events, and more.

36-01 43rd Ave. (at 36th St.), Long Island City, Queens. (℡) 212/784-7700. www.africanart.org. Admission $5 adults; $2.50 seniors, students, and children. Tues–Fri 10:30am–5:30pm (to 8:30pm 3rd Thurs of each month); Sat–Sun noon–6pm. Subway: 7 to 33rd St. Walk north to 36th St., turn left and go 1 block to 43rd Ave.

P.S. 1 Contemporary Art Center

If you're interested in contemporary art that's too cutting-edge for most museums, don't miss this MoMA affiliate museum. The Renaissance Revival building that houses the center was originally a public school (hence the name). This is the world's largest institution exhibiting contemporary art from America and abroad. You can expect to see a kaleidoscopic array of works from artists ranging from Jack Smith to Julian Schnabel; the museum is particularly well known for large-scale exhibitions by artists such as James Turrell.

22–25 Jackson Ave. (at 46th Ave.), Long Island City, Queens. (℡) 718/784-2084. www.ps1.org. Suggested admission $5 adults, $2 seniors and students. Wed–Sun noon–6pm. Subway: E, V to 23rd St./Ely Ave. (walk 2 blocks south on Jackson Ave. to 46th Ave.); 7 to 45th Rd./Court House Sq. (walk 1 block south on Jackson Ave.).

Queens Museum of Art

One way to see New York in the shortest time (albeit without the street life) is to visit the Panorama, created for the 1939 World's Fair, a building-for-building architectural model of New York City complete with an airplane that takes off from LaGuardia Airport. The 9,335-square-foot Gotham City is the largest model of its kind, with 895,000 structures built on a scale of 1 inch = 100 feet. A red-white-and-blue ribbon is draped over the Twin Towers, which still stand in this Big Apple.

Also on display is a collection of Tiffany glass made at Tiffany Studios in Queens between 1893 and 1938. The Contemporary Currents series features exhibits focusing on the works of a single artist, often with an international theme (suitable to New York's most diverse borough). History buffs should take note of the museum's NYC Building, which housed the United Nations' General Assembly from 1946 to 1952. Art exhibitions, tours, lectures, films, and performances are part of the program, making this a strong museum on all fronts.

Next to the Unisphere in Flushing Meadows–Corona Park, Queens. ✆ 718/592-9700. www.queensmuse.org. Suggested admission $5 adults, $2.50 seniors and students, free for children under 5. Tues–Fri 10am–5pm; Sat–Sun noon–5pm. Subway: 7 to Willets Point/Shea Stadium (follow the yellow signs for the 10-min. walk through the park to the museum, which sits next to the Unisphere).

Socrates Sculpture Park *Kids* This former riverside landfill is now the best exhibition space for large-scale outdoor sculpture in the city. No velvet ropes and motion sensors here—interaction with the artwork is encouraged. It's well worth a look, especially on a lovely day. Check the website for the current exhibition schedule—or just let yourself be happily surprised. There's a great view of Roosevelt Island and the Upper East side from this riverbank park.

Broadway at Vernon Blvd., Long Island City, Queens. ✆ 718/956-1819. www.socratessculpturepark.org Free admission. Daily 10am–sunset. Subway: N or W to Broadway; walk 8 blocks along Broadway toward the East River.

12 Spectator Sports

For details on the **New York City Marathon** and the **U.S. Open Tennis Championships,** see the "Calendar of Events" in chapter 2.

BASEBALL With two baseball teams in town, you can catch a game almost any day from opening day in April to the beginning of the playoffs in October. (Don't bother trying to get subway series tix, though—they're the hottest seats in town. Ditto for Opening Day or any playoff game.)

Star catcher Mike Piazza and the Amazin' **Mets** play at **Shea Stadium** in Queens (subway: 7 to Willets Point/Shea Stadium). For tickets (which ran $12–$45 for regular-season games in the 2003 season) and information, call the **Mets Ticket Office** at ✆ 718/507-TIXX, or visit **www.mets.com**. Also keep in mind that you can buy game tickets (as well as logo wear and souvenirs, if you want to dress appropriately for the big game) at the **Mets Clubhouse Shop,** which has two midtown Manhattan locations; see p. 287.

So the **Yankees** haven't won a World Series in 2 years—that only means they are overdue to win their 27th championship in 2003. The Yanks play at the House That Ruth Built, otherwise known as Yankee Stadium (subway: C, D, 4 to 161st St./Yankee Stadium). For tickets ($8–$80 in 2003), call **Ticketmaster** (✆ 212/307-1212 or 212/307-7171; www.ticketmaster.com) or **Yankee Stadium** (✆ 718/293-6000; www.yankees.com). Serious baseball fans might check the schedule well in advance and try to catch **Old Timers' Day,** usually held in July, when pinstriped stars of years past return to the stadium to take a bow.

At Yankee Stadium, upper-tier box seats (which run about $33), especially those behind home plate, give you a great view. Upper-tier reserve seats are behind the box seats and much cheaper ($17). Bleacher seats are even cheaper, and the rowdy commentary from that section's bleacher creatures is free. Most of the expensive seats (field boxes) are sold out in advance. You can often purchase these same seats from scalpers, but you'll pay a premium. Tickets can be purchased at the teams' **clubhouse shops** in Manhattan; see p. 287. If you're interested in taking a tour of the House that Ruth Built, call ✆ **718/579-4531** or check **www.yankees.com** for details (click on "Yankee Stadium").

Minor-league baseball ✮ made a Big Apple splash in summer 2001 when the **Brooklyn Cyclones,** the New York Mets' A-level farm team, and the **Staten Island Yankees,** the Yanks' junior leaguers, came to town. Boasting their very own waterfront stadium, the Brooklyn Cyclones have been a major factor in the revitalization of Coney Island; spanking-new Keyspan Park sits right off the legendary boardwalk (subway: F, N, Q, W to Stillwell Ave./Coney Island). The SI Yanks also have their own shiny new playing field, the Richmond County Bank Ballpark, just a 5-minute walk from the Staten Island Ferry terminal (subway: N, R to Whitehall St.; 4, 5 to Bowling Green; 1, 9 to South Ferry). What's more, with bargain-basement ticket prices (which topped out at $8 for the Cyclones, $10 for the Yanks in the 2003 season), this is a great way to experience baseball in the city for a fraction of the major-league hassle and cost. Both teams have already developed a rabidly loyal fan base, so it's a good idea to buy your tickets for the 2004 summer season—which will run June through September—in advance. For the Cyclones, call ✆ **718/449-8497** or visit **www.brooklyn cyclones.com**; to reach the SI Yanks, call ✆ **718/720-9200** or go online to **www.siyanks.com**.

BASKETBALL　Two pro teams call **Madison Square Garden,** Seventh Avenue between 31st and 33rd streets (✆ **212/465-6741** or www.thegarden.com; **212/ 307-7171** or www.ticketmaster.com for tickets; subway: A, C, E, 1, 2, 3, 9 to 34th St.), home: Allen Houston and the rest of the **New York Knicks** (✆ **877/NYK-DUNK** or 212/465-JUMP; www.nyknicks.com); and the **New York Liberty** (✆ **212/465-6080;** www.wnba.com/liberty) ✮, who electrify fans with their tough defense and All-Stars like Teresa Weatherspoon and Tari Phillips. Knicks tickets are hard to come by, so plan ahead if you want a front-row seat near first fan Spike Lee.

ICE HOCKEY　The **New York Rangers** play at Madison Square Garden, Seventh Avenue between 31st and 33rd streets (✆ **212/465-6741;** www.newyork rangers.com or www.thegarden.com; subway: A, C, E, 1, 2, 3, 9 to 34th St.). The Rangers have been going through tough times, but tickets are hard to get nevertheless, so plan well ahead; call ✆ **212/307-7171,** or visit www.ticketmaster.com for online orders.

8

Shopping for Big Apple Bargains

New York draws bargain hunters from around the globe with its wealth of values, range of merchandise, and unparalleled sales. As with anything, you just have to know where to look.

City **sales tax** is 8.625%, so if you're visiting from out of state, consider having your purchases shipped directly home to avoid paying sales tax.

1 The Top Shopping Streets & Neighborhoods

Here's a rundown of New York's most interesting shopping areas, with some highlights of each to give you a feel for the neighborhood. **If addresses and phone numbers are *not* given here,** refer to the store's expanded listing by category in "Shopping A to Z," later in this chapter.

DOWNTOWN
LOWER MANHATTAN & THE FINANCIAL DISTRICT
The Financial District's shopping scene was devastated by the demise of the World Trade Center, whose underground shopping mall had evolved into the city's best by 2001. **South Street Seaport** (© 212/732-8257; subway: 2, 3, 4, 5 to Fulton St.) carries the neighborhood's torch. Familiar names like Bath & Body Works and the Sunglass Hut line Fulton Street, the Seaport's main cobbled drag, and fill the levels at Pier 17, a barge-turned-shopping-mall. There's nothing here you can't get anywhere else; come for the historic ambience, the harbor views, and to spend a few dollars in Lower Manhattan, which needs all the support it can get. For a complete store list, visit **www.southstreetseaport.com**.

Lower Manhattan continues to shine in the discount department. New Yorkers were thrilled in March 2002 when the king of discount department stores, **Century 21,** reopened its doors (the store is across the street from the World Trade Center site). Electronics megamart **J&R** is still going strong, now occupying a full city block with its great prices on everything that you can turn on, plug in, or use to tune out, from cameras and computers to CDs and software.

CHINATOWN
Don't expect to find the purchase of a lifetime, but there's some quality browsing. The fish markets along Canal, Mott, Mulberry, and Elizabeth streets are fun for their bustle and exotica. Dispersed among them (especially along **Canal St.**), you'll find a mind-boggling collection of knock-off sunglasses and watches, backpacks, leather goods, and souvenirs. It's a fun browse, but don't expect quality, and be sure to bargain before you buy. **Mott Street,** between Pell Street and Chatham Square, boasts the most interesting off-Canal shopping, with an antiques shop or two among the storefronts selling blue-and-white Chinese dinnerware. The highlight is the **Pearl River** Chinese emporium (see "Gifts & Paper Goods" in "Shopping A to Z," later in this chapter).

THE LOWER EAST SIDE

The bargains aren't what they used to be in the **Historic Orchard Street Shopping District**—which runs from Houston to Canal along Allen, Orchard, and Ludlow streets, spreading outward along both sides of Delancey Street—but prices on leather bags, shoes, luggage, and fabrics are still good. Be aware, though, that the hard sell on Orchard Street can be hard to take. Still, the district is a nice place to discover a part of New York that's disappearing. Come during the week, because most stores are Jewish-owned and therefore close Friday afternoon and all day Saturday. Sunday tends to be a madhouse.

The artists and other trendsetters who have been turning this neighborhood into a bastion of hip have added a cutting edge to its shopping scene. You'll find a growing crop of alterna-shops south of Houston and north of Grand Street, between Allen and Clinton streets to the east and west, specializing in up-to-the-minute fashions and club clothes for cutting-edge 20-somethings, plus funky retro furnishings, Japanese toys, and offbeat items. Before you browse, stop into the **Lower East Side Visitor Center,** 261 Broome St., between Orchard and Allen streets (© **866/224-0206** or 212/226-9010; subway: F to Delancey St.), for a guide that includes vendors both Old World and new. Or you can see the list at www.lowereastsideny.com. *Money-saving tip:* Check the website or call the center for details about the **Go East card,** which will score cardholders discounts at neighborhood merchants.

SOHO

People love to complain about superfashionable SoHo—it's become too trendy, too tony, too Mall of America. True, **J. Crew,** 99 Prince St., between Mercer and Greene (© **212/966-2739**), is one of big names to have supplanted the artists and galleries that used to inhabit the cast-iron buildings. But SoHo is still one of the best shopping neighborhoods in the city, and fun to browse. You'll find few bargains, as merchants have to cover those high rents. This is the epicenter of cutting-edge couture, with designers like Anna Sui and British legend Vivienne Westwood in residence. Most of these designer shops are probably *way* out of your price range, but the streets are full of boutiques, some hawking more affordable wares, and the eye candy is tops. End-of-season sales, when racks are cleared for incoming merchandise, are the best bet if you want to buy.

SoHo's prime shopping grid is from Broadway east to Sullivan Street and from Houston down to Grand Street.

NOLITA

Just a few years ago, **Elizabeth Street** was a nondescript adjunct to Little Italy. Today it's the grooviest shopping strip in town, star of the neighborhood known as Nolita. Elizabeth and **Mott and Mulberry streets** are dotted with an increasing number of shops between Houston and Spring streets, with a few pushing south to Kenmare. But don't expect cheap; Nolita is the stepchild of SoHo. Its boutiques are the province of shopkeepers specializing in high-quality, fashion-forward products and design, but a few yield quirkier, more affordable gifts—and the browsing is excellent. It's an easy walk from the Broadway/Lafayette stop on the F, V line here, since it starts just east of Lafayette Street; you can also take the 6 to Spring Street, or the N, R to Prince Street and walk east. **Prince Street** is probably the best stretch for affordable treasures.

THE EAST VILLAGE

The East Village remains the standard of bohemian hip, and is one of the city's best neighborhoods for wallet-friendly shopping. The easiest subway access is the 6 train to Astor Place, which lets you out by **Kmart** and **Astor Wines & Spirits;** from here, it's just a couple blocks east to the prime hunting grounds.

East 9th Street ⭐ between Second Avenue and Avenue A is one of the most fun shopping strips in the city. Lined with an increasingly smart collection of boutiques, it proves that the East Village isn't just for kids anymore. So far, prices have stayed within reach. Up-and-coming designers sell excellent, affordably priced fashions for women here, including **Jill Anderson, a. cheng,** and others, and a small branch of **Eileen Fisher** caters to bargain hunters by serving as the chain's outlet store. This is also an excellent stretch for gifts and little luxuries; see "Gifts & Paper Goods" in "Shopping A to Z," later in this chapter. Most of these shops don't open until around 1pm, and most are closed Mondays. If you're enjoying this 'hood, check out the offerings on surrounding blocks; they aren't as mature, but it won't take long.

If it's strange, illegal, or funky, it's probably available on **St. Marks Place,** 8th Street, running east from Third Avenue to Avenue A. It's like a permanent street market, with countless T-shirt and jewelry stands.

LAFAYETTE STREET FROM SOHO TO NOHO

Lafayette Street has a retail character of its own, distinct from the rest of SoHo. It has grown into a full-fledged Antiques Row, strong in mid-20th-century furniture. The quality is high, but prices are higher. Lafayette is great to browse if you have an interest in design trends—stroll between Astor Place and Spring Street—but bargain hunters are better off elsewhere. Browsers should take the 6 train to Astor Place and work their way south, or get off at Spring Street and walk north. Dispersed among the stores are a number of cutting-edge clothiers; this is where skateboard fashion moved from the street to the catwalks.

GREENWICH VILLAGE

The West Village is great for browsing and gift shopping. Specialty book- and record stores, antiques and crafts shops, and gourmet food markets dominate. Except for NYU territory—**8th Street** between Broadway and Sixth Avenue for trendy footwear and affordable fashions and Broadway from 8th Street south to Houston, anchored by **Urban Outfitters** and dotted with skate and sneaker shops—the Village isn't much of a destination for fashion hunters.

The prime drag for strolling is **Bleecker Street,** where you'll find lots of leather shops and record stores interspersed with interesting, artsy boutiques. **Christopher Street,** just east of Seventh Avenue, is fun and loaded with Village character. Serious browsers should also wander west of **Seventh Avenue,** where boutiques are tucked among the brownstones, and along **Hudson Street.**

MIDTOWN
THE FLATIRON DISTRICT & UNION SQUARE

The epitome of uptown fashion a hundred years ago, **Sixth Avenue** from 14th to 23rd streets has grown into the city's discount shopping center. Superstores and off-pricers fill the cast-iron buildings: **Filene's Basement, TJ Maxx,** and **Bed Bath & Beyond** are all at 620 Sixth Ave., and **Old Navy** is next door; **Barnes & Noble** is at Sixth Avenue near 22nd Street.

HERALD SQUARE & THE GARMENT DISTRICT

Herald Square—where 34th Street, Sixth Avenue, and Broadway converge—is dominated by **Macy's,** the self-proclaimed world's biggest department store, and other famous-name shopping. At Sixth Avenue and 33rd Street is the **Manhattan**

Mall (© 212/465-0500; www.manhattanmallny.com), home to mall standards both national and local, which opened a new food court in May 2003.

A long block over on Seventh Avenue, not much goes on in the Garment District. This is, however, where you'll find that quintessential New York experience, the sample sale; see "Scouring the Sample Sales" on p. 278.

TIMES SQUARE & THE THEATER DISTRICT

This neighborhood has become increasingly family-oriented: with the rollicking **Virgin Megastore; Gap** at 42nd and Broadway; the **Toys"R"Us** flagship on Broadway and 44th Street, with its own Ferris wheel; and the **E-Walk** retail and entertainment complex on 42nd Street between Seventh and Eighth avenues, overflowing with mall-familiar shops.

West 47th Street between Fifth and Sixth avenues is the city's **Diamond District.** More than 90% of the diamonds sold the United States come through this neighborhood first, so there are some great deals if you're in the market for a nice rock or a piece of fine jewelry. The street is lined with showrooms; be ready to wheel and deal with the largely Hasidic dealers, who offer quite a juxtaposition to the crowds. For an introduction to the district, visit **www.47th-street.com**. If you're in the market for wedding rings, there's only one place to go: Herman Rotenberg's **1,873 Unusual Wedding Rings,** 4 W. 47th St., booth 86 (© 800/877-3874 or 212/944-1713; www.unusualweddingrings.com). For semiprecious stones, head to the **New York Jewelry Mart,** 26 W. 46th St. (© 212/575-9701). Virtually all dealers are open Monday through Friday only.

Shopper's alert: You'll notice a wealth of electronics stores throughout the neighborhood, many trumpeting GOING OUT OF BUSINESS sales. These guys have been going out of business since the Stone Age. That's the bait and switch; pretty soon you've spent too much money for not enough MP3 player. If you want to check out what they have to offer, go in knowing what the going price is on what you want. You can make a good deal if you know exactly what the market is, but these guys will be happy to suck you dry given half a chance.

FIFTH AVENUE & 57TH STREET

The heart of Manhattan retail is the corner of Fifth and 57th. Home to high-ticket names like Gucci, Chanel, Cartier, and Van Cleef & Arpels, this neighborhood has long been the province of the uber-rich. In recent years, however, both Fifth Avenue and 57th Street have become more accessible as wallet-friendlier retailers such as the **Niketown** and the **NBA Store** have joined the fold. You'll also find kid wonderland **FAO Schwarz** as well as a number of national names such as **Banana Republic** and **Liz Claiborne,** which have further democratized Fifth by setting up their flagships along the avenue.

High traffic flow and real estate costs keep prices up, and the flagships tend to send their sale merchandise to lower-profile shops. Still, the window-shopping is classic. And if you, like Holly Golightly, always dreamed of shopping at **Tiffany & Co.,** 727 Fifth Ave., at 57th Street (© 212/755-8000; www.tiffany.com), the world's most famous jewelry store is worth a stop. The multilevel showroom is so full of tourists that it's easy to browse. If you want to indulge, head upstairs to the gift level, where you'll find a number of items to suit a $75 budget. Everything comes packaged in the classic little blue box with an impeccable white ribbon.

UPTOWN
MADISON AVENUE

Welcome to Rich Man's Land. Madison Avenue from 57th to 79th streets has usurped Fifth Avenue as the toniest shopping stretch in the city. It's home to the most luxurious designer boutiques: Calvin, Prada, Versace, Valentino . . . the list goes on. Even the sales are ridiculous. ("This $1,200 sweater is on sale for $575? I'll take it!" Yeah, right!) Still, the window-shopping is unparalleled—even if you're not into fashion, the displays are entertainment in their own right. What's more, a stroll along the superchic avenue on a nice day often results in a star sighting. By all means, make a point of browsing even if you don't intend to buy.

For those of us with limited budgets, stores such as **Crate & Barrel** and the **Ann Taylor** flagship, 645 Madison Ave., at 60th Street (℗ **212/832-2010;** www.anntaylor.com), make Madison Avenue a little more approachable.

THE UPPER WEST SIDE

The Upper West Side's best shopping street is **Columbus Avenue.** Small shops catering to the neighborhood's mix of young hipsters and families line both sides of the pleasant avenue from 66th Street to about 86th Street. For comfort over style (these city streets can be murder on the feet!), try **Aerosoles,** 310 Columbus Ave. (℗ **212/579-8659),** or **Sacco** for women's shoes that offer a bit of both, and **Harry's** and **Tip Top Shoes** for men, women, and children. **Maxilla & Mandible** offers groovy natural science–based gifts (see "Museum Stores" in "Shopping A to Z," later in this chapter).

Boutiques dot Amsterdam Avenue, but main drag Broadway is more notable for its terrific gourmet edibles at **Zabar's** and **Fairway** markets, both legends in their own right (see "Edibles" in "Shopping A to Z," later in this chapter).

2 The Best Department Stores for Bargain Hunters

Bloomingdale's   Bloomie's is more accessible than Barneys or Bergdorf's and more affordable than Saks, but still has the pizzazz Macy's and Lord & Taylor now largely lack. Taking up a city block, it has just about anything you could want, from clothing (both designer and everyday basics) and fragrances to a full range of housewares. The frequent sales can yield unbeatable bargains; look for full-page advertisements in the *New York Times.* The main entrance is on Third Avenue, but pop up to street level from the 59th Street station and you'll be right at the Lexington Avenue entrance. 1000 Third Ave. (Lexington Ave. at 59th St.). ℗ **212/705-2000.** www.bloomingdales.com. Subway: 4, 5, 6, N, R to 59th St.

Century 21 *Value*   Despite suffering severe damage in the terrorist attacks on the World Trade Center, Century 21 reopened its doors on March 1, 2002. The designer discount store is back, and it's better than ever. Prices on designer goods are 40% to 70% off what you would pay at a department store or designer boutique. Don't think that $250 Armani blazer is a bargain? Look again at the tag—the retail price is upward of $800. This is the place to find those $5 Liz Claiborne tees, $20 Todd Oldham pants, or $50 Bally loafers—not to mention underwear, hosiery, and ties that are a bargain-hunter's dream. Kids' clothes, linens, and housewares are also part of the stock. Avoid the weekday lunch hour and Saturdays, if you can. 22 Cortlandt St. (between Broadway and Church St.). ℗ **212/227-9092.** www.c21stores.com. Subway: 1, 2, 3, 4, 5, M to Fulton St.; A, C to Broadway/ Nassau St.; E to Chambers St.

Kmart   Kmart is so out of place in the East Village that it has turned the mundane into camp: Japanese kids stare at gargantuan boxes of detergent as if they were Warhol designed; pierced and tattooed locals navigate the name-brand maze alongside stroller-pushing housewives. Kitsch value aside, this multilevel store is a great bet for discount prices on practical items, from socks to shampoo. You'll also find a pharmacy, a food department (sale prices on snack foods are rock-bottom), and even a photo studio. 770 Broadway (between 8th and 9th sts.). ✆ 212/673-1540. Subway: 6 to Astor Place. Also at 250 W. 34th St. (between Sixth and Seventh aves.).

Lord & Taylor Okay, so maybe Lord & Taylor isn't the first place you'd go for a vinyl miniskirt, but you can't deny its elegant mien. Long known as an excellent source of women's dresses and coats, L&T stocks all the major labels for men and women, with a special emphasis on American designers. Their house-brand clothes (khakis, blazers, turtlenecks, and summer sportswear) are well made and a great bargain. Sales, especially around holidays, can be stellar. The store is big enough to have a good selection but doesn't overwhelm. The Christmas window displays are an annual delight. 424 Fifth Ave. (at 39th St.). ✆ 212/391-3344. www.lordandtaylor.com. Subway: F, V, B, D to 42nd St.

Macy's A four-story sign on the side of the building trumpets "MACY'S, THE WORLD'S LARGEST STORE"—hard to dispute, since the 10-story behemoth covers an entire block. Macy's is a hard place to shop: The size is unmanageable, the service is dreadful, and the din from the crowds on the ground floor will kick your migraine into action. The store's one-of-a-kind flair that made it legendary is just a memory. But they do sell *everything*. What's more, sales run constantly, so bargains are guaranteed. And the store provides personal guides/shoppers at no charge. At Christmastime, come as late as you can manage (the store is usually open until midnight in the final shopping days).

Tips for sale seekers: One-day sales usually occur on Wednesdays and sometimes on Saturdays. Call the store when you arrive to find out whether your visit overlaps with one. Or check the *New York Times* any day of the week for full-page advertisements, which sometimes include clip-out coupons for additional 10% to 15% discounts. At Herald Sq., W. 34th St. and Broadway. ✆ 212/695-4400. www.macys.com. Subway: B, D, F, N, Q, R, 1, 2, 3, 9 to 34th St.

3 Shopping A to Z
ANTIQUES & COLLECTIBLES

New York has a wealth of antiques shops, covering everything from ancient to Americana to Art Deco to mid-20th century modern. Prices are astronomical—much higher than virtually everywhere else. Still, traditionalists will love the blocks off **Broadway near 10th and 11th streets,** where the bounty includes Kentshire Galleries (37 E. 12th St.; ✆ 212/673-6644); and **East 59th, 60th, and 61st streets** around Second Avenue, not far from the Manhattan Art & Antiques Center (1050 Second Ave., between 55th and 56th sts.; ✆ 212/335-4400), where about two dozen high-end dealers line the street and spill over onto surrounding blocks. Fans of mid-20th-century furniture and Americana with a twist should browse **Lafayette Street** in SoHo/NoHo. Just about any dealer will have the current issue of the free *Greyrock Antiques Guide* and/or *Antiques New York,* which will lead you to specialty dealers around the city.

Chelsea Antiques Building *Value* More than 100 dealers occupy this 12-floor building, which is open daily. The permanent stalls run the gamut from 18th-century antiques to rare books to early-20th-century radios, jewelry, and toys. Prices are so good that it's known as a dealer's source, and shoppers are the type who love to prowl, touch everything, and sniff out a bargain. 110 W. 25th St. (between Sixth and Seventh aves.). ✆ 212/929-0909. Subway: F to 23rd St.

J. Fields Studio & Gallery This gallery is the place for vintage and contemporary foreign and domestic film posters. A limited supply of music posters is on hand, too (including a selection of psychedelic posters from the '60s). J. Fields is considered the best vintage-poster restorer in the city, so quality is first-rate. Prices are high, but vintage lobby cards start at $15. 55 W. 17th St. (just east of Sixth Ave.), 6th floor. ✆ 212/989-4520. www.avidcollectorposters.com. Subway: F to 14th St.

La Belle Epoque   This shop specializes in original Art Deco and Art Nouveau posters—mostly European advertisements—from the 1890s through the 1950s, as well as conservation framing. If you're a buff with a limited budget, smaller framed pieces in the $100 range means that you can buy rather than just browse. 280 Columbus Ave. (at 73rd St.). ✆ 212/362-1770. www.la-belle-epoque.com. Subway: B, C to 72nd St.

BEAUTY

Kiehl's   Kiehl's is more than a store: It's a virtual cult. Models, stockbrokers, visitors, and just about everyone else stops by this old-time apothecary for its simply packaged, wonderfully formulated products for women and men. Lip Balm no. 1 is the perfect antidote for the winter winds. Kiehl's now has a counter at Saks, too, but stop into the original if you can. 109 Third Ave. (between 13th and 14th sts.). ✆ 212/677-3171. Subway: L, N, R, 4, 5, 6 to 14th St./Union Sq.

Ricky's Urban Groove   This wild emporium of personal-care products is a blast to browse. Goodies run the gamut from chartreuse-hued wigs to temporary tattoos to nail colors you've never dreamed of. But Ricky's also makes a good stop for travel sizes, brushes, hair clips, and anything else you might've forgotten, all at low, low prices. The SoHo location is best. 590 Broadway (between Houston and Prince sts.). ✆ 212/226-5552. www.rickys-nyc.com. Subway: L, N, R, 4, 5, 6 to 14th St./Union Sq. Also at 718 Broadway (near Astor Place; ✆ 212/979-5232; subway: N, R to 8th St.); 466 Sixth Ave. (between 11th and 12th sts.; ✆ 212/924-3401; subway: F to 14th St.); 44 E. 8th St. (at Greene St.; ✆ 212/254-5247; subway: 6 to Astor Place); 988 Eighth Ave. (at 58th St.; ✆ 212/957-8343; subway: A, B, C, D, 1, 9 to 59th St./Columbus Circle).

Sephora   The Rock Center branch of the French beauty superstore is a three-floor bonanza of beauty. You'll find everything you could want, from scents to nail color to skin cleansers to bath salts to makeup brushes to hair accessories—in a phenomenal number of lines that run the gamut from upscale lines Babor, Philip Thomas Roth, and Murad to funky bunches like Philosophy, Urban Decay, and Hard Candy. It's an incredible store, with an encyclopedic staff and testers galore. At Rockefeller Center, 636 Fifth Ave. (at 51st St.). ✆ 212/245-1633. www.sephora.com. Subway: E, F to 51st St. Also at 1500 Broadway (between 43rd and 44th sts.; ✆ 212/944-6789; subway: N, R, S, 1, 2, 3, 7, 9 to 42nd St/Times Sq.); 130 W. 34th St. (between Broadway and Seventh Ave.; ✆ 212/629-9315; subway: B, D, F, Q to 34th St./Herald Sq.); 119 Fifth Ave. (at 17th St.; ✆ 212/674-3570; subway: N, R to 23rd St.); 555 Broadway (between Prince and Spring sts.; ✆ 212/625-1309; subway: N, R to Prince St.); 1129 Third Ave. (at 67th St.; ✆ 212/452-3336; subway: 6 to 68th St.); 2103 Broadway (between 73rd and 74th sts.; ✆ 212/362-1500; subway: 1, 2, 3, 9 to 72nd St.).

BOOKS
THE BIG CHAINS

Barnes & Noble   B&N dominates the urban landscape with more locations than any other chain. The Union Square location is a favorite: The selection is huge and well organized, the store is comfortable and never feels overcrowded, and you're welcome to browse—or nab a chair and read—as long as you like. There's a cafe and an extensive magazine stand. Many locations host an active calendar of readings, often starring such luminaries as Martin Amis and Elmore Leonard. On Union Sq., 33 E. 17th St. ✆ 212/253-0810. www.bn.com. Subway: L, N, R, 4, 5, 6 to 14th St./Union

Sq. Also at 1972 Broadway (at 66th St.; ℭ 212/595-6859; subway: 1, 9 to 66th St.); 4 Astor Place (between Broadway and Lafayette St.; ℭ 212/420-1322; subway: 6 to Astor Place); 675 Sixth Ave. (near 22nd St.; ℭ 212/727-1227; subway: F to 23rd St.); 160 E. 54th St. (at Third Ave.; ℭ 212/750-8033; subway: 6 to 51st St.); 600 Fifth Ave. (at 48th St.; ℭ 212/765-0590; subway: E, F to Fifth Ave.); Citicorp Center, 160 E. 54th St. (between Lexington and Third aves.; ℭ 212/750-8033; subway: 6 to 51st St.); 2289 Broadway (at 82nd St.; ℭ 212/362-8835; subway: 1, 9 to 79th St.); 105 Fifth Ave. (at 18th St.; ℭ 212/807-0099; subway: F to 14th St.); 240 E. 86th St. (between Second and Third aves.; ℭ 212/794-1962; subway: 4, 5, 6 to 86th St.).

Borders The selection of books and music at Borders is extensive, service is great, and the stores host a wealth of events, including appearances from authors to musician Lou Reed to ethereal pup Mr. Winkle. 461 Park Ave. (at 57th St.). ℭ 212/980-6785. www.borderstores.com. Subway: 4, 5, 6 to 59th St. Also at 550 Second Ave. (at 32nd St.; ℭ 212/481-2913; subway: 6 to 33rd St.).

SPECIALTY BOOKSTORES

New York has some terrific specialty bookstores; these are some of the best.

Argosy Books Antiquarian-book hounds should check out this 78-year-old store, with high ceilings, packed shelves, an intellectual air, an outstanding collection of rarities—including 18th- and 19th-century prints, maps, and autographs—and a solid sale table. 116 E. 59th St. (between Park and Lexington aves.). ℭ 212/753-4455. www.argosybooks.com. Subway: 4, 5, 6 to 59th St.

Bluestockings Women's Bookstore & Cafe After this community bookstore announced it would close in early 2003, new owners stepped in at the last minute to keep it open. They've changed the focus slightly to "independent bookstore, cafe, and activist resource center." The small storefront is packed with books to answer literary needs and wants of women, straight and gay, with fiction, nonfiction, memoirs, poetry, self-help, and missives on racism, classism, sexism, empowerment, and more. There's a pleasant cafe, as well as a small but well-chosen section of children's books. A full calendar of readings, meetings, and workshops is always on. 172 Allen St. (south of Houston St.). ℭ 212/777-6028. www.bluestockings.com. Subway: F to Second Ave. (use First Ave. exit).

Bookleaves (Value) This unassuming West Village used-book nook is wonderful for general-interest browsing at hand-me-down prices. Art-book enthusiasts, in particular, should seek out this place. 304 W. 4th St. (near Bank St.). ℭ 212/924-5638. Subway: A, C, E to 14th St.

Books of Wonder You don't have to be a kid to fall in love with this bookstore. Kids will love BOW's story readings; call or check the site for the latest schedule. 16 W. 18th St. (between Fifth and Sixth aves.). ℭ 212/989-3270. www.booksofwonder.com. Subway: L, N, R, Q, W, 4, 5, 6 to 14th St./Union Sq.

Complete Traveller Whether your destination is Texas or Tibet, you'll find what you need in this, possibly the world's best travel bookstore. There are maps and accessories, plus a collection of antiquarian travel books whose facts may be outdated but whose writers' perceptions continue to shine. The staff is attentive. 199 Madison Ave. (at 35th St.). ℭ 212/685-9007. Subway: 6 to 33rd St.

Forbidden Planet Here's the city's largest collection of sci-fi, comics, and graphic-illustration books. The range of products can't be beat, and the proudly geeky staff really knows what's what. Great sci-fi-themed toys, too. 840 Broadway (at 13th St.). ℭ 212/473-1576. www.forbiddenplanetnyc.com. Subway: L, N, R, Q, W, 4, 5, 6 to 14th St./Union Sq.

Tips **An Old Favorite Returns!**

For many years the best independent bookstore in New York City, **Coliseum Books,** known for its informed staff and great selection, drew book lovers to 57th Street and Broadway. High rents and competition from the superstores forced it to close its doors in 2002. But this story has a happy ending: Coliseum will be reborn at a new location, **11 West 42nd Street,** across from the New York Public Library, sometime in late 2003.

Gotham Book Mart   Paris may have had Sylvia Beach, but New York was lucky enough to have Frances Steloff, who opened Gotham Book Mart in 1920. She championed such once-banned works as Henry Miller's *Tropic of Cancer,* and numbered among her admirers Ezra Pound, Saul Bellow, and Jackie Onassis. Frances has passed on, but her aura lives. The emphasis here is on poetry, literature, and the arts. Look for the sign that says WISE MEN FISH HERE. *Note:* The store is scheduled to move, but the location and date were unknown at press time; call before you go. 41 W. 47th St. (between Fifth and Sixth aves.). ℂ 212/719-4448. Subway: B, D, F, V to 47th–50th sts./Rockefeller Center.

Gryphon Bookshop *(Value*   Here's the Upper West Side's best used-book store. It's a browser's delight, stacked with used and rare fiction, nonfiction, and art books, plus the occasional reviewer's copy at discounted prices. 2246 Broadway (between 80th and 81st sts.). ℂ 212/362-0706. Subway: 1, 9 to 79th St.

Hagstrom Map & Travel Center   This bookstore sells travel guides and an incredible selection of cartography to meet about any map need, including some of the best maps around of the Big Apple. 57 W. 43rd St. (between Fifth and Sixth aves.). ℂ 212/398-1222. Subway: B, D, F, V to 42nd St. Also at 125 Maiden Lane (at Water St.; ℂ 212/785-5343; subway: A, C, 2, 3, 4, 5 to Fulton St.).

Housing Works Used Books Cafe *(Finds*   Find your reading material at this spacious yet cozy used-book shop, sporting 45,000 books and records to browse. It's part of Housing Works, a not-for-profit organization that provides housing, services, and advocacy for homeless people living with HIV and AIDS. The collection is terrific and well organized, with lots of well-priced paperbacks, hardbacks, and coffee-table books. There's a cafe that serves coffee and tea, sandwiches, sweets, and light bites, plus beer and wine, and you're welcome to read as you snack. The store often hosts readings as well as occasional music performances; call or check the website for the current calendar. 126 Crosby St. (south of Houston St.). ℂ 212/334-3324. www.housingworksubc.com. Subway: F, V to Broadway/Lafayette St.; 6 to Spring St.

Kitchen Arts & Letters   Here's the ultimate cook's and food-lover's bookstore. You'll be wowed by the selection, which includes rare, out-of-print, and foreign-language titles focusing on food and wine. The staff will conduct searches for hard-to-find titles. The shop is an overstuffed jumble, but if this is your bag, you'll be browsing for hours. 1435 Lexington Ave. (between 93rd and 94th sts.). ℂ 212/876-5550. email: kalstaff@rcn.com. Subway: 6 to 96th St.

Murder Ink   Murder, she wrote, he wrote, they wrote. Murder Ink claims to be the world's oldest mystery-book store. They purport to sell every mystery in print, and also have a huge selection of out-of-print paperbacks, hard-to-find imports, and signed first editions. 2486 Broadway (between 92nd and 93rd sts.). ℂ 800/488-8123 or 212/362-8905. www.murderink.com. Subway: 1, 9 to 96th St.

(**Finds** New York's Most Dramatic Book Shops

At 86 years old, the **Drama Book Shop** (© 212/944-0595; www.drama bookshop.com) at 250 W. 40th St., between Eighth and Ninth avenues, is hardly a newcomer. But since its move from cramped, second-floor digs in Times Square 2 years ago, the performing-arts bookstore has reinvented itself in a large new space, complete with the Arthur Seelen Theatre, an in-house performance venue, and a resident theater company. The the-atre also hosts discussions and book signings with members of the theater community, ranging from playwright Tina Howe to critic Mel Gussow. Offering thousands of plays, from translations of Greek classics to this sea-son's hits hot off the presses, the shop also offers books, magazines, and newspapers on the craft and business of the performing arts, ranging from biographies, criticism, directing, makeup, and lighting to how to get an agent. The shop is open from 10am to 8pm Monday through Saturday, and from noon to 6pm on Sundays.

When they aren't waiting tables or scouring *BackStage* for work, you'll find many actors and other show-biz wannabes perusing the **Applause Theatre and Cinema Books** (© 212/496-7511), at 211 W. 71st. With its vast collection of printed plays, screenplays, reference books, and other related books, both new and used, the store has, for years, been a major source for those in the dramatic arts. Open from 10am to 9pm Monday through Saturday and from noon to 6pm on Sundays.

Oscar Wilde Bookshop   The world's oldest gay and lesbian bookstore was on the brink of extinction until it was thankfully saved by the Lambda Rising chain. The nice staff makes browsing in this landmark a pleasure. 15 Christopher St. (between Sixth and Seventh aves.). © 212/255-8097. www.oscarwildebooks.com. Subway: 1, 9 to Christopher St.

Partners & Crime   This Village shop is as much fun as a good thriller. The new and used collections include signed first editions. Readings by well-known scribes are a regular event, and live actors perform a 1940s mystery radio show, complete with organist and sound effects, on the first Saturday of the month at 6 and 8pm ($5). 44 Greenwich Ave. (at Charles St.). © 212/243-0440. www.crimepays.com. Subway: A, C, E, F, V, S to W. 4th St. (use 8th St. exit).

Rand McNally Travel Store   Sheet maps, globes, city maps, international maps, laminated maps—so many maps that you might never get lost again. A wide range of travel guides, atlases, and such travelers' aids as voltage converters and inflatable pillows, too. 150 E. 52nd St. (between Lexington and Third aves.). © 212/758-7488. www.randmcnally.com. Subway: E, F to Lexington Ave.; 6 to 51st St.

Revolution Books   If you're looking for an alternative viewpoint, you'll find one at Revolution. Books on Marxism, feminism, and just about any other "ism" make up the bulk of this store. But it's not just political lit; fiction, poetry, mag-azines, and newspapers are also on hand. 9 W. 19th St. (between Fifth and Sixth aves.). © 212/691-3345. Subway: 4, 5, 6, L, N, R to 14th St./Union Sq.

Rizzoli   This clubby Italian bookstore is the classiest—and most relaxing—spot in town to browse for visual-art and design books, plus quality fiction, gourmet cookbooks, and other upscale reading. There's a decent selection of foreign-language, music, and dance titles as well. 31 W. 57th St. (between Fifth and Sixth aves.). © **212/759-2424.** Subway: N, R to Fifth Ave.

St. Mark's Bookshop   Established in 1977, this East Village bookshop is a great place to browse. You'll find lots of terrific alternative and small-press fiction and poetry, plus criticism, Eastern philosophy, and mainstream literature with an edge. You'll also find art, photography, and design books as well as an alternative 'zine rack. Lots of spoken-work CDs and cassettes, too. 31 Third Ave. (at 9th St.). © **212/260-7853.** www.stmarksbookshop.com. Subway: 6 to Astor Place.

The Scholastic Store _(Kids_   This mammoth store is at the ground level of the headquarters for children's publisher Scholastic. The 6,200-foot retail space is a veritable interactive playground for kids. Books, toys, and software feature Scholastic's top-selling brands, from Clifford the Big Red Dog to Captain Underpants. Harry Potter and friends are also well represented. A full slate of in-store events, from author signings to craft workshops, keeps kids busy; check the website or call for the schedule. 557 Broadway (between Prince and Spring sts.). © **212/ 343-6166.** www.scholastic.com/sohostore. Subway: N, R to Prince St.

Shakespeare & Co.   This boutiquelike bookstore stocks the latest bestsellers, and has a well-rounded inventory. The displays are enticing if you're looking for something new. 716 Broadway (at Washington Place). © **212/529-1330.** www.shakeandco.com. Subway: N, R to 8th St. Also at 939 Lexington Ave. (at 69th St.; © **212/570-0201;** subway: 6 to 68th St.); 137 E. 23rd St. (at Lexington Ave.; © **212/505-2021;** subway: 6 to 23rd St.); 716 Broadway (at Washington Place; © **212/529-1330;** subway: 6 to Astor Place, N/R to 8th St.); 1 Whitehall St. (at Broadway, next to U.S. Customs House, 1 block from Staten Island Ferry; © **212/742-7025;** subway: 4, 5 to Bowling Green; N, R to Whitehall St.).

The Strand _(Value_   Something of a New York legend, The Strand is worth a visit for its "8 miles of books" as well as its extensive inventory of review copies and bargain titles at up to 85% off list price. It's the city's best book deal—there's almost nothing marked at list—and the selection is phenomenal (there's even a rare-book department). Still, you'll work for it: The narrow aisles mean you're always getting bumped; the books are only roughly alphabetized; and there's no air-conditioning in summer. The Lower Manhattan location is significantly smaller. 828 Broadway (at 12th St.). © **212/473-1452.** www.strandbooks.com. Subway: L, N, R, 4, 5, 6 to 14th St./Union Sq. Strand Annex at 95 Fulton St. (between William and Gold sts.; © **212/732-6070;** subway: 4, 5, 6 to Fulton St.).

Traveler's Choice   This small, friendly travel-book store can meet all of your travel-guide needs, from Antarctica to Zimbabwe. 2 Wooster St. (between Grand and Canal sts.). © **212/941-1535.** Subway: A, C, E to Canal St.

Urban Center Books   Housed in an architectural landmark (McKim, Mead & White's 1882 Villard Houses), the Municipal Art Society's bookstore boasts a terrific selection of new books on architecture, urban planning, and landscape design. In the Villard Houses, 457 Madison Ave. (at 51st St.). © **800/352-1880** or 212/935-3592. www.urbancenterbooks.com. Subway: 6 to 51st St.

CLOTHING
RETAIL FASHIONS
Fashion hounds should check out "The Top Shopping Streets & Neighborhoods," earlier in this chapter, for advice on prime hunting grounds for original designs. Also check out the listing for **Century 21** (p. 269), the biggest and best discount department store.

Fashion Flagships

Some New York flagship stores are an experience you won't find in your local mall. These stores are display cases for the complete line of fashions, so you'll often find much more to choose from than in your at-home branch.

Check out **Ann Taylor,** 645 Madison Ave., at 60th Street (✆ 212/832-2010; www.anntaylor.com); the **Banana Republic** flagship at Rockefeller Center, 626 Fifth Ave., at 50th Street (✆ 212/974-2350; www.bananarepublic.com); **Eddie Bauer,** 1960 Broadway, at 67th Street (✆ 212/877-7629; www.eddiebauer.com), which also carries the AKA Eddie Bauer line and sports and mountaineering line; **Liz Claiborne,** 650 Fifth Ave., at 52nd Street (✆ 212/338-3888; www.liz claiborne.com), carrying all of Liz's lines; and the **Original Levi's Store** at 3 E. 57th St., between Fifth and Madison (✆ 212/826-5957). **Old Navy** has a flag-ship featuring its basics and signature sense of humor at 610 Sixth Ave., at 18th Street (✆ 212/645-0663; www.oldnavy.com).

For Men & Women

Afterlife   This shop sells cutting-edge sportswear and club-wear accessories to downtowners who aspire to Patricia Field's couture club wear but can't afford it. Expect lots of tiny Ts, clingy fabrics, and hip-hugging pants, plus accessories to heighten the hipper-than-thou look. 450 Broadway (between Grand and Canal sts.). ✆ 212/ 625-3167 or 212/625-0787. Subway: N, R, Q, W, 6 to Canal St.

Burlington Coat Factory _(Value_   Burlington has a stash of off-price and slightly irregular designer togs for men, women, and kids, but come for the coats. You'll find an exhaustive selection at excellent prices, as well as a fine selec-tion of discounted leather bags and shoes. 707 Sixth Ave. (between 22nd and 23rd sts.). ✆ 212/229-1300. Subway: F to 23rd St.

Daffy's _(Value_   Long before any of these Johnny-come-lately discounters arrived, Daffy's offered rock-bottom prices. They don't get the big brand names of Cen-tury 21, but you'll come across classic European sportswear (cashmere sweaters and the like) and staples, especially for men. The kids' collection—much of it trendy designer—is a well-kept secret among city moms. 111 Fifth Ave. (at 18th St.). ✆ 212/529-4477. www.daffys.com. Subway: 4, 5, 6, L, N, R, Q, W to 14th St./Union Sq. Also at 462 Broadway (at Grand St.; ✆ 212/334-7444; subway: N, R to Canal St.); 335 Madison Ave. (at 44th St.; ✆ 212/557-4422; subway: 4, 5, 6, 7, S to 42nd St./Grand Central); 1311 Broadway (at 34th St.; ✆ 212/736-4477; subway: 1, 2, 3, 9 to 34th St.); 125 E. 57th St. (between Park and Lexington aves.; ✆ 212/376-4477; subway: 4, 5, 6 to 59th St.).

Filene's Basement _(Value_   This Boston-based institution's Manhattan satellites pale when compared to the mother store. The stock can be hit-or-miss, but you will find discounts on men's and women's clothing, handbags, accessories, shoes, and a few brands of perfume. Every now and then a big-time European label pops up, but don't count on finding the current season's goods, especially in the down-stairs men's store. Inventory turns over lightning-quick here, though, so you never know what a trip through can yield. 620 Sixth Ave. (between 18th and 19th sts.). ✆ 212/620-3100. www.filenesbasement.com. Subway: F to 14th St. Also at 2222 Broadway (at 79th St.; ✆ 212/873-8000; subway: 1, 9 to 79th St.).

H&M _(Value_   The Swedish discounter Hennes & Mauritz took New York by storm in 2000 with its high-style fashions at budget-minded prices. The colorful, loud, bustling stores are mammoth, the departments better organized than most full-retail department stores, the men's and women's wearables ultrachic, and the prices low, low, low. It's a fave with teens, in particular. The main Herald Square store carries all lines, including babies, children's, and maternity wear. 1328 Broadway (at 34th St.). ℂ 646/489-8777. www.hm.com. Subway: B, D, F, N, R, V to 34th St./Herald Sq. Also at 640 Fifth Ave. (at 51st St.; ℂ 212/656-9305; subway: E, V to Fifth Ave.). Smaller location at 558 Broadway (between Prince and Spring sts.; ℂ 212/343-0220; subway: N, R to Prince St.).

Loehmann's *Value* This enormous discount outlet occupies a chunk of the original Barneys, and it has latched on to the stylish vibe. But not the prices, though; here, you'll pay 30% to 65% off department-store prices. Two floors of casual wear by makers such as Liz Claiborne and Laundry lead to one of the city's best finds: The "Back Room," where styles by big names—Versace, D&G, Donna Karan, Max Mara—are offered at a fraction of retail. There's also a floor of men's fashions, the best you'll find in the discount realm. Excellent shoes, too, with great prices on top-quality styles. 101 Seventh Ave. (between 16th and 17th sts.). ℂ 212/352-0856. www.loehmanns.com. Subway: 1, 9 to 18th St.

Roots *Finds* This Canadian sportswear company got worldwide attention for outfitting the best-dressed teams at the 2002 Winter Olympics: Canada and the USA. This is one of their few American shops, and it's worth checking out. Roots sells their top-quality fleece, Ts, sweats, and casual wear—not to mention those Olympic berets—at Gap-comparable prices. 270 Lafayette St. (at Prince St.). ℂ 212/324-3333. www.roots.com. Subway: 6 to Spring St.; N, R to Prince St.

Syms *Value* Syms is the discount store for men and women who need career wear. Designer and brand-name clothes are slashed 40% to 60% off their original retail value. Good buys on kids' clothes, too. *Money-saving tip:* Register at the website for an additional 10% savings. 42 Trinity Place (between Rector St. and Battery Park). ℂ 212/797-1199. www.syms.com. Subway: 1, 9, N, R to Rector St. Also at 400 Park Ave. (at 54th St.; ℂ 212/317-8200; subway: 6 to 51st St.).

Tristan & America This Canadian retailer sells affordable, nicely tailored clothing in muted palettes to men and women who love Banana Republic's clothes but need a break from the high prices there. Look for great men's sweaters, affordable women's suits, and nicely cut trousers and A-line skirts. Excellent sales. 1230 Sixth Ave. (at 49th St.). ℂ 212/246-2354. www.tristan-america.com. Subway: B, D, F, V to 47th–50th sts./Rockefeller Center.

Urban Outfitters The store for basics is sort of a Gap for alternative guys and gals: Jeans, oversize and tiny T-shirts, and bright velours and stretchy polyesters. There's a good selection of funky jewelry, as well as a wonderfully offbeat, affordable housewares section with batik bedspreads, candles, glassware, and mod bathroom accessories. You'll also find lots of silly gifts, from *Mad Libs* books to boxes of genuine *South Park* Cheesy Poofs. 628 Broadway (at Bleecker St.). ℂ 212/475-0009. www. urbn.com. Subway: 6 to Bleecker St. Also at 374 Sixth Ave. (at Waverly Place; ℂ 212/677-9350; subway: A, C, E, F, V to W. 4th St.); 162 Second Ave. (at 11th St.; ℂ 212/375-1277; subway: L to Third Ave.); 526 Sixth Ave. (at 14th St.; ℂ 646/638-1646; subway: F to 14th St.); 2081 Broadway (at 72nd St.; ℂ 212/579-3912; subway: 1, 2, 3, 9 to 72nd St.).

X-Large Your teen will love you for taking him or her to this hot spot (co-owned by Beastie Boy Mike D) for skate and urban street wear. The emphasis is on supercasual, with cutting-edge takes on staples like tees and sweatshirts; it's also big with 20-somethings and hip Japanese. 267 Lafayette St. (between Prince and Spring sts.). ℂ 212/334-4480. www.xlarge.com. Subway: 6 to Spring St.

Just Women

a. cheng   Alice Cheng's retro-modern styles for women are fresh, pretty, and, best of all, affordable. The petite shop is a breezy delight. 443 E. 9th St. (between First Ave. and Ave. A). ✆ 212/979-7324. Subway: 6 to Astor Place.

Anthropologie   Funky-chic and affordable wearables and accessories mix with gifts and furniture. Geared to young women who've outgrown Urban Outfitters. 375 W. Broadway (between Spring and Broome sts.). ✆ 212/343-7070. www.anthropologie.com. Subway: C, E to Spring St. Also at 85 Fifth Ave. (at 15th St.; ✆ 212/627-5885; subway: L, N, R, 4, 5, 6 to Union Sq.).

Eileen Fisher   Making their way around the nation in her shops and through outlets such as Saks and the Garnet Hill catalog, Eileen Fisher's separates are a dream come true for stylish women looking for easy-to-wear classic pieces. She designs fluid clothes in a neutral palette with natural fibers that don't sacrifice comfort for chic. Prices are on the high side, but the quality, fabrics, and style make them worth it. The SoHo shop, at 395 W. Broadway, is Fisher's prime showcase, but bargain hunters should head for the East 9th location, which functions as an outlet store, with sale merchandise and seconds. 314 E. 9th St. (between First and Second aves.). ✆ 212/529-5715. www.eileenfisher.com. Subway: 6 to Astor Place. Also at 395 W. Broadway (between Spring and Broome sts.; ✆ 212/431-4567; subway: C, E to Spring St.); 166 Fifth Ave. (between 21st and 22nd sts.; ✆ 212/924-4777; subway: N, R to

---

⟨Value⟩ **Scouring the Sample Sales**

Welcome to the ultimate New York bargain: the sample sale, where top fashion designers recoup some losses by selling off the sample outfits they make for store buyers. Often, they throw in canceled orders, overstock, and discontinued styles. Prices are rock bottom. What's the drawback? Such sales aren't advertised because designers don't want to alienate the big retailers by stealing their customers.

So how do you get the scoop? The **weekly columns** "Sales & Bargains" in *New York* magazine and "Check Out" in *Time Out New York* list current and future sales; you can find *New York* magazine's sale picks online at **www.nymetro.com**. The free site **NYSale (www.nysale.com)** is probably your best source; it'll let you in on otherwise-unadvertised sales. If you're in the Garment District (especially along Broadway and Seventh Ave.) in the morning, you'll probably be handed **flyers** advertising sales that day.

A few tips as you venture into bargain land:

- Don't go at lunch; you'll be elbow-to-elbow with rushed office workers.
- Bring cash. Some designers do accept credit cards, but don't chance it.
- Few, if any, of these spaces have dressing rooms, so be prepared to try things on over your clothes (or hope it fits). Furthermore, because these garments are samples, they don't always come in a wide array of sizes.
- All items are sold "as is," and every sale is final, so inspect merchandise carefully before you buy.

23rd St.); 521 Madison Ave. (at 53rd St.; ℂ **212/759-9888**; subway: 6 to 51st St.); 341 Columbus Ave. (near 77th St.; ℂ **212/362-3000**; subway: B, C to 81st St.); 1039 Madison Ave. (between 79th and 80th sts.; ℂ **212/879-7799**; subway: 6 to 77th St.).

Foley & Corinna *(Finds)* The Lower East Side's best boutique specializes in affordable original designs with a '70s flair that's retro in a nonkitschy way. You'll find a few reconstructed vintage pieces mixed in (such as vintage Ts with added lace for a sexier look), plus an excellent handbag collection. 108 Stanton St. (between Essex and Ludlow sts.). ℂ **212/529-2338**. Subway: F to Delancey St.

Intermix The place to dress and accessorize like your favorite *Sex and the City* gals, at not-too-expensive prices. The Flatiron location is the original, and remains the best. 125 Fifth Ave. (between 19th and 20th sts.). ℂ **212/533-9720**. Subway: N, R to 23rd St. Also at 210 Columbus Ave. (between 69th and 70th sts.; ℂ **212/769 9116**; subway: B, C to 72nd St.).

Jill Anderson *(Finds)* Finally, a New York designer who creates affordable clothes for real women for real life—not just for 22-year-old size-2s. This narrow, peaceful shop and studio is lined with Jill's simple, clean designs, which drape beautifully and accentuate a woman's form without clinging. They're wearable for all ages and many figure types (her small sizes are small enough to fit petites, and her larges generally fit a full-figured size 14). Her clothes are feminine without being frilly, retro-reminiscent but modern, understated but stylish. If this sounds appealing, don't miss her shop. 331 E. 9th St. (between First and Second aves.). ℂ **212/253-1747**. www.jillanderson.com. Subway: 6 to Astor Place.

Jungle Planet This Village boutique specializes in trendy, affordable young women's casual wear in cotton, synthetics, and knits—print skirts, cute Ts, and the like. Sale prices start at $10. 175 W. 4th St. (between Sixth and Seventh aves.). ℂ **212/989-5447**. Subway: A, C, E, F, V, S to W. 4th St.; 1, 9 to Christopher St.

Liberty House This Columbia University–area boutique is a find. It specializes in women's wear in easygoing styles that transcend age lines and figure types. Great casual sweaters, Ts, cotton pants and skirts, linen separates, and more, all at affordable prices. You'll also find ethnic gifts at the front of the store, jewelry and accessories under the glass-topped counter, and a kids' shop specializing in unique styles that don't cost a fortune. 2878A Broadway (at 112th St.). ℂ **212/932-1950**. Subway: 1, 9 to Cathedral Pkwy./110th St.

Nicolina This charming and sophisticated shop is a Theater District anomaly. Come for fashionable basics in high-quality materials: wide-legged linen pants, flowing A-line and princess-cut dresses in silk and cotton, sweaters from labels like Beyond Threads and Sarah Arizona in fine wools, cotton, and silk. Great accessories, too, plus a small selection of contemporary and vintage gifts. 247 W. 46th St. (between Broadway and Eighth Ave.). ℂ **212/302-NICO**. Subway: N, R, S, 1, 2, 3, 9 to 42nd St./Times Sq.

VINTAGE & CONSIGNMENT CLOTHING

Alice Underground This lovely SoHo shop specializes is cheap-chic vintage wear, from Victoriana to *Mod Squad* era. The goods are displayed in an orderly fashion, and there's a good selection of vintage linens. 481 Broadway (between Broome and Grand sts.). ℂ **212/431-9067**. Subway: N, Q, R, W, 6 to Canal St.

Allan & Suzi *(Finds)* Make it past the freaky windows and you'll find one of the best consignment shops in the city. Allan and Suzi have specialized in 20th-century designer wear for over a decade, and the selection is marvelous. Their vintage and contemporary couture collection—which ranges from Chanel to Halston and Versace—is so well priced that it's within reach of the average shopper. The wild one-of-a-kind pieces are worth a look unto themselves. 416 Amsterdam Ave. (at 80th St.). ✆ 212/724-7445. Subway: 1, 9 to 79th St.

Andy's Chee-Pees   This vintage-clothing store sports two jam-packed levels of retro-chic wearables, including leather, denim, '50s Hawaiian prints, blazers, and much more. Prices aren't exactly "cheep," but the quality is high. 691 Broadway (between 3rd and 4th sts.). ✆ 212/420-5980. Subway: 6 to Bleecker St.

Argosy   This narrow shop offers a small but pristine collection of '60s and '70s fashions, including an excellent collection of stylish leather jackets. Prices are reasonable considering the quality. 428 E. 9th St. (between First Ave. and Ave. A). ✆ 212/982-7918. Subway: 6 to Astor Place.

Encore *Value*   This is one of the city's best resale shops, with two floors of quality women's wear, plus a small men's department and accessories, all sold at a fraction of the original cost. Periodic sales sweeten the deal: The Chanel suit I saw for $650 was the buy of the century, but you don't have to bring that much cash to go home with a bargain. 1132 Madison Ave. (between 84th and 85th sts.), 2nd floor. ✆ 212/879-2850. www.encoreresale.com. Subway: 6 to 86th St.

Housing Works Thrift Shop *Finds*   With consistently low prices (most pieces $25 or less), lots of designer names (Todd Oldham, Calvin Klein, Donna Karan), and clothes in excellent condition, why go anywhere else? Styles range from classic to funky. There's also a good used-jeans area and a miniboutique selling couture-ish items at slightly higher prices. There's furniture, too, but good pieces go very fast. A great place to shop—not only will you get a bargain, but sales benefit homeless people living with HIV and AIDS. 143 W. 17th St. (between Sixth and Seventh aves.). ✆ 212/366-0820. www.housingworks.org/thrift. Subway: 1, 9 to 18th St. Also 202 E. 77th St. (between Second and Third aves.; ✆ 212/772-8461; subway: 6 to 77th St.); 306 Columbus Ave. (between 74th and 75th sts.; ✆ 212/579-7566; subway: B, C to 72nd St.); 157 E. 23rd St. (between Third and Lexington aves.; ✆ 212/529-5955; subway: 6 to 23rd St.).

Ina *Finds*   This designer consignment boutique specializes in used wearables, vintage and current, for men and women from the world's top couture houses. Labels run the gamut from Halston to Calvin to Prada to Daryl K. A beautiful selection of shoes and accessories is on hand. The locations are so close that you can scour both in one trip. 21 Prince St. (between Mott and Elizabeth sts.). ✆ 212/334-9048. Subway: N, R to Prince St.; 6 to Spring St. Also at 101 Thompson St. (between Prince and Spring sts.; ✆ 212/941-4757; subway: N, R to Prince St.

Kimono House   This SoHo shop is an excellent stop for low prices on vintage kimono and *yukata* (cotton kimono, which make great bathrobes). The fabrics alone are worth the price for folks looking to dress up their wardrobes and homes with brilliant jewel tones and Asian patterns. 131 Thompson St. (between Houston and Prince sts.). ✆ 212/505-0232. Subway: C, E to Spring St.

Love Saves the Day   This is the store made famous in *Desperately Seeking Susan* (Madonna bought those groovy boots here). LSD hasn't changed much since, except the prices keep going up. In addition to the entertaining collection of tacky vintage clothes, there's another good reason to come: the impressive assortment of Donny and Marie memorabilia and other collectible kitsch. 119 Second Ave. (at 7th St.). ✆ 212/228-3802. Subway: 6 to Astor Place.

Metropolis   Some of the biggest names in fashion scout this clean, orderly vintage shop for fashion ideas. With good reason: Some of the coolest old clothes in the world turn up here, from skater pants and micro-cords to ging-ham-checked Western shirts—perfect for your very own hoedown or hullabaloo. 43 Third Ave. (between 9th and 10th sts.). ✆ 212/358-0795. Subway: 6 to Astor Place.

Michael's *Value*   This consignment boutique boasts designer wear for women—including such names as Chanel, YSL, Prada, Gucci, and Escada—at a fraction of the original cost. The bridal salon is an unbeatable find for a top-quality dress at an off-the-rack price. 1041 Madison Ave. (between 79th and 80th sts.), 2nd floor. ✆ 212/737-7273. www.michaelsconsignment.com. Subway: 6 to 77th St.

New & Almost New *Finds*   This closet brims with well-chosen contemporary and retro designer wear, all like new and at great prices. 65 Mercer St. (just north of Broome St.). ✆ 212/226-6677. Subway: J, M, N, R, Q, W to Canal St.

Screaming Mimi's *Value*   Screaming Mimi's is as neat and well organized as any high-priced boutique—yet prices are reasonable, especially given the pricey vintage shops that have popped up in recent years. The clothes and accessories are well chosen, and the display is top notch. The housewares department is a cornucopia of kitsch, and includes a selection of New York memorabilia; prices start under $10, so this is a great place to find a special souvenir. 382 Lafayette St. (between 4th and Great Jones sts.). ✆ 212/677-6464. Subway: 6 to Astor Place.

Tokio 7 *Value*   This designer consignment shop features gently used couture from labels like Helmut Lang, Yohji Yamamoto, Vivienne Westwood, and others, at way-below-retail prices. 64 E. 7th St. (between First and Second aves.). ✆ 212/353-8443. Subway: 6 to Astor Place; L to First Ave.

Tokyo Joe *Value*   This cramped boutique is the designer consignment shop for left-of-mainstream hipsters. Browsing can be hellish, but prices are great. The shoe collection is stellar, often boasting barely (or never) worn Manolos and Jimmy Choos, priced at a fraction of what the *Sex and the City* gals pay at the uptown boutiques. 334 E. 11th St. (between First and Second aves.). ✆ 212/473-0724. Subway: L to First Ave. Also at 240 E. 28th St. (between Second and Third aves.; ✆ 212/532-3605; subway: 6 to 28th St.).

EDIBLES

Black Hound   This charming shop specializes in truffles, cookies, and cakes. This is a terrific choice for those who like their chocolates not too frilly or sweet. Just about everything comes packaged in a blond-wood box tied with a velveteen ribbon, making them simple but elegant gifts. 170 Second Ave. (between 10th and 11th sts.). ✆ 212/979-9505. Subway: 6 to Astor Place; L to Third Ave.

Chelsea Market   Located in an old Nabisco factory, this big, dazzling food mall is the city's largest. Come for raw and ready-to-eat foods, including divinely inspired baked goods and cappuccino from **Amy's Bread; Hale and Hearty** for yummy soups; Manhattan's best brownie at **Fat Witch Bakery;** and much more, including the wonderful **Chelsea Wine Vault. Chelsea Market Baskets** is a great place to pick up gifts for home. 75 Ninth Ave. (between 15th and 16th sts.). ✆ 212/243-5678. www.chelseamarket.com. Subway: A, C, E, L to 14th St.

Chocolate Bar *Finds*   Chocolates from chocolatier Jacques Torres and other pre-mier manufacturers stay on the shelves no longer than 2 weeks, keeping the supply always fresh and oh-so tempting. The brownies are worth trekking many blocks for. The espresso courtesy of illy is the perfect complement to the chocolate. 48 Eighth Ave. (between Horatio and Jane sts.). ✆ 212/366-1541. www.Chocolatebarnyc.com. Subway: A, C, E, L to 14th St.

Dean & Deluca   The quality here is superb: In addition to the excellent butcher, fish, cheese, and dessert counters (check out the cakes and the great character cookies) and beautiful fruits and veggies, you'll find a dried-fruit-and-nut bar, a huge coffee-bean selection, a gorgeous cut-flower selection, lots of imported waters and beers, and a limited but quality selection of kitchenware. A small cafe makes a great stop for a cappuccino break. 560 Broadway (at Prince St.). ℂ 212/226-6800. www.dean-deluca.com. Subway: N, R to Prince St.

Dylan's Candy Bar *(Finds)*   The brainchild of Dylan Lauren (Ralph's little girl) and Jeff Schwartz, this beautifully designed 5,500-square-foot shop is nirvana for sweet tooths (sweet teeth?). Two levels boast an endless selection of goodies (they claim to carry more than 5,000 sweets from around the world), running the gamut from dime-store brands to private-label artistic confectionary gifts. This place is a blast—like *Willy Wonka and the Chocolate Factory* come to life. 1011 Third Ave. (at 60th St.). ℂ 646/735-0078. www.dylanscandybar.com. Subway: 4, 5, 6 to 59th St.; E, V to Lexington Ave.

Fairway Market *(Value)*   This unpretentious gourmet-food megamarket is an excellent place to put together a sophisticated picnic for nearby Central Park or an eat-in meal. The fruits and vegetables are glorious, and prices are better than you'll find at similar-quality markets. An excellent section of prepared and prepackaged foods, too—perfect for preparing in your in-room kitchenette. 2127 Broadway (at 74th St.). ℂ 212/595-1888. Subway: 1, 2, 3, 9 to 72nd St.

Gourmet Garage *(Value)*   This SoHo store features a neighborhood-appropriate loftlike setting and some of the tastiest gourmet products in town. The Garage supplies many of the city's best restaurants, and sells to the public at wholesale, about 40% off the retail of fancier stores. This location also boasts a good selection of premade sandwiches and prepared foods. The Upper West Side store features an extensive department of kosher foods. 453 Broome St. (at Mercer St.). ℂ 212/941-5850. Subway: N, R, Q, W, 6 to Canal St. Also at 2567 Broadway (between 96th and 97th sts.; ℂ 212/663-0656; subway: 1, 2, 3, 9 to 96th St.).

Grand Central Market   Gloriously restored Grand Central Terminal now has its own small but terrific gourmet food hall at street level, accessible from 42nd Street, with such vendors as **Adriana's Caravan** for spices; **Ninth Avenue Cheese** for a gourmet selection; and the **Corrado Bread & Pastry.** 42nd St. at Park Ave. www.grandcentralterminal.com. Subway: S, 4, 5, 6, 7 to 42nd St./Grand Central.

Li-Lac Chocolates   Li-Lac is one of the few chocolatiers still making sweets by hand. In business since 1923, this Village shop whips up its chocolate and maple-walnut fudge fresh every day. They also make pralines, caramels, and hand-dipped chocolates, including sweets for the holidays (bunnies and chocolate eggs for Easter, chocolate Santas for Christmas, and so on). 120 Christopher St. (between Bleecker and Hudson sts.). ℂ 800/624-4784 or 212/242-7374. Subway: 1, 9 to Christopher St. Also at Grand Central Market (Grand Central Terminal; ℂ 212/370-4866; subway: 4, 5, 6, 7 to 42nd St./Grand Central).

Zabar's   Zabar's is an institution. This giant deli sells prepared foods, packaged goods from around the world, coffee beans, breads, and much more (no fresh veggies, though). This is the place for lox, and the rice pudding is the best I've tasted. You'll also find an excellent—and well-priced—collection of housewares and restaurant-quality cookware, plus a never-ending flow of Woody Allen stock characters who shop here daily. Prepare yourself for crowds. The attached cafe serves terrific sandwiches and takeout—ideal for a Central Park picnic. 2245 Broadway (at 80th St.). ℂ 212/787-2000. Subway: 1, 9 to 79th St.

ELECTRONICS

J&R Music World/Computer World This block-long Financial District emporium is the city's top discount computer, electronics, and office-equipment retailer. The sales staff is knowledgeable but can get pushy if you don't know exactly what you want. Don't succumb—take your time and find what you need. Or better yet, peruse the store's catalog or website. Park Row (at Ann St., opposite City Hall Park). (C) 800/426-6027 or 212/238-9000. www.jandr.com. Subway: 2, 3 to Park Place; 4, 5, 6 to Brooklyn Bridge/City Hall.

GIFTS & PAPER GOODS

If you're looking for a special gift for a creative spirit, check out the shops that line **East 9th Street** in the East Village; the side streets of **SoHo,** where a good number of unusual boutiques still survive; **Nolita;** and Greenwich Village, especially in the wonderful cadre of one-of-a-kind shops in the **West Village.** See "The Top Shopping Streets & Neighborhoods," earlier in this chapter.

Alphabets This playful shop has two halves: one for cards, toys, and Ts, the other for creative housewares, from dishware to freeform vases. It's all fun and affordable. 2284 Broadway (between 82nd and 83rd sts.). (C) 212/579-5702. Subway: 1, 9 to 86th St. Also at 115 Ave. A (at St. Marks Place; (C) 212/475-7250; subway: 6 to Astor Place; L to First Ave.); 47 Greenwich Ave. (between Perry and Charles sts.; (C) 212/229-2966; subway: 1, 9 to Christopher St.).

Card-O-Mat This big, bright shop stocks the city's most diverse collection of creative cards, notepads, address and date books, photo albums, stationery, and other paper goodies. You'll find styles here you won't see anywhere else thanks to a wide range of European imports. 2884 Broadway (between 112th and 113th sts.). (C) 212/663-2085. Subway: 1, 9 to 110th St./Cathedral Pkwy.

Daily 235 This quirky card and candy store for artsy grown-ups is a great place to pick up creative under-$10 gifts, from small-print books to Buddha-shaped candles. 235 Elizabeth St. (between Prince and Houston sts.). (C) 212/334-9728. Subway: N, R to Prince St.; 6 to Spring St.

Extraordinary* *Finds* This warm, friendly gallery–cum–gift shop is worth going out of your way to discover. Owner J.R. Sanders, an interior designer who has created exhibits at many museums, has assembled a collection of gifts from around the world. Lacquered crackle-eggshell trays from Vietnam, carved mango bowls from the Philippines, rosewood utensils camouflaged as tree branches from Africa, and much more—all eye candy for those who thrive on whimsy and good design. Best of all, prices are reasonable—you'd pay twice as much at any other gallery or boutique—and late hours (usually daily to 10:30pm) make it easy to visit. Truly extraordinary! 251 E. 57th St. (just west of Second Ave.). (C) 212/223-9151. Subway: 4, 5, 6 to 59th St.

H This tranquil shop is a favorite for unusual housewares and gifts. The wonderful collection runs the gamut from Slinky vases to Japanese rice-paper coasters to old French electronics illustrations, suitable for framing. 335 E. 9th St. (between First and Second aves.). (C) 212/477-2631. Subway: 6 to Spring St.

House of Cards and Curiosities *Finds* This jam-packed shop, the West Village's own funky take on an old-fashioned nickel-and-dime, is a joy to browse for kooky trinkets and cards. 23 Eighth Ave. (between 12th and Jane sts.). (C) 212/675-6178. Subway: A, C, E, L to 14th St.

JAM Paper (Value) For stylish stationery at low prices, JAM is the place to go. Most papers are color-block solids, but the spectrum covers the rainbow. You'll also find a large, creative selection of well-priced supplies for your home and office. 111 Third Ave. (between 13th and 14th sts.). © 212/473-6666. www.jampaper.com. Subway: L to Third Ave. Also at 611 Sixth Ave. (between 17th and 18th sts.; © 212/255-4593; subway: F to 14th St.).

Kate's Paperie I could browse for hours in this delightful shop's handmade stationery and wrap, innovative invitations and thank-yous, notebooks, writing tools, and other paper products, including lampshades. Lovely art cards, too—perfect for writing the folks back home. A joy! The SoHo location is best. 561 Broadway (between Prince and Spring sts.). © 888/941-9169 or 212/941-9816. www.katespaperie.com. Subway: N, R to Prince St. Also at 8 W. 13th St. (between Fifth and Sixth aves.; © 212/633-0570; subway: F to 14th St.); 1282 Third Ave. (between 73rd and 74th sts.; © 212/396-3670; subway: 6 to 77th St.). 140 West 57th St. (between 6th and 7th aves.; © 212/459-0700; subway: N, R, W to 57th St.).

Leekan Designs This high-ceilinged shop is packed with Asian, Oceanic, and Moroccan exotica, from beaded jewelry to folk art to tableware to textiles to floor mats. The collection is eye-popping, and prices are quite affordable. 93 Mercer St. (near Spring St.). © 212/226-7226. Subway: N, R to Prince St.

Mascot Studio (Finds) Stop into this rough-hewn custom frame shop for one-of-a-kind picture frames, most extremely affordably priced. The small shop also curates art and photography shows, so you might even find a worthwhile exhibit when you arrive. 328 E. 9th St. (between First and Second aves.). © 212/228-9090. Subway: 6 to Astor Place.

Mxyplyzyk (Value) Come to this unpronounceable Village shop for one of the city's most fun and creative collections of one-of-a-kind housewares, office ware, and gifts. Most everything is reasonably priced. 125 Greenwich Ave. (at 13th St., near Eighth Ave.). © 212/989-4300. Subway: A, C, E, to 14th St.

New York Firefighter's Friend (Finds) Purchase FDNY logo wear, including T-shirts, sweatshirts, hats, and more. The goods are all top-quality, and a portion of profits go in support of the widows and children of the 343 firefighters lost in the September 11, 2001, terrorist attacks. 263 Lafayette St. (between Prince and Spring sts.). © 212/226-3142. www.nyfirestore.com. Subway: 6 to Spring St.

New York 911 (Finds) Next to Firefighter's Friend (see above), you can shop for NYPD logo wear, and EMT, FBI, and NYC coroner gear. The goods include shirts, caps, patches, logo toys, and more. (Not all of the products are licensed by the city; I suggest trying to stick with those that are.) A portion of the proceeds goes to NYPD-related charities. 263 Lafayette St. (between Prince and Spring sts.). © 888/723-3907 or 212/219-3907. www.ny911.com. Subway: 6 to Spring St.

Old Japan Come to this small Village shop for vintage silk kimonos, Japanese dolls, Noguchi lamps, Mingei folk items, and other gifts from the Land of the Rising Sun, including scarves and handbags fashioned out of kimonos and buckwheat pillows covered in kimono cotton. Vintage kimonos run $300 to $1,500, but there's always a year-round sale rack with prices under $100, and small pieces are always affordable. 382 Bleecker St. (between Perry and Charles sts.). © 212/633-0922. www.oldjapaninc.com. Subway: 1, 9 to Christopher St.

Pearl River (Value) Even after moving from tight quarters on Canal Street to a more spacious location, this Chinese mall still overflows with affordable Asian exotica, from paper lanterns to Chinese snack foods to Mandarin-collared silk pajamas to mah-jongg sets to Hong Kong action videos. The new location features a waterfall and a cafe serving 40 different types of tea. This fascinating place can keep you occupied for hours. 477 Broadway (at Grand St.). © 212/431-4770.

www.pearlriver.com. Subway: N, R to Canal St. Also at 200 Grand St., between Mott and Mulberry sts. (✆ 212/966-1010; subway: B, D, Q to Grand St.).

Royale   The cutest card shop in the Village, and a good choice for oddball postcards to send back home. 177 W. 4th St. (between Sixth and Seventh aves.). ✆ 212/929-1029. Subway: A, C, E, F, V, S to W. 4th St.; 1, 9 to Christopher St.

HOME FASHIONS & HOUSEWARES

ABC Carpet & Home   This 10-floor emporium is the ultimate home-fashions and -furnishings store. The goods run the gamut from Moroccan mosaic-tile end tables to Tuscan pottery to Tiffanyish lamps to distressed bed frames made up with Frette linens to much more, all carefully chosen and exquisitely displayed. Prices aren't bad, but these are high-end goods. Some of the smaller items are affordable, and the sales yield substantial discounts. Across the street is the multifloor carpet store, which boasts a remarkable collection of area rugs. 881 and 888 Broadway (at 19th St.). ✆ 212/473-3000. www.abccarpet.com. Subway: 4, 5, 6, L, N, R, Q, W to 14th St./Union Sq.

Amalgamated Home   Looking for brushed-metal switch plates for your groovy new stainless-steel kitchen? How about a purple velvet love seat straight out of a Looney Tunes cartoon? Or the hippest rice bowls in town? You'll find it all and more at this pair of home shops, which stocks eye-catching household goods you won't see anywhere else. 19 Christopher St. (between Sixth and Seventh aves.). ✆ 212/255-4160 (furniture and lighting), or 212/691-8695 (hardware and household sundries). Subway: 1, 9 to Christopher St.

Broadway Panhandler   If you're looking for restaurant-quality cookware and kitchen tools, this is the place. It has the best combination of selection, prices, and service in town. Don't just take it from me—*New York* magazine gave Broadway Panhandler the "Best Pots and Pans" nod in 2000. 477 Broome St. (between Greene and Wooster sts.). ✆ 212/966-3434. Subway: C, E to Spring St.

Details   These fun-and-funky home stores are the place to outfit the coolest pad in town with Day-Glo bath accessories, cool-print shower curtains, glassware, and the like. Everything's cute and affordable! 347 Bleecker St. (at W. 10th St.). ✆ 212/414-0039. Subway: 1, 9 to Christopher St./Sheridan Sq. Also at 142 Eighth Ave. (at 17th St.; ✆ 212/366-9498; subway: A, C, E to 14th St.); 188 Columbus Ave. (at 68th St.; ✆ 212/362-7344; subway: 1, 9 to 66th St.).

Fishs Eddy *(Value)*   What a great idea—selling remainders of kitschy, custom-designed china. Ever wanted a dish that *really* says "Blue Plate Special"? How about a coffee mug with the terse logo "Cup o' Joe to Go"? The store is Browse Heaven, and prices are low enough. Other items include vintage and retro-inspired flatware, bowls, and restaurant-supply glassware that can be hard to find, like soda fountain and pint glasses. 889 Broadway (at 19th St.). ✆ 212/420-9020. www.fishseddy.com. Subway: 4, 5, 6, L, N, R, Q, W to 14th St./Union Sq. Also at 2176 Broadway (at 77th St.; ✆ 212/873-8819; subway: 1, 9 to 79th St.).

kar'ikter *(Finds)*   New York's biggest collection of sleek and playful Alessi housewares from Italy (including Michael Graves's iconic teakettle with bird whistle), as well as European animation cells and toys starring Tintin, Babar, and Asterix. 19 Prince St. (between Elizabeth and Mott sts.). ✆ 212/274-1966. www.karikter.com. Subway: 6 to Spring St.

Leader Restaurant Equipment & Supplies *(Value)*   The Bowery is the place to find restaurant-supply-quality kitchenware, and Leader is the best dealer on the block. This big, bustling shop is a good source for Chinese and Japanese wares—chopsticks, rice and noodle bowls, sushi plates, sake cups, and the like. You'll see a lot of the same styles you'd find at the high-end stores in SoHo or the Village, but at a fraction of the prices. 191 Bowery (between Spring and Delancey sts.). ℭ **800/666-6888** or 212/677-1982. Subway: 6 to Spring St.

Lighting by Gregory *(Value)*   The stretch of the Bowery (Third Ave.) from Houston to Canal streets is considered the "light-fixture district" for its huge selections and great bargains on light fixtures, lamps, and ceiling fans. Gregory's multishowroom shop is by far the best of the bunch, with a first-rate selection of all the name brands (including ultraquiet Casablanca ceiling fans) and terrific prices. 158 Bowery (between Delancey and Broome sts.). ℭ **888/811-FANS** or 212/226-1276. www.lightingbygregory.com. Subway: J, M to Bowery.

LEATHER, HANDBAGS & LUGGAGE

Grace Bags *(Value)*   So you've always wanted a Prada, Gucci, kate spade, or Tod's bag, but your budget's just not up to shelling out the big bucks? Then come to this bargain hunter's delight of a discount shop, where good-quality *faux* versions of the designer styles sell for just $10 to $45. 190 Orchard St. (between Houston and Stanton sts.). ℭ **212/228-6118**. Subway: F to Second Ave.

Greenwood   This Village shop sells top-quality leather handbags, backpacks, luggage, and wallets from famous names like Frye and Latico at reasonable prices. The selection is excellent, and service is professional. 263 Bleecker St. (between Sixth and Seventh aves.). ℭ **212/366-0825**. Subway: 1, 9 to Houston St.

Jobson's *(Value)*   In business since 1949, Jobson's is a great discount source for name-brand luggage and leather goods. Rather than simply offer a cut off the retail price, management marks most items at 10% above cost, which usually amounts to a whopping 40% to 60% break for the buyer. The shop also does a huge airline and professional flyers business, and they'll be happy to tell you what the pros buy. Negotiators sometimes prevail. 666 Lexington Ave. (between 55th and 56th sts.). ℭ **212/355-6846**. Subway: 6 to 51st St.

Jutta Neumann *(Finds)*   If you stop into this shop, you're likely to find the artist herself behind the counter, cutting and stitching her bold-hued leather goods— bags, wallets, boots, and more. Her new mules and strappy sandals have made a big splash. 158 Allen St. (between Stanton and Rivington sts.). ℭ **212/982-7048**. www. juttaneumann-newyork.com. Subway: F to Delancey/Essex sts.

Manhattan Portage Ltd. Store   Come here for the hippest nylon and canvas carryalls in town. Manhattan Portage manufactures its bags in the city, and they're made from hard-wearing materials that can stand up to an urban lifestyle. Popular styles include messenger bags, DJ bags, and backpacks (in standard and one-shoulder styles) in a range of colors from bright yellow to camouflage. Manhattan Portage bags are also sold through other outlets, but you'll find the most complete selection here. 333 E. 9th St. (between First and Second aves.). ℭ **212/995-5490**. www.manhattanportageltd.com. Subway: 6 to Astor Place.

Original Leather   If you're in the market for a leather jacket, pants, or skirt, this is the best of the Village's discount leather shops in terms of quality and price. You'll get good value for your dollar here, and the salespeople aren't *too* hard-sell (comparatively speaking, that is). 173 W. 4th St. (between Sixth and Seventh aves.). ℭ **212/ 675-2303**. Subway: A, C, E, F, V, S to W. 4th St. Also at 176 Spring St. (between Thompson and W. Broadway; ℭ **212/219-8210**; subway: C, E to Spring St.); 552 LaGuardia Place (between Bleecker and 3rd St.; ℭ **212/777-4362**; subway: A, C, E, F, V, S to W. 4th St.); 256 Columbus Ave. (at 72nd

St.; ℂ 212/595-7051; subway: B, C to 72nd St.); 1100 Madison Ave. (between 82nd and 83rd sts.; ℂ 212/585-4200; subway: 4, 5, 6 to 86th St.).

Tip: Compare prices and styles to **Janet Woo,** down the block from the West Village location at 189 W. 4th St. (ℂ **646/638-3035**), another reasonable outlet.

Village Tannery   The cream of the Greenwich Village leather crop, with gorgeous and well-priced handbags, backpacks, wallets, and organizers. 173 Bleecker St. (between MacDougal and Sullivan sts.). ℂ 212/673-5444. Subway: 1, 9 to Houston St. Also at 742 Broadway (between Astor Place and Waverly St.; ℂ 212/979-0013; subway: 6 to Astor Place).

LOGO STORES

Mets Clubhouse Shop   New York's other favorite baseball team has its own logo store in Midtown. Stop in for goods galore—baseball caps, T-shirts, posters, Piazza jerseys, '69 Miracle Mets memorabilia, and much more. You can buy regular-season game tix here, too. 143 E. 54th St. (between Lexington and Third aves.). ℂ 212/888-7508. www.mets.com. Subway: E, V to Lexington Ave.

The MTV Store   This petite boutique sits street-side, just below the MTV studio. There's not much here—but your kids will surely find something they want, whether it's a *Jackass* bumper sticker, an *Osbournes* T-shirt, or one of any number of *TRL* souvenirs. Flyers are sometimes on hand at the register, advertising for audience members for MTV shows. 1515 Broadway (at 44th St.). ℂ 212/846-5655. Subway: 1, 2, 3, 7, 9, N, R, S, Q, W to 42nd St./Times Sq.

NBA Store   For all things NBA and WNBA, go to this three-level store, a multimedia celebration of pro hoops, complete with bleachers for player appearances and signings. 666 Fifth Ave. (at 52nd St.). ℂ 212/515-NBA1. www.nbastore.com. Subway: B, D, F, V to 47th–50th sts./Rockefeller Center.

NBC Experience   This mammoth, neon-lit store sits across from the *Today* show studio and sells all manner of NBC-themed merchandise. Your kids will enjoy the interactive features, like the virtual reality "Conan O'Brien's Wild Desk Ride" or "Al Roker's Weather Challenge," which lets you do the forecast alongside the meteorologist, as well as the candy shop. 30 Rockefeller Plaza (at 49th St.). ℂ 212/664-3700. www.nbcsuperstore.com. Subway: B, D, F, V to 47th–50th sts./Rockefeller Center.

The Pop Shop *Finds*   For affordable and wearable art that makes supercool souvenirs, come here. This groovy store is full of items based on designs by artist Keith Haring, who died in 1990. T-shirts, posters, calendars, stationery, toys, notebooks, and transparent backpacks—all sport the vivid colors and loopy stick-figure drawings Haring made famous. Best of all, the Pop Shop is a nonprofit, offering continued support to the AIDS-related and children's charities that the young artist championed in life. 292 Lafayette St. (between Houston and Prince sts.). ℂ 212/219-2784. www.haring.com. Subway: F, V to Broadway/Lafayette St.

Yankees Clubhouse Shop   For all your Bronx Bombers needs—hats, jerseys, jackets, and so on. Tickets for regular-season home games are also for sale, and there's a limited selection of other New York team jerseys. 245 W. 42nd St. (between Seventh and Eighth aves.). ℂ 212/768-9555. www.yankees.com. Subway: A, C, E to 42nd St. Also at 393 Fifth Ave. (between 36th and 37th sts.; ℂ 212/685-4693; subway: 6 to 33rd St.); 110 E. 59th St. (between Park and Lexington aves.; ℂ 212/758-7844; subway: 4, 5, 6 to 59th St.); 8 Fulton St., in the South Street Seaport (ℂ 212/514-7182; subway: 2, 3, 4, 5 to Fulton St.).

MUSEUM STORES

In addition to these, check out the excellent shops at the **New York Public Library,** the **Museum for African Art,** the **Jewish Museum,** the **American**

Folk Art Museum, the **American Museum of the Moving Image,** and the **Isamu Noguchi Museum;** see chapter 7.

Maxilla & Mandible *Finds*   This shop is not affiliated with the Museum of Natural History, but a visit here makes a good adjunct to a trip there (it's right around the corner). It's a fascinating natural-history emporium. Inside, you'll find rocks and shells from around the world, luminescent butterflies in display boxes, even real fossils containing prehistoric fish and insects that come with details on their history. There's also a variety of natural history–themed toys for kids. 451 Columbus Ave. (between 81st and 82nd sts.). ✆ 212/724-6173. www.maxillaandmandible.com. Subway: B, C to 81st St.

Metropolitan Museum of Art Store   Given the scope of the museum, it's no wonder the gift shop is outstanding. Many treasures from the museum's collection have been reproduced as jewelry, china, and other objets d'art. The range of books is dizzying, and there's a comprehensive selection of posters and children's toys. 1000 Fifth Ave. (at 82nd St.). ✆ 212/570-3894. www.metmuseum.org. Subway: 4, 5, 6 to 86th St. Also at Rockefeller Center, 15 W. 49th St. ((✆ 212/332-1360; subway: B, D, F, Q to 47th–50th sts./Rockefeller Center); 113 Prince St. (at Greene St.; ✆ 212/614-3000; subway: N, R to Prince St.); on the mezzanine level at Macy's, 34th St. and Sixth Ave. ((✆ 212/268-7266; subway: B, D, F, N, R, Q, V, W to 34th St./Herald Sq.).

MoMA Design Store   Across the street from the Museum of Modern Art in Midtown is this shop, whose stock ranges from posters and clever toys to reproductions of many of the classics of modern design, including free-form Alvar Aalto vases and Frank Lloyd Wright chairs. If these high-design items are out of your reach, don't worry: There are plenty of affordable outré home accessories from which to choose. The new SoHo store is equally fabulous. *Note:* The design store will remain open while the museum is closed for renovation. 44 W. 53rd St. (between Fifth and Sixth aves.). ✆ 212/767-1050. www.moma.org. Subway: E, F to Fifth Ave.; B, D, F, V to 47th–50th sts./Rockefeller Center. Also at 81 Spring St. (at Crosby St.; ✆ 646/613-1367; subway: 6 to Spring St.).

Museum of Arts and Design   The nation's top showcase for contemporary crafts boasts an impressive collection of crafts in its museum store, too. Come for exquisite handblown glassware, one-of-a-kind jewelry, original pottery, and other artistic treasures, all beautifully displayed. 40 W. 53rd St. (between Fifth and Sixth aves.). ✆ 212/956-3535. www.americancraftmuseum.org. Subway: E, F to Fifth Ave.

New York Transit Museum Store   Lots of transportation-themed gifts; the cufflinks made out of subway tokens are great! Grand Central Terminal (on the main level, in the passage next to Station Masters' office), 42nd St. and Lexington Ave. ✆ 212/ 878-0106. Subway: 4, 5, 6, 7, S to 42nd St./Grand Central.

MUSIC & VIDEO

Music buffs will find a wealth of new-and-used shops (both CDs and vinyl) in the West Village. Standouts include **Rebel Rebel,** 319 Bleecker St. (✆ 212/ 989-0770), for imports and New Wave and glam classics; **Rockit Scientist,** off Bleecker at 43 Carmine St. (✆ 212/242-0066), a tiny place with a huge folk and psych collection; and **Sonic Groove,** 41 Carmine St. (✆ 212/675-5284; www.sonicgroove.com), which supplies the sounds for many city DJs. **Bleecker Bob's Golden Oldies,** 118 W. 3rd St. (✆ 212/475-9677), has outlived its legend; it's just a hole-in-the-wall with worn, badly organized vinyl.

   St. Marks Place between Third and Second avenues in the East Village is another great bet, especially for used music at low prices. **Joe's CDs,** at 11 St.

Marks (© 212/673-4606), is a standout, as is **Sounds,** at no. 20 (© 212/677-3444), the dirt-cheap granddaddy of the St. Marks shops, and **Norman's Sound & Vision,** around the corner at 67 Cooper Square (© 212/473-6610).

In the Financial District, **J&R Music World** has a big selection of new music, and brand-new releases are almost always on sale; see "Electronics," earlier in this chapter.

Academy Records & CDs   This Flatiron District shop is always filled with classical, opera, and jazz junkies perusing the extensive, well-priced collection of used CDs and vinyl. There's also a variety of other music, from rare '60s pop songsters to spoken word. 12 W. 18th St. (between Fifth and Sixth aves.). © **212/242-3000.** www.academy-records.com. Subway: 4, 5, 6, L, N, R, Q, W to 14th St./Union Sq.

Bleecker St. Records   This sizable, well-lit space is great for one-stop shopping. The clean, well-organized CD and LP collections run the gamut from rock, oldies, jazz, folk, and blues to Oi! punk. You'll find lots of imports, collectibles, and out-of-print records (including singles), a terrific collection of used CDs, and a mix of casual listeners and serious collectors cruising the bins. 239 Bleecker St. (near Carmine St., just west of Sixth Ave.). © **212/255-7899.** Subway: A, C, E, F, V to W. 4th St.

Footlight *(Finds*   A dreamy collection of vintage vinyl—strong in jazz and pop vocalists, soundtracks, and show tunes—for the serious collector. 113 E. 12th St. (between Third and Fourth aves.). © **212/533-1572.** www.footlight.com. Subway: 4, 5, 6, L, N, R, Q, W to 14th St./Union Sq.

Generation Records *(Value*   This store sells mostly CDs and is an excellent source for "import" (ahem!) live recordings. Originally specializing in hardcore, punk, and metal, the collection upstairs still has a heavy edge but has diversified. Downstairs is a well-organized and priced used-CD selection that's not as picked-over as most; there's also a good selection of LPs. 210 Thompson St. (between Bleecker and 3rd sts.). © **212/254-1100.** Subway: A, C, E, F, V to W. 4th St.

Jazz Record Center   *The* place to find rare and out-of-print jazz records. In addition to the extensive selection of CDs and vinyl (including 78s), videos, books, posters, magazines, photos, and other memorabilia are available. Prices start at $5 for vinyl, $10 for CDs, and soar from there, befitting the rarity of the stock. Owner Frederick Cohen is extremely knowledgeable, so come here if you're trying to track down something obscure. 236 W. 26th St. (between Seventh and Eighth aves.), 8th floor. © **212/675-4480.** www.jazzrecordcenter.com. Subway: 1, 9 to 28th St.

Kim's Video & Audio   This funky minichain is New York's underground alternative to Blockbuster Video, but they also stock a decent selection of indie vinyl and CDs as well as books and 'zines at Mondo Kim's, Kim's West, and Kim's Mediapolis. Kim's Video at 144 Bleecker St. (between Thompson St. and LaGuardia Place). © **212/260-1010.** Subway: A, C, E, F, V, S to W. 4th St. Also Kim's West at 350 Bleecker St. (at W. 10th St.; © **212/675-8996;** subway: 1, 9 to Christopher St.); Mondo Kim's at 6 St. Marks Place (between Second and Third aves.; © **212/598-9985;** subway: 6 to Astor Place); Kim's Mediapolis at 2906 Broadway (at 113th St.; © **212/864-5321;** subway: 1, 9 to 110th St.).

NYCD *(Value*   This neat, narrow little store is home to one of the city's best collections of used rock CDs thanks to its off-the-beaten-track Upper West Side location. Downtown trollers simply don't make it this far uptown to prune the selection, so it's easy to find lots of top titles among the pickings. 426 Amsterdam Ave. (between 80th and 81st sts.). © **212/724-4466.** Subway: 1, 9 to 79th St.

Other Music *(Finds*   Head to Other Music for the wildest sounds in town. You won't find a major label here. They focus on small, international labels. The bizarro runs the gamut from Japanese spin doctors to Irish folk; needless to say, the world-music selection is terrific. Fascinating and bound to be filled with music you've never heard. The staff knows their stuff, so ask away. 15 E. 4th St. (between Broadway and Lafayette St.). ℭ 212/477-8150. www.othermusic.com. Subway: F, V to Broadway/Lafayette St.; 6 to Astor Place.

Throb   A popular stop for dance-club DJs, this CD/vinyl shop specializes in electronic genres: house, ambient, jungle, drum-and-bass, loungecore, trance, and trip hop. Imports are big business here. You'll also find record bags and T-shirts. 211 E. 14th (between Second and Third aves.). ℭ 212/533-2328. www.throb.com. Subway: L to Third Ave.

Tower Records   Both locations of the chain are superstores brimming with a huge collection of music—classical, jazz, rock, world, you name it. The Village location has a good selection of indie and alternative labels. Just behind it at West 4th and Lafayette is **Tower Books and Video** (ℭ 212/228-5100), where you'll find videos, books, and magazines (although the video selection isn't as good as you might expect). Look for in-stores by big names. 692 Broadway (at W. 4th St.). ℭ 212/505-1500. www.towerrecords.com. Subway: N, R to 8th St.; 6 to Astor Place. Also at 1961 Broadway (at 66th St.); ℭ 212/799-2500; subway: 1, 9 to 66th St.).

Virgin Megastore   In the heart of Times Square, this superstore bustles day and night. For the size of it, the selection isn't as wide as you'd think; still, you're likely to find what you're looking for among the two levels of domestic and imported CDs and cassettes. Other plusses are an extensive singles department, a phenomenal number of listening posts, plus a huge video department. There's also a bookstore, a cafe, and a movie theater, and you can even arrange airfare on Virgin Atlantic. Look for a busy schedule of in-stores at both locations. 1540 Broadway (at 45th St.). ℭ 212/921-1020. www.virginmegamagazine.com. Subway: N, R, 1, 2, 3, 7, 9 to Times Sq./42nd St. Also at 52 E. 14th St. (at Broadway; ℭ 212/598-4666; subway: 4, 5, 6, N, R, L, Q, W to 14th St./Union Sq.).

SHOES

Designer shoe shops are on **East 57th Street** and up **Madison Avenue,** becoming pricier as you move uptown. **SoHo** is an excellent place to search; the streets are overrun with shoe stores, with **Broadway** below Houston between Spring and Canal streets the place to look for discount prices. Cheaper copies of the trendiest styles are sold in the shops along **8th Street** between Broadway and Sixth Avenue in the Village, which some people call Shoe Row. Most department stores have two sizable shoe departments—one for designer stuff and one for daily wearables—and sales can be terrific. The women's shoe department at **Loehmann's** (p. 277) is well stocked and unbelievably priced.

Harry's Shoes   This large, always-bustling store focuses on selling first-class brands for men, women, and children—from Aerosoles to Timberland—at the lowest retail prices. Expect such brands as Clarks, Sebago, Ecco, Havana Joe, Rockport, and many, many more. You might do well to price-compare with Tip Top (see below), which sells many of the same brands. 2299 Broadway (at 83rd St.). ℭ 866/4-HARRYS. www.harrys-shoes.com. Subway: 1, 2, 3, 9 to 86th St.

Sacco   Mostly Italian-made women's shoes that cross style with supreme comfort. I especially love the fall and winter boots, which are comfortable enough to carry me around the city on even the most arduous of research days. Lots of terrific basic

Value $50 Fabulous: Chinatown's Secret Treasure Trove

You've come to the Big Apple ready to shop. But there's one thing holding you back: sticker shock. Unfortunately, that old adage—if you have to ask, you can't afford it—holds true in many Manhattan shopping 'hoods.

But no self-respecting fashionista would let a detail like a shoestring budget get in her way. You *can* come home with fab fashions and funky housewares, and boasting about that full-body massage—all for less than $50. Head for Chinatown, the mecca for intrepid bargain shoppers.

There's the Rub   Sure, SoHo's Bliss Spa is nice, but Chinatown can't be beat for the best deals on massages. Try **New Land Chinese Reflexology Center**, 234–238 Canal St., between Centre and Baxter streets (© **212/ 966-0306**; subway: J, M, Z to Canal St.), where prices range from $7 for 10 minutes to $42 for a full-hour massage. Reflexology treatments will set you back $28 for 40 minutes. It's open day and night, so you almost never have a wait!

Knock It Off   On the streets of New York, you'll see tables of the newest and finest designer bags that are somewhat less than genuine. Most are convincing imitations, and they function much like the real thing.

Lots of wallet-friendly knockoffs can be found in Chinatown, particularly along Canal Street between Lafayette and Mott streets (subway: J, M, Z to Canal St.), where small shops—usually no more than glorified stalls—offer a dazzling array of Vuitton-like, Prada-ish, and almost-Chanel bags, wallets, shoes, shirts, scarves, watches, and perfume. Why not pick up a not-exactly-Burberry hat for a 10-spot, and tote the savings in the not-quite kate spade purse you got for $15?

Cooking with Fusion   Nothing says fabulous like a cupboard full of exotic foodstuffs. Tucked in between the seafood and meat sellers, Asia **Market Corporation,** 71½ Mulberry St., just below Canal Street (© **212/ 962-2028**; subway: J, M, Z to Canal St.), is no more promising from the outside than an old deli—but appearances can be deceiving. This grocery boasts a dizzying selection of goodies—many of the same brands found in the city's pricey food emporiums. Most of the stock is dedicated to Asian cooking—but these are some of the best prices on wasabi, nori, and exotic spices and rices that you will see.

Got Zen?   The corner of Baxter and Walker streets, just below Canal Street, is home to a variety of sellers hawking housewares, jade, and plants. Stop in **Peony Flowery Bonsai Fountain** at 106 Walker St., between Lafayette and Centre streets (© **212/334-1807**; subway: N, Q, R, W to Canal St.), where lovely bonsai trees start at $16. Then relax at **Dragon Land Bakery,** 125 Walker St., just below Canal Street (© **212/ 219-2012**; subway: N, Q, R, W to Canal St.), Chinatown's answer to Fauchon, where sweets, pastel puddings flavored with mango or green tea, and crisp cookies are available for between 75¢ and $1.75.

—Maureen Johnson

blacks and browns. Good prices and sales, too. 94 Seventh Ave. (between 15th and 16th sts.). ℂ 212/675-5180. www.saccoshoes.com. Subway: 1, 9 to 18th St. Also at 14 E. 17th St. (between Fifth Ave. and Broadway; ℂ 212/243-2070; subway: 4, 5, 6, N, R, L, S, Q, W to 14th St./Union Sq.); 111 Thompson St. (between Prince and Spring sts.; ℂ 212/925-8010; subway: C, E to Spring St.); 324 Columbus Ave. (between 75th and 76th sts.; ℂ 212/799-5229; subway: B, C to 81st St.); 2355 Broadway (at 86th St.; ℂ 212/874-8362; subway: 1, 9 to 86th St.).

Shoe Mania *Value*   Another terrific discount shoe store for men and women; here, the emphasis is on style and comfort, with brands like Kenneth Cole, Dr. Martens, and Steve Madden dispersed among the Birkenstocks, Mephistos, and Joseph Siebels (great European comfort shoes). 853 Broadway (at 14th St.). ℂ 212/245-5260. Subway: 4, 5, 6, N, R, L, S, Q, W to 14th St./Union Sq. Also at 331 Madison Ave. (between 42nd and 43rd sts.; ℂ 212/557-6627; subway: 4, 5, 6, 7, S to 42nd St./Grand Central).

Stapleton Shoe Company *Value*   If Imelda Marcos had been a man, her first stop would have been this shoe store, next to the American Stock Exchange. Stapleton sells men's brands like Bally, Timberland, and Johnston & Murphy, all at discounts so deep it'll feel like insider trading. 68 Trinity Place (at Rector St.). ℂ 212/964-6329. Subway: N, R to Rector St.

Tip Top Shoes   If you find yourself discovering that the shoes you thought were so comfortable just aren't cutting it—trust me, it happens a lot—head over to Tip Top, New York's premier walking-shoe shop (since 1940). You'll find all of the top brands here for men and women, including Rockport, Mephisto, Dansko, Ecco, and hip Campers, plus tennies from New Balance and Puma. 155 W. 72nd St. (between Broadway and Columbus Ave.). ℂ 800/WALKING or 212/787-4960. www.tiptopshoes.com. Subway: 1, 2, 3, 9 to 72nd St.

TOYS

The Enchanted Forest *Finds*   Here's a shop for kids and grown-ups alike. It overflows with stuffed animals and puppets, plus the kinds of simple but absorbing games that parents remember from the days before PlayStation, like Pick-up Sticks and Chinese Checkers. There's also a book nook specializing in reissued classics like *The Phantom Tollbooth*. It's truly a special place. 85 Mercer St. (between Spring and Broome sts.). ℂ 212/925-6677. www.sohotoys.com. Subway: N, R to Prince St.

FAO Schwarz   The best-loved toy store in America was designed with an eye for fun: The elevator is shaped like a huge toy soldier, and there are plenty of hands-on displays to keep the little ones occupied. Entire areas are devoted to specific toy makers (Lego, Fisher Price, *Star Wars* action figures, Barbie). You and the kids will find plenty of affordable gifts to take home. 767 Fifth Ave. (at 58th St.). ℂ 212/644-9400. www.fao.com. Subway: N, R to Fifth Ave.

Toys"R"Us   Geoffrey the Giraffe must be mighty pleased with his home occupying almost an entire city block in Times Square, which boasts its own Ferris wheel that kids can ride for free. The huge collection is well organized and the store's "ambassadors" are abundant and helpful; they'll even point you to restaurants and kid-friendly attractions in the neighborhood. A must if you're traveling with kids! 1514 Broadway (at 44th St.). ℂ 800/869-7787. Subway: 1, 2, 3, 7, 9 to 42nd St. Also at 24–30 Union Sq. (ℂ 212/674-8697; subway: 4, 5, 6, N, R, L, S, Q, W to 14th St./Union Sq.).

9

New York City After Dark

There's so much to see and do in New York at night that your biggest problem is going to be choosing among the many temptations.

There's no way that I can tell you what's going to be on while you're in town. For the latest, most comprehensive listings, from theater and performing arts to live rock, jazz, and dance-club coverage, *Time Out New York* (www.timeoutny.com) is my favorite source; a new issue hits newsstands every Thursday. The free weekly *Village Voice* (www.villagevoice.com) is available late Tuesday downtown and early Wednesday in the rest of the city. The arts and entertainment coverage is extensive. The *New York Times* (www.nytoday.com) features terrific entertainment coverage, particularly in the Friday "Weekend" section; the cabaret, classical-music, and theater guides are particularly useful. Other weekly sources are "Goings on About Town" in the *New Yorker* (www.newyorker.com); and *New York* magazine (www.newyorkmag.com),

whose "Cue" features the latest happenings. *New York's* www.nymetro.com site is an excellent Web source.

Bar-hoppers shouldn't pass up the comprehensive annual *Shecky's New York Bar, Club & Lounge Guide.* Its website (http://newyork.sheckys.com) is even more current, and all the information is free. **Shecky's Bar Phone** at ℂ 212/777-BARS offers up-to-the minute nightlife news for the cost of a phone call.

NYC/Onstage (ℂ 212/768-1818; www.tdf.org) is a recorded service providing schedules, descriptions, and details on theater and the performing arts. The bias is toward plays, but NYC/Onstage is a good source for music (including performances at Lincoln Center), dance, opera, cabaret, and family entertainment.

CultureFinder (www.culturefinder.com) is an excellent site for Big Apple arts and entertainment, with an emphasis on museums, theater, and classical music.

1 The Theater Scene

Nobody does theater better than New York. No other city—not even London—has a scene with so much breadth and depth, with so many alternatives. Broadway gets the most ink and airplay: This is where you'll find the big stage productions, from crowd-pleasers like *Phantom of the Opera* and *42nd Street* to newer phenomena like *Hairspray* and *The Producers.* But today's scene thrives beyond the bounds of Broadway. With bankable stars on stage, crowds lining up for tickets, and hits popular enough to generate major-label cast albums, Off-Broadway isn't just for culture vultures anymore.

Despite this vitality, plays and musicals close all the time, often with little warning. Before you arrive, or even once you get here, check the **publications** and **websites** at the beginning of this chapter to get an idea of what you might

---

Kids Kids Take the Stage: Family-Friendly Theater

The family-friendly theater scene is flourishing. There's so much going on that it's best to check *New York* magazine, *Time Out New York,* or the Friday *New York Times* for current listings. Besides Broadway shows, the following are some dependable—and cheaper—entertainment options.

The **New Victory Theater,** 209 W. 42nd St., between Seventh and Eighth avenues ((C) **646/223-4020;** www.newvictory.org), is the city's first full-time family-oriented performing-arts center and has hosted companies ranging from the Trinity Irish Dance Company to the Flaming Idiots, who juggle everything from fire and swords to bean-bag chairs.

The **Paper Bag Players** ((C) **212/663-0390;** www.paperbagplayers.org), called "the best children's theater in the country" by *Newsweek,* perform funny tales for children 4 to 9 in a set made from bags and boxes, in winter only, at Hunter College's Sylvia and Danny Kaye Playhouse, 68th Street between Park and Lexington avenues ((C) **212/772-4448**). You can also call to inquire whether they'll be staging other performances about town.

TADA! Youth Theater, 120 W. 28th St., between Sixth and Seventh avenues ((C) **212/627-1732;** www.tadatheater.com), is a youth ensemble that performs musicals and plays for kids, teens, and their families.

The **Swedish Cottage Marionette Theatre** ((C) **212/988-9093;** www.centralpark.org) puts on marionette shows for kids at its 19th-century Central Park theater throughout the year. Reservations are a must.

The World Voices Club at the **New Perspectives Theatre,** 750 Eighth Ave., between 46th and 47th streets ((C) **212/730-2030;** www.newperspectivestheatre.org), presents a new puppet show each month based on fables from various world cultures.

While David Mamet hardly seems like a playwright for the kiddies, the "Atlantic for Kids" series is at the **Atlantic Theater Company,** 453 16th St., between Ninth and Tenth avenues ((C) **212/691-5919;** www.atlantictheater.org), which Mamet founded with actor William H. Macy. Two of

---

like to see. One useful source is the **Broadway Line** ((C) **888/BROADWAY** or 212/302-4111; www.broadway.org), where you can obtain details and descriptions on current Broadway shows, hear about special offers and discounts, and ultimately be transferred to TeleCharge or Ticketmaster to buy tickets. There's also **NYC/Onstage** ((C) **212/768-1818;** www.tdf.org), providing the same kind of service for Broadway and Off-Broadway productions. (Don't buy tickets, though, until you read "Top Ticket-Buying Tips," below.)

Many top stars are heading for the New York stage these days: In current and recent seasons you could have seen stars like Antonio Banderas, Kathleen Turner, Kevin Bacon, and Hugh Jackman onstage. But keep in mind that stars' runs are often short, and tickets sell out fast. If you hear that there's an actor you like on the New York stage, check with the box office to find out how long they'll be in the part, or if there are certain performances they don't do (like matinees), before you nail down your travel plans.

their hilariously offbeat productions made *Time Out New York*'s Best of 2000 list, and Mamet's version of *The Frog Prince* entertained crowds in winter 2002, so it's worth seeing what's on while you're in town.

Another excellent troupe that excels at children's theater is the **Vital Theatre Company,** 432 W. 42nd St., between Ninth and Tenth avenues (© 212/268-2040; www.vitaltheatre.org); it's well worth seeing what's on.

If you want to introduce your kids to live opera, check out the "Opera in Brief" program, which runs most Saturdays at 11:30am, at **Amato Opera** (p. 300). For kid-friendly classical music, see what's on at **Bargemusic** (p. 300), which presents chamber-music concerts for kids throughout their season. Look for Young People's Concerts and Kidzone Live!, in which kids get to interact with orchestra members prior to curtain time, at the **New York Philharmonic** (p. 301). Also check to see what's on at **Carnegie Hall** (p. 305), which offers family concerts for a bargain-basement ticket price of just $5, plus the CarnegieKids program, which introduces kids ages 3 to 6 to basic musical concepts through a 45-minute music-and-storytelling performance. Finally, don't forget "Jazz for Young People," Wynton Marsalis's stellar family concert series at **Jazz at Lincoln Center** (p. 305).

Money-saving tip: High 5 Tickets to the Arts (© 212/HI5-TKTS; www.high5tix.org) makes theater more accessible for kids 13 to 18. Teens can buy donated tickets for select theatrical performances for $5 each at weekend performances, or $5 for two (for the teen and a guest of any age) for Monday through Thursday shows. High 5 also offers discount museum passes at the wallet-friendly price of two for $5 (for the teen and a guest of any age). Check out the website for details on theater or museum tickets, which can usually be purchased with proof of age at any New York City Ticketmaster outlet or online. Also check the High 5 website for listings of free and nearly free events going on while you and your teen are in town.

THE BASICS

LOCATIONS Broadway, Off-Broadway, and Off-Off-Broadway refer to theater size, pay, and other arcane details, not location—or, these days, even star wattage. Most of the Broadway theaters are in Times Square, around the thoroughfare for which the scene is named, but not on it: You'll find them on the side streets mostly in the mid-40s between Sixth and Eighth avenues, running north as far as 53rd Street. There's even a Broadway theater outside Times Square: the Vivian Beaumont in Lincoln Center, at Broadway and 65th Street.

Off-Broadway, on the other hand, is not that exacting. With the popularization of off-the-beaten-track productions, the distinction between Off- and Off-Off-Broadway has become fuzzier. Off-Off-Broadway shows tend to be more avant-garde and experimental.

TIMETABLES Broadway shows tend to keep regular schedules. There are usually eight performances a week: evening shows Tuesday through Saturday,

Value How to Save on Theater Tickets

If you employ a little patience, flexibility, and know-how, there are ways to pay less than full price for your theater tickets—sometimes a lot less.

For Advance Planners Your best bet is to try before you go. You might be able to purchase **reduced-price theater tickets** over the phone (or in person at the box office) by joining one or more of the online theater clubs. Membership is free and can garner you discounts of up to 50% on select Broadway and Off-Broadway shows. The deals are available to registered club members at **Broadway.com** (www.broadway.com), **Playbill Online** (www.playbill.com or www.playbillclub.com), and **TheaterMania** (www.theatermania.com). You can sign up to be notified by e-mail as offers change. I like the **Playbill Club** ★ best; its discounts tend to be the most wide-ranging, often including the best Broadway and Off-Broadway shows. TheaterMania's **TM Insider** is the runner-up. Nothing prevents you from signing up with all of them and taking advantage of the best deals.

You can sign up with the **Hit Show Club** (© 212/581-4211; www.hit showclub.com), a free subscription club that offers its members discounts to Broadway and Off-Broadway shows. Once you sign up, you can find offers online or stop by their offices at 630 Ninth Ave. (between 44th and 45th sts., 8th floor; open Mon–Fri 9am–4pm) and pick up discount coupons for theater, dining, and attractions. I recommend calling the info line or checking the website before you leave. One advantage of the website is that it will let you "bid" on tickets for the Broadway and Off-Broadway shows in which you're interested. Maybe you can tell the folks back home how you scored *Phantom* tickets for just 20 bucks!

The Theatre Development Fund, which operates the TKTS same-day discount-ticket booth (see below), also runs the **TDF Voucher** program, which gives participants dirt-cheap access to a world of cutting-edge theater and performing arts that even most New Yorkers don't know about. Sign up for $28, and you'll get four vouchers that you can use at any number of events that will be on while you're in town: theater, ballet, light opera, dance, and more. That's $7 a ticket—cheaper than a movie! You can order your vouchers online at the TDF website (www.tdf.org; click on "TDF Programs," then "TDF Vouchers"), where you'll be able to review a list of current ongoing events that accept vouchers before you buy.

If You're Already Here The best deal on same-day tickets for Broadway and Off-Broadway shows is the **Times Square Theatre Centre,** better known as the **TKTS** booth run by the nonprofit Theatre Development Fund at Duffy Square, 47th Street and Broadway (open 3–8pm for evening performances, 10am–2pm for Wed and Sat matinees, from 11am on Sun for all performances). Tickets for that day's performances are usually offered at half-price, with a few reduced 25%, plus a $2.50 per ticket service charge. Boards outside the ticket windows list available shows; you're unlikely to find the biggest hits, but most other shows turn up. Only cash and traveler's checks are accepted (no credit cards). There's often a line, so show up early for the best availability and be prepared to wait—but the crowd is part of the fun. If you don't have a specific show in mind, you can walk up to the window later in the day and something is always available. Sometimes representatives from Off- and Off-Off-Broadway shows that aren't listed offer discount flyers to the people waiting in line.

Run by the same group and offering the same discounts is the **TKTS Downtown Theatre Centre,** at South Street Seaport (open Mon–Fri 11am–5:30pm, Sat 11am–3:30pm; subway: 2, 3, 4, 5, E, J, Z, M to Fulton St.; A, C to Broadway-Nassau). All the same policies apply. The advantages to coming down here are that the lines are generally shorter, and matinee tickets are available the day before, so you can plan ahead.

Visit **www.tdf.org** or call **NYC/Onstage** at ℰ **212/768-1818** and press "8" for the latest TKTS information.

Many shows, particularly long-running ones such as *Cabaret* and *Phantom of the Opera,* offer **twofers,** which allow you to purchase two tickets for the price of one for certain performances. You can find these coupons at many places in the city: hotel lobbies, in banks, in shops, even at restaurant cash registers. They'll definitely be found at the **Times Square Visitors Center,** 1560 Broadway, between 46th and 47th streets (ℰ **212/768-1560**). They're also available at the **NYCVB Visitor Information Center** at 810 Seventh Ave., between 52nd and 53rd streets (ℰ **212/484-1222**); and at the information window on the main concourse of **Grand Central Terminal,** East 42nd Street at Vanderbilt Avenue, near the ticket-purchase windows directly across from the information kiosk.

For Theater Fans Willing to Go the Extra Mile Broadway shows—even blockbusters—sometimes have a limited number of tickets set aside for **students and seniors,** and they might be available at the last minute. Make sure you have ID. Also, some Off-Broadway houses make "rush" seats available to students 30 minutes to an hour before curtain. On Broadway, *Rent* has offered all kinds of bargains to keep younger theatergoers coming. Call the box office of the show in which you're interested to inquire about their discount policies.

If you don't mind staying on your feet, you can save big bucks—and often gain access to sold-out shows—with **standing-room** tickets, offered by many (but not all) Broadway shows. A limited number are usually sold on the day of show, and cost between $10 and $20. Call the box office in advance and they can fill you in on their standing-room policy.

Some Off- and Off-Off Broadway shows, including such fetching performances as the Blue Man Group, will let you see the show for free if you're willing to be an **usher.** This requires some advance legwork and willingness to put in extra hours, but it can pay off for theater fans on shoestring budgets. Again, inquire with the theater directly.

There are so many options for getting cut-rate tickets that any visitor can fill up a week with cheap shows. But there's never any guarantee that last-minute tickets or discounts will be available to a specific show. If there's one you absolutely must see, splurge on full-price advance-purchase tickets.

plus matinees on Wednesday, Saturday, and Sunday. Evening shows are usually at 8pm, while matinees are usually at 2pm Wednesday and Saturday, and 3pm Sunday. But schedules can vary. Shows usually start on the dot; if you arrive late, you may have to wait until intermission to take your seat.

TICKET PRICES Ticket prices for Broadway shows vary dramatically. The high end for any given show is likely to be between $60 and $100, or higher. The cheapest end of the price range can be as low as $20 or as high as $50, depending on the theater. If you're buying tickets at the low end of a wide range, be aware that you may be buying obstructed-view seats. If all tickets are the same price or the range is small, you can pretty much count on all of the seats being pretty good. Otherwise, price is your barometer. Legroom can be tight in these old theaters, and you'll usually get more in the orchestra seats.

Off-Broadway and Off-Off-Broadway shows tend to be cheaper, with tickets often as low as $10 or $15. In fact, experimental theaters like the award-winning downtown multi-arts venue **HERE,** 145 Sixth Ave. (© 212/647-0202; www. here.org), offer performances at prices that range from free to $17. However, seats for the most established shows and those with star power can command prices as high as $50 or $60.

Don't let price be a deterrent to enjoying the theater. There are ways to pay less if you're willing to make the effort and be flexible, with a few choices at hand as to what you'd like to see. Read on.

TOP TICKET-BUYING TIPS

BEFORE YOU LEAVE HOME If you want to guarantee yourself a seat at a particular show by buying tickets in advance, it's almost impossible to get around paying full price. (The only exception is to register for one or more of the online theater clubs, which may offer advance-purchase discounts to members; see "How to Save on Theater Tickets," below.) Phone ahead or go online for tickets to the most successful or popular shows as far in advance as you can; with shows such as *The Producers* or star turns like 2003's *Gypsy,* with Bernadette Peters, it's never too early.

Buying tickets can be simple, if the show you want isn't sold out. Call such general numbers as **TeleCharge** (© 212/239-6200; www.telecharge.com), which handles most Broadway and Off-Broadway shows and some concerts; or **Ticketmaster** (© 212/307-4100; www.ticketmaster.com), which also handles Broadway and Off-Broadway shows and concerts. If you're an American Express cardholder, check to see if tickets are being sold through **American Express Gold Card Events** (© 800/448-TIKS; www.americanexpress.com/gce). You'll pay full price, but Amex has access to blocks of preferred seating set aside for cardholders, so you may be able to get tickets to a show that's otherwise sold out, or better seats than you would otherwise be able to buy.

Theatre Direct International (TDI) is a ticket broker that sells tickets to select Broadway and Off-Broadway shows—including some of the most popular, like *Cabaret*—to individuals and travel agents. Check to see if they have seats to the shows in which you're interested by calling © **800/BROADWAY** or 212/541-8457; you can also order tickets through TDI via their website, **www.broadway.com.** Because there's a service charge of $15 per ticket, try Ticketmaster or TeleCharge first; but because they act as a consolidator, TDI may have tickets for a specific show if the major outlets don't.

Other reputable brokers include **Keith Prowse & Co.** (© **800/669-8687** or 212/398-4175; www.keithprowse.com) and **Global Tickets Edwards &**

Edwards (© **800/223-6108;** www.globaltickets.com). For a list of other licensed brokers, get a copy of the Official NYC Visitor Kit (see "Visitor Information" in chapter 2 for details). All kinds of ticket brokers list ads in the Sunday *New York Times* and other publications, but don't take the risk. Stick with a licensed broker recommended by the NYCVB.

If you don't want to pay a service charge, call the **box office.** Broadway theaters don't sell tickets over the phone—the major exception is the **Roundabout Theatre** (© **212/719-1300;** www.roundabouttheatre.org), which charges a $5-per-ticket "convenience" fee—but a good number of Off-Broadway theaters do sell tickets over the phone.

WHEN YOU ARRIVE   Once you arrive, getting your hands on good tickets can take some smarts—and failing those, cash. Even if it seems unlikely that seats are available, always **call the box office** first. Single seats are often easiest to obtain, so people willing to sit apart may find themselves in luck.

You should also try the **Broadway Ticket Center,** run by the League of American Theaters and Producers at the Times Square Visitors Center, 1560 Broadway, between 46th and 47th streets (open Mon–Sat 9am–7pm, Sun 10am–6pm). They often have tickets available for otherwise sold-out shows, both for advance and same-day purchase, and charge about $5 extra per ticket.

If you want to deal with a broker, **Keith Prowse & Co.** has an office that accommodates drop-ins at 234 W. 44th St., between Seventh and Eighth avenues, Suite 1000 (© **800/223-6108;** open Mon–Sat 9am–6pm).

If you buy from one of the **scalpers** selling tickets in front of the theater, you're taking a risk. They may be legit—a couple from the 'burbs whose companions couldn't make it for the evening, say—but they could be swindlers passing off fakes for big money. It's a risk that's not worth taking.

One preferred **insiders' trick** is to make the rounds of Broadway theaters at about 5 or 6pm, when unclaimed house seats are made available to the public. These tickets—reserved for VIPs, friends of the cast, the press, etc.—offer great seats and are sold at face value without service charge.

Also, note that **Monday** is often a good day to cop big-name tickets. Though most theaters are dark that day, some of the most sought-after choices aren't. Locals are at home the first night of the workweek, so all the odds are in your favor. Your chances will always be better on weeknights, or for Wednesday matinees.

2 Opera, Classical Music & Dance

In addition to the listings below, see what's on at **Carnegie Hall** and the **Brooklyn Academy of Music,** two of the most respected—and enjoyable—performing-arts venues in the city. The **92nd Street Y** also hosts lots of arts events, usually at low prices. I've listed the operatic and symphonic companies at **Lincoln Center;** also check the center's calendar for all offerings. See "Major Concert Halls & Landmark Venues," later in this chapter.

OPERA

In addition to the choices below, you might want to see what's on from the **New York Grand Opera** (© 212/245-8837; www.newyorkgrandopera.org), which puts on free Verdi productions at Central Park's SummerStage (see the box on p. 306) as well as workshop programs throughout the year.

Fans with an ear for experimentalism might check out **American Opera Projects** (© 718/398-4024; www.aopinc.org), which develops new American operas and other projects and showcases them at venues around town. Tickets generally run $25 to $30, and discounts may be available for students and seniors.

Amato Opera Theatre (Value) This cozy, off-the-beaten-track venue functions as a showcase for talented young American singers. The 100-plus-seat house celebrated its 50th season in 2001. The staple is full productions of Italian classics—Verdi's *La Traviata,* Puccini's *Madame Butterfly,* Bizet's *Carmen,* with an occasional Mozart tossed in—at great prices ($28, $23 for seniors and kids). Performances, usually held on Saturday and Sunday, now regularly sell out, so it's a good idea to reserve 3 weeks in advance.

Attention, moms and dads: On one Saturday a month, "Opera in Brief" offers fully costumed, kid-length versions of the classics with narration so Mom and Dad have a forum in which to introduce the little ones to opera. At $15 or so per ticket, these matinees are wallet-friendly, too. 319 Bowery (at 2nd St.). ℂ **212/228-8200.** www.amato.org. Subway: F to Second Ave.; 6 to Bleecker St.

Metropolitan Opera Tickets can cost a fortune—anywhere from $25 to $275. But for its full productions of the classic repertory and schedule packed with world-class singers, the Met ranks first in the world. Millions are spent on fabulous stagings of new works and repertory favorites, and the venue itself is a wonder of acoustics. To guarantee that its audience understands the words, the Met has outfitted the back of each row of seats with screens for subtitles—translation help for those who want it, minimum intrusion for those who don't. James Levine is the brilliant and popular conductor of the orchestra.

The Met has a number of programs that allow access to cut-rate tickets; for details, see "Lincoln Center Alert: Last-Minute & Discount Ticket-Buying Tips" on p. 302. At the Metropolitan Opera House, Lincoln Center, Broadway and 64th St. ℂ **212/362-6000.** www.metopera.org. Subway: 1, 9 to 66th St.

New York City Opera This superb company attempts to reach a wider audience than the Metropolitan with its more "human" scale and much lower prices ($25–$98). It's also committed to adventurous premieres, new works, the occasional avant-garde work, American musicals presented as operettas (Stephen Sondheim's *Sweeney Todd,* and *Porgy and Bess*), and even obscure works by mainstream or lesser-known composers. Its mix stretches from the "easy" works of Verdi and Gilbert & Sullivan to the more challenging oeuvres of the likes of Arnold Schönberg and Philip Glass. For the 2003–04 season, look for the Hal Prince production of *Sweeney Todd* and Lauren Flanigan in the opera production of Eugene O'Neill's *Mourning Becomes Electra.* At the New York State Theater, Lincoln Center, Broadway and 64th St. ℂ **212/870-5630** (information or box office), or 212/307-4100 for Ticketmaster. www.nycopera.com or www.ticketmaster.com. Subway: 1, 9 to 66th St.

New York Gilbert and Sullivan Players If you're in the mood for light-hearted operetta, try this lively company, which specializes in Gilbert and Sullivan's 19th-century English comic works. Tickets are affordable, usually in the $30-to-$50 range. The annual calendar generally runs from October to April and includes four shows a year, plus winter performances at City Center (p. 303). At Symphony Space, Broadway and 95th St. ℂ **212/864-5400** or 212/769-1000. www.nygasp.org. Subway: 1, 2, 3, 9 to 96th St.

CLASSICAL MUSIC

Bargemusic (Value) Many thought Olga Bloom peculiar when she transformed a 40-year-old barge into a chamber-music concert hall. More than 20 years later, Bargemusic is an internationally renowned recital room boasting more than 100

Value   **Bargain Alert: The Classical Learning Curve**

The **Juilliard School,** 60 Lincoln Center Plaza, Broadway at 65th Street (© 212/799-5000 or 212/721-0965; www.juilliard.edu), the nation's premier music education institution, sponsors about 550 performances of high quality—at low prices—throughout the school year. With most concerts free and $20 as a maximum, Juilliard is one of New York's great cultural bargains. Though most would assume that the school presents only classical music, Juilliard offers other music as well as drama, dance, opera, and interdisciplinary works. The best way to find out about the wide array of productions is to call, visit the website (click on "Calendar of Events"), or consult the bulletin board in the building's lobby. Watch for master classes and discussions open to the public featuring celebrity guest teachers.

The **Manhattan School of Music,** at Broadway and 122nd Street (© 212/749-2802, ext. 4428; www.msmnyc.edu), hosts student concerts as well as daily recitals during the academic year. Most performances are free, and the top ticket price is usually $15. In addition to orchestral and chamber music, the school is highly regarded for its contemporary music and jazz as well as musical theater programs, so performances run the gamut. Look for free master classes, too. Call the box office weekdays between 9am and 5pm for the latest schedule, or check the website (click on "Concert Calendar"); tickets are usually required even for free events, so plan ahead.

chamber-music performances a year. There are three shows per week, on Thursday and Friday evenings at 7:30pm and Sunday afternoon at 4pm. The musicians perform on a small stage in a cherry-paneled, fireplace-lit room accommodating 130. The barge may creak a bit and an occasional boat may speed by, but the music rivals what you'll find in almost any other New York venue—and the panoramic view through the glass wall behind the stage can't be beat. Neither can the price: Tickets cost $35 ($20 students), or $40 for performances by larger ensembles. Reserve well in advance. At Fulton Ferry Landing (just south of the Brooklyn Bridge), Brooklyn. © 718/624-2083 or 718/624-4061. www.bargemusic.org. Subway: 2, 3 to Clark St.; A, C to High St.

New York Philharmonic   Symphony-wise, you'd be hard-pressed to do better than the New York Philharmonic. The country's oldest orchestra is now under the guidance of distinguished conductor Lorin Maazel, formerly of the Bavarian Radio Symphony Orchestra. Don't expect quality to falter one bit. Highlights of the 2003–04 season include "John Williams: The Art of the Score" and performances by flutist James Galway and a guest appearance by former conductor Kurt Masur in January. There's a summer season in July, when themed classics brighten the hall, as well as free summer concerts in Central Park that are worth checking into.

Tickets range from $36 to $68; opt for a rush-hour concert or a matinee for the lowest across-the-board prices. If you can afford it—and if the tickets are available—it's well worth it to pay for prime seats. The acoustics of the hall are such that, at the midrange price points, I prefer the second tier (especially the boxes) over the more expensive rear orchestra seats. Go cheap if you have to; you're sure

> **Value** Lincoln Center Alert: Last-Minute & Discount Ticket Buying Tips
>
> Most seats at **New York Philharmonic** performances are sold to subscribers, but there are ways to get tickets.
>
> When subscribers can't attend, they may return their tickets to the theaters, which resell them at the last moment. These can be in the most coveted rows of the orchestra. Ticket holders can return tickets until curtain time, so tickets that are not available in the morning may be available (at full price) later in the day. The hopefuls form "cancellation lines" 2 hours or more before curtain time for a crack at returned tickets.
>
> Periodically, some **same-day orchestra tickets** are set aside at the philharmonic, and sold in the morning for $25 (maximum two). They usually go on sale at 10am weekdays, 1pm Saturday (noon if there's a matinee).
>
> **Senior/student/disabled rush tickets** may be available for $10 (maximum two) on concert day, but never at Friday matinees or Saturday-evening performances. To check availability for any of these programs at all performances, call **Audience Services** at ✆ **212/875-5656.**
>
> You're also invited to watch the Philharmonic at work by attending an **Open Rehearsal** for just $14. Not only is this a bargain-basement way to see a great orchestra, it's fascinating to watch how the conductor and musicians shape a piece. There are usually 30 or so of these throughout the season; call Audience Services or check the website for the schedule.
>
> Families with teenagers can participate in **Phil Teens,** which allows you and your teen between the ages of 12 and 17 to attend a New York Philharmonic Rush Hour Concert for just $10 each. Rush Hour concerts start at 6:45pm and last an hour. Your Phil Teen ticket also allows you to arrive as early at 5:30pm to meet guest artists, soloists, and special guests.
>
> Lincoln Center's **Alice Tully Hall** (where the Chamber Music Society performs and other concerts are held), **Jazz at Lincoln Center,** the

to enjoy the program from any vantage. At Avery Fisher Hall, Lincoln Center, Broadway at 65th St. ✆ **212/875-5656** for audience services, 212/875-5030 for box-office information or Center Charge at 212/721-6500 for tickets. www.newyorkphilharmonic.org. Subway: 1, 9 to 66th St.

DANCE

In addition to the troupes below, some other venues to keep in mind are the **Brooklyn Academy of Music,** the **92nd Street Y, Radio City Music Hall,** and **Town Hall** (see "Major Concert Halls & Landmark Venues," below).

For innovative works, see what's on at the **Dance Theater Workshop,** in the Bessie Schönberg Theater, 219 W. 19th St., between Seventh and Eighth avenues (✆ **212/691-6500** or 212/924-0077; www.dtw.org), a first-rate launching pad for nearly a quarter-century; and **Danspace Project,** at St. Mark's Church, 131 E. 10th St. (✆ **212/674-8112** or 212/674-8194; www.danspaceproject.org),

Metropolitan Opera, and the **New York City Opera** offer last-minute-purchase and discount programs, as do **Carnegie Hall** and the **Brooklyn Academy of Music.** Policies differ; for instance, the **New York City Ballet** offers Student Rush tickets only, at $10 a pop, while the New York City Opera allows students to buy tickets a week in advance at half-price ($13–$53), as well as offering same-day rush tickets (Rush Hot Line: ✆ **212/870-5630).** In addition to senior and student rush tickets, Carnegie Hall offers some limited-view tickets for $10 (on sale Sat at 11am for the week's upcoming performances), and presents some totally free events through its neighborhood concert series. Check with the venue directly for details on their specific programs. And call the box office first to check on same-day availability before heading to the theater—or, if you're willing to risk coming away empty-handed, be there at opening time (or before) for first crack.

The **Met Opera** offers **standing-room** tickets for $12 to $16, which can be a bargain for budget-minded fans. It's not a bad situation, because you get to lean against plush red bars. (Don't tell the ushers I told you, but if subscribers fail to show, I've seen standees with eagle eyes fill the empty seats at intermission.) Wheelchair-access standing-room places are also available. Tickets go on sale Saturday at 10am for the following week's performances (Sat–Fri). The line sometimes forms much earlier, so plan ahead. Keep in mind that special performances may not be available to potential standees. Call ✆ **212/362-6000** for details. It never hurts to inquire about standing-room availability at other venues as well.

Summer visitors should also keep in mind that both the **Philharmonic** and the **Met Opera** offer **free concerts in the parks** throughout the five boroughs, including Central Park, in July and August. For the current schedule, call ✆ **212/875-5656** or 212/362-6000. The Philharmonic maintains a list of their upcoming park gigs throughout the five boroughs at **www.newyorkphilharmonic.org**; look under "Events and Performances."

whose performances lean toward the avant-garde, with ticket prices usually falling between free and $15, depending on the performance.

In addition to regular appearances at City Center (see below), the **American Ballet Theatre** (www.abt.org) is in residence at Lincoln Center's Metropolitan Opera House (✆ **212/362-6000**) for 8 weeks each spring. The same venue also hosts such visiting companies as the Kirov, Royal, and Paris Opéra ballets.

The weekly *Time Out New York,* available on newsstands, maintains a section dedicated to dance events around town that's an invaluable resource to fans.

City Center   Modern dance usually takes center stage in this Moorish dome-topped performing-arts palace. The companies of Merce Cunningham, Martha Graham, Paul Taylor, Alvin Ailey, Twyla Tharp, the Dance Theatre of Harlem (in residence in Sept, and celebrating its 30th year this season), and the American

Ballet Theatre are often on the calendar. Don't expect cutting edge—but do expect excellence. Tickets generally run $25 to $80, depending on the performance; sightlines are terrific from all corners, and a new acoustical shell means the sound is pitch-perfect, so you won't lose out with cheaper tickets. City Center also presents a limited program schedule at the Cathedral of St. John the Divine (p. 235) at lower-than-average ticket prices ($15–$50). 131 W. 55th St. (between Sixth and Seventh aves.). ℂ 877/581-1212 or 212/581-1212. www.citycenter.org. Subway: F, N, R, Q, W to 57th St.; B, D, E to Seventh Ave.

Joyce Theater   Housed in an old Art Deco movie house, the Joyce has grown into a modern dance institution. You can see everything from Native American dance to the works of Pilobolus to the Martha Graham Dance Company. In residence annually is Eliot Feld's company, Ballet Tech, which WQXR radio's Francis Mason called "better than a whole month of namby-pamby classical ballets." The Joyce has a second space, the **Joyce SoHo,** where you can see rising young dancers and experimental works in a 70-seat performance space. Tickets are usually $38 at the main theater, as little as $10 at the SoHo space. 175 Eighth Ave. (at 19th St.). ℂ 212/242-0800. www.joyce.org. Subway: C, E to 23rd St.; 1, 9 to 18th St. Joyce SoHo at 155 Mercer St. (between Houston and Prince sts.; ℂ 212/431-9233; subway: N, R to Prince St.).

New York City Ballet   Highly regarded for its unsurpassed technique, the New York City Ballet is the world's best. The company renders with happy regularity the works of two of America's most important choreographers: George Balanchine, its founder, and Jerome Robbins. Under the direction of Ballet Master in Chief Peter Martins, the troupe continues to expand its repertoire and performs to a wide variety of classical and modern music. The cornerstone of the annual season is the Christmastime production of *The Nutcracker,* for which tickets usually become available in early October. Ticket prices for most events run $28 to $66. At the New York State Theater at Lincoln Center, Broadway and 64th St. ℂ 212/870-5570. www.nycballet.com. Subway: 1, 9 to 66th St.

3 Major Concert Halls & Landmark Venues

Apollo Theatre   Built in 1914, this legendary Harlem theater launched or nurtured the careers of countless musical icons—including Bessie Smith, Billie Holiday, Dinah Washington, Duke Ellington, Ella Fitzgerald, Sarah Vaughan, Count Basie, Aretha Franklin, and James Brown—and is in large part responsible for the development and popularization of black music in America. By the 1970s, it had fallen on hard times, but a 1986 restoration breathed new life into the landmark. Today the Apollo is renowned for its African-American acts of all musical genres, from hip-hop to Wynton Marsalis's "Jazz for Young People" events. Wednesday's "Amateur Night at the Apollo" is a fun-filled night that draws in young talents with high hopes of making it big (a young Lauryn Hill started here—and didn't win!). Tickets are usually $15 to $27, slightly higher for finalist shows. *Money-saving tip:* For free tickets to *It's Showtime at the Apollo* (www.apolloshowtime.com), call ℂ 212/889-3532 or send a self-addressed, stamped envelope and the dates you'll be in the Big Apple to It's Showtime at the Apollo, 3 Park Ave., 40th Floor, New York, NY 10016. 253 W. 125th St. (between Adam Clayton Powell and Frederick Douglass blvds.). ℂ 212/531-5300 or 212/531-5301. Subway: 1, 9 to 125th St.

Brooklyn Academy of Music *Finds*   BAM is the city's most renowned contemporary-arts institution, presenting cutting-edge theater, opera, dance, and music. Offerings have included presentations of baroque opera by William Christie and Les Arts Florissants; pop opera from Lou Reed; Marianne Faithfull singing Kurt Weill; dance by Mark Morris and Mikhail Baryshnikov; the Philip Glass ensemble accompanying screenings of *Koyannisqatsi* and Lugosi's original *Dracula;* the Royal Dramatic Theater of Sweden directed by Ingmar Bergman; and much more, including visiting companies from all over the world. Tickets run anywhere from $5 to $95, depending on the performance and the seats you choose; most performances offer a $25-to-$75 range.

Of particular note is the **Next Wave Festival,** from September to December, this country's foremost showcase for new, experimental works. The **BAM Rose Cinemas** show first-run independent films, and there's free live music every Thursday, Friday, and Saturday night at **BAMcafé,** which can range from atmospheric electronica from coronetist Graham Haynes to radical jazz from the Harold Rubin Trio to tango band Tanguardia! ($10 food minimum). 30 Lafayette Ave. (off Flatbush Ave.), Brooklyn. ✆ 718/636-4100. www.bam.org. Subway: 2, 3, 4, 5, M, N, Q, R, W to Pacific St./Atlantic Ave.

Carnegie Hall   Perhaps the world's most famous performance space, Carnegie Hall offers everything from grand classics to the music of Ravi Shankar. The **Issac Stern Auditorium,** the 2,804-seat main hall, welcomes visiting orchestras from across the country and the world. Many of the world's premier soloists and ensembles give recitals. The legendary hall is both visually and acoustically brilliant; don't miss an opportunity to experience it if there's something on that interests you.

There's also the intimate 268-seat **Weill Recital Hall,** usually used to showcase chamber music and vocal and instrumental recitals. Carnegie Hall has also reclaimed the ornate underground 650-seat **Zankel Concert Hall** as its newest venue, as of fall 2003. For last-minute ticket-buying tips, see the box on p. 302. 881 Seventh Ave. (at 57th St.). ✆ 212/247-7800. www.carnegiehall.org. Subway: B, N, Q, R to 57th St.

Lincoln Center for the Performing Arts   New York is the world's premier performing-arts city, and Lincoln Center is its premier institution. Whenever you're planning an evening's entertainment, check the offerings here—which can include opera, dance, symphonies, jazz, theater, film, and more. Lincoln Center's many buildings serve as permanent homes to their own companies as well as major stops for world-class performance troupes from around the globe.

The **Chamber Music Society of Lincoln Center** (✆ 212/875-5788; www.chambermusicsociety.org) performs at Alice Tully Hall or the Daniel and Joanna S. Rose Rehearsal Studio, often with such high-caliber guests as Anne Sofie Von Otter and Midori. The **Film Society of Lincoln Center** (✆ 212/875-5600; www.filmlinc.com) screens a daily schedule of movies at the Walter Reade Theater, and hosts a number of film and video festivals as well as the Reel to Real program for kids, pairing silent-screen classics with live performance. **Jazz at Lincoln Center** (✆ 212/258-9800; www.jazzatlincolncenter.org) is led by the incomparable Wynton Marsalis, with the orchestra usually performing at Alice Tully Hall; the "Jazz at the Penthouse" program, where great jazz pianists like Ellis Marsalis and Tommy Flanagan play in a spectacular candlelit setting overlooking the Hudson River, is the hottest ticket in town. In the fall of 2004, Jazz at Lincoln Center is scheduled to move into its new, $128 million, 100,000-square-foot home, Frederick P. Rose Hall in the AOL Time-Warner Center on Columbus Circle. **Lincoln Center Theater** (✆ 212/362-7600; www.lct.org) consists of the Vivian

Park It! Shakespeare, Music & Other Free Fun

As the weather warms, New York culture comes outdoors to play.

Shakespeare in the Park, held at Central Park's Delacorte Theater, is the city's most famous alfresco arts event. Organized by the late Joseph Papp through his Public Theater, the schedule consists of one or two summer productions, usually of the Bard's plays. Productions often feature big names and range from traditional (Andre Braugher as an armorclad *Henry V*) to avant-garde (Morgan Freeman and Tracy Ullman in *Taming of the Shrew* as a Wild West showdown). The theater itself, next to Belvedere Castle near 79th Street and West Drive, is a dream—on a starry night, there's no better stage in town. Tickets are given out free on a first-come, first-served basis (two per person), at 1pm on the day of the performance at the theater. The Delacorte might have 1,881 seats, but each is a hot commodity, so people line up next to the theater 2 to 3 hours in advance (even earlier if a big name is involved). You can also pick up same-day tickets between 1 and 3pm at the Public Theater, at 425 Lafayette St., where the Shakespeare Festival continues throughout the year. For more information, call the Public Theater at ℂ **212/539-8750** or the Delacorte at ℂ **212/861-7277,** or go online at www.public theater.org.

With summer also comes the sound of music. The **New York Philharmonic** and the **Metropolitan Opera** hold free concerts beneath the stars in Central Park, and in parks throughout the five boroughs. For the schedule, call ℂ **212/875-5656** or 212/362-6000. The Philharmonic maintains a list of their upcoming gigs at www.newyorkphilharmonic.org; look under "Events and Performances."

The most active music stage in Central Park is **SummerStage,** at Rumsey Playfield, midpark around 72nd Street, which has featured everyone from James Brown to Patti Smith. Recent offerings have included concerts by Hugh Masekela, the Jon Spencer Blues Explosion, and Marianne Faithfull; "Viva, Verdi!" festival performances by the New York Grand Opera;

Beaumont Theater, a modern venue with great sightlines that has been home to much Broadway drama, and the Mitzi E. Newhouse Theater, an Off-Broadway house that has also hosted theatrical triumphs.

For details on the **Metropolitan Opera,** the **New York City Opera,** the **New York City Ballet,** the **Juilliard School,** the phenomenal **New York Philharmonic,** and the **American Ballet Theatre,** which takes up residence here every spring, see "Opera, Classical Music & Dance," earlier in this chapter.

Most of the companies' **major seasons** run from about September or October to April, May, or June. **Special series** like Great Performers help round out the calendar. Indoor and outdoor events are held in warmer months: Summer kicks off with the **JVC Jazz Festival** in June; July sees **Midsummer Night's Swing** with partner dancing, lessons, and music on the plaza; August's **Mostly Mozart** attracts talents like Alicia de Larrocha and André Watts; the 3-year-old **Lincoln Center Festival** celebrates the best of the performing arts; **Lincoln Center Out of Doors** is a series of free music and dance performances also in August; in cabaret nights; and more. The season usually lasts from mid-June to August. While some big-name shows charge admission, tickets aren't usually required; donations are accepted, however. Call the hot line at ℂ 212/360-2777 or visit www.summerstage.org.

The calendar of free events heats up throughout the city's parks in summertime. You can find out what's happening by calling the **Parks and Recreation Special Events Hot Line** at ℂ **888/NY-PARKS** or 212/360-3456, or pointing your browser to **www.nycgovparks.org/sub_things_to_do/ upcoming_events**.

Also each summer is the **Bryant Park Summer Film Festival,** in which a classic film—think *Dr. Zhivago* or *Viva Las Vegas*—is shown on a large screen under the stars every Monday evening at sunset. Admission is free; just bring a blanket and a picnic. Rain dates are Tuesdays. For the schedule and more information, call ℂ **212/512-5700.**

In Lower Manhattan, Trinity Church, at Broadway and Wall Street, hosts a chamber-music and orchestral **Noonday Concert** series year-round each Monday and Thursday at 1pm. This program isn't quite free, but almost: A $2 contribution is requested. Call the concert hot line at ℂ **212/602-0800** or visit www.trinitywallstreet.org; see chapter 7 for further details.

Most of the city's museums offer free music and other programs on select nights. The **Metropolitan Museum of Art** has an extensive slate of offerings, including live classical music and cocktails on Friday and Saturday evenings. There's lots of fun to be had at others as well, including the **Guggenheim,** whose weekend Worldbeat Jazz series is a big hit; the **American Museum of Natural History,** which features live jazz in the Hall of the Universe in the Rose Center for Earth and Space; and the **Brooklyn Museum of Art,** which hosts the remarkably eclectic **First Saturday** program monthly. For details, see the museum listings in chapter 7.

September there's also the **New York Film Festival,** and more. Check Lincoln Center's website to see what special events will be on while you're in town.

Tickets for all performances at Avery Fisher and Alice Tully halls can be purchased through **CenterCharge** (ℂ 212/721-6500) or at www.lincolncenter.org (click on "Box Office & Schedule"). Tickets for all Lincoln Center Theater performances can be purchased through **TeleCharge** (ℂ 212/239-6200; www.telecharge.com). Tickets for New York State Theater productions (New York City Opera and Ballet companies) are available through **Ticketmaster** (ℂ 212/307-4100; www.ticket master.com), while tickets for films showing at the Walter Reade Theater can be bought up to 7 days in advance by calling ℂ 212/496-3809. For last-minute full-price and discount ticket-buying tips, see p. 302. 70 Lincoln Center Plaza (at Broadway and 64th St.). ℂ 212/546-2656 or 212/875-5456. www.lincolncenter.org. Subway: 1, 9 to 66th St.

Madison Square Garden Monsters of rock and pop fill this 20,000-seat arena, which is also home to the Knicks, the Rangers, and the WNBA's Liberty. The cavernous hulk is better suited to sports than to concerts, or in-the-round events such as Ringling Bros. Barnum & Bailey Circus. End up in the back for U2, and you'd better bring binoculars. You'll find better sightlines at the **Theater at Madison Square Garden,** an amphitheater-style auditorium with 5,600 seats that has played host to some major stars, from Barbra Streisand to Roxy Music. Watch for annual stagings of *The Wizard of Oz, A Christmas Carol,* and such family shows as *Sesame Street Live.* Newest at MSG is the **Comedy Garden** (www.comedygarden.com), the Garden's comedy club at the Theater, where talent runs the gamut from well-known local comics to Robin Williams.

The box office is located at Seventh Avenue and 32nd Street. Or you can purchase tickets through **Ticketmaster** (© 212/307-7171; www.ticketmaster.com). On Seventh Ave. from 31st to 33rd sts. © 212/465-MSG1. www.thegarden.com. Subway: A, C, E, 1, 2, 3, 9 to 34th St.

92nd Street Y Tisch Center for the Arts *(Value)*   This generously endowed community center offers a phenomenal slate of cultural happenings, from classical to folk to jazz to world music to cabaret to lyric theater and literary readings. Great classical performers—Janos Starker, Nadja Salerno-Sonnenberg—give recitals here. The concert calendar often includes luminaries such as Max Roach, John Williams, and Judy Collins; Jazz at the Y from Dick Hyman and guests; the longstanding Chamber Music at the Y series; the classical Music from the Jewish Spirit series; and regular cabaret programs. The lectures and literary-readings calendar is unparalleled, with featured speakers ranging from Lorne Michaels to David Halberstam to Jeff Bezos (CEO of Amazon) to Katie Couric to Elie Wiesel. There's a regular schedule of modern dance, too, through the Harkness Dance Project. Best of all, readings and lectures are usually priced between $20 and $30 for nonmembers, dance is usually $20, and concert tickets generally go for $15 to $50—half or a third of what you'd pay at comparable venues. Additionally, a full

---

(*Moments* Free Music Above and Below the Ground

The noises of car horns, alarms, and sirens are not the only sounds you will hear in your travels around Manhattan. Music is everywhere. In the warm weather, a bagpiper or violinist will set up at a busy corner and play for hours. In the winter, the musicians head into subway stations, where they are legally not allowed to play, but I've rarely seen the law enforced. Many are very good, while others—well, they are just trying to make a few bucks. Some of the very good ones, who actually audition for the opportunity, perform as part of a program sponsored by the New York Metropolitan Transit Authority (MTA) called **Music Under New York.** If they are chosen, they are allowed to perform at designated subway stations including Times Square/42nd Street, 34th Street/Sixth Avenue, 14th Street/Union Square, and 59th Street/Columbus Circle. In the summer, there is a Music Under New York festival at Grand Central Station and Bowling Green Park. The variety of music is amazing and the quality as good as you might see at some of New York's clubs. In subway stations I've heard gospel, blues, Cajun, Dixieland jazz, Andean, Brazilian drumming, rumba, and my favorite, doo wop, the original sound of the New York subways. So take a few moments before boarding your train and listen to the music. If you're so moved, toss some change or a dollar into the hat, guitar case, or donation can. For more information, visit the MTA website (www.mta.nyc.ny.us/mta/aft/muny.htm).

calendar of entertainment targeted to the culturally aware in their 20s and 30s—from poetry readings to film screenings to live music including the debut of a very young, talented pianist and singer, Norah Jones—is offered at the Upper West Side community center **Makor,** 35 W. 67th St. (© **212/601-1000;** www.makor. org; subway: 1, 9 to 66th St.). 1395 Lexington Ave. (at 92nd St.). © **212/996-1100.** www.92ndsty.org. Subway: 4, 5, 6 to 86th St.; 6 to 96th St.

Radio City Music Hall   After an extensive renovation in 1999, this stunning Art Deco 6,200-seater continues to be a choice venue; the setting alone adds a dash of panache to any performance. Star of the Christmas season is the **Radio City Music Hall Christmas Spectacular,** starring the legendary Rockettes (tickets $36–$119). Visiting pop chart–toppers, from Patti LaBelle to Radiohead, also perform here. Thanks to perfect acoustics and uninterrupted sight lines, there's hardly a bad seat in the house. The theater also hosts dance performances, family entertainment, and a number of annual awards shows—including anything MTV is holding in town—so this is a good place to celeb-spot on show nights. 1260 Sixth Ave. (at 50th St.). © **212/247-4777,** or 212/307-7171 for Ticketmaster. www.radiocity.com or www.ticketmaster.com. Subway: B, D, F, V to 49th–50th sts./Rockefeller Center.

Town Hall   This intimate landmark theater—a National Historic Site designed by McKim, Mead & White—is blessed with outstanding acoustics, making it an ideal place to enjoy many kinds of performances, including theater, dance, lectures, drama, comedy, film, and music. The grade is extremely steep, so unless Lurch sits in front of you, fellow audience members shouldn't block your view. Ticket prices vary depending on the show but are usually less than $40. 123 W. 43rd St. (between Sixth and Seventh aves.). © **212/840-2824,** or 212/307-4100 for Ticketmaster. www.the-townhall-nyc.org or www.ticketmaster.com. Subway: N, R, S, 1, 2, 3, 7, 9, Q, W to 42nd St./Times Sq.; B, D, F, V to 42nd St.

4 Live Rock, Jazz, Blues & More

I discuss the top venues, both large and small, below. But there are many more, and new ones pop up all the time. For the latest, check the publications discussed earlier in this chapter.

LARGER VENUES

For coverage of **Madison Square Garden,** the **Theater at MSG,** and **Town Hall,** see "Major Concert Halls & Landmark Venues," above.

Beacon Theatre   This pleasing venue—a 1928 Art Deco movie palace with an impressive lobby, stairway, and auditorium seating about 2,700—hosts mainly pop music, usually for the over-30 crowd. Featured acts have ranged from Bryan Ferry to perennial faves the Allman Brothers. You'll also find such events as the bodybuilding "Night of Champions" on the calendar. 2124 Broadway (at 74th St.). © **212/496-7070.** www.livetonight.com. Subway: 1, 2, 3, 9 to 72nd St.

Hammerstein Ballroom   This midsize general-admission venue is one of the city's most popular rock stages, hosting everyone from Moby and Bush to Belle & Sebastian to Joey Ramone's "Life's a Gas" memorial. The sound system is good, and the stage high enough that sightlines are decent from the main floor. The side balconies are for VIPs, but the main balcony level, graded for good views and boasting comfortable theater-style seating, is usually open to regular folk. You have to have a mezzanine-level ticket to gain access, so request one when you're buying if you want one (there's usually no cost difference), since many events are Standing Room Only on the main floor. At the Manhattan Center, 311 W. 34th St. (between Eighth and Ninth aves.). © **212/485-1534.** www.concerthotline.com. Subway: A, C, E to 34th St./Penn Station.

Tips   Ticket-Buying Tips

Tickets for events at all larger theaters and Hammerstein Ballroom, Roseland, Irving Plaza, B.B. King's, and S.O.B.'s can be purchased through **Ticketmaster** (© **212/307-7171**; www.ticketmaster.com).

Advance tickets for an increasing number of shows at smaller venues—including CBGB, Bowery Ballroom, Mercury Lounge, Village Underground, Tribeca Blues, and Fez Under Time Cafe, plus Brooklyn's Warsaw and North-six—can be purchased through **Ticketweb** (© **212/269-4TIX**; www.ticket web.com). Do note that Ticketweb can sell out its allotted number of tickets without the show being completely sold out. If Ticketweb is sold out, check with the venue directly.

Even if a show is sold out, that doesn't mean you're out of luck. There are usually people hanging around at showtime trying to get rid of extra tickets for friends who didn't show, and they're usually happy to pass them off for face value. You'll also see scalpers, who often peddle forgeries and are best avoided—it doesn't take a rocket scientist to tell the difference. Be aware, of course, that in New York City, it's illegal to sell a ticket for more than $5 above its face value.

Roseland   This old warhorse, a 1919 ballroom, has been under threat of the wrecking ball for years. Everybody has played at this too-huge-for-its-own-good 2,500-capacity general-admission hall, from Marc Anthony to Hole to Busta Rhymes. Bands who inspire mosh pits like to book here (Nine Inch Nails, No Doubt), because there's plenty of space for slamming and surfing. Thankfully, there's also room to steer clear and enjoy the show. *Money-saving tip:* Purchase advance tickets at Irving Plaza (p. 311) sans the Ticketmaster service fee. 239 W. 52nd St. (between Broadway and Eighth Ave.). © 212/777-6800, 212/247-0200, or 212/307-7171 for Ticketmaster. www.roselandballroom.com or www.livetonight.com. Subway: C, E, 1, 9 to 50th St.

MIDSIZE & MULTIGENRE VENUES

For the most part, expect to pay a little more for shows at these venues than you would at smaller clubs—anywhere from $10 to $25, depending on the act.

B.B. King Blues Club & Grill   This 550-seat venue is one of the prime anchors of Times Square's "new" 42nd Street. Despite its name, B.B. King's seldom sticks to the blues; instead, you're likely to find pop, funk, and rock names, mainly from the past. The big-ticket talent runs the gamut from Nile Rodgers and Chic (cool!) to Big Bad Voodoo Daddy to the Turtles (yes, with Flo and Eddie) to the Afro-Cuban All Stars. A few more (relatively) esoteric acts take the stage on occasion, such as Luther "Guitar Junior" Johnson and Shemikia Copeland. Tourist-targeted pricing—$25 to $35, plus minimums—makes for an expensive night, but there's no arguing with the quality of the talent. The Sunday gospel lunch is a genuine slice of joy. 42nd St. (between Seventh and Eighth aves.) © 212/997-4144, or 212/307-7171 for Ticketmaster. www.bbkingblues.com. Subway: A, C, E, Q, W, 1, 2, 3, 7, 9 to 42nd St.

The Bottom Line   The Bottom Line built its reputation by serving as a showcase for the likes of Bruce Springsteen, and it remains one of the city's most well-respected venues. With table seating, waiter service, and decent bar food, it's one of the city's most comfortable. The Bottom Line is renowned for its sound and bookings of the best rock and singer/songwriters in the business. Shawn Colvin, Marshall Crenshaw, Lucinda Williams, Suzanne Vega, Steve Forbert, Emmylou

Harris, Tower of Power, and David Johansen (and alter-ego Buster Poindexter) are among the artists who make this their favored venue for area appearances. There are usually two shows nightly. Tickets usually run $15 to $30, with most $20 or less. 15 W. 4th St. (at Mercer St.). ⓒ 212/502-3471 or 212/228-6300. www.bottomlinecabaret.com. Subway: N, R to Astor Place; A, C, E, F, V to W. 4th St.

Bowery Ballroom   This marvelous space is run by the same people behind the Mercury Lounge (see below). The Bowery space is bigger, accommodating a crowd of 500 or so. The stage is big and raised to allow good sightlines from every corner. The sound couldn't be better, and Art Deco details give the place a sophistication that doesn't come easy to general-admission halls. My favorite spot is the balcony, which has its own bar and seating alcoves. This place is a favorite with alt-rockers like Melissa Ferrick, Shudder to Think, and Toshi Reagon, as well as acts like Warren Zevon, Neil Finn, and Patti Smith, who thrive in an intimate setting. Tickets run $10 to $30, with most under $20. ***Money-saving tip:*** Buy advance tickets at Mercury's box office; you'll save the service charge and up to $2 to $5 on the day-of-show price. 6 Delancey St. (at Bowery). ⓒ 212/533-2111. www.boweryballroom.com. Subway: F, J, M, Z to Delancey St.

Irving Plaza   This high-profile, midsize music hall is the prime stop for national-name rock bands that aren't quite big enough yet (or anymore) to sell out Hammerstein, Roseland, or the Beacon. Think Five for Fighting, Jars of Clay, Super Furry Animals, the Reverend Horton Heat, and Cheap Trick. From time to time, big-name artists also perform—Prince, Bob Dylan, and Trent Reznor have all played "secret" shows here. This is a nice place to see a show, with a well-elevated stage and lots of open space, even on sold-out nights. There's an upstairs balcony that offers unparalleled views, but come early for a spot. Tickets range from $15 to $30, with most between $25 and $30. ***Money-saving tip:*** Buy tickets prior to the day of show to save $2 to $5. 17 Irving Place (1 block west of Third Ave. at 15th St.). ⓒ 212/777-1224 or 212/777-6800. www.irvingplaza.com. Subway: 4, 5, 6, L, N, R, Q, W to 14th St./Union Sq.

The Knitting Factory   New York's premier avant-garde music venue has four spaces, each showcasing performances ranging from experimental jazz and folk to spoken-word and poetry to multimedia. Regulars who use the Knitting Factory as their lab of choice include former Lounge Lizard John Lurie; around-the-bend experimentalist John Zorn; guitar gods Vernon Reid, Eliot Sharp, and David Torn; and Television's Richard Lloyd. (If these names mean nothing to you, chances are good that the Knitting Factory is not for you.) The schedule is peppered with edgy star turns from the likes of Cibo Matto, Gil Scott Heron, Taj Mahal, Faith No More's Mike Patton, and Lou Reed. There are often two shows a night in the pleasing main performance space, so it's easy to work a show around other activities. Prices usually run $7 to $20, with most falling between $10 and $15. The Old Office Lounge offers an extensive list of microbrews and free live entertainment. 74 Leonard St. (between Broadway and Church St.). ⓒ 212/219-3006. www.knittingfactory.com. Subway: 1, 9 to Franklin St.

ROCK & MIXED-MUSIC CLUBS

Arlene Grocery   This casual Lower East Side club boasts a friendly bar and a good sound system; unfortunately, music isn't always free, but the quality of the artists is usually pretty high, and the cover is around $5. Arlene Grocery serves as a showcase for hot bands looking for a deal or promoting their self-pressed record. The crowd is a mix of club-hoppers, rock fans looking for a new fix, and industry scouts looking for new blood. 95 Stanton St. (between Ludlow and Orchard sts.). ⓒ 212/358-1633. www.arlene-grocery.com. Subway: F to Second Ave.

The Baggot Inn *Value*   This easygoing pub has become one of the best show-cases in the city for unknown acts, especially if you like quality acoustic and folk-rock music. Blues, Irish music, poetry, acoustic jams, and open-mike nights also regularly pop up on the calendar. The cover is always bargain-priced—from free to $5—and happy hour until 7pm and nightly drink specials round out the entertainment value. 82 W. 3rd St. (between Thompson and Sullivan sts., below the Boston Comedy Club). © 212/477-0622. www.thebaggotinn.com. Subway: A, C, E, F, V to W. 4th St.

Bitter End   Folk rock's legendary Bitter End has been going strong in the heart of the Village for 40-plus years, and it's still a relevant showcase for acoustic and electric rock and experimental sounds. Admission costs $5, with a few shows reaching $7. 147 Bleecker St. (between Thompson and LaGuardia sts.). © 212/673-7030. www.bitterend.com. Subway: A, C, E, F, V to W. 4th St.

CBGB   The original downtown club has seen better days, but no other spot is so rich with rock history. This was the launching pad for New York punk and New Wave: the Ramones, Blondie, the Talking Heads, Television, Patti Smith, Stiv Bators and the Dead Boys—everybody got started here. These days, you've probably never heard of most acts here. Never mind—CB's still rocks. Come early if you have hopes of actually seeing the stage. Cover usually runs $6 to $10.

More today than yesterday is **CB's 313 Gallery,** a welcome spin-off that showcases alternative art on the walls and mostly acoustic singer/songwriters on stage; cover is usually $5, never higher than $8. Same goes for CB's **lounge,** which has a more cerebral alt edge to its sounds, plus regular poetry slams (cover free to $8). Within striking distance of the history, but more pleasant all the way around. 315 Bowery (at Bleecker St.). © 212/982-4052, or 212/677-0455 for CB's 313 Gallery. www.cbgb.com. Subway: F to Second Ave.; 6 to Bleecker St.

The C-Note   This Alphabet City boîte used to focus on contemporary jazz performers but has branched out to embrace singer-songwriter pop, rock, blues, country and roots, Latin music, and other genres. The quality tunes are almost always worth the price of admission, which ranges from free to $7. 157 Ave. C (at 10th St.). © 212/677-8142. www.thecnote.com. Subway: L to First Ave.

Continental   The cover ranges from free to $5 at this proudly skanky joint, where artists such as Spacehog occasionally surface among the unknowns. It's punk central in the East Village, even more so than CBGB. 25 Third Ave., at St. Marks Place. © 212/529-6924. www.nytrash.com/continental. Subway: 6 to Astor Place.

The Cutting Room   This Flatiron District music club and restaurant is co-owned by actor Chris Noth (*Sex and the City, Law & Order*), so don't be surprised if you spot a famous face or two. That said, the environment is usually easygoing, and the mix of entertainment runs the gamut from experimental synth ensemble Mother Mallard's Portable Masterpiece Co. to the terrific Oingo Boingo-ish Nia-gras. A huge draw is Saturday night's Le Scandal (formerly Blue Angel Cabaret), sort of a feminist take on burlesque, with a dash of Jim Rose Circus Side Show thrown in. The cover is $10 to $12, but can rise to $15 when names like Midge Ure are there. 19 W. 24th St. (between Broadway and Sixth Ave.). © 212/691-1900. www.the cuttingroomnyc.com. Subway: N, R to 23rd St.

Fez Under Time Cafe   You have to reserve a seat a few days ahead for the pop-ular Thursday night Mingus Big Band ($18), when the low-ceilinged basement per-formance space is filled with the cool sounds of jazz. The rest of the week brings an eclectic live-music-and-performance-art mix, which can range from Patti Rothberg to drag grande-dame Hedda Lettuce to tributes to acts like Queen and ABBA from Loser's Lounge. The cover ranges from $10 to $15, and a two-drink minimum

Value   Free Music in the Clubs

Rodeo Bar (p. 314) is the city's top no-cover club, but it's not the only free show in town.

Others worth checking out include the **Living Room,** 84 Stanton St., at Allen Street (✆ 212/533-7235; www.livingroomny.com), an unpretentious bar/restaurant that's good for acoustic acts (the sound system isn't great for electric). The pass-the-bucket policy allows you to contribute to the performers' earnings (the venue suggests a $5 tip); there is a one-drink minimum. Also on the Lower East Side is **Luna Lounge** ⋆, 171 Ludlow St., between Houston and Stanton streets (✆ 212/260-2323; www.lunalounge.com), which usually hosts two bands a night. Monday's comedy night, Eating It, has become so popular that there's a $7 cover (one drink included).

East Village stalwart **Manitoba's,** 99 Ave. B., between 6th and 7th streets (✆ 212/982-2511), features a fun rock-and-roll bar from Dictators frontman Dick Manitoba. **Lakeside Lounge,** 162 Ave. B, between 10th and 11th streets (✆ 212/529-8463; www.lakeslounge.com), also regularly hosts excellent-quality live music with no cover charge.

Jazz fans can try **Arthur's Tavern,** in the Village at 57 Grove St., at Seventh Avenue South (✆ 212/675-6879), a comfortable club and piano bar attracting a mixed gay-and-straight crowd. Beware of the drinks, which can be pricey. In the East Village, "Live Jazz or Die" is the mantra at **Detour** ⋆, 349 E. 13th St., at First Avenue (✆ 212/533-6212; www.jazzatdetour.com), a high-quality club offering no-cover music nightly (two-drink minimum); $3 happy hour from 4 to 7pm maximizes the fun.

Harlem's **Showmans Cafe,** 375 W. 125th St., between St. Nicholas and Morningside avenues (✆ 212/864-8941), hosts free music Monday through Saturday ranging from jazz to funky bebop that attracts music lovers and players from all walks of life, and the service is just as friendly whether you come from the neighborhood, downtown, or out of town.

Also keep in mind that a number of clubs listed in these pages offer free music 1 or more nights a week, such as **Cafe Wha?,** the **Continental,** the **Baggot Inn, Arlene Grocery, Smoke, Chicago B.L.U.E.S.,** the **C-Note,** the lounge at **CBGB, 55 Bar, Tonic,** and the **Internet Cafe;** the **Knitting Factory** offers free music in its Old Office Lounge. There's also free live music every Sunday at SoHo's **24/8 Lounge** (see "Bars & Cocktail Lounges" later in this chapter). **Jazz at the Cajun** lets you listen to the finest old-school jazz in town for the price of a meal—and you have to eat anyway, don't you? The easiest way to check for free events while you're in town is to peruse the weekly *Time Out New York,* which announces no-cover shows with an easy-to-spot FREE! Sunday and Monday are big nights for freebies.

Remember that schedules and no-cover policies can change at any time, so always confirm in advance.

might be required. *Money-saving tip:* Students holding a valid photo ID can usually attend the Mingus Big Band late show for just $10. 380 Lafayette St. (at Great Jones St.). © 212/533-2680. www.feznyc.com. Subway: 6 to Bleecker St.

Mercury Lounge   The Merc is everything a top-notch live-music venue should be: unpretentious, civilized, and with a killer sound system. The rooms are nothing special: a front bar and an intimate back-room performance space with a low stage and a few tables lining the brick walls. The calendar is filled with a mix of accomplished local rockers and national acts like Frank Black, Art Alexakis, and the Mekons. The crowd is grown-up and easygoing. The only downside is that it's consistently packed thanks to the high quality of the entertainment and all-around pleasing nature of the experience. The cover is likely to be between $8 and $10, maybe more for national acts. 217 E. Houston St. (at Essex St./Ave. A). © 212/260-4700. www.mercuryloungenyc.com. Subway: F to Second Ave.

Rodeo Bar *(Value)*   Here's New York's oldest—and finest—honky-tonk. Hike up your Wranglers and head inside, where you'll find longhorns on the walls, peanut shells underfoot, and Tex-Mex on the menu. But this place is really about the music: urban-tinged country, bluegrass, swinging rockabilly, and Southern-flavored rock. Bigger names like Brian Setzer and up-and-comers on the tour circuit like Hank Williams III occasionally grace the stage, but regular acts like Dixieland swingers the Flying Neutrinos, cowpunk goddess Rosie Flores, and BBQ Bob and the Spareribs usually supply free music, keeping the urban cowboys plenty happy. A 10-gallon hat full o' fun. It's happy hour until 7pm; the music starts around 9:30pm nightly, and goes until at least 3am. 375 Third Ave. (at 27th St.). © 212/683-6500. www.rodeobar.com. Subway: 6 to 28th St.

Tonic *(Finds)*   This quirky Lower East Sider has become the avant-garde jazz/experimental rock spot in the Knitting Factory vein, sometimes with big names like John Zorn's Masada, Cibo Matto, and Marc Ribot in the house. Tickets range from $8 to $12. A DJ spins mood music downstairs. Sunday's Klezmer brunch is definitely worth seeking out. *Money-saving tip:* You can usually save a few bucks by buying advance (rather than day-of-show) tickets, either at the Tonic box office, open daily from 8 to 11pm, or at Other Music (p. 289). 107 Norfolk St. (between Delancey and Rivington sts.). © 212/358-7503. www.tonicnyc.com. Subway: F, J, M, Z to Delancey/Essex sts.

Village Underground *(Finds)*   The folks behind dear departed Tramps have opened this intimate, even romantic subterranean venue. Some big-name talent turns up, including Buckwheat Zydeco, Michelle Shocked, Junior Brown, and R&B legend Solomon Burke (on the heels of his Rock and Roll Hall of Fame induction). Even if you don't recognize the names, you can count on quality music. Tickets run from $7 to $25; advance tickets can be purchased at www.ticketweb.com or at © 866/468-7619. 130 W. 3rd St. (between Sixth Ave. and MacDougal St.). © 212/777-7745. www.thevillageunderground.com. Subway: A, C, E, F, V to W. 4th St. (use W. 3rd St. exit).

JAZZ, BLUES & MORE

A night at a top-flight jazz club can be expensive. Cover charges can vary dramatically—from as little as $10 to as high as $65, depending on who's taking the stage—and there's likely to be an additional two-drink minimum (or a dinner requirement, if you choose an early show). Call ahead so you know what you're getting into; reservations are also an excellent idea at top spots.

For those of you who like your jazz with an edge, see what's on at the **Knitting Factory** (p. 311), **Tonic** (see above), and the **C-Note** (p. 312). Trad fans should also consider the Thursday Mingus Big Band Workshop at **Fez Under Time Cafe**

(p. 312), while swingsters should consider **Swing 46** (p. 330). **Smoke** (p. 316) is probably your best bet for quality jazz without a cover. Lovers of Latin and world music can't do better than terrific **S.O.B.'s** (p. 316).

There's also world-beat jazz every Friday and Saturday from 5 to 8pm in the rotunda at the **Guggenheim Museum;** see chapter 7. And don't forget **Jazz at Lincoln Center** (p. 305), the nation's premier forum for the traditional and developing jazz canon.

Birdland   While the legends of Parker, Monk, Gillespie, and other bebop pioneers still hold sway, Birdland isn't a crowded, smoky joint of yesteryear. The big room is spacious, comfy, and classy, with excellent sound and top-notch talent. Expect lots of accomplished big bands and jazz trios, plus occasional appearances by stars like Dave Brubeck. You can't go wrong with the Sunday night show, starring Chico O'Farrell's smokin' Afro-Cuban Jazz Big Band. The Southern-style food is pretty good. At press time, Tuesdays were the domain of the Duke Ellington Orchestra, led by Duke's grandson Paul Ellington every other week. The cover runs a hefty $20 to $35, with a $10 food-and-drink minimum. *Money-saving tip:* You can avoid the minimum by sitting at the bar rather than a table, and you'll also score a complimentary beverage (at press time, anyway; check current policy). 315 W. 44th St. (between Eighth and Ninth aves.). © 212/581-3080. www.birdlandjazz.com. Subway: A, C, E to 42nd St.

Blue Note   The Blue Note has attracted some of the biggest names in jazz to its intimate setting. Those who've played here include just about everyone of note: Dave Brubeck, Ray Charles, B.B. King, Manhattan Transfer, Dr. John, George Duke, Chick Corea, David Sanborn, Arturo Sandoval, Gato Barbieri, and the superb Oscar Peterson. The sound system is excellent, and every seat in the house has a sight line to the stage; however, in recent years, the hard edge that once was the Blue Note has faded. Softer, smoother jazz is the domain now, so if that's your thing, enjoy. Prices are high here, ranging between $20 and $30. There are two shows per night, and dinner is served. 131 W. 3rd St. (at Sixth Ave.). © 212/475-8592. www.bluenote.net. Subway: A, C, E, F, V to W. 4th St.

55 Bar *Value*   This Prohibition-era Village dive hosts high-quality jazz and blues nightly, with guitarists a specialty (think Wayne Krantz, Hiram Bullock). The house guitar trio is definitely worth a listen, and if saxist Ed Palermo is on the bill, go. The cover ranges from free (two-drink minimum) to $15; it's usually in the $3-to-$5 range. 55 Christopher St. (just east of Seventh Ave.). © 212/929-9883. www.55bar.com. Subway: 1, 9 to Christopher St.

Internet Cafe *Value*   Those looking for an affordable jazz fix should visit this casual online cafe, which features well-regarded jazz from up-and-coming acts nightly, plus a full bar. The cover charge is never more than $8, usually less; at press time, legendary bluesman Bobby Radcliffe had a standing gig on Friday nights with no cover. 82 E. 3rd St. (between First and Second aves.). © 212/614-0747. www.bigmagic.com. Subway: F to Second Ave.

Iridium   This snazzy jazz club has relocated from its longtime perch across from Lincoln Center to a heart-of-the-Theater District location. Everything else remains the same, including the talent and big-name acts. Like the Energizer bunny, Les Paul keeps on going, playing every Monday night (tickets $27.50, plus $15 minimum). Other top-notch performers include Nicholas Payton, Mose Allison, McCoy Tyner and Bobby Hutcherson, and the Jazz Messengers. A full, rather sophisticated dinner menu is served. 1650 Broadway (at 51st St.). © 212/582-2121. www.iridiumjazzclub.com. Subway: 1, 9 to 50th St.

Jazz at the Cajun *(Finds)*   This cozy, casual New Orleans–themed supper club is the best venue in town for prewar big-band and Dixieland jazz—think Jelly Roll Morton, Scott Joplin, early Duke. The crowd comes from all walks of life, united in their love of the old school. Cajun is home base for Vince Giordano's Nighthawks, who are masters of yesteryear—a joy to watch!—but the place jumps no matter what crew takes the stage. There's no cover charge, and food is affordable and just fine, with entrees in the low and mid-teens; reserve in advance. 129 Eighth Ave. (between 16th and 17th sts.). ℂ 212/691-6174. www.jazzatthecajun.com. Subway: A, C, E to 14th St.; L to 8th Ave.

Jazz Standard *(Finds)*   Boasting a retro-speakeasy vibe, the Jazz Standard is one of the city's largest jazz clubs, with well-spaced tables seating 150 and a $15 cover ($20 on weekends). The rule is straightforward, mainstream jazz by new and established musicians, including such stars as Branford Marsalis. Now that the restaurant is **Blue Smoke** from Danny Meyer (Union Square Cafe, Gramercy Tavern), serving mouthwatering gourmet Southern barbecue at affordable prices, you really can't go wrong. This makes for one fantastic night on the town. 116 E. 27th St. (between Park Ave. S. and Lexington Ave.). ℂ 212/576-2232. www.jazzstandard.net. Subway: 6 to 28th St.

Lenox Lounge *(Finds)*   One of Harlem's best jazz clubs, the intimate, Art Deco–cool back room—complete with zebra stripes on the walls and banquettes—hosts top-flight jazz vocalists, trios, and quartets for a crowd that comes to listen and be wowed. The cover never goes higher than $15 (one-drink minimum). Well worth the trip uptown for those who want a genuine Harlem jazz experience. 288 Malcolm X Blvd. (Lenox Ave.; between 124th and 125th sts.). ℂ 212/427-0253. Subway: 2, 3 to 125th St.

Smoke *(Finds)*   A rising star in the New York jazz scene and the best place to hear the music on the Upper West Side, Smoke is a welcome throwback to the informal, intimate clubs of the past. It's the kind of place that on most nights you can just walk in on and find some solid jazz. And though it seats only 65, for no more than a $20 cover, Smoke still manages to attract big names like the Steve Turre Quartet, Ron Carter, Eddie Henderson, and vocalist Vanessa Rubin. On Sunday through Thursday there is no cover, and each night has a theme including funk on Wednesdays with the rocking Hot Pants Funk Sextet, Latin jazz on Sundays, and my favorite, Hammond organ grooves on Tuesday. There are three sets nightly and a very popular happy hour. 2751 Broadway (between 105th and 106th sts.). ℂ 212/864-6662. www.smokejazz.com. Subway: 1 to 103rd St.

S.O.B.'s *(★)*   If you like your music hot, hot, hot, S.O.B.'s is the place for you. This is the city's top world-music venue, specializing in Brazilian, Caribbean, and Latin sounds. The packed house dances and sings along nightly to calypso, samba, mambo, African drums, reggae, or other global grooves, united in the high-energy, feel-good vibe. Bookings include top-flight performers from around the globe; Astrud Gilberto, Mighty Sparrow, King Sunny Ade, Eddie Palmieri, Buckwheat Zydeco, Beausoleil, and the unsurpassed Celia Cruz are only a few of the names who have graced this lively stage. The room's Tropicana Club style has island pizzazz that carries through to the Caribbean-influenced cooking and extensive tropical drinks menu. This place is so popular that it's an excellent idea to book in advance, especially if you'd like table seating. Monday is dedicated to Latin sounds, Tuesday to reggae; Friday features a late-night French Caribbean dance party, while Saturday is reserved for samba. The cover runs $10 to $25, but frequently stays at or below the $15 mark. *Money-saving*

tip: Check the website for a $5-off coupon. 204 Varick St. (at Houston St.). ℭ 212/
243-4940. www.sobs.com. Subway: 1, 9 to Houston St.

Terra Blues   This artsy blues club hosts an active calendar of local and
national acts, with a $5 to $10 cover, even on weekends; plan on a two-drink
minimum. 149 Bleecker St. (between Thompson St. and LaGuardia Place). ℭ 212/777-7776.
www.terrablues.com. Subway: A, C, E, F, V to W. 4th St.

The Village Vanguard   What CBGB is to rock, the Village Vanguard is to
jazz. One look at the photos on the walls will show you who's been through since
1935, from Coltrane, Miles, and Monk to Branford Marsalis and Joshua Red-
man. Expect a mix of established names and high-quality local talent, including
the Vanguard's own jazz orchestra on Monday nights. The sound is great, but
sightlines are terrible, so come early for a front table. The crowd can seem either
overly serious or overly touristy, but don't let that stop you—you'll always find
great music. Covers range from $15 to $30; Sunday through Thursday nights are
cheapest. 178 Seventh Ave. S. (just below 11th St.). ℭ 212/255-4037. www.villagevanguard.
com. Subway: 1, 2, 3, 9 to 14th St.

5 Stand-Up & Sketch Comedy

Comedy Cellar *Finds*   This intimate subterranean spot is the club of choice for
stand-up fans in the know, thanks to the most consistently impressive lineups in
the business. He might be the highest-paid sitcom star now, but once an unknown
Ray Romano honed his material here. $10 weekdays, $12 weekends, two-drink
minimum. *Money-saving tip:* Check the website to order free tickets and free
drinks for select nights. 117 MacDougal St. (between Bleecker and W. 3rd sts.). ℭ 212/
254-3480. www.comedycellar.com. Subway: A, C, E, F, V to W. 4th St. (use 3rd St. exit).

Gershwin Hotel *Value*   One of New York's best budget hotels (see chapter 5)
hosts some of the city's best comedy lineups in the Living Room lounge, for a
$5 cover charge. Comedians usually take the stage 4 nights a week; best of the
bunch is Thursday's terrific Great $5 Comedy Show, which regularly hosts the
best funny-men and -women in the biz. 7 E. 27th St. (between Fifth and Madison aves.).
ℭ 212/545-8000. www.gershwinhotel.com. Subway: N, R, 6 to 28th St.

New York Comedy Club *Value*   With a $7 cover charge on weekdays ($10
Fri–Sat) plus a two-beverage minimum, this small club offers the best value for
your money. Despite what the owners call their "Wal-Mart approach" to comedy,
the club has presented Damon Wayans, Chris Rock, and Brett Butler, among
others, in its two showrooms. Monday's Open Mike Night (5pm) is $3 with
unlimited soft drinks, and you're welcome to get on stage for your 5 minutes of
fame. Weekends set aside time for African-American and Latino comics. Come
early for a good seat. 241 E. 24th St. (between Second and Third aves.). ℭ 212/696-5233.
www.newyorkcomedyclub.com. Subway: 6 to 23rd St.

Stand-Up New York   The Upper West Side's premier stand-up comedy club
hosts some of the brightest comics in the business, plus drop-ins like Dennis
Leary, Caroline Rhea, Robin Williams, and Mr. Upper West Side himself, Jerry
Seinfeld. Cover is $10 to $15, with a two-item food or drink minimum. *Money-
saving tip:* Order your tickets for PrimeTime shows (Thurs–Sat) online at the
website and you'll save $5 per ticket. 236 W. 78th St. (at Broadway). ℭ 212/595-0850.
www.standupny.com. Subway: 1, 9 to 79th St.

Upright Citizens Brigade Theater *Value*   You've seen their twisted, highly original sketch comedy on Comedy Central—now you can see the Upright Citizens

Brigade, New York's premier alternative comedy troupe, live. The best of the nonstop hilarity is *A.S.S.S.C.A.T.,* the troupe's extremely popular long-form improv show, which often sells out in advance. The company has supplied a few members of the Not-Ready-For-Prime-Time Players in recent years, including Amy Poehler. You won't pay more than $7 for any show; reservations are a must. 307 W. 26th St. (between Eighth and Ninth aves.). ℂ 212/366-9176. www.ucbtheater.com. Subway: 1, 9 to 23rd St.

6 Cabaret Rooms & Piano Bars

The city's top supper clubs and cabarets are not for the budget-minded. At places like **Cafe Carlyle,** in the Carlyle Hotel, 781 Madison Ave. (ℂ 212/744-1600), home to the legendary Bobby Short (and Woody Allen in the Eddy Davis New Orleans Jazz Band most Mondays), and the Algonquin's **Oak Room,** 59 W. 44th St. (ℂ 212/840-6800), covers usually run in the neighborhood of $75, plus two-drink or dinner-check minimums; count on a $300 night on the town.

But never fear: One of these more casual, less-expensive options will result in a wallet-friendly night. Reservations are suggested for cabaret shows, and are not usually necessary for piano bars (although it never hurts to check).

Brandy's Piano Bar   A mixed crowd—Upper East Side locals, waiters off work, gays, straights, all ages—comes to this intimate, old-school piano bar for the atmosphere and nightly entertainment. The talented waitstaff does most of the singing while waiting for their big breaks, but enthusiastic patrons regularly join in. The sounds tend to familiar adult-contemporary radio hits and cabaret tunes. This place is so unhip that it's downright cool; it makes for a fun and affordable night on the town. No cover charge; two-drink minimum. 235 E. 84th St. (between Second and Third aves.). ℂ 212/744-4949. Subway: 4, 5, 6 to 86th St.

Danny's Skylight Room   You'll find this Theater District showroom tucked away in, of all places, the rear of a Thai restaurant. It offers surprisingly strong lineups, including the fabulous Blossom Dearie and her world-class trio, with a cover that ranges from $12 to $25 (usually $20 or less), plus a $10 minimum; ask about dinner/show packages. There's no cover in the piano bar, where you'll hear first-class tunes from the American songbook. Happy hour (weekdays 4:30–7pm) means two-for-one beer and wine. At Danny's Grand Sea Palace, 346–348 W. 46th St. (between Eighth and Ninth aves.). ℂ 212/265-8133 or 212/265-8130. www.dannys grandseapalace.com. Subway: A, C, E to 42nd St.

Don't Tell Mama   You'll find an evening of torch songs, comedy, and much more in a friendly, and affordable, atmosphere at this wonderful two-room Theater District cabaret. The cover charge ranges from free to $20, depending on the show, plus a two-drink minimum. Drinks only, no dinner. The piano bar is particularly lively, and always free (two-drink minimum). 343 W. 46th St. (between Eighth and Ninth aves.). ℂ 212/757-0788. Subway: A, C, E to 42nd St.

Duplex Cabaret   Expect a high camp factor and lots of good-natured fun in this multilevel space, New York's oldest cabaret. A mixed gay/straight crowd of locals and out-of-towners sit at outdoor tables, gather around the downstairs

---

⟨*Value*⟩ **Money-Saving Tip for Cabaret Fans**

At **Cafe Carlyle,** value-minded cabaret fans can save by reserving standing room (which usually results in a spot at the bar) for just $35.

piano (singalongs from around 9pm), or head upstairs to the cabaret for shows that run from minimusicals to drag revues to stand-up comedy. No cover at the piano bar (two-drink minimum), $5 to $15 in the showroom. 61 Christopher St. (at Seventh Ave.). ℂ 212/255-5438. www.theduplex.com. Subway: 1, 9 to Christopher St.

Judy's Chelsea This lovely cabaret room is one of the top cabaret rooms in town, with a smart, modern look and an easygoing vibe. Talent runs the gamut from rising stars to well-known vets of the cabaret stage. Covers vary depending upon who's on stage, but usually stick between $10 and $15 (no cover for the piano bar); there's also a $10 food-and-drink minimum. 169 Eighth Ave. (between 18th and 19th sts.). ℂ 212/929-5410. Subway: A, C, E, L to 14th St.

7 Bars & Cocktail Lounges

TRIBECA

In addition to the choices below, consider **Walker's,** 16 N. Moore St., at Varick Street (ℂ **212/941-0142**), a holdout from pre-fabulous TriBeCa; see chapter 6.

Grace *Finds* This spacious and unpretentious lounge has made itself right at home with a sophisticated yet down-to-earth vibe; a good selection of cocktails, single-malts, and on-tap beers from the sweeping, welcoming mahogany bar; and an affordable menu of elegant yet unpretentious Pan-Asian–influenced New American dishes ($8–$14) that make great late-night cocktail nibbles. There's an airy dining room in back, too, if you'd like to reserve a nook for yourself. 114 Franklin St. (between W. Broadway and Church St.). ℂ 212/343-4200. www.gracebarandrestaurant.com. Subway: 1, 9 to Franklin St.

Liquor Store Bar Housed in, yes, a former liquor store, this wonderful little oak-and-brass tavern is the best place for an affordable drink with a dash of style in TriBeCa. Come midweek to beat the Friday and Saturday crowds. 235 W. Broadway (at White St.). ℂ 212/226-7121. Subway: A, C, E to Canal St.

99 Hudson Street Restaurant & Sports Lounge The city's best sports bar (rated No. 1 in the *Daily News*) is a guy's joint if there ever was one. The space is big, with giant TV screens at every turn tuned to just about every game on the planet. (Wall Streeters bring their international cohorts here to catch everything from English football to Japanese sumo.) The menu is what you'd expect: wings, burgers, club sandwiches, and *lots* of beer. Reservations accepted (a good idea when the big game's on). When the big games are over, this turns into a surprisingly popular singles place. 99 Hudson St. (between Franklin and Leonard sts.). ℂ 212/ 219-0900. www.thesportingclub.net. Subway: 1, 9 to Franklin St.

CHINATOWN & LITTLE ITALY

Double Happiness *Finds* The only indicator to the subterranean entrance is a WATCH YOUR STEP sign. Once through the door, you'll find a beautifully designed speakeasy-ish lounge with artistic nods to the neighborhood, plus a low-key vibe. The space is large, but a low ceiling and intimate nooks add a hint of romance (although the loud music mix may deter true wooing). Don't miss the green-tea martini, an inspired house creation. 173 Mott St. (between Grand and Broome sts.). ℂ 212/941-1282. Subway: 6 to Spring St.

Mare Chiaro This authentic corner of Little Italy now hosts a bizarro mix of slumming Nolita hipsters, uptown singles, and neighborhood holdovers from an age when this was just a drinking man's bar. But Mare Chiaro still works its crusty magic, transporting you back to another era with its gentrification-resistant vibe.

Tips ... No More Smoke-Filled Bars in NYC ...

As of April 1, 2003, New York City adopted tough nonsmoking laws pro-
hibiting smoking in all bars and restaurants. At press time, the shock of
the new law was still taking effect, and many bars and lounges had not
figured a way around the law. The only exceptions were cigar bars, private
clubs, and specially ventilated smoking rooms where employees do not
enter (the law was proposed to protect employees of bars from the harm-
ful effects of second-hand smoke). So our only advice at this moment is,
like in California, where a similar law has been in effect for years, if the
urge arises, expect to huddle outside the bar with your cigarette or cigar.
Don't worry; you won't be alone.

A great place for a cheap beer at a crossroads of city life. 176½ Mulberry St. (at Broome
St.). ② 212/226-9345. Subway: 6 to Spring St.

THE LOWER EAST SIDE

Also consider **Le Pere Pinard** (p. 147), 175 Ludlow St., south of Houston (② 212/
777-4917), an affordable, terrific, and *très français* wine bar. There's also **Mercury
Lounge,** 217 E. Houston St. (② 212/260-4700), which has a casual, comfortable
bar up front; see p. 314.

Barramundi   This nice lounge is notable for its fairy-tale outdoor garden,
friendly staff, and settled-in feel in a neighborhood overrun by hipster copycats.
Come on a weeknight to snare a table in the little corner of heaven out back. A
fireplace makes Barramundi almost as appealing on cool nights. 147 Ludlow St.
(between Stanton and Rivington sts.). ② 212/569-6900. Subway: F to Second Ave.

Good World Bar & Grill *(Finds)*   Don't worry about running into your fellow
tourists here; this former Chinese barbershop is completely off the beaten track.
Despite the location and utter lack of decor, it draws a young alterna-hip crowd
with its refreshing lack of pretensions, low prices on good on-tap beers, and surprisingly good—and affordable—Scandinavian eats. 3 Orchard St. (between Division
and Canal sts.). ② 212/925-9975. Subway: F to E. Broadway.

Idlewild *(Finds)*   It may look unapproachable from the street, with nothing but
an unmarked stainless-steel facade, but inside you'll find a fun, easygoing bar
that's perfect for lovers of retro-kitsch. The interior is a larger-scale repro of a jet
airplane, complete with reclining seats, tray tables, and too-small bathrooms.
There are booths in back for larger crowds, and an *Austin Powers*–style bar to
gather around at center stage. The crowd is a mix of downtown locals and hip
tourists, and the DJ spins a listener-friendly mix of light techno, disco in the
funkadelic vein, and '80s tunes from the likes of the Smiths and the Cure.
Drinks are affordable. 145 E. Houston St. (between First and Second aves., on the south side
of Houston). ② 212/477-5005. Subway: F to Second Ave.

Rivertown Lounge *(Value)*   This spacious, low-key neighborhood boîte is an
excellent place to hang with the locals and nurse a beer. Happy hour lasts all day:
Enjoy $3 wine and drafts Monday through Friday from 1 to 8pm. There's a dart-
board and a pool table. DJs speed up the vibe most nights. 187 Orchard St. (south of
Houston St.). ② 212/388-1288. Subway: F to Second Ave.

Whiskey Ward *(Finds)*   Here's the second-best bar in town for serious whiskey
fans (only behind the East Village's dba): first-class single malts and bourbons

from which to choose, and no pretensions. Decor is kept to a minimum in traditional saloon style, but the jukebox rocks and a pool table provides additional entertainment. Nice on-tap and bottled beer selection, too. 121 Essex St. (between Rivington and Delancey sts.). ℂ 212/477-2998. Subway: F to Delancey St.

SOHO

Also consider old-world **Fanelli's Cafe** (p. 148), 94 Prince St., at Mercer Street (ℂ 212/226-9412), for a brew and a burger—but come early to avoid the crowds. Another terrific choice for a pint-and-plate combo is **Puck Fair** (p. 149), 298 Lafayette St., just south of Houston (ℂ 212/431-2100).

Ear Inn   This far-west SoHo pub has been a local fave since before the Civil War, thanks to its casual ambience, huge selection of beers, and bartenders who aren't looking for their big break. This is the kind of place where bikers can pony up to the bar next to bankers, and everybody gets along. 326 Spring St. (between Greenwich and Washington sts.). ℂ 212/226-9060. Subway: C, E to Spring St.

Merc Bar   Notable for its long tenure in the fickle world of beautiful-people bars, upscale Merc Bar has mellowed nicely. You'll still find a good-looking crowd in the superbly appointed lounge, but now it's a confident rather than trend-happy one. The decor bespeaks civilized rusticity with warm woods, a canoe over the bar, copper-top tables, and butter-leather banquettes. A great place to nestle into a comfortable couch with your honey, splurge on a classy cocktail, and enjoy the scene. The European martini (Stoli raspberry and Chambord) is divine. Look carefully, because there's no sign. 151 Mercer St. (between Prince and Houston sts.). ℂ 212/966-2727. Subway: N, R to Prince St.

THE EAST VILLAGE & NOHO

In addition to the choices below, also consider **Fez,** 380 Lafayette St., at Great Jones Street (ℂ 212/533-2680; www.feznyc.com), a dimly lit Moroccan-themed bar and lounge that I prefer to the downstairs performance space; see p. 312.

Burp Castle *Finds*   This theme bar is a must for serious beer lovers. It's styled as a "Temple of Beer Worship," complete with medieval-inspired decor, choral music on the sound system, and soft-spoken waiters in monkish garb. Before you have time to let the weirdness sink in, you'll be distracted by the incomparable beer list. There are more than 500 bottled and on-tap beers from which to choose—including a phenomenal collection of Trappist ales, of course. The staff is courteous but a bit too studiedly monkish in its behavior; I couldn't wrest an actual recommendation out of them. 41 E. 7th St. (between Second and Third aves.). ℂ 212/982-4576. Subway: 6 to Astor Place.

dba *Finds*   dba has completely bucked the loungey trend that has taken over the city, instead remaining firmly and resolutely an unpretentious neighborhood bar. Everyone is welcome in this beer- and scotch-lover's paradise, which posts a massive drink menu on chalkboards. Owner Ray Deter specializes in British-style cask-conditioned ales (the kind that you pump by hand) and stocks a phenomenal collection of single-malt scotches. The crowd is a pleasing mix of connoisseurs and casual drinkers who like the choices and egalitarian vibe. Ray has enclosed the back garden, transforming it into an East Village beer garden. Excellent jukebox, too. 41 First Ave. (between 2nd and 3rd sts.). ℂ 212/475-5097. www.drinkgoodstuff.com. Subway: F to Second Ave.

Drinkland   This Alphabet City boîte boasts a retro-futuristic pop-art interior by the designer for *Austin Powers* and DJs from around the world, who spin techno, house, jungle, trance, and other electronic sounds Tuesday through

Sunday nights for a crowd that really comes to listen. There's almost never a cover (usually $5 on Sat only), but call to confirm. 339 E. 10th St. (between aves. A and B). ✆ **212/228-2435.** www.drinkland.com. Subway: L to First Ave.

KGB Bar This former Ukrainian social club still boasts its Soviet-themed decor, but it now draws creative types who like the low-key boho vibe. Sunday nights are the biggest draw, thanks to the success of KGB's excellent reading series, where an increasingly talented pack of up-and-coming and published writers read their prose to a receptive crowd starting at 7pm. Past readers have included Rick Moody *(The Ice Storm)* and Kathryn Harrison *(The Kiss).* 85 E. 4th St. (between Second and Third aves.). ✆ **212/505-3360.** Subway: 6 to Astor Place.

McSorley's Old Ale House In business for more than 140 years, McSorley's window proudly claims WE WERE HERE BEFORE YOU WERE BORN. Only McSorley's Ale is served, light or dark, and two at a time. Come to bask in the old-time New York vibe, not to nurse a Diet Coke. This is an ale-sodden frat-boy madhouse most nights and an Irish Armageddon on St. Patrick's Day, but everybody seems to love it. Although it's also a McSorley's tradition to urinate on the wall outside, they prefer you honor that one in the breach, not in the commission. 15 E. 7th St. (between Second and Third aves.). ✆ **212/473-9148.** Subway: 6 to Astor Place.

Tom & Jerry's (288 Bar) *Finds* Here's a pleasing neighborhood bar minus the grunge factor that usually plagues such joints. The place has an authentic local vibe, and the youngish, artsy crowd is unpretentious and chatty. The beer selection is very good and the mixed drinks are better than average. Flea-market hounds will enjoy the vintage collection of "Tom & Jerry" punchbowl sets behind the bar, and creative types will enjoy the rotating collection of works from local artists, which changes monthly. There's no sign, but you'll spy the action through the plate-glass window on the east side of Elizabeth Street just north of Houston. 288 Elizabeth St. ✆ **212/260-5045.** Subway: 6 to Bleecker St.

GREENWICH VILLAGE & THE MEAT-PACKING DISTRICT

Bowlmor/Pressure *Finds* Supercool Bowlmor isn't your daddy's bowling alley: DJs spin, martinis flow, candy-colored balls knock down day-glo pins, and strikes and spares are automatically tallied into the wee hours. Frankly, Bowlmor is a blast. Once you're finished with your 10-pin—or while you're waiting for your lane—head upstairs to the rooftop lounge Pressure, housed in a 16,000-square-foot inflated bubble and boasting designer-mod furnishings, a sexy cocktail menu that includes a luscious chocolate martini (infused with Godiva chocolate liqueur), a fleet of pool tables, and always-on movie screens adding an arty-party flair. 110 University Place (between 12th and 13th sts.). ✆ **212/255-8188** (Bowlmor), or 212/352-1161 (Pressure). www.bowlmor.com or www.pressurenyc.com. Subway: 4, 5, 6, L, N, R to 14th St./Union Sq.

Chumley's Many bars in New York date to Prohibition, but Chumley's still has the vibe. The college-age crowd doesn't date back as far, however. Come to warm yourself by the fire and indulge in a once-forbidden pleasure: beer. The door is unmarked, with a metal grille on the small window; another entrance is at 58 Barrow St., which takes you in through a back courtyard. 86 Bedford St. (at Barrow St.). ✆ **212/675-4449.** Subway: 1, 9 to Christopher St.

Hogs & Heifers This roadhouse-style bar is it: a *Coyote Ugly*–style bar, complete with "bra tree," bar-top hip-shaking, and free-flowing shots. It's pretty much devoid of its original rough-and-tumble local appeal, but still offers fun for those who don't mind the tourist trappings. The bridge-and-tunnel, frat-boyish crowd gets wild as the night wears on, especially on weekends. 859 Washington St.

(at 13th St.). ✆ 212/929-0655. Subway: A, C, E, L to 14th St. Also at 1843 First Ave. (between 95th and 96th sts.; ✆ 212/722-8635; subway: 6 to 96th St.).

White Horse Tavern Poets and literary buffs pop into this 1880 pub to pay their respects to Dylan Thomas, who tipped his last jar here. Best enjoyed in the warm weather when there's outdoor drinking, or at happy hour for the cheap drafts that draw in a big frat-boy and post-frat yuppie crowd. 567 Hudson St. (at 11th St.). ✆ 212/243-9260. Subway: 1, 9 to Christopher St.

CHELSEA

Chelsea Commons ★ The trendy bars come and go in this fashion-conscious neighborhood, but time stands still at Chelsea Commons. This old pub hosts an assortment of locals; artists trying to avoid the pretentiously hip, and workers from the nearby warehouses and depots. A fireplace gives it a homey feel in the winter and an outdoor patio, an urban escape in the summer. The jukebox has a nice mix of R&B, rock, country, and jazz. A great place for conversation and a pint of beer. Food is also available, but don't get fancy; stick with the basic pub fare. 242 Tenth Ave. (at 24th St.). ✆ 212/929-9424. Subway: C, E to 23rd St.

Gaslight The ideal cross between a cozy English pub and an elegant Victorian lounge. No taps, though—but a dependably good hangout nonetheless. 400 W. 14th St. (at Ninth Ave.). ✆ 212/807-8444. Subway: A, C, E to 14th St.

Serena *(Finds)* This plush and popular basement boîte has managed to stay fresh by reinventing itself. Done in deep, sexy reds, Serena is again as hip as can be— I've even spotted Moby here. It's relatively unpretentious considering its hot-spot status; still, dress the part if you want to make it past the doorman. The crowd is young and pretty, and the music mix is a blast—think Fatboy Slim meets ABBA meets Foghat and you'll get the picture. In the basement level of the Hotel Chelsea, 222 W. 23rd St. (between Seventh and Eighth aves.). ✆ 212/255-4646. Subway: C, E, 1, 9 to 23rd St.

THE FLATIRON DISTRICT, UNION SQUARE & GRAMERCY PARK

Also consider the **Old Town Bar & Restaurant** (p. 165), 45 E. 18th St., between Broadway and Park Avenue South (✆ 212/529-6732), a genuine tin-ceilinged 19th-century bar that's a terrific place to soak up some Old New York atmosphere. Sleek noodle house **Republic** (p. 165), 37 Union Sq. W. (✆ 212/627-7172), boasts an up-front bar that's popular with a wallet-watching cocktail crowd who come to enjoy such creative libations as the Sake Dragon martini (sake and Chambord) and a Fuji apple Cosmopolitan.

Dusk *(Finds)* This casual, artsy lounge is a great choice for a cocktail. There's a fab mirrored mosaic wall, banquettes opposite, a friendly bar serving affordable drinks, a pool table, and mostly U.K. tunes—from drum-and-bass to Super Furry Animals to Blur to Enya—on the sound system. Expect an easygoing, youngish crowd that stays relaxed and unpretentious into the evening. No sign, but look for the three blue lights attached to a dark storefront. 147 W. 24th St. (between Sixth and Seventh aves.). ✆ 212/924-4490. Subway: F to 23rd St.

Gramercy Park Hotel Bar Who says a hotel bar can't be a dive? But this one is a dive in the best definition of that term. It has a loungey feel to it, with its quasi-antique furnishings and lush red drapes. But it's distinctive, even comforting, in its gauche retro-80s look. The bar was used in the movie *Almost Famous,* about a young journalist covering a rock band for *Rolling Stone,* maybe because rock-and-rollers like Sting, Deborah Harry, and The Clash have frequented the

Moments The Dive Bar Experience

Watering holes in New York are many and diverse: There are bars and clubs with cover charges, outrageously expensive cocktails, elegant finger food, beautiful people, and velvet ropes to keep you waiting in the cold until someone determines you are worthy to enter. And then there are places in this city where you should be rewarded for braving, old, dark places where the drinks are cheap and the characters colorful. These are the dive bars, and they are just as much New York as the hottest, trendiest club you've read about back in your hometown. Here are some of my favorite dive bars; stop in one for a real New York experience.

Jimmy's Corner, 140 W. 44th St., between Broadway and Sixth Avenue (© 212/221-9510). Owned by a former boxing trainer, Jimmy's is a tough-guy's joint that has been around for more than 30 years and survived the Disneyfication of Times Square. Pictures of boxers adorn the walls and the jukebox plays lots of R&B and 70s disco. In the pre-smoking-ban days, the smoke would get so thick in Jimmy's you needed night-vision goggles to see through the haze. Beer is cheap and drinks aren't fancy. Skip the theme bars and restaurants and go for an after-theater pop at Jimmy's.

Rudy's Bar & Grill, 627 Ninth Ave., between 44th and 45th streets (© 212/974-9169). This Hell's Kitchen establishment is no secret; its happy hour is legendary, and the small place is usually packed with slackers sucking up cheap beer including the house brand, Rudy's Red, a weak, watery brew served in a huge plastic cup for $3. My advice is to get there before happy hour, grab a seat on one of the few broken banquettes, and keep your eyes open for the hot-dog guy, who gives out

place, as have actors Matt Dillon, Ethan Hawke, and Peter O'Toole. And if Peter O'Toole gave it the thumbs up, who are we to argue? 2 Lexington Ave. (at 21st St.). © 212/475-4320. Subway: 6 to 23rd St..

Heartland Brewery   The food leaves a bit to be desired, but the house-brewed beers are first-rate. Great American Beer Festival three-time award-winner Farmer Jon's Oatmeal Stout is always on hand, as are three or four handcrafted ales and a lager or two. A good selection of single malts and tequilas, too. The two-level bar is big and appealing, but expect a loud, boisterous after-work crowd, plus a good number of Germans and Brits (testament to the quality of the brew). 35 Union Sq. W. (at 16th St.). © 212/645-3400. www.heartlandbrewery.com. Subway: 4, 5, 6, L, N, R, Q, W to 14th St./Union Sq. Also at 1285 Sixth Ave. (at 50th St., across from Radio City Music Hall; © 212/582-8244; subway: B, D, F, V to 47th–50th sts./Rockefeller Center); 93 South St. (at Fulton St.) © 646/572-BEER; subway: 2,3 to Broadway/Nassau; 4, 5 to Wall St.; 6 to Brooklyn Bridge.

Pete's Tavern   The oldest continually operating establishment in the city, Pete's opened while Lincoln was president. It reeks of history—and more importantly, there's Guinness on tap and a terrific happy hour. The crowd is a mix of locals from Gramercy Park and more down-to-earth types. 129 E. 18th St. (at Irving Place). © 212/473-7676. www.petestavern.com. Subway: 4, 5, 6, L, N, R, Q, W to 14th St./Union Sq.

free hot dogs. You'll need one to balance out a bucket of Rudy's Red. In the summer, Rudy's opens its cement garden for drinks "alfresco."

Subway Inn, 143 E. 60th St., at Lexington Avenue (© 212/223-9829). My all-time favorite dive, the Subway has been around for over 60 years, and I believe some of the regulars have been on their stools that whole time. The red neon sign beckons from outside, while inside, no matter what time of day, it's midnight dark. The bartender is ancient, and until recently, served Schaeffer on tap. The demise of Schaeffer was troubling, but thankfully not much else has changed. The booths are still wobbly and the models of Godzilla and E.T. along with assorted other dusty junk continue to decorate the shelves behind the bar. The last time I visited, I was kept from going into the men's room by police who were rousting one of the regulars during a drug bust. You might find workers from the upscale stores in the neighborhood and writers searching for "material " slumming at the Subway, and occasionally a celebrity "discovers" it, but this joint remains the epitome of a dive.

Tap a Keg, 2731 Broadway, between 103rd and 104th streets (© 212/ 749-1734). The Tap a Keg calls itself a "Hell of a Joint." And hell can mean two things here: very good fun or a nightmare. That's the happy contradiction. There are a few wooden tables and televisions; a great jukebox with jazz, reggae, and R&B; and a popular pool table. But it's the 7-hour happy hour with pints of beer around $3 and the regular gathering of wizened, disheveled characters that give the Tap a Keg its well-deserved dive status.

TIMES SQUARE & MIDTOWN WEST

Joe Allen (p. 171), the legendary Broadway pub on Restaurant Row, 326 W. 46th St., between Eighth and Ninth avenues (© 212/581-6464), is great for an after-theater cocktail. A branch of **Heartland Brewery** (p. 324) is across from Radio City at 1285 Sixth Ave., at 51st Street (© 212/582-8244).

Algonquin Bar   The oak-paneled lobby of this venerable literati-favored Arts and Crafts hotel is the comfiest and most welcoming in the city, made to linger over pre- or post-theater cocktails. You'll feel the spirit of Dorothy Parker and the Algonquin Round Table that pervades the room. Try the Matilda, a light blend of orange juice, Absolut Mandarin, triple sec, and champagne, named after the Algonquin's feline in residence. Adjacent is the clubby **Blue Bar,** home to a rotating collection of Hirschfeld drawings. Well worth a few spare bucks if you want to soak in Old New York atmosphere at its finest. 59 W. 44th St. (between Fifth and Sixth aves.). © 212/840-6800. Subway: B, D, F, V to 42nd St.

M Bar *(Finds*   This library-style lounge transcends its hotel-bar status with a cir-cular bar, a first-rate cocktail menu, comfortable seating, a dark and romantic Art Deco mood, and a warmth that will make pretension-phobes feel right at home. Prices are reasonable, too, considering the neighborhood. The weekly Wednesday jazz night has turned into a big hit with locals—so much so that the calendar has expanded to include cabaret nights and wine tastings. A real gem! Adjacent to the Mansfield hotel, 12 W. 44th St. (between Fifth and Sixth aves.). © 212/944-6050. Subway: B, D, F, V to 42nd St.

Mickey Mantle's   Before Mickey Mantle's officially opened several years ago, I was walking past the restaurant, peered into the window, and there was my boyhood idol, the Mick, sitting at the bar by himself. Through the window I waved—and he waved back. It made my day. And though the food's not very good and the drinks are overpriced, I still have a soft spot for Mickey Mantle's and always will. With plenty of Yankee memorabilia on the walls and sports on all the televisions, it's an ideal place to watch a game, but stick with the basics: beer and burgers. 42 Central Park S. (between Fifth and Sixth aves.). © 212/688-7777. www.mickeymantles.com. Subway: F to 57th St.

Russian Vodka Room *(Finds)*   This old-school lounge is a Theater District find. It's not going to win any style awards, but it's comfortable and knows what's what when it comes to vodkas. More than 50 are on hand, plus the RVR's own infusions; you can order an iced rack of six if you can't decide between such yummy flavors as cranberry, apple-cinnamon, ginger, horseradish, and more (the raspberry makes a perfect Cosmo). The 30-something-and-up crowd is peopled with post-Soviet imports as well as New Yorkers in the know. A martini or Cosmo is about $10, but you could do the backstroke in it. Come early if you want to snag a bar table. 265 W. 52nd St. (between Broadway and Eighth Ave.). © 212/307-5835. Subway: C, E, 1, 9 to 50th St.

Tír Na Nóg   This festive place is a standout among the Irish pubs that line Eighth Avenue near Penn Station. The decor lends the place a genuine Celtic vibe, as does the Murphy's on tap and the lilt of the bartender. The bar has established itself among both locals and bridge-and-tunnel types for its unpretentious, lively air. There's good, upscale pub grub; a dance floor; and live, foot-stompin' Irish music Friday and Saturday nights. The ideal place to celebrate St. Patrick's Day. 5 Penn Plaza (Eighth Ave. between 33rd and 34th sts.). © 212/630-0249. www.tirnanognyc.com. Subway: A, C, E to 34th St./Penn Station.

MIDTOWN EAST & MURRAY HILL

Bull & Bear   The name speaks to its business-minded clientele; there's even a stock ticker in constant service for those three-martini lunches. The Bull & Bear is like a gentlemen's pub, with leather chairs, a waistcoated staff, and a troika-shaped mahogany bar polished to a high sheen at the center of the room. Still, it's plenty comfy for casual drinkers. Ask Oscar, who's been here for more than 30 years, or one of the other accomplished bartenders to blend you a classic cocktail. Or just order a beer—either way, you'll be right at home here. An ideal place to kick back after a hard day of sightseeing. At the Waldorf-Astoria. 301 Park Ave. (between 49th and 50th sts.). © 212/872-4900. Subway: 6 to 51st St.

The Ginger Man   The bait at this appealing and cigar-friendly upscale bar is the 66 gleaming tap handles lining the wood-and-brass bar, dispensing everything from Sierra Nevada and Hoegaarden to cask-conditioned ales. The cavernous space has a clubby feel, as Wall Streeters and the young men and women they flirt with lounge on sofas and chairs. The limited menu is well prepared, and prices are better than you'd expect from a place like this. 11 E. 36th St. (between Fifth and Madison aves.). © 212/532-3740. Subway: 6 to 33rd St.

King Cole Room   The birthplace of the Bloody Mary, this spot may just be New York's best classic hotel bar. The Maxfield Parrish mural is worth the price of a classic cocktail (ask the bartender to tell you about the "hidden" meaning of the painting). The sophisticated setting demands proper attire, so dress for the occasion. The *New York Times* calls the bar nuts "the best in town," but there's an elegant bar-food menu if you'd like something more substantial. Avoid the after-work hours at holiday time, when the crowd can ruin the mood. At the St. Regis hotel, 2 E. 55th St. (at Fifth Ave.). © 212/339-6721. Subway: E, F to 53rd St.

P.J. Clarke's After being closed for a year, this 120-year-old saloon/restaurant was renovated, preserving most of all the original detail, and re-opened in 2003 under new ownership (one of the owners is actor Timothy Hutton). P.J. Clarke's is a New York institution, a late-night hangout for politicians, actors, and athletes. This is where Ray Milland went on a bender in the classic 1948 movie *The Lost Weekend*. Maybe if Milland stopped drinking and had one of P.J. Clarke's legendary hamburgers, he wouldn't have ended up in Bellevue. 915 Third Ave. (at 55th St.). © 212/317-1616. www.pjclarkes.com. Subway: E, V to Lexington Ave.

THE UPPER WEST SIDE

The subterranean **All State Cafe** (p. 179), 250 W. 72nd St., between Broadway and West End Avenue (© **212/874-1883**), is one of the best workaday pubs in town, with a loyal and easygoing grown-up crowd, great burgers, a terrific jukebox, and a cozy fireplace.

Also consider the dive **Tap a Keg,** 2731 Broadway, between 103rd and 104th streets (© **212/749-1734**). Closer to Columbia, there's also a terrific bar that rollicks well into the wee hours at **Nacho Mama's,** 2893 Broadway, between 112th and 113th streets (© **212/665-2800**).

Café del Bar *Finds* A tiny, casual reggae lounge in the northern hinterlands of Columbus Avenue. Roots music provides the friendly vibe here, along with $4 Red Stripes and the special of the house, Mango Mimosas. If you get hungry, Jamaican beef patties and curried lamb pies will satisfy the craving. 945 Columbus Ave. (at 106th St.). © 212/531-1643. Subway: C or B to 103rd St.

Dublin House For years, like a welcoming beacon, the Dublin House's neon harp has blinked invitingly. This very old pub is a no-frills Irish saloon and the perfect spot for a drink after visiting the nearby Museum of Natural History or Central Park. There's a long, narrow barroom up front and a bigger room in the back that's good for groups. Original wood-veneer detail remains, adding to the pub's charm. The Guinness is cheap and drawn perfectly by the very able and sometimes crusty bartenders. Best enjoyed in the late afternoon or early evening when the regulars populate the bar. Stay away on weekend nights and St. Patrick's Day when the place is overrun with amateurs: frat boys and sorority girls on pub crawls. 225 W. 79th St. (between Broadway and Amsterdam Ave.). © 212/874-9528. Subway: 1, 9 to 79th St.

Eden *Finds* A sleek downtown cocktail lounge has finally found its way uptown. This French-owned lounge features a sleek granite-topped bar, a dark comfy back room with couches, and plush chairs. Happy hour here is happily an extended 4 hours, 5 to 9pm 7 days a week. The DJ comes on after happy hour, and spontaneous dancing has been known to occasionally take place. There is live blues on Wednesday and reggae on Thursday. A belly dancer entertains late on weekends. Bites are available like *quesadillas* and *croque monsieurs*. A fashionable refuge in an unfashionable neighborhood. 2728 Broadway (between 104th and 105th sts.). © 212/865-5565. Subway: 1, 9 to 103rd St.

Shark Bar This popular, upscale spot is well known for its good soul food and even better singles' scene. It's also a favorite hangout for sports celebs, so don't be surprised if you spot a New York Knick or Ranger. 307 Amsterdam Ave. (between 74th and 75th sts.). ℂ **212/874-8500.** Subway: 1, 2, 3, 9 to 72nd St.

THE UPPER EAST SIDE

There's an outpost of the Meat-Packing District roadhouse **Hogs & Heifers** (p. 322) at 1843 First Ave., between 95th and 96th streets (ℂ **212/722-8635;** subway: 6 to 96th St.). Despite its offshoot status, this one's slightly more laid-back and boasts more genuine saloon style. Also consider New York's number-one dive: **Subway Inn,** 143 E. 60th St., just east of Lexington Avenue (ℂ **212/223-8929,** see the box "The Dive-Bar Experience" earlier in this chapter.

Great Hall Balcony Bar *Moments* One of Manhattan's best cocktail bars is only open on Friday and Saturday—and only from 4 to 8:30pm, to boot. The Metropolitan Museum of Art transforms the lobby's mezzanine level into a cock-tail-and-classical music lounge twice weekly, offering an only-in-New-York experience. The music is usually provided by a grand piano and string quartet. The setting couldn't be grander, especially when the hall is transformed into a Christmas paradise at holiday season. You'll have to pay the $10 admission, but the galleries are open until 9pm. At the Metropolitan Museum of Art, Fifth Ave. at 82nd St. ℂ **212/535-7710.** www.metmuseum.org. Subway: 4, 5, 6 to 86th St.

Mo's Caribbean Bar & Mexican Grill The poor man's Cancun Spring Break vacation can be found at Mo's, where "Beach Party" nights are common along with live reggae on Tuesdays, sweet and strong rum drinks, a half-price happy hour every day, and disgusting but satisfying munchies such as jalapeño poppers, nachos, and jerk chicken wings to keep you fortified while you drink. 1454 Second Ave. at 77th St. ℂ **212/650-0561.** Subway: 6 to 77th St.

HARLEM

Lenox Lounge More famous for its status as Harlem's best jazz club (p. 316), Lenox Lounge also boasts Harlem's best bar scene. This old-world throwback (scotch comes Johnnie Walker, not single-malt) is warm, cozy, and immensely popular with grown-ups from all walks of life. 288 Malcolm X Blvd. (Lenox Ave., between 124th and 125th sts.). ℂ **212/427-0253.** Subway: 2, 3, to 125th St.

8 Dance Clubs & Party Scenes

No slice of New York nightlife is as mutable as the club scene. In this world, hot spots don't even get 15 minutes of fame—their time in the limelight is usually more like a commercial break.

First things first: Finding and going to the latest hot spot is not worth ago-nizing over. Clubbers spend their lives obsessing over the scene. My rule of thumb is that if I know about a place, it must not be hip anymore. Just find someplace that amuses you, and enjoy the crowd.

"Clubs" as actual, physical spaces don't mean much anymore. The hungry-for-nightlife crowd follows events of certain party "producers" who switch ven-ues and times each week. A number of bars and lounges listed in the preceding section—like **Idlewild** and **Drinkland,** to name just two—host DJ parties and "club" scenes on various nights of the week.

I've concentrated on a wide variety of scenes below, from performance-artsy to perennially popular discos, most of which are generally easy to make your way into. You can find listings for the most current hot spots and movable parties in the **sources** listed in the introduction to this chapter.

New York nightlife starts late. With the exception of places that have scheduled live performances, it's almost useless to show up anywhere before 11pm. Don't depend on plastic; bring cash, and plan on dropping a wad. Cover charges start out anywhere from $5 to $30 and often get more expensive as the night wears on. *Time Out New York* is a great source to check, as it lists cover charges for the week's big events and clearly indicates which are free.

Money-saving tips: Additional online sources that might score you discount admissions to select clubs include **www.promony.com**. No matter what, **always call ahead,** because schedules change constantly and can do so at the last minute. Even better: You also may be able to put your name on a guest list that will save you a few bucks at the door. You can also check **http://newyork.sheckys.com** for VIP guest-list access. And always check the clubs' websites directly for special deals.

Baktun   This club has been hot since the word *go*. Sleek Baktun was conceived in 2000 as a multimedia lounge, and incorporates video projections (shown on a clever double-sided video screen) into its dance parties as well as live cybercasts. The music tends toward electronica, with some live acts. At press time, Saturday's Direct Drive was still the key drum 'n' bass party in town. The cover runs $3 to $10. 418 W. 14th St. (between Ninth Ave. and Washington St.). ℂ **212/206-1590.** www.baktun.com. Subway: A, C, E, L to 14th St.

Cafe Wha?   You'll find a carefree crowd dancing in this casual basement club any night of the week. From Wednesday through Sunday, the stage features the house's own Wha Band, which does an excellent job of cranking out crowd-pleasing covers of familiar rock-and-roll hits from the '70s, '80s, and '90s. Monday night is the hugely popular Brazilian Dance Party, while Tuesday night is Classic Funk Night. Expect to be surrounded by lots of Jersey kids and out-of-towners on the weekends, but so what? You'll be having as much fun as they are. Reservations are a good idea. The cover runs from free to $10, making Wha a good value to boot. 115 MacDougal St. (between Bleecker and 3rd sts.). ℂ **212/254-3706.** www.cafewha.com. Subway: A, B, C, D, E, F, V to W. 4th St.

Centro-Fly   This swank Op Art club is so fab that Mary J. Blige used it as a video set. The sunken bar must be the coolest in town. Despite its fabulousness, Centro-Fly is quite welcoming. Two mondo sound systems and a four-turntable booth lure in top-notch DJ talent ranging from Junior Sanchez to Dimitri from Paris to Paul Oakenfold. Depending on the night, look for deep house, hip-hop, or another edgy music mix. The Friday-night funky-soulful British house party GBH (www.gbh.tv), New York's longest-running house party, may be the best reason to come. *Money-saving tip:* Sign up for Centro-Fly's weekly e-mailer for access to reduced $10 admission. 45 W. 21st St. (between Fifth and Sixth aves.). ℂ **212/627-7770.** www.centro-fly.com. Subway: F to 23rd St.; N, R to 23rd St.

Club Shelter   House heads flock to this old-school disco. The big draw is the "Saturday Night Shelter Party," when late-80s House music takes over. The crowd is racially and sexually diverse and dress is not fancy; wear whatever is comfortable for doing some heavy sweating on the dance floor. At press time, live acts such as Patti LaBelle were set to be added. 20 W. 39th St. (between Fifth and Sixth aves.). ℂ **212/719-9867.** Subway: B, D, F, Q, V, 7 to 42nd St.

Don Hill's   This long-lived, eccentric, divey club draws a heavily integrated gay-lesbian/straight crowd that comes for rock, glam, and punk some nights, campy parties on others. Röck Cändy is a fun neo-glam resurrection, featuring live hair-metal bands (for whom there is still a scene in New York). The cover always falls between $5 and $10, and drinks are affordable. 511 Greenwich St. (at Spring St.). ℂ **212/334-1390.** Subway: 1, 9 to Canal St.

Nell's *Finds*   Nell's calls itself "The Classic New York Nightclub," and it has earned the moniker. It was the first to establish a loungelike atmosphere years ago. It has been endlessly copied. Nell's attracts a grown-up crowd that ranges from homeboys to Wall Streeters, and it's as marvelous as ever. Although the entertainment can run the gamut from comedy and spoken word to Cuban sounds, most of the parties have a soulful edge. The gem of the New York nightlife scene! The cover is a well-worth-it $7 to $15, depending on the night. Dress nicely—Nell's deserves respect. 246 W. 14th St. (between Seventh and Eighth aves.). ℂ **212/675-1567.** www.nells.com. Subway: A, C, E, 1, 2, 3, 9 to 14th St.

Swing 46   Swing is still a nightly affair at this jazz and supper club (supper not required). Music is live nightly, and runs the gamut from big band to boogie-woogie to jump blues. Don't miss Vince Giordano and His Nighthawks if they're on the bill, especially if sharp-dressed Casey McGill is singing and strumming his ukulele, too. The Harlem Renaissance Orchestra is another great choice. Even first-timers can join in the fun, as free swing lessons are offered nightly at 9:15pm. The cover is $7 Sunday through Wednesday, $12 Thursday through Saturday. No jeans or sneakers. 349 W. 46th St. (between Eighth and Ninth aves.). ℂ **212/262-9554.** www.swing46.com. Subway: C, E to 50th St.

13 *Value*   This little lounge is a great place to dance the night away. It's stylish but unpretentious, with a steady roster of fun weekly parties. Sunday night's no-cover Britpop fest Shout! lives on, as popular as ever—and with no cover, to boot. The rest of the week runs the gamut from '70s and '80s New Wave and glam night to progressive house and trance to poetry slams and performance art. If there's a cover, it's usually $5, occasionally $7 or $10. Happy hour offers two-for-one drinks (and no cover) from 4 to 8pm. 35 E. 13th St. (between Broadway and University Place), 2nd floor. ℂ **212/979-6677.** www.bar13.com or www.bar13.com. Subway: 4, 5, 6, N, R, L, Q, W to 14th St./Union Sq.

Vinyl *Finds*   No alcohol is served at Vinyl—but that doesn't keep the rapturous masses at bay. This TriBeCa club welcomes a big, mixed black/white, gay/straight crowd to the best roster of weekly parties on the planet—mainly hip-hop- and house-flavored party nights ruled by a first-rate crop of DJs. The now-legendary Body and Soul (www.bodyandsoul-nyc.com) is a Sunday-afternoon party extra-ordinaire. Even better is Friday's Be Yourself, superstar DJ Danny Tenaglia's weekly rave, which doesn't relent until the Saturday-morning cartoon hours. 6 Hubert St. (between Hudson and Greenwich sts.). ℂ **212/343-1379.** Subway: A, C, E to Canal St.; 1, 9 to Franklin St.

9 The Gay & Lesbian Scene

To get a thorough, up-to-date take on what's happening in gay and lesbian nightlife, pick up copies of *HX* (www.hx.com), *New York Blade* (www.nyblade.com), *Next* (www.nextnyc.com), and *Gay City News* (www.gaycitynews.com), available for free in bars and clubs all around town, at news boxes throughout the city, or at the **Lesbian, Gay, Bisexual & Transgender Community Center,** at 208 W. 13th St., between Seventh and Eighth avenues (ℂ **212/620-7310;** www.gaycenter.org). The weekly *Time Out New York* boasts a terrific gay and lesbian section; another great source is the legendary free weekly *Village Voice.* Always remember that asking people in one bar can lead you to discover another that fits your tastes.

In addition to the choices below, be sure to see what's happening at such clubs as **Vinyl** and **Don Hill's,** which cater to gay and/or gay/straight mixed crowds; see "Dance Clubs & Party Scenes," above. You might also wish to consider **Duplex** and **Don't Tell Mama** if cabaret's more your style (p. 318). Women might wish to see what's on at **Bluestockings** bookstore and cafe (p. 272).

Barracuda   Chelsea is central to gay life—and gay bars. This trendy, loungey place is a continuing favorite, voted "Best Bar" by *HX* and *New York Press* for 2 years running, while *Paper* singles out the hunky bartenders. There's a sexy bar for cruising out front and a comfy lounge in back. Look for the regular drag shows. 275 W. 22nd St. (between Seventh and Eighth aves.). ✆ 212/645-8613. Subway: C, E, 1, 9 to 23rd St.

Big Cup   Big Cup isn't a bar, but a coffeehouse. Still, you'd be hard-pressed to find a cooler, comfier pickup joint, or a more preening crowd. This is where all the Chelsea boys hang; just think of it as a living room–style lounge without the alcohol. By the way, it also happens to be a fab coffeehouse. 228 Eighth Ave. (between 21st and 22nd sts.). ✆ 212/206-0059. Subway: C, E to 23rd St.

Boiler Room   This East Village bar is everybody's favorite gay dive. Despite the mixed guy-girl crowd, it's a cruising scene for well-sculpted beautiful boys who love to pose, and a fine hangout for those who'd rather play pool. 86 E. 4th St. (between First and Second aves.). ✆ 212/254-7536. Subway: F to Second Ave.

Chase *Finds*   This serene and stylish multiroom lounge on the northern fringe of Hell's Kitchen is symbolic of how far this neighborhood has come over the last half-dozen years. The pretty-boy staff is welcoming to locals and visitors alike. The relaxed weeknight ambience transforms into quite a party scene on weekends. 255 W. 55th St. (between Broadway and Eighth Ave.). ✆ 212/333-3400. Subway: A, B, C, D, 1, 9 to 59th St./Columbus Circle.

The Cock *Finds*   This gleefully seedy East Village joint is the most envelope-pushing gay club in town. A self-proclaimed "rock and sleaze fag bar" is dedicated to good-natured depravity. Head elsewhere if you're the retiring type. 188 Ave. A (at 12th St.). ✆ 212/777-6254. Subway: L to First Ave.

Crazy Nanny's   This lesbian bar and club is huge, friendly, and perpetually trendy. There are two floors, two bars, a groovy jukebox, dancing, a pool table, video games, and a variety of theme nights, including Dance Party on Thursday, and karaoke on Sunday and Wednesday (free cover). Out-of-towners are welcome. There's usually an $8 cover; drinks are half-price Monday through Friday from 4 to 7pm. 21 Seventh Ave. S. (at Leroy St.). ✆ 212/366-6312. www.crazynannys.com. Subway: 1, 9 to Houston St.

The Eagle   Everybody's favorite leather bar has been beautifully re-created in this far west Chelsea bi-level space. 554 W. 28th St. (between Tenth and Eleventh aves.). ✆ 646/473-1866. Subway: C, E to 23rd St.

Hell   This glamorous lounge is a sexy haven for a predominantly gay weekend crowd in the hipper-than-hell Meat-Packing District. The cocktails are well mixed, and plenty of comfy sofas are on hand for getting cozy. Ahead of its time in the 'hood, Hell is not quite as ultrahot as it used to be, but that just means there's more room for you. 59 Gansevoort St. (between Washington and Greenwich sts.). ✆ 212/727-1666. Subway: A, C, E to 14th St.

Henrietta Hudson *Finds*   This friendly, popular, and sometimes raucous women's bar/lounge is known for drawing in an attractive, upmarket lipstick lesbian crowd that comes for the jukebox and videos as well as the pleasingly low-key atmosphere. There's a $5 to $7 cover on weekends, when DJs spin tunes (Fri–Sat) and live bands are in the house (Sun). 438 Hudson St. (at Morton St.). ℂ 212/924-3347. Subway: 1, 9 to Houston St.

Meow Mix   Owner Brooke Webster has made this funky, divey East Village bar a great hangout since 1994. It draws in a young, attractive riot *grrrrl* crowd with nightly diversions like DJs and live bands, a pool table, and an authentic Ms. Pac Man machine in the basement lounge. It's the place to watch New York Liberty away games on the big-screen TV. Two-for-one happy hour daily from 5 to 8pm. 269 E. Houston St. (at Suffolk St.). ℂ 212/254-0688. www.meowmixchix.com. Subway: F to Second Ave.

Rubyfruit Bar & Grill   This cozy bar and restaurant is a popular hangout, and less raucous than most of the other all-girl party scenes listed here. Choose a romantic dinner downstairs, or head upstairs for the playful, friendly pickup or hangout scene—whichever you prefer. 531 Hudson St. (between Charles and W. 10th sts.). ℂ 212/929-3343. Subway: 1, 9 to Christopher St.

Splash/SBNY   After 10 years, this campy and fun dance club still manages to be one of the hottest scenes on the men's circuit. In fact, an end-of-2001 rebirth has breathed new life into the scene; *New York* magazine even chose it best gay dance club for 2002. Beautiful bartenders, video screens, New York's best drag queens—Splash has it all. Theme nights are a big deal. Best of the bunch is Musical Mondays, dedicated to Broadway video clips and music. Musical Mondays' famous singalongs are such a blast that they draw a crossover gay/straight mixed crowd as well as celebs like Nathan Lane and the cast of the ABBA musical *Mamma Mia!*. 50 W. 17th St. (between Fifth and Sixth aves.). ℂ 212/691-0073. www.splashbar.com. Subway: F, V to 14th St.; 4, 5, 6, N, R, L, Q, W to 14th St./Union Sq.

Stonewall Bar   Where it all started. A mixed gay and lesbian crowd—old and young—makes this an easy place to begin. At least pop in to relive a defining moment in queer history. 53 Christopher St. (east of Seventh Ave.). ℂ 212/463-0950. Subway: 1, 9 to Christopher St.

Townhouse Bar   Here's a first-class watering hole for men who want to relax rather than cruise. Friendly and open to all. 236 E. 58th St. (between Second and Third aves.). ℂ 212/754-4649. Subway: 4, 5, 6 to 59th St.

Ty's Bar   This friendly, unassuming gay bar has been a part of the Village men's scene for about a million years. The second Tuesday of each month is Firemen's Night, if you want to chat up some of New York's bravest. 114 Christopher St. (between Bleecker and Bedford sts.). ℂ 212/741-9641. www.tys.citysearch.com. Subway: 1, 9 to Christopher St.

View Bar *(Finds)*   Up front is a very attractive and comfortable lounge; in back is a pool room with the name-worthy view; throughout you'll find friendly bartenders, affordable drinks, and Kenneth Cole–dressed boys who could pass on either side of bi. A welcome addition to the scene. 232 Eighth Ave. (between 21st and 22nd sts.). ℂ 212/929-2243. Subway: C, E to 23rd St.

Index

See also Accommodations and Restaurant indexes, below.

ACCOMMODATIONS

Great Trips Like Great Days Begin with a Plan

FranklinCovey and Frommer's Bring You *Frommer's Favorite Places*® Planner

Classic Size Planning Pages $39.95

The planning experts at FranklinCovey have teamed up with the travel experts at Frommer's. The result is a full-year travel-themed planner filled with rich images and travel tips covering fifty-two of Frommer's Favorite Places.

- Each week will make you an expert about an intriguing corner of the world
- New facts and tips every day
- Beautiful, full-color photos of some of the most beautiful places on earth
- Proven planning tools from FranklinCovey for keeping track of tasks, appointments, notes, address/phone numbers, and more

Save 15%

when you purchase Frommer's Favorite Places travel-themed planner and a binder.

Order today before your next big trip.

www.franklincovey.com/frommers
Enter promo code 12252 at checkout for discount. Offer expires June 1, 2005.

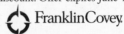

Frommer's is a trademark of Arthur Frommer.

FROMMER'S® COMPLETE TRAVEL GUIDES

Alaska
Alaska Cruises & Ports of Call
Amsterdam
Argentina & Chile
Arizona
Atlanta
Australia
Austria
Bahamas
Barcelona, Madrid & Seville
Beijing
Belgium, Holland & Luxembourg
Bermuda
Boston
Brazil
British Columbia & the Canadian Rockies
Brussels & Bruges
Budapest & the Best of Hungary
California
Canada
Cancún, Cozumel & the Yucatán
Cape Cod, Nantucket & Martha's Vineyard
Caribbean
Caribbean Cruises & Ports of Call
Caribbean Ports of Call
Carolinas & Georgia
Chicago
China
Colorado
Costa Rica
Cuba
Denmark
Denver, Boulder & Colorado Springs
England
Europe
European Cruises & Ports of Call

Florida
France
Germany
Great Britain
Greece
Greek Islands
Hawaii
Hong Kong
Honolulu, Waikiki & Oahu
Ireland
Israel
Italy
Jamaica
Japan
Las Vegas
London
Los Angeles
Maryland & Delaware
Maui
Mexico
Montana & Wyoming
Montréal & Québec City
Munich & the Bavarian Alps
Nashville & Memphis
New England
New Mexico
New Orleans
New York City
New Zealand
Northern Italy
Norway
Nova Scotia, New Brunswick & Prince Edward Island
Oregon
Paris
Peru
Philadelphia & the Amish Country
Portugal

Prague & the Best of the Czech Republic
Provence & the Riviera
Puerto Rico
Rome
San Antonio & Austin
San Diego
San Francisco
Santa Fe, Taos & Albuquerque
Scandinavia
Scotland
Seattle & Portland
Shanghai
Sicily
Singapore & Malaysia
South Africa
South America
South Florida
South Pacific
Southeast Asia
Spain
Sweden
Switzerland
Texas
Thailand
Tokyo
Toronto
Tuscany & Umbria
USA
Utah
Vancouver & Victoria
Vermont, New Hampshire & Maine
Vienna & the Danube Valley
Virgin Islands
Virginia
Walt Disney World® & Orlando
Washington, D.C.
Washington State

FROMMER'S® DOLLAR-A-DAY GUIDES

Australia from $50 a Day
California from $70 a Day
England from $75 a Day
Europe from $70 a Day
Florida from $70 a Day
Hawaii from $80 a Day

Ireland from $60 a Day
Italy from $70 a Day
London from $85 a Day
New York from $90 a Day
Paris from $80 a Day

San Francisco from $70 a Day
Washington, D.C. from $80 a Day
Portable London from $85 a Day
Portable New York City from $90 a Day

FROMMER'S® PORTABLE GUIDES

Acapulco, Ixtapa & Zihuatanejo
Amsterdam
Aruba
Australia's Great Barrier Reef
Bahamas
Berlin
Big Island of Hawaii
Boston
California Wine Country
Cancún
Cayman Islands
Charleston
Chicago
Disneyland®
Dublin
Florence

Frankfurt
Hong Kong
Houston
Las Vegas
Las Vegas for Non-Gamblers
London
Los Angeles
Los Cabos & Baja
Maine Coast
Maui
Miami
Nantucket & Martha's Vineyard
New Orleans
New York City
Paris
Phoenix & Scottsdale

Portland
Puerto Rico
Puerto Vallarta, Manzanillo & Guadalajara
Rio de Janeiro
San Diego
San Francisco
Savannah
Seattle
Sydney
Tampa & St. Petersburg
Vancouver
Venice
Virgin Islands
Washington, D.C.

FROMMER'S® NATIONAL PARK GUIDES

Banff & Jasper
Family Vacations in the National Parks

Grand Canyon
National Parks of the American West
Rocky Mountain

Yellowstone & Grand Teton
Yosemite & Sequoia/Kings Canyon
Zion & Bryce Canyon

FROMMER'S® MEMORABLE WALKS

Chicago	New York	San Francisco
London	Paris	

FROMMER'S® WITH KIDS GUIDES

Chicago	Ottawa	Vancouver
Las Vegas	San Francisco	Washington, D.C.
New York City	Toronto	

SUZY GERSHMAN'S BORN TO SHOP GUIDES

Born to Shop: France	Born to Shop: Italy	Born to Shop: New York
Born to Shop: Hong Kong, Shanghai & Beijing	Born to Shop: London	Born to Shop: Paris

FROMMER'S® IRREVERENT GUIDES

Amsterdam	Los Angeles	San Francisco
Boston	Manhattan	Seattle & Portland
Chicago	New Orleans	Vancouver
Las Vegas	Paris	Walt Disney World®
London	Rome	Washington, D.C.

FROMMER'S® BEST-LOVED DRIVING TOURS

Britain	Germany	Northern Italy
California	Ireland	Scotland
Florida	Italy	Spain
France	New England	Tuscany & Umbria

HANGING OUT™ GUIDES

Hanging Out in England	Hanging Out in France	Hanging Out in Italy
Hanging Out in Europe	Hanging Out in Ireland	Hanging Out in Spain

THE UNOFFICIAL GUIDES®

Bed & Breakfasts and Country Inns in:
- California
- Great Lakes States
- Mid-Atlantic
- New England
- Northwest
- Rockies
- Southeast
- Southwest

Best RV & Tent Campgrounds in:
- California & the West
- Florida & the Southeast
- Great Lakes States
- Mid-Atlantic
- Northeast
- Northwest & Central Plains

- Southwest & South Central Plains
- U.S.A.
- Beyond Disney
- Branson, Missouri
- California with Kids
- Central Italy
- Chicago
- Cruises
- Disneyland®
- Florida with Kids
- Golf Vacations in the Eastern U.S.
- Great Smoky & Blue Ridge Region
- Inside Disney
- Hawaii
- Las Vegas
- London
- Maui

- Mexio's Best Beach Resorts
- Mid-Atlantic with Kids
- Mini Las Vegas
- Mini-Mickey
- New England & New York with Kids
- New Orleans
- New York City
- Paris
- San Francisco
- Skiing & Snowboarding in the West
- Southeast with Kids
- Walt Disney World®
- Walt Disney World® for Grown-ups
- Walt Disney World® with Kids
- Washington, D.C.
- World's Best Diving Vacations

SPECIAL-INTEREST TITLES

Frommer's Adventure Guide to Australia & New Zealand
Frommer's Adventure Guide to Central America
Frommer's Adventure Guide to India & Pakistan
Frommer's Adventure Guide to South America
Frommer's Adventure Guide to Southeast Asia
Frommer's Adventure Guide to Southern Africa
Frommer's Britain's Best Bed & Breakfasts and Country Inns
Frommer's Caribbean Hideaways
Frommer's Exploring America by RV
Frommer's Fly Safe, Fly Smart

Frommer's France's Best Bed & Breakfasts and Country Inns
Frommer's Gay & Lesbian Europe
Frommer's Italy's Best Bed & Breakfasts and Country Inns
Frommer's Road Atlas Britain
Frommer's Road Atlas Europe
Frommer's Road Atlas France
The New York Times' Guide to Unforgettable Weekends
Places Rated Almanac
Retirement Places Rated
Rome Past & Present

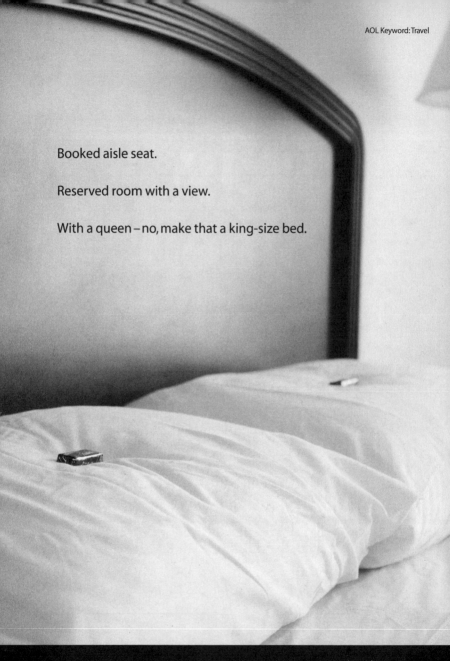

Booked aisle seat.

Reserved room with a view.

With a queen – no, make that a king-size bed.